When I Say Read, Read:
One Fella's Journey Through *Doctor Who*
Volume 1: 1963-1979

By Daniel R. Budnik

THROCKMORTON PRESS

MINNESOTA | INDIANA

Copyright by Daniel R. Budnik

All Rights Reserved

Printed in the United States of America

Cover Design by Taylor Productions

First Printing: 2025

ISBN # 979-8-218-58784-0

This book is not authorized by the BBC. Doctor Who and the TARDIS are trademarks of the BBC.

THROCKMORTON PRESS LLC
240 ORCHARD RDG
HUNTINGTON, INDIANA

To Roger Budnik, for introducing me to The Doctor a long time ago.

Table of Contents

Introduction	**13-15**
Season 1	**16-62**
Season 2	**63-101**
Season 3	**102-146**
Season 4	**147-189**
Season 5	**190-229**
Season 6	**230-271**
Season 7	**272-295**
Season 8	**296-320**
Season 9	**321-344**
Season 10	**345-370**
Season 11	**371-395**
Season 12	**396-415**
Season 13	**416-441**
Season 14	**442-465**
Season 15	**466-490**
Season 16	**491-515**

7

When I say "Read"...

Read.

READ!

Introduction

The first episode of the British science fiction television show *Doctor Who* aired on November 23, 1963. The day after the assassination of U.S. President John F. Kennedy. It went out late Saturday afternoon. The hopes for the show's success were not terribly high when it started. Then, some strange aliens called The Daleks appeared. And here we are, almost 900 episodes later. The show still airs. The show still lives and breathes. If you want a guide to the history of the show, this book isn't it. I would suggest you go online. There are histories scattered all over. You might also try any of several books about the show. Or any of the documentaries about its history that have appeared on DVDs and Blu-Rays. Suffice it to say, this book anticipates that the reader knows the basics of the show. However, here are a few of those basics just to keep us all on the same page before the fun begins:

The Doctor – A being that travels time and space helping other beings out. They take on many different forms. They have lived for thousands of years. They may be a Time Lord or they might be a timeless child. It all depends on when you're joining the show.

TARDIS – Time and Relative Dimension(s) In Space. This is The Ship in which the Doctor travels. It is shaped like a London police box. It's blue. It's rectangular with a little light on top. Inside, it is a vast multi-dimensional space. Far bigger within than without. In theory, it is indestructible.

Companions – This is the name given to the people/ aliens that travel with the Doctor. It seems to arise from the Doctor saying, "Fear makes companions of all of us" in the third episode of the show "The Forest Of Fear." I could be making that up though. Throughout the run, people have tried to change the name from "Companion" to whatever else seems to fit. In the end, Companion works fine. The companion is generally the Doctor's best pal. Sometimes there are more than one.

Sonic Screwdriver – The generic name for a device that the Doctor carries in their pocket that does all sorts of things. Readouts of alien planets, repairing barbed wire, unlocking doors, tightening screws. It was originally an actual screwdriver that worked sonically. It now does much more than that. But, like the name "Companion," it still sticks. If you hear people loudly complaining about the sonic screwdriver because it does too many things, you should wrap a warm towel around their brain and give them a paper bag to breathe into.

Earth – The third planet from the Sun in the Milky Way. The Doctor's favorite planet. But then, they don't have to live here all the time.

Gallifrey – Possibly the Doctor's home planet. It is the planet of the Time Lords. In recent seasons/ series of the show, the Doctor may be from Places Unknown.

Series/ Seasons – The first is more prevalent in Britain. The second more so in America. These words are referring to television shows. In this book, the original run from 1963-1989 will be called "Seasons." The current run will be "Series." For reasoning behind this, write to the author in care of the publisher's dog.

Original Run – November 23, 1963 to December 3, 1989. "An Unearthly Child" to "Survival" Episode Three. The 1996 TVM is lumped in at the end.

Current Run – March 2005 to ?. I consider the current run to be a continuation of the original. In the same way the "Dallas" or "Twin Peaks" or "The Gilmore Girls" returns were.

Episodes – In the original run, most episodes were 25 minutes long. (One season had 45 minutes.) In the current run the episodes are in the vicinity of 45-50 minutes each.

Daleks – Xenophobic race that live inside an ambulatory armory with some charming design features. They're not very nice.

Cybermen – Mechanically augmented human/ humanoids. Unlike the Daleks, they'll convert anybody to their way of life.

The Master/ Missy – The Doctor's friend from school who is now a 100% Crazy Person. The Doctor and the Master have clashed many times.

I'm going to stop there because I could go on for ages. Those are the very basic tenets of the show. There are so many more. Before the book begins, I wanted to do two more things; 1) introduce myself and 2) tell you how this book works.

Hello, It's Me.

I am a writer. My last three books were Pop Culture related. (The one before that was a novel.) I co-wrote a book on rather obscure 1980s horror films. I wrote a book on low budget 1980s action films. I wrote a book on The Henningverse. That book was a deep dive into three 1960s American sitcoms. Back in 1986, when I was 13, I wrote a long essay for Mrs. Hiller's English class on "Doctor Who: The Early Years." I got 100 percent on it. "A joy to read." Ever since then, I've wanted to write a definitive (for me) book on my favorite show. What you're holding in your hand is the first volume in a two volume (to be updated as time goes on) journey through the show from 1963 to 2025. It is a dream come true. It is a labor of love. It is all those cliches. I also think it's a fun journey through a very long running show spanning decades of pop culture history. This dream is accomplished. Enjoy reading it.

How To Use This Book

The book is divided into seasons/ series. Within each chapter/ season/ series, I review each individual episode. I give the title, writer, director, air date and episode number. Then, there is a brief plot synopsis followed by my review. The reviews are very subjective. There have been so many books on *Doctor Who*. I have read many of them. I know the history of the show and all the episodes by heart. When I read another book on it, I want to know what that author thinks. Where that person is coming from and what they have to say. And if they have any good jokes. That's how, I believe, you should treat this book.

The book is split in two volumes. This first volume is pretty much set in stone. The second volume is shorter so additional reviews can be added over time.

Episode numbering: "Shada" is not included. "Resurrection of the Daleks" is counted as two episodes. "The Five Doctors" is one episode. I hope that I have got the numbering right. For some reason, that was the toughest thing to do. I kept losing track of numbers. Almost as if the show didn't want me to get the number right.

The stories throughout the first season have individual episode titles. You will see the generally accepted overall title for each serial in all caps before the first episode of each serial. Then the individual title underneath the overall title for the first one. The remaining episodes for that serial will feature just the actual title.

I tend to write in a cumulative manner. As the show shows us, so I will mention it to you. For example, "The Brain of Morbius" could contain a long discussion about the Doctor possibly being The Timeless Child. But it doesn't. Because that was a glimmer in no one's mind but Chris Chibnall's when that aired. We will talk timeless children when the time comes. (See the episode "The Timeless Children.") If something important isn't mentioned in a review, it could be because it doesn't get a reveal until later.

(The last paragraph holds true throughout the book. Except when it doesn't.)

That's all you need. Now, please, turn the page and begin your journey through my thoughts on one of the best TV shows (one of the best THINGS) ever. And if you have any complaints, please write to me in care of the publisher's cat.

It's November 23, 1963. It's around 5:15 to 5:30. (Depending on where you look.) The screen goes white and hazy and some odd "music" that would have bothered your grandmother begins…

DOCTOR WHO

SEASON ONE

(1963-1964)

AN UNEARTHLY CHILD

An Unearthly Child

Written by Anthony Coburn

Directed by Waris Hussein

Episode 1: (November 23, 1963) Two English Schoolteachers (Ian and Barbara) investigate the home life of an intelligent but odd student of theirs (Susan). It turns out she lives in a junkyard in a police box with her grandfather, a strange old gentleman known only as The Doctor.

Cliffhanger: The TARDIS has landed on a strange desolate world. The shadow of a man (?) appears and stares at the newly arrived blue box.

The surprise of this episode is that it still holds up well today. Now, someone raised on MCU movies will probably be bored out of their skulls. But someone with the willingness to sit down and use a little patience will find that this is an excellently made piece of 1960s television. Keep in mind that when this was shot it was done pretty much live. The actors treated it almost as a piece of theater with the cameras moving around them. There's one big break in the center. (Barbara entering the TARDIS) and one obvious break earlier on (after Susan says she likes walking in the fog in close-up and it cuts to the three shot). Apart from those moments everything is live. The viewer must remember that there are going to be awkward moments. Bits that are a little bit off. Once you can come to grips with those, you'll see a fast-paced episode.

The first half of the episode weighs heavy on the "mysterious" Susan Foreman of 76, Totter's Lane who apparently lives in a junkyard. The first time we see her she is dancing/ moving oddly to the generic rock of John Smith and The Common Men. ("They went from 19 to 2.") And the rest of the first half is the two schoolteachers, Barbara Wright (history) and Ian Chesterton (science) becoming so curious about her that they follow her to her home: the junkyard.

Parts of the first half have the feel of a bit of an Afterschool Special. The strange student who knows some things and doesn't know others. The young woman who seems to live under the sway of her grandfather, a Doctor. A young woman who lives in a junkyard. The two concerned teachers try to find out more about her. They want to help her, bring her a better life. It feels very much like a *Play For Today*, dealing with some sort of social issue. What if Susan's grandfather was an evil man who kept her under his thumb? What if Susan was alone and living rough in the junkyard? What if Susan and her grandfather were time travelers from another world living inside a dimensionally transcendental space/ time machine that looked like a 1960s police box?

Well, maybe that last one wouldn't have been as Ken Loach as the others but it's what is happening here. The second half is one long scene in the control room of the TARDIS. (Time and Relative Dimension in Space.) Ian and Barbara are amazed at where they are. It was a police box and now it's a huge futuristic room. Well, they're amazed until they start to insist that this is all in Susan's imagination. Meanwhile, her grandfather, the Doctor, laughs at them and patronizes them. It all ends in tears as the TARDIS is sent on a very evocative journey to a very desolate place.

And it's all handled with great aplomb by Director Waris Hussein and the actors. William Hartnell became known for fluffing lines but here he's in complete control. His first appearance around 12 minutes in is wonderfully iconic. The Doctor here is not pleasant to the humans. (He has several Shakespearean asides that I've always found a little odd. Surely everyone can hear him.) One wonders what it is he does all day. (We'll learn some of that in the future.) William Russell and Jacqueline Hill are excellent as the two teachers (who may have a bit of a thing for one another) that become private investigators of a sort. They hold their own well against the Doctor in the long scene that dominates the second half. Carole Ann Ford is the perfect mix of average teen (age 15 or so) and a bit odd, a bit unearthly. There's something I've always found so wonderfully incongruous about her outfit when we enter the TARDIS for the first time. Nothing is alien about it. She's just hanging out in some 1960s fashion enjoying dinner.

The episode is helped along by Hussein's direction The camera moves a lot. He has prevented the story from ever becoming static due to the movement and his use of framing. From the opening scene with the police officer to the POV shots of Susan in class, he keeps the episode alive. The POV sequence with Ian and Susan discussing the five dimensions is a favorite moment of mine. The opening with the cop is another favorite moment and the perfect opening for the show. I've always loved the way the music keeps going and going until we see the police box. When the doors swing open on their own, I know Douglas Camfield didn't like it, but I do. Anthony Boucher's script isn't a world beater but, in this episode, at least, his dialogue is sharp, to the point and gives us everything we need to know without going overboard.

Overall, it's an excellent opening episode for the show. The eerie, what's going on with Susan? first half opens with a beautiful and unexpected twist in the second half. As perfectly structured as something shot live like this could be. It pulls the viewer in and then completely upends them. And then, just when you think you're getting a grasp on it, we're not in London anymore. We're in a strange, sandy place... and who is that staring at the TARDIS?

THE DOCTOR WHO PILOT EPISODE

Never aired in the context of Doctor Who itself

The pilot for *Doctor Who* was shown to Sydney Newman, Head of Drama at the BBC. He's one of the people who is always considered one of the co-creators of the show. (When I was young, it was CREATED BY: Sydney Newman and Donald Wilson.) His was the final word. And that word was: No. Followed by: Do It Again. Also: Here's a list of things you should change.

The episode was shot again and that's the one that aired on the BBC. The Pilot Episode (I know. It used to be easy to refer to "The Pilot." Now, you must specify "The one without the Puddle Girl.") aired in the

1980s during a BBC Special celebrating the studio in which it was shot. But it did appear on the "The William Hartnell Years" VHS from the mid-1990s and it is on the DVD for "An Unearthly Child" in "The Beginnings" box set. (Also, the box set includes the "complete" Pilot. They had to shoot the second half twice. So, you get the TARDIS scene in two different takes.) It's an interesting viewing. Terribly similar to the episode that aired but with a bunch of differences. In general, I prefer the episode as aired. Although there are at least two things that got changed that probably shouldn't have been.

I'm not going to review the Pilot Episode because at its heart it is the same as the episode aired. I just wanted to point out some of the changes.

-In the Pilot Episode, there is far less fog in the opening shot with the police officer and the junkyard. The camera also, I'm not sure why, suddenly turns to the left and looks at some garbage on the ground. In the Actual Episode, there is lots of fog and the camera follows the police officer. (The officer feels more like Dixon of Dock Green in the Pilot.)

-In the Actual Episode, the camera rounds some junk, and we see the police box. The camera pans up slightly. We hear the hum and see the episode title. In the Pilot Episode, the camera wobbles around some junk and goes up to the TARDIS. Then, it backs away so we can see more of it. (And a lot of the surroundings, including a clown mannequin of some sort that could have been from the 1960s version of *Killer Klowns from Outer Space*.) Then, it steadies itself on the box. We see the title and it pulls back in on the "PULL TO OPEN" sign.

-In the Actual Episode, Susan looks through The French Revolution book (which we will see again tomorrow, sort of) and proclaims that something isn't right. In the Pilot Episode, she does a sort of impromptu Rorschach test and looks very pensive afterwards.

-Carole Ann Ford's performance is much more "alien" in the Pilot Episode. Watch her face and her eyes. She seems like an alien pretending to be a regular girl. While in the Actual Episode, she seems more like a normal teenage gal who just happens to live in a trans-dimensional space/ time machine.

-The camera in the junkyard and the doors in the TARDIS seem very unsure of themselves throughout the Pilot Episode. (Plus, that mannequin almost falls on Ian when he loses his torch.)

-Susan is not wearing the cool striped shirt in the Pilot Episode. She's wearing a shiny and obvious "I'm From the Future!" vest.

-The big one: Susan says explicitly that she is from the 49th Century in the Pilot Episode. That is changed to vagueness in the episode as aired. (Could you imagine if they left that in?)

-There is a lot of sci-fi sound effect whirring and screeching and noises in general when they first enter the TARDIS and when they go on the trip. It's alternately properly alien and properly annoying. Mainly because it's just too loud.

-In the final shot of the Actual Episode, the shadow approaches... there is a long pause as the person playing the shadow stands still. then the credits roll, and we quickly fade to black. In the Pilot Episode, the credits begin to roll quicker... but it doesn't fade to black for a long time. There is a 1960s *Doctor Who* activity called "Pretending You Are in A Freeze Frame as The Credits Roll." (It's the sort of thing *Police Squad!* made fun of in its closing credits.) This is the first example of it.

The two changes I don't think help:

-The Shakespearean asides in the Actual Episode aren't in the Pilot. They're rewrites. I don't really think they work.

-In the Pilot Episode, the Doctor mentions Napoleon and the Romans as people who wouldn't be able to assimilate knowledge that was beyond their reckonings. (a la Ian and Barbara's confusion) I like that. In the Actual Episode the Doctor mentions the "Red Indians" seeing a steam train and their "savage minds." It makes the Doctor sound like an old racist uncle, which is too bad. Why on Earth they thought that was a clever idea I can't begin to imagine.

You don't need to watch The Pilot Episode. But it is fascinating to see the tweaking that went on. Let's get to the Cave of Skulls.

The Cave of Skulls

Episode 2: (November 30, 1963) The Doctor, Susan, Barbara and Ian are captured by cave dwellers trying to make fire at the year "Zero."

Cliffhanger: Trapped in the Cave of Skulls, they notice that all the skulls have been split open.

The BBC rescreened the first episode right before the second episode. The first episode got much better ratings the second time around, but the rating dipped slightly for the second episode. I'd like to give you a one-word reason for that: cavemen. The previous episode was in two halves. This one is sort of the same, but the two halves overlap one another and occur one scene after another.

The scene in the TARDIS is excellent. Even though they've just travelled through time and space, even though Ian and Barbara got knocked out, it's like the previous episode's conversation never ended. Barbara is becoming less skeptical. Ian and the Doctor are arguing about what's outside. We get a great "Doctor Who?" gag when Ian refers to the Doctor as "Doctor Foreman." We get a discussion of what time is like. The Doctor delivers a short speech about seeing alien skies, which is lovely. Then we step out onto a barren landscape.

The last three episodes of "An Unearthly Child" are sometimes referred to as "100,000 B.C." But the doctor does say that the yearometer reads Zero. What all that means is that prehistoric humans dominate this episode after a couple of scenes with the TARDIS crew. In my mind, I always remember the opening scene with the cave dwellers being interminable and bringing the whole story down. From travel through time and space, to a bunch of British actors in furs watching a guy interacting vigorously with a stick. The Stick Man is Za, head of the cavepeople. There is a rival from another tribe named Kal. There is a young woman who is the "prize." (She's a greasy prize but she's a prize.) And there's an old guy named Horg.

Everyone does their best with the caveman shtick. Some of it works quite well. They were originally meant to speak in grunts. But they were given flowery speeches about fire and that the maker of fire rules the tribe. The opening scene (right before the TARDIS scene) lets everyone know what's going on. It's about 2 ½ minutes. It makes its point and goes. But, the second scene, after Kal has kidnapped the

Doctor, goes on for quite some time. They make their point and then make it again. And again. They're very sincere until Horg speaks. He sounds a bit like he's goofing around.

On one end, we have two "modern-day" schoolteachers trying to come to terms with space/ time travel. On the other end, we have freezing cave dwellers trying to make fire. There's a parallel to be drawn there. Unfortunately, the prehistoric humans are never that interesting. And they get in the way of the TARDIS crew's interaction, which has become quite interesting. None of the cave people are nice. So, there's no one to be sympathetic towards. When Kal captures the Doctor, the Doctor legitimately looks terrified and a little pathetic. Surrounded by these cave dwellers, unable to make fire. (Kal saw the Doctor light a match but the matches are lost.) When the rest of the crew enter the cave and they brawl with the cave people, that's good stuff. As is the closing scene in the Cave. There's a feeling of desperation. We've gone from wonder and discovery to a group of savages ready to kill them. One almost thinks "Surely this can't be right. To introduce us to such a wonderful concept and then have them die in a rotten little cave filled with skulls?" Well, it's not going to be the end but it's so early in the show that there is a feeling that anything could happen.

Including many more scenes with the cavemen talking and talking and talking.

Oh, both Susan and the Doctor mention that the TARDIS hasn't changed its shape. It's still a Police Box. Hmm, first I've heard of it.

The Forest of Fear

Episode 3: (December 7, 1963) An old cavewoman lets the travelers go leading to a frantic chase through the forest.

Cliffhangers: The crew think they've made it back to the TARDIS safely. They have not.

This episode is better than the previous one. Apart from a slow scene at the end where Kal talks about what he sees in his mind, it's a hysterical episode of television. Za is attacked by a panther and is left covered in blood, Susan and Barbara seem to be constantly shrieking. The Doctor almost loses it on more than one occasion, physically trying to hold Susan back when she goes to help the injured Za. There's the very discussed moment where the Doctor picks up a rock. It looks like he is going to club Za to death, but Ian stops him. And the Old Woman who frees our gang from the cave is brutally murdered by Kal. It's not a light episode.

Luckily, it only rarely carries over into histrionics of an "Oh dear" nature. When they're trapped in the cave, The Doctor is alternately sweet ("Fear makes companions of all of us") and a real jacakss. Once they are set free, there is a hysteria and fever pitch to their mad dash for the TARDIS that doesn't really appear a lot in *Doctor Who*. Once the show becomes an institution, we know they'll get away. The fun is in "How" they do it. At this point, we don't even know if they will do it. There's a frisson to this episode that the Doctor's hair seems to reflect. The Doctor is rarely this disheveled, usually only at regenerations or in The Matrix. There's also some wonderful back and forth comparing the survival instinct to compassion. The Doctor favors abandoning the wounded Za and his lady Hur. But the others will not do it. It's working that theory a lot of fiction has that compassion will beget compassion.

The moments when it doesn't quite make it is in those weird moments when the cave dwellers act like cavemen. In the previous episode, they were given flowery speeches. I mentioned Kal's speech earlier. But, in this episode, Hur confronted with the travelers acts much more like how I imagine a caveperson would. Pensive, violent, confused and forgive me, dumb. I'm not sure why she can't respond to the TARDIS crew the way she responds to Kal or her father. In the future, we will learn of the TARDIS's translation circuits. (That's for another story, a distant masque.) I wonder if the cave dwellers have something similar. When they are together, to them, they are eloquent and speak grandly. But, on their first encounter with others, their translator dumbs them down a shade. Makes them seem more like the way people think they should be. Maybe to give the caveman some sort of advantage? Or maybe just to make things go quicker? The TARDIS crew wants to get out of there. Not be pontificated at.

The clashes between the Doctor and Ian scatter throughout the episode. The Doctor is not pleasant here. Ian, as the nominal hero, must deal with this old man who may be a genius but is also a jackass. The Doctor's constant slowing them down is what causes Kal and Hur to catch up with them. Susan tries to be as helpful as she can but is too deferential to her grandfather. Barbara is just trying to get through this while keeping her humanity and her sanity. The moments when they think they're away, the moments when they see the TARDIS, you can see the joy and relief in their eyes. Then, the nicely composed shot of the TARDIS with the cavemen rising behind rocks shatters it all. And the episode ends on the cold, steely face of Za. (Who does a particularly excellent job of not moving as the credits roll.)

This episode mostly works fine and ups the ante incredibly. It doesn't even bother me that I can't logically figure out how Za and the small army of cave dwellers got so far ahead of the Tardis crew, Kal and Hur. Every Caveman Knows a Shortcut. They probably invented the shortcut, after all.

The Firemaker

Episode 4: (December 14, 1963) The Doctor and his friends end up in The Cave of Skulls again. This time they must make fire.

Cliffhanger: The travelers land on an unknown world. They think the radiation level is normal. It is not...

And the first adventure ends. The Tribe of Gum gets their fire. Kal gets Hur and oversees the tribe. Kal and Za get in a big brawl (on film as opposed to video). That brawl is violent and ends with a head being smashed in. The Doctor, Susan, Barbara and Ian run for their lives again, just barely escaping. In fact, the climax of this episode is the same as the climax of the previous one. The crew races through the forest towards the TARDIS. (This time, the forest is on film so there's more expanse.) The cavepeople are there (using the shortcut). But, in this episode, the tribe are behind them, rather than in front.

I do love the cavepeople's reaction to fire. It's been missing from their lives for so long that they really do worship it. Kal is the only one who seems wary of it. He sticks a finger in just to see if it's real. (It is.) Hussein's direction is as strong as ever here even as the story is running itself in some circles. The way they assemble around the torch gives a real feeling of awe mixed with some craziness. They've been cold for some time.

The Doctor, as irascible as he is, turns out to have been right all along. Ian, Barbara and Susan showing compassion for Za and saving his life (and giving him fire) winds up with them locked in the Cave of

Skulls forever. (There is a chat between Hur and Za that is interesting, once it gets past explaining what happened last week. Za believes that these people are a new tribe. The next round of evolution. He knows he can't let them go because they can provide him with insight and knowledge that will keep him as leader.) The Doctor wanting to leave Za was the right thing to do, according to the story. They would have got away just fine and none of the 4th episode would have happened. In future episodes, kindness and compassion will find a way to victory. In these early episodes, things don't always work out quite like we'd expect. For example, I don't think we expected to see Ian and The Doctor stoning Kal. I know I didn't.

The episode moves at a decent pace. Occasionally it moves a little too quick. But I think all of us knew where it was going so let's get there rather than dawdle. It is nice to see the travelers produce a way to get out of the Cave rather than having someone let them out. But, about halfway through the episode, I always kind of feel like I'm done with the cave dwellers, and we can get out of here. Luckily, that's kind of the way the makers of it think too. And it begs the question: Was this adventure the right one to use at the start of the show?

Producer Verity Lambert and Script Editor David Whitaker didn't think so. They felt the premise betrayed the creativity and imagination of the first episode. The original first story was meant to be the crew getting shrunk in Coal Hill School. But the budget wouldn't allow it. So, they went with the cave dwellers. It is lacking in imagination and creativity. Episode 1 is capture. Episode 2 is escape, chase and capture. Episode 3 is escape and chase. Would it have worked better if the second story had been made first? Possibly. In the end, I tend to think that the simplicity of this story (and the grime and the blood) heightens the travelers' excitement, hysteria and general worry. So, I don't mind it but I'm glad when it's over. If you gave the show all the budget it needed, should this have been the first? No way. The first one should have been an imaginative adventure that also has the character moments that this one does. But this is what we have. Let's enjoy it, shall we? And besides, who knows where we'll go next?

One question: Right after the travelers light a fire, we cut to a little girl. A drumbeat starts on the soundtrack. She looks up. Then we cut to all the cavepeople, and they are all sort of looking up and around. Horg says "Orb strikes the old stone and Za does not bring them out." Can they hear that drumbeat? It's implied that they hear something. Who's hitting the drum or making the noise?

THE DALEKS

The Dead Planet

Written by Terry Nation

Directed by Christopher Barry

Episode 5: (December 21, 1963) Barbara, Susan, Ian and The Doctor land in an odd, petrified jungle. (Not a forest. It's also very radioactive but they don't know that yet.) There is a brilliant futuristic city nearby. Thanks to the Doctor being a jerk, they explore it. It seems deserted. Until Barbara makes a friend.

Cliffhanger: Is Barbara being threatened by a madman with a sink plunger?

It's just the four main cast members in this episode. First exploring the jungle. (The Magneton!) Then, exploring the city. They hold their own very well. It's an intriguing, suspenseful episode that shows the TARDIS crew bonding together under adversarial conditions (the fluid link being spilled) but also showing the Doctor being incredibly selfish. (He empties the fluid link so they can see the city.) No one knew when this originally aired how big it would be. How crazy things would get. So, to see the four of them just exploring and learning is something that always brings me a lot of joy. There is trouble here, obviously. But let's explore for an episode. Let's check it out. Kal isn't going to show up. Everything's dead.

Not all of it works. Some of it might seem a trifle quaint. The "Space Food" sequence is the sort of thing that Terry Nation loved. It will either strike you as goofball to the extreme or quite delightful. (Like watching toy commercials from the 1950s.) I love it. I feel like the current Doctor has an actual working cafeteria of some sort. But, in 1963, you had a big clunky machine that expelled bars tasting of food.

There are some lovely scenes with Ian and Barbara keeping up the continuity. They discuss whether the Doctor can get them home and how he can be a jerk. 1960s shows weren't always big on the continuity. (Unless you had a show that became semi-serialized at times like *The Beverly Hillbillies*.) It's nice to see it continuing here. It's also nice to see Ian and Barbara getting closer. Like Sarah Jane, I googled "The Chestertons." More about that later.

The initial spectacle of the Dalek City is the first big special effect of the show. It is primitive but it is gorgeous. The actors on the right side of the screen. The Dalek City model on the left. You can see why The Doctor gets so excited. I'd want to go there too. And isn't that tree branch over the top left of the screen a fantastic touch? It adds a Sleepy Hollow feel to the city below. The wonderful pulsating music that plays and the Doctor's fun field glasses only add to the excitement. And that shot of the city, shrouded in mist, with the pulsating music really rewards anyone who spent the cave dweller episodes thinking "This isn't that imaginative."

Overall, it's kind of one of my favorite episodes. When you realize that epic revelations are being set aside for future episodes and this one is about exploring, it becomes delightful. The Doctor scheming. Barbara and Ian worrying. A hand touching Susan's shoulder. (Mike Ferguson, what are you doing?) The contrast between the city and the jungle. The mystery behind it all. And then the slow realization that the city is not dead. That something is watching them. That something is closing off Barbara from everyone else. That something is very much alive… and it is not nice.

Note: This episode was shot twice. There was an issue with talkback from around the studio seeping into the episode's sound. So, we are watching the second version of it, like the first episode.

The Survivors

Episode 6: (December 28, 1963) The Doctor meets The Daleks for the first time. But the Doctor is a bit too sick to really enjoy it.

Cliffhanger: Susan has the anti-radiation drugs from the TARDIS. She knows something is out there, in the jungle. Bravely she steps out of the TARDIS…

The Daleks are here! Hooray! *Doctor Who* would never be the same. By the end of this serial, the show had gone from being one that was due to be cancelled after 13 episodes to something that could run forever. Terry Nation's script here, like almost all his scripts, is good, fun Saturday morning serial style adventure. The crew is dying of radiation sickness. The Daleks, the beings inside this moving mechanism with the eye stalk and the ray gun and the plunger and the bumps, only care about the travelers if the travelers can assist them in some way. The story of Skaro's (the planet) history is told. A neutron war 500 years ago between the Daleks and the Thals. The Daleks mutated and lived in their city. The Thals... well, the Daleks describe them as horrible mutations, but we don't see them. The Daleks and The Doctor have their first conversation. But, as mentioned, he has been hit hard by radiation sickness and is not at his best.

The futuristic city is such a major change from the dirty caves of the previous serial. When you see the Daleks and the way they're shaped, suddenly the doorways and a lot of other bits of architecture make sense. The city is built specifically for them to survive in. Whether or not it's better than the cave is tough to say. The cave was obviously a set, but it looked like a cave. The futuristic city interior looks futuristic enough but there are some joins and seams visible that cry out "Check out this set!" In the end, it doesn't bother me because, finally, we have that imaginative/ creative burst that was promised back in the first episode. We have these strange creatures with flashing lights on their domed heads speaking in monotone. They shoot Ian in the legs when he tries to run away. Apart from that, they just seem like scientific observers. Watching these strange beings that may or not be Thals.

After spending a good portion of their last story captured, the addition of the radiation sickness is a nice touch. It ups the ante here. It isn't just sitting around and waiting. The travelers need something to happen. (When they realize that the box left outside the TARDIS was the drugs they need, they metaphorically kick each other in the pants.) Ian and Susan are doing OK. The Doctor and Barbara are not. They need to get out and get cured. Fast.

Susan makes a mad dash through the jungle at the end. Much like the mad dash in "The Forest of Fear", it's a mix of her running through the set, people scrapping branches against her face in close-up and a great POV of the camera moving through the jungle model. Susan is a teenager. I understand that. But boy she whimpers and screams a lot. One would have thought she might have encountered things like this before, travelling with The Doctor and all. These sorts of adventures do seem to be part of the Doctor's MO. Maybe they just went to nice places before this?

I can write all I want. This episode is so especially important because it introduces the Daleks. Is it a great episode? No. But, it is darn good, and it keeps the viewer wanting more, which is exactly what it should do. It even keeps the viewer hanging on at the beginning with a little trick that *Dallas* did in 1980. Remember when J.R. got shot? It was the big cliffhanger through the Summer of 1980. A writer's strike delayed the next season beginning. And then, when it did begin, it took four (I believe) episodes before we learned Who Done It? People had to keep tuning in. In this episode of *Doctor Who*, it's almost 5 minutes before the Daleks appear. The Doctor and Ian are knee deep in an argument. I almost forgot that we were waiting for the Dalek arrival. And then it happens... and it all changed.

Note: This episode was taped on November 22, 1963. The cast and crew found out about the assassination of JFK right before shooting began.

The Escape

Directed by Richard Martin

Episode 7: (January 4, 1964) We meet the Thals. They're better looking than the Daleks. But they are a bit too Caveman Chatty for my tastes.

Cliffhangers: The travelers escape with Ian hidden inside a Dalek. We see the cloak that they put the Dalek mutant under. Slowly, a claw pokes its way out.

There are going to be some episodes where I don't have as much to say as I do about others. This could be one of them. Susan meets Alydon, a Thal. We spend several scenes with the Thals. Susan has the first big scene with a Dalek. The travelers plot their escape from the cell. That's about it. It's the first directed by Richard Martin and he handles himself well here. The larger scale the episodes got, the more they seemed to get away from him. But this one is genuinely sharply done.

The Doctor has their first scene with the Daleks. But Susan gets the first scene with them. She seems perfectly at home amongst the Daleks. I'd mentioned previously that she screams and laughs nervously a lot. This sort of thing is the sort of thing she's more used to from the past. Maybe she was the negotiator. The Doctor was the genius who could figure out the problems. But Susan was the one that went in and figured out how to work with people, The Squirrel Girl of her time.

The scenes with the Thals, apart from Susan meeting Alydon, do resemble the cave dweller scenes. But whereas the cavemen were all about survival and violence, the Thals are pacifists. They've been wandering across Skaro for four years looking for food, hoping for rain. There's some interpersonal stuff that goes on. It's superficial, like a lot of Terry Nation's characterizations of secondary characters. The scenes aren't terribly interesting. But they advance that portion of the story. They become even less interesting alongside the Daleks (who use the word "exterminate" for the first time) and the travelers. But at least their costumes are amusing enough to keep you wondering why they're wearing them.

The best parts in the episode, apart from Susan's scene with the Thal and the Daleks, are watching the TARDIS crew using their intelligence and reasoning to figure out how to catch a Dalek. It's a less frenetic version of the scene in 10 Downing Street in "World War Three" when the Ninth Doctor, Rose and Harriet Jones, MP are trying to figure out what makes the Slitheen tick. And it's fun to watch. It's a Terry Nation thing and it comes up aces for the gang when they catch a Dalek.

This leads to the removal of the Dalek Being from its machine. There is a great moment in Terry Nation's original script where we learn that the Daleks *think* they are still humanoid. If you've seen 21st Century *Doctor Who*, you know they are anything but. I like the concept that this race is just an inch away from absolute, complete insanity. "Yes, we look human. All humans have these weird claws and tentacles. Don't you?" It's a great cliffhanger for, I think, quite a good episode. If the focus had stayed specifically on the travelers rather than time spent with Thals, it might have been the best one yet.

The Ambush

Directed by Christopher Barry

Episode 8: (January 11, 1964) The TARDIS crew can't stop the Dalek's ambush of the Thals. But they do escape the Dalek City. One wishes they'd remembered to bring the fluid link with them.

Cliffhangers: The fluid link is back in the city. The TARDIS cannot travel without it. So, the travelers must go back in, maybe they can get the Thals to help them.

Terry Nation's titles are being particularly literal here. This is about an ambush and Ian trying to stop it. Spoiler: he fails. There is some great escape chicanery in the limited hall and lift sets in the first half. Even though they're only in a couple of very similar rooms there is a real excitement to the scenes here. Once the ambush is over, yes, the pacing drops. It becomes a bit of a Love-In hanging out with Thals and chatting. But it's setting up the second half of the serial.

By this point, the TARDIS crew are working very well as a team together. From the Doctor forcing open the door to Susan's diversion to keep the real Dalek from being suspicious. Yes, they're still ticked at the Doctor for getting them into this mess, but they work well together. The looks on their faces when they realize that they must go back in the Dalek city are priceless and should maybe have a horn going "bwah bwah!!!"

This really does feel like the end of the first half of the story with a calm interlude before the second half commences. The first three-and-a-half episodes, although they spend a large chunk of it imprisoned, have had a real feeling of excitement to them. A real feeling that we really don't know what is going to happen next. Granted, most things ended up resolved with serial-style adventure tropes but it's more exciting than the stuff with the Tribe of Gum. And the Dalek city really comes across as being a vast place, especially with all the travel in the lift. There is also something very nice about the moment when they finally look out a window and see daylight.

The one slight drawback, which really isn't a drawback, is that that closing scene with the Thals, until the reveal of the missing fluid link, feels like an extended ending. We know the Daleks are jerks. We know they won't help. The Thals know they must carry on. The TARDIS crew is back with The Ship and the Daleks can go fly a kite. After watching the four episodes here in close succession, the scenes in the jungle made me kind of sleepy. I expected the credits to roll and a new adventure to begin. That is technically what happens but it's all a part of the same adventure.

In the early days of the show, this will be what keeps the travelers within the adventures. It's not that they want to be there or that they feel the need to stay and fight. It's some extenuating circumstance. It's something that is out of their control. Whether they're captured or something is lost, or they are separated from the TARDIS, the early crew were unwitting adventurers, but they always dove right into the fray when they were needed. We'll track the moment when those attitudes change. For now, suffice it to say, this adventure isn't over. We've got to get that fluid link.

The Expedition

Directed by Christopher Barry

Episode 9: (January 18, 1965) The TARDIS crew must convince the pacifist Thals to help them break into the Dalek City to get their fluid link back. The Daleks discover that they need radioactivity to survive and come up with a not very nice plan.

Cliffhanger: Thal Elyon is about to get pulled into the Lake of Mutations by some sort of lake mutation.

I have probably said this on more than one occasion, but I like a good swamp. Hanging out in them, looking at them, whatever. I like a swamp. In this episode, we have the Lake of Mutations. Not a swamp but darn near close enough. My favorite moment of the episode happens at the lake. That involves Ian splashing his face with water by the edge of the lake and a strange thing appearing in the water. It's sort of a flat octopus that rises out of the water. It's covered with gunge, and it has two glowing eyes, almost like light bulbs. Is it fake looking? Sure. Do I believe that it is 100% real? Definitely. Why couldn't a mutation in a lake look like a fake monster of some sort? (Remember when we learned about the Daleks' genesis, we found out that Davros experimented a lot and loved making giant clams.) I only wish the monster at the end of the episode, that goes after Elyon, was visible. And not just a whirlwind.

Well, that's my favorite moment in the episode. Now that the crew is away from the Daleks, the episode spends its time jumping back and forth between the two groups. The Daleks come to the revelation about the radiation. The Thals spend a lot of time figuring out if it's worth fighting (and possibly losing their lives) to help the Doctor and his gang. (The promise of all the food the Daleks have stored is an incentive.) There is a long discussion between the crew (with Susan and Ian on one side and The Doctor and Barbara on the other) about whether the Thals should fight for them. For much of it, The Doctor and Barbara seem oblivious to the fact that they want the Thals to fight and die for them and their fluid link. (Until the script has them remember it.) Ian seems to be against it until he starts treating the Thals belligerently to get them to fight.

I can't say I've always been enamored by these scenes. There's something about Ian's solution that strikes me as distasteful even if it's not real. He grabs Dyoni, the young, virginal blonde female, and says he's taking her to the Daleks. That makes Alydon, her love, punch Ian out. (I just recently watched *The Virgin Spring* and that movie sprung to mind right here.) Ian basically wanders around the Thals saying "I'm doing this! I'm taking her to the Daleks!" Until he gets punched. I guess we can thank Heaven for small favors that the scene didn't go on longer. "What about this rock? Do you all love this pair of sandals? Woe betides the man who stops me from taking a packet of your hot cocoa!" The whole sequence goes on too long and feels like a foregone conclusion. We know that the Thals are going to help. I wish Terry Nation had come up with a better batch of scenes here. Because it is hilariously selfish of the TARDIS crew to ask the Thals to do this. (Even with the possible promise of food.) It never sits well with me and I'm always glad when I see monsters in lakes. Those I can understand!

And, if the Thals are so close to starvation after 4 years of wondering, how come they all look so great. At least, some of the cavemen looked desperate. Susan calls Alydon "Perfect" when she first sees him. That's not what you call the member of an emaciated, starving group of people. I get the feeling that they'll do just fine without the TARDIS crew being around. But that's not what happens. I'm probably complaining to much. Part of it is that this sort of philosophy is something the show really wouldn't follow as time went along. Everyone is still finding their feet.

Luckily, it's not a slow episode. The cutting from the Daleks to the Thal encampment keeps things moving, even when the discourse is not that grand. And there's always those darn mutations in the lake. I wish the next episode was called "The Lake" and was about them encountering monsters in it. Instead, it's called "The Ordeal" and I hope you like caves and people jumping across gaps. If you do, this next episode will be your favorite.

The Ordeal

Directed by Richard Martin

Episode 10: (January 25, 1964) The Daleks have a plan. You won't like it. The Thal expedition goes into some caves. Jumping is involved.

Cliffhanger: Antodus is hanging from the rope and threatening to drag Ian into the crevasse with him.

Just a quick note: At this point, the show was pulling in more than 10 million viewers per episode. It's a hit! It's a hit!

Let's not diddle about. We've got spelunking today. A lot of spelunking. This is a semi-infamous episode in the annals of *Doctor Who*. The show has been known at times for using padding. That is, scenes (visual or verbal) that don't really push forward the story. They keep wheels spinning and use up time. They're there to fill out an episode. This episode has probably one of the best known (I call it "beloved") samples of padding ever: The Thals, Barbara and Ian jumping the crevasse. The episode is a little over 26 minutes long. It should be about two minutes shorter. For some reason, nearly half the episode is devoted to examining, exploring and leaping across (one by one) a big hole deep in the caves.

To pull back to the bigger picture, the episode does spend its time (in the first half) cutting between The Doctor, Susan and the Thals trying to bother the Daleks surveillance equipment with The Daleks preparing to bombard the planet with radiation while our gang messes about in the cave. (In the second half, it's all cave jumping except for a minute-and-a-half to two-minute-long scene with the Doctor and Susan captured by Daleks.) The episode is trying to keep things moving along. Unfortunately, the stuff the Doctor is doing isn't terribly interesting. His ego is really getting in the way. (And does he destroy the TARDIS key at one point? How are they getting back in The Ship?) The stuff in the cave is...

Critics before me have commented on the sequence in the cave. *About Time* calls it filler beyond belief. Other places have pointed at that sequence as being one where stuff happens, but the story does not advance an inch. They examine the drop. Ian jumps to a ledge on the other side. The others jump across and join him one by one. (There is another cave around the edge that they go into.) Then, Antodus jumps, and all hell breaks loose. Is it filler? Yes. I think it is. Several minutes could have been trimmed and wouldn't have bothered the overall running time of the episode. We don't need to see each person jump across. We could cut from the first jump to the last jump and get the point. With the Daleks so close to bombarding the planet, they need to move a little quicker than this. Personally, though, I like it. I'm convinced by the cave set. There are some very good angles in and around the rocks that must have been tricky to get. And, after a time, I just go with it. If the episode wants to give me 12 minutes of this, I will enjoy it. But, then I, sometimes, enjoy odd things. I can completely understand anyone's dislike for it.

It's not helped by the character of Antodus. He is Ganatus' brother. He is marked earlier as being a coward. And yes, he sure is. But not an endearing coward. Not a funny coward with a yellow streak down his back. But a whiny, self-pitying coward that you want to knee in the groin. When he tells his brother that the two of them should turn back because the others are dead anyway, he loses all sympathy that we had for him. Granted, his dead, sad eyes staring down the cliff as Ian tries to get him the rope works well. You know things are going to go poorly. But all I can ask is: Why are you here? (There is a slight implication that his brother made him come but Antodus is a grown Thal.) You should have stayed behind. This sequence is long enough without your complaining.

The Rescue

Directed by Richard Martin

Episode 11: (February 1, 1964) The final confrontation between the Daleks, the Doctor and the Thals. For now.

Cliffhanger: After leaving Skaro, there is some kind of odd explosion within The Ship. The travelers are knocked unconscious.

Doctor Who always seemed to have problems ending stories with a bang and structuring long stories well. The first four episodes of this story (we like to call it "The Daleks") build nicely. But, once the fifth episode begins everyone seems a little lost. Episode 6 is fun (although some might call it an ordeal) but is way too long. (Literally.) It spends much of its time advancing the main portion of the cast about 15 to 20 feet in a Cave. In contrast, this episode underruns, it's barely 22 and a half minutes long. It should be about two minutes longer. And it moves very, very quickly. Until it slows down for about three minutes of "We can't get through these doors!" shenanigans. Plus, there's an extra-long coda, which the show didn't always indulge in. It makes for a lopsided closing pair of episodes. The one with the actual conclusion of the story is too short. The one without much of anything in it is too long. This will happen again.

Is it a good finale? Yeah, it's pretty good. There are a couple of odd moments. Ian, Barbara and their gang spend 2 ½ days trying to sneak in the back. Yet, as they're approaching the main Dalek control room, they run into the Thals who just walked in the front door. It reminds me of the cop in the movie *The Stepfather* who spends the whole movie hunting down the killer. Then, at the very end, he finds the killer and is instantly killed by him. Everyone thinks "What was the point of all that then?" The reuniting of the Thals here echoes that point.

Richard Martin had the great idea to have a constant loudspeaker countdown going during the climax. The nuclear reactor is going to poison the atmosphere of the planet when we reach zero. The steady Dalek voice counting down is nicely incorporated into the final brawl. What doesn't quite work in the climax is something they handled better in "The Firemaker." In that, the final fight between Kal and Za and the final run through the woods is shot on film in a film studio. By doing that, they can use more angles, get more varied shots and make things more exciting. Because things are done shot by shot. In the studio, when they're basically shooting live, everything is happening live. The brawl in this episode is well done but has a few awkward moments. (The main one being when Susan, The Doctor and a couple other people clearly get a late cue. They're standing still when the camera cuts to them and then they start running.) The awkward moments come from assorted people, Daleks, lots of odd movement and the huge awkward cameras shooting everything. If the scene had been shot on film, it would have been more exciting.

And the end would have made sense. The countdown suddenly stops. One of the Thals rolls a Dalek into a machine. It explodes and then the Daleks die. So, that machine was their power source. You'd think it wouldn't have been that easy to stop them. I would have preferred a giant red On Off switch. It would have given me something to look at like a finish line in a race. As it is, we see a few minutes of people and Daleks scrambling around on the set… and then it ends. The good guys won! Hooray! I'm pretty darn certain they couldn't have done it any better at that time. I don't dislike it. It is well done. It's just awkward and a bit inconclusive. However, it is true. The Good Guys won! So, although the climax could have been more epic, it closes out the story well enough.

The TARDIS crew leave the Thals to revive Skaro. The Doctor mentions that he was a pioneer on his own planet. Barbara and Ganatus kiss. (Oh, Antodus falls down that cliff, whining all the way.) Their next adventure begins. So, many stories end with the Doctor immediately leaving or running away at the end, that it's nice to see a few minutes of peace and pause before the next adventure begins. The next adventure that involves an explosion in the TARDIS! And even though they just left Skaro, Susan now has a skirt on! How did she do that?

THE EDGE OF DESTRUCTION

The Edge of Destruction

Written by David Whitaker

Directed by Richard Martin

Episode 12: (February 8, 1964) After the explosion, the TARDIS crew begins acting very weird. Becoming paranoid and violent. Has something got into the ship?

Cliffhanger: As the Doctor works at the console, a pair of hands wrap around his neck.

This is the first time the show's script editor will have to rush in at the last minute to write a stopgap story. It will happen a lot in the future. Here, David Whitaker, allowed only the TARDIS sets and the TARDIS crew concocts a strange, mysterious character piece. A character piece that has the characters not acting like their characters about half the time. But that's part of the fun.

I've always had a very soft spot for this story. Two things in pop culture that I always will walk a long mile for: double albums and bottle episodes. They're sort of the opposite thing, but it doesn't matter. One is about expansive creativity and stretching beyond the point where you normally go. The other is about limiting your resources and coming up with something imaginative. Back then, they weren't called "bottle" episodes. Something like "Edge of Destruction" and its companion would simply be the "very cheap" episode. But, whenever you must do very cheap on purpose, you bring in your best writers. David Whitaker is a hell of a writer.

From the opening moments, this episode feels weird. There is no TARDIS hum during the opening moments. Susan stumbles around in some continuity-confusing clothes and seems concussed. Barbara isn't much better. Ian sounds like a child, speaking slowly and deliberately. The Doctor has a big gash on his head, which they fix with some neat bandages. Most of the first half of the episode is a deliberately paced (but not slow) return to some sort of normalcy after the explosion.

The Doctor and Barbara, honestly, don't seem that far off from their regular characters. Ian and Susan do, though. Susan's infamous scenes with the scissors (jabbing them into the bed as she screams with each stab) brought the show grief. (Never use something a child can find around the house and imitate.) But that scene is well-played and (odd for TARDIS scenes back then) well-lit. The long shadows of Susan and the scissors on the wall accentuate the danger and the dementia that have overtaken the ship. (In fact, at one point after discussion of possibly something else on the ship, Susan rushes into the control room and you can see the shadows of what look like two people on the wall for a moment. Evil within the ship or our own active imaginations?)

In the second half, the TARDIS starts throwing out odd clues. Clues about what? Who knows? Melting clocks. Bits of the TARDIS console that give people pains in the neck. And odd images of a universe exploding on the scanner. When the TARDIS became a woman, it could be tough enough to gauge what she was saying and what she was up to. It's a lot less easy when she's simply The Ship. Everyone seems bewildered and/or frightened by what's happening around them.

This leads to the best scene in the episode: Barbara yelling at the Doctor. Well, the old jerk deserves it. Everything that happened in "The Daleks" was because of his chicanery with the fluid link. His unwillingness to help them while they went up against The Tribe of Gum may have proved correct in some ways but showed him up as being a jerk. And he is a jerk in this episode. Sarcastic towards the schoolteachers at first and then downright nasty when he accuses them of causing the troubles. Even the normally uxorious Susan seems taken aback by his accusations. The explosion does make them act contrary to what we've seen in the past. But that makes the first half so odd and eerie. Then, when their characters begin to come back into place, we see the distrust and it isn't pleasant. There is an implication that the Doctor may have drugged Ian and Bárbara so he can get work done. Regardless, he's getting strangled at the end. So, somebody is awake. Unless they're floating phantom hands.

The Brink of Disaster

Directed by Frank Cox

Episode 13: (February 15, 1964) If there had been no Daleks, this would have been the last episode of *Doctor Who*. Think on that for a bit. (But don't stop reading.) The TARDIS crew learn why The Ship is acting so weird. But it might be too late to do anything about it.

Cliffhanger: Somewhere in the snow, Barbara and Susan find a giant footprint.

The episode begins with more distrust, more fear. Ian seems to definitively be strangling the Doctor. He's still a little bit concussed. The Doctor decides to put Ian and Barbara off the Ship. Luckily, leveler heads prevail, and the group begins figuring out the clues that the TARDIS has left them. One of my favorite moments as a child watching this was when the Doctor wished they had a clue. After a pause, Barbara puts forward the theory that they've been given nothing but clues... by the TARDIS. The Doctor does say that it is a machine, and it is not living. We know that is not true now. But this is the "First" Doctor. Heck, he doesn't seem to have a second heart in the previous episode.

Some people think the TARDIS's complicated system of clues is a bit much. They think it's Whitaker over-complicating everything. But he is meant to be showing the way a semi-sentient machine would work on a budget of nothing. So, it doesn't bother me. I like the pictures, the clocks, the doors opening again and again and so on and so forth down the line. When Barbara, with the Doctor, explains what is happening, it's fun to watch. It all comes down to that Fast Return Switch.

Yes, the Fast Return Switch has "FAST RETURN" written above it in black marker of some sort. Well, that's so the Doctor can always remember where it is. OK, it does look odd. But, as a kid, I don't remember seeing that and thinking "Oh, that's foolish." I remember thinking "Oh, there's the Fast Return Switch!" I like the fact that such a small thing (a spring out of place) is plummeting the Ship back towards the Big Bang. That's a fun concept. And it works completely in the confines of the TARDIS itself. Maybe I'm easily convinced but this story convinces me easily.

The Doctor is all over the place in this one. Nasty at the start. Then apologetic when he realizes that something else (not schoolteacher-related) is going on. He goes kind of hysterical during his big speech. The light is shining down on him and the console. William Hartnell gives it his all. I think it almost completely works. And then, of course, there is the scene with Barbara. He plays the humbled older intellectual man who is wrong very well. His chat with Barbara is sweet. They're trapped in this space together. Try and get along. By the end of the episode, they've landed in snow. The guys are getting dressed. The gals are frolicking in the snow. And the show has changed slightly. It's not a big shift. It has adjusted the lead character. He will still be irascible and stubborn. But he's a bit more lovable now. A bit less cold. Which is wonderful. Now, if we could only calm some of Susan's hysteria and screaming down.

MARCO POLO

The Roof of The World

Written by John Lucarotti

Directed by Waris Hussein

Episode 14: (February 21, 1964) The TARDIS crew meet Marco Polo! He commandeers the TARDIS as a gift for Kublai Khan. Win some, lose some.

Cliffhanger: Tegana gets very excited about poisoning Marco's water supply. Hey, this guy isn't so nice!

It is 1289 AD. The gang have landed in the Himalayas, way up high in the mountains. They meet the Warlord Tegana (jerk) and Marco Polo (sometimes a jerk) along with their attending entourage. All on their way in a huge caravan to see Kublai Khan at Peking. Several minutes before meeting them all, the TARDIS decides to fall apart. It happens so quickly and so oddly that it feels a bit contrived. They were just in the TARDIS, and everything was fine. Now, as they stand out in the snow, the Doctor keeps going in and out with worse news every time he emerges.

As mentioned earlier, they use the idea of the TARDIS getting separated from them or breaking down to keep everyone in place. This one casually breaks down the TARDIS and then has it separated from the crew by Marco commandeering it. I kept wondering if maybe there was another switch that the Doctor had hit that maybe went awry like the Fast Return Switch. Maybe there's some sort of clue in the fact that everything was crazy, everything was fine, everything fell apart. The serial is an intelligently written one, with a few problems, but this kick starter to get it going is mega-contrived.

It is a very leisurely first episode. Sort of the opposite of "The Dead Planet," which was a constant series of reveals across a strange planet. Once we see Marco Polo several minutes in, we know that we are safe in history. Maybe not a particularly nice part of history but one that is certainly easier to deal with than the land of the cave dwellers. We can see very quickly that Tegana is plotting and that underneath his suave charm, he's a real threat. It is going to be some time before the threat comes out to the forefront. (Trust me.) Learn to enjoy having him around.

I will say the "do something to the TARDIS" thing has stuck with me more than previous viewings of this episode. The TARDIS crew are now travelling with Marco. Not because they want to, but because they've been forced to. Heck, the Doctor breaks into hysterical laughter at one point because he cannot fathom how they're going to get out of this. Well, the stories up to this point do seem to kind of run into one another. So, one might think he's going a bit 'round the bend and needs a vacation.

The episode feels a bit vague. A bit "OK, where are we going now?" Part of that is because this is the first of the Lost Episodes. The episode was destroyed by the BBC. We are listening to the original audio. It has been matched to a visual reconstruction. There are animated reconstructions. Reconstructions that use photos from the shooting of the episode, images of the sets and the actors. (Heck, there are so many images for Marco Polo that one of Loose Cannon's Reconstruction is in color.) Fans (and eventually the BBC) have used the scripts and created images to match the audio. Some have professional BBC-commissioned animation. This one does not. I've always found that there is a bit of a disconnect when watching these recons. They're not quite as "here" as a regular surviving episode. So, my discussions might go occasionally vague. That doesn't mean I don't appreciate the heck out of these things.

The Singing Sands

Episode 15: (February 29, 1964) More adventures with Marco. This time, there's a sandstorm. Then, all their water gourds are drained. It doesn't look good.

Cliffhanger: At the oasis, Tegana pours his water into the desert sand, laughing. (Comedy can be very subjective.)

Did I mention (I know I didn't) that this serial is narrated by Marco Polo as it shows a map detailing their journey across China? It's an interesting touch. It takes the point of view out of the hands of the travelers and puts them in the hands of Marco, a well-known historical figure. (Or at least, we all know the game you play in a pool using his name.) The serial covers a long period of time, it takes some time to travel across a desert. So, having Marco give a little travelogue and update every few minutes is a clever idea. But, at the same time, it takes the story away from the main characters. This will happen in future historical stories (more about that in a moment) but it really happens here. The story becomes Marco Polo's journey where he encountered some strange people. Rather than the Doctor and his companions on an adventure with Marco Polo. Sometimes it works, sometimes it doesn't. It is the sort of a thing a show does when it and its characters are very well established. (*The X-Files* episode "Hungry" is an excellent example.) Here it sometimes feels like it is too soon. We need more time with the main characters.

Especially here where the Doctor, apart from one line, is completely absent from the episode. William Hartnell got sick, and they had to write him out of it. So, he is talked about throughout the episode. He is sulking. He won't eat. He is insulting Marco. But we don't encounter him. Frankly, all the character development we got from the previous episodes kind of gets flushed away here. The Doctor is a stubborn, obstinate old fool again. I was hoping we'd moved past some of this. But, per this episode, we have not. And there's the weird thing here where The Doctor needs to rest in the TARDIS and is going to die. Like when radiation affected him the most. This isn't the Doctor we will know later in the series. Luckily, Susan gets more to do then she has... well, so far.

Susan and Ping-Cho make a charming team. They are fun to watch engaging in shenanigans, even if they wind up in trouble often. When they get lost in the desert and the sands started singing, it was honestly harrowing. Even though, I will mention this many times, we're watching a recon of the whole thing. The audio for that section is crazy. Susan does go hysterical, as she is prone to do. But the whole thing is presented as if it were as alien as the Daleks or the Tribe of Gum. That makes it worth the time. I also love Susan's use of 1963/4 slang. She hasn't really used it before, and it feels like a thing she's acquired simply for this episode, but it works.

Apart from Susan, the travelers don't do much here. The Doctor, apart from a scene, is sulking. Ian hangs out with Marco. Barbara has one great scene with Susan. (Susan says that one day her and her grandfather will stop travelling. It's a lovely moment. I don't think it portends anything specific right there. It simply happens to keep continuity between previous stories. In the over-arcing journey of the show, it does seem to foreshadow a future visit to somewhere...) Barbara's other main scene is being hysterical during the sandstorm, which is probably the way I would have acted. It does seem like they didn't have Susan there, so they'd have the other leading lady act hysterical.

There is a palpable charm to this episode. Just the thrill of travelling in adverse conditions. Coming up against problems. Dealing with them and carrying on. It's a bit pedantic but quite delightful. It's not as much fun as the best of "The Daleks" but it keeps you interested and keeps you looking ahead. Yes, it is a bit long. Yes, it is audio only. So far, it's fascinating.

Five Hundred Eyes

Episode 16: (March 7, 1964) The gang takes a trip to the Cave of Five Hundred Eyes. Trouble ensues.

Cliffhanger: Eyes in one of the caves paintings move and Susan screams. And screams. And screams.

The original remit of *Doctor Who* was that it should be semi-educational. Sydney Newman was big on that. The gang should travel the cosmos and learn and teach. This episode is probably the biggest example of that with two segments (one brief, one longer) devoted to teaching the kids. The first segment regards condensation. Knowing what we know about the TARDIS today this seems impossible, but condensation forms on the walls of the TARDIS. The water is collected to drink. It is explained to us. Then there is the hashish segment of the episode. Ping-Cho has a presentation telling a story. We learn that that word "hashish" is now assassin. My favorite teaching moment is: Ian saying to Susan "Do you know that that word is still used in English?" "Really?" "Assassin." See! We all learned. The ratings were pretty darn high for this story. I would have thought teaching kids on a Saturday evening would have been troublesome. (*In Search Of* never tried to do that. Well, properly.) But the ratings don't reflect that.

Again, the TARDIS crew seem very secondary to everything going on. Even with the condensation scene and Barbara strolling through the Cave of Five Hundred Eyes, this still feels like Marco's show. Which, I guess, is fine. Barbara has her doubts about Tegana. Ian's response is sort of "What?! No?" to her. To me, Tegana is doing everything but twirling his mustache to show he's a bad guy. Marco not seeing it, I get that. Probably a little cognitive dissonance going on there. But the TARDIS crew not seeing it feels not quite right. Lucarotti's scripts are very good. They're just not quite grasping how to bring the TARDIS crew into it. He's more interested in the historical characters and the teaching.

Something I haven't brought up is how they treat the Asian characters here. Ping-Cho is handled well. Zienia Merton does an excellent job. Tegana is clearly not Asian but the great weight and self-importance he seems to have carry him trough. (Again, there is no existing footage from this episode. I am going off photos. For all I know, Tegana's performance could be high camp.) This episode though does have one guy who I feel like we've been given the wrong recon image of. The bandit who meets Tegana in the cave looks as Asian as I do, and my family came over to the U.S. from Poland in the 1950s. Have you seen his picture? He looks like he'd be playing Electric Piano in a Southern Rock band from the 1970s. That can't be the way he really looked. Can it? What about the paintings on the walls of the Cave? We see them in color in the recon. Hopefully in black and white, they looked better. They look like an 8th grader's drawing for a Marco Polo-related Role-Playing Game Monster Manual. I quite love them.

The story continues to be a good one. But it's becoming a bit repetitive in its structure. It could use a little more pizzaz. Because it really is starting to feel like nothing big is going to happen until we reach the climax. It feels a bit like we're biding time. It's fun... We're biding time.

Lastly, I'd like to point out Marco's rages. He has a couple of them in this episode. "WHAT ARE YOU DOING?" "YOU LIED TO ME!" and so on. He's a man who keeps his calm. He'd have to be doing all that he does. You can tell by how loud he yells when something doesn't go his way how on the edge he is. The guy wants to go home.

The Wall of Lies

Episode 17: (March 14, 1964) They hunt for Barbara in the cave. Assassins lurk...

Cliffhanger: Ian goes to speak to the guard but finds he's been murdered.

I just thought of something. These past 24 episodes must have really been something for Ian and Barbara. Not just the travelling in time. Not just being so far from home. Not just all the other races and everything they've encountered. But all the killing. The caveman life is about survival. You're alive today. You might be dead tomorrow. Being killed is something that happens as often as you have dinner. The Daleks would kill them before they'd even care to find out who they are. All these beings out in the universe that would kill let alone look at you must be something that you can get used to but must always stick with you. "I explored the universe. And all it did was try to kill me over and over." Ian and Barbara were schoolteachers. What's the worst that might have happened to them in a day? A couple of kids argue. Someone drops their lunch tray. I honestly can't think of what might have been difficult for them at that time. (In that realm, of course. I'm sure Barbara had to deal with sexist horse dung daily.)

Look at this episode. They save Barbara from being killed by a Mongol warrior who rolled dice with his friends to decide who would take her life. They save her in the nick of time. And Marco kills the Mongol. In front of everyone. To me, that would be something hard to accept. I used to hate when I was in school and someone in class didn't like me. Imagine a world where everyone pretty much hated you and wanted you dead. That's where Ian and Barbara are. The Doctor seems to treat it as par for the course. In this episode, he calls Polo a savage, which seems very inappropriate since Marco holds all the cards. But The Doctor does it. Susan doesn't seem to be very adept at this kind of thing either. One feels like she probably should be though. It's Ian and Barbara I worry about most. I hope they're going to be OK.

Aside from that, this is quite a good episode. Tegana is a bad guy. We know that. Well, he's a bad guy in the world of Marco Polo. In the world of the Doctor, Ian, Barbara and Susan, he's no worse than Marco. Marco will not let the TARDIS go. Tegana simply wants to kill. Which is worse? Who knows? This episode has a great scene where the Doctor is spotted leaving the TARDIS and Marco goes ape. The TARDIS crew are now the enemies and Tegana is a stronger ally than ever. (It doesn't help the TARDIS crew's case when Marco asks Ian what he would do in his place. Ian waffles the answer.) I find it entertaining that Marco complains in his narration about the TARDIS crew giving him trouble. He took the TARDIS from them. He took their home from them. You can bet your life I'd respond in the same way if I was The Doctor et al. To act like he's done them some sort of favor is ludicrous. But, under the influence of the Khan and Tegana, he seems convinced of this.

The story is falling (or has already fallen) into a formula that I will discuss in the next review. So far, it's keeping itself moving. The TARDIS crew comes a bit more to the forefront in this episode than previously. This simply isn't one of those historical serials where they will take too much control of the narrative. It's basically them trying to get away. Heck, check the gang's chat in mid-episode where the Doctor declares that the TARDIS is almost fixed, and they can leave. All of them are very, very excited to leave Marco Polo. As "Marco Polo" is the unofficial name of this serial, the viewer can make their own call as to what this means in context.

Rider From Shang-Tu

Episode 18: (March 24, 1964) The caravan repels some thieves. Then, it rests at a waystation run by a gentleman named Wang-Lo. The TARDIS crew almost escapes.

Cliffhanger: Susan is grabbed by Tegana on her way to the TARDIS.

This episode has a scene in it that could only appear in a story like this. A story that ebbs and flows. A story that builds to the climactic moments, such as the bandits attacking the caravan, and then calms down and lets everyone have a few minutes to themselves at Wang Lo's waystation. It's the scene with the Koi in the pond. Susan and Ping-Cho watch them. One by one, they compare the fish to people they are travelling with. It's a scene that I feel would have been quite lovely in its original form. In the reconstruction, it still works, even if it isn't as strong. The joy of it is that it doesn't have anything to do with the story. There isn't going to be a sequence later where the fish become important. It's just a fun scene between two young women from very different backgrounds sharing a laugh. I think, more so than the design and costumes (which we really can't fully appreciate anymore) or the story itself, this is why "Marco Polo" is still beloved. Because it can encompass a wealth of dramatics within itself.

I had mentioned Terry Nation's apparent love of Saturday Afternoon serials. (It will come up again shortly.) The thrill of the capture and escape and the Perils of Pauline (or the Doctor and his goof troop). This serial is structured more like a 1930s/ 1940s/ 1950s serial than "The Daleks." In those serials, there would be a general setup in the first chapter. Then, we would get variations of that until the end. An episode would begin with a big cliffhanger, resolve itself and then set up the next big thing leading to the next cliffhanger. (I would recommend *Daredevils of the Red Circle* for an almost perfect example of this. It's on Blu-Ray and it is so, so good.) "Marco Polo" is set up exactly in this fashion. The previous episode ended with the discovery of the dead guard and bandits on the way. This one begins by repelling the bandits (using bamboo, suggested by Ian and not The Doctor) and then gets to the waystation. Then, the travelers trying to fully escape... This serial is the most serial-like of all the serials and what we talk about when we talk about serials.

Tegana's machinations may be becoming repetitive by this point, but the serial keeps up enough interesting moments. The rider from Shang-Tu feels like an educational moment. But a very specific moment. He has travelled 300 miles on horseback over 24 hours. Changing horses every 3 miles (apx. 1 league). It's an interesting scene. But, like the koi, not essential to the plot, which kind of makes it more interesting. In this episode, the TARDIS crew comes a bit more to the forefront. Ian and the Doctor have some great lines at the opening. Their scene where Marco asks if they plan on escaping again and they don't respond is great. The closing scene feels like *Doctor Who* again, rather than "Marco Polo and the Strange Explorers." I don't mean to sound like I'm belittling this serial. The wonder of the show is that it does all sorts of things. And that's not just travelling to different places. But finding ways to tell stories differently. This is one of those. Lucarotti is using the "long journey" to be expansive. If it's becoming a bit repetitive, well, maybe it is a little too long. Maybe 6 episodes would have sufficed. As mentioned, reconstructions can put us in the driver's seat, but sometimes vision is obscured, which is unfortunate. Luckily for us, we are moving towards the finale.

Mighty Kublai Khan

Episode 19: (March 28, 1964) The caravan meets up with Kublai Khan. Ping-Cho goes missing.

Cliffhanger: Ping-Cho and Ian encounter Tegana. The warlord is not happy.

A great episode. At a point where the repetitive quality of the story has reached its height, the TARDIS crew and everyone else arrives at the court of The Great Khan. (KHAN!!!!) And, in a lovely bit of comedy, the Khan is old and decrepit. He becomes fast friends with The Doctor. After a long horseback ride, Our Hero is old and decrepit too. It's such a lovely twisteroo. A lovely turn in expectations. After 5 ½ episodes of talk about the Khan, when we see he's an old guy with, probably, a bad case of gout, it's a nice switch. It cushions the rest of the episode, which is a little sharper and darker than the previous ones.

The rest of the episode is tense and exciting. Ian looking for Ping-Cho, followed by Tegana, is nicely done. The character of Kuiju, with his monkey, is as sleazy as it gets. When Ian arrives, there is a real sense that a Hero has arrived. But then that cliffhanger hits and the episode freezes solid as the closing credits roll. No one at that time knew that this was portending the final episode. We know though. And it's chilling. Are we finally at the point where Tegana will be exposed? Without Marco there, will anything that happens even matter?

The revelation that the Khan is nearby does boost everything. It brings an added impetus to the episode. Brings an oomph in. The moment where Susan declares that she is glad that Ping-Cho got away portends the next Lucarotti serial "The Aztecs." Arranged marriage is not a huge topic in *Doctor Who* but it certainly came up on occasion. This episode does a nice gear shift and really begins to feel like we are moving towards the end. (The Khan's mention of the Mongol warriors amassing nearby, which is a surprise to Marco, boosts this. A great sense of menace is right on the periphery of this episode.)

I will end this by saying that the scene between Ian and Marco, where Ian tells Marco what the TARDIS is, is superlative. It is a big moment for the show. Telling a well-known character from history what the TARDIS is is big. Marco's response is wonderful. I believe that he believes Ian but since Ian has lied Marco cannot go forward. His closing remark to Ian is so lovely. If he believed Ian, Ian would have the TARDIS key. If Marco felt it was true, his own freedom would not be as important as the freedom of these four people. These four people he met at the top of the mountain several weeks ago and who truly mean nothing to him. (Read Marco's Journals. All the TARDIS crew related material has been redacted.) But he accepts and values them. They reciprocate (maybe The Doctor doesn't) but here must be the point where the paths spread out. Away from one another. As beloved as Marco might be, the travelers need to do what they need to do to go free.

Assassin At Peking

Episode 20: (April 4, 1964) Everyone arrives at Peking. The story ends but goes on.

Cliffhanger: The Ship escapes Peking and heads off on its next adventure.

Genghis Khan is mentioned by Kublai. Remember that.

The funny thing about a serial is that it goes on and on without an ending in sight until the ending is in sight. Tegana tries to stop the caravan. He fails. The TARDIS crew try to get the ship back. They fail. It happens repeatedly. Until it doesn't happen anymore. Until we reach the end of the story. Then, events begin to matter. Then, an end can be seen just beyond the horizon. Finally, Tegana is up against Kublai Khan. The Mongols are approaching Peking. The Doctor loses the TARIDS in a game of backgammon. Ian is on trial for stealing the TARDIS. Ping-Cho is set to be married. Suddenly, after six episodes, after almost two-and-one-half hours of drama, elements begin to matter. Things that were fluid begin to become concrete. And "Marco Polo" comes to an end.

After all the preceding events, the TARDIS crew has very little to do with it. Yes, they realize that Tegana is going to kill the Khan. It's Marco who saves the day. The travelers get themselves to the point where they can run away. (And even the ending isn't a cliffhanger to another story, it is Marco in his journal wondering where the gang will go next.) Everything seems to be OK in the end. Well, the Mongols are still on the way, but history takes over once the TARDIS leaves the scene.

Despite the main characters doing so little, the episode works. It's an excellent closing episode. Granted, some of that comes from the fact that we can't see it. The climax is a prolonged swordfight between Marco and Tegana. I don't believe it was shot on film like the Kal and Za brawl. So, it wouldn't have been as dynamic. It would have relied on the choreography skills of the two actors. As it stands, I'm convinced. Regardless of that, the whole story finally falling in place around Susan, Barbara, Ian and The Doctor makes for good drama. The Doctor playing backgammon with the Khan is quite funny. Ian and Ping-Cho do well together. Susan has less to do here. Barbara never had much to do. It still works though. The fact that we are at the end of the journey tightens the dramatic strings wonderfully. Lucarotti had us dancing around for the last five -ish episodes. Now, he closes the dramatic doors. Luckily, Our Gang is on the outside.

Overall, this is an excellent serial. As far as we can tell. Other serials can be dragged down a bit by what we see. This one has the definite advantage of invisibility of a sort. All the stills in the recon are helpful and push the story on. Lucaortti's script meanders but then it's meant to. It's about a journey. A long journey. This is the longest real time story of the show until "The Power of Three." (Let's not count "Heaven Sent.") It feels like it takes a lot of time. It has the ebb and flow of life. Moments of importance, moments of feverish behavior, followed by languid moments. Moments of life where we can look around and enjoy the world. Whether you like it or not (whether I like it or not) might be immaterial. There isn't really a *Doctor Who* serial like this before or after. That puts it in a special place. I do wish that the TARDIS crew had been more involved in the overall story. But, overall, I like the story and I think it puts another set of tricks in the narrative storybox of the show. Like Marco, I wonder where they will go next. Unlike Marco, I know.

THE KEYS OF MARINUS

The Sea of Death

Written by Terry Nation

Directed by John Gorrie

Episode 21: (April 11, 1964) The Doctor and friends land on an island where the sand is glass, and the sea is acid. Inside a giant pyramid, they meet a guy named Arbitan. He is the caretaker of the Conscience of Marinus. (More later.) He is under siege by the rubber fetish-y Voord. The travelers are sent around Marinus to find four keys, which will activate the Conscience.

Cliffhanger: Ian, Susan and the Doctor arrive at their first location. Barbara got there before them. They find her travel dial on the ground with blood on it.

Terry Nation is back. This time he's writing in an even more serialized fashion. Specifically, that is what he and script editor David Whitaker concocted. This story would take the Doctor and his friends to assorted locales around a very eclectic planet named Marinus. A planet ruled by a machine that sits on the island. A machine that, frankly, I don't like the sound of one bit, and I'm surprised the Doctor isn't more unhappy about it. A machine that takes away the free will of everyone on the planet. (Is this a joke about TV viewing?) No wonder the Voord decided to take advantage of it.

Anyway, much of this episode is like the wandering around we saw in "The Dead Planet." The crew explore the surface of the island, discovering assorted facts. Including the submersibles that brought the Voord across the acid sea. (With a particularly gruesome moment being when they find a Voord rubber suit inside one of the submersibles and realize that the Voord didn't get out. The acid got in.) Then, they find the pyramid, like the Dalek city, and explore it. With its long-painted hallways and spinning/ sliding doors, it feels a bit like the Dalek city.

Except it's all a little clumsier than what we saw in the previous Nation story. It all feels like it's being done with a little less care. The drawings of the hallways in the Dalek city are cool. Overuse of them makes them obvious but they're still workable. In this episode, they are used for outside halls stretching along the sides of the pyramid. They never stop looking like well-painted attempts to expand the space. Then, that's followed by an array of odd moments and mishaps.

When a Voord first appears, the music goes very dramatic as we see his rubber outfit and flippers. Then, there is the trill of a flute. Suddenly, it seems like we're in an S&M remake of *Peter and The Wolf*. There's a boom mike shadow in one shot. When one of the doors spins, you can see a stagehand doing it. When the Doctor is pulled into a door, the camera spends an inordinate amount of time not cutting to the next shot. So, we can see William Russell's foot enter the frame when it's not supposed to. Then there's that odd two-dimensional Voord cut out falling into a pool of acid. The episode almost becomes comedic when you look for the goofs.

Then, there's the question of What Happened to Susan? In Marco Polo, Susan seemed like a mature young woman, occasionally having some silly fun with Ping-Cho. In this episode, she's constantly screaming and sniveling. Carole Ann Ford mentions it on the DVD commentary. She asks the Director if he had been told to make Susan seem younger. The director has no recollection of that. But, boy, it does seem obvious. I don't think that was a goof though.

We can talk more about The Voord and their leader Yartek when we get to episode six of this story. But I will say that when I was growing up, the question was always: Are those rubber suits meant to be the Voord themselves? Or are they more humanoid looking and these are simply suits? I think the answer is the latter. However, we never see one out of the suit, even when they should be, like in the last episode.

Let the adventure begin! It is one of those strange starts where the Voord are trying to kill everyone and Arbitan isn't very nice. The TARDIS crew seems less annoyed than they should be, and they're really excited about their travel dials. Heck, if they're excited, I am too. Let's follow Barbara to…

The Velvet Web

Episode 22: (April 18, 1964) In the city of Morphoton, everyone is content, and everyone gets everything they desire. But there is a price to pay.

Cliffhanger: Susan lands in the middle of a jungle that seems to be screaming at her.

This episode contains one of my all-time favorite comedy moments in *Doctor Who*. We know that the brains of Morphoton convince people that they are getting whatever they want when they're just being given garbage. The brains basically sap all their will (are they offshoots of the Conscience?) and then the brains use the people as their slaves to do something or other. The Doctor asks for a laboratory. Ian and he are shown inside. Their eyes light up as they look at all the equipment. They are in awe of what has been done. Except we can see that there is no lab. It's a small, white room with a table and a dirty mug on top. The way the Doctor admires the mug always makes me laugh and laugh.

This is pure B-movie plotting all the way. Giant brains with eye stalks using their superior mental power to subjugate the smaller brained people. Making them think they have everything they want when they have nothing. The thing that makes it work well here is the time spent on it. In the 1950s or earlier in the 1960s, this would have been a feature film, probably around 70 minutes long. Parsing out the info over a longer stretch of time. If this was an episode of an hour-long show, say *Star Trek* (which wasn't around yet), they would have had to slow things down to get it to meet the running time.

But here, because the episode is just a touch over 25 minutes, the pacing cooks. There are no pauses. (Well, maybe some of the scenes with Barbara and Sabetha in that little room might go on a bit.) The conditioning doesn't work on Barbara. We meet the brains. Barbara hides a bit. Then, Ian takes her to the brains and it's all over. Cramming it into one episode means we don't dwell too much on anything. The elements happen and then we move on. I was always very happy that it was done so quickly. Again, it gives the lie to those who say that the 1960s episodes were paced slowly. This is breakneck B-movie plotting.

Not that there's a lot going on here to get too in-depth into. The scenes that contrast the fantasy sets with the reality sets are nicely done. We see the reality from Barbara's point of view. Then, it cuts to everyone on the opulent fantasy set. Nation doesn't seem interested in why any of this is happening. Just what is happening. And Marinus does seem like an odd place, doesn't it? From that island and the sea of acid to this strange city where everyone is enslaved to a group of large brains. Where is this city in relation to Arbitan's island? The other side of the world? Nearby? We never find out. It's almost like we went to another world when really all we did was go to a slightly different subgenre of science fiction that happens to exist on the same planet.

One more thing: The brains mention the various places to send the TARDIS crew to work. I wonder where the brains get the people they're using from. The implication is that all their own people are enslaved. When one realizes that Altos and Sabetha are both sent by Arbitan, one wonders if the brains just sit around and wait for that dummy Arbitan to send a couple more people their way. If this is the first stop on everyone'd travel dial, then that makes a lot of sense.

One final thing: All the clothes are rags, and the laboratory is a room with a table and a dirty mug, When the TARDIS crew arrives in the city, they eat fruit and truffles. There is poultry of some sort. If everything else is a filthy sham, what are they eating?

The Screaming Jungle

Episode 23: (April 25, 1964) Everyone, but the Doctor, lands in dense jungle surrounding an old building. The key must be in there. But what is that screaming?

Cliffhanger: Suddenly, Ian and Barbara land in a frozen tundra. This won't go well.

On Monday, April 20, 1964, BBC 2 premiered! That meant that there was another channel for *Doctor Who* to go up against when this episode aired. Its ratings, though, seem to indicate that all as well, for the moment.

Also, I love that Ian is still wearing his "Marco Polo" togs throughout. There's a nice mix of wardrobe stuff going on in this story. Not enough to spend paragraphs on but enough to mention. Anyway…

This episode is 100% B-movie serial. More so than the others. The cast, mainly Ian and Barbara, are trapped inside a building being encroached upon by the screaming jungle. By vegetation, by vines. They learn that the scientist who lived within accelerated the growth spurts of plants causing them to envelop the building. The scientist himself is seen, briefly, within the building. He has set up a series of deathtraps to keep people who are after Arbitan's key away. That is super cool. But begs a few questions.

The scientist does expect The Voord, so he has all these death traps set up. But he also says that no one from Arbitan has come to him before. So, how did he know the Voord were on their way? If a friend said, "Here's a key. One of my pals will be by soon to claim it." I'd say, "All right." And wait. Maybe do a little biology on the side. I don't think I'd set up a RAIDERS OF THE LOST ARK-style obstacle course for people to go through. Unless I was a paranoid nut. Maybe Arbitan needs to vet his people better.

Let's imagine that I am waiting for someone to show up to get the key. Why am I experimenting on the growth rate of vegetation in the middle of a jungle? I've already set up death traps. I have nets, bars, spikes and a statue with odd hands and a fake key in it. Why would I accelerate the creepers around me to the point where they kill me? Surely, there must be another hobby I can take up.

None of these questions are answered within this episode so we must go with what we see. And what we see is a cheap but cheerful episode with death traps, a creeping jungle and an odd statue. In the DVD commentary, they discuss the statue. If you haven't seen it, do an online search for it. A huge Indian-style idol with two human arms that move. Why the human arms? They didn't have the budget. Is it goofy? Oh yes. Does it work? Yes, it works just fine.

I love the early moment where Susan and Barbara have a bit of a chat. Altos, Sabetha and Ian have gone into the jungle near to the building. The other two stand outside and have a sweet talk about Ian and how cool he is and, briefly, about life. It's nothing extended. It may be filler. But it's nice. The episode however is at its best when everyone goes away except for Ian and Barbara. That's when it becomes apparent how cool a Wright and Chesterton show would have been. It's obvious from the first moment. They have great chemistry together, dealing with the old guy and his strange ways. Then, as they search for the real key, it becomes a bountiful revelation. These two need more time to be together. It's the *Hart to Hart*, *Remington Steele* couple that we needed from *Doctor Who* that we never thought we got but almost did. I love all the creeping vines, but I love this more. I do hope they don't freeze to death.

The Snows of Terror

Episode 24: (May 2, 1964) Frozen tundra. Ice Warriors. (Not those.) And feverish trappers. Somewhere in there… there's a key.

Cliffhangers: Ian lands in a room with the final key. But things go wrong. Fast.

I will begin with two things: This episode introduces us to Vasor. A big, beefy hairy trapper living in the tundra area of Marinus. (I don't understand this planet at all.) He's a jerk. He puts raw meat into Ian's backpack. He clearly has eyes on Barbara but not in a good way. It won't be until Peri that we encounter a companion (well maybe Jamie) that gets so many anti-amorous looks. Vasor is sleazy. We don't get a lot of truly sleazy characters in the 1960s. Welcome Vasor!

The other thing is Susan. She has a scene where she inches across several huge icicles that are stretched across a chasm. She's heroic and awesome there. Way to go, Susan! But there are some other scenes where… Oh, My Lord!... who asked her to scream that loud? I imagine it was just Carole Ann Ford doing what she was told. But, again, if she's been travelling with The Doctor, her grandfather, for a long time, stuff like this shouldn't be that terrible. Sabetha doesn't scream when the ice warriors come to life. And she spent a good portion of her life in Morphoton with no free will. The production crew needs to decide on Susan's age and go from there.

Besides all that, it's another super fun episode. The great *Discontinuity Guide* says that the problem with this serial is that the settings/ storied aren't developed. I would say "Who cares? Terry Nation sure didn't." These episodes are about arriving in a recognizable setting. (*The Gold Rush* without Chaplin) and having them work through some tropes. This one begins in a cabin with a horny trapper and ends in a cave with ice warriors and a chasm. Bring it on, Mr. Nation! It's OK if you repeat yourself. Just ring some changes.

I think the episode is a joy. Now, this could be because I am one of 1700 people on the planet Earth that loves the cold. So, to me, this episode is a fun jaunt. Wolves? Love 'em! Horny trappers? That's why I bring the cat o' nine tails. Ice warriors guarding ancient keys? I'm ready for it. One thing: Why is this key in such a tremendously elaborate hiding place? Deep in a frozen cave. Across a precarious chasm. Guarded by several "ice warriors." Suspended within a block of ice. Did John Dickson Carr plan this? Arbitan should have requested fewer death related scenarios for the people he sent. Although, per the last episode, Ian, Barbara, Susan, Altos and Sabetha may be the first people to get to this point. So, maybe, Arbitan was overdoing it because he thought no one would ever get there. Maybe he was just having a laugh. Who knows?

This is a great middle of a serial episode. I'm glad this Doctor isn't here because he would have held everything up. It's pure thrills and chills and chasms. I can't find much fault with it. OK. The icicles look like giant Halloween candy corns. And I want to eat them. Are you satisfied?

Also, I know what you're saying "Dan, I flipped a few pages back in your delightful book and… I found a write-up about another Terry Nation story where people go across a chasm." Yes, yes you did. But in "The Ordeal" it was chasm to leap across. Here it a chasm with a bridge but Vasor dismantles the bridge, so they must use large icicles and… Look, it's all from the same realm of cliffhanger serials. Heights. The main characters having to traverse some great heights. Its standard stuff from the moment Harold Lloyd wound up on those girders back in *Never Weaken* in 1923 to now. The heroes rarely ever fall to their deaths. But I'll be darned, it's always fun to watch them up there. Always. Like eating very tasty ice cream, it's never not good. Speaking of that, we're heading over to some courtroom drama now. It's a drier ice cream. An ice cream without anything mixed in. Still tasty.

Sentence Of Death

Episode 25: (May 9, 1964) Ian has killed some guy! The people of Millennius are going to kill him! (Guilty until proven innocent.) But Ian gets the best lawyer in the land: Perry Mason? No, The Doctor who currently thinks he's a lawyer. Let's see how this goes.

Cliffhanger: Susan has been kidnapped by the killer. Susan screams.

All right, the first thing to ask is: What the heck was Arbitan up to? The people in Millennius (a place that the Doctor really wanted to go to) are very possessive of the key. They know someone will come to get the key. Then, when someone shows up to get the key. They act very confused and convict Ian of murder. This society kind of stinks. I appreciate the Doctor wanting to go there. But this version of the Doctor has his on and off moments. The city is an off moment for me.

Did the Conscience hit this city? Throughout this adventure, there's no sign that the Conscience of Marinus has been up to anything. One begins to think that Arbitan was full of garbage. No one seems under control of anything. They all seem to be doing their own thing. Have you seen that gamey map that he shows to the TARDIS gang back in the first episode? I am starting to think that he is a goofball. Maybe Arbitan is some rich weirdo on an island who has his own concept of life. He sent out these keys to people with some sort of reward involved and he's just having fun. In a few seasons, we shall meet the Celestial Toymaker. He is immortal. Notice how lame Arbitan's death was. Could he be playing? Could he be having fun? The history of the show won't help. And I can't help. Think about it. Won't you?

The episode is mainly a Perry Mason-style courtroom drama but with a weird twist. Ian has been found at the scene of a murder. The key is involved. In this evolved society, the courtroom assumes guilty before innocent. The exact opposite of what we think. The courtroom drama becomes odd at that point. Everything we know of in courtroom drama flips slightly. Ian is always guilty. He is never innocent. As much as the Doctor might do, Ian is always losing. In one way, it is a fascinating twist. In another way, it is slightly annoying.

I applaud The Doctor's attempts to win in it. I had felt… maybe mischievously… that having the Doctor gone for two episodes was like having your supervisor on a two-week vacation. I thought I could do my work and rest for a bit. It was nice having Ian and Barbara lead the show. But it is the Doctor's show. He is doing his best in this world that is opposite to the way he works. I feel like a later version of the Doctor might have rejected this, grabbed the key and gone on their way. We are early on. Let's see where it goes. I do love the moment at the end where Susan says she has been kidnapped. We see Barbara's face and the "The Keys of Marinus" as the next episode title. Suddenly, things go worldwide again.

The Keys of Marinus

Episode 26: (May 16, 1964): Ian's trial hangs in the balance. Also, Marinus's fate hangs in the balance.

Cliffhanger: The TARIDS leaves Marinus.

This Millennius seems like a dippy place to me. I don't know that Earth justice is much better but the "guilty until proven innocent" thing seems like a way for them to be just plain lazy. If they catch you and they think you've done something, then you're guilty of that thing according to them. So, if you're not guilty, the people who are guilty can do everything in their power to continue to make you look guilty even if you're not. It happens here. The guard's wife kidnaps Susan and is going to kill her. Barbara and the gang catch her. She confesses and says Ian was her accomplice. That just makes Ian's guilt even worse. But how? She has been working with an accomplice. Susan overheard them. Ian's been under guard the whole time. How could she have talked to Ian? It makes no sense but those goofballs on Millennius are all for that. The Doctor looked forward to going to that place. He can't get out of there fast enough.

Back on Arbitan's island, the Voord have taken over, led by their leader Yartek. And they become even more confusing. If they've taken over the island and are awaiting the gang to return, why are they still in those things we thought were wetsuits? One of them trips over his own flipper so they're not convenient to wear. Yartek pretends to be Arbitan by putting a white hood over his head. But his head is three times the size of Arbitan's head. Also, Yartek refers to the other Voord as his "creatures." Is he just being a jerk and demeaning his fellow Voord? Or are the other wet suited things actual creatures of some sort, like Yartek monster clones? There have been few *Doctor Who* villains that have been as confusing as The Voord. In fact, I think I've just spent way too much time thinking about them.

So, this episode wraps up our adventure. I kind of wish the court intrigue had been more intriguing. For the third time in less than 1 and a half episodes, a character incriminates themselves by saying something out loud that they shouldn't have. That seems to be Terry Nation's only ace up his sleeve. Could you imagine if he had written a real murder mystery? Every ten pages someone would do something like this until the whole thing became so confusing you just set the book down and walked away from it. I do wish we'd gone to more high adventure. The weird legal system makes the whole thing a lost cause until the big twisteroo at the end.

The Conscience blows up with the fake key. The Doctor says it was a rotten machine anyway. He's not wrong. I do wish the show ended with some sort of excitement. It all kinds of fills up the running time and then ends. The best parts of this serial (and there were some fine parts) are long behind us. The pyramid set ends up being as boring as we remembered it and the Voord are awful villains. Oh well, not all the final episodes can be good ones. Maybe there will be a better pyramid in our future?

THE AZTECS

The Temple of Evil

Written by John Lucarotti

Directed by John Crockett

Episode 27: (May 23, 1964) The TARDIS crew land in an Aztec tomb in Mexico around the 15th Century. Barbara is declared to be the reincarnation of the high priest Yetaxa. Everyone else gets to hang out for a bit before the sacrificing begins.

Cliffhanger: Tlotoxl says that he will destroy Barbara. He gives the camera a good hard stare.

John Lucarotti's second serial for *Doctor Who* has much sharper plotting than "Marco Polo." Well, I guess it "actually has plotting" is a better way to describe it. Whereas Polo meandered along until they met the Khan, this episode jumps right out of the chute giving the four leads something to do and moving the stories along. Ian is to be trained as the head warrior. (Although, there's already a head warrior so this could be trouble.) Susan doesn't do much, but she is sent to a seminary. (Sounds like someone may be going on vacation.) The Doctor schmoozes with a lady named Cameca in the Garden of Peace to try and find a way into Yetaxa's temple. And Barbara takes her reincarnated role very seriously.

Lucarotti also gives us two excellent Aztec characters in Autloc and Tlotoxl. One regal and calm. Autloc has a very regal bearing and seems like he'd be an interesting guy to shoot the breeze with. The other, Tlotoxl, is a bit grotesque and always seems mistrustful and scheming. Obviously, we know which side the TARDIS crew needs to keep on with these two. But, at the end of this episode, Barbara (and Susan) is testing them all.

In "The Keys of Marinus," Barbara mentions the Aztecs as she is admiring the construction of Arbitan's pyramid. Now here she is in one of her favorite periods of history. A beautiful city with great traditions that had a basis of human sacrifice at the heart of it. You know right off the bat that Barbara/ Yetaxa isn't going to go for that. It's The Doctor's response that is interesting here and is always the moment that is really remembered.

You cannot rewrite history. Not one line. That's the Doctor's credo in this episode. I also think that was David Whitaker's too. You can't change what's already happened in history. If Barbara tries to stop the sacrifice, it's not going to work and may cause them a lot of problems. Barbara has a good point: Cortez only saw this side of the Aztecs. He believed they were barbarians and he slaughtered them. Maybe if she can stop them from sacrificing that might change something. But, The Doctor knows, try as she might, it's not going to work.

At this point, still very early in the show, this philosophy might still work. It begs the question: Why Earth's history? Why not Skaro's history? Or Marinus's? When Polo had the TARDIS, why didn't the crew just hang around until they got their ship back naturally? Surely that was bound to happen because there is no record of a time travelling blue box at the Khan's palace. Why did they keep trying to get it back? Well, maybe we're still formulating this theory. It certainly doesn't seem to ring true to later *Doctor Who*. At the cliffhanger, things certainly don't go well for Barbara. We'll see how this plays out over the next three episodes.

The Warriors of Death

Episode 28: (May 30, 1964) Barbara and Tlotoxl continues to clash. The Doctor meets up with the son of the man who built the temple. He gives the warrior something to help him win his next fight. That could be problematic.

Cliffhanger: Ixta is about to kill Ian. Tlotoxl demands that Barbara save his life… if she is Yetaxa.

The second episode develops the story nicely. Susan only gets one scene, but Carole Ann Ford is on vacation. (Oddly enough, her scene involves mentioning arranged marriages. That was a Lucarotti theme.) Ian and Ixta have a brief scuffle in the beginning, which Ian wins. Then, they reconvene at the climax for a much lengthier brawl where Ixta cheats. (Thanks to the Doctor.) The Doctor tries to get info from Ixta about his dad's temple. (Not realizing who Ixta is.) Barbara is being doubted by Tlotoxl every which way. There's a lot going on here.

This is really the first story we've had that develops itself across its episodes. Rather than the norm, which is more serialized styles of storytelling. And it feels good to watch. One could be forgiven for thinking that the show might always stick with the Saturday Serial style. It will not. Quite a few stories in *Doctor Who* will sort of wax and wane dramatically. The best are the ones that can develop the story across the episodes while also including the cliffhangers. This one has another excellent cliffhanger and it's an important point within the episode.

Poor Barbara. She is trying her best. She carries herself regally. She gets in some arguments with Tlotoxl. She has a few chats with Autloc. But there is a sinking feeling, only halfway into the story, that all she is up to will amount to very little. The Doctor may be right here. She can't re-write history. And as she tries, she just makes things worse for them. If you think about it... if Barbara is Yetaxa's reincarnation, they're safe. (Ish.) Once that goes away, what the heck will happen to them? I can't imagine it will be pretty.

As all this is happening, The Doctor continues chatting with Cameca in the garden. The Doctor finds her charming, but I can never quite tell if he's flirting with her. Or if he's just being kind. Or if he just cares about getting back to the TARDIS and he'll do whatever. There are a lot of great close ups throughout this episode and Hartnell gets several strong ones.

In fact, the direction is quite good. After the clumsiness of bits of "The Keys of Marinus," we get the occasional camera wobble here but far more interesting shots. The moment Tlotoxl approached Barbara and suddenly we realized that the camera's on a crane is a great moment. Several bits of framing are fantastic. Especially some Shakespearean type moments. Such as Ixta telling Tlotoxl that he is getting help to defeat Ian. The two Aztecs are up close right in the screen. In the background, you can see Ian looking over at them with a "What the heck are they talking about?" frown on his face. Mix that with the music, which I quite like, and you're getting an above average serial. Some of the viewing figures and the Appreciation Index dropped off during this episode. But, hey, I can't vouch for the Great British public and their tastes.

The Bride of Sacrifice

Episode 29: (June 6, 1964) Things heat up in Mexico. They don't get much better for the TARDIS crew.

Cliffhanger: Ian is in the tunnel leading into the tomb. It starts to fill with water.

The strands of the story weave ever stronger around the throats of our travelers. The constant references to the Perfect Victim and the upcoming Day of Darkness don't make anything any lighter. It really is a breath of fresh air to have a story that is constructed across the available episodes rather than going one episode at a time. It ratchets up the drama and makes it more watchable. Now, I know that the, as mentioned, British public's interest waned. And I suppose if I were eight or nine when I saw this, the drama might have bored me a bit. Where are the pepper pots with the ray guns? Where are the screaming jungles? Heck, where did those cavemen go? I understand, British Public. And I forgive you. Much in the same way that there are several moments in the dialog that seem more Christian than Aztec, I look out from the midst of this story and forgive you for sort of abandoning it as it went along.

A lot of things happen here but the most interesting is probably with the Doctor and Cameca. The Doctor gets engaged! That won't happen again for a very long time. The scenes with the two of them are very sweet. She seems much enthralled by The Doctor. Her discussion with Autloc about making cocoa is delightful. (There is a wonderful extra on the DVD about making cocoa.) The cocoa shared is the bond forged. The Doctor does it without fully understanding what he's doing. This isn't going to end well for Cameca but it's sweet, nevertheless.

Meanwhile, as Tonila and Tlotoxl try to disprove Barbara's godhood, things do begin to start to feel dark for our main characters. So much so, that Ian and The Doctor in the Garden of Peace breaking into the temple seems like a small bit of light. The direction by John Crockett is strong throughout. Compare this one with the previous serial. This is how you do the drama. The scene where Tlotoxl is trying to get Barbara to drink poison is so well-framed. So intimate and powerful. They may have been using large, clunky cameras that seemed to run into everything but when they had a director that really tried… it showed.

I do love both Autloc and Tlotoxl as characters. Obsequious Tlotoxl trying to get what he wants and using whoever he must to get there. And noble Autloc. The scene where Barbara and he discuss the fate of Susan (who refuses to marry the Perfect Victim) is beautifully acted and written. "Would you betray our culture to save your handmaiden?" There's the rub. If these were the cavemen, yes. I believe she would have. But this is a culture that she has always admired and studied. She must be being torn apart inside. Also, she must be wishing that Susan (who has travelled the universe) would stop whining and grow up a bit. Sorry. Watched as I normally do, one episode a day, week off in between seasons, I really like Susan. Watched for this book (several episodes a day and then writing), her character's flaws become very apparent. The show's makers really didn't seem to 1) know what age she was or 2) know what to do with her. This will happen again.

The Day of Darkness

Episode 30: (June 13, 1964) It is the day of sacrifice. What shall become of our heroes?

Cliffhanger: Spoiler! They're OK. And they seem to have landed but they're still moving…

"We failed." "Yes, we did." Essentially, they did. Sort of. Autloc loses his faith and leaves for the wilderness. He's an old man. If the "wilderness" means the desert, he probably won't last long. Tlotoxl keeps his power. The Perfect Victim is killed. Tonila becomes High Priest of Knowledge. And Ixta… well, Ixta's doing OK until he gets in a fight with Ian and falls off a temple. (Prior to that, he frames Ian and gets away with it.) Saddest of all, Cameca is left broken hearted when the Doctor leaves. Aztec culture will continue. Until the arrival of the Conquistadors and then it will end in blood.

Ian's entering the temple speeds things up. After the quick movement of the first episode, setting everything in place, and the calmer machinations of the past two episodes, this episode goes through a lot with Susan's return being a part of it. Relationships end. People die. People lose faith. The TARDIS crew decide that they can do nothing here and basically Run Like Hell at the first chance they get. I'm glad that Lucarotti mixes the escape plotline with the Sacrifice finale and does it well. I think if the focus had been on the travelers' failures, this would have been too much. As it stands, the scenes with the Doctor and Cameca are sad. But the rest of is so mixed in with them trying to escape that it isn't quite as all-encompassing as it could be. And, honestly, I don't know if I'd fully want that. It doesn't make for much fun. Watching the crew running damage control as they try to leave works better for me.

As it began, it ends with Barbara talking to someone in the tomb. First time, it was Susan. They were having fun. They were exploring history. Here, however, it is the Doctor and Barbara. A palpable sense of sadness and failure does linger over the scene. The Doctor does his best by saying she changed Autloc's mind. But it doesn't seem like enough. The scene has a lovely capper, though. The Doctor leaves behind the brooch Cameca gave him. Then, he shrugs, puts in his pocket and they leave 15th Century Mexico.

The acting is excellent throughout. The costumes are fine. The sets are excellent, even the obvious backcloth at the top of the temple isn't a problem for me. (On PBS a long time ago, you knew it was a backdrop, but you couldn't really tell. On the DVD, it's obvious. That just makes it more like a play to me.) The direction and the writing keep up their strengths until the end. Overall, this is the strongest story so far. And it does beg one question from me…

They have failed. I understand. But, technically, didn't they kind of fail with the cavemen and Marco Polo too. Chaos, a fight (generally on film instead of VT) and everyone running to the TARDIS and leaving ASAP. It's what makes "The Aztecs" work so well. We just want to get away from the cavemen. The crew gave them what they wanted and received nothing but imprisonment in return. So, run! Tegana has been exposed. Marco fights him and yells the crew away. But what have they accomplished? Marco took care of Tegana. Marco still won't be able to go home. The ending of that one seems more of a failure because there's a stronger feeling of almost nothing accomplished. But "The Aztecs" is the one that veers into tragedy. It's the one to point to in this first block as the highlight of what *Doctor Who* could do. Unless you wanted *Doctor Who* to do nothing but aliens and ray guns and jumping around on cliffs. (Heck, this episode not only has a closing fight, but Ian is found with a murder weapon in hand near a body. Did Nation and Lucarotti have a little confab before putting together their scripts?) Anyway, the crew have escaped and now something else weird might be happening. They are about to meet some "Strangers in Space."

THE SENSORITES

Strangers In Space

By Peter R. Newman

Directed by Mervyn Pinfield

Episode 31: (June 20, 1964) The TARDIS crew land on a spaceship in the far future. The crew seems to be dead. They're not, just a bit boring. They are trapped in orbit around the Sense-Sphere, home of the Sensorites.

Cliffhanger: The Sensorites have arrived. We see one of them outside the ship.

Well, we're back to wandering about for a first episode and then a big cliffhanger revealing something. Except it's less visually interesting than both "The Daleks and "The Keys of Marinus." It basically takes place in a grey spaceship control room and a grey hallway. There is some threat (from the unseen Sensorites and a crew member who may be crazy). Overall, it's 25 minutes spent with two dull 28th Century astronauts and the TARDIS crew. The TARDIS crew all seem to have gotten lobotomies since the last episode. After the previous first episode ("The Temple of Evil") that threw us right into the story, this episode goes very slowly.

It's pre-Apollo rockets so it has that 1950s *Destination Moon/ Rocketship X-M* sort of vague "space" feel to it, which generally I find charming. The shot where the TARDIS crew move from the TARDIS console room to the control room on the ship in one shot is delightful. Mervyn Pinfield is an aggressively undynamic director but occasionally he has a good moment. (When Barbara and Susan head down the hall and the camera glides up to the electric eye and we see a hand, that's nice. It's too bad the door gets stuck coming down.) There's something about Maitland and Carol here that makes them seem so dull.

The TARDIS crew are doing their best to keep it lively. The music is trying hard. And yes, I think the cliffhanger is very good. But this is a disappointment compared to the previous story. It feels very childish. (I think that's the word I want.) OK. I like the opening scene in the TARDIS. The gang quickly recap their previous adventures. It's nice to have that continuity. And it's nice to have a moment when they can calm down between adventures. It's sweet. The Doctor's random story about Henry VIII just seems confusing to me, though. But then, there's the discussion of how the ship isn't moving but it says they're still moving. How could this be?

Oh, they're in a spaceship! That's why! Oh, for fun. The Doctor's look of utter confusion when Barbara says they maybe materialized inside of something seems odd. (Didn't they just materialize inside an Aztec tomb? I know that's not moving like a spaceship. But, technically, if it's on the surface of the Earth it is moving.) Ian, Susan and The Doctor all express great confusion. "Inside something?" Frankly, you're hoping they'll break into laughter because they look stupid. This hope strikes the viewer more than once in the episode.

The introduction of John does add a little tension but it's kind of too late. One can feel that we're getting a Sensorite reveal at the end of the episode and maybe it would be best if we moved towards that rather than this constant low-key faffing around. Also, Barbara and Susan are going to look for water. They pass a huge sign marked "WATER" and wander out into the possibly dangerous hallway instead. Why? Why are they doing that? I'll stop.

The thing at the end of the day though: I quite like this episode. It has a low-key, almost dull, charm that is a nice difference from the previous four episodes. Critically however, it's not up to much. Way too generic with only some hints of Susan having psychic power to keep things interesting. Maybe the Sensorites will liven things up? Maybe we'll get another hallway to wander down? Let's have a look.

The Unwilling Warriors

Episode 32: (June 27, 1964) Our gang meet the Sensorites face to face. They learn why they're being kept here.

Cliffhanger: Susan must go down to the Sense-Sphere with the Sensorites or else all will die.

It is great to see something happening with Susan again. She is the person in this episode who can communicate telepathically with the Sensorites. They do a lot of their communicating via their minds and Susan can join them. She has otherworldly discussions with no one at certain times in the episode. It confuses most people and angers the Doctor. I think, mainly, it's because she's a young woman that she can do this. Regardless, it's good that they give her something to do. Although, when her and Barbara defy the Sensorites telepathically, I wish Susan would have come up with what to say rather than Barbara (who isn't very telepathic).

In the previous review it may have come across as if I didn't like this story. Not true! I love the claustrophobic feel of it. Apart from the TARDIS set at the start of the previous episode, it's all taken place inside this one large set, including the control room and the hallway. (We see several hallways. I imagine we're seeing one.) I love when the Sensorites enter and slowly begin their movement through the space of the control room. I like the Sensorites. With their big orange heads, the strange hair in front of their mouths and their big disc feet. I don't mind that they step on each other's feet the first time they appear. And I love the Sensorite that stares defiantly into the spaceship from outer space. I also love the long moments with no dialogue. I think Ian and Barbara's first encounter with the Sensorites is nicely done. There's a lot to enjoy in this episode. The knowledge that with Susan being taken things will open out means there's more fun to be had.

I also like that we quickly get the reasoning behind why the Sensorites are keeping the astronauts here. Why the TARDIS crew is going to be held here. It's all in the Molybdenum! The Sensorites were burnt once before by humans regarding their MO. (Their molybdenum. Not their modus operandi.) Sometimes these serials have soap opera style pacing. Pacing where it takes forever and a day to get a plot point clarified or for something to happen that advances everything. I like knowing right now what's up with these big-headed goofballs with the odd eyes. (We're going to learn a thing or two about the Sensorites that feels as counter intuitive as some of the things we learn regarding the Conscience of Marinus. I'll tell you later.)

Setting aside all that, it still isn't terribly dynamic. It doesn't move quickly. It isn't boring but you can feel the 25 minutes. Now, that's not necessarily a bad thing because it is 25 minutes. But sometimes it's nice when you can't feel each minute. If you love this episode, you can luxuriate in it. For me, it still feels a bit too childish. The description that the TARDIS crew just follows the Doctor may be true-ish but doesn't seem quite right. And the Doctor is kind of a jerk in bits of this episode. The moment that really sticks out is when he yells at Barbara to "Do As Your Told!" when he tells her to talk to John. If I were Barbara, I'd knee that old jerk in the groin right there. Overall, it's one of these episodes where the interesting stuff is balanced out by the stuff that doesn't really work. I guess that makes it an average episode. Let's see what happens when we go down to the Sense-Sphere.

Hidden Danger

Episode 33: (July 11, 1964) Ian, Susan and The Doctor go down to the Sense-Sphere. Ian has a bad reaction to some working-class water.

Cliffhanger: Ian passes out after drinking poison water. Oh well, he's dead.

Here we go. Upon reaching the Sense-Sphere, the story begins to expand. Once we see the world of the Sensorites, things become more interesting. More or less. The final scenes on the ship are good ones. Probably the best scenes there. But it's the planet scenes that expand the story nicely. Although, oddly enough, it still retains the rather childish atmosphere from the ship. Maybe the Sensorites are a kind of childish race.

The thing about their sashes and collars kind of brings that out. It will become sharper in later episodes but each of the Elder Sensorites wear some sort of different reminder of who they are. Double sashes for the First Elder. One sash for the Second Elder. A large collar for the City Administrator. In the next episode, this will become a big thing. In this one, it's something the viewer sees and the Sensorites mention. We are going to discover the weird facts about their sashes and such shortly. But for now...

I love how the City Administrator is immediately villainous. He'd be twirling his mustache if he had a proper one. He points a disintegrator gun at the TARDIS crew when they arrive. But he knows they are there to try and help save all the Sensorites from dying. He's a jerk. I love that there is at least one Sensorite who will follow the City Administrator to the ends of the Sense-Sphere. Why? Who knows?

Let's hop back to the ship: The Doctor is angrier than we have ever seen him. Susan wants to be grown up. She wants to go down and negotiate with the Sensorites. He will not let her. He treats her like a child. It's an intense sequence within this rather childish story. It comes off making the Doctor look like a jerk. Not trusting Susan. One can see why Carole Ann Ford got tired of playing the character. It's too bad because I really like Susan. But writing these reviews in quick successions shows how woefully underdeveloped her character was.

Anyway... one of the best moments here is Ian's cough. It's been spoken of in *Running Through Corridors* and mentioned in the DVD commentary. Ian does that thing where he clearly does something wrong, but we're not supposed to spot it... he sips some of the plebs' water. Soon after, he begins to choke. So many fluffs and so many goofs over the weeks makes the viewer shrug and carry on. But it is part of the narrative. Ian is in trouble. That is very nicely done. Almost kind of meta in a way. And it sets up a nice cliffhanger. The TARDIS crew just wanted to solve the problem of the deaths of the Sensorites and go. Now, they're personally involved.

I'll wrap this up by saying that I love the scene where the Sensorite explains how everyone is in the class they're supposed to be in, and everyone does what they're best at. When it is mentioned that their society means that some live a lot better than others, the Sensorite is simply confused. Maybe if it had been a female Sensorite there would have been more empathy?

A Race Against Death

Episode 34: (July 18, 1964) Ian is poisoned. The Doctor must find a cure.

Cliffhanger: The Doctor investigates the aqueduct from whence came the poisoned water. But there seems to be a monster in there.

Most of this episode has its focus on the racism of the City Administrator. A jingoistic gentleman who believes that all humans should be destroyed. He believes that all Sensorites that don't hate all humans are garbage. He treats the humans in the episode with condescension. And, per the previous episode, he realizes that no one (not even other Sensorites) can recognize each other without the sashes. That's a bit weird to me. But it is a big thrust of the episode. Is that still xenophobia?

The City Administrator's distrust and hatred of humans is clearly xenophobia. But what is going on with the sash and collar thing? It's one thing to say, "White people can't tell the Chinese people apart because they all look alike." Racist? Sure. But it's another thing to say that we can't tell ourselves apart because we all look alike. What does that even imply? As we watch the episode, we can see that they look alike. Except for the fact that some are slim, and some are a little chubby. Some are tall, and some are short. Why can't they tell each other apart? Maybe there is some racial thing going on. The First Scientist can't tell the difference between the City Administrator and the Second Elder. That's like saying that I mistook the President for the Vice President. I don't know if it makes sense. But it is the basis of this episode and now this story.

The Sensorites were presented as being a people who did not want anyone else coming to their planet. And, via their stories of the Earth people who came to see them, this makes sense. So, this is a strong element of the story. Barbara isn't here but the rest of the TARDIS gang take care of themselves just fine. Ian is sick. Susan is assisting. The Doctor gets a fun montage. I like that he's trying to save the Sensorite people, but they always think he is misleading them. The Doctor and Susan and Ian are all put within the vicinity of death due to the crazy politics of the Sensorites.

The Episode works. The story that seemed a bit stunted in its first episode has expanded out. It may be a bit childish. The way the first Administrator acts is like a kid who has got some power and is abusing it. But, I think, this is a success. And it has one of the most important moments in the show…

The Doctor has cured the disease. He has saved Ian. But, instead of saying, as he would have in previous stories, "Well, let's get out of here" he says, "We need to find out what is going on here." He doesn't go away. The TARDIS is available to him. Everyone can go. He decides to risk his life to find out why the Sensorites are dying. In the episode, it's treated casually. It's treated a bit as a whim. But it is the Doctor we will know and love. Here is the first moment when it happens. The Doctor we have loved for so many years begins to become themselves here. Now, let's keep a watch on this guy and see what he does.

Kidnap

Directed by Frank Cox

Episode 35: (July 25, 1964) There is something down in the sewers. But there's also trouble up top. The City Administrator has a cunning plan. Everyone could be in trouble now.

Cliffhanger: Carol has been kidnapped!

I like the beginning of this episode. The Doctor in the aqueduct. Something down there with him. Growling and howling. The Doctor attacked! The Doctor's coat is shredded. It's a great way to start it off. Gives a nice feeling to everything. The fact that the Sensorites can't go down there because they hate the dark means it's really a place only for humans or humanlike people. Let's keep that in mind.

I like John and Carol. I think they'll make a nice couple. I liked the character of John when he was a bit crazy and dangerous. There was a sadness in there, mixed with the slight tinge of crazy. I liked when he was getting treatment to clear out his brain. I'm not sure what that device was on his head. But I think I saw something like it in a *Green Acres* episode about a hairdresser. It is nice to see him cured. (The First Elder has a lovely, if too curtly delivered, line about John being returned to Carol.) This was a nice little storyline running through the episodes. I'm glad Carol's not with Maitland. He was dull.

The City Administrator (First Elder by the end of the episode) is a good villain. Pompous, overbearing, devious, violent and chubby, he has the perfect traits of what we need and love in a villain. To me, he's clearly devious from the beginning. It takes a lot longer for our TARDIS friends to spot this, but they get there in the end. It is interesting to see how easily the First Elder is killed. He's basically hit in the shoulder and dies. Maybe the Sensorite shoulder is like the probic vent on a Sontaran?

The episode clearly doesn't have almost 26 minutes of material in it. Richard Cox replaces Pinfield. In the same way that his direction on "The Brink of Disaster" mirrors Richard Franklin's, his direction here mirrors Pinfield's. More or less. Pinfield has some more interesting framing going on throughout. But Cox keeps the same pace as Pinfield. It's not dull, but it's certainly not going anywhere fast. It keeps up the same childish vibe.

The First Elder is beginning to feel like the only grown-up in a group of disc-footed big headed old child men. Watching the City Administrator, his assistant and the Second Elder in the room with the disintegrator gun begins to look like some sort of meeting of a bunch of Teletubbies from an alternate world. Their look sometimes gives off a bit of gravity. But the tighter their outfits, the goofier they are. This episode seems to go out of its way to accentuate their goofiness. Of course, even the TARDIS crew isn't as up to their game as they should be. As I said, the City Administrator is clearly a jerk. But the crew go out of their way to try to get him made the Second Elder. Then, he's immediately curt and rude with them. I almost expected the humans to look at the camera and shrug their shoulders in confusion.

Ian, Susan and The Doctor do make a decent team. One can never forget Barbara though. And one really can't because they mention her every two minutes. Her vacation is almost over. She'll join us next week. With Maitland? We can only wish.

A Desperate Venture

Directed by Frank Cox

Episode 36: (August 1, 1964) Lots of plot elements come together very quickly, including the crazy humans in the aqueduct. Suddenly, we're at the cliffhanger.

Cliffhanger: The Doctor takes completely random offense at Ian. He says Ian and Barbara will be let off The Ship at their next stop.

We leave the Sense-Sphere. We leave it sort of not having done much. We saw a lot of aliens who all looked the same. We met some crazy humans who were poisoning the water. The First Elder is OK. (But not that OK.) The Sensorites themselves come off as "Don't call us. We'll call you." types of aliens. On more than one occasion, the show has presented us with something that it really wants us to believe is interesting or worthwhile. But they come off rather lame. Arbitan and his Conscience were one. The justice system on Millennius is another. The Sensorites follow that. An incredibly xenophobic race that I guess have learned to trust a bit by the end. But there's something about the First Elder's confusion over the fact that humans can feel compassion for one another that makes me throw up my hands. It's a good thing this episode moves fast because if it went slower, I'd be rolling my eyes. And that thing where they can't handle noise tips over from "Hmm, interesting" to "Hmm, kind of dumb."

The Episode does move fast. Sort of. The first half deals with Carol's kidnapping by the Second Elder (previously the City Administrator). Then, we meet the humans from that previous expedition who are in the aqueduct poisoning things. At least with their fun beards and pointy sticks, they're more interesting than Maitland. (What happened to Maitland? We don't see him again.) But all of it is wrapped up so quickly. So quickly, in fact, that the main villain, The City Administrator is dealt with mostly off screen. I don't mind that it's wrapped up quickly though. I like the fact that if you hit play on the episode... when it ends, this story is over. That cliffhanger is foolishness, but this story is over.

As I mentioned before though, I don't dislike the story. It almost has enough stuff going on to fill six parts. Well, the first two episodes have enough for one and the last one has enough for one and a half. "The Aztecs" is the only story that really is structured well across its episodes. The Sensorites are OK. From a distance, I think fondly of them. (Although, I might be thinking of the Ood.) Watching them in real time they alternately interest me and then annoy me. I get what the creative team is trying to do. Give us an alien race that is more shaded than the Daleks. Somehow, they just ends up feeling more childish than the Daleks ever were.

John and Carol are going to live happily ever after! Susan gets to use a lot of her telepathic powers. The Doctor has some nice moments with the humans and some jerk moments. Barbara takes charge. And it all moves along very quickly. There were a few points where I thought "Are they going to finish on time?" Thank Goodness, they did. "The Sensorites" is important in the history of the show for its different type of alien and, mainly, being the first story where the Doctor stays on a planet to find out what's wrong after we know he can leave. That's enough. (Plus, there's that wacky stuff with the lock that I didn't really get into. Maybe another time.)

THE REIGN OF TERROR

A Land of Fear

Written by Dennis Spooner

Directed by Henric Hirsch

Episode 37: (August 8, 1964) The TARDIS crew land outside of France during the French Revolution. Things don't go well.

Cliffhanger: The Doctor is unconscious inside a farmhouse that is burning down.

I want to start this review by talking about Stanley Myers. He does the music for this serial, all the episodes. The music has a kind of a big orchestral sound to it. Occasionally moments that are clearly French-like. (Their national anthem, for example.) When the farmhouse is burning in the end, and we're cutting from shots of a large model burning and the Doctor unconscious on the floor within, the music helps the excitement mount until the "Next Episode" credit appears and we know that the *Doctor Who* theme will be kicking in in a moment.

One of the fun things about this show is that if you keep an eye on the people involved all sorts of names that will either make you go "Oh them!" to "That name sound familiar..." pop up. If you go outside of the show, to the comics and the books and so forth, even more names appear. From Terry Nation (as a kid I knew him more from seeing his name on *MacGyver*) to Carey Mulligan appearing in "Blink," the show is covered with important creative names. Stanley Myers is one of them. He wrote tons of movie scores throughout the 1970s into the early 1990s, including *The Deer Hunter*. The "Cavatina" theme is his. He also scored several Nicholas Roeg films, including the crazy *Eureka*. He scored the nutty sci-fi action film *Nightmare at Noon* with Hans Zimmer. *My Beautiful Launderette, Lady Chatterley's Lover*, several Peter Walker Films, *Paperhouse, The Incubus, The Great Tycoon, The Great Train Robbery, The Witches* and a lot of others. "The Reign of Terror" is near the beginning of his career. It's a heck of a beginning.

Oh, the episode. It's a good one. It starts off rather leisurely. Ian and Barbara must get back in the Doctor's good graces. Then, they discover they're in France and it's The French Revolution. I always find it odd that Susan says the Doctor loves this time so much. (Maybe that's why she took home that book in "An Unearthly Child?" Maybe her grandfather was reading it?) The sense of evil and foreboding really kicks in when all the soldiers show up. They're looking for two noblemen within the house. The soldiers are uneducated, dangerous and scary because they seem like the sort of rednecks that were shooting zombies at the end of the *Night of the Living Dead*. Except these redneck French soldiers are killing people. (The word "Citizen" becomes rather chilling as this story goes on. It should mean something, but it becomes a word of contempt and confusion.)

The casual way that life is wasted here seems to signify the way life was treated during this period. Or, indeed, any time when life becomes almost useless. Almost superfluous. The two noblemen are casually shot after being introduced to us. When the soldiers haul away Ian, Susan and Barbara, there's talk of the guillotine. I'm not sure why it is... but in most future/sci-fi stories (this is another historical), when things seem like they should be at their worst, somehow there's always hope somewhere. Or it never quite feels as dark as one would think. Here, however, in the middle of The Reign of Terror, there is a real feeling of "How will they get out of this?" When they burn down the farmhouse, with the Doctor inside, that feeling intensifies. Helped by the fact that director really lingers on the model of the house burning, the Doctor in danger, everyone watching it all... as that music builds. It's an excellent cliffhanger. And it's an interesting opening episode for a writer who will be more known for silliness than tragedy.

Guests of Madame Guillotine

Episode 38: (August 15, 1964) Ian, Barbara and Susan are locked up awaiting decapitation. The Doctor begins a long walk to Paris.

Cliffhanger: Ian watches Susan and Barbara taken to the Guillotine.

From the opening image of the guillotine coming down and the two old crones knitting and laughing as the new prisoners arrive for the chop to rats infesting Susan and Barbara's cell and Ian watching the ladies being taken to their death, this is a grim episode. Probably the grimmest since "The Forest of Fear." That makes sense as we are now in the final serial of Season 1 as broadcast. Heck, this episode has a moment where the Doctor violently wallops a prison work party overseer over the head. (They add a sound of the man snoring as the Doctor leaves. Originally, you couldn't tell whether he was dead or alive.) It's all very grim. Ian gets a cellmate who dies within minutes. (Not before revealing important information, though.) Everyone seems to be either for the chop, doing hard labor or laughing at and taking advantage of those in those positions. The cavemen were awful. But they were cavemen. These are the French. They should know better.

The separation of the TARDIS crew is done cleverly. Ian is put in a cell by himself. This is because William Russell is enjoying his vacation of two weeks. Barbara stayed in that spaceship with Maitland for two episodes and you remember what happened with The Doctor and Susan. But Ian (once you know what's happening) is very obviously but smartly kept separate. He meets the spy. He has important words about a "James Stirling." As the DVD production text notes, "Stirling" is related to a "Stirling bond." And in a spy-related adventures in 1964, who was the world's biggest spy? James Bond. Well done Mr. Spooner.

The gals get the roughest part of the episode. There's never any hope that they're not going to the guillotine. It's simply a matter of when. And when it happens at the end of the episode, it's done rather casually. Taking the next group to the chop. Losing their heads in a little bit. It's become such a part of these people's lives that they cannot see how horrible it is, living like this. Poor Barbara, she must deal with Susan at her whiniest. We've had Susan go from little child to mature young woman. Here she is simply whiny and shrieky. Even Barbara admits that she's never seen Susan quite like this. Granted, the prison is awful and when the rats show up, I can understand not becoming happier. But they've gotten out of worse than this. Susan seems to be a bit tired of it all.

The Doctor gets the side trip. Apart from the violent part, there's some humor. The overseer is obese and lazy and just yells at people all the time. The Doctor, almost stupidly, gets the man's dander up. The Doctor has no papers. (Always a bad sign of a country in trouble. When you can't walk down a street minding your own business without having to show your papers.) There is a funny line about the Doctor knowing he's clever. The overseer calls the Doctor "skinny" and then the Doctor's on the chain gang. There's not much humor here but there are little bits. The kind of thing that Dennis Spooner would throw in more of when he takes over as script editor and the kind of thing that would make the show interesting and idiosyncratic.

I'll leave here with the jailer. Is there a more sycophantic character around? Well, yes, I can think of a few. Gatherer Hade comes to mind. The jailer is almost funny. But his wishy-washy behavior with Lemaitre and his abuse of the prisoners makes him more of a character one wants to see get clubbed with a shovel rather than laugh along with. We'll see how he develops. And we'll see if Susan and Barbara keep their heads.

A Change of Identity

Episode 39: (August 22, 1964) Susan and Barbara DO NOT get their heads cut off. Ian is still on vacation-ish. And the Doctor puts on a very elaborate disguise to get into the jail. Enjoy live action. We're about to get animated in a different way.

Cliffhanger: The tailor turns in the Doctor's ring to the jailer.

Hooray! Susan and Barbara keep their heads. They are rescued by a bunch of the noblemen who have a safe house hidden away in the countryside. So, let's think about that for a moment: They are in the French Revolution. It's overthrowing the decadent aristocracy. The people who take advantage of all of those who are not well-off, born into wealth. But the Revolution has gone so bad that Barbara and Susan (not French royalty) are about the be killed for no reason other than the soldiers of the Revolution caught them and they're going to die. They are freed by the very people the Revolution was being fought against. Like if they were rescued by the British somewhere in the American colonies during the Revolutionary War. This will become more important in a bit.

The Doctor is delightful in this episode. He gets to dress up like some sort of French officer. (The revolutionaries must have realized something had gone wrong when they saw the way all their leaders were dressed. Once a Frenchman, always a Frenchman.) He has a ridiculous feather on his head. He befuddled a tailor, and he befuddled a jailer. But, when he tried to befuddle Lemaitre, his face couldn't be paler. Maybe this is why the Doctor is said to like this period so much. During all this terror, he's getting a couple of laughs in. Why not? I do wonder why the tailor has all this stuff in his shop. I'm trying to remember a movie where a character impersonates, for example, a general. They buy a general's uniform at a costume store and that's all they need. What movie was that?

Anyway, Ian only appears briefly before he "escapes," under Lemaitre's eye. This makes for a slightly confusing moment a little later. Several of the hidden noblemen speak of a stranger at the local tavern asking about something. It's never said what the tavern is, and it's never said who this stranger is. Presumably, it's Ian. But, if you had missed the previous episode, this conversation would come off as just confusing because they keep so vague about what's happening. They're so vague I feel like maybe they're confusing themselves. But it doesn't matter. Susan and Barbara are currently safe. Ian is on a mission. The Doctor is having fun. And, next episode, everything will become far more animated.

Final note: The director passed out during final rehearsal for this episode. So, someone was called in to direct the episode. Some say it was Tim Coombe. Some say they don't remember who it was. But they all knew Henric was out for the count in this episode. Apparently, he wasn't fun to work with until he passed out. Then, he became more delightful. Unfortunately, his next two episodes are lost, and we will be watching someone else's interpretation of his directing.

The Tyrant of France

Episode 40: (August 29, 1964) Ian is properly back in France. The Doctor meets Robespierre. Barbara makes a "friend," if you catch my meaning. Susan gets sick.

Cliffhanger: Leon has set a trap and caught Ian.

Somewhere within the foundations of this episode the whole serial starts to become Much Ado About Nothing. As with "Marco Polo," one wonders what the TARDIS crew are fully accomplishing in this space. Capture, rescue, capture. The Doctor is goofing but a wicked tailor may be ending his fun soon. Susan gets sick to add some drama to her and Barbara's story and they meet a wicked physician. As this goes on, the bubbling revolution goes on underneath them.

We meet Robespierre. The Doctor charmingly picks on him and his reign of terror. Robespierre does that thing where he says more or less "You're right." It's a nice scene. Even animated. It's nice to see the Doctor meet up with the big people in history like this. Poor Robespierre. He really was a terror. But the story has him lamenting the fact that the Revolution really has ended up being a huge mess. Every day a new enemy pops up. Every day someone else wants power. Every day they must kill more and more people. He laments it but he can't stop it. It's never ending. I get the feeling that he knows this has all gone wrong. I think they all probably know that. But, if you can stay in power for another day, everything will be OK. That's another day where things might become all right. The Doctor thinks it's nonsense of course.

It's nice to have Ian back. He has a long chat with Jules about James Stirling and the English involvement in things. They drink some wine and chat. Ian really seems intent upon finding this Stirling. I applaud his need to get involved but he seems to have lost sight of the fact that they're time travelers and shouldn't be there. And what is supposed to happen when he finds James Stirling? I'm a little confused about that. It is nice to know that we were talking about Ian in the last episode.

I do like the way the episode begins with some sort of feeling of hope. The Doctor successfully meets Robespierre. Susan and Barbara are safe. They are reunited with Ian. But, as the episode goes along, all the hope leaks away. The Doctor cannot get out of the prison and the watchful eye of the jailer. Susan is sick and getting worse. So, her and Barbara must go to a suspicious doctor. Ian seems to be safe for the moment. But, very quickly, that changes. It's not super-fast like the last episode of "The Sensorites." It's got a more organic feeling to it. (Although, the final scene with Ian just sort of happens.) What started as possible hope, possibly leaving soon, by the end, puts them back almost where they were at their worst a few episodes ago.

This is a lost episode. But this one, unlike "Polo," is animated. It is nice to see things moving when the picture has been lost. The animation here is good. It's not Pixar but it moves enough and gives us plenty of detail. To be honest, I think we get a few too many close ups. But then designing the rooms and layouts of spaces is probably more complicated and expensive than using faces. So, I can't fault them for that. The episode is not paced very quickly but they handle the images well.

A Bargain of Necessity

Episode 41: (September 5, 1964) Chicanery of all kinds goes on. Will this be the episode where the TARDIS crew lose their heads?

Cliffhanger: The Doctor and Lemaitre enter Jules's house.

I am so glad that we have this animated. Unfortunately, the animation doesn't quite pick up all the nuances of the episode. Barbara, Ian and Jules have two scenes where they discuss the Revolution. They discuss the people on either side. They discuss right or wrong. We learn that Jules is in the middle. He's not an aristocrat. But he doesn't like what the Revolution has done. These are a couple of well written scenes but they're a little tough to gauge without seeing the actors.

The animation does its job to show us the places we're in and to let us see the faces of the people. But, during these scenes, the loss of facial expression hinders the story. Leon holds Ian captive to get information from him. Ian will probably die. He might be tortured beforehand. Jules saves him and shoots Leon in the process. Barbara, who took a shine to Leon, is pissed at Jules and Ian. And she is very surprised when they act like he was an enemy. She points out that the Revolution did a lot of great things. She's speaking like Yetaxa/ Barbara here. She knows her history and she's treating these real people whose lives they have become involved with as if they were just figures from a distance. Ian points out that they have taken a side. I mean, Jules saved her life. Leon's people would have laughed while she was decapitated. Barbara takes some real high ground here. And it seems a bit ridiculous. (Especially as she is given the capper line in the first scene.)

Unfortunately, it's tough to gauge the performances without seeing their faces. Cartoon Ian scowls and frowns. Cartoon Barbara gets upset. We know the actors are capable of more nuance. I would love to see how they look as they talk like that. I asked what Ian thought he was getting up to in the last episode. He is so serious about finding Stirling. Well, here you go. They have become involved, whether they like It or not. I feel like this is a very Dennis Spooner way of looking at things. Different from David Whitaker who doesn't want the TARIS crew to become involved. Spooner is saying "They're there. They are involved. Now, we must deal with that." It's nice to see the show evolving like this. Something which sounds so easy to say at the start becomes tougher to deal with as the series evolves and grows.

The rest of the episode is fine. The Doctor frees Barbara, tricking the poor jailer again. He has a tougher time getting Susan out. In fact, it does seem to take quite a bit of time before he finally gets Susan free. I feel like this may have been more fun to watch live than animated. It sounds like everyone's enjoying themselves and it has a bit of a touch of farce to it. (Shades of Episode Three of "The Romans.") But, after a time, if we can't see it, we should get on with it.

Oh, so Susan's not sick anymore? Last episode, she was in such dire straits that they went to a physician. This week, she's fine. That's Susan for you! She is an alien, I guess.

The Doctor's talk with Lemaitre near the end is a good one. Some nicely written dialogue scenes in this episode lead us towards the final cliffhanger. This comes right after Jules says that anyone who is a traitor should be shot, or words to that effect. Immediately, the Doctor walks in the room with Lemaitre and a horn goes off... Wah Wahh!! (I'm kidding there. But it is set up in that way.) Now, we're heading into the last episode of this story and the last episode of Season 1. Let's see what the TARDIS crew will finally accomplish in the French Revolution.

Prisoners of Conciergerie

Episode 42: (September 12, 1964): We meet a very famous guy. The TARDIS crew continue their journey amongst the stars.

Cliffhanger: It's the end of Season 1. The Doctor is given a lovely goodbye speech. (Not too distant from the final words of "Survival.") And the journey continues…

Now, we learn what the TARDIS crew can bring to the adventure: They can watch an historically inaccurate, but fun, meeting between Barrass and Bonaparte. At the inn that Webster mentioned back in Episode Two. It's a fun scene. But others have got here before me. *Running Through Corridors* mentions it and, way back, *Doctor Who: A Celebration* mentions it. That the crew (Ian and Barbara) are basically reduced to staring through a keyhole as history happens. This, surely, can't be fun for them. It reminds me of an episode of the wonderful 1980s *Voyagers!* TV show. Bogg and Jeffery going through history fixing things. And occasionally, monitoring things to make sure they go as planned. I love that show. I prefer *Doctor Who*. But we're at a strange point here. David Whitaker is still in charge of scripts and his theory on historical intervention is well-known. Dennis Spooner takes a freer hand but won't (or can't) until he takes over the scripts in a few serials. So, while there is some drama at the very start of the episode and near the end, most of the story seems to be over and done with. We're just filling in a gap and signposting the future of France.

The opening scene with the reveal of who James Stirling is nicely done. It explains a lot of things that happened over the previous four episodes. In fact, if you go back and watch Lemaitre knowing who he is, it's a lot of fun. It's fun watching The Doctor manipulate the jailer. But Stirling does the same thing. And in the same way the Doctor does. A weird thing though is that as awful and as sleazy and gross as the jailer is… he ends up alive and well in the end. He's last seen welcoming the wounded Robespierre into the cells. He'll be fine if the guillotine keeps going. (In the original script, Ian mentions to Jules that the guillotine should be put away now.)

We know that the TARDIS crew will reunite. But it does get a bit hairy there at the end. The scene with Robespierre when they shoot him is pretty harrowing for *Doctor Who* at any time. It is apparently historically accurate though. So, we can be happy about that. It's all so depressing though. I mean, we know what happens. Napoleon takes over and we go from there. But… I guess the question I have is: Who would have thought the Reign of Terror would have ended so unpleasantly?

The first season ends. I absolutely love it. Even at its low moments, it's going out there and giving us so much entertainment. The direction is varied, which is probably the biggest bump in the road. Some stories were directed well. (This one, Chris Barry's episodes of The Daleks, Warris Hussein's existing episodes and John Crockett). Some were directed in confused fashion or not so great. (Pinfield, Martin, Gorrie.) But it's like the first season of 1966's *Batman*. This is kind of new ground. Some people get it. Some don't. Unfortunately, the "some don'ts" will be hired for the show until the mid-1980s. We will survive.

The closing scene is a lovely (but slightly awkward) goodbye to what has come before and a signpost to what will come next. I think it's a great end for the season. It sort of really isn't the end. Or it wasn't meant to be. The production will continue making episodes until the end of "The Dalek Invasion of Earth." But this is where we get a break. This is where we don't get a new episode for a while. So, a deep breath before we dive back in. (And, keep in mind, that the show's future was still up in the air at this point. If the powers that be got what they wanted at this moment, this book would only be about another 20 pages long.) (If it is only another 20 pages long, then you live on Earth-2. I thank you for buying a copy! Go online. Someone from Earth-1 might sell you a full version.)

SEASON TWO

(1964-1965)

PLANET OF GIANTS

Planet of Giants

Written by Louis Marks

Directed by Mervyn Pinfield

Episode 43: (October 31, 1964) The TARDIS crew gets shrunk in someone's garden. Oh, and the garden had a murder occur in it. Oh, and a deadly insecticide may have been released in it too. Welcome to Season Two!

Cliffhanger: A cat threatens the TARDIS crew.

Trouble with QR18 and A14D!

Omitted from the script: "QR18 is the atmospheric pressure outside the Ship at the point of travel." "A14D is the weight of the Ship." That's the problem we're having today when the TARDIS doors open in mid-flight. You know that can't be good. But all seems well. Wouldn't it be fun if they started their 2nd season with no problems? A bit of a hiccup but no real trouble. Well, it ain't going to happen when DN6 is in the area.

"Let's shrink the TARDIS crew" was originally meant to be the very first *Doctor Who* adventure. But they couldn't pull it off. Now, they felt they could. With Ray Cusick's great miniature designs, they do a pretty fine job of it. The story bases itself deep in the worry about poisons in insecticides at that time, especially DDT. It's littered with dead bugs. Dead bugs that look great. It's also got my favorite kind of businessman: The kind who says he will be ruined if someone doesn't do something for him. Then, he pulls out a gun and shoots that person.

I firmly believe that Corporate/ Capitalist America is awful. I firmly believe that it ran its course a long, long time ago. All it does now is keep wealthy families wealthy and occasionally churn out a new billionaire who immediately acts awfully. I know now that the United States is not a democracy. The wealthiest dictate what happens. The rest of us must deal with it. But, as far as all that goes, I don't think evil businesspeople carry around guns and kill as much as TV and movies would lead us to believe. The guy in this one is fun. Trying to intimidate the scientist who won't be intimidated and then just shooting him. That's one way to do it.

There have been complaints with this story that the mix of shrunken TARDIS crew mixed with a very basic murder-type thing don't match. People seem to want there to be something larger going on here. (No pun intended.) (OK. I lied. There is a pun intended.) To me, this is the perfect balance. The TARDIS crew are tiny. They're not Ant Man and the Wasp. What could they possibly do if, for example, the full-sized Daleks were here? (If they were both shrunk though...) We'll get more into the story with the next episode. I wanted to mention that here because it seems like a bit of strangeness.

The TARDIS crew encounter a giant worm, a giant bee and giant ants. There's a giant match, matchbox and seed packet. In the world of regular sized people, it's the same old crap. No sense of wonder there. Maybe that's what people find blah about this story. I think it's a grand way to spend the first episode. (Plus, I could watch the four leads do their thing without anyone else all day.)

Dangerous Journey

Episode 44: (November 7, 1964) The crew winds up in a lab. A lab with giant flies, poisoned seeds and a murderer.

Cliffhanger: The Professor has finished washing his hands and pulls out the stopper from the sink.

The giant cat is a fun cliffhanger. This one is even better. The scientist slowly washing his hands in the sink. The Doctor and Susan under the stopper. And then the casual removal of the stopper. The credits begin to roll as the water slowly drains away. It doesn't fade to black until the water is gone. Oh no! The Doctor and Susan got washed down the drain, into the grate! Well, that's the end of *Doctor Who*.

Louis Marks does a nice job coming up with inventive shtick for this episode. Like previous Pinfield episodes, it doesn't go anywhere fast. But there is enough happening to, generally, make one forget that it's going slowly. And yes, the more we get to know the big humans, the less interesting they become. A gullible professor. A dead guy. An evil businessman. I stand by what I said earlier. Anything more would have been too much. The less time spent with the big humans, the better.

Luckily, Pinfield does know how to shoot all of Raymond Cusick's fantastic sets. The sink is wonderful, especially from Barbara and Ian's POV. The Doctor and Susan are already small. They look so much smaller down in that sink. I love the chain for the stopper. The openings in the drain look kind of terrifying to me. I'd be afraid to fall in or drop something in there. Same with the grate at the other end of the pipe. Watching the characters peer over the top of the grate with that huge pipe behind them is darn amusing.

I'm always kind of amazed when I watch this story. It always kind of goes a bit on the back burner. Maybe because Louis Marks's other stories are generally more well-known to me. But they really pull off the miniature sets here. Check out that freakin' fly! Oh, my goodness. That is a gross thing. I wonder where that went after the shoot was done. I'd like to think Cusick hauled it out for Halloween. Let's not forget the fun briefcase. It's another great moment when they crawl out of that huge case and peer around.

The scene where Barbara touches the poisoned seed is noticeable for 1) Ian's lack of vision. Doesn't he pay more attention normally? He saw Barbara's ankle was swollen. How come he couldn't see that she touched a seed? 2) Barbara's slightly odd behavior. She acts like a child who has done something wrong rather than a grown woman who might be in some sort of trouble. It does up the ante though. Not only are they tiny. Not only is there a murderer. But Barbara has been infected and might die soon. Keep piling it on.

It's funny that I mention all the incidents because the next episode is an infamous one. Just keep in mind, that the big humans are going to have to do more now. They haven't really done much. So, the next episode (which is the last one of this serial) will feature more of their chicanery and less of the miniature stuff. Let's get out of here and get to a Crisis.

Crisis

Directed by Mervyn Pinfield & Douglas Camfield

Episode 44: (November 14, 1964) The TARDIS crew must stop a killer, prevent DN6 from being distributed and get back to the TADRIS before Barbara dies.

Cliffhanger: The scanner is broken and the Doctor wonders where they were.

One could be forgiven for thinking "Wow! This episode crams in a lot." There's the silliness with the switchboard operator and her cop husband. There's the bit with the DN6 formula. There's the enormous telephone and the cork. There's the stuff with the gas jet. There's… there's a lot of stuff. And you're right. You're completely right. This feels like two episodes worth of material because it is two episodes worth. The fact that there are two directors gives it away. Verity Lambert decreed that episode four ("The Urge to Live") and the third episode did not have enough material for two episodes, so they became one. Yes. There are a few moments that seem a little off because of the editing but, overall, it works.

Could you imagine more time spent with the switchboard operator and the cop? I do love that the TARDIS crew is going through such crazy agony being so small and then… we cut to the lady and her husband. Living their lives in this small country village. Doing their thing, day in and day out. He walks his beat like *Dixon of Dock Green*. She answers the switchboard and distributes the mail. Nothing big ever happens around here. Until the tiny people show up, then all heck breaks loose.

Of course. That's not as great as the businessman putting a hankie over the phone to sound like Smithers. It's hysterical and no one buys it, except for the fact that the people that need to buy it do. Imagine being so boring that your boss can't even tell your voice sounds completely different when you call them up to tell them something important. There's an episode of *Police Squad!* where Lt. Frank Drebin does the same thing. When it cuts to the person listening, they dubbed in the voice of the actual actor being impersonated. I'm glad they didn't do that here. I kind of wished they had. It's very 10-year-old style plotting. It doesn't make sense. So what? It needs to happen so it's going to happen. The fact that he does it twice is really the best part.

I giggle at those bits because the rest of the episode is quite good. The giant props continue to be excellent. The struggle of Barbara is great. She chooses trying to save the world over her own life. That's our Barbara! I love Ian and Susan running with the giant match and the Doctor uselessly giving them instructions. The only part that really confuses me is how quickly (and how exactly) they get back to the TARDIS. It's a heck of a long walk. (Most of them were carted there in a briefcase.) Surely Barbara must be in terrible shape by time they arrive?

In the end, it's a fun opening to the second season of the show. It does one of the things *Doctor Who* does best. It melds the fantastic to the mundane to come up with something all its own. I always wonder if the mundanity of the cliffhanger is meant to match the seemingly mundane previous cliffhangers. "The scanner's not working. Why? We've landed. Maybe I can find out." That doesn't make sense but maybe it's meant to belie the return of something. Something big…

THE DALEK INVASION OF EARTH

World's End

Written by Terry Nation

Directed by Richard Martin

Episode 46: (November 21, 1964) The TARDIS crew land by a river. It's London. But the future. And things aren't very nice at all.

Cliffhanger: A Dalek rises out of the Thames.

Terry Nation strikes again. With another episode that lands the TARDIS crew in a place for them to investigate. Unlike "The Daleks," it's not an alien landscape. Unlike "The Daleks," they meet other beings by the end and have conversations with them. (Like "The Keys of Marinus.") Like "The Keys of Marinus," they are separated from the TARDIS. They get split up. They meander around. Eventually, they begin to discover bits and bobs of what is happening around them. He may have his best first episode here in some respects because the crew have landed on Earth.

For a while, it seems like, finally, The Doctor has gotten them home. (Although, technically, he got them home in the last story, but they were too small to enjoy it.) Unfortunately, we have seen a strange man with an odd metal thing on his head drown himself in the river. And we have seen the sign saying that it is forbidden to dump bodies in the river. So, we have our doubts. Unless it's a Parallel Earth. (It's not.) It's nice to see them positive and happy about being on Earth. That fades quickly. (Although, I do wonder what that last cliffhanger was about as it comes to nothing here.)

I kind of wish maybe we hadn't seen the big sign and the Roboman go into the water. I almost think it would have worked better if we honestly thought they were home. The location footage certainly helps. Prior to this, our only location footage was Brian Proudfoot walking around in France pretending to be William Hartnell's Doctor. Seeing the river. Seeing the Dalek rise out of it. Seeing the urban decay of the warehouse. Watching Barbara, Susan and their rebel friend run through rotten buildings and areas really does add to the realism of the episode. I do wish we had learned, as they did, that we were somewhere wrong. Maybe seeing the sign. Maybe the flying saucer. Maybe the dead Roboman in the river. I don't know. It's just a thought.

This is one of those episodes that kills on first viewing, especially if you don't know what's going on. Think about it. It's called "World's End." That might shake some up a bit but there is a place in London called "World's End." So, it's not that crazy. If you recognized Terry Nation's name, you may have thought "Daleks." But some of you with an inclination towards leather may have thought "Voord." There's no sign of Daleks until the very last minute. The flying saucers could belong to anyone. (Even Ed Wood.) Richard Martin's direction isn't as interesting as Christopher Barry's, but it doesn't have as many goof ups as Gorrie's. It's not fast paced but it slowly builds until… a Dalek rises out of the Thames!

That's a great cliffhanger. Unlike, though "The Dead Planet," which I can watch over and over, something about "World's End," the more I watch it, makes me want it to speed up a bit. You can feel every minute of it. I don't quite remember that the first time I saw it. But it does feel a bit like Terry Nation is padding things out a bit. The addition of the mercury link shenanigans and going to the city helped him the first time. Here it's Barbara and Susan running with rebels and Ian and The Doctor going through an interesting warehouse. This is me just moaning. I mean, it's an iconic episode with an iconic ending. So, what if the pacing is a bit off. We have a Dalek invasion to deal with.

The Daleks

Episode 47: (November 28, 1964) Susan and Barbara work with the rebels. Ian and The Doctor have been captured by the Daleks.

Cliffhanger: The Doctor is about to be operated upon.

The Daleks here are much more assured of themselves compared to that scared batch we saw on Skaro. Hiding in their great big metal city. Scared of everything. These Daleks are the "Masters of Earth," as they say several times. They have some sort of dish-type thing on their backs that helps them move over non-metal surfaces. The Doctor says to Ian that we must be millions of years before "The Daleks." Implying that the Daleks were a world-conquering force of some kind before their war with the Thals. Although, that's not really what is implied in the first story. We'll roll with it for the moment. It's not like the history of the Daleks becomes easier to figure out from this point on.

Let's talk about the Robomen: First, the Robomen seem dumb. Don't they? Their helmets don't seem terribly secure. Do they? Why do the Daleks need to test their intelligence? They're just dumb guards. Why do they test the Doctor the way they do? Did all these Robomen pass that lock test? Why do I think "No" is the answer? It is said that eventually their programming is rejected, and they die. Later in the story, they are called "walking corpses." That explains why they talk the way they do. They sound like Daleks on a slow record speed and talking with deep voices. (They sound dumb.) My question is: if they are programmed until they die, what does the Dalek by the Thames mean when he says to a Roboman that he will be punished later? How do you punish someone you've completely programmed to your will and who dies when the programming breaks? What on Earth could that punishment be?

Anyway, The Doctor in the cell with Ian and Craddock is a fun scene. Craddock keeps razzing the Doctor and the Doctor keeps razzing him back. (Surely, this guy can't be someone the Daleks are trying to make into a Roboman.) It all ends abruptly with the Doctor being thrown on an operating table. I will say the scene where the Doctor and Ian first encounter a Dalek isn't, for me, one of the Doctor's best moments. His arrogance here is at a ridiculous level. He knows what the Daleks can do. They don't know who he is. They can just shoot him dead and shut him up. He speaks heroically but it always seems ridiculous to me. I'm kind of glad when that scene ends.

The exterior of the Dalek spaceship is a nice size set. After so many cramped sets in previous serials, it's good to see a larger space. Although, during the battle at the end, I wished Richard Martin had picked a few more interesting angles. We've got, basically, an overhead shot with everyone doing their best to stay choreographed and in place. Then we have this weird long shot behind some scaffolding where it's kind of tough to see what's happening. I'm not sure what that's about. But there is a feeling of epic that is not in, say, the closing battle of "The Rescue." (The episode of "The Daleks" called "The Rescue." I'm not speaking about the next serial "The Rescue." And when I mention "The Daleks" right there I'm not speaking about this episode but that serial.)

I do like the rebels. It has a WWII spirit to it. As they struggle along, Barbara cooks, Susan makes sad faces, and they listen to the Dalek propaganda over the radio. It all sems very bleak. Luckily, they have Dortmund, the scientist, with his Dalek-destroying bomb to keep morale up. We also have Jenny. Jenny has become a tough broad in the face of adversity. It's understandable. But maybe Barbara should give her a slap. Overall, this gang is far more interesting than the Thals. Probably because they're closer to us. (And, if we're talking Nazis, the Thals are very Aryan, which kind of throws comparisons off a bit.) They're humans struggling to survive against overwhelming odds. It's a very good episode. I also love the way the invasion story is told, overlapping the two groups. (Like the moment when everyone realized they were small in the previous serial.)

Day Of Reckoning

Episode 48: (December 5, 1964) The Doctor and Ian get freed from the Dalek ship but separately. Barbara and Jenny and Dortmund go on a fun run. Susan and David begin to get a little close... if you know what I mean.

Cliffhanger: The Daleks have left a bomb. It's about to go boom.

I think throughout the previous episodes we can see moments where Carole Ann Ford would have gotten annoyed/ fed up with the way Susan was being portrayed. In the original outline for the character, she was meant to be much more interesting. That's not quite the way she comes off in the show. She has had some good moments. The first episode, her moments with Ping-Cho, her scenes in "The Aztecs," much of "The Sensorites." The rest of the time things have been rough. Crying, screaming, always afraid, worried, depressed and just generally kind of a downer. Ian and Barbara bring their own brand of verve to the show. The Doctor is The Doctor. He's more arrogant here than we'll see him until Jon Pertwee takes over the role. He is still, however, The Doctor.

Susan, however, is just tiresome. Think about "The Reign of Terror." She's useless in the jail cell. She leaps up on a bed when there are rats around. She's a sad sack to the Power of 100. Then, upon arriving at Jules's house, she gets sick, which causes them to end up back in jail. I know she can't help being sick. But the way she goes from sick to Not Sick so quickly is suspicious. She then spends about two episodes in a cell accomplishing nothing. If you ever hear people complain that the 13th Doctor had too many people in her TARDIS because they never got enough to do, let's journey back to this season, shall we?

Anyway, you can see the start of a budding relationship with David here. You can see the Doctor (not at his best but he has been drugged and dropped) realizing that this young man is competing for her affections in a way that he can't. The beginning of Susan's departure is happening here. But, for me the moment when I think I can see Carole Ann Ford say "I'm outta here" is when her and David are hiding from the Dalek. It trundles by them, looks around and goes away. The two of them are hiding in the bushes. And David... has his hand clamped over Susan's mouth. What?! I understand he's the hardened rebel. But a few days ago, Susan almost got her head cut off. She travelled through the desert with Marco Polo. She's been kidnapped. She's been imprisoned by cavemen. She travelled up a drainpipe because she was only about an inch tall. And, oh yes, she helped defeat the Daleks once before! Why is his hand over her mouth? What is she going to do? Yell out or what? I don't get it. It seems very condescending. (Although maybe she likes when David does that? She is an alien, after all.)

The rest of the episode is about everyone separating out and heading North to the big Dalek mine. The best sequences involve Jenny, Dortmund and Barbara wheeling Dortmund in his wheelchair through the streets of an empty (pretty much) London. A constant incessant percussion track plays as we see them flying by landmarks of all sorts. Barbara and Jenny are really cooking. It ain't easy running from the Daleks! It's a lovely, iconic location scene that really gives scale to the whole epic feel of the story. Dortmund sacrifices himself to test a new Dalek bomb. (The first one failed and so does the second.) So, the episode ends with Jenny and Barbara on the run, heading north. Ian doesn't do much in the episode.

The Doctor (because of an injury to William Hartnell, which I will mention shortly) seems mostly annoyed and Susan seems ready to go. But, as I said, we're all heading North. Who knows who we will meet along the way?

The End of Tomorrow

Episode 49: (December 12, 1964) The journeys continue. Except for the Doctor and his bunch because William Hartnell has the week off.

Cliffhanger: The Slyther is about to eat (?) Ian and his pal on the edge of a deep hole.

William Hartnell was dropped during the attack on the Dalek ship in the previous episode. He was given a week off to recuperate. In this episode, the Doctor stands up at the start and falls right over. The rest of the cast is allowed to advance the story as far as they can without the Doctor. Starting with David Campbell becoming a demolitions expert. (These rebels can do anything!) Barbara driving a bus. And Ian eating some baked beans. Right from the can!

The story divides off nicely with each of the groups at different spots. Susan and friends are still in London. They spent most of the episode scouting out sewers. (Susan mentions that one smells like an old goat farm. A Coal Hill School Field trip? Or is there a story about Gallifreyan Goats that I've been missing?) They meet up with Tyler. They get into trouble with some alligators, and we see another of Richard Martin's little goofs. (They add up if you watch out for them.)

Martin was a young director trying to give it his all in this multi-camera studio setting. Sometimes he succeeds. Sometimes he doesn't. In the second episode, you can see a crew member in the background of a shot with Ian, The Doctor and some Robomen. In this one, you can see something about the ladder that Susan is trying to use to get her out of the sewer that you shouldn't. There's a rung missing. Susan grabs above the rung. She begins to climb onto the ladder and it swings back out over some stagnant water with an alligator in it. In poorer prints and on 425-line TVs, I wonder if this would have been visible. I feel like "yes" but maybe it wouldn't have been quite as obvious as it is on the DVD. That part of the ladder is not supposed to be in shot. The less said about the Slyther, the better.

The Slyther is probably the first full-on goofy monster in Doctor Who. An amorphous shambling blob that makes a strange noise and eats people. It's first appearance is nice. It's in the background and you're not sure what you're looking at at first. Then, it moves a bit, and you think "Huh? What on Earth might that be?" It's a monster that should be shrouded in darkness but, like that rung and that crew member, it's too clearly visible. Also, the description of it as a pet for the Black Dalek doesn't make much sense to me. But, hey, it's the Slyther!

Barbara and Jenny get the most boisterous part of this episode, again. Their sequence in the bus is a lot of fun. Barbara trying to deal with the negative Jenny is interesting because a good slap might do wonders. Although Jenny's excitement when they run over a Dalek with the bus is great. The flying saucer and toy bus are less great but workable. (You can always put on the CGI effects on the DVD. I think they work well.) Ian and his friend took a spaceship. These two took a bus. They're getting there. (It's almost like "The Five Doctors" for a bit. In the air, on land and underground. I wonder if Terrance Dicks wanted to use the Slyther in that?)

It's definitely a middle episode. But it has a lot more going on it than "The Ordeal." It feels far more expansive. It keeps an epic quality to the serial throughout. The shot of the Daleks, Robomen and 30-odd slaves at the entrance to the cave mouth only helps. *Doctor Who* with a bit of a budget is always something to be reckoned with. But now, let's welcome back The Doctor and see how he feels about his granddaughter's new friend.

The Waking Ally

Episode 50: (December 19, 1964) The Doctor is awake. We're finally beginning to learn what the Daleks are up to on planet Earth. Plus, Barbara and Jenny meet some mean ladies.

Cliffhanger: Ian finds himself trapped inside the Dalek bomb heading to the center of the Earth.

Everyone is slowly drawing closer. By the end Ian is down in the mines, literally. He hides in a bomb that's going down towards the center of the earth. Barbara and Jenny are being interrogated by the Daleks with a little quick thinking going on. And the Doctor, Susan, David and Tyler are moving ever closer. The episode continues to follow the path of the previous two with the travels but there is finally a feeling like we are closing in on the ending. Earlier on in the story, one couldn't quite see how any of this was going to go. At this point, the convergence is palpable.

We do learn more about what the Daleks are up to. They want to use the magnetic core of the Earth for some sort of chicanery. You think they might have found a less populated planet to use. But I guess they needed the slave labor. Or something. Best not to think about it too much. The Daleks know what they want and it's not for us to question.

The best moments in this episode are the fish kissing scene and the scene with the two old "witches" in the house. The fish kissing scene is a return to romance after the Doctor and Cameca's brief dalliance so long ago. David and Susan kiss for a moment. It's a sweet scene. Maybe flirting by slapping a fish in someone's face isn't the most romantic thing in the world but I've seen worse. I like how the Doctor knows right away what's going on. He mentions Susan being a good cook. Unfortunately, there's some confusion over how hot a pan of cooked rabbit is. Tyler wraps a coat around his hand to handle the pot. David just grabs the handle. Maybe he has asbestos hands. Maybe that's why Susan is attracted to him.

The scene with the two old ladies in the shack is one of my favorites. There's a storm coming. Barbara and Jenny stumble into this shack. There's an old woman who looks like a witch and a young woman who looks a little goofy. (Sorry.) They make clothes for the slaves in the mines, so the Daleks leave them alone. Barbara offers them food and they act like crazy scavengers. I love the old woman grabbing a huge knife and piercing the top of the baked beans can. She takes a good long sniff. This broad is nuts. Obviously, immediately, they betray Barbara and Jenny to the Daleks. They're nasty people who get no comeuppance for what they've done. However, story-wise, they've done the right thing. It puts Barbara and Jenny right in the mine so Barbara can get them into Dalek Control.

Terry Nation's script is building nicely. The scene with the guy and his brother who has become a Roboman is a good one. Rather poignant, even though the Robomen are still goofy. I won't miss them when this is over. Martin still has some trouble with action. The fight with the Slyther is a little awkward. And the scene in the very, very wobbly cart descending into the Earth alternately looks all right and a little silly. Plus, I always wonder why Ian climbs on top of the cart to jump down to the mine floor. Why not hang out of the cart and drop down? You're just adding like 4 feet onto the height of your jump. At least, he didn't hurt his kneecaps I suppose.

Flashpoint

Episode 51 (December 26, 1964) The Dalek invasion is over. And Susan leaves.

Cliffhanger: The stars and the heavens.

Richard Martin does his absolute best here. He takes that chaotic couple of minutes from the last episode of "The Daleks" and he makes it into about 10 minutes. It works much better here. The Dalek POV as it approaches the defiant Doctor and then dies is beautifully done. It won't be topped until "The War Machines." Barbara's idea of sending out the order to the Robomen to destroy the Daleks is great. I do like that Barbara impersonates a Dalek voice by waving her hand in front of her face. But the Doctor speeds it up by just trying to sound like a Dalek.

From the opening moments with Ian in the bomb, sabotaging it, to the volcano eruption and the burying of the Daleks on Earth, this episode does the absolute best it can within its budget and the fact that it was basically recorded live. I've little to argue with here. It's lovely to see the group get together, as it always is. It's great to see the Daleks banished from the planet. Hearing Big Ben toll and hoping for the Earth to become non-Dalek again is a peaceful and hopeful moment.

There are a few bits of troubles here and there. Ian is stuck halfway down the mineshaft. He has sabotaged it. So, the Daleks get a team of Robomen to haul the bomb back up the shaft to try again. Several times during this scene, we cut to half a dozen Robomen hauling on a rope. Each time we see them they yell "Pull! Pull!" repeatedly. Look, it's been tough enough treating the Robomen seriously. Every time it cuts to them here, I can't keep from laughing. The Robomen are what they are, but this is humorous. The other odd moment is around 13 minutes in when the Robomen and humans are storming the Dalek headquarters. In one shot, you can clearly see a brick wall and a bit of a sign in the background. That's the Kew Bridge set where the closing scene takes place. They didn't cover up a portion of the set and it is so distracting (and such a goof) that it is funny.

Take away all that though and we are left with a strongly mounted, exciting closing episode to a truly epic *Doctor Who* adventure. The other long stories have felt long. This story feels big. I think they pulled it off. One of the ways they made it so big was the human (ish) story mixed in. The fact that the last 7 to 8 minutes deal with Susan and the Doctor and David is smartly done. We know Carole Ann Ford is leaving. We know Susan is going away. We're losing one of our main characters after 51 episodes. This episode treats it with the gravitas it deserves.

I have seen critics complain about the ending of this episode. Basically, they're saying that it's wrong because Susan isn't allowed to choose. The Doctor locks her out of the TARDIS when he sees how much her and David love each other. He says goodbye and then leaves. I think those critics need to pull their heads out and have a look around. Even David says that The Doctor knew that Susan would never leave him no matter what. That's what is heartbreaking about the scene. The awkward moments regarding her shoe. (I do feel bad that she's in post-Dalek invaded Earth with only one shoe.) The Doctor watching her and David together. The moment Ian and Barbara see what he's doing and let him do it. All strong, strong moments. Susan's face, the Doctor's speech, David holding out his hand. *Doctor Who* is loaded with affecting moments. (Most of them post-2005 but there are plenty before that.) This is the first big moment like this. The first moment that shows what kind of show this is and can be. We lose the ones we love but we continue. Hey, it's like life right. To me, to say that The Doctor is somehow being a jerk here or not letting Susan choose, implies that he's deliberately leaving her. He ain't, Jackson. Watch the show and learn. Both hearts are being broken. But it is time to move on. The Doctor made the right choice. I just feel bad that they never got back to see Susan properly. I hope Susan thrived in this place.

Building a new world out of the wreckage of the old. I do hope she doesn't regenerate though because David is going to be very surprised. And what about their kids?

Well, Susan is gone. She will return a long time from now. The Daleks are gone. They'll be returning before you know it. But first, a rescue mission.

THE RESCUE

The Powerful Enemy

Written by David Whitaker

Directed by Christopher Barry

Episode 52: (January 2nd, 1965) The TARDIS crew lands on the planet Dido. There is a crashed UK spaceship and a ruined village. There seem to be only three inhabitants: an injured man named Bennett, a strange man in elaborate ceremonial robes named Koquillion and a young girl named Vicki. (Not short for Victoria. Just Vicki. V-I-C-K-I.)

Cliffhanger: Spikes appear out of a wall. Ian is being pushed towards the edge of a cliff. The drop puts him right next to some sort of ferocious looking monster.

This is the first episode of the second production block of *Doctor Who*. Like the Doctor, at the beginning, a lot of the cast and crew have been able to take a rest. Two major members are, of course, gone: Carole Ann Ford as Susan. David Whitaker as Script Editor. This episode introduces us to the new Script Editor Dennis Spooner. He wrote "The Reign of Terror" so we have a bit of a clue as to what his writing is like. Maureen O'Brian is here as Vicki. The new gal. In fact, this is David Whitaker's sort of goodbye (because he'll be back) to everyone that also says hello to Vicki.

Let's start with Vicki: She's charming and energetic. Her excitement over thinking that a rescue ship has arrived three days early (It's the TARDIS that's arrived.) is infectious. She and Bennett have been involved in a terrible series of events. The ship crashing. The people of Dido inviting everyone to a banquet. (Vicki couldn't go because she was sick.) The Dido inhabitants killing all the passengers. Bennett fighting back. And now it's just the two of them, lorded over by this odd Koquillion with his spanner that causes cave ins. Throughout it all, Vicki keeps perky and positive. The only time she really loses it is when she talks to Barbara. She doesn't want anyone to feel sorry for her and the weight of what they've been through seems to overwhelm her. But, generally, she's strong and kind of a, to be honest, breath of fresh air. As you may have noted, as much as I like Susan, her inconsistent character was truly getting on my nerves. Hopefully, Vicki will be more consistent.

The rest of the episode is sneaking around in caves. Don't let that bother you. It's fun. So, is the opening TARDIS scene. William Hartnell is at his funniest throughout this episode. The line about Barbara's trembling, the moment where he points out he can hear everything Ian and Barbara are saying and the great line when he has his back to the wall are all classics. Then, he has that moment where he asks Susan to open the doors and his face drops. He is sad. They all are. Ian and Barbara reminisce on where Susan might be. It's nice that the show hasn't forgotten her. I guess that's why the previous script editor was brought in to do this. He can keep the continuity and move the story/ show along here.

I always like a good cave. This one has Koquillion in it. The cave has spikes and strange rings on the walls. It has a little ledge. It has some sort of monster skulking around. This is a fun cave! Somehow, even though the shenanigans in here are not high tech, it's fun to watch. It's that old Saturday Afternoon serial kind of thing, tweaked slightly. In fact, Whitaker tweaks the now almost standard *Doctor Who* first episode template here. The TARDIS crew meander around not knowing where they are at first and discovering assorted things. It's intercut with these other characters, mainly Vicki, who give us the whole story and mainly give us this new character. Only a future TARDIS member would be able to subvert the template like this. We don't just focus on Barbara, Ian and Susan. Vicki's importance here spearheads that she will be a big part of this. Then, Whitaker tweaks it some more by having the Doctor know what planet it is… and it's a planet he's been to and likes. Just enough subversion of that formula to keep it fresh. Let's see what Desperate Measures we're getting ourselves into next.

Desperate Measures

Episode 53: (January 9, 1965) We learn the secret of Koquillion and get a new member of the TARDIS crew.

Cliffhanger: The TARDIS falls off a cliff!

People have complained in the past that this a "murder mystery with one suspect." I would suggest those people should read more murder mysteries. In most of the best murder mysteries, everything that happens is beholden to the mystery. (OK. Occasionally there may be character stuff in a long-running series, like Holmes and Watson chatting, but generally things happen because the mystery needs them to.) To me, "The Rescue" is never about a "mystery." It's a story that introduces a new companion. And it's the story that does it for the first time.

It is about us meeting Vicki. Having the crew meet her. They get to know one another. It's about some confusion, such as Barbara shooting Sandy the Monster. It's about Vicki wanting them to go away. It's about The Doctor being one of the most charming beings in the universe. Watch how nothing is really happening with Koquillion until the Doctor has befriended Vicki. It's a sweet scene. The Doctor brings some of The Doctor's arrogance in but it's not bad here. Vicki clearly takes to him. Yes, the Doctor may be thinking of Susan when he's talking to this young woman. There may be some selfishness there. But he's acting from his hearts. Once befriended, he begins to try to figure out what's going on immediately.

I think the fact that The Doctor figures out the "mystery" almost immediately means that the mystery is second place to the meeting. Look at "Partners in Crime." That episode aired 33 years later. No one has ever clamored for The Adipose to return. To most people, that episode is the one where Donna returns to the show and joins the Doctor for travelling. (Obviously "Rose" is an even more extreme version, but it must do the companion thing AND introduce the show to people.) The "mystery" in "The Rescue" is simply some weirdness, some intrigue, some conflict: all to bring Vicki into the fold.

I think it's a great episode. It has a nice pace. Bennett is clearly a jerk. Then, when you learn why he's pretending to be Koquillion, you really kind of hate him. He killed a crewmember on the ship. Vicki didn't know. Now he's killed so many people to cover up his crime. The Doctor is disgusted, and I'm disgusted. In the Dido Hall of Judgment, the two meet. It's a hell of a set for only being on the screen for a few minutes. Daunting scene. I love to see the Doctor defending himself against Bennett. It's an exciting moment. The appearance of the Didoians (?) promises hope for the future. Although, 1) they look like they could be ghosts and 2) what happens to Bennett? He steps through a door at the back of a hall and falls off a cliff. Should there have been a plank there or something? Is that where they execute people when they've been found guilty in the Hall of Judgment? I never had the novelization for this one. I feel like that may have helped.

Anyway, it's a sharply written, funny, exciting and sweet two-parter. It's clearly a piece of a longer story. The fact that the whole thing ends with the TARDIS dropping off a cliff immediately following them leaving Dido means that it really is one darn thing after another, Vicki had a rough time for a while there. But she's going to have a wild time now.

THE ROMANS

The Slave Traders

Written by Dennis Spooner

Directed by Christopher Barry

Episode 54: (January 16, 1965) The TARDIS crew are relaxing in a villa outside of Rome in AD 64. They've been resting for a month before the story starts. But now it's over. The Doctor and Vicki talk a walk to Rome and get involved in an assassination. Barbara and Ian are kidnapped by slave traders.

Cliffhanger: Ascaris the tongue-free assassin is about to kill The Doctor.

Dennis Spooner ladles in his concept of what *Doctor Who* should be. We know what David Whitaker was up to. Dennis seems to have a more playful concept of what the show can do. Steven Moffat may see Dennis as his patron saint. David was awesome and brought the show through its gestation period, but Dennis will keep the show going. This is his second story as Script Editor and a story he wrote himself. So, there is much of his template all over this.

I love the concept of the main characters of a show based around adventures having a grand time when they can take a vacation. When Douglas Adams oversaw the show around 1978, he pitched a show where the Doctor retires. There would have been an episode where the Doctor does very little. Graham Williams said no. But it's a beauty of a concept. Dennis Spooner gives the crew a month of relaxation before this episode begins. It isn't something one would expect of a show at this time. It's great, though.

So, when the problems start, they feel a little more problematic than they did. Because they had been resting. There isn't a star in the heavens that says that they should be under siege all the time. That's what happens though. And to watch them relaxing, luxuriating in this space isn't a bad thing. It's something that should make the viewer happy. They know that garbage will happen soon. They know that life will become insane again

The Doctor and Vicki prove to be a fun couple in a way that Susan and the Doctor never could. The Doctor has no control over Vicki. So, there is a fun camaraderie when the two of them are together. I love that the episode mixes them up in Nero's court so quickly. Vicki, at this point, is the perfect version of the *Doctor Who* viewer. Young and energetic and willing to engage in whatever.

Dennis Spooner does have a problem making the darker portions as flippant as he wants them to be. Barbara and Ian are grabbed by Slave Traders and the sequence is slapstick, but the implication is not. The two conflicting tones don't quite work.

The main takeaway… The TARDIS is indestructible. It falls from a cliff and it is ready to go. The crew has been broken up into bits. The slave stuff is unpleasant. The Doctor and the Vicki are in the proximity of Nero. Who knows? Maybe this time they won't all meet up again. Maybe this time it will be the end.

All Roads Lead to Rome

Episode 55: (January 23, 1965) We meet Nero! Ian winds up on a slave ship. The Doctor must prepare for a big lute concert.

Cliffhanger: Ian and Delos have been told that they will be fighting in the arena. They see some very hungry lions.

Nero enters with a burp and a lyre.

You can see exactly what kind of story Dennis Spooner has cooked up in the middle of the episode. (Well, the assassin attacking the Doctor kind of gives it away too.) The Doctor and Vicki are strolling through some sort of Roman town square. A slave auction begins. Women begin to walk up onto the stage. The Doctor drags Vicki away. The moment they're out of eyesight... Barbara steps onto the stage/platform. Ahh, it's a farce! The assassin scene and the first meeting with Nero cement this. The Doctor is having such a good time that Vicki seems a bit worried about him. She must keep bringing him back down to Earth. He does a good job of not getting in trouble with Nero and Hartnell goes super energetic when he's sending Ascaris the Assassin out the window. (I think the time off must have done William Hartnell a world of good.)

Barbara has less fun. What with being sold as a slave at auction. But she doesn't seem to have it terrible once she's sold. The man who buys her works for Nero and she will be the Empress's handmaiden. That's not bad. Much better than the extremely sick woman that Barbara spends time in a cell with. What an odd world. You're just walking down the street and suddenly you're captured and sold into slavery. The slavers even go so far as they did in the last episode. A home invasion! This time there's no murder or thievery, just kidnapping and slavery. I don't think I would have done well in Ancient Rome.

Ian has somehow spent five days on a ship, down in the galley rowing. I'm wondering if the timelines all match here. It took five days to walk Barbara to Rome. During that time, Ian was immediately put on board a ship to row. At the same time, The Doctor as Maximus and Vicki are in Rome. I can see that Barbara thing going five days. But the Maximus timeline only takes a couple of days. Surely. That timeline seems to be going along OK. Then, Ian says, "5 days" and everything goes mental. It is a time travel show so having a parallel story be in a slightly different timeline isn't crazy. (It's kind of cool.)

Rowing that boat constantly seems like a terrible thing. But surely being the gallery master must stink just as much. Yelling "In" and "Out" repeatedly. Trying to be a tough guy all the time. All that shouting. I wonder if there were any nice galley masters. Guys who weren't real jerks. "He doesn't yell at you, really. He just wants to make it fun for everyone." Of course, he's dead and the ship has sunk before we can think about it too much. In fact, that whole ship rowing portion feels a bit less detailed than it could be. We only know how long it's been because Ian told us. And we only know what happens to the ship because Delos tells us. It's a very abrupt portion of the episode.

Regardless, the Doctor's having a good time. So is Vicki. Her excitement when Nero shows up is delightful. Their responses to the strange bald man who keeps whispering to them is fun. And The Doctor is now going to have to figure out how to put on a concert in the court of Nero when he can't play the lyre to save his life. It's all building quite nicely. Thank goodness Christopher Barry is back.

Conspiracy

Episode 56: (January 30, 1965) Full out farce. The Doctor puts on a concert. Barbara gets chased around by an amorous Nero. Ian and his pal end up fighting in the arena. Vicki is just marveling at how silly ancient history is.

Cliffhanger: Ian is about to be killed by his friend in the arena, at Nero's command.

I really should let the farce speak for itself here. There's a lot of great running through corridors. Nero chasing Barbara. The Doctor appearing here and there. Poppaea, Nero's wife, always seeing things she doesn't like. There's a court poisoner who takes a shine to Vicki. And it's all crazy. Culminating in The Doctor's big performance for Nero. Stolen directly from "The Emperor's New Clothes." Followed by a final, real fight between Ian and Delos as Barbara and Nero look on. The episode is over 26 minutes, which is overlong for the normal timeslot. But, as it focusses almost all its farce here, it's OK, I think. It's clearly an experiment.

One of the joys of the second block of episodes (that began with "The Rescue") is that it's clear that the production team are pushing the boundaries. Throughout their first block (52 episodes made, 51 aired), they were getting piecemeal episode orders from the folks in charge. 13 here, 13 more, 13... But, at the start of this block, they were given 26. Those episodes will take us to the end of the story "The Chase." It will take us to the end of Barbara and Ian's time on the show. As they had these episodes available, they felt they could experiment. Verity Lambert, with new guy Dennis Spooner, decided to try things out. Obviously, "introducing a new companion/ lead" is big. And in this episode, they're pushing the comedy. Very soon, they'll push the weird. People of the time weren't thrilled on the comedy. I believe they thought it was stupid and many didn't fully get what the show was doing. Nowadays, with hindsight, we can see the comedy and we see what they're trying,

The thing that always impresses me is that they only have one long hallway and a couple of rooms. Yet during that rush of scenes with Nero after Barbara, it, generally, feels bigger. They're still doing that thing with the cloth hanging on the back wall simulating endless hallways. It works better here than it did on Marinus and about as well as it did on Skaro. Luckily, there's always someone running past or by it, so attention isn't as drawn to it. Christopher Barry does an excellent job of making it work even though it is done basically live in the studio. Whatever Verity wanted from this episode; it works.

We do get to see The Doctor and Nero in a Roman sauna together. Possibly the first time we'll see the Doctor this nude until "Spearhead from Space." So, drink it in! There's some fun business in the sauna with a sword and that poor servant of Nero's. He has a rough day. Although, I do feel like the Doctor should have anticipated Nero's response at dinner. Nero thinks he's the best everything in the world. The Doctor playing but not playing is only going to bother him. It's a clever trick of the Doctor's but it does cause Delos and Ian to have to fight.

I always forget that Delos is played by the great Peter Diamond one of the best stuntman, fight arrangers in the business. He worked on the original *Star Wars* films, *Raiders of the Lost Ark*, *The Princess Bride* (he choreographed the fight scene) and a ton of others. Also, he's a pretty good actor. There's some real ferocity to the fight between Ian and Delos in the arena. (I know the arena is not that large. I always thought of this as a small private room that Nero had off to one side. When he wanted to see someone get hurt, they brought the gladiators to him.)

The episode spends so much time keeping Barbara from Vicki and the Doctor that it's with a great sigh of relief that Barbara and Ian see each other at the end. Now, Ian is fighting for his life but still... It gives one a little hope that the next episode will reunite everyone peacefully. And then we catch the title.

Inferno

Episode 57: (February 6, 1965) Nero fiddles while Rome burns. The TARDIS crew gets the heck out of Dodge.

Cliffhanger: Some force is dragging the TARDIS towards it. (It might be on a Web Planet of some variety.)

Rome burns while Nero plucks at his lyre. And it was the Doctor who gave Nero the idea! Even Vicki is astounded. After being told for so long that you cannot interfere with history, it comes as a bit of a shock. Vicki says she got a lecture about it. After all that happened in "The Aztecs," The Doctor causes the burning of Rome. He seems a bit upset by that at first but after a few moments he's quite amused. Maybe he honestly thought he couldn't do it. He gave the speeches to keep people from trying. Maybe someone he used to travel with told him that. Regardless, things have changed.

Since Dennis Spooner is our writer and script editor here, he would be the culprit. He already added touches of comedy to "The Reign of Terror." Here he goes for full on farce. He reverses everything David Whitaker had set in stone for the show. Let's be honest: I think that's for the best. Under Whitaker's hand, the show would be like the aforementioned *Voyagers*. A TV show teaching us about history where the characters can't really do much but guide history onto its path. *Voyagers* is a lot of fun. The 20 episodes of it are very entertaining. But it needed more of a kick to keep going and going, I believe. Spooner has given *Doctor Who* that kick. History is up for grabs!

I love the closing scenes where they have returned to the villa. Ian and Barbara get some good flirting in. (I think they shared a sauna together, if you know what I mean.) (Can I just say here? I think Barbara should have better hair. That hair doesn't say 1965 to me. It says "My best friend's grandmother's hair from a long time ago".) The realization from Ian that everything that happened over the past week or so was because Barbara beaned him with the vase is cool. Then, the Doctor arrives and is hilarious as he chastises them for being bone idle. The Doctor really does love the sound of his own voice sometimes. Did anyone ever write fan fiction about the family returning to their villa later and finding it in a very odd state? I bet someone did.

There's an interesting moment where Tavius is seen saying silent goodbyes to Barbara, Ian and Delos. While he's doing so, he clutches a crucifix. I guess that's to imply that he is not part of this barbarous Roman culture. He's part of the new wave of Christians on the way. Per the DVD information text, the Romans blamed the Christians for the burning of Rome. I wonder how they pulled that off when we specifically see Nero hire a group of men and tell them to tell people they're burning Rome because Nero commanded it. Well, I guess you can spin anything when you put your mind to it.

Overall, a super fun story. Stories like this are probably my favorite kind of historical. The more pedantic ones are certainly interesting but sometimes don't have things for the TARDIS crew to do. This one gives everyone something to do, let's them meddle with history and gets them all back to the ship in time for the next round of adventures. In the end, the climax is basically "Let's all get out of here!" as fast as they can. But it's had enough incident and fun behind it to make it exciting and feel like they have had a heck of an adventure. Now, take a deep breath. Things are about to get weird.

THE WEB PLANET

The Web Planet

Written by Bill Strutton

Directed by Richard Martin

Episode 58: (Feb 13, 1965) The crew land on a strange, hazy planet inhabited by giant ants and God knows what else.

Cliffhanger: The TARDIS is gone. Barbara is about to step in an acid pool. All is not well.

This episode got 13.5 million viewers. The highest numbers of viewers the show would get for a very long time. Luckily, the serial keeps up that number of viewers. It never goes below 11.5. I love the fact that the largest number of viewers for a 1960s episode turned out for this one. As it's one of the weirdest episodes of the show. It takes the template of "The TARDIS crew land on a new planet and wander around" and tweaks it a bit. Just enough to make it weirder.

In the past, the gang met up with somebody or something. They glean little clues as to what's happening and where they might be. Here it's different. Vicki and Barbara stay in the TARDIS. Ian and the Doctor put on ADJ's (Atmospheric Density Jackets) and explore the surface of the planet. They don't see any life. There's an enormous temple with a statue way up at the top. The whole surface is shiny and smeary. (Some sort of Vaseline was placed over the lens while they were on the surface.) it makes the planet look very different from previous ones. We see a giant ant and a small grub of some sort. They are trying to claim the TARDIS, or something. Yes, that's right. A giant ant and a giant grub. The main characters don't meet them, but they hear them. Trust me, you'll know their sound.

I love the episode because at the end we are as in the dark as the TARIDS crew. What is that noise exactly? What is the supersonic noise Vicki keeps hearing? There's an acid pool. But, when the credits roll and the Doctor realizes that the ship had vanished, we realize that we have no idea what just happened. The chirruping ants and the grub haven't been discovered. The planet isn't really giving up its secrets. In *About Time*, the authors point out that for the first two episodes it's tough to gauge what exactly is happening. And it's true. It's giving the audience a lot of credit. It's going to take a while before we figure exactly what's happening.

I like the scene between Vicki and Barbara where Vicki won't take her medicine. Vicki talks about the future and education. Barbara is a bit amazed and treated a bit condescendingly but it's fun, nevertheless.

Poor Ian! He loses his gold pen and his Coal Hill belt! I love the Doctor experimenting on things by having Ian take off some potion of his clothes. It's a fun investigation scene.

I also quite enjoy the TARDIS under siege. That hasn't really happened yet. It's good to know that there are aliens who go after the TARDIS. Aliens that don't care what it is or who the Time Lords are.

Overall, it's a pretty good but strange episode. The lack of other humanoid beings is not a problem here. It just expands what the crew end up looking at. They mention that they feel like they're being watched. They're not wrong. It all wraps up with a multiple event cliffhanger. Everyone's in trouble! I'm hoping someone or something can come along and help for a bit.

The Zarbi

Episode 59: (February 20, 1965) They're still goofing around on the planet Vortis. This time giant wasps show up.

Cliffhanger: The Doctor has a tube lowered over his head. A woman's voice speaks to him.

The episode keeps the weird level going high. Ian and the Doctor are still wandering the surface of the planet. They're getting a little bit cross with one another. I mean, if the TARDIS has dematerialized, then they're pretty much trapped here. If something dragged it away, what was it? Plus, those jackets they're wearing aren't being particularly helpful. At least they know they're on the planet Vortis in the Galaxy of Pictos. (Why Ian doesn't just claim the Doctor is making stuff like this up sometimes is beyond me.)

Barbara gets the most mind clearing portion of the episode. She meets the giant wasps who used to live on the planet and who used to rule the planet. The Zarbi were the servants. Then, one day, this evil appeared. It's described as being like a plague being spread. A sickness laying waste to the planet. Forcing the Menoptra to leave and, hopefully, return some day. That sickness is the Animus, the voice we hear at the very end.

How are the Menoptra? Well, they're a touch better than the guys running around in the ant suits. (I'll mention them again in a moment.) They're a bit on the pretentious side. They're a bit, let's face it, on the goofy side. They have a weird way of moving that is supposed to say "alien." It generally ends up saying "What the heck are they doing?" There is a credit in the episode for the movement of the Menoptra. One of the wasps is played by the choreographer. I give the production high praise for trying it. But even Barbara seems to have a "This is too much" look on her face sometimes.

It is nice that the mind is beginning to clear a bit re: what the heck is going on here? That constant noise the Zarbi makes whenever they're onscreen, coupled with the smear on the lens really begins to create a sort of disconnect in this viewer's mind. As I mentioned in "The Romans" reviews, Verity Lambert was really shooting for the stars with this production block. She was really attempting to push the show as far as it would go. Luckily, it happens during some of the highest ratings the show ever had. I can only imagine what a viewer in 1965 thought of this.

Back then, a British TV screen had 405 lines on them. That's 405 lines of information. I'm watching this via a Blu-Ray on a 50" HD TV at a 1:33 aspect ratio. There are moments in this landscape, as the Zarbi clomp around as their noise goes on and on and the lens is smeary, when I feel a little bit like I am in another world. I can't imagine what this looked like on a 1965 TV. Smaller screen. Low definition. Sound not quite the best. I wonder if it may have all gone on too long. Possibly to a point where viewers threw up their hands and said, "Bring back Nero and all that goofiness!"

Even if I have trouble connecting to the episode, I do love the bravery of it. It's quite bold in the way it refuses to give up any of its answers until it's time to do so. That does make the previous episode a lot of wandering. Some of the wandering is reminiscent of previous episode wanderings. But it's still worth the watch. We are finding out what's up. We'll find out where this journey is taking us.

Escape To Danger

Episode 60: (February 27, 1965) The TARDIS crew (minus Barbara) meet the Animus. Ian escapes from the Carsinome and meets Vrestin, a Menoptra. The invasion is about to begin.

Cliffhanger: Some Zarbi and a Larva gun run by the entrance to a rockface. Previously, Ian and Vrestin fell through it somehow. It's tough to say.

I applaud that they're still going for it with all the giant insects. The Zarbi meander around. The gun things speed along. A Menoptra flies onto the set. They look odd. Yes. They look unreal. Sure. But let's keep going with it. As the Doctor says to the Animus when he's under the Animus's hair dryer, "they come from a different astral plane." So, who knows? Maybe the Zarbi are thinking "Those humanoids don't look quite right to us. They look a little fakey. Also, the older one is wearing a wig." We're deep into the day at Vortis here so all bets are off.

I love the scenes in the Animus's lair with the Doctor and Vicki. (Ian's great too but he gets out of there quickly.) They really make a good team. They were great in "The Romans" and here, under a much stranger form of danger, they hold together well. The moment they put that control thing over Vicki, and she goes zombie-like is a bit disconcerting. Such a lively companion now suddenly with dead, dead eyes is a sight. I like their fiddling around with the astral map. It's kind of a goofy looking thing. I love that it must remain plugged in. The time and relative dimension link will break if it gets unplugged. (I remember Barbara mentioning in the first episode that she was going to give the place a jolly good spring clean. I can see the high hilarity when she accidentally unplugs the astral map to get the vacuum cleaner going.) I do hope the Doctor has that hooked up to a surge protector. One burst of energy through the TARDIS and that thing is useless. I wish the Doctor still used the Astral map. I would have loved to see 13th using it with her gang.

There's one moment that I always wonder about here. (There's also a moment that confuses me but that will come later.) The Doctor sends Vicki into the TARDIS for a box. When she hands it to him, he says its wrong and sends her back. But, not before taking out its contents and letting Vicki hold it. The content is a spider in amber or something. And it scares the heck out of the Zarbi. The Doctor doesn't look like he's up to tricks here, but is he? Did he send her to get the wrong box? I'm guessing he did. But why lie? The Animus doesn't know what's in the boxes. Why not just send her for the box with the spider? No one would know. Why the chicanery? Unless it's a mistake. But if it is a mistake, it's a heck of a coincidental mistake to make.

Ian gets a lot of excitement in this one. He gets to run through the odd halls of the lair. He gets to brawl with a Zarbi. He kicks the Zarbi onto its back and, of course, it can't get up. Larvae guns shoot at him. He befriends a Menoptra. It's in that scene with Vrestin that we finally learn what's going on. The Menoptra in the previous episode gave some clues. But here it is fully established that this is the wasps' planet and the force that now rules and keeps the surface dead is the intruder. (Not that we became convinced that it was the on the side of good when it was talking to the Doctor. But, apparently, it convinced Ian.)

My favorite moment in this episode is the moment (it is brief) where everything seems to work well. Now, we know that they're on small soundstage sets. The designers do their best to give us some real depth. I love the giant buildings painted on the backdrops to give us a sense of a big, big world. But try as they might, there are definite moments when the spatial limitations are obvious. That's why I love that first shot when Ian escapes out onto the surface. A Menoptra flies over. Ian runs by. And the guns and the Zarbi go flying past. For one moment, none of this seems silly at all. It all looks pretty darn cool. I'm convinced anyway.

I'll close with the confusing moment: What's going on in the cliffhanger? Vrestin and Ian are going to the Crater of Needles. Zarbi and Larva are chasing them. The duo hides in a crevasse in the rock face. Suddenly, dirt starts falling on Ian. They let out some yells and apparently they fall and fall... into the Crater of Needles (?). (We don't see them do so.) But then, we linger on as the Zarbi and the larva guns pass the crevasse and keep on moving. Wasn't the cliffhanger when they fell into the wherever? Is it really these goofy insects running by? That could be one of those Richard Martin moments when something just kind of goes wrong. Maybe it was meant to end right before but everyone was so caught up in emotion that it got missed. Maybe.

Crater of Needles

Episode 61 (March 6, 1965) Barbara is back. The invasion is still approaching.

Cliffhanger: The Zarbi attack Barbara.

If you're not used to the gauzy, hazy look on the planet by this point, you're just going to have to deal with it.

This episode has another odd moment with The Doctor. He is holding a piece of recording equipment. The Animus asks him what it is, and the Doctor waves it away. It's just some broken equipment. But then, the device begins to play the recording from the Menoptra invasion force on a nearby plateau. The Doctor doesn't turn it off. He lets the whole message play and lets the Animus hear everything. He looks angry that it's happening, but he doesn't do anything. Did The Doctor mean for that to happen? If he didn't, why didn't he stop it? He just gave the game away. Why Doctor, why?

And another confusing moment, again at the cliffhanger. Well, let's talk the battle first. The Menoptra invasion begins! But their position has been given away and their weapons are ineffectual. I love the first appearance of the flying Menoptra with "Code Word: Electron!" I'm not sure why the Menoptra require other Menoptra to give code words. Are there spies within the giant wasp community? Do they not recognize each other immediately? "This fella looks like a wasp… but he could be a Zarbi! Better use the code word." I don't know. I'd be offended if a fellow Menoptra didn't trust me. There must be spies, that's it. Menoptra in Larva gun outfits back in the Carsinome. Anyway…

It's a sizable invasion attack for *Doctor Who*. Shot on film, lots of flying around. Lots of shooting and chaotic action. It looks like the Menoptra are not doing so great. But then, the Zarbi, and Larva guns are a bit goofy looking so it's a little tough to gauge precisely what's happening. It's fun though. The confusing moment comes right at the end. Barbara and a Menoptra are backed up against a piece of rock. The Larva and Zarbi approach, poised to fire. Barbara closes her eyes. Then, it cuts to a longshot of the two of them running away while the "Next Episode" caption appears. Almost as if they didn't want to leave that week with too much jeopardy going on. They've already escaped from the life-or-death moment. Thank goodness. I do wonder if that was a mistake or not.

Ian and Vrestin get a slightly better recap of their confusing cliffhanger. We sort of see them falling. But, like a few moments in this serial, it's a little tough to figure out what is happening and why. Something happens and then we see the aftermath. What we couldn't understand took us from one point to the other. Then, Ian and Vrestin meet the Optera. They are basically woodlice. Menoptra who never had wings and burrow around underground. This species was added at the last minute. I'm not 100% sure why. I'm still getting used to the Menoptra. We really didn't quite need another confusing race. This one looking kind of goofier than the ones before it and talking like a slightly more intelligent Roboman. It is interesting to see a variation of the main race who have adapted themselves to the underground. But, at this moment, I'm not terribly enamored of the Optera. Although, I do like Vrestin's wings extending and bringing awe. That's a cool moment. (And makes the Menoptra who have had their wings removed even sadder. It's too bad they don't grow back.)

The Doctor and Vicki are still back in that one room in the Carsinome. My favorite moment: When the Doctor is trying to retrieve the control unit thing, Vicki is scaring a Zarbi with the spider. She lets out a quick whistle and a wave at the Doctor for him to slide the control thing over. I like this Vicki. It does bother me when both her and the Doctor are fitted with those gold devices and their faces go blank and dead. Things don't look so great for the good guys right now. If I more fully understood the bad guys, maybe I'd feel worse. But luckily, the story is still confusing me just enough to keep me on tenterhooks.

Invasion

Episode 62: (March 13, 1965) Two different groups are approaching the Carsinome. Trying to reach the center of the Web.

Cliffhanger: The Doctor and Vicki are captured. An organic gun in the wall covers them in thick, white webbing.

That cliffhanger is a harrowing one, huh? As much as the ending is starting to seem exactly like the ending of "The Daleks," this is like when Susan and the Doctor are captured. They are pinned to the wall with Dalek restraints. Here, it's much nastier. Caught in that white web where the Doctor's face does not look happy, and you can't even see Vicki. That's a good cliffhanger.

Before that Vicki and The Doctor get a charming scene where they reverse the polarity of the retaining gold necklace thing and get a Zarbi under their control. The Doctor treats it a bit like a dog. Vicki calls it "Zombo" and pats its head. They make a great team these two. I like Vicki more and more with each episode.

Yes, this episode keeps some elements of strangeness. (One of those moments mentioned later.) But, basically, becomes the last few episodes of "The Daleks." The Doctor, Vicki and Barbara above ground trying to figure out how to get in. They have a Menoptra weapon (or something) called the Isop-Tope, which can destroy the Animus. They must get to the center of its web to use it properly. One of the Menoptra has a great speech about how he felt like giving up when his wings were taken but meeting Barbara has given him courage again. The description of how they didn't notice the Animus was there until it had leaked into their world, and it was too late is excellent. The set they're in is fantastic. The perspective up that chimney is nicely done. I wish there were fewer fluffed moments in here but it works. (The camera can be seen at the edge of a shot. It runs into the scenery in another.)

Underground, Ian and Vrestin and the Optera are going on a variation of the journey Ian took in "The Ordeal" so long ago. Except this time instead of with tall, blond Thals, it's with odd little woodlice things who grunt and bounce around. William Russell does seem to have trouble keeping a straight face on occasion. Or maybe it's Ian caught up in the general energy of the Optera. I can't quite tell. As others go above, they go below. All to the same destination. If I had to pick the direction this serial would have gone back at the start, it wouldn't have been "replicating the last two episode of 'The Daleks'."

There is a scene in this episode that I always find odd. It's the scene where Nimini, the female Optera, plugs the gap in the wall with her head. The Optera are picking through the walls and using some nice flowery language to describe what they're doing. Nimini hits one spot and acid begins coming out. Immediately, she jams her head into the hole and starts screaming. A few moments later, she's dead. The head Optera says that this kind of thing happens all the time and that's just what they do. But it's horrible. At least, in theory. In practice, it's a little underwhelming. Her scream is wrenching but it's treated so casually that one almost forgets about it. Ian lingers over her body for a few moments. But it's tough to gauge what he's thinking. He doesn't look sad or horrified or disgusted. He's just looking. Maybe he's stunned. Maybe he just wants to get back to the TARDIS. It's a scene that I always feel should have more said about it. It underplays itself so much that I'm not sure it cares.

The Centre

Episode 63: (March 20, 1965) The final battle in the Carsinome for the heart of Vortis.

Cliffhanger: We see the moon Pictos. We see the caption "Next Episode THE LION."

Well, The Menoptra have Vortis back. The Zarbi are their servants. The Optera have come up to the surface. The Animus has been banished back to its dimension. Water flows freely once again. And, like several previous stories, this one has the big climax at The Centre and then about another eight minutes after that. Another eight minutes with the Menoptra, Optera and Zarbi. Your mileage may vary. Personally, after the TARDIS crew leaves, I think there's a sitcom in there somewhere. (I also forgot that after the TARDIS leaves we get several minutes without them there, ending on a close up of the moon Pictos. I'm not sure we needed that scene. I'm good with Vortis.)

One thing I always forget at the end is when the Menoptra thank The Doctor for all he's done. I don't mean to be rude but what did he do? He gave away the position of their Strike Force. He figured out how to get a Zarbi under their control. And then he... spent the climax lying down amongst the Animus's tentacles while other people did things? At least, The Doctor formulated the plan in "The Daleks." Here he does almost nothing. It's Barbara who saves the day when everyone else fails.

I do love how everyone converges on the Centre for the climax. That giant parade float-like spider/octopus Animus hovering above a giant light with tentacles everywhere is a sight to see. They keep whatever strings hold it up just out frame so even though it is clearly fake (like, say, the man-sized ants running around for all six episodes) it could be real. Remember, we're on a different plain of reality here. Why shouldn't the Animus look like that? It's almost Nestene-esque. But, I think the Animus, the Nestene Consciousness and the Great Intelligence all come from somewhere other than here. If you know what I mean. And I'm not sure I do.

This really is a serial that needs to be watched over time. Normally, when I watch it, it's one a day over six days. That's perfect. Watched several a day, as I did for this book, it's a bit much. The noise that the Zarbi makes becomes overbearing. The Optera have some lovely dialogue, but they look kind of dumb. And The Menoptra's movement and patterns of speech drive me up the wall. Vrestin calling Ian "Heron" really bugged me during this episode. "Ian! It's Ian!. Why are you putting an 'h' in there?" And is there anything funnier/ more embarrassing than the "Zarbi!!!! Come here!!!!" scene. That's a cringer. I can watch almost everything *Doctor Who* can throw at me. (Even "The Doctor's Daughter." Usually.) But this scene always sneaks up on me and always makes me want to hide.

Then, there are all the little goofs and errors and bits of confusion. I've mentioned the two cliffhangers. This episode has the obvious power cord going out of that web spraying gun on the wall. It has the doors not closing properly when The Doctor and Vicki enter the Centre. It's only with this viewing that I realized one of the Menoptra has been doing Zarbi impersonations. They present it in such a way that you need to be told what's going on. Barbara fires the Isop-tope at the Dark Side of the Animus. Where might that be exactly? She just stands there, and the Animus dies. Why add the "Dark Side" thing at all if no one makes sense of it? There are quite a few things throughout this serial that don't fully make sense and needed clarification. Maybe that's why it's so odd to watch?

Overall, it's an experiment that works as often as it doesn't. As an experiment, I always have a soft spot for it. I realized the Doctor's best moment here: The way he seems to be in real pain after getting sprayed with the webs. The Animus is talking to him. The slightest movements seem to hurt him. I like that. (Not the Doctor getting hurt. William Hartnell's acting.) If you're a fan of the show, do not skip this one. You've probably never seen anything quite like it.

I would make a joke about the crew leaving an insect planet and the next episode being called "The Lion." But Rob Shearman made that joke in *Running Through Corridors*. And it was a good one.

THE CRUSADE

The Lion

Written By David Whitaker

Directed by Douglas Camfield

Episode 64: (March 27, 1965) The TARDIS lands in Palestine during the 12th Century. The Third Crusade is underway. They meet Richard the Lionhearted and get in some fights.

Cliffhanger: King Richard will not allow Ian to go after Barbara, who is being held prisoner by Saladin.

I do like some good Shakespearean dialogue. I don't expect to see King Richard appear and say something like "Hey, my knights. What up?" But did they all actually talk like this? (Didn't King Richard speak French?) It takes so long to make a point. During the big fight scene at the start of this episode, if they spoke so flowery, they'd be dead before they could finish their sentences. Just wondering. Because some of the most eloquent dialogue in all of *Doctor Who* pops up in this episode. David Whitaker really went to town here. Luckily, his words are matched by the sharp direction of Douglas Camfield. Thank goodness, a director who can do a fight scene. (I did notice that the Doctor gets into the theatrical talk. His aside while in the clothing merchant's tent is very Shakespearean.)

Watching "The Crusade" (the title for this serial) is for me like a watching a film made by a very high-quality filmmaker. It looks good. The acting is excellent. The dialogue is first rate. Everything is top quality. But, for reasons beyond the control of the makers, I never fully get into it. I never 100% get on board with it. We've seen the TARDIS crew separated so many times. We know they'll get back together in the end. It's just a question of when. When the serial first aired, viewers would have had no idea how long this would go on. They've seen 2-part stories all the way up to 7-part stories. So, this could last 2 weeks or almost 2 months. And it is good viewing. But I'm never fully engaged by it. Previous books have asked "What exactly would the TARDIS crew do here?" Well, get captured, steal some clothes and talk to the King. We know what they're not going to be doing is altering history greatly. The joy in "The Romans" was that the Doctor indirectly started the Great Fire of Rome. What could they possibly do here? The Third Crusade did not end with total victory for the Brits or the Saracen. That's why there was a Fourth Crusade. All the crew can do is instantly try to reunite and get the heck out of here. (If Barbara hadn't been captured, this could have been one part.) I will let you all know that this story is 4 parts. We will see how it develops from here.

The Doctor and Vicki do get a comedy scene. A variation on the scene with the tailor from "The Reign of Terror." My favorite part of that scene is the opening shot. The Doctor is talking to the stall owner. In the background, slightly out of focus, is the hooded face of Vicki. It's a cool moment. As mentioned, the Doctor "borrows" their clothes. He's not giving anyone his ring again.

The one thing that elevates the element of danger here is Barbara's capture. Ian, Vicki and The Doctor are fighting when they realize they lost Barbara. Cut to: Barbara, gagged, being held down by two Saracen who are tying her up. That's harrowing. When she is with Saladin, as intelligent and kind in his own way as he seems to be, one can only think that women were not always treated well in this society. What's next for Barbara? Being put in a harem? Some sort of torture? Or worse? The episode doesn't dwell on it. But, if you know the history, all you can think is "Get Barbara out of there now!" The episode leaves us hanging. That's a cliffhanger.

The Knight of Jaffa

Episode 65 (April 3, 1965) Court intrigue continues! But this time, we can't see it. Only hear it.

Cliffhanger: Barbara is grabbed by a man lurching out of an alley towards her.

The plotlines seem a little unbalanced here. Barbara is kidnapped by El Akir who wants to torture her and put her in his harem. (Possibly not in that order.) She's on the run in the streets of the city. If she gets caught, she's going to be in a lot of trouble. Ian is knighted and sent to get her. The knighting scene with King Richard is fun. The Doctor and Vicki giggle away at him. Meanwhile, Vicki dresses up like a boy. (It's a theatrical contrivance. She looks nothing like a boy.) The Doctor has a run in with the Court Chamberlain and the clothing vendor, which he wins through some clever confusing wordplay. So, basically, Ian does nothing. More or less. The Doctor and Vicki engage in shenanigans. And, if Barbara is caught again, she will be mistreated. Probably brutally. I mentioned earlier *Doctor Who* being able to change moods, but this is a little much.

Apart from worry for Barbara, all the good stuff here goes to the supporting characters. (Thank the Lord they're not cavemen!) El Akir is sleazy. Saladin is wise. King Richard is hotheaded. Joanna is lovely. Their scene together in Episode Three is one of the best acted scenes in all the show. It's too bad this episode is lost because they seem to have another great scene here. Yes, this is one of two episodes missing from Season Two. (Luckily for all of us.) Unluckily, both episodes are from this story. We only have half of it to enjoy. Which does dent it sadly.

The reconstruction I watched was a little light on the helpful subtitles. So, there are moments near the end when Barbara is hiding among houses on the street where I was a little lost. For all the great dialogue throughout, one forgets how much visual stuff is going on here. I would love to see an animated version of these two lost episodes. It didn't happen on the Season 2 Blu-ray set but hope springs eternal.

I'm a little short on things to write for this episode. Barbara is the one who has things happen to her that aren't just silliness. But she gets kidnapped and then escapes and then, possibly, gets kidnapped again. It's harrowing. I mean, I would think this might be the most scared she's been since the Cave of Five Hundred Eyes. I think in the next episode, when I can see more, I will say more. I do like how Saladin thinks Barbara is some sort of travelling actress. He thinks she is going to tell him stories, like Scheherazade. I do enjoy *The Tales of a Thousand Nights and One Night*. Sadly, El Akir grabs her before she can tell her story. (Maybe she would have told that one Ping-Cho told so long ago. More or less.)

The Wheel of Fortune

Episode 66: (April 10, 1965) Barbara makes a friend. The Doctor and Vicki gain an enemy. Ian is on vacation in the desert.

Cliffhanger: El Akir has re-captured Barbara and promises death as her only escape. Death is a long way away.

El Akir is a real piece of work, a real villain. A man who came into town one day and, basically, went door to door taking what he wanted. I know he has dealings with Saladin. But I've missed exactly what it is he does. Apart from being a jerk with a slew of guards and a harem. He is, unfortunately for this show, not the sort of villain where Ian can walk in, flip a switch, watch all the guards slow down and then give El Akir a trashing. El Akir is too entrenched in this world, in this space. I feel awful for the man who rescues Barbara. Telling his story about El Akir burning his home down with his wife and son inside, just so he could take one of the man's daughters as his sex slave. In a serial, where the lines of good and evil are very grey, El Akir is true evil.

That's why Barbara's plight in this episode is so harrowing. When the father gives her a knife, saying that if El Akir finds them to kill his daughter and herself, Barbara is clearly stunned. "Life is better than this!" she yells. In the current run of *Doctor Who*, I think they would find a way to back up that line. In this episode, you hear her say that and think "Is it?" When Barbara and the daughter are hiding from El Akir and his guards, the daughter looks at the knife to protect themselves. But Barbara is looking at the knife in absolute terror. This is now officially worse than the Five Hundred Eyes caves and the thieves. It's one thing to have thieves and criminals be horrible. But when you'd rather kill yourself than let the bigwig in the area find you, things are screwed.

I'm always very glad that Barbara gets this storyline. Well, "glad" isn't the right word. I'm glad she gets a proper storyline. William Russell is on vacation, so he does almost nothing. (Strange that this would happen in the last two episodes of a story rather than in the middle two.) He's mentioned a few times. When we cut from Barbara in distress, to Ian taking a nap, one does want him to get a bit of a move on.

The Doctor and Vicki get a few strong scenes. One with the clothing merchant. One with Joanna. They're well written and well-acted. But, in the end, they do very little for the story. The biggest giveaway is the Doctor's attitude towards Joanna. She wants The Doctor (she's very persuasive) to give her info on what her brother is up to. The Doctor says sure. He finds out that King Richard is sending Joanna to marry Saladin's brother, Saphadin. But he won't tell her, and she finds out from someone else. All heck breaks loose. And the Doctor just sort of "tsk tsk tsks." He complains about court intrigue. Really, it looks like he and Vicki are just keeping everyone as placated as they can keep them until Ian and Barbara show up and they get the heck out of there. It's a variation of the argument from Episode 5 of "The Reign of Terror." They are part of history now and these are real people around them. You play with their emotions and feelings at your peril. Because that's what the Doctor seems to be doing (vamping until they can go) it increases the "Why couldn't they think of something for the TARDIS crew to do? Why send them somewhere where they do nothing, and the guest actors get almost all the best stuff?"

The Doctor gets a good scene with the Earl of Leicester. But the Doctor's insistence upon how wonderful his brain is over the soldier who knows that he must fight when diplomacy breaks down makes our hero look like an ass. Because, generally, the soldier is right. The Doctor's anger towards him should probably be directed inward. Talk is cheap. Especially when everyone has lots and lots of weapons. It's a good scene that is a little tough to read. Luckily, the best scene here (and one of the best scenes ever) is Joanna and King Richard arguing after she finds out about the marriage arrangement. I'm so glad this episode exists, if just for that scene. Three of the four main characters may be in superfluous positions but the writing and acting keeps this episode high quality. One of my all-time favorites.

The Warlords

Episode 67: (April 17, 1965) The TARDIS crew get the heck out of there at the first chance they get.

Cliffhanger: Something wiggy is happening inside the TARDIS.

A weird episode. It's missing so it's kind of tough to say if it's as slapdash plotted as it seems to be just from hearing it and seeing some images. Everything wraps up very quickly. But even as that happens, there's a long sequence when Ibrahim ties Ian to the ground, puts honey on him and ants approach. It seems late in the game to introduce such a (well, I think he is) overbearing character. He helps Ian out and helps get Barbara and the father's other daughter away from El Akir. But couldn't time have been better spent on some of the other characters? I mean, there's no Joanna, there's no Saladin or Saphadin. There's one scene at the beginning with King Richard. What happened to the story? Did half the cast not show up for part four?

Then there's the harem, which I'm kind of glad we don't see because I don't think it would be a happy place. I do like the bit where the traitor slave girl is surrounded by her fellow harem occupants, and we hear a scream. I forgot that El Akir is killed by the father rescuing his daughter. How'd they get there so easily? (Let's not dwell on the fact that the daughter has had her virginity taken from her by El Akir. Dad's doing his best but I'm not sure how he'll take that.) In fact, there are two big parts of the previous cliffhanger that get thrown out quickly. 1) Barbara almost immediately escapes from El Akir. We can't see how because the picture isn't there but shame on El Akir for the lax security. 2) Joanna is mad at The Doctor. (So, they say as we don't see her.) But King Richard knows The Doctor did not tell her, but he sends the Doctor and Vicki away anyway. The previous cliffhanger was such a good one that this really does feel thrown away.

What happened to David Whitaker here? The first three episodes moved calmly and deliberately and this one is almost bonkers in the amount of incident. And isn't it lucky that everyone meets up at the TARDIS in the end? The Doctor and Vicki don't even escape. The King lets them walk back. (The Duke of Leicester isn't happy but still.) Did David Whitaker lose his original fourth episode? Did they just throw this together at the last minute? As I said, maybe when viewed, this is really something. But, hearing it, it feels like everyone reached the end of Episode Three and threw up their hands. "Let's just get them back to the TARDIS." When they're back in the TARDIS, they're making "knight" jokes and laughing it up. Barbara has forgotten her ordeal already.

As I said, it's an odd episode. It feels like the last 20-25 of *National Lampoon's European Vacation*. (I'm sure you didn't expect to see that mentioned here.) The original script like the first *Vacation* is a series of vignettes all the way to the end. The studio decided that they wanted more of an "ending." So, they brought in another writer who re-wrote the final act into a wacky chase scene with a burglar. There are a few laughs. Sure. But it feels like we all suddenly wandered into a different movie. That's what "The Warlords" does. Gone are the most interesting characters. It's all about wrapping it up. (Except for a long stretch of Ibrahim.) There is the occasional nice moment, like the discussion of King Richard seeing Jerusalem. But even that feels a bit thrown off. Most of the great dialogue and speeches are gone. In fact, when Leicester delivers one, I almost got the feeling Richard was going to say "OK. OK. Knock it off. Keep moving." I wish I'd read the novelization. I wonder if it has a better flow.

THE SPACE MUSEUM

The Space Museum

Written by Glyn Jones

Directed by Mervyn Pinfield

Episode 68: (April 24, 1965) The TARDIS lands on the planet Xeros. It's jumped a time track. That means, well, it means they're there and they're not there. If you know what I mean.

Cliffhangers: The time track realigns itself and the TARDIS crew officially arrives. Now, their lives are in real danger.

Another great episode. But, very different in the "why" it's great than "The Wheel of Fortune." That was wonderfully written, well-acted and well directed. "The Space Museum" is clearly cheaply made. We see Mervyn P's name on this, so we know it's going to be drab in the direction department. It's sort of another variation on "Our four main characters land somewhere strange and wander around." But, this time, it's because something strange has happened in a bland place that this episode becomes so darn intriguing.

This is one of those "sideways" stories, like "The Edge of Destruction" or "Planet of Giants." This one however, deals with time and time travel. While the episode itself is far from dynamic, the premise always gets me. Something makes time go all wonky when the crew tries to land. Suddenly, they go from their Crusade clothes to their regular clothes… but they haven't moved. Vicki drops a glass, and it leaps right up back into her hand. When they step onto the surface of the planet, they leave no footprints. They can't be seen by the inhabitants. They can't be heard by the inhabitants. Their hands pass through walls and exhibits… They're there but not there. And the most intriguing and frightening thing of all comes near the end. They see themselves basically stuffed and mounted as exhibits in this space museum.

What the heck? Well, I mentioned a time track. Somehow the TARDIS landed off center. It's showing them what they are going to have happen to them in their future. As they explore, they also wait for the TARDIS to correctly align itself, so they are there for real. It's an eerie and silent episode, that even has a Dalek thrown in. it's unlike anything (idea-wise) that the show has done before, and it expands upon what the show can do.

After the flowery language and the lovely costumes (but strange lack of story) to the previous four episodes, this does have a cheap air. Long, white, sterile highways. Older guys with goofy wigs and outfits. Younger men with bad eyebrows. All speaking but not audible. Several museums displays of random, well, things. Yes, there is a Dalek there, which is awesome. But it has the feeling of chintz to it, which is why a conceptual story works well here. They will go into greater detail in the next episode, but this all brings up the concept of free will and are they able to stop the future they've seen from happening. That's what the story is going to be, and this episode sets it up beautifully. The real story begins when the displays disappear and the closing credits roll. Let's find out who all these goofy looking guys are and why on earth they want to put the Doctor and his crew in displays.

The Dimensions of Time

Episode 69: (May 1, 1965) The TARDIS crew meet the Xerons and the Moroks and try to figure out what needs to be done to prevent themselves being made into exhibits.

Cliffhanger: The Doctor is about to begin Stage One of the Taxidermy process.

This is a tricky episode. In theory, it should be a fascinating and rather harrowing episode covering the TARDIS crew honestly not knowing what to do to stop the future they saw from happening. They can leave the planet but that doesn't change the future. It simply implies that they'll come back again another time. So, they decide to go into the museum and try to figure out what's up. They have some interesting discussions about what they could do that might be right or wrong. And, no matter what the Doctor does, he winds up in the Museum Director's special interrogation chair. Followed by the start of the preservation process. (The Moroks, who run the museum, don't really seem to know how a museum works. They get their first visitors in ages and their first inclination is to make them into exhibits. That's not usually the way it works.)

There are a few small problems that get in the way of the episode fulfilling itself: First, I feel like there's something off in the way the written material is presented to us. I have read Glyn Jones' novelization and it is funnier and sharper than the televised serial. Dennis Spooner did some re-writing. All in all, the feeling that this should be really something special is deadened in the presentation. Second, the Moroks and the Xerons are really two of the blandest and most boring races ever on the show. The Moroks are blustery older men in bad outfits who used to have a great empire but are now just bored. And the Xerons are a bunch of wet young men who it is almost impossible to keep interest up for. Third, Mervyn Pinfield's directions really doesn't seem to capture any excitement at all here. A good script has been deadened by so many odd choices.

Vicki's doing OK, I think. Ian and Barbara are all right. The Doctor's scene where he fools the Mind Probe of the Xeron Commander is funny. But, once the initial conversations are done and we meet all the other characters, it becomes a bit of a chore. One really must focus to keep interest. Now, through some of the dialogue and the fascinating premise, I think one can keep a strong focus. But this is one of those weird stories where I honestly can't tell if it's better watched all in a row or with gaps. With gaps, you can stave off most feelings of dullness. But, watched all in a row, especially after Episode 1, there is a feeling of the characters rolling towards something inevitable and unpleasant. With no way to escape. I'm watching them close together for this book and it does seem to work slightly better than spacing everything out. Not enough happens in each episode for an entire episode so rolling them together kind of works here.

In the end, the premise of an episode like this was explored much better in the BBC Past Doctor Adventure Novel *Festival of Death* by Jonathan Morris. In that one, the Doctor, Romana 2 and K9 help save a ship full of people. Only to learn that they'd been there before, more than once in fact. And the Doctor learns that the last time he visited there he died. That book goes whole hog on the time paradoxes and strange timelines and completely succeeds. I wish "The Space Museum" had made it there. But we do have two episodes to go.

The Search

Episode 70: (May 8, 1965) With the Doctor being prepped, the remaining three travelers resort to more desperate measures to save lives. As the Moroks resort to more desperate measures to stop them.

Cliffhanger: Ian sees the Doctor and gasps. We don't see the Doctor.

No Doctor in this episode.

There are some nice moments here. The two best ones being 1) Ian's realization that if they are going to end up in the cases then any guns the Moroks pull on them are deterrents not to be used to kill them. So, he goes after a Morok holding them at gunpoint and he's right. That's some nice use of the premise there. There is less of that in this episode than the previous one but it's still there.

2) One of Vicki's best moments. When she re-programs the armory computer guard to let the Xerons into the armory. The Xerons are, like I said, wet and ineffectual. Vicki takes charges immediately. Mainly because if they overthrow the Moroks then no one winds up in the cases. But, also, because she wants to help. Her proud recitation of the answers to open the armory is a great moment.

I just wish the Moroks weren't so dopey. I mean, yes, the Xerons aren't up to much, but they've got the dynamic Vicki with them. So much of this episode seems to involve Moroks trying to get into the TARDIS, one Morok asking another who is on guard at a certain spot, one Morok yelling at another, a Morok giving another Morok boring orders. Oh, Moroks creeping around with guns. They're huge guys with huge hair and huge outfits. They don't really creep as well as they think they do. In the original script, Glyn Jones made the Moroks more obvious jokes. Tired fighters who were now bored bureaucrats lording over a museum that was basically nothing more than a big shrine to what they used to be. The show as televised doesn't seem to realize how goofy they are. They're not as goofy as the eyebrows of the Xerons but they should be.

By the time you reach the end of this episode, unfortunately, you do have to strain to keep the original premise of the show in sight. All the similar looking Moroks and Xerons and all the similar looking hallways kind of deaden the mind a bit. (Is this place even a museum anymore? It just seems like a series of hallways.) The Zaphra gas is a fun addition. They pump the halls full of this gas to drive out Barbara and a Xeron. The unfortunate thing there (this flows into the next episode) is that what they say the gas does doesn't seem to actually be what it does. It's odd. Anyway, Barbara and Ian don't do a lot here really. But the fear of what is happening to the Doctor and Vicki's awesomeness makes it worth viewing. Let's see how they wrap this up.

The Final Phase

Episode 71: (May 15, 1965) It looks like no matter what the TARDIS crew did will not be enough.

Cliffhanger: Oh boy. The Daleks have a time machine. They are after the TARDIS crew.

It's nice to have The Doctor back. I wasn't terribly worried when it looked like he might not come back to life at the beginning. I was certain he was in some more episodes. For a few minutes at the beginning, the episode meanders a bit. Someone is over here. Someone is over there. What's happening? And then, the story does a nice little turn and suddenly… The whole TARDIS crew has been captured and it looks like it's over.

Now, we know that they're not killed and made into exhibits. So, the question comes down to: How do they get out of this? And it is well handled. It's very much a solution that the current run of the show takes to heart. The concept that the Doctor doesn't always save the day. What happens is the people they influence throughout the story learn how/ build up the courage to win the day. The people they have influenced get in there and somehow win. That's what happens here. Vicki is the one who realizes it. As Ian, Barbara and a still recuperating Doctor are feeling bad, she still has the feeling that something will happen. It must happen.

Yes, they're safe in the end. The time spent with the Xerons has caused them to bring the revolution. The adventure ends and the Space Museum is shut down. This was an interesting "sideways" *Doctor Who* story. There's not much to say here. The episode is basically what I've just described. Like many from this time, it ends several minutes before the credits roll. The crew is given a Time/ Space Visualizer that they get inside the TARDIS. We learn that the brief appearance of the Dalek on the Visualizer is a piece of great Portend.

I quite like "The Space Museum." But, in some respects, it's like a low-budget movie with a great concept behind it. A great concept that the filmmakers can't quite flesh out. They can't quite get it to fully work. Here, it's because of budget, direction and possible script interference. You can see the good story in here. I feel like this fourth episode had more to it at one point. But it basically does what it needs to. And I think it's entertaining enough.

THE CHASE

The Executioners

Written by Terry Nation

Directed by Richard Martin

Episode 72: (May 22, 1965) The Daleks have a time machine. (The DARDIS?) A crew of time-travelling Daleks are dispatched to exterminate the TARDIS crew. A chase through time and space begins.

Cliffhanger: A Dalek rises out of the Aridian sand.

Terry Nation brings back the Daleks in a format very similar to "The Keys of Marinus." Over the next six episodes, the TARDIS crew will jaunt around time and space being chased by those goofy pepper pots. When it ends, only one group will remain standing. But that group will no longer be the same. The Chase!

"The Chase" is a fairly silly romp taking us from late spring to early summer. At this point, the production crew knew what people wanted the most: the Daleks. So, from here and through the next two seasons, basically, we would get a "big" Dalek story with all the "regular" stories scattered around it. I applaud Nation for doing something different with the Daleks here, even if the story is something he's already done.

Speaking of "something he's already done," this episode begins differently. The TARDIS crew are watching the Time/ Space Visualizer from the Morok Museum. It can show them anything that happened in the past. We see Shakespeare and The Queen. We see Abraham Lincoln. We see the Beatles on a Top of the Pops performance recorded especially to air on *Doctor Who*. (Warning: The U.S. DVD/ Blu edits that scene out.) There's a lovely laziness to this scene, especially after the crazy running around and existential worrying at the end of "The Space Museum." Watching Ian sing along to The Beatles is a joy. But then those darn Daleks appear on the screen, and they know they are being chased. That's a nice way to start it off. But then, they land on Aridius, a desert planet, and we basically go through the motions of "The Dead Planet" and "World's End" but this time in sand. We know the Daleks are going to appear from somewhere.

It isn't quite the same though. The Doctor and Barbara decide to sunbathe. Ian and Vicki go investigating. They find weird things in the ground. We see a tentacle wave around. (That's not good.) They find a ring in the sand. Vicki has a great moment where she laughs hysterically upon seeing the ring. (She remembers a childhood story about a ring in the sand.) They enter a sandy underground cave and… more tentacles! I love good tentacle things. *SH! The Octopus* is one of my favorite films. Even though these tentacles aren't the most realistic things, I love them anyways.

To be honest, of the three "explore the terrain" scenarios so far, this one is the toughest to keep a handle on, interest-wise. Skaro was our first (as far as we know) alien planet. It was a cool landscape with the huge futuristic city in the distance. World's End was a return to Earth but one a bit twisted. Aridius is a desert. It's like the surface of Vortis but without the random crags and rock outcroppings. The difference between desert long shots and interiors is obvious. Not in a bad way just in a "We're back in the studio" kind of way. The endless desert isn't terribly compelling. So, creepy tentacles and going underground is a sharp idea.

The Dalek crew that has been assembled do seem to a bit dippy. Maybe they're hopped up on a time travel drug that makes them act odd. I don't know. There was always something a bit "What was that Dalek doing in there?" about the Dalek rising out of the Thames. But it was impressive. The Dalek at the cliffhanger here is less so although the concept is great. The Dalek slowly rises out of the sand to face the time travelers it has been sent to execute. But it's a model. They couldn't bury a real Dalek in sand and then get it to rise out of the ground. The sand was too heavy. So, it's clearly a model. And it's clearly a model that, for whatever reason, they've dubbed some grunts and groans over. That's a bit of silliness to me. Which shall fit the overall vibe of the serial. Mostly.

Overall, despite a few pacing issues, this is a good way to start the adventure. The TARDIS crew are fun here, especially their enjoyment of the Visualizer. We've got the lay of the land/ desert. We know the Daleks are there/ arriving shortly. Unfortunately, the crew have all separated so this may not be as easy as it should have been. Plus, tentacles!

The Death of Time

Episode 73: (May 29, 1965) The crew meets the Aridians, the Mire Beast and tangle with some Daleks.

Cliffhanger: The Daleks vow to hunt the crew through eternity.

Well, of all the people the crew ends up with after their initial first episodes exploring in this era, the Aridians are the toughest to pay attention to properly. They are an amphibious people who live underground on a desert world. They rival the Xerons in being the most useless alien race we've encountered so far. There's nothing to recommend them. There's nothing to them that is interesting. They turn the crew over to the Daleks immediately, which is understandable but not the best way to make them worth much. The best thing about the episode is that it's the only one they're in. Hooray! Every once in a while, *Doctor Who* will have a race or a something or other show up and the first thing I will think is "Wow. I can't wait until they're gone." This is one of those races. I think one thing that really nails it for me is when the Aridians say something like "The Elders have decreed that you be handed over to the Daleks." All I could think was "The Elders? What Elders? Let me see these clowns." My total disbelief that this race exists anywhere else but right on the screen makes me think this isn't the best thought-out group.

Now, the Mire Beasts are a different story. Yes, they go around eating the Aridians. They're tentacle-y and they're blobby. And they're not particularly realistic looking but I love them anyway. Why are they the bad guys? All they do is follow their instincts. On a planet with, clearly, no mires, they are scuttling around getting their food where they can. I applaud that. They're not quislings like the Aridians. Maybe they're cool. Maybe if they simply got a good meal every now and then, things would be different. I'm not saying I want a Mire Beast companion travelling in the TARDIS. Wait. I am saying that. Awesome!

The Daleks have arrived. That one gets out of the sand and gets up to business. They do exactly what you'd expect. The TARDIS crew hangs out down in the caves waiting to get sentenced to death. It's all a bit perfunctory. I know Terry Nation was big on saying how quickly he could write these things but sometimes a second draft or a little re-think wouldn't kill you. It's not a lively episode. It feels like a space holder. And it makes so little sense. A planet called Aridius is a desert planet inhabited by aquatic life. There is an explanation given, I know... but come on. Isn't this more than a little goofy? I mentioned that the story is a bit deliberately silly. I don't believe this part is meant to be.

The TARDIS crew do get at least one great scene. After they've escaped their Aridian captors, there is a Dalek guarding the TARDIS. I love how silly the crew acts when they're distracting the Dalek. "Oh, Dalek! Cooey!!" Things are very serious, definitely. The most evil and persistent race in the galaxy wants you dead. That ain't no laughing matter. But it is nice to get a few yuks in and try to enjoy yourself. And they do end up sending the Dalek over a sand hill to its sandy doom. Nice. I like that scene. It has a fun inventiveness that the rest of the stodgy episode really doesn't. And, tricky enough, one becomes more reminded of who directed this episode as it goes along.

This episode has several of those Richard Martin moments that are becoming prevalent. Especially during the big Mire Beast attack. There's a very awkward moment involving a collapsing wall, Barbara and some Aridians with a Mire Beast. It looks mighty amateurish. I imagine there was no way they could have done it again. But still, it would have been nice if they could have. There will be more of these odd moments as we carry on. I do feel like the bigger the story, the more everyone loses sight of the smaller details. And they come back to bite you in the bum.

Flight Through Eternity

Episode 74: (June 5, 1965) The TARDIS lands on the Empire State Building. The TARDIS lands on a ship out on the high seas.

Cliffhanger: The Doctor announces that each stop brings the Daleks temporally closer to them

This episode is much better than the previous one, mainly because it's very different. There are no groups of fighting alien races, no drawn-out drama. Just silliness. Even when silliness doesn't quite fit in. The episode is in two halves: Empire State Building and the ship. Now, I'm positive you know what the ship is, but I'll keep things hidden for a while. It's fun to have spoilers hidden in a review sometimes.

The Empire State Building sequence is a classic in comedy. No, not really. It's only a few minutes long and it features the great Morton Dill. He's a Southerner of some sort who talks about Hollywood and is a bit of a rube. An apple knocker. He encounters the TARDIS crew as they briefly appear. Then, he encounters the Daleks. Most of the things about this scene and Morton have been mentioned in other books. If this is meant to be the world's tallest building, why are there other buildings just as tall in the background? Why did they hire a Columbo impersonator to be the tour guide? Although, this is before Columbo on TV, so maybe Levinson and Link saw this and drew inspiration. What exactly is Dill doing when he is trying to take a picture. Is he steadying his camera? If so, he's doing it in a weird way. The big question is: Why Ian and Barbara don't stop and realize that they're back on Earth in their time? One doesn't think they'd stop and leave the chase, but they might acknowledge it.

It seems a bit odd to suddenly have this super hick character appear. Until you realize when this was made. It's mid-1965. The BBC used to import over American shows. What was one of the biggest American shows (if not the biggest) of the first half of the 1960s? You got it. *The Beverly Hillbillies.* The Paul Henning produced show about the hillbillies from Bug Tussle who strike it rich and buy a mansion in Beverly Hills. And who is one of the main characters? Jethro Bodine. A super hick. Just like Mr. Morton Dill. That's who we're channeling here: Jethro. And Peter Purves, the actor, does a decent job. He doesn't seem to fully understand what exactly he's doing. It's more of an impersonation than a character. But it's fun. I wish he'd got his own spinoff. I would have liked to see him appear in the Jago & Litefoot audio series.

In the second half of the episode, they land on a ship. They get accused of being stowaways. Chicanery! They leave. The Daleks appear and either kill everyone or drive them off the ship leaving it deserted. It's all presented in a bit of a wacky way with even a Dalek misjudging something and falling into the ocean. Now, the shot of a woman jumping into the ocean with her baby isn't terribly funny. OK, it's good for some laughs. But it's an odd moment where you think "Did they think this through?" It's basically the set up for a historical joke. The ship is the Mary Celeste. The famous ship that was discovered in 1872 completely abandoned in the Atlantic Ocean. (Arthur Conan Doyle wrote a story about it calling it the *Marie Celeste* and that has become a better-known spelling.) Get it? It's a bit of time travel comedy. What caused the mystery? The Daleks? The Doctor from the time of "The Aztecs" would be spinning in his grave. But, watching it as a kid, it's a decent joke.

The episode is a fun one. It's nothing profound but if you're in the middle of a long serial you want to keep things moving. This does that. Again, Terry Nation doing comedy isn't the funniest thing for me. I know he wrote for Tony Hancock but when Terry does funny it ain't so great. But it's charming enough. The ending of the episode is a nice moment though. The Doctor does admit that the DARDIS is too hot on their trail. It's drawing ever nearer. Sooner or later, they will have to stop and fight. After a frivolous episode, it's nice to have that nailed down. Could the next location be the spot of the final standoff?

Journey Into Terror

Episode 75 (June 12, 1965): The TARDIS lands in a Gothic mansion. The Daleks fight the Frankenstein Monster. Things have gone a little crazy.

Cliffhanger: Vicki was left behind! The Daleks have created an "exact" duplicate of The Doctor.

This is one of my favorite episodes of *Doctor Who*. Not because it's a great episode. I honestly can't say it is. It has the same sort of sloppiness that "The Web Planet" overflows with. It has the same kind of "Oh, that'll do" that Richard Martin brings to those episodes. "Good evening. I am Dracula…" That makes sense, kind of, in the end. But, throughout it just seems weird and like a mistake. Some of the haunted house paraphernalia isn't thrown at us in the best way either but it's not without its charms.

The TARDIS crew look forward to having to fight the Daleks here. Ian points out that they will probably have trouble with stairs. Everyone goes exploring and discovers assorted bits of stuff that scares them. When the Daleks arrive, they're just confused by all of this. They don't have the same horror film references in their mind that I do. And I pity them for that. The whole episode has a fun, slightly silly, gothic atmosphere. The cast seem to be enjoying themselves. Apart from the Daleks, there's never really a sense of danger, which is charming. You can be scared but not to the point of anxiety and worry. Overall, this might be my favorite episode of this serial. The Doctor would fight vampires and Frankenstein Monster variations later in the series. But this is his first real tussle with them. (Re: the stairs and Daleks. The first Daleks we saw couldn't go off their metal floors. The second round we saw had satellite dishes on their backs that allowed them to move anywhere. Why wouldn't other Daleks use something to adapt themselves to steps? Heck, this group has a time machine. All is possible.)

The thing that makes it great is the Monster Mash fun of the episode. A screaming woman, cobwebs, gothic mansion Frankenstein Monster, Dracula... I miss a werewolf but that's a lot of makeup. This is the mid-1960s. Bobby "Boris" Pickett's "Monster Mash" had been a huge hit about a year-and-a-half before. Plus, even though the monster Golden Age ended in the mid-1940s... even though we were more sci-fi than horror in the past 15 years... people still love their monsters. People still love to get scared and creeped out.

I mentioned the "Monster Mash." There were many, many other songs about monsters and monsters having parties or just hanging out over the prior 7 to 8 years. "Rocking Monster Ball," "The Monster's Ball," "Rocking Monster Hop," "Monster Party," "Frankenstein's Den," the list is endless. I, myself, have put together a 100-song playlist/ 3 CD-R set of the best horror music that time had to offer. It was charming. It was mostly in mono. I have no idea whether anyone related to *Doctor Who* would have heard any of it, but I think they might have.

Let's also have a quick look at 1964 and 1965 horror films. Remembering that much of *Doctor Who* rooted itself in the world of horror and horror tropes. Not so much in these early seasons but as we go along. So, 1964: *Dr. Terror's House of Horrors* has a vampire tale in and amongst its anthology storytelling. Hammer had out *The Evil of Frankenstein*, their 3rd Frankenstein film. We get voodoo/ zombie films, including *I Eat Your Skin* and *The Incredibly Strange Creatures Who Stopped Living and Became Mixed-Up Zombies*. We get Italian films like *Castle of Terror*, with Barbara Steele creeping us all out. Hammer does *The Curse of The Mummy's Tomb*. The gory and fun *The Flesh Eaters* attacks us. (Let's not forget H. G. Lewis's *2000 Maniacs* and *Color Me Blood Red*.) We get the incredible *Kwaidan*, some of the most stylish ghost stories ever. (Also, *Onibaba*!) We get a German film called *Night of the Vampire*, that I would like to watch. We get several *Psycho* rip offs including *Nightmare*. The Wrestling Women met the Aztec Mummy. *The Masque of the Red Death* was going full scale. I have not seen *The Vampire of The Opera*, but I think I need to. Jess Franco brings Dr. Orloff back. Mario Bava begins to go giallo with *Blood and Black Lace*. And Don Sharp brings us *Witchcraft*.

In 1965, Santo fought some witches. One of my favorites happened down at the beach... *The Beach Girls and The Monster*. Yes, Billy the Kid met Dracula! *Devils of Darkness* was the first contemporary British vampire film. *Bloody Pit of Horror* strikes out and makes us feel delighted. More Jess Franco. Hammer brings us *Dracula, Prince of Darkness*. We get *Hush... Hush Sweet Charlotte*. Rasputin appears. Polanski repels. *The Skull* screams. Vampires, witches, blood... it's all here.

Well, that list may have been a bit self-indulgent. But it's fun to see *Doctor Who* do a horror episode. And it's also fun to remember that there was a lot of horror going on at that time. The Hammer renaissance was spreading.

The Death of Doctor Who

Episode 76 (June 19, 1965): The gang lands on the planet Mechanus. The Daleks create an exact double of the Doctor. What can our gang do?

Cliffhanger: Deep in the cave, a wall opens. A strange robot tells them (I think) to join him. So, the TARIDS crew gets in with this odd robot to escape the wrath of the Daleks.

You know there is one pedant out there saying: "Well, as their name isn't 'Doctor Who,' then that means that nobody dies. Nice try, Nation!" That's also the kind of person one can freely kick in the nuts without too much worry.

I suppose there's a chance that viewers originally might have been thinking "Oh no. Finally, the episode where we lose The Doctor. I'm going to miss that irascible sonofabitch." There's a chance that that happened. But mostly, I think folks are thinking what I did: "Hey, that guy doesn't look like the Doctor." Yes, he's an older white guy with long hair but that doesn't make him the Doctor. As the episode goes along, the way Richard Martin handles this "duplicate" becomes kind of more and more ridiculous.

There are just weird moments where we get long shots of the "duplicate" and then cut to close ups of William Hartnell. They're meant to be the same being. It's confusing and it really doesn't work. Of course, a lot of times throughout my *Doctor Who* journey things happen that just don't work, and I roll with it. But this one is kind of egregious. It's almost daring you to say "Yes, yes. That works." And during the fight scene when it's cutting back and forth between them and it becomes impossible to tell what's happening. And the duplicate has Hartnell's voice dubbed over his... well, there is a good moment. The disgust that Barbara and Vicki have when they discover that they're shielding the "duplicate." It's almost over-exaggerated but I quite like it. I suppose in an episode with all the other things going on in it a robot double isn't a bad thing. It's just an odd thing.

The rest of the episode I quite like. The jungle is fun. It's not great. It's clearly a bunch of goofy looking "fungoid" fake trees on a studio floor. I don't mind the floor. It makes me think that the Mechanoids not only built the giant city, but they also set up the floor. You can see a camera at one point, which lends to my "What was Richard Martin up to here?" confusion. But I don't mind it. The fact that the TARDIS crew have chosen this place to fight gives the episode some gravitas.

I especially like the scenes in the cave. The Doctor pretending to be the robot is very brave. I like when they trap themselves in there keeping themselves as positive as they can but it's clear that once the Daleks get in the whole thing is over. There is a wonderful darkness to those moments. It really does feel like the end of the big battle between the Doctor, his friends and the Daleks. Then, that door opens, and the oddly shaped robot speaks unintelligibly. There is a new lease on life! The final episode can begin. And it's going to take place in that wonderful city we saw overlooking everything.

The Planet of Decision

Episode 77 (June 26, 1965): The Daleks meet the Mechanoids. We meet Steven Taylor. Ian and Barbara say goodbye.

Cliffhanger: Ian and Barbara make it home as the Doctor and Vicki watch on the Space Time Visualizer.

And the Daleks are defeated. Not by our gang. This group of Daleks is an extermination squad. They get defeated by the round and tough to understand Mechanoids. They're an interesting group of robots. They were sent by humans to create a world where we could live. But, in the end, the humans never showed up, so the Mechanoids run it on their own. For some reason, they've taken a human hostage: Steven Taylor. An astronaut whose best friend is a teddy bear and who revels in the fact that more humanoid beings have arrived.

The TARDIS crew enter this narrative of the Mechanoids and Steven near the end. Just in the same way that the robots and Mr. Taylor join the TARDIS crew and the Daleks at the very end of this long story. I don't know, in real time, how long the crew have been on the run. They got to rest at the end of the last episode but only for a bit. This endless Saturday Afternoon serial style living can be a bit much. Luckily, because there's a lot to do in this episode, we don't dwell on any one spot for too long.

The crew is brought up to the Mechanoid city. I love that the Daleks enter the cave and are so confused. The gang is no longer there, Daleks. They are about 200 feet above you. It's more annoying than the TARDIS. Here the crew fell into some dumb luck. I do like seeing our gang in the Mechanoid Zoo. There's a great *Twilight Zone* episode where a human ends up in an alien zoo. (I won't tell you which one.) This has some of that. But it's not a twist ending. It's just a moment. A moment in a packed episode. Luckily, they've left the fungoids and the "duplicate" behind and given us a space up in the sky. Sort of a *Doctor Who* Cloud City.

I love the concept that the moment that the crew gets up to the top of this sky city... they immediately look for a way to get back down again. Vicki has vertigo. Barbara almost falls over and Ian almost pulls her pants off. Steven runs back into fire to save his mascot, the teddy bear. The episode always moves much faster than I thought. Morton Dill is one joke. Mary Celeste is one joke. This episode is a dozen jokes, as it were. And it nails them one after the other. Every spot the TARDIS crew arrive in is not a spot to linger. It's a spot to look and decide "How do we get out of this?" Is it a problem that the Mechanoids left enough wire to get off the roof? I don't know. Steven has nothing to go to when he gets to the ground. He's got no working ship. So, why not leave those wires? They don't know about the TARDIS.

The episode has a lot of fun in it. It's an excellent closing episode with two classic sequences. The final battle between the Daleks and the Mechanoids. Their only battle. It feels like the right thing to say though "Their Final Battle." It is very kinetic, very exciting. Lots of cuts, lots of angles, lots of camera movement, animated moments. It's a fantastic scene that truly feels like the end of the Mechanoids and the end of this round of Daleks. That leads to the even better sequence.

Saying goodbye to Barbara and Ian. Saying goodbye to companions is something that happens on the show a lot and something we accept. Like the previous Nation stories, there's a long stretch after the ending. (We'll talk about Steven when we begin the next serial.) And that deals with the DARDIS still being active and Ian and Barbara using it to get home. The Doctor is belligerent. He is angry and he is upset, losing his friends. Risking their lives on this journey. Vicki convinces him that it is for the best. Their final scene together happens in the time machine, and we don't see it. It's poignant and lovely.

And we close this first era, as it were, we see Ian and Barbara in a lovely photomontage returning to London, blowing up the DARDIS and cavorting. Then, there's one last scene with them on a bus realizing they lost 2 years, but they are so happy together. (And, possibly, they are immortal. More of that later or in another book.) It's beautiful. There was sadness when Susan left. There is such joy here. We will miss them, as we do all the companions and all the Doctors. But it's nice to see that they are alive, well and so happy. The capper of Vicki and the Doctor watching them on the bus just brings out the last of the tears. Such a silly story. Such a beautiful ending. And the show shifts again. Where to now?

THE TIME MEDDLER

The Watcher

Written by Dennis Spooner

Directed by Douglas Camfield

Episode 78: (July 3, 1965) The TARDIS, with Steven in tow, lands on the English coast in 1066. There are Saxons. There is talk of Vikings. And there's a strange monk watching it all.

Cliffhanger: The Doctor finds the gramophone playing a record of monk chants. He is immediately trapped in the room by the Meddling Monk who laughs at him. The Doctor clearly knows who he is.

I really like this episode. It's slowly setting something up. Something that, as *Doctor Who* fans at this point, we wouldn't have quite expected. (Although, seeing Dennis Spooner's name on the script might lead you to believe something's up, like Darin Morgan's name on an *X-Files* episode.) The Monk who is lurking around is clearly up to something. It isn't until late in the episode that we get a clue. But it's a clue that doesn't make complete sense when we see it. What this episode does instead, and what I love about it, is it's a series of charming and/or funny scenes between our main characters (including new boy Steven), each other and a Saxon woman. The guiding premise is not discovery. Like many first episodes up to this point. But The Doctor trying to prove to Steven that the TARDIS is a time machine. And it's all the better for its utter lack of danger or worry. (Note: Vicki says the "D" in TARDIS stands for "Dimensions" rather than "Dimension." This will last for a long time.)

William Hartnell is at his most delightful in this episode. (Maybe it's because he knows he has a vacation next week.) He has some great jokes with the "space helmet for a cow" one being an all-time favorite. He has a lovely scene where he talks with Vicki. It's just the two of them now and it seems like they'll probably have a good time travelling the universe on their own until Steven bumbles in with his panda and his skepticism. The scenes with the three of them are great. The Doctor almost treating Steven with contempt. Steven thinking the Doctor is a daft old man. Vicki trying to moderate between them. Very funny and, as I said, the machinery that gets this episode rolling.

I like the scene with Edith and The Doctor quite a bit. Yes, it is Althea Carlton who played the main lady caveman so long ago. There's no reason her family line couldn't be some sort of *Blackadder*-esque journey through history where she generally plays a slightly dirty woman. She's charming here. Casually chatting with the Doctor about the Vikings and fishing and mead. The Doctor is at his most charming. Even when he's doing that thing where he asks odd questions that only a time traveler would ask. He never does it so poorly that she catches on, but she has a few "What the heck?" moments. He does go off on a long tangent when he realizes that this is 1066 and that the Battle of Hastings looms. In fact, it's the big educational moment in the episode. The Doctor basically looks at the camera (more or less) and rattles off a history lesson for everyone.

The best moment of the episode though comes near the end. It's not Steven getting excessively violent with a Saxon and then recovering a modern-day wristwatch. It's not even the Doctor finding the record and getting caught by the Monk. It's that great moment when the Doctor is standing by the fire and the monk's chants waft through the forest. Then, suddenly, everything slows down weirdly and then speeds up again. That's great *Doctor Who*.

The Meddling Monk

Episode 79: (July 10, 1965): We learn that the Meddling Monk has a plan of some sort involving the Vikings. The Vikings show up and attack Hilda. Steven and Vicki learn that the Monk is not from this time.

Cliffhanger: Vicki and Steven discover that the Doctor has vanished from his cell.

With William Hartnell on vacation, the episode's title character really becomes the focus. We see Peter Butterworth doing some fine comedy business with toast. He gets water thrown in his face. He tries to act as Monk-like as he can but there's something about him that makes me think camp/ pantomime no matter what he's doing. Obviously, he was in a slew of Carry On films so that's where most folks know him. This was shot several weeks before his first one: *Carry on Cowboy*. He's fun to watch, especially as you try to figure out what exactly he's up to here. Has anyone else noticed that there are moments, especially when he's carrying the breakfast tray, when Butterworth resembles Rondo Hatton's little brother?

Anyway, Vicki and Steven continue to make a great double team, looking for the Doctor, getting in trouble with Saxons and generally being a fun couple. It breaks my heart that we only have two more stories with the two of them together and all, but one of the eight episodes is lost. (Although, as I write this the animated Blu-Ray of "Galaxy 4" has just come out and looks darn good.) I like watching them together. Vicki the more seasoned traveler who is a bit more cautious. Steven who wants to be the leading man but isn't always the best at it. They get lucky, as does Butterworth, that Hartnell is gone.

May I point out how much I like the sets here? The forests look spacious, even though they're crammed int the studios. The stock shots of Viking ships don't really work. But the way the Vikings arrive sort of up and over the cliff face convinced me. I also love the monastery with the building in the background. I know it's a fake building, but I find it quite adorable. Not that I want to live there but I like the design. I'm not 100% sure how big the monastery set was but it looks expansive. There seems to be a lot of space there. Granted, the big fight between the Saxons and the Vikings should maybe have been shot on film elsewhere. It's the scene where this all feels too cramped and, Boy, is this fighting awkward. Watch the one guy vaguely stab Gunnar the Viking in the leg sort of. I don't think those swords and spears are as sharp as they look.

Overall, the episode is one of great fun. Holding off The Doctor and The Monk doing anything together must come into play with the next episode. I'm going off the title. But there is one moment in the episode that is exceptionally dark. Hilda hears a noise outside. She steps out with her spear. A Viking leaps on her. Chaos. Later, her husband and the other Saxons return to the huts. Hilda is on the ground, pretty much comatose. Her husband pats her face with a wet cloth and declares that they will find the Vikings who did this. Of course, what do we all know about the Vikings? The pillaging and the raping. The intimation here is that that's what happened to Hilda. The show never comes right out and says it. But that's what happened. It's a dark moment mixed into what is a mostly comedic story. It makes the Vikings an actual proper threat. I'm not 100% sure if it works but it's here.

A Battle of Wits

Episode 80: (July 17, 1965) We learn what the Monk is up to, and the Doctor isn't happy.

Cliffhanger: Vicki and Steven make a heck of a discovery.

The writer does a fun thing here where the Doctor goes missing for half the episode. We know that William Hartnell is back but where is he. He escaped in a tunnel under the monastery that Vicki and Steven travel. The Monk can't find him. Much like the upcoming episode "The Destruction of Time" and the much later episode "A Good Man Goes to War" there is fun to be had in wondering when the Doctor will return. (Granted, folks originally watching it probably thought he was gone for this episode too. We know a little bit more now.) When he does show up, it's a great moment. A wounded Saxon is at the monastery. The Vikings are approaching it. The knock at the monastery door surely must be the Vikings. But it's The Doctor.

I don't know if there's a full-on Battle of Wits here. (Unless that's meant to be Saxons vs. Vikings) The Doctor pretends to have a rifle, but he really has a big stick. They get attacked by some Vikings but there are some nice slapstick shenanigans around that. The Doctor really is in control here. William Hartnell is commanding the screen in a way the Doctor never has yet. Possibly it's knowing the villain here. (Or whatever the Monk is supposed to be.) They know one another and the Doctor knows that this man is going against the established rules of the show. Doesn't the Monk watch *Doctor Who*? Did he miss Dalekmania? Come on. It's nice to that as the episode ends, we're one episode away from the closing of the story and the season. So, this will not get abnormally drawn out.

Before I forget: I love how many times the phrase "beacon fires" is used in the scene where the Monk asks the head Saxon to light them. "Beacon fires." "Beacon fires?" "Yes, beacon fires." "…beacon fires…" Every time there's a pause you just know someone is going to say, "beacon fires."

Anyway, The Monk wants them to light beacon fires. Beacon fires? I'm kidding.

The Doctor has a chat with Edith about what's happening. In it, the Doctor delivers the rest of the history lesson for the episode. Yes, everyone this is around the time of The Battle of Hastings. But is the Monk planning on doing something very naughty? What's with that bazooka/ cannon thing up on the clifftop? Won't that be close to the beacon fires?

Beacon fires?

I will say that they make these Saxon women as sturdy as anything. It's only a been a few hours since her encounter with the Vikings and she's up on her feet, moving around. I guess there's really no time to sit and worry it out. Especially when there's Vikings around. I kind of wish the Doctor was a little more observant here. But, with the Monk and the Vikings he's feeling excited. Something is about to happen with history! Still maybe Edith should have got the evening off.

Steven and Vicki continue to be very entertaining together. They're trip through the tunnel is good fun. Steven's admitting that "OK, maybe the Doctor does have a time machine" is great. I love Vicki going into a sort of sulky mode when she realizes that the TARDIS was carried away by the tide. Steven's obliviousness to that is slightly odd but he has a lot on his mind too. The guys in this episode maybe aren't as observant as they should be.

Steven and Vicki do however get to take part in the game-changing cliffhanger. In the first episode, "An Unearthly Child," Susan says that her grandfather built the TARDIS, and she named it. It's presented as a one-of-a-kind machine. Well, apparently, that was a fib Susan liked to tell. The cliffhanger here, as you read, is the discovery that the chapel altar is the Monk's TARDIS. That's a big moment. The Doctor, Susan and The Monk are from the same race. And there is more than one TARDIS out there.

Checkmate

Episode 81: (July 24, 1965) The Monk's plan is revealed. But the Saxons put a stop to it while the Doctor puts a stop to the Monk. For now.

Cliffhanger: The second season ends.

This is a strong ending to a great story. The stuff with the Vikings and the Saxons is a bit too pat. A bit too obvious. Steven says it himself. The Vikings have tied him, Vicki and the Doctor up. The Doctor has his eyes closed and is ruminating upon what the Monk wants to do. Vicki is trying to get free. Steven is questioning the way this time travel thing works. If the Monk changes the course of history, if there is a different victor at the Battle of Hastings, what will happen? It's not what the history books said. So how can it happen? Well, time will bend around them, and it will be like what they knew never happened. It's a bit of a time paradox kind of chat that would be accentuated and worked out with more precision in the Steven Moffat years or *Back to the Future 2*. But it is a good question.

Prior to this story (and a bit of "The Romans"), meddling in time was forbidden. That's why a story like "Marco Polo" can be well-acted and look great but feels static. Because they can't change anything. They remind me of a newspaper comic strip nobody remembers called "Dick's Adventures in Dreamland". In it, a Little Nemo type boy dreams himself into the American Revolution. It was one of those comics that took up like a half page of the Sunday color section. They were these gloriously written, epic adventures with this kid right in the middle of the Revolution. The whole thing was to teach American History. Occasionally, he would give George Washington a good idea or something like that. But mostly it was teaching. Try as they might, it was never very interesting. So, we have Dennis Spooner to thank for bringing us an episode like this. One where there is a "time meddler," as the Doctor calls the Monk. (The Doctor knew the title of the serial even if we didn't.) One where time travel isn't just a vehicle to get us from one story to another but where it is part of the world of the show and an element of the show that is fascinating. Something that adds to the show's big bag of tricks.

The Saxon and Viking thing, as mentioned, gets wrapped up very quickly. In fact, if you're following the Doctor and his gang and the Monk, that plotline almost occurs off to one side. That bit of history is resolved. But the more interesting stuff happens with our time travelers. The scenes where Vicki and Steven pick through the Monk's TARDIS is delightful. The bank thing, The Leonardo thing, all good stuff. The Doctor learning about the Monk's plan is so good. Mainly because the Monk seems to be kind of doing it just for fun. He's kind of bored so he thought he'd advance human civilization. The Doctor is appalled. And that is super amusing. The Doctor strands the Monk in 1066 but I feel like the Monk may not be gone forever.

The second season ends with the TARDIS dematerializing (safe from the tide). We see a starscape. Steven, Vicki and The Doctor appear in the stars. It's the visual equivalent of the Doctor's speech from the end of the first season. And it's beautiful. We know that the third season is looming but... this is not the end of the second shooting cycle. There are 5 episodes left, which would be the first 5 of S3. The last episodes with Verity Lambert onboard. (Donald Tosh is our new script editor.) So, with the start of S3, the old guard, apart from Hartnell, is completely gone. Let's see where the show goes from here.

SEASON THREE

(1965-1966)

GALAXY 4

Four Hundred Dawns

Written By William Emms

Directed by Derek Martinus

Episode 82: (September 11, 1965) The Doctor, Steven and Vicki land on a desolate planet populated by some women known as The Drahvin and some robots called The Chumblies.

Cliffhanger: They do not have fourteen dawns. They have two.

So begins Season Three. It begins with a story that gets short shrift in the annals of *Who*. For many years, it was put forward as a very straightforward "don't trust to appearances" type of story. But the story was lost. For many years, we had nothing to go on but plot synopsis and descriptions by people "who were there" and told us what went down. Then, William Emms's excellent novelization showed up. The story suddenly seemed less straightforward than we thought. We thought it was "The Doctor and gang meet these supposedly evil robots and these ugly things called The Rill. They also meet the beautiful Drahvin. However, after a time, it becomes obvious that all is not as it seems."

Just watching the existing 6 minutes of this episode shows you that this is a very simplistic description of this episode. The TARDIS crew are not scared of the Chumbley. (Vicki names it that, for Heaven's Sake.) They are wary of it but curious. But, because it can't speak and the Drahvin can, the ladies get to explain what's happening and the Rills don't get to give out their side. Luckily, the more Maaga, Head Drahvin and the only one who is not some sort of clone, speaks, the more the TARDIS crew seem wary of her. It's nowhere as near simplistic as it was presented to us for decades. No, the crew does not immediately say the Drahvin are evil, and the Rills are good. They reserve judgment. But Maaga's rhetoric is convincing. And, as Steven says, the Rills sound like they're trying to help. There's no way to prove it yet.

Other than that, the episode, I think, is a strong opener. The TARDIS crew lands on this unnamed planet ready to explore. Vicki is cutting Steven's hair, which is charming. Steven is still a bit antagonistic, still a bit pushy. But it fits in fine here. The first arrival of the Chumbley on this rather dead planet. (Xeros is mentioned) is a nice moment. The arrival of the ladies who seem like strong warriors, but not the brightest bunch, shifts everything again. So, the episode keeps you moving. It's got good dialogue. Good performances and a great cliffhanger. Plus, because we never see the Rills, it keeps that important reveal in its back pocket.

Let's dive right in here and say: This is the third animated episode we're watching here. There is a 6-minute segment of Episode 1. In 2011, a copy of episode 3, Airlock, was discovered. For some reason, I think because it has decent sound, "Galaxy 4" was chosen to be the first full-length animated Hartnell story. I think it's a wise choice. It's not an obvious classic. It's one that beings a season but then gets sort of lost when "The Daleks' Masterplan" begins in a few weeks. But it's also, I think, a sharp story. It's got a nice pace. It gives over its reveals at good moments. And it has the ticking clock of the end of this world always going on behind it. I just got the Blu-Ray of this serial animated a week before I'm writing this. So, this is new for me and, after episode one, I'm quite enjoying it.

A final note: One of my favorite things here is the odd misdirection in the titles. This planet is not in Galaxy 4. Maaga and her ladies are from Galaxy 4. They left that Galaxy, four hundred dawns ago. That's not the number of dawns this planet (even with three suns) has left. I always like that bit of oddness. I'm not sure why they're called what they're called but they're just confusing enough for people who aren't paying complete attention.

Trap of Steel

Episode 83: (September 18, 1965) The Drahvins are not as nice as we thought they were. We finally see a Rill.

Cliffhanger: We finally see a Rill.

Now, as I mentioned, I am watching this in animated form. They've done a lovely job and I'm quite enjoying it. But something comes up here that never occurred to me before. That's the scene where Maaga is eating her plate of greens. Vicki is staring at them in disgust. In my mind, Maaga was eating some weird stuff, which justified Vicki's displeasure. In the animated images, it looks like a green salad. Vicki says they're leaves. Maaga agrees. And Vicki is disgusted. Vicki is from the 25th Century. I would love to know what they're eating at that time. Is it food pills? Or TARDIS-style food bars? Because eating a salad shouldn't make someone so disgusted. In the 25th Century, do they eat nothing but meat? Are there no more trees? I'm trying to think of Buck Rogers and what he used to eat. The Drahvins aren't nice, but I can't fault their diet. Anyway…

We now know that there are only two dawns left. The Doctor tries to hide it. But, in these cases, the people with the large guns always seem to have the upper hand. Although I think the show is still going strong, there is something odd after the Doctor reveals this to Maaga. So, Vicki is left with the ladies first. The Doctor and Steven go to the TARDIS and come back. Then, Steven is left with the ladies while The Doctor and Vicki go to see the Rills' ship. It makes sense, of course. But it does feel like an odd way to structure things. In the next episode, will the Doctor be held captive while Steven and Vicki go to do things?

The moment when the Chumbley sets off the explosion around the TARDIS is a nice one. It seems hostile but I don't believe it is. It's just trying to access this strange device, presumably because of The Rill, the robot's master. The animated scene in this is done nicely. They use some angles and shots that probably wouldn't have been in the original, but I don't mind. Derek Martinus is one of the best directors *Doctor Who* had so I think he'd handle it well. But maybe not crazy 2023 animated well.

The scene with Steven and the Drahvin is a good one. He basically slowly convinces her that she is worth as much as Maaga and almost gets her to turn sides. She doesn't though. Maaga catches her before it happens. The weird thing about the scene is that it was originally written for Barbara, not Steven. And if you think of Barbara saying the lines, they make sense. Steven handles himself well, but it does feel like he's saying someone else's words.

Then there's the Rill ship. On the animated edition, it is as big as Arbitan's hideout in "The Keys of Marinus." I love the interior of it. In the next episode, which exists, it has a strange, abstract almost stage-like quality, which is still cool but looks a little inexpensive. If I can be kind. I love The Doctor and Vicki's journey through the ship. I love the contrasts of the two ships. The Drahvin ship looks like a crock pot with legs. The Rill ship is this gorgeous thing in the wild with a weird smell to it. We do get to see a Rill at the end. Things are going to heat up now.

Air Lock

Episode 84 (September 25, 1965): We meet the Rills. They're odd but not bad. Just a bit aloof.

Cliffhanger: Trapped in the airlock, Steven begins to have regrets.

This is an excellent episode. We get the Rills side of the story. We get Maaga delivering a speech that borders on complete insanity. We get the Doctor being contrite and then delivering one of my favorite lines. We get a race for the climax ending as Steven is dying in the airlock. I'm so glad that this episode exists. Having one full episode of this one really helps it out.

Let's start with Maaga's speech. Steven is asleep and she is talking to three of her soldiers. Being able to see the dull looks on the soldiers' faces is a real plus. Maaga has real feeling on her face. It's a weariness. It's a loneliness. It's a craziness. I'm not 100% certain where exactly she comes from, but it sounds like a crazy place. The Land made of nothing but women is a classic trope since the Amazons. This one, though, is kind of the saddest. How many actual people like Maaga are there back on her world wherever that is? (Isn't it odd that she says the galaxy they're from but not the planet? Is that because their planet is so well known for being awful that she doesn't want to name it?) Maaga's soliloquy is lovely. Especially because Stephanie Bidmead keeps staring at the camera, which makes it all rather unsettling. Her bemoaning the fact that she is surrounded by these clones, thought-free soldiers, is one thing. The end of the speech where she describes knowing that the Rills and the TARDIS crew will die on the exploding planet is quite chilling. She is insane. This will be backed up by the Rills' story in a few moments.

Vicki's first scene with the Rills, surrounded by the Chumblies that provide the voices of the Rill is quite endearing. We can clearly see something in the ammonia gas behind the big door. But we are led to believe that it is much larger and much more substantial than just what we can see. Vicki handles herself well here. Learning the other side of the story. The episode doesn't specifically equate their "ugliness" with the Drahvin's "loveliness." The Rills do seem like an aloof race. It might be because they must lock themselves away. But their aloofness contrasts with the Drahvin's. There is only one Rill that we see and only one "real" Drahvin. It's quickly obvious who should be trusted.

The flashback to the Rills attempting to speak to the Drahvins is nicely done. We usually don't get that kind of thing. We're usually just told the story and go from there. But the Drahvin with blood on her face is rather harrowing. Maaga, in cold blood, killing her soldier to anger her other soldiers is frightening. In a story that seems almost fairy tale like at times, moments like these are darker than one would expect. I think it's our new script editor, Donald Tosh. He script edited "The Time Meddler" and that has a woman clearly being pillaged by Vikings. As we will see as the season goes along, he has a darker view of what the show does. (Not the same sort of thing as, say, Eric Sward who believed that the universe was simply very violent and someone like the Doctor really didn't have a place in it.) Moments like Maaga's murder of her own soldier are one of these moments. There will be more over the next two dozen episodes.

Overall, quite a good episode. Time is running out. The Doctor is going to help the Rills, but the Drahvins seem to be going crazier. Maaga's face as she's killing Steven in the air lock is another chilling moment. She's quite a villain. An overlooked one in the history of the show. But, to combat the darkness there, we have the Doctor being completely charming while talking to the Rills. His response to the Rills claims that they are too terrifying for someone like him to look at is classic Doctor. "Nonsense. We're not children." He really is coming to his own as the hero here. It took a while but it's a good arc.

The Exploding Planet

Episode 85: (October 2, 1965) The planet explodes. But who survives?

Cliffhanger: Something weird happens very far away. In the jungle.

I do hope that the actual episode as aired is as strong as the animated episode is on the Blu-Ray. The whole episode has a sense of urgency to it. The episode speeds along. The Rills ship is being powered up. The Drahvin have become desperate and are trying to storm the Rills' ship. The Doctor and friends get to meet the Rills face to face. There's some lovely dialogue. Some great action. And the world explodes in the end.

The concluding moments as the planet rips itself apart are quite harrowing. I think we already knew they were from the audio, from the reconstructions, from the novelization. But the animation makes it very visceral. The ground shakes. It tears apart. Huge cracks appear revealing molten lava flowing and spewing up into the air. The Chumbley falls in, sinking calmly. Maaga is seen pushing her last soldier away from her and her soldier falls into the lava. Then Maaga is alone staring into the sky. And then she disappears from shot and lava flies into the air. We never knew the name of this world. We never will. (Maybe it's Trenzalore.)

Then when we cut back to the TARDIS, the scanner is on but we're light years away from the planet. As the Doctor at this time has no idea where he's going, it is implied that we will never go back to there. We will never learn what this planet was. Did it have a history? Was it just an uninhabited planet that happened to be visited in its final days? We'll never know. Unless someone writes a sequel or a prequel. Call it "Galaxy 3" or "Galaxy 5." (Hey! We already have a Galaxy 5 in the show's history. You can link them together somehow.)

I think the scenes with the Doctor and pals chatting with the Rills are quite enchanting. I think Steven's opening scene with the Rills is excellent. Where he distrusts the Rills as much as he distrusted the Drahvin. Even after they saved his life. It's a well-written scene and well-directed in the animated version. Steven eventually does trust them. But he does spend the entire time when the Rills ship is powering up complaining. Maybe he could calm down a bit. Maybe he should trust the Doctor a bit. Because the Doctor does have this under control. The dialogue between him and the Rills is delightful. When they all say goodbye to one another, there is a feeling of a friendship (no matter how brief) ending. I think it's quite well written. I don't think I've ever said this before, but I wish William Emms had done another one. He's got the storytelling and the pacing down perfect. This one is just right at about 100 minutes. I have no problem with any of the episodes or any of the pacing. It's too bad he never came back.

Anyway, one final thing: I love the Chumbley at the Drahvin ship with the Rill voice. As the Drahvin stand there with guns raised, the commanding voice shuts them down fast. It does question simply why they didn't accept their help? You see why the Rills are so reluctant to reveal their forms to the Doctor and friends. It's because of these Drahvin. They are a horrible bunch, aren't they? And yet, when Maaga is standing on the planet alone, it reminded me of that Twilight Zone episode, which aired two years before this "On Thursday We Leave for Home." The image of the man who was too proud for his own good left alone, standing solitary on a planet. Knowing that if he could have stopped being a jerk for one minute, then he would be free. But it didn't happen and he's alone. Maaga standing on the edge of the precipice, a second before falling, I would like to think had the same thought. Who knows? Maybe a future Doctor hoped for her repentance. Maybe in a future story, when she falls into the crack in the earth, the TARDIS will be there, door open, to save her and allow her a second chance.

MISSION TO THE UNKNOWN

Written by Terry Nation

Directed by Derek Martinus

Episode 86: (October 9, 1965) Special Agent Marc Cory, license to kill, lands on the planet Kembel with several confused astronauts. He discovers the Daleks and several allies planning to take over the galaxy.

Cliffhanger: All the good guys die.

Two things before we begin:

1) I have no idea which delegates are which. For that information, I recommend Volume 1 of *About Time*. It has a very in-depth discussion of who is who. The guy who looks like the Thing (*Marvel Two-In-One* Forever!) is the main talker. The guy who looks like an odd black bellows Muppet thing is my favorite. But, as far as names go, you're on your own.
2) Please do not pay attention to all the mentions of Solar Systems and Galaxies. You will just get a headache. The episode is lost and all we have is a reconstruction. So close to Galaxy 4, every time they mention a "galaxy," I think "Which one? 3 or 4 or 5? Who lives in 1?" Don't let it bother you. Terry Nation and Robert Holmes had all kinds of trouble with this sort of thing. It's used to make the story seem more epic. It works when it doesn't give you a headache.

The only *Doctor Who* episode that features neither The Doctor, the TARDIS or his/ her travelling pals. (Although William Hartnell is listed in the closing credits.) The story behind this episode is related to the abbreviated "Planet of Giants" episode. This is the end of the second cycle of episodes. Verity Lambert owed an episode. (Although, if she hadn't done it, what would the BBC have done? Charged her for it? These episodes were so cheap she would have probably laughed.) The head of the BBC loved the Daleks. So, Terry Nation wrote an episode with Daleks and without the main characters to see if it would work. In the history of the show, it's a gloriously strange interlude. When the episode ends and it promises "Temple of Secrets," surely people must have expected some Daleks. I wonder if they told Donald Cotton what was happening? I wonder if someone could please help and not destroy all the episodes around this time period?

It's tough with this one. Marc Cory is posited as James Bond. At this point, we are all waiting for *Thunderball*, the first truly epic James Bond film to come out. (Over 2 hours. Shot in scope. Takes over a half-hour for James to get properly involved. Super fun film.) Terry Nation, who is as pulp as the creator of Tarzan, brings in a solar System Secret Agent. He brings onboard a bunch of astronauts. They meet some strange flippin' plants called Varga plants, from Skaro. And they all die. The Daleks win. All Marc Cory can do is leave a tape recording hidden in the bushes. If this episode existed, I feel like Derek Martinus would have ably mixed the claustrophobia of the jungle with the expansiveness of the Dalek delegate room well. On a reconstruction, it's tough to gauge and it can get a little dull. The push, the verve, the locomotion of the story isn't quite there in just the audio and some pictures. The Galaxy 4 Blu ended with a bit of animated Mission, and it made it quite expansive. I do hope someone animates this soon.

The episode is interestingly told. The first half is almost all the two guys and the horrors of the jungle. In the second half, it segues into the Dalek delegation and killing the humans. By the end, one might think that we are in deep doodoo. The Dalek delegates all seem a bit goofy, but they are colorful enough to warrant more time spent with them. (I guess, like the Rills.) When it ends, at that point, I think one thinks "Hey! Where are the main characters? Is this a backdoor pilot? What's going on?" It was a brave move. I think it probably confused the British public. They do seem to get confused easily though. The next episode definitely doesn't help. Although, I like it very much.

THE MYTH MAKERS

Temple of Secrets

Written by Donald Cotton

Directed by Michael Leeston-Smith

Episode 87: (October 16, 1965) Contrary to the previous episode, the TARDIS crew gets embroiled in the end of the Trojan War. Homer is nearby.

Cliffhanger: The TARDIS, Zeus's temple, has vanished.

It is time for a new producer. Our third script editor has been here for a while. Donald Tosh has brought a darker tone into the show. Now, John Wiles has taken over. The Received Wisdom is that he didn't want to do this. He tolerated it. During his time, there is a very definite shift in tone. It doesn't quite come through in this episode. But there is a touch of it about. This is the first multi-episode story where we have nothing existing since "Marco Polo." It's been a long time. And it's another historical. But this is a different sort of historical. Marco takes facts (more or less) and uses them to enhance and tell the story. "The Myth Makers" is exactly what its title says. It is mythical. It is epic. It is also very down to earth. It is also very fun.

The painful thing about the episode is that it is lost. The whole story is lost. So, we have the audio and lots of images. Do the images do the story justice? I don't know. I can say that there are some wonderfully odd and funny moments in here. Including Hector and Achilles' fight, As the Doctor says, they are doing more talking than fighting. I love the TARDIS appearing during this epic historic fight. I love that no one really seems to mention it until the Doctor walks out and is mistaken for Zeus. He's missing the beard, but he could be. I wish we had these episodes. The novelization (more later) is so good and so sharp and so wonderful. The episode seems to be delightful.

The main thrust of all of it is the Doctor (rather negligently) walking into a fight. I don't know why he does it. Is the TARDIS so rotten right now that he can't gauge what's happening outside anymore? Does he think The War Lord has a war game going and he wants to check on it? I think this is a great story. I think the way the Doctor enters it is a bit risible. Once it gets going though, it's fun.

Odysseus is awesome. *The Odyssey* is a hell of a book. (Is that underselling it?) I love that he is presented as a bit of a lout. As a bit of a jerk. He knows immediately that the Doctor is not Zeus. And the Doctor is doing his best. Agamemnon is tired. The Doctor's attempts to be prophetic don't work. But they do somehow believe that he might be Zeus. Even when Steven shows up as a "Traveler." It's all quite satirical. It's all quite humorous.

The tricky thing is that Vicki doesn't really become involved. She hurt her ankle running from the exploding planet, wherever that was. But, as the TARDIS is gone, (and I presume Zarbi didn't take it), she will become an important part of things soon. This is her last story. John Wiles joined and wanted to get rid of her. Donald Cotton's script is sharp. But the treatment of Vicki is subpar. She was an important part of the show. The first new companion. And to start her last story like this is not ideal. Mr. Cotton will do his best, but the outcome is predetermined.

Overall, this is a good episode. It's witty. It's interesting. It promotes later episodes and it's fun. I wish it existed because the reconstructions we have give me almost nothing. But let's see how the rest of the story goes.

Small Prophet, Quick Return

Episode 88: (October 23, 1965): Vicki, now known as Cressida, meets the royal family of Troy. Steven fights Hector. The Doctor is given two days to find a way to take down Troy.

Cliffhanger: Cassandra orders the death of Vicki and Steven

King Priam declares that Vicki isn't going to work as a name. He names her Cressida. A moment later, Vicki meets Troilus. I think I can see where this might be going.

Another great episode. There are some very funny moments sprinkled throughout. Hector is pretty amusing as a spineless coward who is completely ill-equipped for fighting. When he is looking for Achilles and quietly whispering his name, I laughed out loud. His fight with Steven is fun, especially when you see that Steven is pretending to lose so he will get taken into Troy. Now, granted, that doesn't go well when he gets in there, but it does provide for a nice cliffhanger.

It's nice to meet the royal family of Troy. King Priam seems a practical and rather weary man. He takes a shine to Cressida quickly. He's like the King version of The Doctor, I guess. Paris, as mentioned, is a self-aggrandizing coward with a nice sense of humor. Troilus is a hunk. And Cassandra is exactly how Cassandra should be. She's always prophesying and nobody's listening. She foretells that Vicki, and her friends will somehow cause their downfall. She calls out the TARDIS as basically being a Trojan Horse, although that's not actually a thing yet. She is quite strident. But it's got to be tough to be always right and never have anyone listen. Also let's take a moment and enjoy that episode title. The Small prophet is Vicki who quite clearly states that she knows the future but never quite gets around to telling Priam about it. They are nice scenes in Troy. Priam bemoaning Hector's taste in woman is very funny.

Meanwhile, the Doctor must come up with a plan to get the Greeks into Troy. I've always liked that he immediately dismisses the Trojan Horse as an imaginary idea thought up by Homer. (I will more than once recommend the wonderful novelization written by Donald Cotton. It is told from the point of view of Homer relating part of the Iliad that he did not decide to include.) When The Doctor says to the hilariously gruff Odysseus, "Have you ever thought of flight?" And Ody responds with "I can't say that I have," I always laugh. Watching (or really listening to) the Doctor struggling here is great fun. And really makes me bemoan the fact that we have so little from this story. The funny thing with the novelization is that I think it's one of the best. Like all 3 of Cotton's novelizations, it's atypical. But, because we don't have "The Myth Makers" anymore, I almost wish there was a straightforward novelization just to relate the story as easily as possible. (I won't give up the actual novelization though.)

The cutting between the Greek camp and the Trojan royal family keeps the pacing of the episode moving along nicely. It feels like they're figured out something for the TARDIS crew to do in a historical, even if, technically, they're not doing a whole lot more than they did in "The Crusade." It helps that these are real people whose stories are based in myths. Everyone can have a little more fun with them. They make them seem far more modern (for the time) than the people of King Richard's court or any of Saladin's men. Not to say that it's better. But it is always nicer to give our gang something to do.

Death of A Spy

Episode 89: (October 30, 1965) Troilus and Cressida are falling in love. Steven sits in a cell. The Doctor comes up with the idea of a giant horse.

Cliffhanger: Paris announces that he has ordered the giant Horse to be brought into the city.

The comedy keeps flying at us here. But Cassandra's histrionics are starting to mean something. She knows, as does Cressida and Steven, what this horse means. It's what she thought the TARDIS might be in the previous episode. It is the end of Troy. As per Cassandra's MO, no one will believe her until it's too late. If only she wasn't so shrill. She yells at one point near the end of the episode, and I had to turn the volume down. Maybe seeing the actress performing these OTT lines would work. But just hearing them makes me as tired of her as her family is. Too bad she's right.

Even as the story is moving toward its inevitable conclusion, the episode takes a lot of time out for Cressida talking to her guy, Troilus. It's quite sweet. They flirt well together. They speak casually with each other. They clearly are in love. It feels a bit like a summer romance. You know when you meet someone at camp or something. You hit it off immediately. You want to be together. The end of summer looms and there's a feeling of bittersweet sadness mixed in with everything. There are plenty of times in the history of *Doctor Who* where a companion (Oh, and The Doctor too) falls in love. The love is doomed by the nature of the show. Here, however, Vicki seems to be bucking against that trend. She seems to be convincing herself that this is the place to stay although she knows full well what's going to happen shortly. At one point, she says to Steven that she could really get to like living here. Now, she's saying that as she's locked in a cell. And King Priam has given her a day to solve the problem of the war or else she's in trouble. Steven doesn't imply that she's a loony, but the thought must pass his mind. Regardless, the scene between the two lovers is just the right length to show how well they get along. And that, depending upon the way the next day goes, they might be together for a while.

Meanwhile, The Doctor is still trying to get the Greeks within the walls. He comes up with hang gliders and has Greeks flying around with catapults. But even he isn't convinced, Odysseus certainly isn't. In the end, he mentions the idea of the Trojan Horse and it goes down like gangbusters. I do love that Odysseus forces him to ride inside the horse. It's funny to think of the Doctor in there with all these soldiers. Part of him believes this will work. Another part of him still believes that this idea is Homeric nonsense. (The original title for this episode was "Is There a Doctor in The Horse?" I think that's brilliant.) So, the Doctor and the troops hide inside the horse. The Greeks pretend to leave. And the story is moving toward its inevitable climax. At least it has a climax, unlike say "The Reign of Terror" or "The Crusade." Both of those kind of flounder a bit and then end. I think Donald Cotton has a bit of a shift in styles up his sleeve for the finale.

That leads us to the spy: The Cyclops. A mute man with one eye who spies for the Greeks. The caption from last week leads you to think that Vicki will be killed. But it's The Cyclops. Goodbye Cyclops! We hardly knew ye. He is played by Tutte Lemkow though. We certainly know him.

Horse of Destruction

Episode 90 (November 6, 1965): Troy falls. Steven is badly wounded. Cressida says goodbye.

Cliffhanger: With handmaiden Katrina in tow, the Doctor needs to get Steven medical attention ASAP.

John Wiles is now the producer with Donald Tosh as the script editor. I mentioned the darker aspects of the last few stories that had Tosh onboard. Here, with Wiles running the show, things get even darker. The story up to about halfway through this episode has been relatively light. Then, the Greeks pour out of the horse. They throw open the gates. During the last ten minutes or so, on the soundtrack, there are constant screams as the Greeks storm and burn the city. Cassandra is dragged off to be a plaything for Agamemnon. I don't want to know what happens to the rest of that family. Troilus is wounded in a fight with Achilles. Odysseus is so power mad and crazed that he goes after the Doctor at the end. The violence is unseen because the episode is lost. But we know it was not nice. During all this, Vicki stays with Troilus.

That's an interesting moment. Now, we know that Ian and Barbara are safe. They were watched on the Space/ Time Visualizer. We know, eventually, that Susan is OK. She was left to rebuild a world. But Cressida and her man are in the dirt outside burning Troy. Aeneas shows up so not all the Trojans are dead. But my oh my, it is bleak. The Doctor's final moment when he hopes she'll be OK has a very different feel from previous departures. We never learn how Vicki wound up, until the Season 2 Blu-Ray set was released. And I'm not sure if that's canon. She's a brave gal, our Vicki. I'm not sure why Wiles felt he had to get rid of her so quickly. It's going to be a long time before there's a female companion that I like as much as her. Certainly, the next regular one isn't one of the best. I do think it was a mistake to break up this group. But it happened and we carry on.

I do applaud that the attack isn't sugar coated at all. It is violent. It is unpleasant. Back in "The Romans," the Doctor accidentally causes the burning of Rome. That's treated as a joke. Here, The Trojans believe Vicki brought the horse and The Doctor suggested the Horse. I don't know if the Doctor can ever rightly claim to not interfere in history again. This is high scale interference. Donald Cotton's next script will pull a similar trick in its final episode. But that's not a war. It's a gunfight between some decent men and a bunch of jerks. Here, it's more resonant. This is a new path the historical stories can take, I think. When they're not going pseudo, like "The Time Meddler."

Did I mention that I'll miss Vicki? Did I mention Steven is badly wounded? Did I mention Katarina? She's one of Cassandra's handmaidens. She helps Steven onboard the TARDIS and gets whisked off. Katarina is convinced she's dead. I wish we could see the episode so we can see the way the Doctor reacts to her being there. He sounds slightly amused by her belief that she is in limbo. But I think he's still hurting from Vicki going. And Steven never really got to say goodbye. It's a sad, mad rush of an episode. Keep this Donald Cotton around.

It was Rob Shearman in *Running Through Corridors* who pointed out something about this episode that really strikes a viewer. After all the chaos, after all the violence of the second half of this episode, with Steven's wound, Vicki's rushed goodbye, the closest call yet getting back into the TARDIS, when chaos seems like it can't get worse, we see the caption "Next Episode: The Nightmare Begins." The nightmare hasn't started yet. The Doctor needs a vacation but it ain't happening anytime soon.

THE DALEKS' MASTERPLAN

The Nightmare Begins

Written by Terry Nation

Directed By Douglas Camfield

Episode 91: (November 13, 1965) The Doctor, Katarina and Steven land on Kembel. Right in the middle of a Dalek attempt to invade the solar system in 4000 AD.

Cliffhanger: The Doctor sees that the TARDIS doors are open. There are Daleks moving around outside.

The combination of the cliffhanger from the previous episode and the cliffhanging excitement from "Mission to the Unknown" throws us full into the nightmare beginning on the planet Kembel. There is a short scene with the Doctor, Steven and Katarina (!). Troubled, they need to rest, they need somewhere to take Steven. He has been poisoned by the sword that cut him in the previous episode. But then, we go to the year 4000, sometime after Mission. We meet Mavic Chen, the ruler of the solar system. We see some soldiers on Kembel, including Bret Vyon, who are in peril. We get a whole world laid out before us as we see our TARDIS crew in need of some medical help.

Before I get back to the episode proper, isn't the turmoil we're caught in here rather odd? There have rarely, in the history of the show, been moments like this. Vicki is gone. Steven is badly wounded. Someone new is onboard the TARDIS who truly doesn't understand what the heck is happening. And the Doctor is lost for words and actions. Pure craziness.

Luckily, we are in one of Terry Nation's best written episodes. * I know you just saw that asterisk. Read on for a bit. Or hop ahead. It's your call. The way he lathers in the year 4000 political stuff is well done. Several security agents discuss their leader Mavic Chen. One likes him. One not so much. But he is the leader, so we don't go that crazy. Politics! The way the two soldiers on Kembel fight to survive is great. The one who lets Bert get out of there has an iconic moment... He is looking around, desperate. And then he turns... and a Dalek looms over him and fires. That is classic Dalek. No longer the Daleks of the previous stories. But crazed predators who destroy. It begins here, in this nightmare.

Overall, it's a great episode. The Doctor being hoodwinked by Bret is exasperating but happens. Bret winding up in the magnetic chair is tit for tat. I love the Doctor sneaking around the Dalek encampment as Mavic Chen arrives in his delightful Spar. This is not the Doctor of about two years ago. This is a very different person. He knows something is wrong and he investigates. That's where we needed the show to go. And the cliffhanger, of the Daleks around the TARDIS with open door, is quite chilling. I just wish we could see it. But maybe we'll see something soon. Just wait a few minutes.

*The story goes that Nation was hired to write around half of the episodes for this story. But he was thinking about taking the Daleks elsewhere. Getting them away from *Doctor Who*. Trying something new to make some more money. So, it is said, that Donald Tosh had a knock on his door one night. He opened the door, and a cab was driving away. Nation left an envelope full of in-depth character and ship descriptions plus the basic story outline. Awesome. But there was almost nothing related to actual scripts. The episodes credited to Nation were dreamt up by Nation but, possibly, written by Tosh. I believe Tosh. The increase in general quality of these episodes, compared to "The Chase," makes me think that Nation suddenly became a much better writer or someone else was doing the writing.

Day of Armageddon

Episode 92: (November 20, 1965): We learn about the Daleks' plan. The Doctor comes up with a way to thwart it, at least for a while. It involves some fun disguise work.

Cliffhanger: The Spar is taking off. The Doctor, in disguise, has not shown up.

I love this episode. The mix of growing intrigue between the Daleks and their menagerie alongside the Doctor and his bunch trying to stop them really works. It's a fast paced, exciting episode that boils down to a great cliffhanger that hopefully will not leave the Doctor out in the cold. Remembering that this is the Doctor who used to say, "Let's get out of here" and run as soon as he could. In this episode, he masquerades as a vegetative representative of the Dalek council. He goes in there specifically to learn what the heck they're up to.

This is a moment in the story that I adore. Watching the Doctor go into that meeting with all the other unpleasant delegates to learn what's going on always surprises me. He keeps his non-vegetable hands hidden away. When all the other pound upon the tables, he keeps his hands hidden. But, in the end, he does grab the taranium core. That's the core that the Daleks need for their time destructor that Mavic Chen brought. There's the real jerk.

Chen is so good. Kevin Stoney's performance is brilliant. I so wish we had all the episodes. He is slightly odd. He has long nails, and he writes in a weird way. He is always so sincere and so interested in everything going on. He is a great villain. The Daleks are awesome throughout. Their yelling and demanding is as strong as ever. But, when we think they are going to take over everything, that makes them stronger. They will get stronger as we go throughout the serial. Chen is so good. He is betraying the entire Solar System. (Bret isn't happy.) For whatever reason, he has cultivated this taranium core. This bit of element that will activate the Daleks' Time Destructor. Why would a nice person do this? The answer: He's not a nice person. Mavic is a gloriously effective and theatrical character who will tear us all apart for his gain.

Luckily, the episode gives us Bret, Katrina, Steven and The Doctor. They're a surprisingly exciting group trying to find out what's going on. The Varga plants, luckily, don't seem too bothersome. The jungle is horrible, but it isn't anything Marc Cory had to go up against. I love their movement through it all. Their discovery of the Daleks. And I love the Doctor here. On the DVD commentary. Peter Purves (Steven) says that he thinks William Hartnell it at his best here. I've said before that I believe that. I believe that more now. This is The Doctor that we love. The fact that we are wondering whether he can do what the other Doctors have done is interesting. It's hindsight. I think it might be irrelevant. But it is good.

Watching Bret, Steven and Katarina go to the Spur as the Doctor tries to figure out what's going on is great. I don't know why we have this episode and not the others around it. Sometimes I feel like someone is controlling the episodes we get and giving us just enough to keep us moving. This one was gone until 2007. When it reappeared, it gave us just enough of the delegate and the show itself to keep us going. Just enough to keep us fully wrapped up in this story. And, frankly, this story is incredible. It's very much, at this point, a modern-day type of story. Where will it go? Where will the Doctor end up? Is Bret an ancestor of someone else we know? What is happening? 2 episodes into a 12-episode story and things are thrilling. Everything is pushing us to see what's next.

Devil's Planet

Episode 93: (November 27, 1965) The good guys, in the stolen Spur, are chased by the Daleks.

Cliffhanger: Not so much fun.

The whole episode plays itself as a bit of dark but fun adventure. The Spur escapes from Kembel. They may get to Earth. They need to because Mavic Chen is betraying them. Not having the TARDIS there is worrisome (the episode is lost. So, I think in the novelization it is more worrisome.) But Bret and Steven and The Doctor and Katarina (doing her best) seem to push everything ahead.

The problem is the Daleks. At this point in the show, we've never encountered the Daleks like this. They kill a delegate because that's what they do. They manage Mavic Chen's arrogance because they need the taranium core. They seem slightly incompetent, even at the end where they're landing on Desperus. But they are ruthless, and they are only out for themselves. The show kind of lets that go for a bit as they team up with others. But, when worst comes to worst, they link up with each other and are nigh on unstoppable.

It's a straightforward episode. They try to escape. They are pulled down on a prison planet. Things go wrong. Some of these reviews must be shorter than others.

I love the Doctor's optimism in this episode. I feel like he's doing that just for Katarina. He wants everything to be OK although this is darker than they've been. How would he have dealt with Susan in this? I feel like he may have fought harder. But he fights with a real gung-ho spirit. When we see the prisoners, when we know that the planet is nothing but lifetime prisoners who just want to get away, the episode tries to make it not as horrible as it is. That might just be the reconstruction though. I feel like the episode is as horrible as it seems to ne.

Dragging them down from a horrible jungle planet with the Varga plants to a horrible prison planet is a rough trip. This ain't Galaxy 4! All we had to deal with there where the ladies with issues. Here we have poorly shaven criminals who did... who knows what?

It's such a desperate episode. It's such a dark episode. The show has never quite gone to this space before. I think it might be John Wiles and Donald Tosh. Think back to "The Chase." That, in theory, was very dark. But this, in practice, is dark. The Doctor seems a bit strange here. I never fully believe that he can save the day. That element of the show has gone away. At least, for a while. One must always think that the hero will save us. When she/he/they can't, there's trouble. Where do we go?

This episode doesn't give us that answer. After an existing episode, it's always tough going back to the reconstructions. It works. And it's exciting. But it's not fully what we need. Steven is trying. Bret is trying. (Hell, it's the Brigadier!) Katarina is trying as best as she can in her frame of mind. I do like her. But this is the wrong time for her to be a companion. The Doctor is working it and trying to save everyone.

Once you see the cliffhanger... there is a moment that we really haven't had yet. A moment of "The Doctor didn't save us." What do you do when the hero can't save you? We will find out in the next episode. And it's not going to be fun.

The Traitors

Episode 94: (December 4, 1965) Katarina is killed. Bret is killed. The Doctor and Steven are on Earth in 4000 AD being chased by the world's best secret agent, Sara Kingdom.

Cliffhanger: After Killing Bret, Sara declares that the other two must be killed. Shoot them in the head.

This is a weird episode. Possibly one of the very weirdest episodes of the 1960s. Much of it involves Mavic Chen and a cohort convincing people that they have done nothing wrong. That Bret Vyon and others are the terrible ones. Convincing them completely. And then discussing how awesome things will be when the Daleks and Chen take over the solar system. It's oddly relevant today and yet just so gross. That thing of the person in charge being a traitor who can manipulate their followers to believe exactly how they want to believe makes me a bit sick. Especially seeing Sara Kingdom, who seems to be an intelligent woman, believing it all and falling for it all.

So much of the episode revolved around Mavic Chen. Around the Daleks and their delegates and their machinations. The story does really have an epic feel. It does feel like all the people in the Solar System are truly in trouble. That comes out even in a reconstruction. Whatever this Time Destructor is... the Daleks must not get it. The Doctor is the only one stopping it from happening. There's so much chaos happening. And some of it feels like regular *Doctor Who* kind of stuff. But we know it's not. The Doctor and everyone are separated from where they need to be. The TARDIS is planets away. So worrisome. But they keep going and they keep fighting. I love this episode. I wish we could see this episode. I wish it existed. A few moments do... but they're not happy moments. We will be there shortly.

The main portions of this episode are almost sort of forgotten when one piles on the accumulated incidents. Mavic Chen is going to get his core back. Sara Kingdom is going to kill whomever she needs to. Chen has an underling who is bald. I imagine that's not his fault, but it looks weird. The Doctor and gang talk to a guy who seems to be trustworthy. But a Nation story specialty ruins him. The guy mentions something that the others haven't mentioned yet. And that makes things tricky. Because this episode has two moments that we haven't encountered before in the show. But they are so important.

Katarina dies.

Someone who travels in the TARDIS with the Doctor dies. A crazed maniac holds her hostage in the airlock of the Spur. She ejects herself and him to save the others. There is a feeling here that the Doctor has not experienced anything like this. We see (in recon) her body floating through the vacuum. She's only been here for 4 episodes and change. Is this truly her fate? She left Troy to have this happen to her. I'm sorry but I truly feel like this is a Tosh and Wiles thing. The universe is much, much darker than we have encountered it before. Someone who the Doctor takes on as a replacement Susan or Vicki dies violently a little bit later. Life isn't fair. I feel like Tosh and Wiles are here to rectify some problems they saw in previous stories. Or they're just telling the stories they think should be told.

And yet, Bret dies at the end, killed by Sara Kingdom. Steven is still not quite onboard as a full companion of the Doctor. But Bret is in another realm. However, he does seem to trust the Doctor. And when Sara kills him it's a distressing moment. He seemed like someone who would last for a while. If he and Katarina died in one episode, what might happen in the next one? Luckily, that one exists. So, we can see what's going to go on.

Counter Plot

Episode 95: (December 11, 1965): Sara, Steven and The Doctor go to Mira. As do the Daleks.

Cliffhanger: The Daleks catch our gang. It looks like the end.

Once the deaths are left behind, we get a nice groove going. The Doctor and Steven running around maniacally. Bret is dead. Their so-called accomplice is dead. What on Earth are they going to do? There is a real lovely feeling of "How are they going to get out of this?" but it's not at a cliffhanger. It's at the start of an episode. They're already so far from the TARDIS. They've lost two of their own. This looks bleak. Luckily, a bit of silliness, which doesn't quite fit the new Tosh/ Wiles regime, saves them.

There's a lot of fun back and forth throughout this episode. The Daleks know Chen has screwed up but they're going with it because he is the only one who could get them the taranium core. Chen and his sidekick are trying to work damage control, especially when the travelers go to the planet Mira. And they get as lucky as The Doctor and Steven do. It is kind of a fun mix of the desperation of the travelers and the damage control/ fal-der-al of Chen's actual incompetence.

When I first encountered this story, it was this episode. It's on the *The Daleks – The Early Years* VHS tape. (They did one for each of the first four Doctors but only the Tom Baker one survives in the digital realm. They also did this one for the Daleks and one for the Cybermen) That was a 120-minute VHS tape with random straggler episodes. Two episodes of this serial and an episode of "Evil of The Daleks' and something else. So, this was the first real contact I had with this serial. And it just seemed weird to me. There was a strange looking man conniving with a bald guy who was almost camp. There were Daleks in another space doing something. There was a female secret agent who gets a big character moment. She was chasing the guys. There were mice. There was a teleportation scene that I knew Stanley Kubrick had seen. There were invisible creatures.

I had seen "The Chase" and I had seen "The Keys of Marinus." But this was nuttier and more harrowing at the same time. No TARDIS and being chased by Daleks is never a good thing. The whole space hopping element of it really caught my attention. I mean, Sara Kingdom is about to kill Steven and The Doctor. Suddenly, they and some mice are transported across the galaxy (or the Solar System or whatever the heck we're calling it.) And it's such an odd thing. The vastness of the universe becomes something so easily traversable, even without a TARDIS.

Then, there's the Sara Kingdom thing. She joins the Doctor and Steven by the end. But she has that big reveal about Bret. About him being her brother. I don't feel like sibling stuff is terribly important to the people of that time. Bret may have mentioned it before she killed him if it was. Sara is great here. Steven's anger is justified. But it's the Doctor who is so good. This is a heroic Doctor. A Doctor unlike the previous seasons. Possibly through the loss of many close to him, he's lost his self-aggrandizing tactics and he's just as good. Hartnell is on fire here. I hate the fact that when he seems to be at his best (before his sickness will cause trouble) we're missing so many episodes. Like the next one. But the next one's a big one. And we'll see how it goes. Have the Daleks finally won? It's not for me to say.

Coronas of the Sun

Teleplay by Dennis Spooner

From an Idea by Terry Nation

Episode 96: (December 18, 1965) One more desperate ploy (stealing the Dalek spaceship on Mira) leads to another desperate ploy (Steven trying to charge the fake taranium core) leading to one more desperate ploy.

Cliffhanger: The TARDIS has landed but the atmosphere is poisonous!

This is the end of the first half of the story. What was a madcap chase through space is now going to become a madcap chase through time? (Yes, I know. The first half was like a more serious version of "The Chase" without the TARDIS. This second half is like "The Chase" and is just above the seriousness level of "The Chase." But sometimes not by much. The serious level that the story had in its first four episodes returns in the last two.) This episode is a harrowing and fun resolution to all the initial runarounds. And, boy, do I wish we could see this one! It uses a variation of a trick that the episode "The Parting of the Ways" would use 40 years later. It's funny. Yes, the comedy all comes from The Daleks arguing with Mavic Chen. It's suspenseful. The only thing that keeps everyone alive is the fact that the

Daleks can't shoot them when they have the core. In the end, there is a feeling of triumph. But Steven's complaining and the Doctor acting like he's back in "The Sensorites" kind of mars that slightly.

Dennis Spooner is back! (Although, as mentioned, Terry Nation may not have really been back. As I mentioned, this story does have a distinct feeling of being "The Chase" in two discrete sections. But, better written and better directed than "The Chase.") Dennis Spooner will write most of the rest of the story. There really isn't much difference, writing-wise, between this one and the previous ones. As I said, it's a series of gambits from the Doctor, Steven and Sara. A fake taranium core. Steven almost killing himself to charge it. The Doctor being as strong as he can to stop the Daleks from doing anything before he wants them to do it. And the joy of Mavic Chen wondering who the heck this old man with the cane (who Sara Kingdom trusts) is. Mavic hasn't seen the show. (What would life have been like if Chen was familiar with the elders on the planet with the Savages?)

I do like that, at this moment, we have The Doctor as our main character, a guy from who knows where. We have Steven from the 25th (?) century. And we have Sara from the year 4000. Many claim that the Doctor always must have someone from modern day Earth with them to give the audience an identification figure. I've never thought that to be true. But here it definitely is not. There is a big argument between how primitive Steven (born 400 years in my future) is from Sara and The Doctor. Which is kind of an amusing Dennis Spooner type conversation that makes me giggle whenever I think about it.

The highlight of this episode though must be the great arguments between The Daleks and Mavic Chen. Chen's arrogance is hilarious. The Daleks get in some great lines. They still need each other right now. It is odd to see The Daleks be deferential to someone who is being sarcastic towards them. But they give it right back. "You make your incompetence sound like an achievement" is one of the funniest Dalek lines ever. I'm not sure people watching today would go for funny Dalek lines. But who knows? After episodes like "The Witch's Familiar," we may be dialing back on their absolute terribleness. Now, having said that, they are absolute terrible but that doesn't mean we can't goof with them. And Chen has a heck of a time berating them as they mess things up. At the end, they seem triumphant. We know they're not. But we hope our gang can get a break. Because things are going to get rougher before they get better. Even if Yuletide looms.

The Feast of Steven

Written By Terry Nation

Episode 97: (December 25, 1965) It's Christmas. It's crazy. And at the end we're all loaded.

Cliffhanger: The Doctor wishes the viewers a Happy Christmas.

Terry Nation says goodbye to the program until Season 10. And he leaves with maybe not his best episode. It's certainly one that screams "I do comedy!" But, after that is screamed, we get "But, maybe not that funny!" Or "Donald Tosh's script (if he wrote the majority of this) is not that funny!" * Then, after these things are screamed, all we can hear is the constant yelling that goes throughout this episode, especially the second half. The informed viewer can see exactly what the episode is meant to be doing. Nowadays Christmas TV specials are huge business on the BBC and in Britain. When we get to the later portions of this book we will be discussing all the Christmas Specials in detail. Some very Christmassy, some not. Just like this episode. "The Feast of Steven" was a regular episode. It just happened to be 1) in the middle of a huge Dalek story and 2) set at Christmas for a portion of it.

So, the plan was to make a standalone episode with very little reference to the outside story and some references to Christmas. In the middle, they discuss the Daleks and Mavic Chen. The Doctor suggests that they find a way to damage or drain off or destroy the taranium core but that's about it really. The rest consists of two vignettes. One set at Christmas at a British police station. Originally, it was meant to feature cast members from the popular cop show *Z-Cars* but that didn't work. So, it's a generic police station with the TARDIS appearing outside it and confusing the cops. (The least likely place for a police box is in front of the police station.) The Doctor is detained. Steven pretends to be a cop. Sara is confused. And then, it's over as soon as it began.

The second half is even more strident. Set in a silent movie studio in Hollywood in the 1920s (I think. Does it matter?) There's a woman being tied to a log to be cut in half with a buzzsaw. There is a "The Sheik" styled romance. And there's a lot of yelling. A lot. It's a weird segment because the first one has cops. They can get our gang in some trouble. Here it's just people in a movie studio. Sure, they can throw them out. We know the show wouldn't do that amount of outside material. Why drag it out any longer? The problem is that we can't see what's happening so we've no idea how far they are from the TARDIS at any time. They just keep running and running and where are they? I don't know. But, eventually, they run back into the TARIDS. That's a good thing.

Maybe if we had the images from this one that would help. We know for certain that this episode never made it outside of Britain. "The Daleks' Masterplan" was syndicated around the world but they left this episode out because it was Christmas-specific, and it can be lifted from the story without much trouble. I mean, the thing is that they're clearly trying. No one seems to be shirking their duties. But, without the images, it's all so much yelling. It really becomes much ado about nothing. I wish we had it so we could judge it properly. It's so difficult now.

However, we have a great moment from the closing scene. The Doctor brings Sara and Steven champagne. They toast. Then the Doctor toasts all the viewers at home. That moment I love. I could certainly get into more of that. Maybe The Doctor could have some "strange interludes" in future episodes.

*When we go through (as we've been going through) the Wiles/ Tosh era, the show is darker than it was. And yet during this time the silliest episode the show has done so far is put into play by these two guys. One would think that they were trying to put the nail in the coffin of the show ever doing comedy again. "Let's try a comedy!" "Remember the Christmas episode?" "Oh, yeah. I've changed my mind."

Volcano

Written by Dennis Spooner

From an Idea by Terry Nation

Episode 98: (January 1, 1966) More shenanigans at holiday time. But it is funnier and more interesting.

Cliffhanger: Happy New Year, everybody! The Daleks are on their way.

Overall, this is a much more entertaining episode than the previous one. We can't see it. That stinks. But there's less constant running around and screaming. The vignettes are far more interesting and, in at least one case, very funny. Mix that in with the Daleks slowly discovering what we know about the Taranium core and it's a pretty good interim episode.

The scenes with the Daleks and the delegates aren't the fastest things around. More bickering between the delegates. The one who looks he like has Oreo cookies taped to him is my favorite. More wild claims of greatness from Chen. As the Daleks move meticulously around them. I think the reason why it's so slow is because once they discover that the core is not the core they will chase the crew. So, they're leavening in a little suspense to the whole deal. To keep us wondering. To keep us on the edge of our seats. But, one can be certain, that they won't figure it out until the end. That's soap opera-style plotting for you.

The best sequence here is possibly the cricket sequence. Yes, I am A Douglas Adams fan. Yes, I have read *Life, The Universe and Everything* which has a great sequence involving cricket commentators and aliens. Yes, that probably was something based off a wonderfully silly scene like this. It's a kind of hidden scene. Because the episode is lost, because we know so little of it, the charming scene with the cricket commentators trying to find anything in the books about a police box landing on the field is great. I read John Peel's novelization when it came out. (I still have it nearby.) But, for whatever reason, I don't remember that scene at all. It's such a charming, weird bit that I kind of don't feel like it's Terry Nation-related at all. But it could be.

In a very modern bit of storytelling, we cut from the Daleks learning the taranium core isn't working to the Doctor realizing that something is following them through the time stream. Steve and Sara are convinced that it's the Daleks. The Doctor is not. Since we're getting the parallel plotting, we know it's not... more or less. For a moment, I truly felt like it was the Daleks, and the editing was playing tricks. Well, it's not. When we see who it is, it's awesome.

It's the Meddling Monk! Hooray! You know, he may not be the nicest guy but he's not a bad guy. He's just a meddler. I am so glad to see that he didn't end up in 1066. I'm imagining it didn't take him a ton of time to fix things. You knew the Doctor would never get back to 1066 to see him. (Well, not the 1st Doctor anyway.) So, it's great to see him here. And he gets his revenge on The Doctor, sort of.

I love the scenes with the Monk here and wish we could see them. Volcanos and ice planets. So epic. But, so out of the reach of my eyeballs. There's something so exciting about the thought that the Meddling Monk and The Daleks will be teaming up shortly. Or, at least, meeting up. Again, I would love to know who came up with this. As it's the Monk, I would warrant a guess: Dennis Spooner. And it is a super fun way to continue to stretch out the story. I mean, we have four episodes left. A team-up! That's always cool. I'm sure if I checked Marvel Comics for this month there would have been some fun team-ups with heroes or villains. Anyway, it looks like the story is getting underway again. What does the journey have in store for us next?

Golden Death

Episode 99: (January 8, 1965) Let's all go to Egypt.

Cliffhanger: A mummy! No way!

It is fun to have the Daleks meet up with the Meddling Monk. Although, if I were the Monk, I would have taken off the moment I saw the Daleks. He can chase the Doctor later. Getting himself involved seems like the wrong kind of meddling. But he does meet them. And the Daleks and Chen force him to look for The Doctor. I'm not terribly thrilled that he must do that. He does get a great scene with the Doctor. Because the poor Monk thinks he's ahead but as always he's slightly behind.

The Doctor kind of fits right in here, into Ancient Egypt. He wears a Panama hat. He strolls around with his cane. He keeps away from the Daleks and Chen. He fiddles around with the Monk's TARDIS. Things are going to get bleak. But, in this episode, the Doctor's having fun. I like that. Steven and Sara don't have quite that much to do. There are Egyptians in this episode. (It is set within the construction site of a great pyramid.) They don't do much. Dennis Spooner doesn't seem interested in them anyways. Which is fine. There's so much else going on.

Except there kind of isn't. When you focus on the episode, there isn't much happening. Everybody arrives. They kill some Egyptians. The Monk meets the Daleks. The Monk talks to the Doctor. Sara and Steven get tied up and untied. Then, the episode ends with a strange mummy arm appearing out of a sarcophagus. For the first time in the "Masterplan," I feel like we've hit some padding. The fact that it comes after two episodes that are basically goofing is a bit problematic. I prefer Dennis Spooner's writing to Terry Nation's. But this isn't as good as any of the first six episodes. It feels like it's running in place. A location we haven't been to is nice. But something must happen soon. The next episode is in Egypt too. Maybe they should have folded them into one episode and given us another location. It's running in place when it needs to pick up the pace that they (deliberately) set aside for two episodes. This episode needed to rock. It doesn't quite roll.

As I'm finding so little to say about the episode, I thought I'd just mention that I now have "reconstruction fatigue." Before the animated "Galaxy 4" and finding "Day of Armageddon," this was much worse. The first 25 episodes of this season were all lost except for 2. Now we have 4 existing and 3 more animated. I miss the actual episodes. This happened back with "Marco Polo." It seems easy to do a proper review off of a reconstruction. But the more there are, the harder it gets. Luckily, the next episode exists. But then, we have 6 more missing ones. Oh BBC! I saw someone on YouTube comment that they think all this missing episode stuff is "garbage." How do they have the audio? How do they have the pictures? How do they keep finding them if they're supposed to be so lost? I have answers for all those questions. I wish this person were right. Maybe for the 70th Anniversary we will get a big happy bundle of lost episodes from the BBC. I'll pay whatever.

Escape Switch

Episode 100: (January 15, 1966) More running around in Egypt. But this time something decisive happens.

Cliffhanger: One trip: to Kembel! The TARDIS dematerializes. Then there's an explosion.

The Doctor isn't in this episode for quite some time. One would be forgiven for thinking that Hartnell was on another vacation. But it is a tactic that they have used before. When the Doctor is not around, there's a vacuum in the story. The tension is building throughout the moments when he's not there. It's fun watching the Monk trying to finagle his way into the TARDIS. It's interesting watching how close a Dalek gets to Mavic Chen to talk to him. (It looks like they're dancing.) The tension builds... until the point when the Doctor does reappear. And it's a great moment. He's in charge. He's powerful. He's the Doctor. And I love that hat.

The story does something clever with its use of the indigenous people. They're, again, not that interesting. But every few minutes, we see a brief scene with them. They are debating what to do with the "war machines" they've seen. Eventually, they decide to fight them. And now during the Core exchange, the Egyptians attack. Things were already crazy enough. But, at that moment, all heck breaks loose. The Egyptians turn out to be a pretty bad attack party. I do like them here though. They mention

"Hyksos" at one point. I'm all for that. They were one of my favorite one-and-done heavy metal bands of the 1980s.

Overall, it's a good episode. Not great. But, the end, with the loss of the taranium core and the use of the Monk's directional unit, lifts it and implies that greatness is approaching. Because we are (or maybe we're not) heading back to Kembel for the final battle. The Doctor did what he could, but his compassion causes him to lose in the end. However, he does have a trick up his sleeve.

We say goodbye here to the Meddling Monk, at least in the series. He will be back in other media. He doesn't do a whole heck of a lot here, but he is fun to watch. And the fact that the Doctor zinged him again (twice!) is great. Seeing his TARDIS transferred from a building block to a police box is funny and seeing him on the ice planet is funny too. He's not stranded, like previous. He just doesn't know where he's going to go next. Suddenly, we've got more than one "Doctor Who" flying around the universe. (I wonder if he ever encountered Clara and Ashildr.)

In the end, this stops the slightly aimless rambling of the last four episodes and sets us up for the climax. We're going back to Kembel. It really does feel epic at this moment. Having this episode in existence is perfect because it gives us just enough to keep us moving through the final two episodes. I wish those episodes existed. I'm certain they're awesome. But this one is a good one. Douglas Camfield really makes it feel like everything is much bigger than it is. It's a pyramid after all. While this isn't the pyramid scene from *The Spy Who Loved Me*, it ain't half bad, babe.

The Abandoned Planet

Episode 101: (January 22, 1966) We're back on the planet Kembel. But things have gone a little weird. Just what we needed.

Cliffhanger: Mavic Chen leads Steven and Sara, at gunpoint, into the hidden underground Dalek base.

This one does the opposite of the previous episode. The Doctor is in it for the first half or so. He thinks they're still in Egypt. Then, he proclaims they're on Kembel. Then, something weird happens, Sara and Steven go to investigate. And we realize, as they realize, that the Doctor has vanished. He's nowhere to be found. They thought he was following behind them. He's gone. He keeps coming up throughout the episode. He's not here though. He's literally gone for half the episode as he was in the previous one.

Again, it's not Hartnell on vacation. What it does is build up a "What is the Doctor is up to?" feeling. It's so important that the show doesn't show us. It spends time goofing around with those fun to look at, but incompetent, delegates. The show is up to something. Now, we know that John Wiles and William Hartnell didn't get along. After a time, we know that John Wiles was considering trying to do episodes of the show without him. If that's true, that's not very nice. I don't know if that's what is happening. The Doctor is missing, certainly, but I'm not sure if it's malicious. At least, I'd like to think it's not.

What about the rest of the episode? I love that the directional unit did bring the TARDIS to Kembel after all just before it burned out. From what we know of the TARDIS in the future, we know she has a special link with the Doctor. I like to think that she boosted her power as much as she could to get them where they needed to be and then cut out the directional unit. She says in "The Doctor's Wife" that she didn't always take him where he wanted to go but where he needed to go. I think that's what she did here. Thank goodness too because the Daleks are close to starting up their plan in earnest.

Chen is quite hilarious in this episode. His egotism is full-blown. The other delegates are astounded at how full of himself he is. I wish this episode existed because I would love to see the Daleks reactions to Chen. I know they don't have faces, but they can usually express themselves a lot with how they move. He finally, of course, goes too far and he gets locked away with all the other delegates. Scarcely believing how this could have happened.

The moment where Steven realizes that the once teeming with Varga plants planet is now rather silent is great. The title kind of gave it away to us but it's still a shock. The scenes with the delegates and the Daleks are so close to their exploration. To see everything suddenly so deserted is harrowing. And what do the Daleks have in mind for the delegates? They lock them in a cell in the original building and then they go underground. Are they going to experiment on them when the Time Destructor is working? Are they going to just leave them there when they take over everything? It's intriguing and rather scary.

Overall, it's an excellent penultimate episode. Again, Sara and Steven make a good team. Yes, I still miss Vicki but these two have chemistry. I like their talk with the delegates in the cell. Chen still has his ego on overdrive. Also, there's a good cliffhanger. For the final episode, we are moving into a bunker that the Daleks have had prepared for some time. The story has had its longueurs. It would have probably been better at eight episodes, but it's still exciting as we approach the climax

.

Destruction of Time

Episode 102: (January 29, 1966) The Time Destructor is activated, and the Masterplan draws to a close.

Cliffhanger: The Doctor and Steven leave the eradicated Kembel. Nothing but death and destruction behind them

The epic ends. And it ends with ten minutes of the Time Destructor ululating over and over and over as the Planet Kemble and everything around it is destroyed. When I first heard about this story, the Time Destructor seemed like a rather abstract thing. A MacGuffin. A thing everyone was working to start or stop. But never really took over the story. Imagine my surprise.

Where has the Doctor been for the last episode? Inside the Dalek base, examining the Destructor. His plan to put a stop to the Daleks, who have amassed in the thousands on the planet: Activate the Time Destructor and let it roll. Let it roll until it burns out the taranium core and stops forever. It's a hell of an idea. * The Doctor doesn't go this crazy that often. Generally, like in "The Parting of the Ways," something stops him from doing it. Here, there's nothing. It's a final gambit on a horrible planet to save the universe. And the universe will never know. Mavic Chen does have that one guy who was helping him back on Earth. Maybe he'll crack. If not, Chen is gone, and Sara is gone. A jungle planet no one cared for has been reduced to the state of the planet in "Galaxy 4," prior to explosion.

It's been a story filled with desperate moments, in and amongst the silly ones. I don't know how much of this was Nation's and how much was Spooner's, but they did a great job. I wish we got to see it so I can judge the direction. But the audio is relentless. The first 10 minutes is Mavic Chen teetering over into insanity. He's so wonderfully nuts in the episode. And his demise is great. The Daleks simply stop talking to him. They no longer pay a lick of attention to him. That drives him insane and gets scary at the same time. The casual way the Dalek Supreme asks the other Daleks to kill Chen out in the hall so they don't damage the Time Destructor is chilling. He was a great villain, Mavic Chen, and he goes out as crazy as he came in.

I love the Doctor's confrontation with the Daleks and the Time Destructor. They are on equal footing here. They have been for a couple moments during the story, but this is the ultimate one. At this point, one can truly see how the Daleks are terrified of the Doctor. He's an old man who can destroy them by sheer bravery and intelligence. Speaking of "old" man, we of course don't know what age the Doctor is here. But the Time Destructor must age him, I don't know, 60 years or 70 years. Or more. We don't know how old this incarnation of the Doctor is so that could be nothing to worry about or very bad. (Hint: Pay attention to future stories.) His shriek at Steven when he wants him to go back into the TARDIS is the Doctor as we've not heard him before, and it is startling and terrifying.

And then there's Sara. We'll close this review with Sara. We didn't really get to know her that well. But she was brave, smart and strong. She and Steven made a good team. Her and the Doctor might have become interesting pals as time went on. In the end, she wastes away to a skeleton on the surface of Kembel. She wastes away saving the Universe but it's a horrible way to go. As with Katarina, losing her life to save others, another travelling companion in the TARDIS has died. The face of the show has changed quite strongly over the last 16 or 17 weeks. What else do Wiles and Tosh have in store of us? (When one dies of old age from a machine like this one, how does the body know when to die? Does it die at the age it's supposed to die at? Or does it just age until the body can age no longer and then die and decay? I've always wondered. If you know, write to me care of the publisher.)

*A very bracing and crazy one with a desperate Doctor putting his life and the lives of his friend's way behind everyone else's. But there was always one moment that confused me, and the reconstruction doesn't really help. The Doctor activates it. And time goes forward, faster and faster. Somehow, it gets put in reverse. (I think Steven does it.) So, the Doctor can recover a bit and Steven is not affected. And, before it burns out, the Daleks are reduced to embryos. I know what happened but I'm a little vague on how it happened.

THE MASSACRE

War of God

By John Lucarotti

Directed by Paddy Russell

Episode 103: (February 5, 1966) It is 1572. The Catholics in France hate the Protestants and vice versa. Something horrible is brewing. Steven winds up right in the middle of it. And the Doctor goes missing. (But this time he doesn't have a Time Destructor.)

Cliffhanger: The Protestant hating/ killing Abbot of Amboise looks just like The Doctor.

John Lucarotti is back for his final story. And it's another very serious historical. This one, unlike the others, is set in a very specific time. But, unlike others set at specific times, I had to look this one up. A lot was happening in 1572. A lot of intrigue between the Huguenots and the Catholics. None of it was what I would call pleasant. As others have pointed out, Lucarotti succeeds in making an intriguing historical because this is not an immediately recognizable historical moment. Steven becomes the viewer. As more and more exposition is doled out to him, he keeps responding with "I really don't understand. I'm just passing through." He's hoping on the Doctor coming back from visiting a scientist called Praslin. He may be hoping in vain.

It isn't going to be until 1979's "City of Death" that *Doctor Who* can make France appealing. The Doctor is supposed to love the French Revolution. He also seems quite keen on being here now. When you learn what's about to happen, it seems like madness that he would stay and absolute insanity that he would leave Steven on his own. The whole episode is filled with paranoid people being paranoid and it's alternately fascinating and so tiring.

Don't all these guys in the bar have somewhere else to go. They sit there, laughing at Catholics and hoping that their Protestant prince will help them to some power. But the people in charge still seem to be Catholics and we learn of a massacre of Protestants in the past. And it all sounds so awful. One crazy fanatic religious group in charge and giving itself the full rights to subjugate another. Setting up curfews to keep everyone inside. The other side isn't so great either. The main man is a complete jerk. His friend is OK. But the whole thing is so tiresome. How can you live in a world like this? I thought the revolution was bad. Well, maybe that was worse because you could tell everyone apart from how they dressed. Here, you must ask them what their religion is. And all this death over religion? You can just feel that something horrible is going to happen. Anne Chaplet and what she overheard adds to that. (And the title of the serial, or at least what we call the title, adds to that.)

So, the Doctor forgets history to see Praslin and talk to him about his discovery of germs. We learn that scientists are generally convicted of heresy and probably killed. Can you imagine a so-called civilized society that treats its scientists like that? One would imagine that the leaders are probably pig ignorant fools leading groups of pig ignorant fools. But you never can tell. It's nice to see the Doctor have a chat with a fellow scientist but it doesn't detract from (even in a recon) how uncomfortable the scenes with Steven are. He is being as calm and charming as he can be. But it's clear that he can't sit there like an ignorant dope forever. He's going to have a pick a side soon if the Doctor doesn't show. And, as the cliffhanger suggests, the Doctor may have some other plans.

The Sea Beggar

Episode 104: (February 12, 1966) The Abbot looks exactly like the Doctor. Is he? Steven gets more and more embroiled the less he tries to become embroiled.

Cliffhanger: De Coligny is declared The Sea Beggar.

One could be forgiven for thinking that they're going to OD on intrigue in this episode. The constant switching back and forth between the Huguenots and the Catholics. The code names for the assassin of The Sea Beggar and The Sea Beggar being a code name that we don't use until the very end. (And when we hear it used we think "What?") Steven's being called out as a spy because he recognizes the Abbot as the Doctor. Or maybe he's not? Maybe he is the Abbot? Where is Preslin? He hasn't been there in years says a rotten old lady who hopes they burned him. There is talk of a possible looming "something" happening. But the Catholics are holding the cards close to their chests and the Huguenots seem to believe it won't happen because the Prince is one of them. Through it all, Anne Chaplet recognizes the kindness in Steven. Steven walks around slightly dazed, wondering where in the name of the gods is the Doctor?

We only see the Abbott very briefly in this episode. We learn that he just arrived. We learn that only one other person has seen him, and the recollection isn't great. And we also learn that the other people in charge don't seem to trust him. A cardinal sent him. But the others seem to think he's a bit, well, incompetent or he's deliberately messing things up. For example, he goes to the house of the Admiral when he should have stayed hidden. That draws a lot of attention to him and makes no sense. After dwelling on previous historicals, one might begin to think "Hey! Is that the Doctor? Has he taken on the role of this man that nobody knows and started trying to sabotage things?" Possibly. But, in this episode, it is hard to tell. We only see him briefly and we only hear about him. In the original script, apparently, the Abbot has more to do. But Donald Tosh rewrote it (possibly to fit John Wiles' plan of seeing how much Who they could do without Hartnell) and kept things deliberately vague. This is the 4th episode in the last 5 where William Hartnell has been there but deliberately hasn't been given much to do. Doing that once was fun. Four times? It feels a bit disrespectful to me.

Poor Steven. If things weren't so dangerous, it would be amusing. He's trying hard to prove that he's not a spy. But everything that happens seems to make him even more of a spy. I really don't know why the Doctor has done whatever it is he's doing. After what they've just been through on Kembel, it seems heartless of him. Granted, the Doctor did get a hefty dose of the Time Destructor so for all we know his mind could be a bit wonky right now. I wish we could see this episode because I really feel like Peter Purves would have pulled this off. The fact that so many of the Catholics think he's a spy when he just wants to go away, again, could be amusing if things weren't so dangerous. Well, it's been two episodes. Each episode covers one day. So, he's got two days until the massacre begins. Here's hoping someone figures out what's going on.

One more thing: You'll note that I'm not using a lot of the characters names. Trust me. You're better off this way. Remember The Admiral, The Abbot and Anne. The Three A's. The others will do just fine on their own.

The Priest of Death

Episode 105: (February 19,1966) The Sea Beggar is almost assassinated. Steven meets The Abbott and is no longer sure. The Queen Mother is insisting that her son attacks the Huguenots. And then, the Abbott is killed.

Cliffhanger: The angry mob are told Steven killed the Abbott. They chase Steven into the night.

The cliffhanger on this one is quite harrowing. The body of the Abbott is basically more or less lying in the street. A mob of louts stand around it yelling and damning the Protestants. They're worse than any mob *The Simpsons* has ever given us. That obnoxious old lady from the previous episode seems to be there too. When Steven pushes through the crowd to get to the Abbott/ Doctor, he is immediately called out and chased. We have had some desperate cliffhangers in the show. It's one thing to have a monster howl in an aqueduct or a Dalek threaten to shoot you or anything else... A full-crazed mob storming at you ready to tear you apart is the worst. If the Abbott is the Doctor, then it's all over. Steven can run as much as he wants but his time will be up soon.

I noticed something in this episode that makes this story a bit unique. Well, two things: 1) I mentioned this. Each episode tales place over the course of one day. 2) The episodes don't have cliff hanger recaps. They just begin the next morning. So, if you've been paying attention, you know that the next episode will begin the next morning, which is St. Bartholomew's Eve, and Steven will either be dead in the streets of the city or he'll be hiding out somewhere. I wonder how many people spotted that. It's a little tough to gauge in the recon but it might be easier if we had the episodes.

Again, Hartnell doesn't do much. He has a brief scene with Steven. Then, a long scene with Tavannes who doesn't trust him at all. Tavannes begins to mention, as we thought, that everything started to go wrong when the Abbott showed up. They had plans set and they had everything ready to proceed. But little moments here and there have fouled things up and they are all related to the Abbott. When he hears the Sea Beggar was not killed by the Abbott's assassin that is the last straw and he has the Abbott killed. Isn't that a bit harsh? When Tavannes tells his guards to do it, even they are like "Um, really." But they do it. And it is startling to see The Doctor (?) dead on a street.

In this episode, we see a lot of the young King and the Queen Mother. He's basically one step away from being a flibbertigibbet. And she seems horrible. She doesn't like Huguenots and that's all there is too it. They're going to die. How on Earth do all these horrible, horrible people get put in charge of anything? Isn't that most of history though? The people who want to rule the most, or are put into a position of power, generally should not be allowed anywhere near it. Something horrible looms for the next episode.

One of the weird things with the episode is how idiotic Steven can seem. We know what he's up to. He thinks the Doctor is pretending to be the Abbott and everything is OK. But he ends up looking mighty foolish. He turns in Anne. He approaches the body when there is clearly a mob there waiting to kill. He basically browbeats Anne until she's ready to go back to the Abbott's house with him. From our knowledge of the show, if the Abbott is the Doctor, then he's going to be OK. But the story is playing very coy with us and, consequently, making Steven look like a bit of a dope. Even though, in a regular *Doctor Who* story all this behavior would work in his favor. What does he do now? There's going to be a massacre very soon.

Bell of Doom

Written by John Lucarotti and Donald Tosh

Episode 106: (February 26, 1966) The Massacre begins. The Doctor and Steven run away. Then they make a new friend.

Cliffhanger: Dodo is welcomed onboard the TARDIS.

One of the darkest episodes of *Doctor Who*. An episode where we think the Doctor is dead. Then, we realize he's not. Hooray! Then, the Doctor learns what day it is, sends Anne away (probably to her death) and gets him and Steven out of there. An episode where the Queen Mother casually announces to her main man that tomorrow all the Huguenots shall die. All of them. Records say 5,000 to 30,000 people were killed over the next few days. Families were dragged from their homes and slaughtered. The Admiral is properly killed. The episode used a famous painting of the Massacre, and the recon uses it too. It is harrowing. Death and destruction everywhere. If you look close enough, you see the Queen Mother standing by a pile of bodies staring at them. Sick, sick, sick.

I do love how the Doctor knows what the event is as soon as he learns the date. But Steven doesn't know it. He wasn't taught it. It's a big moment in history but it's not one that everyone knows. So, even the viewer is hanging in the dark waiting to learn what's going to happen. That's why the title we used for years "The Massacre" wasn't great but the title they use now "The Massacre of St. Bartholomew's Eve" is even worse. We're not supposed to know exactly what's happening. We're not given the year. The Saint is mentioned casually. The massacre looms but we're supposed to be where Steven is... a little lost. If you go into it without that knowledge, it really works.

Running away from history isn't the most heroic thing to do but it does feel like the only thing to do here. Knowing that all of the Protestants we met in this story will be dead shortly makes the whole story feel like a variation of a slasher film where everybody dies. We spent this time learning about them, getting to know them and it gets cut short. And there's nothing we can do. I do wish the Doctor had asked for the year earlier. It makes the whole enterprise seem slightly pointless, which is too bad. The story is great. It's confusing. It's dark. It's bewildering and it's sad. But it also feels like "Doctor, you shouldn't have been there in the first place unless you were planning on helping someone."

The way I grew up knowing of this serial was that it was 3 ½ episodes and then the ending was kind of a different thing. It's the bit written by Donald Tosh. Written by him as he's no longer script editor. Gerry Davis has taken over. The episode is John Lucarotti's up until the TARDIS. Well, we know now, that Tosh re-wrote a lot of the story anyway. So, who's to say which bit is which bit. But the scene with the Doctor and Steven in the TARDIS, and the Doctor alone is excellent. Steven's outrage over the Doctor's behavior seems justified to me. The Doctor's long speech about why he does what he does is lovely. When he mispronounces Ian's name one last time, it's a moment for a tear. From the screams and destruction of the massacre to the quiet hum of the TARDIS console room is a jolt. And this episode handles it well and gives us the Doctor in turmoil.

Then, Dodo walks onto the TARDIS and all that stops. Two things: 1) Tosh's script edited shows have been harrowing at times. Darker and more unpleasant than previous shows. 2) This is the first and only story under his watch with a prolonged ending like this. Obviously, it's here to shoehorn in Dodo. But is it also here to add another harrowing ending? Is Dodo meant to be as terrifying as a massacre or the Sacking of Troy? Well, she could be. We'll have to see. But she's so stuck in here (and her last name is Chaplet! Like Anne's... oh boy) that she could add to anything. Let's see what.

THE ARK

The Steel Sky

By Paul Erickson and Lesley Scott

Directed by Michael Imison

Episode 107: (March 5, 1966) They land on a huge Ark-like spaceship, far in the future escaping the destruction of Earth.

Cliffhanger: Dodo's cold is spreading. None of the humans have antibodies so they begin dying.

Oh, it's so nice to have movement again. And for a whole serial! Four full episodes. Hey look! A Monoid! Even he looks awesome. (Named "monoid" because he has one eye. That worked out nicely.) Plus, there's an elephant in the studio. The cutting between video and film in the jungle scene is obvious now but I think it was far less so back in the day. Especially before VidFire diddled with the picture to give us the proper textures. Hey look! There's Dodo! The Doctor asked it and I must too: Why is she dressed like that? Well, we've got a new companion. The last two people who travelled in the TARDIS died horribly. Let's see what happens here.

I'm kidding, of course. Dodo's going to be with us for a while. With her fun wardrobe, her changing accent, her use of the word "Gear!" and whatever else it is she does. The character gets zero setup in the previous episode. We know she has no family except an aunt who doesn't care for her. But she's pretty lackadaisical about all of this. They tell her she might never get back home ever again. And she shrugs it off. A half-hour ago, she was looking for a policeman. Now, she's in the 57th Segment of Time on an Ark while the world explodes. Kids! They take it all in stride. (Except, of course, she's a young woman. Not a kid.)

If you were watching this on PBS back in the day, you had previously seen "The Time Meddler." The Doctor, Vicki, newly arrived Steven and the Meddling Monk. Now, Vicki was gone and there was a rather annoying gal in her place who went out of her way to show you she had a cold. One thing you would also notice is that the director is really going for it. Crane shots, elephants, lots of camera movement, the Monoids rising from the plants. Big backdrops implying huge amounts of circular space around us. It's 1970s comparison would be to "Warriors' Gate." But "Gate" comes after *Alien* and *Star Wars* and *Dark Star*. This is still the land of 1950s/ early 60s sci-fi. Remember that there is no *Star Trek* or *2001* yet.

The story itself is nothing that special. In fact, the writers seemed to have used the Xerons and Moroks as the template for their characters. The humans are a bit goofy. (Maybe that's a requirement if you're going to lead the race to a new world.) They certainly have lost their dress sense even if they are futuristic sophisticated. The Monoids are no better. They do, indeed, have mop top Beatles wigs and one eye. It's starling at first. But, when one of them is seen driving an airport buggy thing around, it becomes less startling and sillier. In my heart, I like to think that the story was written very basically so the visuals could stand out. Maybe that's true. Dodo giving everyone a cold and possibly killing humanity and the Monoids is a wonderfully simple idea. Let's see where we go.

Oh, and is the Doctor getting sloppy after his attack by the Time Destructor? Not figuring out where they were in the previous story and not thinking about the consequences of Dodo's cold here. He needs a vacation.

This story begins within another bit of behind-the-scenes turmoil. Donald Tosh is gone, and Gerry Davis is now full-time script editor. John Wiles, who never got on with William Hartnell, is leaving. His successor, Innes Lloyd, is there throughout. According to the DVD Information Text, Wiles felt like he never really put his stamp on the show. But he kind of did. Taking it to darker spots than we had been to before. Innes Lloyd and Gerry Davis will put their stamp on the show. Although, it will take a few stories. In the meanwhile, the last of humanity and their pals, the Monoids, are about to die of the common cold. Like the Martians in *War of the Worlds*!

The Plague

Episode 108: (March 12, 1966): The cold spreads. The TARDIS crew is put on trial. The Doctor begins trying to find a cure for the common cold. He discovers it comes from contaminated water from their aqueducts, so he goes down there and… wait a minute…

Cliffhanger: The TARDIS leaves the Ark. The TARDIS reappears on the Ark 700 years later. Something has gone weird with their giant human statue.

I don't always say how much I like or dislike the episode here. There's a lot to say so some time there isn't time. I will say here: I quite like this episode. Once you can get over the Guardians fashion sense and their inability to wear their face masks correctly, the episode moves quickly. The courtroom scene is quite good. Steven is excellent. His calling out humanity for not having changed is correct. Remember, not too long ago, a mad, misconceived crowd chased him all night long. Here, another one is condemning him to be jettisoned into space. (Reminding me of "Planet OF Evil.") Some people won't listen. When the Doctor takes over trying to find a cure, the episode cooks along until that incredible cliffhanger, which we shall talk about in a moment.

One of the things that Russell T Davies (RTD) did in his first series was address what this cliffhanger does. What happens after the Doctor leaves? What about the fallout? He does it from two different directions.

"The Long Game" to "Bad Wolf." "World War Three" to "Boom Town." In this serial, we get a bit of great narrative joy. As with the current run, we don't always know when a story begins and ends. So, the average viewer would have imagined this story ended. The TARDIS materializes and we fade to black. But then it returns and we're in the same spot. That's great. And it's 700 years later and that's better. Dodo's delivery of "The statue... it's finished." is excellent. The slow pan up as "The Return" appears on the screen and then we see the Monoid head on the statue that should have a human head is so good. The music. The pan up. The model. Everything is right in place. And that's my favorite kind of cliffhanger. The "What in the hell?" cliffhanger. It's perfect because at this point who knows what might happen next.

The episode, apart from the cliffhanger, isn't anything revolutionary. I think it's the direction that lifts it. Peter Purves gives it his all during the trial scene. They have him in a cage. He's getting sick. The cage seems to be lined with some sort of plastic wrap. Bu, he is strong and convincing. Now, granted, if they had never arrived there, none of this would have ever happened. But, as I mentioned, I think the Doctor was harmed more by the Time Destructor than he cares to say. Plus, there's his "sweat out a fever" advice. I'm told this is very bad advice. If someone is burning up from fever, make them warmer. They will sweat it out. I'm no doctor. (If I was, this book would be an exciting medical thriller about clones or dinosaurs or something.) But that's what they always used to do me when I was a kid. And it always seemed to work. Maybe it affected my brain somehow. I'm not sure. Maybe it's Gallifreyan medicine and you're all wrong?

Anyway, this episode moves at a nice pace. It doesn't break any new ground. The crew on trial. Fighting to stop a disease. Being disbelieved by one and all. What it does, when we aren't looking, is throw the format of the show into a bit of disarray. If we can't believe that the Doctor always gets it right, what are we going to do? I will say this: I like Dodo more in this episode. She's quite good in the first scene where she's sniffling and then crying. And I like her taking the Doctor's hand when things go wrong. I do wish the main human guy was a bit less wispy. But, hey, maybe that's the Guardians for you?

The Return

Episode 109: (March 19, 1966) It is 700 years later. The Ark is approaching the planet Refusis. A further outbreak of the cold crippled the Guardians so the Monoids took over.

Cliffhanger: The shuttle is destroyed. How will Dodo and The Doctor get back to Earth?

The best moments in this one are the first few minutes. Watching the TARDIS crew stroll around the sets we'd been on for the last two episodes that are now completely deserted is disconcerting. We know it's 700 years later. We know they are almost at the planet Refusis. But why has the statue got the wrong head? And where is everyone? * Those moments are great. Then, when they start to see the subjugated humans and the Monoids in charge, it makes sense. But that doesn't quite prepare one for how goofy everything is going to get.

If the first episodes had a faux seriousness to them, with the pompous Guardians and their mute friends/ servants, this episode dives right into some kind of camp blender. The Monoids can now talk using some sort of translator devices. The humans now understand them. Oddly enough, they need those devices to communicate with each other. That seems odd. They can't communicate with each other. It's strange.

But what might be stranger is the "security kitchen" where they keep the humans to make them meals. It's the first subjugated race we've seen who are kept prisoner in a kitchen and just keep making meals. I'm not sure if that's the dumbest or funniest thing I've heard in a while. Suffice it to say, it's fun to watch. There are some very nice effects with food appearing.

The humans are the same wet and wishy-washy group as before. There's even a quisling, who is referred to in WWII terms. But it's the Monoids that surprise. First, they have no names. But, unlike the Sensorites, they don't even have titles. Just numbers. Does that make sense? Second, apparently, they eat a lot. See the previous paragraph. Third, they act like children who got put in charge of school. They're petty. They're stupid. They give away their plans in the most ridiculous fashion. But the best moment is when they arrive in the big home that the Refusians have prepared for them. (The DVD information text does say that this is something Nazis did.) The Monoid, to draw out the Refusians, begins smashing items on tables like vases. (I didn't say it wasn't stupid. It was just something Nazis did.) Dodo thinks it's childish. The Doctor does. The Refusians, big, invisible beings, think it's stupid too. Never before have we had such an idiotic bunch leading the way. And, apparently, they're going to kill all the humans after the leave the Ark. We'll get to that later.

I'll end this by mentioning the Refusians. Invisible beings on a different plane of reality who build a very 1960s style home for humans to live in. They have big booming voices. They're not like the Visians at all. Remember them? My other favorite non-Monoid moment in the episode is the Doctor talking to the head Refusian. The Doctor is on one side of the screen, with Dodo in the background, having a very casual conversation with an invisible gentleman who takes up the other side of the screen, invisibly. It's very charming. The Monoids have nothing on these guys. I think the script knows that too.

*In the first episode, a Guardian is miniaturized as punishment. My first thought was: Did everyone accidentally get shrunk down? Are they stepping on crowds of tiny people whose screams they can't hear? Remember that only the Doctor got shrunk down previously. And he's been a little off as of late.

The Bomb

Episode 110: (March 26, 1966) The Monoids have a bomb planted in the statue. All humanity will perish if they can't stop it. Maybe the Refusians can help?

Cliffhanger: The Doctor turns invisible. There's a lot of that going around.

The Monoids, in the end, aren't too tough to defeat. They end up fighting among themselves. They end up getting in pitched battles with each other. If there was no bomb on the Ark, the humans could have probably sat it out and watched them get rid of themselves. The Monoids are certainly up for that. They're such an odd race. See my previous review for all the confusion. The cross fighting here only adds to that. What do they want exactly? In the end, when the Refusians insist that the Guardians make peace with the Monoids, how is that going to go?

Anyway, this episode has a lot going on in it. A lot of shuttles taking off and landing. A lot of forced perspective shots. Models flying through space. Statues being thrown out of the Ark. All sorts of stuff. I would highly recommend putting on the DVD information text during this episode. This was the first episode of the show that was shot extremely out of order because of so much technical stuff happening. Normally, the shows run though from beginning to end. But here, we go all over the place. In fact, the closing scene was the first one shot. I do wonder how everyone handled it. Being so used to doing things in order must have thrown some people off.

How big are the Refusians, I wonder? They can fit in one of those little comfy shuttles. They can also pick up the giant statue and throw it out of the Ark. I don't know. The thought of going to a planet where giant, super strong invisible people live and can always watch me. And then moralize from on high kind of freaks me out. I'll pass.

Overall, it's not a great serial. Its best moment is the twist in the middle. Both stories on either side of the twist are very average. The common cold storyline is decent. The Monoids in charge portion is funny, possibly unintentionally. But, throughout it, the direction is quite impressive. Mr. Imison is doing everything he can to spruce things up. (The 4th episode is just crazy in how advanced it was over other stories of the time.) I wish he had had a better story at his disposal.

I will say that the ending is weird. The Doctor's moralizing speech strikes me as misplaced. They should have just left. All these problems came out because of Dodo's cold. So, why is he giving the speech? I don't mean to be rude, but the Monoids don't seem to be treated as slaves in the opening episodes. Everyone is quite differential to them. They are seen doing work. But, unless something is happening that we missed, I think the Doctor is overdoing it. Maybe to justify the Monoids doing what they did. I always thought the Monoids were kind of jerks. I simply don't see the proof of what the Doctor says. As I mentioned though, he has been a bit off since the Time Destructor hit him. The closest I can get to the humans being awful is when one of the Guardians says that it will be a real tragedy when a human dies. At that time, it's only been Monoids dying. That's not very nice. But that's one person saying it. The whole crowd doesn't nod their heads in agreement. Maybe the novelization can help. Feel free to send me a copy c/o the publisher.

THE CELESTIAL TOYMAKER

The Celestial Toyroom

Written By Brian Hayles

Directed By Bill Sellars

Episode 111: (April 2, 1966) The Doctor, Dodo and Steven land in the realm of the Celestial Toymaker and are forced to play his games.

Cliffhanger: Dodo and Steven head to the next game after reading a poem.

I love that poem thing. Episodes one, two and three end with them. They add a nice eerie touch to the upcoming episode. Unfortunately, those episodes are lost. The fourth one doesn't have them. So, I always wondered if the episodes end with them or whether that's something the recons added to make it a little more interesting. Regardless, the poems are one of the really eerie things about the Toymaker's lair.

In the next reviews, I'll talk about the "received wisdom" behind this story and the one that follows it. The "wisdom" that held true for quite some time. But, for now, what is this story like? We enter another dimension where some sort of omnipotent person holds sway over assorted beings. He makes them play games. He pulls people from time to play. He makes the Doctor invisible and intangible. He has met the Doctor before and the Doctor does not seem particularly thrilled about having to play a game with him. He also dresses like a Chinese Mandarin, which seems an odd choice.

In *Tardis Eruditorum*, Elizabeth Sandifer presents some very convincing theories about the racist basis of this character. Dressed in "Oriental" garb, the novelization goes out of its way to bring out the "Oriental" feel of his world. Plus, the word "celestial" once meant "Oriental." I recommend Elizabeth's books highly. Volume 1 is where you'll find this essay. I feel disappointed if "celestial" isn't meant to mean what I always thought it was meant to be. Something related to stars, something about the Heavens. I always imagined the Toymaker was some sort of misplaced god, a Loki in his own right. But, boy, you can't ignore that Mandarin outfit. I'm going to let that ride for now so we can talk about the episode.

Very disconcerting beginning. Something is getting inside the TARDIS and making the Doctor invisible and intangible. That's not happened before. Usually, the interior of the TARDIS is a safe-ish space. But something so powerful that it can do this doesn't come our way that often. We believe the Doctor when he reveals that he is worried about this. Dodo and Steven don't seem as convinced but they roll with it.

I applaud everyone's enjoyment of the clowns Joey and Clara. Steven and Dodo are quite taken with the sad sack clowning of Joey and the high-pitched whine of Clara. Possibly, if we could see them, they might be awesome. As it stands, they're just some creepy, cheating clowns. In my mind, the snakes and ladders game they played was an epic board stretched across the studio floor, covered in danger. But, from the pictures I can see, it looks about the size of a California King bed. And, unfortunately, so much of the game is visual that the recon, doing its best, can't keep up, nor keep it interesting. Let's not talk about The Trilogic Game, which doesn't seem that interesting to begin with. Once the Doctor Is made invisible apart from his hand, what are we do to?

That's the problem here. Some of the dialogue is fine. But much of it is so visual that the episode drags when we can't see it and only hear it. That's not the makers fault. That's the fault of the people who chucked the episode. But still... I think I liked it. I think. This one is tough to say.

The Hall of Dolls

Episode 112: (April 9, 1966): Dodo and Steven have to play musical chairs with living playing cards. The Doctor is made intangible and unable to speak as the Trilogic game continues.

Cliffhanger: Onto the next game!

When I was a kid, the people who had seen this one described the games Dodo and Steven played as absolutely terrifying, even as they had a bit of silliness to them. The Trilogic Game was some sort of epic game that the Doctor plays, pitting his wits against the Toymaker. This is why you never trust people who watched something when it originally aired but haven't seen it since to give you any clue as to what's going on. Because the episode is lost, it's tough to speak to the game of musical chairs although I will try. However, the mighty Trilogic game is another thing altogether.

The Trilogic Game is a variation of a game called The Tower Of Hanoi. One pile of shapes. Three spots to put them. You need to re-create the pile on the first spot exactly on the third spot. There are a few other rules that I won't go into but the Toymaker does. I had imagined some sort of enormous room with the Doctor having to do something huge. Instead, there is a pyramid on one corner of a triangle. He has to move the shapes to the third corner and have them look the same. Surely, that's not interesting for viewers to watch? The answer is: Yes, surely it isn't. We never get a concept of how the Doctor is doing or where he is. We see a counter showing the move count. He gets 1052. Dodo and Steven have to win first. That's all great.

Then the Toymaker yells out "Go to Move 412!" and the pieces all begin to move on their own. Look, I know the Toymaker is a cheater. I got that. Those clowns cheated like crazy in the previous episode. Is he cheating here, or isn't he? When I first saw episode four and he did that, I imagined he was advancing a natural path that the Doctor was taking. But he does it several times throughout the story. If he and the pieces know exactly where the Doctor is going, what is the point of having him go there at all? If The Toymaker knows that the Doctor will win but The Toymaker's just cheating until he wins, then what's the point of us watching it? I get that he cheats and I get what he's doing there. It completely ruins any sort of suspense and creates a strong pungent feeling of "Why should I care about this?" I imagine the Toymaker might be able to see into the future and that's why he's acting like this. Regardless, every time he yells to advance the moves, it gets on my nerves.

Meanwhile, Dodo and Steven play their game of musical chairs. They find closets full of dolls that they throw onto the chairs. The playing card people walk around looking goofy and possibly being creepy. It's impossible to say from the recon. The chairs seem to be horrible enough. I remember thinking they were in the novelization. One chair electrocutes. One chair freezes. (The one Dodo goes in but Steven gets her out.) One shudders you to death. One makes you disappear. One cuts you in half. It's pretty gruesome stuff. In the recon, it's a bit dull. It's fun to imagine what the chairs are doing to people. I wonder if the effects would have been as interesting. The game does take a very long time. I wish I could see it. All we're left with is our imaginations and Dodo constantly misjudging everything. After the game with the clowns, she seems unable to take this as seriously as she should. I know we've had almost zero-character development with Dodo. But surely, someone could give it a try. I like her skirt. (Mini?) And her hat is fun. Her character, though, is bringing me down.

The Dancing Floor

Episode 113: (April 16, 1965) Dodo and Steven go hunting keys and dancing. The Doctor doesn't do much.

Cliffhanger: Onto the Final Test.

You knew, I think, that eventually, I wasn't going to be able to write a full-length review about one of the episodes. If it's good, there's always a lot to write about. If it's bad, there's always a lot to write about. Sometimes indifference can be entertaining to go over. But, what about an episode like this? A missing episode consisting of mostly visual adventures. Mostly visual adventures that are a step down from last week's visual adventures, which weren't terribly enthralling to begin with. Suffice it to say, this review's going to be a bit short.

The Doctor is still invisible and silent. The Toymaker can see him and hear him but we can't. But we can hear the Toymaker as he talks and talks and talks. And he does that thing three more times! That "Go to Move whatever!" thing that drives me up the wall. He has the audacity to say to the Doctor that he hopes he's been making the moves right. What?! When The Toymaker keeps jumping everything ahead? I don't get it.

Quick note: I realize that one of the reasons why this story and the John Wiles's produced stories are so low on overall verve is 1) most are missing and 2) he didn't use John Cura's telesnaps. Telesnaps were a thing Cura did for hire for the BBC. He had a special camera that would take clear pictures of a TV screen every few seconds. Then, he would sell the images to the production team for further stories/ episodes or just to remember them. *Marco Polo* is lost but well-curated because Waris Hussein bought the telesnaps. Wiles never did. So, we're working off meager publicity photos and that's about it. Anyway...

Dodo and Steven have two adventures: 1) Hunt the key in the kitchen and 2) Cross the dancing floor to the TARDIS. Don't get caught by the dancing dolls! Again, in the novelization, I think these bits are fun. In the recon with no visuals and just lots of music playing and people screaming, it is super obnoxious. The problem with the Hunt The Key game is that it's not a proper game. Each game is supposed to lead them to a TARDIS. This one is about finding a key to a door that leads to a game that leads to a TARDIS. Come on! Visually, I'm sure this scene is a delight. But mainly it's the cook yelling, Dodo flirting with the Major, the Major blustering and Steven being cheesed off. It wastes time that they need to get to the next game but there's no danger. It's just annoying.

After that game, the dancing floor thing is just too easy to play and too tough to really enjoy without the visuals. The final moment with the dolls, the Major and the Cook all with dead faces is a bit haunting. But why is the dance floor so small? I was expecting a huge dance floor stretching across a room. This is an upraised triangle that looks crowded with four people on it. Who designed this? Were they out of money? I wish this sequence was exciting but it just sort of happens and then Dodo and Steven move on to the next game, involving a fat schoolboy named Cyril. He should be nice. I don't foresee any problems there.

One more thing: Dodo and Steven spend much of the episode going back and forth chastising each other for their various beliefs in the fictional characters. Steven is bothered by the Major egging him on. Dodo keeps wondering how they're doing when they're not real. They keep giving each other sass about it. Although, in the previous episodes, it was all Dodo. She seems to think she's getting back at Steven by bringing up the Major thing but then she gets wistful as she wonders if they'll ever meet any of them again. Steven says it best when he says that they must get out of there because this place is getting to her. Agreed.

The Final Test

Episode 114: (April 23, 1966) Dodo and Steven play Cyril on a life-sized board game. The Doctor is back. I hope he played the game right.

Cliffhanger: The Doctor bites down on one of Cyril's sweeties and howls in pain. Toymaker!!

And The Doctor, Dodo and Steven make it out of the Toymaker's dimension but just barely. The Doctor makes use of the Toymaker's own ego to wrap everything up and get them out of there. (I won't ruin what he does it but suffice it to say "Hoisted by his own petard" works nicely here.) We never saw the Toymaker again in the original run of the series but we almost did around 1986. When he returns in 2023, he's very different. He's in our world. But for now. How is the one episode of this serial that exists?

It looks just like we imagined it would. An invisible Doctor plays the game on one set. The Toymaker stands nearby, gloating. It looks like they're on an empty white set mostly. I guess that's part of the dimension. We do see little doll beds with Steven and Dodo's names on them, which I like. The Toymaker continues nattering on. The Doctor, finally with his voice back, cracks wise at this man in the mandarin outfit. I liked that too. The game still isn't very exciting, and The Toymaker really needs some patience but it's nice to hear the Doctor again. It's too bad I never was able to gauge if the Doctor was winning, how long anything was actually taken or anything that was kind of important to the story like that. Without those important elements, when we're specifically given a time limit, the outcome becomes rather pointless because the makers can do whatever they want whenever they want.

Dodo and Steven play Cyril on a large board game. A series of numbered triangles. They roll dice, heading towards the TARDIS. They can lose a turn or be sent back or whatever. The concept is great. The execution is almost great. But it's all so small. What studio were they in when they did this? There's the toymaker's room, this room and the TARDIS control room. Surely, they could have made this more expansive. It's almost so much fun. Cyril is scheming away. Steven is getting cross. Dodo is acting stupid about these characters... AGAIN. It could have been a joy. There's no sense of danger from the electrified floor. Some of them jump precariously from space to space. Others (Cyril) steps from space to space. When Cyril slips in his own slippery powder and hits the floor, you just hear a yell and a noise. Then, you see a giant Cyril doll. Why is this so underwhelming? It's not boring. It just is... there. Intercut this with the Toymaker and The Doctor and, by the halfway point, I really wanted it to end. How did this serial become so beloved in the minds of the people watching?

Maybe because it was different from others around it. Seeing in it 1966 and then talking about it 15-20 years later, with no episodes existing, can greatly exaggerate things in your mind. "And then there was this huge dance hall and a dozen dancers moved slowly towards them. It was terrifying!" When really they meant, "three ladies stood on a triangle about the size of a small office and everyone pretended like everything was really difficult when it was just really cramped and small." Back in the 1980s, this serial was considered *Doctor Who* at its most imaginative and haunting. The next serial "The Gunfighters" was the show at its worst. Neither show had the chance to defend itself. Toymaker was missing three episodes and "The Gunfighters" wasn't syndicated. And there were no novelizations. Then, Donald Cotton' novelized "The Gunfighters." And it was delightful. Funny, exciting, well written and charming. Then, Gerry Davis and Allison Bingeman novelized the Toymaker. The people who praised the serial spent a lot of time putting the book down because it really wasn't representative of the serial. (A serial they hadn't seen in over 20 years.) Davis was the final script editor on it. What the older critics did was point out that Gerry Davis hadn't been well and this Allison whoever must have screwed it up. (Thanks, guys!) Then, "The Gunfighters" was syndicated. People saw it. And people liked it. People with no sense of humor didn't get it but we don't need to worry about them. "The Final Test" made it to VHS. All the older critics began scrambling around and making excuses as the reputation of this story steadily dropped. It hasn't risen since.

Last Minute Note: A few days before this book was published, I saw the 3-D animated version of this on Blu-Ray. The animation alternately works perfectly for the story being told and is distracting. The animators have gone all out. Expanding the spaces and making the toys and dolls quite frightening. They still can't do much with the Doctor and his floating hand. They don't make the story more exciting. For example, the game with the chairs still feels like it goes on for days. However, they present the sort of world that, I think, was in my imagination as a child. What I hoped the serial might look like, even with a script that needed one more good rewrite or four fewer rewrites.

THE GUNFIGHTERS

A Holiday For The Doctor

Written by Donald Cotton

Directed by Rex Tucker

Episode 115: (April 30, 1966) The Doctor, Dodo and Steven land at the O.K. Corral to get the Doctor's tooth pulled. Unfortunately, they get embroiled in the upcoming gunfight

Cliffhanger: Steven begins singing the "Last Chance" song as The Doctor stumbles towards the bar with Doc Holliday's gun.

Look, if you are going into this thinking this is the "worst" *Doctor Who* Story ever, then I think you're wrong. We're allowed our opinions. As social media has demonstrated over the past decade or more, many people's opinions are crap. Based on nothing, sometimes not even on actual experience. "The Gunfighters" was pilloried in *Doctor Who: A Celebration* back in 1983. Several years later, *Doctor Who Magazine* did a Top 10 stinkers. And, yes, this story was the token Hartnell story.

The problem with all the negative thoughts is that they don't match the actual episodes that we have. I will be the first to say that the story goes a little vague for a bit in episode three. But that's no crime. Almost every Pertwee story goes vague in the middle no matter how long it is. The main thing I see in reviews that make no sense is something I mentioned earlier: People don't seem to see that, until the ending, much like Donald Cotton's previous story, it's a comedy. It's a Post-Western comedy. In America, at this time, theatrical Westerns weren't big. We were shifting, because of Spaghetti Westerns, to a sort of Post-modern Western. We weren't there yet. On American TV, things were still going strong. The Big Three were still beloved: *Bonanza, The Virginian* and *Gunsmoke. Doctor Who* doing a goof on westerns was perfect. Is it problematic that it's made by Brits? Well, was it problematic that westerns were reinvigorated by Italians? It's a genre. Take it as it comes or take off.

This episode is great. Rex Tucker may not have been particularly nice to the regulars, but he does a heck of a job directing the episode. It's obvious from the get-go that this isn't a huge space. But it seems larger than anything we saw in the land of the Toymaker. (You're saying, "It's supposed to be." I say "The Toymaker, like Omega, has his own dimension. Everything should be endless. This is a street in an Old West town. If it were endless, you'd never get anywhere.") And he uses all sorts of different angles. He puts the camera way up high and looks down at everyone. He puts the camera at low angles and looks up. At one point, the camera floats along the ground, from the sidewalk into the street and it's very impressive. Certainly, better than anything from the previous episode. Tucker is trying to give it a real western feel, which I love.

The Doctor and the gang are hilarious. Chris Chibnall has obviously been watching "The Gunfighters" when he had Yaz dress Dan like a goofy pirate in "Legend of the Sea Devils." Steven is doing his best here but he ends up almost as bad as Marty in "Back To The Future Part III." Dodo looks great though. She was annoying throughout much of the previous story. She had some good moments in "The Ark." But, it's here, tinkling the ivories, that she really takes off. Her enthusiasm is perfect here. I don't think she gets better than this.

And, of course, the episode is loaded with funny moments. Wyatt Earp's first scene. "Mr. Wearp." The scene with the two "Docs." Steven and Dodo trying to be cool Westerners. The Doctor with a gun. So much good stuff in here. I do wish Donald Cotton had written more for the show. But we have three episodes left... and another one of his great titles.

Don't Shoot The Pianist

Episode 116: (May 7, 1966): The Doctor is mistaken for Doc Holliday. The intrigue builds.

Cliffhanger: It looks like they're going to lynch Steven.

One of the things I love about this episode is how Dodo, Steven and The Doctor are (more or less) assembled near the beginning in the saloon but then they're all off in different places later on. Dodo is with Kate and Doc getting out of town. Steven is stuck with the Clantons. He's doing his best to be genial but it ain't happening. And the Doctor is in a jail cell with Bat and Wyatt. It's not as concretely done as it was in previous Historicals. Here it just kind of happens and it works.

Poor Steven. He sings for ages in the beginning and then he plays some piano for Kate. Dodo plays well. Steven does too. I'm surprised. Or maybe I'm not. The TARDIS can translate languages for you. Maybe it can give you basic musical skills too. Steven really is doing his best. He's surrounded by the Clanton Brothers. They don't seem like the smartest of guys. But they have the guns. Those are usually the people in charge.

Dodo has some fun. She helps Kate with her hair at one point. They have a sweet chat about Doc Holliday and whether Kate should marry him. I think it's delightful. As the tension is building up all around (isn't Tombstone empty?), these two women have this chat. Dodo isn't fully buying it. This is Kate's life though and I'm all for it. Dodo's interactions with Doc are lovely. And the moment the Doc is recognized is fantastic. The bartender gives that away and Doc proves himself as a great draw. Now the three of them are going on a little trip.

The Doctor gets the funniest moments. His chat with the Clantons is very funny. His realization of what's happening is great, especially when it's obvious that nothing he's going to say will convince the brothers. Hartnell is in top form here. I know that Innes Lloyd and Gerry Davis were beginning to send him away, to clear the decks as it were. He's so good here that it seems like they're being unpleasant. The Doctor has one of my favorite moments in this episode. It's the bit where he's spinning the gun and asking Mr. Wearp if he can do this. It's a lovely moment. Followed by the Doctor saying that people keep giving him guns and that he wished they wouldn't. He's great in this episode. Really feels at home.

None of the regulars are involved in the best situations here. Steven is being led on, sometimes foolishly, by the Clantons. Dodo is stuck with the Doc. And the Doctor is accomplishing nothing but keeping himself from getting killed. So, this isn't a historical where they are really part of it. The Doctor's mistaken identity is pushing the episode forward and it is leading us towards the big moment in the next episode. Prior to this one, the good guys were good gunfighters and the Clantons were a bit inept. Have a look at the title of the next episode. Things are going to tilt towards the side of the bad guys.

I haven't really mentioned the "Ballad of the Last Chance Saloon" much. It's sung by Lynda Barron. Wrack from "Enlightenment." And Val from "Closing Time." It's a constant punctuation on what's happening. Sometimes it is a bit aloof. Sometimes it is having fun with the narrative. I enjoy it no matter what it's up to. Is it a bit too much? Possibly. When Kate breaks into it in the saloon and everyone dances along with her, I got lost a little bit. I didn't think it was bad. I just thought maybe we were overplaying our hand. But then, the show is still experimenting with comedy so some weird moments don't really bother me.

Johnny Ringo

Episode 117: (May 14, 1966) Johnny Ringo arrives. Things get a little darker.

Cliffhanger: The gunfight looms.

Now, the real bad guy shows up. Johnny Ringo. He shoots Charlie the barman. He has had a romance with Kate. He's generally a tough guy. And he's a full-on proper killer like Doc Holliday was. He adds just the right bit of oomph to the serial at this moment. Because after the lynching scene, the pace drops a little. Dodo, Doc and Kate have gone away. Pa Clanton shows up. This is the perfect zing the serial needs to pick itself up. Not that it was in trouble. But one would prefer to have the show kicking along and get rescued as it's teetering towards losing some pace, rather than losing the pace and picking it up again.

The opening scene with the lynching is nicely done. Again, Rex Tucker (isn't that a great name for a guy who is directing a Western?) may have not been so great to the regulars but he knew where to put the camera. The framing throughout that scene is perfect. From inside the police station, up above the crowd, to the other changing angles, he keeps that scene exciting and interesting. A scene involving Steven and The Doctor where they do nothing really. It's all Wyatt and Bat doing their thing. Still a very good scene.

I like Dodo out and about in the world with Doc and Kate. They're not gone for a tremendous amount of time. Ringo finds them relatively quickly. But they are fun together. And there is the questions: Doc has a room. Dodo has a room. Where is Kate sleeping? That's for a more late-night version of the show that we're not getting here.

I'm not sure, at the end of this episode, how anyone thinks that the show couldn't pull off a Western. The constant use of the song might bother you. However, even that is going kind of meta. When they carry the Clanton boy who was knocked out to a cell, the song goes very scene specific right there, which is cool. And, frankly, it was a bit unexpected. The rest of the serial has been so nicely done. Unlike "The Myth Makers," which shifted to serious in the second half of the final episode, once Ringo is introduced there is a definite element of darkness brought in. Heck, look at the death of Charlie. He's weaselly. He's probably not a fun guy to hang out with but he doesn't deserve what happens to him. That's the Old West. And the show gets that moment down perfectly. This is the way the world was at this time. This is the kind of thing that could happen. Even to the innocent. Or the innocent-ish.

Now, we know that Innes Lloyd and Gerry Davis oversee the show right now. We also know that they didn't like the historicals. We also know that the Audience Appreciation figures for this serial were in the toilet. However, if you've ever spent some time examining those figures and the comments that go with them, you can, like me, accept that they were important. Then, you might also want to pat the Great British Public on their heads and ask them if they're tired and if they need anything before sleep. They're nonsensical, mainly. We don't know who they're talking to but boy is it annoying. But these comments did lead, in the next season, to the cancelling of the Historicals, which is too bad. Anyone with a modicum of critical acumen can tell that this is better than the last two stories combined. Is it because it's a bit cheap? I don't think so. You saw "Toymaker" right? Is it because of… I don't know… the accents? A few are dodgy but I can't say that I care. If funny dialog delivered with a slightly dodgy American accent bothers you and yet you find Dodo and Steven spending ten minutes in a kitchen looking for a key with absolutely no dramatic drive a real hoot, then I can't help you. You won't like the next review. But you will like what Lloyd and Davis did to the show.

The O.K. Corral

Episode 118: (May 21, 1966): The Gunfight occurs.

Cliffhanger: They land on a new planet and are interested in checking it out!

A great ending to a great serial. Rex Tucker stages the gunfight nicely. It's all on film. He's able to vary the angles and adjust the editing in a way that he never could have in the studio with the multiple cameras. I love the moment when the Clantons fire at the Earps. And the Earps just walk down the street towards them, fearless. Someone's been watching "The Untouchables." It's great seeing Dodo in there. She's really come into her own in this story, which is fantastic. (Especially considering she only has about six episodes left.) It's a rather violent scene. Men gunned down. Bodies on the ground. The sequence shows that Tucker knows his westerns and is having a good time. Subsequently, so do we.

The rest of the episode is the slowly approaching gunfight. The dead Earp brother gets a lovely dying scene. Ringo turns out to be a bit of a snake. The Clantons aren't so smart. The closing scene as the TARDIS crew leaves and everyone is perky does seem odd. They used to shoot the film scenes long before the studio video stuff. I think sometimes they goof up certain things. (Think of Dr Taltalian in "The Ambassadors of Death.") Here, they get the tone wrong. In the shootout, things are grim and violent. Then, suddenly, it's the end of a *Scooby Doo* episode and everyone is having a swell time. Apart from that, though, the episode works well. Very well. And its reputation as "the worst" *Doctor Who* story seems more and more like baloney as time passes. Yes, the constant song may be overused. However, if you watch the show one episode a week or one a day, that problem gets cut down.

There is a moment in the DVD information text where it says that Innes Lloyd and Gerry Davis were not thrilled by this story. (No "base under siege" must have let them down.) So, they encouraged Rex Tucker to play up the comedy. That makes no sense to me. First off, the script is already very funny. There are a few moments when the cast oversell it but, generally, they're playing it correctly. Donald Cotton's previous script was very funny. Until it wasn't. As you will see over the remainder of this season and into Four and Five, Lloyd and Davis aren't big on laughs. Any comedy forthcoming is probably all because of Patrick Troughton. So, to claim that they asked the director to feature the comedy doesn't fit with the writer used or the rather humor-free gentlemen in charge.

The shift from comedy to serious action in the end is less jarring here than it was in "The Myth Makers". First off because we can see it and it's pretty much a tour de force. "The Myth Makers" could either be brilliant or not so much. It's tough to say. Second, because we never like the Clantons or Ringo. When Troy was sacked, we watched two groups of people we'd come to respect rip each other to pieces. It's the extreme version of the sides we see in "The Reign of Terror." In "The Gunfighters," it's a good guy vs. bad guy thing and works much better. In one way. The chaos of the sack of Troy is effective but maybe not pleasant.

I'm a big fan of this story. It always strikes me as odd that people watching it today don't like it too. I was looking at *Doctor Who: A Celebration* again. There's a great picture of the Doctor, Dodo, Steven, Wyatt and Bat. The Doctor has his hands on his lapel and is wearing a cowboy hat. He looks awesome. The caption complains that the Doctor looks ridiculous. At age 11, I agreed completely. At age whatever I am now, I dislike when critics do that. Don't present something cool and then denigrate it to fit your theory. Get a better theory. "The Gunfighters" is a good one.

THE SAVAGES

Episode 1

Written by Ian Stuart Black

Directed by Christopher Barry

Episode 119: (May 28, 1966) The crew lands on a planet where the people are waiting to meet the Doctor. Everyone seems very nice. Something might be very wrong.

Cliffhanger: Dodo has gone down a hallway she's not supposed to. She sees a depleted "savage" stumble towards her.

Nanina, Flower and Dodo. The ladies aren't making out so great with the names when it comes to this story.

The big thing with this episode is that the individual episode names have ended. It won't be until "Rose" that we go back to that. It makes it easier for pedantic people, sometimes like me, to name the stories. But it's kind of less fun. We will not see a "Don't Shoot The Pianist" around here again. I always wondered why they chose this point to change it. Lloyd and Davis are now ensconced. This is the last of the stories from the previous regime but, although it's tough to tell, a Lloyd trademark appears here: gals in short skirts, including Dodo. I know that the shows all have production codes and that "The Gunfighters" was Z. "The Savages," or "Doctor Who And The Savages" as the previous week's caption read, is AA. So maybe it's just as simple as that. Or maybe Innes Lloyd was trying to make the show more uniform in what it did and how it tells its stories. That will certainly begin to happen with the next serial.

This is a cruel serial, right off the bat. It reminds me of "Galaxy 4" in some respects. We see something awful. Then, we meet the "beautiful people." They seem too good to be true and slowly (or quickly) reveal themselves to be something unpleasant. Meanwhile, we learn that the thing that scared or confused us in the beginning is the "good" thing but something is keeping us from it. Dodo is the only one who seems curious here. Steven isn't particularly interested either way and seems to be written out of character. The Doctor is flattered but keeps himself on track.

This episode is the first one where we meet *Doctor Who* fans! A group of people, the rather darkened Elders on this unnamed planet, have been following the Doctor's adventures for some time. (Are they catching TV signals beamed out from Earth from thousands/ millions of light years ago? Maybe.) They know the Doctor is going to visit and they're ecstatic. Although, oddly enough, they expect him to be alone. What season are they watching? I like the Doctor being flattered by these people who are his fans. But, like most fans of this show, they're a bit off-putting and not all that graced with the social niceties and they're a bit weirder than they should be. It's obvious that something is happening with the "savages." Something which the Doctor wouldn't approve of. I like the calm build towards how advanced these people are and how they refill their lifeforce when needed. The Doctor slowly trying to get them to say what it is that makes them this way. This is intercut with a guard capturing Nanina with a light gun and bringing her in to have her life forced drained. I'm not sure if the Elders want some kind of Doctor endorsement but surely they must know that he isn't going to like this. We'll see.

And what's going on with the characters of Steven and Dodo. Dodo acts nothing like herself and she accuses Steven of doing everything the Doctor says. There hasn't been an ornerier companion than Steven. It's odd. It's almost as if they're setting up another change. Well, it would be par for the course for this season.

The Savages

Episode 2

Episode 120: (June 4, 1966) The secret of the Elders' perfection is revealed. The Doctor isn't happy.

Cliffhanger: The Doctor is having his lifeforce drained.

The music is rambunctious in this one, isn't it? Lots of strings going wild. Has the feel of a 1950s sci-film that's really trying to get you revved up. I'll admit: Sometimes it works. Sometimes it's a bit much. The opening scene is tough to gauge without the visuals. The music makes it seem like something insanely exciting is happening. But who knows? Dodo's in the scene. I can't say whether that's good or bad.

Did I mention this is a nasty story? It doesn't get better. It's tough to figure out who is the worst here. Jano, the guy in charge. The man who considers himself so superior that the exploitation of other lives literally means nothing to him. To the point where the moment the Doctor disagrees, he's willing to drain the Doctor's lifeforce. (Jano claims the Doctor is not a very good scientist. But the Doctor is a great scientist. A scientist though who has compassion and who has a heart. The surprise with this society is how much the "younger people," as they refer to themselves, are completely complacent and don't care two jots about who gets hurt so they can have fun.) He's a nasty person.

Exorse might be worse. He's a guard with a gun. He's not even one of the smart people who set up this monstrosity. He's just armed. And with the light gun, he feels strong enough to lord it over the Doctor, which I don't like. When he shoots the Doctor with the light gun, I get very cross with this episode. I can't see them draining the life force from him. But there's lots of noise and lots of scientists talking. And it all rises and rises until the theme begins. All I can think of is "The Destruction of Time." The Doctor was aged badly there. What is this doing to him?

The whole thing is a basic morality play about people who are super advanced but are that way through the exploitation of something else. Jano thinks it's perfectly reasonable. The Doctor does not. I'm unhappy that we're missing the big moment here where the Doctor yells at the leader. Jano has that calm, patronizing feel of jerks who don't realize they're jerks and are humoring someone who calls them out on their horse dung. It's frustrating. And it's going to hurt the Doctor and I don't like that.

Dodo and Steven are still written a little off the mark. Steven keeps making claims about Dodo's character that we haven't seen her exhibit. Steven seems a bit slower than usual. Now, after they help the "savage," they begin to make friends and they being to see what's happening. And yes, the story, at this point, might be on a rather obvious path. But I think it has an idea or two up its sleeve. I wonder if Ian Stuart Black had originally written this for different companions. It has been a hectic season.

I'm pretty good at parsing out episodes of the show. (Not counting as I write this book.) I do one episode a day. Sometimes a little longer between episodes. This is one of the few serials I almost always try to race to the end of. The nastiness of it, the injustice of it, the horror of it. It doesn't make me happy. I know there is a happy ending. So, I like to move towards it as quick as I can. Keep reading with me and we'll get there.

The Savages

Episode 3

Episode 121: (June 11, 1966) The Doctor is drained. Steven gets control of a light gun.

Cliffhanger: The Elders try and gas out Dodo and Steven.

This one gets even darker before it gets lighter. And I'm not referring to the light ray. Although I might be. (Actually, I'm not.) The Doctor is put though the life force draining. It is said that he will never be the same. It seems pretty extreme to me. To put the lead through something like this. Talk is made of all the "savages" who were drained to the point of death. It's never said that the Elders or the people who use the life force give a darn. From what I can tell, William Hartnell was not on vacation during this episode. He was just presented as drained and exhausted. They take him away until he can build up enough juice to go again. That's horrible.

Some say, and this could be true, that this was part of John Wiles's belief that Hartnell didn't have to be part of the show. Watch the Doctor vanishing in the second half of "The Daleks' Master Plan." Watch his small involvement in "The Massacre." Look at the fact that he does almost nothing in "The Celestial Toymaker." But then, watch him in "The Gunfighters." He is marvelous. In some ways, this could be warming up to Lloyd and Davis plan to replace the ailing Hartnell with someone else. Jano's acting in the end seems to portend this.

Yes, the leader of the Elders is given the Doctor's lifeforce. Presumably, because it could be dangerous. Really, who wouldn't want a blast of the Doctor's lifeforce? (It just occurred to me that Doc Holliday has one of The Doctor's teeth. Surely that's an important artifact if the great novel *Alien Bodies* is anything to go by. Or "The Impossible Astronaut." If the Doctor's body is a universal wonder, one of his teeth must be great to have. Even with a cavity!) Anyway, Jano immediately begins to do a William Hartnell impersonation of the 1st Doctor. And I wish we could see it because it seems to be very amusing. It is too bad that to get to this amusing point they must haul the Doctor through the wringer. This is kind of one of the darkest eras in the show's history. But it's not one that is gone into in great detail because so much is missing. One day, we'll re-evaluate it. As I'm doing right now. Good for me!

Much of the episode is spent with Dodo and Steven and the Savages. We have to use our imagination but it's interesting to have them encounter a temple of great beauty. To hear the Savages say that they used to be a very creative and intelligent people, but the Elders drained them to the point where they have nothing left is so depressing. How did the Elders get control of everything, I wonder? If the "savages" were such a prosperous, intelligent people, how did this group of inhuman monsters get to the point where they could shunt these people off to the caves? (There is always the chance that the "savages" are lying. They might have been like this forever and are trying to get some sympathy. I'd like to think that's not true, though. The serial really doesn't go into details. We simply see what is.)

I do love that Exorse is flashed by his own light gun. That moment made me smile. He's so gung-ho about hurting everyone. It's great when he gets zapped himself. Am I being cruel? Maybe. He's a jackass raised on violence. How else are you going to get to him except in the same way? Talking will accomplish nothing. Zap him with the gun and make him dance.

The Savages

Episode 4

Episode 122: (June 18, 1966) The Elders plan ends due to the exchanging of life forces.

Cliffhanger: Dodo and The Doctor leave Steven in charge of the planet we never got the name of. Steven The Planet?

So, that's goodbye to Steven. I always thought Steven was an excellent companion. Much of his oeuvre is missing, which stinks. Back when they used to show just the complete stories on PBS, you would see him at the end of "The Chase." Then, he's properly introduced in "The Time Meddler." Then, suddenly Vicki was gone, and Dodo was there for "The Ark." Then, they went to Tombstone. Then, he was gone. If you can sort of wallow in his era, he's a good companion for the Doctor. He never quite has the hero thing of Ian. He never feels like he must be the leading man, running the show. He's there with his friend, the Doctor, and some ladies. They're having a good time. I've never (and others have felt this way) thought that he would be happy to stay on this planet and run it. But, if it's a life with Nanina... I would gladly teach her what "kiss" means. Godspeed, sir! I hope your life was a good one.

This story/ this episode was known for two things back in the day. 1) No monsters. The elder statesmen of *Doctor Who* would insist that this episode would be better remembered if it had monsters. I insist it would be better remembered if it existed. I have "recon fatigue" big time. I'm so looking forward to watching "The War Machines," even if it isn't a favorite. But simply because things move around. 2) They destroy the laboratory set in the end. The Doctor mentions how satisfying it is and it must have been. That set, which we can't really see, was built to be torn apart in the end. That's cool. And you can hear the excitement as they rip it up, but you can't see it.

The "not seeing it" thing does affect this episode. (Yes, when they find these episodes (in a Youth Club basement in Bergen) I will update this book. And I will have more positive things to say. But it really is like you're making me listen to early stereo albums from the mid-1950s but only giving me one channel. Early stereo jazz albums would put instruments in one channel. So, you could miss an entire solo if you didn't have both sides. Hopefully, the fellows on bass and drums were kicking it.) I do want to see Jano act like the Doctor. I do want to see the Doctor come out of his "coma."* I want to see him taking control, even at his weakest, and lead the charge on the laboratory. I want to see this horrible regime torn down. Somehow the first two episodes are much stronger on recons than the first. I know the ending is there, but it isn't as satisfying as the first half, which is depressing.

An interesting story this one. I do feel like it would work best watched all together, rather than in chunks. Some of the stories do work like that. Dodo starts off strong but then fades away. Steven is just there. And the Doctor is adversely affected. Of course, with the previous Time Destructor problem and now this, I think our friend, The Doctor, should maybe take a bit of a vacation. He doesn't want to get worn out in the middle of an adventure.

*Shades of the self-induced coma they would put themselves into several times in the 1970s.

THE WAR MACHINES

Episode 1

Written by Ian Stuart Black

Directed by Michael Ferguson

Episode 123: (June 25, 1966) Dodo and the Doctor land in 1966 London! (They haven't been there since they picked Dodo up in March) We meet Ben and Polly. We meet WOTAN, supercomputer that may not be very nice. Will Operating Through Analogue, by the way. Things ain't digital yet, baby.

Cliffhanger: "Doctor Who is required." And we will all be confused for some time.

Here we go. Innes Lloyd and Gerry Davis are finally putting their official stamp on the show. It immediately feels more up to date, more hip, cooler than possibly it has been before. It seems very "of its time" and "in the now." The music, the location work, the music, the club, the giant computer. It screams out to the viewer that this is set in...

The Swinging '60s! No place was more swinging than London. In this episode, we go to the Club Inferno, which is, of course, underground. Somewhat. They play hip music. We get overhead shots of dancers.

We get Polly and we get Ben. Polly is secretary to the man who runs supercomputer WOTAN. Sadly, she takes the limelight away from Dodo almost immediately. While they're in the club, Dodo looks a bit like a fifth wheel. Hanging around in the background. They don't even really notice here when she goes. Note how the first scene with Polly does not really feature her much. She walks by. We see her from the side. It's almost as if the director was like "Once everyone sees Polly, who's going to care about Dodo?" (What's with all the bird related names?) I do like the way they treat the Doctor and I do like how bemused the Doctor is by this. He hasn't really spent any time in London since late 1963. If this is 3 1/2 years later, things have really changed, especially those skirts. It's great to have the Doctor land in "modern day" and for it to be so casually done.

Although, I do have one question and maybe this is meant to be something thematic: In "The Ark," Dodo's first story, she points at the statue and says, "It's finished." And we see the Monoid head. In this one, she points at the Post office Tower and says "It's finished" as we pan up it. Is that meant to be a full circle thing? The first time she's far, far from home and she sees something and makes that exclamation. Now, she's home again and she says it. I don't know. I just noticed it and I'm convinced it means something. (Also, the last time they landed here was at the end of "The Massacre." So, the universe may be a huge place but the TARDIS knows what it likes.)

I do love the Doctor in this episode. He looks pretty hip with his cloak and hat. He somehow gets himself talking to all the important people in and around the world of WOTAN. I'm not sure how he does it exactly but I'm not going to put him down. He's a swinging 1960s older gentleman. I'm sure there were plenty of them about. He does evolve this weird cognitive ability to sense danger in this episode. Maybe it's something from the Savage planet? We have no concept of how much time has passed between episodes here. For all we know, it could be 6 months or more.

As mentioned, we meet our next duo of companions: Ben and Polly. Ben is a sailor and not very hip. Polly is as posh as all get out. Unfortunately, like Steven's run, most of their episodes are lost but quite a few have been animated. Anyway, let's see if WOATAN gets this Doctor Who, whoever that's meant to be. I'm sure WOTAN just wants to be friends. He/ It did know what TARDIS meant, if you remember. Maybe he has access to BBC scripts.

The War Machines

Episode 2

Episode 124: (July 2, 1966): Dodo goes bad and then goes away. WOTAN begins assembling his war machines.

Cliffhanger: The War Machine has found Ben. This might not go well.

Mr. Black has a bit of a line in stories with a cruel streak to them, doesn't he? This one has big 1960s computers, which look foolish to us now but I don't mind them. It's got hip 1960s young people doing whatever it is they did. It's got mind control. It's got the hero as an older gentleman dressed rather fab and hanging out with the youngsters and government people. At the same time, it has the scene with the tramp.

An old gentleman down at Covent Garden who decides to doss down at an old warehouse. Only, he discovers, it is filled with people working for WOTAN. Building WOTAN's "kind of interesting looking but oh so cumbersome" War Machines. The men, just regular guys who have been hypnotized, murder the tramp. (The tramp does get a front-page article about his death in the paper the next day. So, it's not all bad.) Later, they test the War Machines steam weapon thing. A man stands blank faced in front of the Machine while it shoots him (more or less) and he drops dead. I don't want WOTAN taking over everything because he's a jerk.

When did Ultron first appear? I was reading a Marvel-Two-In-One comic from the early 1980s with him the other day. Ultron is the cool version of WOTAN. (I did enjoy *Avengers 2*.) Oh, Ultron appeared in 1968. OK. WOTAN was first. Using the phone lines to control the great people of Britain. If he could have put himself in a cool robot form, then he would be something. The world of crazy super computers that want to exterminate humanity expands over the course of about two years. I always wonder why WOTAN went with such large War Machines. It needs a lot of space, especially if it's going to turn around. It makes sense that the Cleaners in "Paradise Towers" look like the War Machines. They're meant to be filled with trash and cleaning products. But why do the War Machines look like the cleaners from "Paradise Towers?" I never fully got that.

Ben and Polly seem to be getting along OK. They're flirty but sort of modern flirty. They may like each other, or they may not. Who knows? I like that Polly asks Ben to lunch and he says he won't be a "Deb's Delight." That's basically a "Debutante's Delight." When wealthy gals take out "lower class/ working class" gentlemen so they can be seen as... I don't know. Worldly? Enjoying a bit of rough trade? I'm not sure. The 3AM scene with the Doctor, Ben, Polly and Dodo at the Inferno is fun. Especially when you hear that it's 3 AM! What!? Doesn't the Doctor have to sleep? He just had his lifeforce sapped from him a few episodes before.

Basically, what I'm doing throughout this review is: trying not to say goodbye to Dodo. 17 minutes into the episode, she is gone. We will get a goodbye from her in episode 4. But she is gone. She tried to turn Doctor Who over to WOTAN. She failed. And then she's gone. We know that Lloyd and Davis were sweeping the show clean as soon as they could. But at least Steven got a decent (well...) leaving scene. Here, Dodo is sent to the country, and she's gone. During her final episode, she's not even herself. She's hypnotized. There's a good chance that no one ever quite figured out what they were supposed to be doing with Dodo. Apart from the fact that she looks like Susan a bit, she was kind of a waste. But then, not everyone who travels with the Doctor must have a long series of magical journeys. Some blow in and out and we ask, "Who's next?"

Oh, one more thing: what is WOTAN's problem? Has it never watched the show? The main character is "The Doctor," not "Doctor Who." I know they made jokes about it (most recently in "The Gunfighters") but it's incorrect. Come on, supercomputer. Get on the stick.

The War Machines

Episode 3

Episode 125: (July 9, 1966) The War Machine roll out approaches. Polly is taken over. Ben and The Doctor must save the world! Because Dodo is still taking a break in the country.

Cliffhanger: The Doctor stands up to a War Machine.

I love the opening of this one. We get the Doctor Who images and the theme. We get a recap of the cliffhanger. Then, we get some classic "computer" numbers on the screen spelling out the title, the author and the episode number. It's always fun when they goof with the titles like this. It doesn't happen enough. When it does, I'll bring it up. I think it's a cool way to keep a show that has gone on for so long fresh.

Ian S. Black may be a bit rough. May be a bit heartless. A lot of soldiers do die near the end of this. But he knows how to pace a 4-part story. You need to have the build to the cliffhanger, but you always need to have a story that moves forward. The story can't stop with the cliffhanger and then build its way up to the next one. That makes for good individual episodes but not so great in the over-arcing story department. Both this and "The Savages" shows that he knew how to structure a 90-minute story and hit those cliffhanger marks. We will see plenty of writers, as time goes on, who work episode to episode. Is one better than the other? I don't know. But this one, like the previous one is a story I can watch all the way through. While, say, the next one, I can't really do that.

Ben and Polly get some great scenes here. Probably better than almost any scene with Dodo except for some of her scenes in Tombstone. Polly has been taken over. Ben is trying to get out of the warehouse. Polly is working under WOTAN hypnosis. There are some great moments between these two. Ben trying to help her. (He's starting to call her "Duchess.") But not sure if he can. Polly working hard for WOTAN but helping Ben twice because he's a friend. That's a nice bit of byplay in the middle of the third episode that keeps the episode interesting and begins to build these characters. (Presumably, we were pretty positive that Dodo wasn't coming back, and Sir Charles was too old to be a companion. Someone must be a replacement.) All we need, all the show needs, is a few minutes. Just a little time. You don't need a full episode or hours to establish characters that people care about. Five minutes. That's all. Dodo never really got that. So, she always seemed strange in the TARDIS. Here, Polly and Ben get that time and it will help.

Michael Ferguson will direct a bunch of *Doctor Who* episodes over time. One of his big things was a pitched battle. He loved being in a warehouse, being in a field, and just letting the guns go, letting the guys punch each other. In this one, it's not quite as fluid as later work but it's still fun. Lots of shooting. Lots of boxes. Lots of steam. We're hampered slightly by the fact that some moments are still missing from this episode. If you read the DVD information text (always some of the best places to find info about the show), you'll see how they restored the scene and made it look as good as it does. I applaud them. I don't think I would have noticed the changes and additions that allowed them to keep it going. Ferguson battles = Awesome. Doctor Who Restoration Team = Awesome. I'm hard pressed to think of another show that has received this much love on home video or in general. (*Star Trek: The Next Generation* with its Blu-ray set is the closest I can come.)

Oh, can I get a shout out for one the best closing shots in *Doctor Who* history? William Hartnell may have decided he's leaving. (Or however you want to frame the story.) But his Doctor is stronger than ever right here.

The War Machines

Episode 4

Episode 126: (July 16, 1966) "The battle of the Computers comes to a climax." Thank you, Radio Times. You're not Dodo!

Cliffhanger: Ben and Polly step into a police box. Their lives will never be the same. Even with a few weeks off.

All right, here's the big question: Who is that couple that see the TARDIS dematerialize at the end of the episode/ season and then look at the camera? Has some fiction been written about them? Do they have a backstory? Is this meant to close a circle? The cop at the start of S1. These people at the end of S3.

Does Torchwood eventually kidnap them and put them away somewhere "safe" where they won't talk about The Doctor? Do their grandchildren start a website devoted to this strange being who appears throughout time and space? Or are they just two goofballs who walked in front of the camera and no one noticed it until it was too late? I feel like the latter is correct. I hope my other thoughts are better. Are they agents from the CIA on Gallifrey? Monitoring the Doctor's adventures?

Dodo is gone. Ben and Polly join the TARDIS. Oddly enough, he doesn't invite them onboard. He shoos them away. I get the feeling like maybe he's looking forward to having some time alone. But they stumble in right at the moment of dematerialization. They may be gone some time. Or they may not be gone any time at all. That's time travel for you.

All in all, this is a good 4th episode. Unfortunately, what stops it from being great is that it expands its scope. "The Dalek Invasion Of Earth" did that but it did the thing the show always does. It keeps the focus on a few meetings and conversations while the bulk of the craziness goes on elsewhere. This one, and I think this is probably from Mr. Ferguson, tries to go huge. It uses actual newscasters (which the modern show has done). It uses large crowds. It uses regular people dealing with a possible catastrophe. In general, it holds up well. But try as it might, it's still mostly shot in a studio as if it were Live.

They go on location. Those moments are awesome. They do give the show effective expanse. They make it feel like this is an epic attempt by the Computers/ the Machines to take over London. In the end, the battle is set in that main control room in the Post Office Tower. It's a little awkward but it gets the job done. Everyone is safe again and we get to see a lot of people snapping out of it.

Throughout it all, the Doctor is excellent. Ben is a great companion right from the get-go. Moreso, in some respects, then Steven. Ben being a sailor treats the Doctor with respect and works with him. The only time he gets angry is when the Doctor is iffy about saving Polly. Is this a good companion? We'll see. The Doctor clearly likes him (and Polly). Ben clearly appreciates the Doctor. Sir Charles is a slightly stuffy bureaucrat. The minister who is called in is a blueprint for much of the Pertwee era. Other people have said this, my thoughts are not original, but they are obtained by close viewing and a lot of writing: This is a new blueprint for *Doctor Who*. It's less imaginative than the previous one but it is sustainable. And it does have interesting places it can go. Overall, it's a well-done story in a setting we never thought we'd see: Modern Day Britain.

Season 3 ends. Complete change from the start of the season except for William Hartnell. If you know what's next, he won't be around for long. Lloyd and Davis have put their stamp on the show. The 1st Doctor works quite well here, I think. But with what they have planned, Hartnell is not going to be up for it. They need someone younger and someone more able to run. The Doctor can't always stand still in the face of an enemy. Sometimes, they'll need to run. Before all of that, we have two more adventures. We have the start of the Fourth Season.

SEASON FOUR

1966-1967

THE SMUGGLERS

Episode One

Written by Brian Hayles

Directed by Julia Smith

Episode 127: (September 10, 1966): The Doctor, Ben and Polly get involved with some pirates looking for lost treasure and some smugglers in 17th Century Cornwall.

Cliffhanger: Captain Pike, the hook-handed pirate, threatens the Doctor's life.

These episodes are very lost, which stinks. But there are telesnaps existing for them, so we do get a decent feel for the sets and the places and the faces. There are also, I find this fascinating, Australian censor clips. This story has a bunch of violence in it that Australia edited out. The episode is lost. The clips survive. So, when things start to move, quite often something violent happens and then everything stops again. Also, in about one minute they use the word "hell" and "damn." *Doctor Who* is getting a bit "adult" for its fourth season. (Although, the episode was shot at the end of the previous production block.) That's Innes Lloyd for you. This is one of two historicals that he commissioned for the show. And it's basically *Treasure Island*, which is fine. It means the travelers can get properly involved because these aren't specific historic events being covered. I do wish the episodes existed though. It's not a much talked about story (although there is one weird thing, I will mention in Part 4). And Terrance Dicks' novelization is not one of his best. So, I'll try hard to keep my focus here and give the best review I can.

Ben and Polly are now part of the crew. It's been since Vicki when we had someone the Doctor invited onboard. (He seems wistful when he thinks about the fact that he was going to be alone for a bit.) Ben is very skeptical. Moreso, I would say, then Steven. It made less sense with Steven as he was from the future and his skepticism just seemed like maybe his mind couldn't take it. Whereas Ben doesn't believe the TARDIS can do anything. Then, when they are suddenly on the Cornish coast, he adjusts his mind again. Thinking "We'll just catch a bus back." Polly is somewhat skeptical but gets onboard quick. Ben takes some time But, he is brave and is willing to fight if needed, which is good. And they make Polly dress like a "lad." And everyone seems convinced that she is a lad. Near the end, the local Squire shows up. A rotund man with a long white, powdered wig on. So, maybe everyone was gender confused at this time. I don't know. Vicki could pass for a nice-looking boy in "The Crusade." Polly with her long hair and her big false eyelashes, not so much. Maybe in person it worked better.

The episode itself is paced nicely. Their initial time on the TARDIS sets everything up that we need to see. It is the start of a new season. Previous stories weren't repeated so giving everyone a bit of a remit on the show isn't a bad thing. I like the Doctor's presence in this episode, whether it be with the churchwarden or the pirate Cherub. If William Hartnell's health was deteriorating, you can't see (or hear) it here. He seems as sharp as ever. (Maybe he knows what the future holds and that's why he wished he was alone. So, he could face it.) The Doctor throughout is generally cool and collected, except for a few moments when he's not. And it's nice to see the TARDIS crew separated in a way that doesn't seem arbitrary. The Doctor was given a clue to Avery's treasure by the churchwarden. Cherub and some pirates kidnap the Doctor leaving Ben and Polly. It seems a bit more natural than previous stories. I think it's probably Brian Hayles' writing. He had "The Celestial Toymaker" re-written by others so often it was impossible to tell whose contributions were whose. This feels more like his writing. Assured and telling a good story. Let's see if he can carry it through to the next episodes and let's hope the telesnaps and clips can keep us tuned in.

The Smugglers

Episode Two

Episode 128: (September 17, 1966) Smugglers, pirates, revenue men. There's a lot going on here. But, somehow, the cliffhanger is remarkably like the previous one.

Cliffhanger: The Squire re-captures Ben and Polly.

Well, I'm starting to get a little lost here. I thought I had everything down with the pirates. Then, I got a little lost with the smugglers. I didn't recognize the innkeeper until someone said his name. Then, the pirates meet with the squire and they're setting up some sort of arrangement. Then, the revenue guy shows up. And… Everyone's looking for Avery's gold! No, not really. Most people are smuggling, and our TARDIS crew just want to get out of there. There are a quite a few characters in this. I'm keeping my overall grasp on things but it's losing me a bit. Plus, this episode isn't what I would call fast paced. It goes from scene to scene to scene to scene and then it ends where it began: the TARDIS crew have all been captured. Kind of wasting time a bit.

The telesnaps aren't quite helping. The scene with the Pirates and the Squire and Polly is particularly weird. The Squire is in full regalia with his long wig on. Pike is dressed like a full-on pirate. And Cherub with his big, bald head looks… also exactly like a pirate. And yet, no one ever mentions anything about that. Is the Squire so corrupt that having two obvious pirates in his living room doesn't confuse him? But there is the fact that they still think Polly is a boy. How? Maybe no one can see anything. Maybe it's a story full of farsighted people who are too vain to wear glasses. I don't know. It is straining credibility. In print, I think it would work. On the screen, I don't know. Plus, Pike has a pike instead of a hand! How many normal merchants have pikes instead of hands? Very few, I would reckon.

Meanwhile, the Doctor has some good moments with Pike at the start. They speak like gentlemen. The Doctor butters him up a little. Cherub acts like a maniac. Jamaica (yes, he's the black guy) shows up and keeps an eye on him. The only problem there is that they're holding the Doctor because he has heard the riddle from the churchwarden. So, if he doesn't give them the info, what can they do? He's the only one that has it. Maybe seeing the episode would have made it a little more exciting. But, as it is, it doesn't really go anywhere.

Then, there's the scene with Tom. He's Polly and Ben's jailer. He seems like he might be a little slow. So, Ben and Polly perform some sort of magical thing that scares Tom and they get away. I've seen some that don't like when Doctor Who companions do this. Taking advantage of the superstitions of people from the past. I don't have a problem with it. Polly and Ben are innocent. They shouldn't be there. They need to prove their innocence. Do what you must do. Plus, this is their first adventure. I would think all is fair when you're wrongfully locked up for murder in a 17th-Century prison when about 6 hours previous you were in 1966 London. But then, I may be too broadminded. (Polly does mention that she finds it relaxing. Maybe she hasn't accepted everything as well as we thought.) At least they didn't do the "You pretend to be sick, and I'll hit the guard over the head thing." The Doctor uses a card trick later so let's revel in the new and exciting ways to get out of being locked up.

The Smugglers

Episode Three

Episode 129: (September 24, 1966) The plots thicken!

Cliffhanger: Avery is killed! The TARDIS gang are in trouble now.

Well, I kind of lost it here. The Doctor escapes. They begin to try to figure out what the churchwarden said. There's some yelling. And then the episode ends. Kewper really likes The Squire. That's why he's a dope. Poor Jamaica. He gets fooled by the Doctor. But, not in the way Tom did in the previous episode. More or less. The Doctor is reading the cards and giving out fates. You think that they'll have Jamaica learn his fate. Then, he'll let a scared Doctor and Kewper go. Instead, the Doctor drops the cards and Kewper wallops him. I'm not sure if that's using the "primitive" nature of someone from the past or not. I didn't quite expect a wallop.

It is nice to have someone believe Ben and Polly. The revenue man, Josiah, does and it's a breath of fresh air. By the time he takes Ben and Polly away, everyone has accused the two of them of doing everything and it does feel a bit foolish. I'm glad we've reunited everyone, and we've begun the treasure hunting by the end. I'm sure it would be more fun to see it than just hear it.

We are moving towards an exciting ending. Some sort of pitched battle. Discovery of the treasure. All that great stuff. I'm also a little worried because once we get to that we won't see it. And it will be tough to gauge. There's an example here that shows how the loss of the picture can hurt an episode: The Doctor and Kewper tie up Jamaica. We see a telesnap with a bunch of pirates on the deck. We see a caption that says the two of them sneak into Kewper's waiting boat. Then, they're back at shore a few minutes later! Hooray! How exactly do they do that? Surely the other pirates must be paying some attention. I know the boss is gone but come on. The image we're seeing doesn't seem to match the nonchalant-ness of the caption. And it kind of takes you out of the moment, which is too bad. Luckily, we are really on the road to No More lost episodes. Granted, it doesn't really start until Season 7. But there are a lot of animated episodes coming up and those are always better, especially when we have a lot of visuals or a lot of characters. So, hold on for a bit more.

Oh, The Squire and Pike still look ridiculous when they stand together. Or at least I can't stop giggling whenever I see them.

Anyway, a shorter review here. As the story goes along and more and more is happening, and more and more can't be seen, I fear that I'm repeating myself. Let's go to the final episode and see what it has in store for us.

The Smugglers

Episode Four

Episode 130: (October 1, 1966) They find a treasure. The revenue men show up. There's lots of fighting and then it ends.

Cliffhanger: The TARDIS has landed at the coldest place on Earth.

That cliffhanger is exciting. Now, granted, one episode ended with the Doctor saying that if they went outside the TARDIS, they'd die… and it was a joke about pollution. The Doctor likes the hyperbole a bit. But it's what we have to look forward to in the next episode. Remember that this episode is the last one of the Third production block. So, the next story is the first of the Fourth production block. Hartnell leaves after the fourth episode. So, "The Smugglers" is the last story he is under contract for as The Doctor. In the next story, he is a guest player. That's an odd thing to think about. The man who got us so far in the show reduced to that in his last story. Well, it does make some sense. It's only four episodes. Still, it doesn't seem very nice to the man who helped make the show so big.

Why am I talking about production blocks? Because I'm completely out of it on this episode. Yes, I do own the novelization. I can read that and let my imagination soar. But it's not watching the episode. Liberties are taken. Things are changed. So, I can but I won't. Unless I'm specifically talking about the differences in the two. The book isn't here to take the place of the two. Or at least it shouldn't be. Not anymore. Which leaves me with much confusion.

They are still looking for the treasure. They talk about it a lot. There are some decent telesnaps of them looking around. It all seems like it might be fun. But, boy, is it kind of dull. The recon is letting me down here. There's action aplenty happening. Heck, there are pirates! It never takes off in the recon and the audio recording though, which is too bad. I had said that people consider this one of the least remembered shows in the original run. They could be right. Darnit, it's not like I'm not trying.

It hits the lowest point when the revenue men arrive and there's an exciting, pitched battle. And we see pretty much none of it… NOTE: THIS IS NOT THE ACTUAL STORY'S FAULT! I blame the BBC and junking everything. But then, they didn't know that jackasses like me and other jackasses would sit around writing things like this book. Suffice it to say, currently, the climax is impossible to watch. So, you sit there, looking at random images and reading captions and then it ends. You hear the TARDIS dematerialize and you let out a sigh of relief because the next three episodes exist. And the seven after those may be lost but they're animated.

This happens every time I watch "The Smugglers." I'm good for the first episode. I go a touch hazy in the second. The third begins to lose me fast. The fourth is a strange, wicked haze that I'm forgetting now even as I'm writing about it. I may return to it before the book is published and see if I can pull anything else from the wreckage. Let me get back to you.

One last thing: Even though this story is tough to watch in its current state, there is one interesting tie-in to modern *Doctor Who*. In "The Curse of the Black Spot," the Captain of the ship is Avery and he has tons of treasure. In the end, his crew is killed. He and his son take the alien ship that's been holding them captive, leaving the treasure behind. I believe the "Avery" spoke of in "The Smugglers" is the Avery who is now travelling the stars and joined The Doctor at Devils' Run in "A Good Man Goes To War."

Final Note: As this was going to press, rumors of "The Smugglers" being animated soon are spreading. Fingers crossed.

THE TENTH PLANET

Episode One

By Gerry Davis and Kit Pedler

Directed By Derek Martinus

Episode 131: (October 8, 1966) The TARDIS bunch land at the South Pole in 1986. They stop off at a multi-national base that is suddenly under siege from… Wait for it…

Cliffhanger: The Mondasian Cyberman arrive at the base.

Innes Lloyd and Gerry Davis finally fully put their stamp on *Doctor Who*. Oddly enough, it doesn't have much to do with the Doctor. Throughout most of the episode, The Doctor, Ben and Polly stand around watching General Cutler and his very, very ethnic Snow Base South Pole crew monitor a rocket and an approaching planet. The Doctor does reveal that he knows what is going to happen. Apart from that, they don't do diddly. To me, that doesn't seem to bode well for the future of the show or, at least, the future of this Doctor. Trust me, we'll be seeing this setup a lot over the next couple years.

It's called a "base under siege" story. Pretty self-explanatory. It is some sort of base, usually military or scientific or both, isolated in some fashion that is attacked by something-or-other. This is the first. The second will be here soon with a slightly different cast but more or less the same story. There's a problem with the base under siege theory in this one. (Part of it is "Hey! We don't know what to do with the main cast!" Eric Saward did that in the 1980s but he knew he was doing that. Here, it feels like the new production team doesn't know what to do with their leading man. More on that later.) The main problem is that this format is more "Action-oriented." I think we can see the problem here. William Hartnell hasn't been "action-oriented" since he fought Koquillion so long ago. They've reformatted the show around the lead but didn't take the lead into account. They've figured out a way to deal with that though. It's not very nice for Mr. Hartnell. (Who, despite some flaws, is one hell of a Doctor.) It does, however, mean that the show can go on and on forever.

Anyway… the base under siege will become the first time the show really gets dredged down in a formula. And it is a formula that carries it through the next few seasons. I, for one, am not a big fan of the show with a formula. RTD's four seasons had a formulaic structure to them that I became less thrilled with as time went on. Mr. Moffat tried something different with every season, which was cool. But, here, we have a formula setting in. Luckily, it's not every story but it's quite a few stories.

That's not to say that I don't enjoy the episode. I think it's quite good. Derek Martinus is one of the best directors the show had. He uses the sets well. The South Pole surface looks extremely cold and daunting. He paces everything well. The capsule has a real feeling of being an actual thing and not just a set. Plus, there are things like the girly pictures next to the bunk of the Italian guy reading Sgt. Rock. We all love The Rock. General Cutler may be a bit of a douchebag, but the episode moves nicely and feels fairly real. When they call Geneva, and we go to Geneva, that's awesome. I didn't expect that. The time spent looking at Mondas spinning like an upside-down Earth is intriguing enough. The parts where the serial breaks down, as I said, are during the "Oops! We forget to give the Doctor, Polly and Ben something to do" bits. And that's, sadly, not a little problem. That's a real stinker.

Is it all made up for when the Cybermen arrive? These are the Mondasian Cybermen with their cloth faces, their holes for mouths and their "human" hands. Some find them silly. Others find them fascinating and weird and scary. (Mr. Peter Capaldi, for example). When they appear at the end, there is a real feeling of "What the heck is happening now?" Maybe the one with the cloak on standing by the TARDIS is gilding the lily a bit. But it works. And it makes one want to, no matter how much The Doctor was left out, find out what might happen next.

The Tenth Planet

Episode Two

Episode 132: (October 15, 1966) The Cybermen take over the base. Their planet, Mondas, needs assistance. Pronto.

Cliffhanger: The Cyberfleet is approaching Earth.

I'll start from the end because I just watched it. General Cutler's son is put on a ship to fly to Mondas. We know that this won't be good. General Cutler, the star of the show, not something I'm thrilled about, yells at the Doctor and commends Ben for killing a Cyberman. Polly says that the general seems to be enjoying this. Cutler says his son is up there. Polly apologizes. Why does she apologize? His son volunteered. His son is a soldier. That's the kind of thing they do. Cutler won't let the TARDIS crew go so for almost all the episode they're in the exact same space. I'm not sure why the writers thought it was a good idea to get sympathy for the obnoxious Cutler by belittling Polly. All it makes me think is "When is this story ending?" Even though I do enjoy the story.

And here is the "base under siege" in a nutshell. Basically, a bunch of jerks in charge of a space belittling our lead cast until they need their help. There are some who absolutely love this format. For me, we're entering a tricky era. I am a big Troughton fan but, boy, these base under siege stories get on my nerves. At least, they'll work out where the Doctor fits in soon. Here, he does nothing apart from argue with a Cyberman. It's a good scene. Probably the best in the episode. But it's stopped with some Cybergun shooting and Cutler yelling.

Lloyd and Davis and Pedler have decided to make General Cutler the leading man. If I was a fan, I'd applaud them. But Culter is an obnoxious Canadian/ American who insults and threatens our leading man who we know is not well. It doesn't endear him. And we're pretty darn certain that he is not going to be in the show after this serial. So, one would prefer having our leads be the leads. This isn't an anthology program. This isn't *Wagon Train*. We're following a specific group of characters as they are engaging in adventures. To neglect and denigrate them in this way, isn't nice. Especially if we know what's coming. I don't think the great British public knew. So, they may have forgiven some of it. But, watched in context, it ends up being a bit unpleasant. Ben goes into another room in this episode. The Doctor and Polly stay in the same place the whole time. Why?

They are re-setting the series. They are preparing for Hartnell's leaving. They are changing things. For the better? Maybe? The ratings have been down. We'll see how it goes. It just seems a bit unpleasant now. The way they did everything wasn't nice. They don't have to be. But we'd hope the people making *Doctor Who* might be as nice as the Doctor and their friends. Oh well. What about those Cybermen, huh?

The Cybermen aren't in this very much. They make a few speeches. They talk about emotions. They vaguely threaten. Then, they're all killed, and the fleet is sent in. They are threatening but do little. Ben has a big moment with them when he's locked up. As mentioned, The Doctor's chat with the Cybermen is nice. They certainly bring an odd feel to the serial. They are inhuman and weird. But they're gotten rid of so easily. Now, the fleet, of course, is huge, but those initial ones go out quick. When the Doctor speaks to Cutler, we know he's right. Cutler won't listen. So, we all must sit around waiting for Cutler to admit the Doctor is right. It's not fully tiresome here yet. But it will become so as we go along. I do applaud though the production team's gumption in making everyone as varied and multi-cultural as possible to contrast with the Cyberman. I just wish the story was better. It's never boring. It's just a wee bit condescending towards the characters we care about. That's never a way to do a show.

The Tenth Planet

Episode Three

Episode 133: (October 22, 1966) The Doctor is unconscious. General Cutler decides to hit Mondas with the Z Bomb rather than risk the death of his son. He yells.

Cliffhanger: The Z Bomb countdown continues! What will happen?

The story goes that Hartnell wasn't happy about his last days on set. The producers weren't being nice to him. So, he called in sick for this episode. At the last minute, Gerry Davis had to do a re-write to distribute his dialogue. He is missed but the episode goes quickly. The only bump in the road is that the Doctor has realized that Mondas will absorb too much energy and blow itself up. All they need to do is wait. But we get that mostly second hand from Ben and Polly because the Doctor is worn out. (Probably by the energy draining from Mondas.) It doesn't matter anyway because Cutler has his own ideas.

The best thing I can say about General Cutler is that we've only got one more episode with him in it after this one. The only person who he is in any way decent too is his son on the space capsule. His son's a bit of a doofus who doesn't really recommend himself as a character. General Cutler is going to explode a bomb that may spray radiation across one half of the Earth. He makes sure that his son won't be affected, and he begins to go ahead with it. Is this a South Pole thing? Some sort of madness. Polly brings up at one point that they should do what the Doctor suggested. If the son dies, that's terrible. Rather him than millions of people. The general doesn't care. Great. That's not good drama. That's dumb drama. Especially because only Ben and Polly will stand up to him and they can't do much.

Ben does try his best to sabotage the rocket. He gets some good ventilation shaft crawling around here. Second only to Corridor Running as a Doctor Who sport. His double does a great stunt over a railing when the insane Cutler knocks him over. There's something oddly rough about this episode, more so than future base under siege episodes. That's because the violence is all being perpetrated by the humans. The Cybermen appear for a few minutes. They're all shot down. The Doctor passes out. Ben is thumped hard. And it's all under the auspices of General Cutler.

This is the penultimate episode of the First Doctor's era and he's not in it. As I mentioned, his presence is felt. He knows what's going to happen, but the general's psychotic behavior doesn't really allow anyone to partake of the wisdom. There's almost no Cybermen. Polly does very little. It's mostly the General Cutler show w/ Ben! And that's not tremendously satisfying, especially because I'm starting to get tired of that main control room. I wish they had treated Hartnell better. I mean, it does lend itself to the Doctor's change in the next story. We know what he's been through over the last season. We know the effect the Mondas drain is having. That's great. Hindsight makes this work to some extent. The problem is that the next episode is lost. It's been animated. So, no more original First Doctor. Makes me kind of sad. I wanted him to go out more heroically than being yelled at by a psychotic general. It would have been far more satisfying. (Heck, for a time in this episode, it looks like the Cybermen have called in sick too. Maybe it would have been better if they had.)

Anyway, the episode moves at a decent pace. Whether you like it or not, it all comes down to how much of Culter's yelling you can put up with and how much you can put up with small dumb moments like this one: Cutler asks his boss if he can use the Z Bomb. -No, you cannot. -Do you give me authority to do whatever is needed to stop the Cybermen? -Yes. -Thanks. All right, everyone. We're using the Z Bomb. -He said you couldn't. -He said I could do whatever I needed.

Oh brother.

The Tenth Planet

Part Four

Episode 134: (October 29, 1966) The Doctor wakes up and was right. But now he's gotten too old and worn out to care. Something is about to happen. Something big.

Cliffhanger: The Doctor changes.

The episode keeps itself moving at a nice clip. It disposes of Cutler early on. But then does something weird with one of its characters soon after. The Doctor is strong at the start, but something is clearly happening to him. As the whole premise of defeating the Cybermen is "Let's wait a little bit longer," it's never quite as suspenseful and as exciting as if they actually had to do something to stop them. But the episode has enough going on to lead us to the big moment at the end…

Before that, I want to mention the character of Dyson. We've had characters like Cutler and Dyson in the show previously but never ramped up to this level. Cutler is the person who bullies and yells. In certain eras in the show, the Doctor doesn't really do that well standing up to them. It's obvious here that the 1st Doctor can't really deal with this sort of person. Cutler pulls a gun on the Doctor and is going to shoot him. The Doctor is, literally, saved by the Cybermen. This Doctor is out of place here. A more mischievous Doctor who doesn't need to be in charge or who just laughs at this sort of character would work better. (Which is what Lloyd and Davis do. It isn't until the 5th Doctor that we once again get a Doctor who really can't quite handle the yelling, bully leaders.)

Then, there's Dyson. One of the faceless members of the team who, along with Barclay, the scientist, and Ben are put in the radioactive room with the Z Bomb to fiddle with it. If you've seen the story, you know the plot element. Suffice it to say, Ben figures that the Cybermen can't enter because they can't handle radiation. So, he wants to delay until Mondas disintegrates. Barclay agrees. Then, there's Dyson. (If you want a quick example of what Dyson is like, think of S19 Tegan or early Donna Noble.) Dyson disagrees with almost everything Ben says and/or complains about everything Ben says. I'm not sure why the writers thought this was an interesting character trait to give someone in the last episode. (Even after the Cybermen are stopped, he still sounds skeptical.) What Dyson is is the first in a long line of characters in *Doctor Who* that will act and talk like this. Disbelieving the Doctor. Disbelieving the companions. Maybe coming around in the end, maybe not. It's a character trait I've always found annoying. And I'm glad when they're not in one of the shows. (Not that I'm saying people can't question the Doctor or whoever. I'm just saying "Shut up after a bit, huh? If you've got nothing helpful to contribute, go sit in the corner.")

The Mondasian Cybermen become history for a long time after this episode. They were odd. They were memorable. They had fun names like Krang and Gern. (I love the name Gern.) They made an impression on Peter Capaldi. They don't do a whole heck of a lot. It feels like they do or like they almost do. But they never quite do. They will be back soon enough though. William Hartnell, however, won't.

The First Doctor doesn't get a big speech like modern day Doctors do. He spends most of the episode looking very sick. His final words are "Keep Warm." I always like that moment and wish I could see it. The animation is excellent on the DVD. He puts his coat on. He looks at Ben and Polly and says, "Keep warm" and then he leaves for the TARDIS. It looks like he's abandoning Ben and Polly. He doesn't. But it does. We know now that in between when he leaves and when the companions reach the Ship the First Doctor has his final adventure in "Twice Upon A Time." We didn't know that then, though. So, it makes the whole closing sequence much more alien and weirder. Who really knew that the Doctor would collapse (remember he did that in the previous episode), the TARDIS would go nuts and suddenly he'd have a new face? I'm tempted to watch "Twice" before I carry on. I'm tempted to stop this story when Ben and Polly start to follow the Doctor, watch "Twice" and then return. Actually, I may do that. You'll have to go to the review of "Twice" to read about that. Suffice it to say, the man who brought The Doctor to life is gone. This last story wasn't his best but he had some good moments. He went truly alien in the end. And then he went full Troughton.

THE POWER OF THE DALEKS
Episode One

Written by David Whitaker

With Dennis Spooner

Directed By Christopher Barry

Episode 135: (November 5, 1966) On the planet Vulcan, an earth colony is experiencing unrest. In the TARDIS, the Doctor has had a bit of a change.

Cliffhanger: The Doctor introduces Ben and Polly to the Daleks. Meanwhile, a Dalek outside of its casing slithers under a door.

The last story was the New Guys putting their big stamp on the show. "This is Doctor Who now!" It's telling that for the first story re-introducing the Doctor they did two things 1) brought back the Daleks and 2) brought back the first two script editors. (Dennis Spooner is uncredited but he is a part of it.) As others have said, the trick of bringing back the Daleks is that they were so popular. They were guaranteed to bring in a certain number of viewers even with a new Doctor. As the serial goes along, if we were worried that the Doctor was actually the Doctor, if we saw that the Daleks knew he was the Doctor, then we would be convinced. As far as the writers, David and Dennis are excellent writers who know how to tell and build a good story. This is as unlike the previous story as you can get. (Starting with the settings. We go from the chill of the South Pole to the hot, mercury-strewn surface of the planet Vulcan.) The first episode takes place slowly inside the TARDIS. Ben is very wary. Polly a little less so. But the Doctor is acting weird. He won't put away that recorder. His ring doesn't fit him anymore. And he's wearing a goofy hat. Can this be The Doctor?

I love the way the episode is structured. There's the long scene in the TARDIS. Things are not resolved by the end of it. They still need time to talk things out. But the Doctor goes out walking and they get involved in the colony and its petty intrigues… and its scientist who has found this capsule preserved in the mercury swamps. Instantly, the TARDIS crew becomes part of this intrigue. The Doctor is impersonating an examiner. Ben and Polly are confused. The whole time, we're thinking "Let's resolve this. We don't like seeing the main characters in confusion this way." However, the story has started us moving in a different direction. It's like if you're going into a workplace one day. You're on the phone with someone important to you. Maybe arguing, maybe trying to figure something out. Suddenly, you're in the middle of a group of people you work with. They only care about work. They don't care about you or your problems. There's something so anxiety provoking about having to leave one thing hanging so abruptly to get involved in another that seems, frankly, less important. This episode does that well.

I'm so glad this was animated. Hearing it, seeing a recon, reading the novelization are all good. But, seeing some movement, seeing the characters helps it work better because as we go along there will be stretches where there's lots of human intrigue, which becomes a bit labored when we can't see what's happening. It can veer towards dull. The movement keeps things hopping, even if it is a cartoon. To see the spaces re-created in the animation and to get the real feeling for the pace makes the show that much better. Some have said this is one of the best Dalek stories ever. For once, "some" might be right.

Let's be honest: animated or not, the closing scene "Ben, Polly, come and meet the Daleks." is chilling. The show has restarted itself and so far, so very good.

The Power of the Daleks

Episode Two

Episode 136: (November 12, 1966) The Doctor keeps examining. Lesterson, Janley and Resno bring a Dalek to life.

Cliffhanger: The Dalek, who has recognized The Doctor, chants "I am your servant" repeatedly.

Another strong episode. The show has a slow build up. The Doctor, Ben and Polly sit amongst this colony, which is obviously filled with intrigue. I'm not sure of the history behind this colony. I'm not sure where Vulcan is exactly. I'm not sure when this is meant to take place, although some places have given a very early date for it. Some of these things do date strangely over time. I'd love to know the purpose of this colony. We never see a lot of people. The ones we see always seem to be bickering or having a rough time with one another. They're either obsessed with their bureaucracy or their scientific endeavors. I don't get the feeling like they're there to explore the place and take advantage of the land. They must wear gas masks when they go out of doors. They did find the capsule but that almost feels like some sort of stroke of luck to me. At the end of the day, the purpose of the colony (or lack thereof) doesn't really bother me. It's just a little niggling factor in the back of my mind.

The moment when the Dalek recognizes the Doctor at the end is a great moment of frisson. The Dalek's gun has been removed. (It shot Resno. Not Fresno, as I kept originally typing.) So, it knows it won't be able to take these people out. Its constant repetition of "I am your servant" is as chilling as the Daleks chanting "I am your soldier" so many years later in "Victory of the Daleks", which is clearly a homage to this scene. The Dalek slowly being revived works nicely in the animation. Previously, you just heard the scientists and saw nothing but telesnaps, which didn't really give one the proper appreciation for the scene. We know what the Daleks can do. The Doctor knows what the Daleks can do. No one else does, not even Ben and Polly. So, the wacky and slightly befuddling Examiner isn't going to get the same kind of excited treatment that this "robot" servant will. Things may start to go badly soon. Again, with a new Doctor, the Daleks are the perfect villains to push the show along. The egos of the scientists are being gently massaged to allow for it.

The pace, as I mentioned, is calm. The story isn't going anywhere fast. The behind-the-scenes machinations are building up. The Dalek is slowly coming to life. And the Doctor, Ben and Polly talk. There's a great scene where the Doctor seems to be acting barmy with some fruit (as Ben speaks some Cockney rhyming slang, which I always find confusing but charming. See "The Time Monster" for TOMTIT). It turns out he's not as barmy as they thought. (He does still have that hat and recorder.) He found a bugging device in the room. Ben wants to leave. Polly isn't so thrilled with being on Vulcan. But the Doctor knows that they must stay, simply because of the Daleks. The Doctor is becoming more and more interesting with each passing minute.

Patrick Troughton is excellent, from what we can hear. He's a bit cheeky. He's very curious. And he doesn't mind being a bit obnoxious. He's very different from his predecessor who would be more demanding and chastise people for not doing what he wanted. This new Doctor can push himself to the front when need be, but he also watches. And waits. And looks. And learns. I kind of forgot that Innes Lloyd and Gerry Davis were still in charge of the program at this point. Subtlety is not really their big thing. I'm glad they went for it here, though. It really helps the program.

The Power of the Daleks

Episode Three

Episode 137: (November 19, 1966) The Governor approves Lesterson teaching the Dalek. The Dalek immediately brings the other two to life and gets access to power.

Cliffhanger: The three Daleks chant that they have their power.

I don't normally get a huge kick out of watching too many episodes in a row. I'm not a big binger. I prefer to space out episodes of shows I love because they are finite. If I'm binging a show, then I'm OK with that and will probably never come back to it. I binged *Parks & Recreation* during the pandemic. I had a hell of a good time. I couldn't wait to do another bunch of episodes. When it ended, I was satisfied. I'll probably never watch it again. I recommend it highly. But it's not like *D Who* (which is what I call it). I tend to prefer to savor episodes.

However, in this viewing, as I focus on the animated episodes, I'm loving it. I got to the end of this episode and immediately wanted to watch the next one. The drama is building so nicely. The Daleks are insinuating themselves beautifully into everything. The Doctor, near the end of this episode, spots the intrigue. He points out that greed and ambition are all over this colony. And the Daleks don't care. Like Jason Vorhees in a *Friday the 13th* film, everyone will be wiped out when the stronger force gets itself in place. It's a slow, inevitable build. They don't know what's up. Only we and The Doctor do.

Several moments here mirror later Dalek stories. The Doctor telling the Dalek to immobilize itself is like the 9th Doctor giving the Dalek orders. Treating it vaguely like a servant that can help is reminiscent of other Dalek stories where they are completely underestimated. I love the moment where Lesterson says the Dalek can reason like a human. And the Dalek almost says that it's better than a human. It's very modern, the way this story is told. It's slower than a modern story. But it has a modern feel to it. It's the serialized story that does it. Having David and Dennis in charge really works here.

Then, the ante is upped when the "rebels" (they think of themselves as rebels but they're probably just jerks) kidnap Polly. Ben and Polly have been kind of on the outside of much of this story. But that's OK. They are the regulars. They are the ones who will be back. They're not obnoxious yellers, like Cutler. They are all pretending to work with one another. In reality, they sure ain't working with each other. They're so much more interesting than the characters in the previous story. Which makes one a little worried because David and Dennis aren't permanent fixtures on the show anymore. Gerry Davis, though, is. We'll see how that goes.

This serial is the first one to bring us the vague Dalek titles that we'll grow to know and love over the years. "The Power of the Daleks" doesn't seem to mean much apart from the fact that we know they're powerful. But their "power" stretches to the humans who feel like they can use them. The Daleks, of course, chant about their power. Also, the power of the Daleks does bring in viewers. And the power of the Daleks will cause this colony some troubles, sooner or later. As titles go along, they may become goofier and less relevant to what's happening. Here, however, it ties in decently. We know that the Daleks are terrible. When we see three of them, it doesn't matter whether they have guns. We know that bad stuff is looming. We only hope the Doctor, with his limited power, can stop them and save Polly and get out of there and make sure he's OK. Let's not forget he hasn't been here long.

The Power of the Daleks

Episode Four

Episode 138: (November 26, 1966) The Doctor and Ben visit a rebel meeting and get in trouble because Bragen, head rebel, is now in charge. Lesterson discovers that the Doctor was right about the Daleks.

Cliffhanger: The Dalek assembly line is in full force.

Beauty of an episode. I like how Janley takes charge of the first half of the episode. It's nice to have a female villain here. We can't see her, of course, but she feels wonderfully in charge and manipulative. We've seen her wrap Lesterson around her finger, very casually. We know what she's capable of and it's fun to watch. The moment when she offers to stand in front of the Dalek to prove it is their servant and won't shoot her is excellent. I love the control she has over the other rebels. Yes, Bragen is sitting off to one side, ostensibly the leader. But Janley takes the spotlight. The best bit: Who knows if she's good or bad? We don't know enough about the colony to really gauge if she is the bad person or not. The Governor seems like a doofus. So does everyone else around him. Bragen and Janley seem power hungry. But we never learn the full extent of what this colony is or does. (Mention is made in the previous episode of helping Earth but that seems very much a tertiary concern.) Janley could be the good one here. Yes, she's using the Dalek. But that doesn't make her bad if she doesn't know what the Dalek is. She's never watched *Doctor Who*. She can be forgiven. In a little while, though, it won't matter. When the Daleks take over, all is levelled.

The centerpiece of this episode is the wonderful closing sequence. Telesnaps and brief clips exist of the Dalek conveyer belt. I remember first reading about this scene in John Peel's novelization and really feeling the excitement and the terror. I remember first seeing the clips and thinking, out of context, "Cool." But the animation really brings it to life. (I'm alternating between black & white and color episodes. I watched this one in color.) It may take a few liberties. I think some of the overhead shots may not have appeared in the original story. I think the full expanse of the assembly line was smaller. To be honest, I'm not watching the show animated to see exact replicas of what happened in the series. It's going to be re-imagined to some extent. That's just natural. Animation has more ability to indulge than the series did. So, for heaven's sake, indulge. I insist. The final moment with a hall full of a couple dozen Daleks is a great one. It's like the huge Dalek reveal at the end of "Bad Wolf." It's a "Oh Hell. We're dead" kind of moment that makes me smile and hope all will be well. (It might not be.)

I also love watching Lesterson creep through the capsule. Because, to me, the word "capsule" implies a small space for a few beings to sit in. The Monoids travelled to Refusis in a "capsule." In *Monster A Go-Go*, the astronaut returns to Earth in a "capsule." The implication here is that this is some sort of (sorry) DARDIS. Lesterson walks and walks. There's room after room before him. The assembly line room is two levels. How on Earth did the Vulcan colonists get this thing out of the swamp and into this room? At this point, it doesn't matter. How did the capsule crash here? Doesn't matter either. It is and it shall be. Now what shall we do?

And the Doctor? He casually figures out a code when Ben is yakking. He figures out a lock is working while casually chatting with someone else. He's becoming the master of doing one thing while he seems to be doing another. (Listen to that recorder as an example.) Let's see what he does next.

The Power of the Daleks

Part Five

Episode 139: (December 3, 1966) Bragen and the rebels quietly take over the colony. In the background, the Daleks finalize their preparations.

Cliffhanger: Daleks conquer and destroy.

Another fantastic cliffhanger. The Daleks, after four episodes of slow preparation, are ready. Ready to kill all the humans in the colony. (Again, I've no honest idea of how big the colony is but they keep trying to make it large in our minds. One of Bragen's guards is from the "Interior," which implies a bigness.) It's like a great slasher film. You set up all these lives. (*Final Exam* is a good one.) You set up all these relationships. You intermingle them. You give them hopes and dreams. The good, the bad, the ugly. And then you set something in motion that doesn't care. Something in motion that destroys them all. And none of the world we just saw means anything anymore. Everything changes in a moment. If they'd only listened to the Examiner-- sorry, the Doctor-- things would be different. Isn't it odd that the words "examine" and "exterminate" are similar?

The story also does a clever thing that I didn't notice, and I didn't think about even though it happened in episode 3 of "The Tenth Planet." Polly gets kidnapped in part Three. She's not in Part Four but her presence is felt because we're worried about her. She's back in this episode but now Ben is gone. His presence is felt too because I kept thinking "Where'd Ben go?" And then someone will mention him. Everyone gets a bit of a break here. I'm trying to think if Steven ever took a break. I'm pretty sure Dodo didn't. It's nice that everyone can get a rest when they need it.

The Doctor doesn't do a heck of a lot in this episode. Probably for the best. Because, as the human machinations continue, the Daleks are always sort of in the background laying cable that we know is going to cause trouble very soon. He gets free just in time to get arrested again. This time with Polly. I understand what they're doing here. The jig is up. They know he's not the Examiner. But he is going to have to get out sometime soon. The Daleks will have to be stopped.

Poor Lesterson. He's gone a bit round the bend. More or less. The problem is he sees the Daleks creating new Daleks and everyone he goes to is a rebel who wants to use the Daleks, including Bragen's guards. Who are these guys? Where did he hire them? Why don't they know who the Governor of the colony is? I'm always fascinated by types like this. How much money does Bragen have where he can hire his own guards? Surely that's not cheap. Anyway, Lesterson is locked away. Janley gets another great moment where she outright lies but the man she's lying to is completely convinced and someone gets in trouble. We can enjoy them now. Because in the next episode, if memory doesn't cheat, they'll all be dead. It's much ado about nothing but it's not as lighthearted as *Much Ado About Nothing* because the crazy chaos is about to begin.

The episode contains the absolute classic moment: Bragen has a Dalek kill Hensell. Now, Bragen is in charge and declares martial law. Right after the killing, there is a pause. The Dalek turns to Bragen and asks, "Why do human beings kill human beings?" Bragen has no answer and tells the Dalek to go on its way. It's a good question. I have no answer either.

The Power of the Daleks

Episode Six

Episode 140: (December 10, 1966) Come and see the power of the Daleks.

Cliffhanger: A Dalek seems to have been guarding the TARDIS. (They did know it was him!) As the Ship dematerializes, it looks up.

The first Second Doctor story ends. And it seems like the Doctor saves the day by goofing around. There's an auxiliary hidden power source the Daleks are using to access their static electricity. He diddles with it, and they all explode. The Doctor claims not to know what he did. He seems a little vague about the whole thing. The recorder speaks for him. Plus, he knocks out the power supply of the colony. Oh well. They live to fight another day.

It's a great climactic episode. It might be a bit too claustrophobic. I'm not sure if that's the animation. It's probably the overall story. The feeling of certain people in certain rooms while the colony is being slaughtered really comes out here. Bragen siting at his desk the whole time, impotent, is amusing. The laboratory. The room everyone hides in early on. They contrast with the assumed masses of people and guards attacking each other and then the Daleks. It mostly works. The feeling of destruction was slightly stronger when I could just hear it. But that might be just me.

Oh Bragen. He gets control of the colony. His first declaration is to kill all the rebels. The rebels he just led because he doesn't want them rebelling against him. (I just thought of "The Zygon inversion" speech the Doctor gives where he asks Zygella what will happen to people like her when the next regime takes over. Someone like Bragen kills them.) Bragen seemed a bit uptight at first. Now, clearly he's a nut. I thought this might happen; I fell for Janley in the end. I knew what she's been up to, but I thought she was a more humane rebel. And when she goes out (fighting), it is a sad moment. I like that the animation has her having lost one shoe, on the ground, eyes open. It's striking and certainly something to remember.

Ben and Polly don't do much. What can they do? By the time they reunite, it's all too far gone. Bragen is killing rebels. Daleks are killing everyone. All that can be done is trying to stop it all. In setting up the new Doctor and using the Daleks as the ever-increasing threat, the two companions have been left a bit behind. It's OK. They'll get stuff to do in the next story and everything will be fine.

One thing I forgot to mention: David Whitaker goes back to basics with the Daleks. They are powered here by static electricity. That was a thing in "The Daleks." In "The Dalek Invasion of Earth," that is circumnavigated by the discs on their back. Presumably, the time travelling Daleks of "The Chase" don't need static electricity or have access to a supply in the DARDIS. In "Masterplan," I imagine those Daleks are sufficiently advanced to have left static behind. These Daleks are presumably from a past time. Who knows exactly how long they've been in that swamp? They may have been earlier travelers from Skaro. Sent to travel around the galaxy and... what? Kill everybody? Probably. They sure weren't sent to explore. That's not the Dalek thing. Anyway, they're static like the original ones. Whitaker likes that kind of thing, I think.

Overall, the animated version of this is solid. Occasional moments look a little awkward. There's a sort of fight scene in the previous episode where I couldn't figure out what was happening. And, in this episode, when the Daleks shoot at the Doctor, it does seem like the Doctor should be dead. Also, I'm not sure what's going on with Bragen and that little TV/ radio thing he has. But, overall, having the show animated was fantastic. I wish they would do this for every lost episode. "The Smugglers," anyone? Probably not. Or maybe? (Late Note: Written before my note at the end of "The Smugglers.")

THE HIGHLANDERS

Episode One

By Elwyn Jones and Gerry Davis

Directed by Hugh David

Episode 141: (December 17, 1966) The TARDIS lands in the aftermath of the battle of Culloden, Scottish Highlands 1746. They get involved with some Scottish "rebels". Then, they get taken prisoner by the Redcoats. We meet a piper named James McCrimmon.

Cliffhanger: Polly, refusing to spend any more time with a stupid peasant. Wanders out in the dark and comes across someone armed with a dagger. (End of Chapter 5 of the novelization, by the way.)

First thing is the interesting note that Elwyn Jones was hired by Davis and Lloyd to write this one. Imagine their surprise the day the scripts came due. Apparently, Jones simply hadn't had time to write any of them. Can you imagine that? I've spent years of my life trying to get to a position where I could write something with some sort of prestige, some sort of importance. Not what you're reading right now, which is a bit of fun. Imagine getting to that point, getting hired and then simply not writing it. That's audacity that I can't even comprehend. But, apparently, Elwyn Jones was so beloved that he even though he wrote very little to none of this, he's still credited and is still on all the sites. Well done, Elwyn! Gerry Davis basically wrote the script in a hurry. I don't know. Maybe you can tell.

The Doctor doesn't really do much. He mentions wanting a hat like a beret he sees. He mentioned wanting a hat in the previous serial too. He likes hats, this Doctor. He tries to help the ailing Laird, who was wounded in the Battle. Then he pretends to be a German Doctor named Wer when the Redcoats show up. I'm hoping in the actual episode that this was a lot of fun. Here it seems like the Doctor really is in a different story from everyone else. It doesn't help that this is his 7th episode, and we haven't actually "seen" him do anything yet. It kind of damages his character. We can read about him, hear him, look at pictures and use our imagination to conjure him up. But he simply isn't here. We need him to show up soon.

Ben and Polly are here. Ben doesn't seem to understand how history works. When you're in a house full of wounded Scottish rebels, don't keep saying how awesome it is to have the Redcoats showing up. I'm not well versed on this time period either (the Doctor chastises Ben for that) but I can read a room. It's like "The Massacre," where we didn't fully get it, but with Ben yelling and being kind of obnoxious rather than Steven's trying to figure out what's happening. Polly escapes with a young woman named Kirsty. Polly is a beloved companion of the show even though most of her episodes are lost. I fear if we had this one, she'd be less beloved. Polly is clearly posh. The way she berates the "stupid peasant" Kirsty is gross. Much more gross than using the supernatural against Tom in "The Smugglers." Kirsty has been through a horrible battle, and she's scared. Polly just showed up. So, what is Polly's approach to assist the scared and scarred Kristy? Insult her. Criticize her upbringing. Generally, treat her as a complete social inferior. (Remember Gaston in "The Massacre" insulting Anne Chaplet. It's that, except we're supposed to like Polly.) I don't like it. In a story that is barely keeping my attention, that's not helping.

It is another completely lost story. We've only got the telesnaps. They don't help much. It starts out with a battle. There's an exciting scene where Ben and Jamie and others are going to be hanged. Polly escapes with a "stupid peasant" named Kirsty and they sneak around a cave. All great stuff, I imagine. We can't see it. Finally, after the struggle of "The Smugglers," I find myself kind of giving up. This episode, through the reconstruction, felt like it went on for an hour, but it didn't. I watched time go by as the episode ran. It was less than 25 minutes. So, I tried something. I grabbed the novelization.

It's written by Gerry Davis. It was published in 1984, the year of Season 21. (*Warriors of the Deep* through to *The Twin Dilemma*) I can't imagine there was a huge crowd waiting for this one. A non-descript, lost historical that not a lot of people remembered wasn't as interesting then as one of the better-known sci-fi stories. (Trust me.) However, I know people were interested in buying it because 38 years ago I bought it. Davis does a nice job of keeping the story flowing. It seems to work much better on the page than on the screen. But I can't quite see what's on the screen. The story isn't terribly interesting. It's a standard "Separate everyone" thing. It takes a full episode to do it. I'm going to go back and forth between the recon and the novelization throughout the next three episodes. Neither one the "proper" version.

The Highlanders

Episode Two

Episode 142: (December 24, 1966) Polly and Kirsty rob Ffinch. Ben and Jamie are taken onto the slave ship *Annabelle*. The Doctor dresses as a washer woman.

Cliffhanger: A body is sent down the plank to show the new slaves the only way they will ever leave the *Annabelle*.

Reading the novelization for this episode (Chapters 6-9, over halfway into the book) and then watching the recon works nicely. I had the images in my mind and then just hearing them with the limitations of the telesnaps really worked well. I should have done that with "The Smugglers." (This is a *Doctor Who* book. All I need to do is find the time.) The novelization isn't the most stimulating adventure. But that's down to the story I think and doesn't have much to do with the writing.

Polly and Kirsty fall in a hole. Then, they make scary noises and Ffinch (Algernon) falls in a hole, and they rob him. I do like Polly calling Finch F-finch. It almost makes me forget how much of a jerk she was towards Kirsty. Ben and Jamie do little. Obviously, Jamie is still a new character and not yet a companion. Ben basically sits around as a captive the whole time. The Doctor gets to have some fun being the crazy German Doctor. I wish I could see the slapstick in this. He smacks the clerk Perkins's head against a desk. He does a bunch of crazy stuff in the name of "medicine." Then, he dresses up as a washer woman and lurks around. I'd like to think these bits were hilarious. Troughton really having some fun. I can't really say.

And this is so unlike the way his Doctor will be. It feels like the goofing that Sylvester McCoy does early on in "Time and the Rani." Trying to find his footing in a new place. Now, Troughton, obviously, was in totally new waters here. He wasn't particularly goofy in the previous story. He was just sometimes weird. He seemed like he was on a slightly different plane of reality from everyone else. In this story, maybe because things are immediately more dangerous, he begins improvising quickly. Plus, hopefully, his brain has calmed down a bit. He does act in ways that his previous self never would have. That's part of the fun. And it is Christmas Eve. Remember the last Christmas episode? Remember how silly it was? Maybe the Doctor is doing that same sort of thing here.

Not much happens in the episode, which makes me think maybe they were doing a similar Christmas thing? The Doctor isn't much farther ahead. Polly and Kirsty move ahead slightly. Jamie and Ben are where we were told they would be at the end of the previous episode. I might be making all this up though. The problem with the episode is that it doesn't feel like much of anything happening. Unless the images are completely revelatory (and I do love the river under the floor reveal), then this story is kind of dull.

I almost feel like this is Davis and Lloyd sabotaging the historical stories. "The Smugglers" was OK. But this one, without historical characters but at a historical moment, ends up feeling inconsequential even if stakes are high. It ends up feeling arbitrary. It ends up feeling like a story that should have been an audio or a novel. If Jamie wasn't in it, why is this one important enough to be in the main canon? The first two episodes don't give us much. The historicals from the previous season were so good, so dramatic, so funny. Even when lost. This is just kind of passing the time until the next story. I hope episodes three and four prove me wrong.

The Highlanders

Episode Three

Episode 143: (December 31, 1966) The Annabelle is getting ready to leave for America with Ben onboard. The Doctor, Polly and Kirsty are trying to find a way onto it to free the indentured servants.

Cliffhanger: Ben is dunked. Rather permanently.

The adventure picks up here nicely. Thanks mainly to my reading of the novelization. This episode covers Chapters 10-13. But not quite the end of 13th. About a page and a half before the end of chapter 13 (page 97) is where the episode ends. Most novelizations put cliffhangers at the end of chapters. Davis plays it a little odd here (but it does make for a better reveal) and puts the resolve of the cliffhanger at the end of the chapter, which I like.

I think the next thing to say is that I forgot how long the Doctor stayed dressed as a woman. Pretty much the entire episode. Surely that's something for the record books. Crossdressing for the entire episode is something that should be marked off. He's not a particularly attractive lady. He looks like Troughton dressed as a lady, your mileage may vary. Even the not terribly attractive Perkins doesn't seem taken with her. I do like how the Doctor does seem to have a plan here. What might it be? I don't know.

The storyline has now come through. The solicitor Grey and his clerk Perkins are in cahoots with Captain Trask. They have captured a group of rebels. They offer the rebels this: become traitors and you go free as hunted men. Or you get hanged. Or Trask will take you to America for 7 years as an indentured servant. After the 7 years, you go free. But, of course, no one goes free. They work themselves to their deaths. They're basically slaves. Slaves that have been told that they are done after a certain time. So, they work hard to get to that time and not let anyone down. They're dead by then though. It's all over. One gets the distinct feeling that Trask and Grey are doing their own thing here. The King offered them traitor or hanging. The indentured servant angle is to make themselves cash. So, in a nasty time, this is about ultra-nasty people.

Thinking about it: if this is the last "pure" historical until "Black Orchid," if this is what they have to offer, I'm OK with it. I'm a little tired of them landing in places where they end up in pubs or inns or similar spots where, if they try to leave, someone will tattle on them, and they'll get arrested. Surely, in the history of Earth prior to 1966, there must be a place they could land where this didn't happen. Where they could wander freely? We almost never see it here. And, because sometimes they can't change anything, it makes for tiresome storytelling. I like that we now have the story down here. Plus, there is the addition of the mysterious ring on Kirsty's finger. But I'm tired of going back into history where everything is like this. I'm not saying I want the show to become nothing but "base under siege" stories but this type of story isn't sustainable.

I will say Ben might be at his best here, though. The scene where he looks at the contracts making him an indentured servant is great. He pauses and then he rips them up. Well done, sir! They immediately beat him senseless and then dunk him in the water. But that's a great moment. The bits with Polly and Ffinch are fun too. Steven had a rough time with his missing episodes. Dodo too. Polly and Ben are suffering the most. It's tough to gauge their characters just from the audio and some images. They are beloved companions, but the restorations aren't that helpful.

The Highlanders

Episode Four

Episode 144: (January 7, 1967) Everyone is safe who needs to be safe. Say goodbye to the Highlands.

Cliffhanger: The Doctor, Ben and Polly leave. With Jamie.

All right. I was happy with the way this ended. There's a pitched battle between the Highlander prisoners and Trask's crew at the end that we can't see. That's too bad. I like the fact that the actual ending is sneaking back across the land with Jamie, and then Ffinch, to get back to the TARDIS. I'd forgotten that. It shows that the makers knew what the real ending was. It works well. It does mean that there are no huge new stakes in the history of the world. It's all about escaping and getting back into the TARDIS. But it's nice to see.

I do quite like the way Polly and Ffinch's relationship ends. She's befuddled and bewildered him throughout. But now, in the end, they've kind of become friends. She even gives him a little kiss. He stands up to Counsellor Grey and everything seems like maybe it will be all right. (We leave in the TARDIS so it's a little tough to say.) However, I like it. I like that on their journey to the ship they become friends. That's cool. I didn't think he was a bad guy, even though he was a Redcoat. That's a sweet storyline resolved well.

Overall, not a favorite, but boy reading the novelization alongside it really helped. Look, when you're writing a book like this with a deadline and a full-time job 5 days a week, you must maximize your time. Maybe I should have been doing this since the start with some of the lost ones. It may have helped. Gerry Davis's book isn't great, but it tells the story clearly and cleanly. It eliminates some scenes, simplifies others and makes for a stronger overall experience. I can't argue with that. One day, upon its return to us, we shall watch it and decide properly. Until then, we do the best we can.

Anyway, so ends the historicals. The pseudo historicals will be a big part of the series from this time out. Overall, they kind of work better with this show. This historical was not bad. It has strangely low stakes throughout. It starts off seeming like it might be something big and somewhat epic. Something covering a battle of something. In the end, it's about a bunch of jerks who try to kidnap two of our main characters. The stakes are low here. There's not even a treasure to hunt, which is always disappointing. I don't dislike it. Not all the stories can be huge stakes adventures.

Everyone gets something to do. Ben gets to be proper heroic. Polly gets to have some fun goofing with Ffinch, although Kirsty disappears pretty quick from the thing. Jamie gets a decent enough introduction. Although, there's nothing really in it until the end to indicate that he might travel with them. He's just a guy who is part of the adventure. The Doctor gets to be clever. He dresses as a sentry. He steals Grey's contracts. He gets to be the Doctor. But this, "we got here and we immediately need to get out" thing needs to evolve. It's been going on a bit too long ago. We need a more serious menace next time. We need a menace that we can really believe in.

THE UNDERWATER MENACE

Episode One

Written by Geoffrey Orme

Directed by Julia Smith

Episode 145: (January 14, 1967) It is circa 1970. Off the coast of Mexico, the TARDIS crew are brough to Atlantis where they're almost sacrificed to the goddess Amdo, Polly is going to be made into a fish person and we meet Professor Zaroff.

Cliffhanger: Polly is about to be turned into a fish person.

I really, really wish we had this episode. For about the first 10 minutes or so, it's quite intriguing. Jamie is now part of the crew. He is generally confused. Ben and Polly are doing their best to convince him that all shall be well. There's a great moment where we get to hear all four of their thoughts and the Doctor wishes for "prehistoric monsters," which is lovely. This is a more playful Doctor than the previous one. Their examination of the coastline is amusing. Although, this is the second story this season where they land on a coastline. Third one since "The Time Meddler." At least this one isn't in England, which is a nice change of pace.

The story starts off with some nice mystery behind it. When they're sent underwater, that adds to it considerably. We have the title. We know there's a menace and we know it's underwater. It's only once they get there that things start to go a little dippy.

It's been said before that this is the serial where *Doctor Who* goes full on B-movie. Technically, the sci-fi era of the 1950s continued into the early 1960s. So, the show was being made as its theatrical counterparts were being made. This story however seems to be Mr. Orme reusing a script that never got made. Maybe by Hammer. Or A.I.P. or someone cheaper.

It starts with the Atlanteans and their outfits, The outfit that the gal is in isn't bad. It's the guys, especially the camp High Priest, who lose out here. Oh, also the guy wearing the fish head. The Doctor figures out that the missing Zaroff is here because of the edible plankton they nosh on. So, we know how important fish is to these people. Why the fish hat/ helmet thing though? It's silly enough hearing your High Priest who sounds like he's escaped from a John Waters film go on and on without having to look at that goofy fish hat thing.

Let's not begin with the Fish People. The scientists wanting to convert Polly into one with plastic lungs is a horrific and it's a dark cliffhanger. Another set of scientists as bad as the ones in "The Savages." But the Fish People themselves... boy they sure look goofy. We can't see them moving yet. Hold on for that.

Let's end with Zaroff. He's teetering on the edge of overacting every moment. He seems like the classic B-movie mad scientist. He lets the Doctor (or "Doctor W") live because he's a fellow scientist. But, after all this, the man has a pet octopus. Where are we know? What show is this? Are we completely off the rails yet? If we do go, I'll join you. I was just wondering.

Keep in mind, after all that: This is the 11th episode of the Troughton era and we still have not seen one that exists. It's all been voices and pictures. One begins to despair of ever seeing the era move properly. We saw Ben and Polly in "The War Machines" and a few episodes of "The Tenth Planet." But, they've done a bunch and we've seen so little. And the Second Doctor? Who is he? All these hats and his recorder. All these outfits. All lost. Isn't it time we saw something properly? Yes. Thank goodness, here we go.

The Underwater Menace

Part Two

Episode 146: (January 21, 1967) The Doctor learns that Zaroff plans on destroying the Earth to raise Atlantis from the depths. The Professor must be stopped.

Cliffhanger: King Thous turns the Doctor and Ramo over to Zaroff.

The very first Troughton episode that currently exists! He doesn't wear a fun hat here but he's having a good time. He does get to put on an Atlantean High Priest outfit near the end, which he clearly gets a kick out of. I feel as if some of the craziness of earlier episodes might have been gone a bit. That's OK. It's been replaced by the craziness of the story. Also, it's great to see Ben, Polly and Jamie moving. Jamie looks good in his kilt. Ben looks butch enough in the caves. And Polly... well, she's Polly. I'm not complaining.

The best stuff in this episode (discovered in 2009) is the Doctor with Zaroff. Zaroff seems like he might be somewhat sane, at first. The more he talks to the Doctor and the quieter the Doctor gets the more insane the man becomes. I love his justification for why he wants to destroy the world. Because it's the dream of all scientists. Well, let's not get too crazy there. (The Doctor does say, "He's mad as a hatter" when describing Zaroff to Ramo.) I love the concept that he's going to empty the ocean into the center of the earth. Steam occurs and the planet cracks apart. I'd say more than a menace, actually.

The rest of the episode is people escaping and running around. Some of it's fun. Ara and Polly make a nice team. I'm not sure who Ara is exactly, but she's delightful. I'd let her lead me around Atlantis any day. The opening with the scientists trying to inject Polly but constantly being stopped by the lights going out is a bit awkwardly done, to be honest. She's almost injected several times, but they keep stopping right at the injection moment. At least once, they seem to anticipate the light about to go dim. That could have been a bit sharper. Plus, the Doctor does know exactly which plugs to unplug to stop the power to the hospital/ operating room area. That seems a bit much to me. (Maybe I need to find my novelizations and check it out.) The direction in the rest of the episode is fine. Don't get me wrong. The direction overall is fine. From the temple to the operating room to the laboratory to the caves, everything moves along decently. In fact, the cliffhanger sneaked up on me. I thought there were a few minutes left.

It's a good cliffhanger, I think. Thous, the leader of the Atlanteans, clearly isn't listening to the Doctor and Ramo. He says he is but you can tell it's baloney loaf. I like that the ending is simply the Leader expressing his disbelief in The Doctor's theory by turning him into Zaroff again. It's been said that Zaroff has really helped the people and that he's given them a lot of advantages. So, one can see what the leader is up to. Although, at that point, I honestly think going to someone else (anyone else) would have worked better. Thous doesn't listen to what the Doctor has to say, which is a sign. He just says he'll think on it. I was expecting the Doctor to say "Think on what? I haven't said anything yet."

We meet the guys who work in the mines. They're threatened with becoming Fish People, so I guess that's a job that no one wants. What are they mining? (Where is my novelization?) They're not mining the plankton. They're just standing around rocks. Are they eating rocks? These miners are captive prisoners so the viewer is getting an overview of everyone in the society here. The shot-on-film cave sequence looks nice. And I do like everyone having a snack in the temple of Amdo. It's, overall, a pretty good episode. Whether the story gets better from here (as we know what's happening) I couldn't say, yet. But it's not a full-on stinker as many have said.

The Underwater Menace

Episode Three

Episode 147: (January 28, 1967) Zaroff's plans look to be going according to schedule. Is this the end of planet Earth?

Cliffhanger: Nothing in the world can etc. etc. and so forth.

I stand corrected and chastened. They are not wearing fish hats or heads. They are fish masks that are being held in front of their faces. Thank goodness this episode exists. Also, we'd never get a good look at the Fish people if it wasn't for this episode. Dreams do come true.

This was the episode that's existed from this serial for the longest. I first saw it on "The Troughton Years" VHS tape released in the early 1990s. It did indeed seem as silly as people claimed. It has a weird kind of free-for-all feeling to it. Big Lolem, who sounds like Cyril from "The Celestial Toymaker" and looks a bit like Divine, hams it up. Everyone hides in the giant shrine. Thous stares intently into Zaroff's eyes (to see the madness) but we didn't know why. The Doctor and his friends hide in the marketplace and play a game of chase with Zaroff until they capture him. Then, Zaroff escapes. And then he escapes again. Then, he's suddenly in control of Atlantis speaking the final line of the episode, which isn't as over the top as people claim. (Received wisdom. I think he undersells it slightly from what I'd been led to believe for years.) Amid all this, everything stops for a Fish People video.

First: Why are some of the Fish People like Fish People? (And why do they keep getting called "fish." Aren't they genetically engineered humans who were forced to be like this?) And why are some of the Fish People just ladies with face masks. Surely, having a huge water grotto area like that must have cost the production a bunch of money. Luckily, they don't send the regulars. They send those two guys from the mines whose names I don't remember. The Fish People stop collecting food. (Then, what were the guys in the mine doing?) They go on strike. We get a very long couple of minutes as a very early synth plays and plays while the actors dressed as Fish People "swim" around a large set. The big thing with all the missing episodes is that it's tough to gauge whether this set, which looks elaborate, hogged space for some other sets, making for chintziness elsewhere. "The Underwater Menace" does seem to have a bunch of money behind it. Which begs the question: Did they read the script beforehand?

The episode is nicely paced. The marketplace scenes expand the world and shows citizens apart from guards, priests, leaders and Ara. There is mention of lots of strangers being around here lately. Is that just small talk not meant to mean anything? Or is it true? How big is Atlantis? I know it's big. But where are the out of towners coming from? The scene expands the story but it's also kind of confusing everything. And, oh… it's nice to see the good guys fall for the "I'm sick. Help me! Haha! I'm not sick and I'm punching you!" ploy.

Apart from "The War Machines," this is the first time we've seen Polly out in the field. In "Machines," she is hypnotized for a good portion of everything and she's in her environment for the rest. Here, she looks nice but boy she's annoying. During the fight with Zaroff, she screams a lot, and her retaliation is useless. She's kidnapped, freed, almost kidnapped again and screams a lot. One would be forgiven for thinking that Polly is a super stereotypical screaming female companion from this. It's not helped that the next episode we see her in has her making coffee for everyone. (Although, I don't mind making coffee for people myself.) Her uselessness (in this episode) is not great. To add to the companion problem issue, Ben and Jamie are interchangeable throughout. Maybe, the build towards the big climax will change things. But the next episode doesn't exist. Oh well.

The Underwater Menace

Episode Four

Episode 148: (February 4, 1967) Zaroff is set to crack the Earth. So, the Doctor comes up with a crazier plan.

Cliffhanger: After some good-natured ribbing from the three young people, The Doctor tries to get the TARDIS to Mars. Things go wrong.

Wow! I wish we had this episode. The animated version and the audio and the novelization imply epic destruction. They imply Atlantis slowly flooding. People moving up and up, closer to the surface. The Doctor racing to try to convince Zaroff to leave. Jamie and Polly sitting on the shore, thinking their friends have passed. The world is saved. But at what a cost! It seems mighty. It seems like a hell of an ending.

The premise is: The Doctor, to save the world, floods Atlantis. In doing so, Zaroff won't be able to set off his explosion. It also will destroy most of Atlantis. It will cause the population to have to move themselves closer to the surface. * If not, on the surface. But, of course, not "on the surface" of Atlantis. On the surface of wherever this story began. Mexico? So, the Doctor floods everything.

It's odd to think that they've been in Atlantis for what? A day? And the Doctor has taken it upon himself to flood and basically destroy the city. He's a very quick decider is our Doctor. Plus, it's the craziest climactic thing he's done since "The Destruction Of Time." Now, that was a different Doctor and that was a far more serious story. Yes, if Zaroff does what he wants, the Earth will be destroyed. But, if the Daleks get the Time Destructor, it's a Time War without the Time Lord. So, the First Doctor does something rather unlike himself (but maybe like other parts of their personality) and the final episode is one big ticking clock.

The Time Destructor must burn itself out. We don't have the episode, but we have the constant sound of the Destructor going off. We know it's terrible. We know it's damaging. And it hangs over so much of the final episode. "The Underwater Menace" goes the same route. The Doctor announces what he's doing at the start. The episode is everything flooding. In the recon, you can feel it building. You can feel it happening. So much of it is imagination rather than what happened. Those Fish People grottos looked nice. So, maybe when Zaroff's laboratory fills up with water, it might have been awesome. Tough to say.

Overall, this episode could be one of the best. It's apocalyptic. It does a wonderful thing where, gazing at the veneer, we can't quite tell what's happening. So, there's a great back and forth between chaos and stillness. And the TARDIS crew gets a fun closing scene in the control room before things go wrong. I like this episode. I wish it existed because it feels like a crazy ending to a crazy story.

*Although, if they can get to the surface of the Earth so easily, see the first episode, what do they care if they get raised to the surface? I would think an existing continent in the water would be safer there than on the surface of a world they are hardly going to understand. Remember what happened when the Silurians showed up? That didn't occur to me until just now. Why risk everything to put yourself back up there when you seem to be living fine under the water? This story is goofy.

THE MOONBASE

Episode One

By Kit Pedler

Directed by Morris Barry

Episode 149: (February 11, 1967) To the Moon! It's the year 2070. The Moonbase holds the Gravitron, which controls the tides on Earth and the weather. (It also contains a very familiar looking group of guys). But all is not well.

Cliffhanger: Jamie sees the "Phantom Piper." We see a redesigned Cyberman.

I discovered this story through the very exciting novelization. The desolated base helping the Earth filled with an assortment of people from around the world. Something strange going on. The Doctor and his companions getting caught up in it. "Doctor Who and the Cybermen" was the name of Gerry Davis's print adaptation and was the third one I owned. I didn't know what Cybermen were but they sure scared me. Unlike the rather juvenile "Doctor Who and the Zarbi," this book was exciting, scary and kept building and building as it went. I remember loving it. (I have not re-read it for this.)

Watching it now, it still has that feeling. To an extent. The first and third episodes are lost so we are watching animated episodes. They look pretty good and I get swept up in them. It's great to have more episodes existing of this gang, because there are very few for the remainder of the season and Ben and Polly are all gone by then. The setting is cool. I love the Gravitron. The crew seems generally amiable. Yes, some sort of strange virus has started its scourge but we're not yelling at the Doctor and the gang yet. Yes, Jamie is knocked unconscious but that's because he wasn't in the original script. There's only one thing wrong with all of it.

It's a remake of "The Tenth Planet." That's "The Tenth Planet" that just aired three years ago!

I'm kidding. It's "The Tenth Planet" that finished airing three and a half months prior to this episode. Also set on a base in the middle of nowhere. The difference? That group was military. This group are scientists. General Cutler was a madman from the get-go. Hobson, the commander/ physicist here, seems much more reasonable and rather casual. In fact, he seems more casual about how four people just show up on the Moon than Cutler did about how three people arrived at the South Pole. "The Moonbase" is set up more like a mystery. "The Tenth Planet" is set up almost immediately as if something big and epic is about to happen. (Heck, it almost does.) "Moonbase" has worry about the weather in it, which is also big. And, of course, they also have the Cybermen.

Now, this one keeps our Cyber pals in the dark and only reveals one briefly at the end. If you remember the Cybermen, you might think "Well, they don't want to storm in because you remember what happened twice last time." But you also might think, "What is that?" because it does look very, very different from the previous Cybermen. Maybe people did think it was a "Phantom Piper." Having said all that, it's not a bad episode. It moves better and is less annoying than "The Tenth Planet." Taking out the caustic, self-serving Cutler helps. Making the atmosphere more laid-back helps. Adding the mysterious virus helps. Also, and this is Lloyd and Davis for you, having a more active Doctor helps. The First Doctor did seem very out of place at the South Pole. His arrogant "I want to be in charge" thing was a bomb. The Second Doctor's willingness to calmly see what's up helps immeasurably. What also helps is that the structure and set-up of "The Tenth Planet" felt at times like it was being written by someone who didn't fully understand what writing and stories were. For this one, Mr. Pedler and his pal Mr. Davis have upped the ante and learned a thing or two. Let's see where we go from here.

The Moonbase

Episode Two

Episode 150: (February 18, 1967) The virus is getting worse. Polly keeps seeing Cybermen. Some men take sugar with their coffee, others don't.

Cliffhanger: A Cybermen hiding under a blanket in the sick bay slowly (wobbly?) approaches everyone.

In a place that they constantly say is so small that you couldn't hide a cat, the Cyberman does a nice job of keeping hidden. He's underneath a sheet in the sick bay. One would have thought they'd have seen him there earlier. But everyone's been busy.

And yes, the episode exists, which is good. It's a fun episode. Hobson is better than Cutler. As a scientist, he's able to see reason when need be. There may be a few too many minutes of "everyone's looking for the fault" but that's fine. We get to see the main set of the episode, which is the Gravitron/ main control room set. This was a Gerry Davis thing. One big set and "base under siege." Here it's still fresh and fun. Although, there is a strange feeling that the base consists of the main room and then the sickbay immediately next to it. Not a lot of hallway work in this story.

The production team was only a week behind air dates at this point. Normally, they'd have a few weeks of hang time. You know, an episode recorded this Saturday is worked on throughout the week. It airs two or three Saturdays later. This episode was recorded on February 11th. That is cutting it hilariously close. No one looks overwrought or crazy here so someone was keeping everyone nice and calm.

I take that back: Polly seems a touch overwrought. She's very screamy in this episode. This is, in fact, one of the episodes that people point to show the show's sexist strain of the 1960s. Yes, Polly does get asked to make coffee. But there's no one else there, they're trying to distract Hobson and the Doctor can't stop looking for a cure to the "virus" to make coffee… but still, it does feel a bit disappointing. There were plenty of great moments, I bet, in lost episodes that we'll never get to refer to for rebuttal purposes. Oh, and about that screaming… She lets off a few hysterical ones at the start of the episode. They seem un-Polly-like to me. According to the commentary text on the DVD, the writers and director were parodying all the "tough gals" of the day, like the ones on *The Avengers*. Emma Peel and such. OK, I can kind of see that. The problem is that it had to be explained to me. It looked like Polly screaming like a scared woman, not a parody of a trend on TV of the day. And to someone watching today, that reference may make zero sense so it works even less well. I don't know. I think some of the producers liked their ladies screaming more than others.

Other things to enjoy and/or watch for: The chat Hobson has with the completely disinterested ambassador about the Gravitron problem. That's a bureaucrat for you. The guys who go out on the surface and their fun moon outfits. (People were nuts for this kind of thing at this time.) The Doctor being a nuisance in the Gravitron room. Jamie doing very little. Ben doing very little. Again, Kit and Gerry don't always seem interested in their leads. Also, please enjoy the giant Cyberman-sized hole in the wall behind the sacks. That's a good time. I wish the next episode existed. But the last one does! Let's watch some cartoons.

The Moonbase

Episode Three

Episode 151: (February 25, 1967) The Cybermen take over the Gravitron control room. The Polly Cocktail is whipped up in defense.

Cliffhanger: An army of Cybermen move across the surface of the moon.

Here's where we can really see Ben's dialogue getting handed around. He's an expert on atomic generators. He's an expert on the epoxy they'll need to destroy the Cybermen's chest units. However, he can also take time to take credit for Polly's work and tell Polly that what they're doing is men's work. Hooray Ben! Hooray Jamie! I do love that there is some tension between the boys here. They both seem to be trying to impress Polly. (Well, she is a cutie.) They both seem to be shorter than Polly in the animated version. (Ben was in live action.) That amuses me. Ladies can go out with men shorter than them. There's something very *Doctor Who* about these two short guys fighting for the tall gal.

I don't quite like the way the episode treats Polly. She comes up with the way to stop the Cybermen. But then, the guys fight over it. Then, when they must bring it to the vacuum of space, Ben has to explain to her the way it works. I don't like that so much at all. I do like that she is part of the attack group though.

However, the rest of the episode is great. I do feel weird regarding the "base under siege" concept. The first two episodes have the Cybermen lurking around and then they take over the Gravitron control room. It's very nicely done. It's very tense. The Cybermen want to destroy all life on Earth. We get some great discussion of emotions. Clearly, clearly, the Cybermen here are loaded with emotions. Someone told them not to act like they did. And it's funny. Or it's clever. * I love the Cybermen here. They are very robotic. Their voices are very robotic. They are emotional in a way that the Mondasian cybermen never were. Kit and Gerry updated them a bit and made them amusing.

I get a kick out of how the Doctor almost immediately knows how to take care of the Cybermen. Polly and her gang destroy the Cybermen on the bridge, as it were. But they spot a Cyber UFO. And the Doctor begins to ask how far down they can tilt the Gravitron. I love that. He's dismissed but he has asked that. I would love to see the actual episode and see how Troughton plays it. He knows what will save the day but he's being coy. In a way that his previous self would not have been. It's interesting.

I really like this episode. I think it builds the suspense and excitement nicely. The Cybermen have an inability to hold onto a space. It's tough to siege a base if you keep getting killed quickly. But that seems to be a thing Kit and Gerry are into. Bases will be sieged more deliberately later. We are still working it out here. It's a good time. The end moment-- the Cybermen moving across the surface-- is such a good cliffhanger. I am very happy that the next episode exists.

*Clever, Clever.

The Moonbase

Episode Four

Episode 152 (March 4, 1967) The Cybermen slowly march on the base. The humans inside do their best to keep them away. It's an exercise in suspense.

Cliffhanger: I have crabs.

They figured out the structure here. What was weirdly paced and oddly structured in "The Tenth Planet," mostly works here. In "Tenth," Kit and Gerry had the Cybermen arrive, get killed, arrive again and then get killed, with an episode in between. Here, the humans have dispatched the Cybermen that were in the base. And now, a UFO full of them is slowly attacking the base from outside. It's nicely done. It's great that we have this episode. In general, the whole thing is pieced together very well. There's a sense of building tension. A laser is used. (They were relatively new in 1967.) The Doctor's question in the previous episode is followed up here, which saves the day.

For the first time, we get a very Second Doctor-like response to the ending. He leaves. The Gravitron repels the Cybermen and their ships. It sends them flying off into space. The Doctor, Polly, Ben and Jamie leave. They don't say goodbye. The Doctor apologizes for any trouble with the Gravitron. That's it. They vanish and Hobson and his gang don't seem to care. The previous Doctor wouldn't have done this. He probably wouldn't have helped clean up. But he would have delivered a speech and he wouldn't have run away. When I say run away, I might be overselling it. They simply leave. We still haven't seen a complete existing story with this Doctor. But what we've seen here is excellent.

With the new Doctor, we have someone here who can dive right in and be a hero. A more familiar hero. This Doctor is in the thick of things. Coming up with stuff. Rescuing people. All the sort of thing that would have had the previous Doctor sort of hanging in the background and maybe not becoming fully involved. With this new format, it works. Granted, if we were still in the original format of the show, this Doctor might look a little odd. But, here, perfect. And, let's be honest, an army of Cybermen slowly approaching the Moonbase and firing lasers at it is good sci-fi stuff. As interesting as "Do nothing! Mondas will destroy itself!" may have been, it's clearly not as exciting. It's brave. Not that exciting.

The Cybermen are repelled again. The serial handled them well. The creepiness of the first two episodes. The assault on the control room in the third one. The final attack from the moon surface itself in this one. They're more robotic here. They're slightly less scary/ silly than their predecessors. I still think they were lying about having no emotions in the last episode. But, regardless, I'm ready to see them again. They're always good for some excitement and a laugh. In fact, I'd say they're as good as gold.

Oh, one of the Cybermen is played by John Levene. Sgt. Benton! What are you doing out there? What is the Brigadier going to say when he finds out?

Oh, one more time: I love using the coffee tray to plug the hole in the base. That's a good coffee tray! Remember what Chekov said about a coffee tray in Act One.

THE MACRA TERROR

Episode One

By Ian Stuart Black

Directed By John Davies

Episode 153 (March 11, 1967) The TARDIS crew land in a futuristic Earth colony where music constantly plays and everyone acts very content. Except one person, Medok. The Doctor isn't content when one person isn't content.

Cliffhanger: Medok and The Doctor meet the Macra…

This is one of the completely lost stories that has been fully animated. In fact, I'm watching it for the first time from the DVD as I'm writing these reviews. This is exciting. I've read the novelization. It's a good one. The recon is not a good one. There isn't a lot of existing material. There are an excessive number of captions and silent film style intertitles. The more of those there are, the tougher it is to keep the focus on the story. So, hooray for animation! Here we go…

The Doctor's face appears for the first time in the opening credits! Prior to the Second Doctor appearing, there wouldn't really need to be any need for this. There was only one Doctor. But now, we need to differentiate. It reminds me of the Target books that used to have, at the bottom of the title page, a little disclaimer telling you which Doctor was in the book. Before we had online episode guides or in-print episode guides, this was mighty helpful.

Overall, it's an interesting episode. The Holiday Camp atmosphere is perfectly obnoxious. The fact that the people who are working constantly as happy music plays don't seem to fully understand what they're working for is always good and ominous. The character of Medok is excellent. He seems like a crazy hobo kind of guy early on. You gradually begin to switch to his side mainly because the Doctor right away is on his side. The Doctor (and Jamie) can feel that something is not as it seems. The Doctor risks their freedom several times to try and figure out what is what.

The Second Doctor is well and truly ensconced in the show now. Yes, maybe the companions don't have as much to do as they possibly should but that's kind of been the way with this group. I like all three of them. Ben can be a bit abrasive but that's his character. I love the animation design of Polly. Jamie almost has stuff to do. They never quite have enough though. The Doctor does a lot here. In fact, he kind of does maybe too much (or maybe it's the animation). He's going to get cleaned up. Then, suddenly, he's at the cells. Then, he's with the group again. Is he bilocating? Is this the original version of him and the bi-generation version teaming up? I don't know. Regardless, the Doctor is strong in this episode.

I like Ian Stuart Black's work on the show. I wish he'd written more. This one is sort of in the realm of "base under siege" but not quite. The colony seems to extend over quite some space. It's a little tough to gauge the actual space involved here, especially when they chase Medok around some sand dunes or something or clay pits or you know what I mean. It's obvious that the people in charge of the colony are covering up something. Whenever we see The Controller, we see a picture and a hear a voice. The mouth never moves. That's not good. And then there's that cliffhanger. Creeping, crawling things infecting the colony. What are they?

The Macra Terror

Episode Two

Episode 154: (March 18, 1967) The Doctor causes more trouble. Jamie and Polly resist mind control. Ben doesn't end up doing so well. Also, there is no such thing as Macra.

Cliffhanger: The Controller is attacked by Macra causing Polly to freak out and getting the TARDIS crew sent to the Pits.

The old recon of this one was rough because there's a lot of visual stuff happening. At the beginning, with the Macra. During Ben and Polly's scene, with the Macra. When the TARDIS crew are being brainwashed by the voices. Having the animation is a godsend. Although some bits I don't fully understand. How do those new houses work? They are like two stacked on top of each other but no visible way into the top floor ones. I think I had a dream about houses like that once. There's a moment where Polly thinks Evil Ben has gone away but he sneaks up on her that really works here. I didn't think Polly, Ben and Jamie were sleeping so close though. I thought they were in cubicles or rooms. Instead, they're on cots/ beds right next to one another. If the voices are coming out of the speakers, surely everyone can hear everyone else's voices? Regardless, it's great to see the story.

It's always been one of those (from Mr. Black's previous stories and the novelization) that seemed quite good. But it was always tough to go that extra mile. First off, I'm pretty certain the giant crabs may not be the best-looking things. We only have brief clips of the Macra. They look like they could be cool if they're in the darkness. But sometimes we know that can be tricky. Giant claws are always fun. Like giant spider legs in *Robot Holocaust* or *Ator The Fighting Eagle*. The Doctor is doing great here. I do fear the monsters might have let the side down. Sadly, no one can really remember or truthfully give us good answers.

Alongside the Doctor being at his anarchic best, we get Ben completely taken over. He acts like himself when he needs to but the moment there's any calm, he becomes a Fake Ben parroting back the colony's nonsense. The big one being the constant repeating about how there is no such thing as Macra. I love that. We know the Macra are a part of the story because that's what the story is called. But how does everyone else know? I like the fact that everyone seems to say Marca but as they say it they forget it. Cognitive Disassociation is fun!

Poor Ben. I have read critiques of this story who dislike it because Ben is the "working class" one so he's the one who gets brainwashed. Hey, they're probably right. Jamie is close to Scottish royalty. Polly is super posh. The Doctor would never have fallen for it. So, it's Ben. The thing about all this is that Ben under control isn't too far gone from regular Ben. He's in the Navy. He's always saying "sir" and following orders. He does well at this. His first moments where he tells The Doctor to knock it off building into them almost getting into a fight is strongly staged. It's different from Polly being controlled by WOTAN. That's a straight up "invade your brain." This is more subliminal, more insidious more like the Morphoton brains in "The Velvet Web." (Gosh, remember that.) This insidiousness turns one of our characters against the others. Always a frightening prospect. I don't know if it is because he's "working class." I just thought the military training might make him a little more susceptible to that kind of thing. I could be wrong though.

The Macra Terror

Episode Three

Episode 155: (March 25, 1967) The TARDIS crew is sent to the Danger Gang mine. They are harvesting a gas from the planet. Jamie breaks away. And he meets…

Cliffhanger: The Macra.

In this episode, our leads spend almost the entire time in the Danger Gang. That's the nastiest part of the mines. (Remember when Jamie and Ben got put in a mine some time ago? In Atlantis, I believe.) And they're all there. Although Ben is in the capacity of the "guy who meanders around looking at people." Having been someone who had to work in Corporate America for more years than they would like, I know that person. The person you think is friendly but then they turn out to be awful. But it's not usually a great friend. I like the Doctor's response to Ben. Very matter of fact, very real. Very "You shouldn't treat your friends like this." The Second Doctor is quickly becoming a brilliant Doctor. It's the missing episodes that get in the way. It's tough to gauge from the animation or the reconstruction. But I'll be darned, Troughton is fantastic.

The Doctor gets really in deep here. He has the great scene, which is wasted on the recon, where he figures out the formula for the gas and why it might be needed. He has scribbled the formula across a huge clear board. The Pilot can't figure out how he found it out. I love that the Doctor's response is that he figured it out with the help of some measurements. The moment he gives himself a 10 out of 10 and then brings it up to 11 is great. I love how the Doctor knows something is wrong. I love how he seems to be working towards a solution. (Remember the Gravitron.) I also love how most people think he's being goofy.

Jamie has some great material here. He goes through the big metal door that the brainwashed can't quite figure in their minds. He goes through it and encounters the Macra. Huge Macra. I think they know that things are going wrong. I think that they don't know how to deal with it. Jamie's wander through their underground space is going to tear everything apart.

Ian Stuart Black tells a hell of a story here. Almost all of this is in the mine. The head of the mine is a rather interesting character. He sounds like he's pleasant at first. But he becomes more unpleasant when things go against what he's been told. Against what the Macra want. Of course, he doesn't know what the Macra are or his brain has been taught to reject them. That's life. He does seem kind of pleasant though.

The TARDIS crew are knee deep in the crazy throughout this episode. It's quite enjoyable. Especially because they don't know the people of the Colony. They're helping these people because they're people who need help. That's what the TARDIS crew does. Helping people who don't want to be helped or people who don't know they need to be helped. Now granted, sometimes the crew is idealistic. In this one, they seem very much like that. Think about "The Savages." The Elders and their people didn't want to be freed. But the Savages sure did. The Doctor and his group helped them all. It's almost assumed that this is what they do. "Always do what you're best at." Even when the people involved don't care. Medok is here. And he still believes it's all wrong and he expects to die in the mines. One person in a civilization wants this. We need to see where this goes.

The Macra Terror

Episode Four

Episode 156: (April 1, 1967): The giant crabs are taking advantage of the humans. What should we do?

Confusion is best left to the experts.

Oh... the early synth score is incredibly good. Synths were very futuristic at this time. (Like moon landings and lasers.) These sounds add an extra kick to the show. Dudley Simpson does the score for this serial. He's our main man for the 1970s. He gives this episode some fun colony tunes and some wonderful atonal bits of music as the Macra terror draws ever nearer. The show is still in a wonderfully weird place. It doesn't matter how big the audience. Weird keeps slipping in here.

The story ends nicely. Ian Stuart Black is one of those writers who understands that even though the story is in four parts, it needs to be a complete story. Schedule your important cliffhangers at the right moment. Make that story stretch properly across the episodes. Let the character arcs go. Let the story build. Make the climax worth something. If you're familiar with, say, "The Tenth Planet," you may have encountered the opposite. That story lurches and lumbers along with no concept of anything but the episode it is part of at that moment. (I know it had its troubles. But still, if you're making money writing, then write and write well.) This is Black's final story for the show. Luckily, Mr. Black novelized all three of his stories. (All very late in the run. "The War Machines" came out in 1989.) He does a nice job with all three of them, tweaking the televised versions when needed.

The Doctor, after several stories where he acted rather oddly, is now fully the hero of the show. And he's doing it in such a different way from his predecessor. He never wants to take charge. He's always sort of off to one side. You can tell when he figures something out. He gets quieter. He becomes more focused. The companions work nicely with him here. It's great to have Ben back. The only heartbreaker is that Ben and Polly only have two more episodes and a scene left. And only one of those episodes exist. We can talk more about them during the next serial. But this story does a nice job of balancing them. They don't have a ton of stuff to do and, certainly, no one is getting modern day story arcs. If Polly and Ben are in love, we don't know about it. The last serial had rivalry between Ben and Jamie over Polly. That never comes up again. Ben and Polly will be mentioned far in the future. But that's for another story.

The tricky thing with this serial comes out here; Ian Stuart Black had apparently wanted the Macra to be less literal. More like some sort of germs. Less literally giant *Attack of the Crab Monsters* crabs; more real figments of the mind that take over and gradually destroy it. Now, that does sound a little tough to pull off. But, also, giant crabs might be even tougher to pull off. Even though, in theory, everyone knows what the crabs looks like. "We've got crabs!" I know, I know. The problem isn't all that in theory. What happens is that we see these giant crabs. We see them running some sort of refinery. We see them taking over this human colony. But we never learn where they came from. If they're some sort of germ, then they could be from anywhere. They look like a race of giant crabs though and the thought is: They live here. This is their home. The humans landed and took it over. The Macra are just trying to take it back. (A Silurian variation.) So, if the Doctor kills them all and they're the original inhabitants, isn't that genocide? And horrible? The answer lingered for years until the episode "Gridlock." RTD said that he wanted to add an old monster/ villain that no one remembered so he has Macra appear on Earth. If so, then they're not all dead and the Doctor didn't commit genocide. Hooray! Let's go to the airport.

THE FACELESS ONES

Episode One

Written by Malcolm Hulke and David Ellis

Directed By Gerry Mill

Episode 157: (April 8, 1967) The gang has landed at Gatwick Airport. On the Runway. They see a murder. They get separated. Something weird is happening.

Cliffhanger: A strange burned (?) man sits up and breaths heavily.

This episode is fantastic. At least for most of it. Near the end, it becomes a bit of a "We saw something! Look there." "There's nothing there. Who are you?" "It was there. Don't worry about who I am." kind of thing. With the bad guys laughing at the good guys derisively. When did *Scooby Doo* start? Anyway. There's another moment where the Doctor and Jamie are sitting waiting to be punished and they see Polly. But Polly this woman is not. She looks like Polly. But the bad guys have got to her. So, our heroes get zinged twice. This is very much the Davis and Lloyd style. This is very much like so many other TV shows. It's OK here because there are other questions to answer and we believe that Doctor will come up with something. It is still a bit of a sigh. "Let me show you a body... Where did it go?" Oh well.

Apart from that, I love the first half of this episode. It breaks my heart that Ben is immediately separated from everyone. Because we won't see him together with them until he leaves. Polly gets a lovely moment or two with The Doctor and Jamie. But, when she is kidnapped and they don't notice, I think the viewer can see that Polly (and Ben) may not be a part of the crew for much longer. That's too bad because I like them. It's too bad because so many of their episodes are lost.

The episode moves nicely. I don't know who those guys are in Chameleon Tours but their main activities seem to be murder and stamping postcards. I don't get it! But I love it. It's an odd villain choice. Then there is that weird burned (?) character that they bring through the airport. I love that they are so ensconced in whatever it is they're doing and that the Doctor and Jamie got thrown in hard.

The airport scenes are lovely. The Doctor, Polly and Jamie discussing what's happened by the wheel of a jet is a joy. This show can keep going for ages and something like this reminds us of that. Keeping in mind, that travel on airplanes at this time was a big thing, Most people went to holiday camps, a la "The Macra Terror." You drive there. You do whatever for a holiday and it's over. Plane trips were slightly out of touch for most people. So, the show is almost in a futuristic place. Which is awesome. Especially with laser-welding crazy Chameleons.

We are back in Modern Day. But while that happens, we're clearly losing two of our family members. "My Fam!" I feel kind of sad here. We're going to another era. Polly and Ben had their charms. Ben was almost Tegan-like in his ability to be bothered. With Polly included, they were a fun duo. Jamie is still not quite the Jamie we know. That will happen shortly. It's a weird run of episodes. I wish the next one existed.

Oh, Malcolm Hulke joins us here. He wrote a story called "Beyond The Sun" some time ago that never got made. He will become a big part of the first half of the 1970s. He's a hell of a writer. A hell of an interesting person. I never met him but I met Terrance Dicks. n the brief time, I talked with him, I showed him my Dinosaur Invasi3on novelization. Terrance smiled and said that Mac was a good guy. I said that that book was my intro to the show. He looked at me and said "Perfect." Another major name arrives. And he gets an animated episode.

The Faceless Ones

Episode Two

Episode 158: (April 15, 1967) The Doctor, Ben and Jamie continue looking for Polly. Samantha Briggs shows up looking for her brother.

Cliffhanger: The Doctor is in the Chameleon Tours hanger when they release the gas.

The pace slackens slightly here. There's a reason for that. There seems to be an abnormal amount of time spent outside the Chameleon Tours kiosk looking at the woman who looks like Polly but isn't. When Samantha shows up, she adds a nice kick to it. She's very Scouse. Polly (or whoever this is) is very posh and they make a fun couple. I wish we could see them. We love Polly but whoever this is that looks like her is acting weird. As annoying as Sam is, she takes our attention. Also, she takes a sharp shine to Jamie, which is delightful.

The Doctor and the Commandant go through several lengthy, pointless chats together. I applaud the Doctor for trying. But it does seem as if it's overdoing it. Have you ever seen "The Night Strangler?" It's a TV Movie from 1974 with Darren McGavin as Kolchak? He's in Seattle working for a newspaper. He is tracking down a strange... I won't ruin it. His boss is a hotheaded charmer named Vincenzo. Throughout the movie and a previous movie they were in and a TV series they shared, the two of them argue a lot. The arguments are always judiciously placed. There are two versions of "The Night Strangler." The original 74-minute version and a 90-minute version. The latter is the one we all see on home video. It's extended for possible theatrical release. In it, Kolchak and Vincenzo have too many arguments. That's what this *Doctor Who* episode feels like. The main characters go back to spots they've already been and run over the same ground again. It's tricky to watch. Because one can imagine everything being much sharper and much more forward moving, narrative-wise. It's not bad. But it should be better.

Overall, it's a good episode. We have the vastness of the airport around us. We have the Doctor being very Doctor-like. We have Ben being Ben for the last time. (He never fully recovered after being controlled by the Macra.) We have Jamie becoming the Jamie that will travel with us for the next two seasons. And we meet Sam. She's fun! Ish. I love the Polly Chameleon. Still posh but not friendly like Our Polly. We will only see Ben and Polly for a couple of minutes from this point on. My heart breaks because I want to see them and know them more than we do. If you're as bugged as I am, feel free to contact the BBC care of The United Kingdom and call them jerks. Because every missing episode from a missing story is so good. Every missing episode seems to remove so much. They do deliver when we can find them. But, lost... we can only conjecture.

The weirdest thing about this episode isn't apparent until the next episode. And maybe not even then. Faux-Polly is called away. So, she leaves near the end. Ben is injected with something by the Chameleons. The Doctor can't get to him. From now on, up until the closing, Ben and Polly are gone. This is now the Jamie, Sam and Doctor show. Innes Lloyd and Gerry Davies did something similar with Dodo. But they didn't introduce Dodo. Ben and Polly were their creations. Maybe it was a contract thing? I don't know. It feels weird when you realize the weird you're feeling is the weird you're feeling. And I can't help because I'm as weird as you're feeling.

The Faceless Ones

Episode Three

Episode 159: (April 22, 1967) The Doctor, Sam and Jamie continue investigating. They get help from a policeman. Yes, the Chameleons are up to something.

Cliffhanger: The young people have completely vanished from the plane.

The Doctor is so good in this episode. The fact that it exists helps. He gets the Commandant of the Airport and the police officer to believe in him long enough to go and investigate. It works brilliantly. The opening scene where he seems to have frozen but zoinks the bad guy is great. The scene where he (with his unkempt hair) looks at the air traffic controllers trying to gauge who is the fake human is so good. And, well, Troughton, is perfection in this episode. There will be a point where we have a lot of his episodes and it kicks ass. But here, we're meandering in a sloppy lost space. We wish we could get more of what's happening. When we see him, though, it's good. And in this episode, he's very good.

I don't just mean because he has a few scenes with the great Wanda Ventham. She plays Ms. Rock. Which is a kickass name. She will appear in the show two more times over the next twenty years. Her son will know when the game is afoot. She's delightful. I don't think she's flirty with the Doctor. But they have nice moments together. The first Doctor had a very specific type, a la Cameca. This Doctor looks younger (about 10 years younger) so the type of person attracted to him would be different.

The Chameleons have a nice scheme going here. Well, we don't really know what it is but they're up to something. The planes full of young people vanish in the end. We see the staff handing the postcards to all the passengers. I'm worried about the way that they seem to have gotten some sort of franchise in the airport. Is that the way airports work? It seems a bit odd to me. Especially when Ms. Rock explains the way the Chameleons do their thing. It all sounds very suspicious. But they are a great villain, or whatever. We saw them in that weird, burnt state earlier. Yes, it is through animation that they become what they are but I won't argue. I think it works. It's a very different kind of villain here. We're only beginning to learn why and what they are. And how they're doing whatever.

Overall, the episode is excellent. The Doctor is great. Doing his thing, sneaking around, making people suspicious but making others interested. Jamie and the Doctor have some nice scenes together, especially tearing up the storage room. This feels like the kind of thing that we will see all over Season Six. It's getting birthed and freshened here. Troughton and Hines clearly enjoy working with each other. There is such a whirlwind of episodes happening in the 1960s. You need to get hold of someone who works with you and who has the same vibe you do. It is visible, really for the first time, here. I do hope you like it because this is our premise for the next two years.

Oh, no Ben and Polly here. They are mentioned. The vibe has really shifted to Jamie, Sam and the Doctor. I wish we had the next few episodes. Animation does its best. And the Chameleons have some tricky and creepy tricks up their creepy sleeves. The moment with the disappearing passengers (even though the Doctor and friends are not involved) is so good. Well shot and very eerie. Those poor kids. I don't know what will happen next. Let's dive in.

The Faceless Ones

Episode Four

Episode 160: (April 29, 1967) We learn more about the Chameleon Tours. But not quite what they're after. Jamie sneaks onboard one of their flights. There's also a bit with a laser. Yes, they use a mirror to stop it.

Cliffhanger: The Chameleon airplane becomes a spaceship and flies onto a space station hovering far above the Earth.

The story strains a little here. It's never boring but it sure could move quicker. More time spent at the Chameleon Tours kiosk. More of Samantha talking and talking. More of the Commandant not believing the Doctor. A long sequence with Jean Rock pretending to be sick so the nurse leaves the First Aid room and the Doctor can investigate it. A lot of stuff which seems OK. Until you really start thinking and you think, this seems like padding. Why the side saga with the sick bay? Even the opening section with the laser seems a bit like padding. There is a reason why.

You'll notice that in this season and the previous one all the stories are four parts, except for those that are Dalek-related. This was a conscious decision of the previous production team. The Dalek stories would appear every six months (ish) and those were the big events. The four-part stories could get the maximum out of the budget and keep people coming back every month for a new non-Dalek story. (Looking at the ratings, it's obvious that the Daleks boost things. At their best, the ratings carry on high into the next few stories and then gradually fade away. So, the Daleks every six months will hopefully boost the show when needed.)

Anyway, this story is six episodes. Why is that? Looking at the history of *Doctor Who*, the Chameleons have certainly never reappeared. They're not a much beloved monster or villain or whatever the heck they are. So, why does this story get the boost and how did that happen? It's the standard story really. Another story fell apart and two episodes need to be added on somewhere. At the point this happened, "The Faceless Ones" was the only one that could be fiddled with. It was a 4-part story. David Ellis had never written for the show before. Malcolm Hulke had almost had a story made back in Season 1. ("Behind The Sun") More or less, at the last minute, Hulke and Ellis were asked to expand their four-part story by two more episodes. Take a 100-minute story and make it 150. Said that way one can't imagine how it would work well.

Elizabeth Sandifer in *Tardis Eruditorum* described it best. The story is in three chunks. The opening to when Ben is taken. From that point to the plane entering the station. And from that point until the end. What the writers did was expand each chunk by about 2/3 of an episode each. So, that meant adding another 16 minutes or so of running about in the first two episodes. Another 15 minutes or so of investigation in episodes three and four. And 16 more to the resolution episodes. So, there isn't one spot that's slower than another. Each segment is just a bit slower than it should be. And most of the extra material is added in the studio. So, keep an eye out. Whenever we're in the studio, you can decide: "Padding or not?" I have the novelization here somewhere. I should read it again. Unless I ate it.

Overall, a good episode. The padding is starting to show. Malcom and David are doing their best. But stuff like this rarely works to everyone's advantage. Let's see how the remaining two parts let the story go and flow. We can do a padding check, if need be.

The Faceless Ones

Episode Five

Episode 161: (May 6, 1967) The plan of the Chameleons is finally revealed. There was an explosion and they lost their identities. So, they are stealing the identities of young people. They're on the last round of collections before leaving.

Cliffhanger: The Doctor and Nurse Pinter are captured by Captain Blade on the Chameleon satellite.

Nurse Pinter! Captain Blade! The Commandant! Jean Rock! The Doctor! Sam! Boy, I kind of miss Ben and Polly. They've only got one more episode left so hopefully we will get some quality time soon.

Anyway, we finally learn what's up. And, yes, "we lost our identities in an explosion" is not the greatest of explanations. Plenty have giggled at that over time. However, the info is being provided by Chameleon Meadows. So, I always looked at it this way: This Chameleon doesn't know where all the bodies are hidden. (Not a euphemism. The bodies of all the missing people involved in the airport are stashed on the grounds of the airport. The rest of them are miniaturized on the satellite.) So, why would he know the full story behind what's happening? Maybe they didn't tell him. "He's not the smartest one. Tell him there was an explosion."

Of course, we call them the Chameleons. They can't really be called that. That's what they became after the "explosion." Unless they really were Chameleons? Maybe that's why it's so tough for them to keep their identity. They don't really have any. I don't know. Maybe we'll learn more in the next episode.

Thank goodness for animation. There are several minutes were Jamie hides on the airplane and then sneaks around. In the telesnap recon, that run of minutes goes on and on and it's tough to gauge what's happening. Here, it's nice to see. I also like that the one who sees all the minutiae of the plan is Jamie. The one least likely to understand any of it sees everything in full.

It's nice to have everyone on the Doctor's side finally. Although, I feel like we're less and less in an airport as the story goes along. It's a strange moment to watch the Doctor take Chameleon Nurse Pinter to the sick bay with two burly police officers assisting him. But then, he is trying to save the day. The First Doctor could take control like this, as he did in "The War Machines." I somehow feel like the Second Doctor is more equipped for this because he can run for his life if need be and generally be more active. Troughton has settled in beautifully now. Again, I wish we could see more of the episodes. The rest of the season isn't going to help that much. Season 5 will be spotty. I am pretty interested to see how this serial ends, even though I know it already. The easy movement between the satellite and the airport is becoming quite charming.

One of the best bits here (and the padding delays it for quite some time) is the Controller who looks like the Inspector constantly insisting that humans are animals and the Doctor has met his match. He's got that smugness that Sensorite Three (The City Administrator) had so long ago. I find it amusing. The only problem is that we want to see the Doctor and The Controller meet up and match wits. But the spacing/pacing of everything keeps keeping that away from us. Come on! Let's all meet up. Well, we know it's going to happen in the next episode, if it happens. Let's see.

The Faceless Ones

Episode Six

Episode 162: (May 13, 1967) The hunt for the hidden bodies begins. The Doctor and the Controller finally meet.

Cliffhanger: We say goodbye to Ben and Polly. Then someone steals the TARDIS! If it's not one thing...

Blade calls the Doctor "human." And that seems odd. At this point in the show, we still haven't fully established what the Doctor is. But, in the previous episode, Chameleon Jamie says the Doctor is not human. Why the confusion? The Chameleons have already lost their identities. Now, they seem to be losing their minds.

A nice closing episode. Mainly made up of a very tense scene where a very relaxed Doctor sits in the Chameleon's control room bluffing and bluffing. While, down on the Earth's surface, everyone is hunting for the bodies. Yes, it does seem a little odd. The bodies are all in cars in a parking lot. Presumably, they dissolve or something soon. I imagine there are going to be some angry people when they come to examine the cars and find a lot of wet, oozy clothes. Anyway, Sam and Jean and some cops hunt for the bodies. There's a nice fight between Sam and the Chameleon.

Let's talk about Sam. She's from Liverpool. She picks on Jean Rock for being rather posh at one point. She's loud. A precursor to Donna Noble? Maybe. She's possibly less annoying than Donna was at the start though. Sam kind of hovers around the edges of the story. She seems like she might become a companion at one point. But then, she just says goodbye to Jamie. It's fun to have her here…

Until Ben and Polly reappear for a very brief scene. Just long enough to say goodbye. I thought, "Oh no, even though many of their episodes are lost, I shall miss them." The Doctor and Jamie do their best to keep their brave faces on. But everyone's close to tears when they leave. It's not a bad leaving like "Where did Dodo go?" I can't say it's a great leaving through. Especially because they're only on film for this episode. Location film footage was done before the other episodes. So, the last scene where they were actually in the studio was Episode 2. Sigh. Is it sexist that the Doctor says to Polly that she should take care of Ben when he becomes an Admiral? Possibly. But I've got tears in my eyes. If you don't, go back to "The War Machines" and watch Dodo leave. That's more your speed. I've always thought that when the Doctor said that to Polly there is an underlying feeling of "You're the tough one here, Polly. Keep it going. Please." The way he leans closer to Polly when he speaks to her speaks volumes to me.

The Chameleons are gone too. The Doctor mediates with them and they go away. Not a normal way to end an episode. One that feels very Malcolm Hulke. We will hear more from him soon. I do hope the Chameleons found some way to survive. MEDIATION! It's the way to go! The Controller is very lofty and superior throughout. The Doctor defeats him by simply not paying attention. By simply carrying on what he's doing regardless. Their plan was epic and would have worked if that pesky Doctor and his friends hadn't butted in.

Others have said this but it's true: Jamie without the Scottish accent is a bit unnerving. I have met Mr. Hines at a few conventions. Just briefly. Saying "You're awesome, Jamie!" and stuff like that. He almost always wears a kilt. Seeing him here, even when animated, feels strange with that voice. The Doctor comments on it so we all know it's odd. Enough of this: Let's find the TARDIS.

THE EVIL OF THE DALEKS

Episode One

Written by David Whitaker

Directed by Derek Martinus

Episode 163: (May 20, 1967) The Doctor and Jamie are led on a convoluted journey to try and find the TARDIS.

Cliffhanger: A Dalek appears in the teleporter.

Right away, please check the second volume of *About Time*. It has a very good essay in it about how one sets a trap for someone like the Doctor. This whole episode is an elaborate plan by Mr. Waterfield, expert in Victorian timepieces to get the Doctor to him. It begins with stealing the TARDIS. It involves a matchbook, a strange clipboard, fake Scottish names and all sorts of guys. But one needs to ask themselves, how did they plan this elaborate ruse when the Doctor never knows where he's going to be next? Read the essay for some insight into that.

The plan, by the way, is hopelessly overelaborate. The Doctor and Jamie spend most of their time just being confused by an endless array of clues. In the end, I'm not sure if any of this is needed. The reason why Waterfield is doing this is to get the Doctor to his shop. Then, get the Doctor to the teleporter to send him back in time to help the Daleks. Obviously, the Doctor is not going to help the Daleks. But the Doctor doesn't know they're involved. (He doesn't know the name of the story.) So, why not send someone to talk to him? "This gentleman would like to talk with you." "What's with all the fal-der-al?" All this chicanery makes for a fun episode. But one that feels a bit drawn-out. Especially as it spends so much time cutting away from the Doctor and Jamie to Waterfield and his cronies.

That's one of the things that does confuse the episode. Waterfield is a very specific "Edwardian Grandfather" type character. Then, we get his helpers: Bob Hall, Perry and Kennedy. It's tough enough keeping every character straight in your head during the next episode, which survives. In this animated episode, I honestly got lost in all the names. Why are there so many people involved? I guess, again, to keep the Doctor and Jamie guessing all the time. But, if you want to meet the Doctor, why go through all this?

It is nice to start the story at Gatwick airport. It makes one think, for a moment, "Hey! Maybe they'll run into Ben and Polly one more time!" It's nice to hear mention of the Commandant. But, to the Doctor, that story is closed. We are now in a brand-new adventure. The continuity is sweet though, especially because the new adventure seems so odd. Extra especially with the title. People spending 25 minutes waiting for Daleks to show. Presumably, they knew the show would make them wait a week. And they keep it convoluted enough that I forgot about Daleks until I first saw Waterfield's teleporting room. (Hey! The first season of *Star Trek* just wrapped a little while ago in the U.S. Did someone on *Doctor Who* see their teleporters?) I would really love to know what made Whitaker decide to begin the story like this. When everything really gets going, one is tempted to call it filler. I'd like to think Whitaker was just doing a "first episode" of a Dalek story in a completely different way then we're used to. Be honest. Did you expect "Evil of the Daleks" to begin like this? No. Neither did I. I'm going with "Mr. Whitaker was a clever man." I believe that.

Sad Note: When Jamie and The Doctor are waiting at the coffee bar, in the original audio The Beatles play. In the animated version, we get some generic Muzak. That's too bad. Because they were playing "Do You Want To Know A Secret?" I think that's a good laugh.

The Evil of the Daleks

Episode Two

Episode 164: (May 27, 1967) The Doctor and Jamie are sent back to a Victorian mansion in 1888 where they meet up with their nemesis and encounter some weird ideas about time travel. (June 2, 1866)

Cliffhanger: The Daleks are ready for the Doctor to begin experimenting on Jamie.

Please note: This is the last existing episode of Season Four and only the 10th episode from the season overall. The animated episodes have been a godsend but it's still rather shocking how little of Troughton's first season survives.

The first 10 minutes take place in 1966. And then we're back in 1866. Bye bye 1966! With "The War Machines," "The Faceless Ones" and the first episode of this story, I think we've spent more time in that period than any other. And, yes, it was swinging! And, yes, miniskirts are here and some of us rejoice. The jump from one century to the other is interesting. The Doctor and Jamie handle it well. Of course, they may be 100 years away from the TARDIS, which would stink. But the difference between Polly in her short skirt and white go-go boots two episodes ago and Victoria Waterfield in her huge Victorian dress with bustle and everything is something. (Although, Mollie Dawson, the maid/ serving girl, has a cheeky streak to her that I like. Some wish she had been the companion instead of Victoria.)

We get to meet Maxtible in this episode. He's a blustery strange man with an interest in the "sciences" and a glorious beard. Seeing him next to Waterfield is like seeing the Bizarro Earth version of Laurel & Hardy. (Although, I think these guys probably never got a laugh together in their lives.) They're a fun duo in their own way. I love how Maxtible is so blustery, like Zaroff. We know that the blusterier we get towards the Doctor, the more this Doctor gets quiet and more studied, which is what happens here. The gradual reveal of their mad plan involving mirrors in a cabinet and reflections and then the mention of static electricity makes the Doctor's eyes go wider and wider. Let's give the Dalek props here. It knows the exact moment to pop out of the cabinet to announce itself.

The Daleks here are interesting ones like they have been in the past few stories. The Dalek who badgers Victoria is rather funny. Sounding like a belligerent prison guard. The Daleks talking to Maxtible and Waterfield are great. I like when the Daleks aren't doing the standard "trying to take over the world" kind of thing. In both Whitaker's stories, they're up to something a little different, a little odd. The Human Factor element of this one is certainly a novel Dalek approach to the destruction of all humanity.

Jamie doesn't do much. He flirts briefly with Mollie. Confuses her. (The Doctor confuses her too.) Then, he gets knocked out by a wide-eyed man who comes in through the side door. This Victorian era is less safe than I thought it was if ruffians just stroll into mansions and beat people over the head. I expected a Dalek eyestalk to poke out of his forehead at one moment. (That does not happen.) Jamie will have a lot to do in upcoming episodes so he could use the rest.

Oh, that portrait above the fireplace. It's Waterfield's wife. She's dead but Victoria, his daughter, is the spitting image. They make sure to tell us that twice. I was hoping it would happen a third time and that there would be some sort of punchline. (There isn't. Not in this episode anyway.)

The Evil of the Daleks

Episode Three

Episode 165: (June 3, 1967) It takes some time but the test of the Human Factor has begun.

Cliffhanger: Jamie is about to meet Kamal.

Boy, there are a lot of people in this story. I think just hearing them on audio or maybe even reading about them in John Peel's novelization doesn't fully give them to you. This one introduces Terrel the schizoid fiancé of Maxtible's daughter. And some random thug. And Kamal, the giant Turk who will crush Jamie! (Yeah, that's a bit unfortunate. Not as unfortunate as what the next serial holds for us but nothing great.) In fact, if the next episode or two is going to be Jamie trying to find Victoria, then all these characters seem superfluous. They do give us a real feel of the country home. A bit of *The Forsythe Saga* with Daleks. But, at the same time, they do all seem to slow the story down.

Not too much though. Jamie begins his quest at the end. He goes on his own accord, being tricked by The Doctor and Waterfield. He does have a heck of an argument with The Doctor. We've had people argue with the Doctor before. But it hasn't been since Barbara yelled at the First Doctor during "The Brink of Disaster," that there's been anything like this. And Jamie is right. He is being lied to. He is being sent to do some dirty work. I'd be pissed too. The Daleks mention that the Doctor is more than human. The way he treats Jamie here attests to that. Yes, he wants the TARDIS back. But he almost seems a little too gleeful when they get Jamie to go after Victoria.

The episode doesn't have a lot of incidents. It's just laying down the track for the upcoming episodes. Mollie and Jamie have a nice flirty scene. Maxtible seems very proud of bringing in Kamal. Arthur acts weird. Ms. Maxtible is tough to pay attention to and Victoria does very little but get moved from one room to another. However, at the end of the episode, it has all paid off. Everyone is in their place. Everyone is set to go. Let's find the Human Factor!

I like the Arthur character. He shows up acting one way. A sound goes off in his head and he acts another way. Soon after that he's acting another way. I always forget this character is in here but he always makes me giggle. Mainly because I don't know what purpose he serves. He reminds me of a Bob & Ray character called Captain Wolf Larsen. The Captain has his own seafaring vessel and he's a decent guy. But then, the boom swings around the deck and hits him in the head. Suddenly, he's a mean guy who goes around punching everyone. Then, he gets hit again and he's fine. That's Arthur Terrel. But Arthur's kind of not meant to be funny.

It's not a stopgap episode because it is setting things up. It is interesting how this new group of characters come out of nowhere to hog the spotlight here. The Daleks are back. The Doctor is going up against them. So, let's spend fifteen seconds watching Victoria pack her shoes. Let's watch Terrel and that other guy argue about how much one of them should get paid. It's not padding but it feels odd. Like introducing a slew of characters in a slasher film that you just know are going to get killed shortly. You must meet them. There's no getting around that. And yet, we know they won't be around long so it kind of feels like someone's time is being wasted. At least, Jamie has begun his journey by the end. Now, we can see what happens next. (Unless there are 4 more characters waiting in the wings.)

The Evil of the Daleks

Episode Four

Episode 166: (June 10, 1967) Jamie and Kamal search for Victoria. Arthur is a jerk. Alchemy comes up.

Cliffhanger: A Dalek glides behind Kamal and Jamie.

Patrick Troughton was on vacation for this episode so he only has one scene. But it's a good one. We watch (well, we hear/ watch animated) Jamie and Kamal fight to the death. It ends with Jamie saving the "big Turk." The Doctor is in a control room with a Dalek. The Dalek is confused about this. The Doctor points out that this is part of the Human Factor. Mercy. There must always be mercy. Which mirrors, so long from now but also kind of in the past, when the Doctor speaks to young Davros in "The Witch's Familiar." When he tells Davros, that heroes and villains don't matter. As long as there's mercy. That's a major plot point of that story. That's the plot point that resolves the story. Here it's a quick moment amongst many other moments but it shows that the Doctors are all the same no matter when they are.

Much of the episode is Jamie and his new buddy sneaking around looking for Victoria. There are a couple of death traps, Indiana Jones-style and Dalek-style. We're meant to know that the Daleks are monitoring every moment. While that is occurring, the Doctor is accruing Human Factor info for them. So far, it all seems to make sense and be OK.

There's some more stuff with Arthur Terrel. Boy, I hope this has some kind of big payoff. He spends about two minutes yelling at and berating Mollie. It's not fun to watch. He may be under the control of something or other but that doesn't mean I have to like him. (I like him when he's not under anything's control, if that helps.) That scene isn't very nice. It certainly gets your dander up. If you're the sort of person who wants their dander up. But it seems like petty garbage alongside everything else.

My favorite scene after the mercy one is with Maxtible and Ruth, his daughter. I applaud the animators toning down Maxtible's beard. It's much calmer here than it is in the actual story itself. (Unless he gave it a big trim in between episodes.) Maxtible begs the Dalek for something. Then, he tells Ruth what it is. Good old-fashioned alchemy at its basest form. Alchemy is the sort of science (utterly fascinating by the way) that involved transmuting baser elements into more powerful/ more valuable ones. Really, that's all metaphor. It's about achieving some sort of higher plane for the human body and soul using the elements as a starting point. But, for many, it was about one thing: turning lead into gold. That's what Maxtible is after. He has seemed a bit like a nut. Maybe it was the crazy beard. Maybe the animators kept it under control because anyone with a beard like this must obviously be screwball. I don't know. But that's what Maxtible is after. He wants the formula to turn lead into gold, which the Daleks say they have. And you know what? I believe they do.

The episode works all right. It's no classic but mixing the house drama with the great escapade keeps it alive. So, there's never a point where it's boring. However, we do need the Doctor back. This could all grow wearisome quickly.

The Evil of the Daleks

Episode Five

Episode 167: (June 17, 1967) The Human Factor has been collected. It is going to be placed in three Daleks.

Cliffhanger: The three Daleks with the human factor in them begin to play with the Doctor.

This is a great episode, mainly because we finally get the Human Factor completed and the Doctor is back. For some reason, I always remember this episode being full of padding. I always remember the trials and tribulations with Kamal going on for a very long time. Well, they don't. At least not anymore. I think it's due to the animation. I remember when this serial came out on cassette back in the early 1990s. Frazier Hines did the narration for it and he did his best. But during the first episode, the last episode and this one there are long stretches of silence. Well, the music is going but much of it is creeping around or fighting. Here we have the opening with the Dalek on the balcony. Then, we have the swordfight in between Jamie and Arthur. You can only imagine how nice it is to see the movement here. It helps the episode flow in a way that it never has before. I don't even remember the novelization working this well.

Anyway, the Doctor is back and he gets several excellent scenes here. His opening scene with Arthur Terrel is a great one. Arthur is not very nice. But the Doctor refuses to act like he's being anything but nice. The angrier Arthur gets, the more infuriating the Doctor becomes towards him. I think it's a very funny scene. Especially when Arthur pulls out a sword and the Doctor figures that he's somehow magnetic and full of electricity. It all ends with the Doctor's line about being a professor of a larger university of which human nature is only a part. Arthur, you have been zinged!

The Doctor also has an excellent chat with Waterfield. He is terrified about the Human Factor being put into the Daleks. From what I can see, the Doctor isn't too keen on it either. (Heck Waterfield tries to knock the Doctor out. They're a violent bunch around here.) And his calm, low key explanation of why they need to keep doing what they're doing and see what happens is excellent. As I've said before, it's a heartbreaker that we're missing so many of Troughton's episodes, especially the earlier ones. But I like this animated business. It's working for me.

Victoria, Kamal and Jamie make a decent team here. The reveal of the hidden door in the small room is nice. There's a sense of adventure and excitement here, especially as they try to keep away from the Daleks. Although, what exactly are the Daleks doing with the door they're trying to break through? I get that they want to keep them alive but surely something less vague would work better. Or maybe not.

And hey, Arthur, Ruth and Mollie all leave at the end of the episode. Arthur was under someone's control. They're getting out of there because things are going all screwy. Oddly enough, the last moments with Arthur here are kind of nice. He generally seems contrite and a little bit like a nice man for a moment. I want to see "The Arthur Terrel Show!"

The only part of the episode that does seem a bit like filler is Maxtible hypnotizing Mollie to get her to forget about seeing Victoria. Somehow it seems unnecessary to me. Yes, Maxtible can do another zany thing but I feel like we all could have got by just fine without seeing that, unless Maxtible hypnotizes a Dalek later, of course.

The Evil of the Daleks

Episode Six

Episode 168: (June 24, 1967): Everyone goes to Skaro! The Doctor has been tricked.

Cliffhanger: The Doctor will take the Dalek Factor throughout the universe and spread it.

The Dalek Supreme finally makes an appearance. I don't remember if he/ they/ it has been mentioned before. But The Doctor recognizes it. The gigantic Dalek with the huge voice strapped in with tubes and wires into the mainframe of Skaroine technology. And he's played the Doctor for a fool. From the stealing of the TARDIS to the creation of the three "human" Daleks, the Doctor has been led right to this moment. The Evil (and the Power and the Glory) of the Daleks has begun! Even despite the Victorian mansion stuff maybe going on a bit long, at this point, the story is huge. David Whitaker was asked to write this as the final saying "goodbye" to the Daleks. * (I forgot that Gerry Davis is gone as script editor. Peter Bryant has taken over.) He's has done a heck of a job. It's a beauty of a buildup.

The Doctor gets a lovely scene with the "human" Daleks. He names them Alpha, Beta and Omega. He plays with them. They call him and Jamie "friend." There's a lovely moment in the animation where the Daleks suddenly must leave and they go to the mirror cupboard. The final one tells the Doctor that they've been called away to Skaro. Right before it goes, it looks at the Doctor and says "Friend." That's nice. That's not a moment one expected.

Maxtible, of course, is going nuttier and nuttier. We can see why they cleared everyone out in the last episode as we're blowing up the mansion. I hope there was no one else in it. They just took Mollie the

Maid. I feel like a place this big has a whole upstairs/ downstairs thing going and we just blew up the servants. Maybe that's an idea for a future novel or audio adventure?

So, we get an episode and a half set in 1966, five episodes in 1866 and then an episode and a half on the Planet Skaro. Date unknown. That's *Doctor Who* for you, folks. No one else back then is doing this kind of thing.

To wrap up this episode, I want to mention something that I really noticed in the animation: Now, when they shoot these episodes, they're shot at once. Over the course of a couple hours on a Saturday evening. Anything on film is played into the studio. All the sets are in the studio and everyone does their acting on them. The way one can sort of tell that something big is happening in this episode, location-wise, is to count the sets they're using. You'll notice that until they go to Skaro the whole thing takes place in the lab. We never leave it. Everyone goes in and out of the set like it's a stage play. When the Daleks tell Maxtible to get the Doctor, he doesn't leave. He just goes to various doors and yells the Doctor's name. When the Doctor and Jamie leave after the Daleks do, Maxtible and Waterfield come in. That's the giveaway that "We're using most of the studio for non-mansion sets. We have this one still but the others are Skaro." It's a little claustrophobic and strange. Because we keep thinking "Someone should go out of the room." But they never do. Because they can't. Because they'll be on Skaro. So, presumably next week, we'll get a relatively biggish set to take the place of the mansion. Let's find out.

*Terry Nation owned the rights. He was taking them to America to try to get them their own show. *My Favorite Dalek*. It would be 4 ½ years before the Daleks would be on *Doctor Who* again. Luckily, the team had another great villain/ monster standing by. And maybe a few others.

The Evil of the Daleks

Episode Seven

Episode 169: (July 1, 1967) The Dalek Factor is harnessed. It's given to Maxtible and it works. Luckily, the Doctor has a trick up his sleeve.

Cliffhanger: Victoria is taken onboard the TARDIS. In the rubble, there seems to be one Dalek left alive.

And the epic ends! And the season ends! And the Daleks are done for… for now.

The story ends well. Big, loud and lots of explosions. All of it predicate on the Doctor pulling a little trick. Always keep some Human Factor handy in your pocket. You never know when you'll need it. Again, the animation sells a lot of the visuals of the episode here. I've always thought that Maxtible's voice when he's a human Dalek was laughable. But it works in the animation. (It helps that they have toned down that beard.) The desolate sort of feel of Skaro is in such stark contrast to the beauty of the Victorian mansion. The Daleks aren't after the good things in life. They just want to kill you if you're not a Dalek.

The episode has a dark streak to it. (I thought Kamal getting pushed into the lava pit was a bit much.) Luckily, the darkness is pointed at the Daleks. The Emperor's booming voice encouraging warring Daleks to not fight in his control room is alternately funny and frightening. All the images, all the sounds, of the Daleks fighting is something. It's pretty much the perfect ending to the Daleks. For many years, chronologically this was kind of the end of the Daleks. All the other stories could be slotted in behind it. But then, we got "Genesis of the Daleks" and then we got a Time War. Who knows where this story is now in the whole scheme of things? It is a final though. If *Doctor Who* had ended in the 1960s, the Daleks would have been remembered for going out with a bang.

It's odd. The Doctor doesn't really do much in the episode. Yes, he does change the Dalek Factor to the Human Factor and convince the Emperor to send Daleks through it which creates and army of Human Daleks that fight the regular Daleks... maybe he does do a lot. His main thing was already done two episodes ago. Giving Alpha, Beta and Omega their human emotions spreads through the Daleks (in varying ways). The chants of "Obey!" mixed with the chants of "Why?" are wonderful.

Maxtible, of course, becomes a Human Dalek. He's last seen wandering off chanting "Kill! Kill!" Waterfield dies saving the Doctor's life in the sweetest moment of the episode. "You saved my life." "Good life to save." Very modern line. Very modern moment. It breaks Victoria's heart but she has a new family now. And, yes, we will see her in the TARDIS soon.

Overall, it's an action-packed crazy Dalek finale that does have a lot of the heavy lifting story-wise done in previous episodes. So here, they slot a couple bits into place and the story ends. Like many Doctor Who stories, the huge fighting happens off to one side. The Doctor and his companions are up to something else. Here though, we do get to see the Daleks fight. I think, the animation probably beats out the original fight. The original episode used actual Dalek toys to simulate the armies. I've seen pictures and some behind the scenes photos. It's sure fun to watch. The verisimilitude factor is low.

I do like the moment when the Doctor steps through the "Dalek Factor" archway. His body buckles and shakes. When he steps to the other side, he seems to be a Dalek. Oh no! But he's also gesturing to Jamie and not fully acting like a Dalek. Is he one, or isn't he? One could be forgiven for thinking Jamie might not trust this man anymore, after all those shenanigans in the mansion. The story does something cool. Through many of these serials, the Doctor has been referred to as human. The show seems to have trouble pinning down whether this guy is human or alien or what.

Here, finally, we get the definitive proof. Earlier, the Doctor is told he can't participate in the adventures because he is more than human. Then, the Doctor tells Terrel that he is a professor of an academy much wider than humanity. Now here, the Dalek Factor does not affect him. Because he is not human. What is he? Who is he? Questions for the future. For now, the Daleks are gone. And an alien Doctor is taking his two friends on more adventures. Onto Season Five!

SEASON FIVE

1967-1968

THE TOMB OF THE CYBERMEN

Written by Kit Pedler and Gerry Davis

Directed by Morris Barry

Episode One

Episode 170: (September 2, 1967) The Doctor, Jamie and Victoria land on the planet Telos. They meet up with an archaeological expedition that is looking for the famed Tomb of the Cybermen.

Cliffhanger: Jamie and that one guy's fiddling around results in that one guy dying and the first appearance of a Cyberman. I think.

The season begins! And it starts with a wonderful sequence shot on film, where the camera follows The TARDIS crew through the doors into the control room. They have a lovely chat. The fact that it's on film makes it feel more spacious when they enter. Victoria asks some questions. And the Doctor reveals that he's about 450 years old. Then, adventure begins! In a quarry.

Again, some lovely stuff here on film. The expedition moving through the hills of sand, dirt or whatever it is. The shot where we follow Toberman as he walks up to the edge of the clifftop is excellent. It really gives the feeling of extra production value. The place feels expansive. It isn't until we blow open the entrance to the Cybertomb that we finally say "Oh look! We're back in the studio." Suddenly, everything feels smaller. Even though the Cyber doors are huge.

The doors have a great image of a cyberman next to them. That's kind of the Cyberthing here: branding. There will be constant reminders throughout the next four episodes that this is a Cybertomb, even when there are no Cybermen around. Of course, there's the Cybermat, but more about that later. Suffice it to say, the opening of this story gives it a nice big feel. Then, we enter the control room and that becomes our main "base under siege" set. Get used to it. We'll spend a lot of time in it.

The expedition might be well-meaning but they're inept. Of course, we start with the guy who rushes the doors and gets electrocuted. Come on, my friend. You're going to have to do better than that. And, once they get in, there's a weird feeling that the Doctor is the one doing everything. You have to wonder: why? What is he up to? He's acting very curious about everything but is there an ulterior motive. Surely it can't be "I'm trying to see if the Cybermen are really here." Who else would have set this up? Is it a joke tomb that the Dalek's put together? Let's find out.

It is nice to have Victoria with the group. She comes to terms with going from wearing the huge Victorian outfit to a miniskirt fairly quickly. But I applaud her adaptation. Now, we've got two lovelies in the TARDIS showing off their legs.

We'll talk more about the archaeological group in the next episodes when we learn more about them. Suffice it to say, that's it's the third multinational group of scientists and soldiers given to us by Pedler and Davis in as many months. It's tough yet to say whether they're better or worse than the other two. But, having a look at Klieg, Kaftan and Toberman… "Worse" might be the immediate thought. At least in this story we're exploring a place that no one knows. It's like the setup of their other stories but just sort of reversed. Somehow, as mentioned, it ends up in one big room. But where are the Cybermen? I think this episode works better in the novelization. For some reason, once they enter the tomb, the pacing of the episode slows way down. It seems to take much longer than it should. I'm trying to remember the first time I saw it in 1992. (It would have been in omnibus form.) I think the suspense kept me tuned in a little more intently. Multiple viewings don't help.

The Tomb of the Cybermen

Episode Two

Episode 171: (September 9, 1967) They go underground and find the tombs. They're frozen. Not for long.

Cliffhanger: The Cyberleader announces that everyone there shall become like them.

One thing: It just occurred to me that we are in the third variation of the Pedler/ Davis Cyberman/ base under siege type story within the course of a year. (Less than a year.) And, in a space where the writers and the producers are running the stories in circles, they introduce a character named Victoria. As I watched her in this episode, I called her "Vicki" at one point. My immediate reaction was: No. We have a Vicki. A Vicki who specifically said she was not a "Victoria" but a "Vicki." So, the new team chooses as their new companion name: Victoria. What? It's a "The Seeds of Death" and "The Seeds of Doom" sort of thing. Why are they so similar? (I do note that Victor Pemberton is script editor on this story. His one and only script editing job with the show. But he will re-appear later. His story that he re-appears with is very similar to so many stories of this period.) I feel like the production crew was really trying to limit what the show could do at this point. Whether they did it on purpose or whether they did it accidentally, the character name choice seems to highlight the lowered creative bar for this era.

Even though, I do love it. The show goes through so many cycles, so many twists and turns, so many changes in its decades on the air, that this isn't the ruination of the show. It's another way to try and do the show. For example, I firmly believe that the Whitaker/ Chibnall era will be looked at quite fondly in the future. As it aired, it wasn't what people wanted. Let it ride.

As for the episode, it has a huge iconic moment. The tombs. As "Space Adventure" plays on the soundtrack, the Cyberman slowly leave their giant tomb. It's a huge set shot on film and it is magnificent. Of course, most of that room is in another set and on video. But they do a nice job of cutting between the two. And, especially on the original VHS, which is all from a film print with no manipulation, it looks great. The DVD re-jiggers it a bit to make it look more obvious, more the way it would have looked as aired. It's still a huge moment though. Although, I have always thought it a bit amusing how quickly everything freezes and then unfreezes and then freezes again. That's Cyber tech for you! (Also, they don't go that far down. Yet they're on the same level when they meet the tombs, which go four or five stories up in the air. Did no one notice an odd jutting out of the ground when they were exploring the quarry?)

The villains in this one are interesting. Klieg is almost competent. He releases the Cybermen from the tomb. But he requires some surreptitious help from the Doctor to get the hatch open to get them from the tomb. Kaftan has a big black man by her side to rough people up. (That's unfortunate.) She also looks so constantly smug throughout. Her and Klieg aren't the brightest bulbs in the bunch. They have Toberman rip up the controls of the ship to keep them there. (Why wouldn't this be obvious to everyone? It's so obvious to the viewer. And there's something about that "American" astronaut that always makes me giggle. What part of America are you from, sir? The 1760s?) I love incompetent villains who have some money and strength who believe themselves superior to everyone else. I'm thinking of The Chameleons here. Or some of the evil Sensorites. They're like 6-year-olds on the playground bullying other kids who suddenly come across kids twice their age. They can pull of subterfuge for a bit. It's going to fall apart. I think the Cyberleader's appearance at the end might be a sign of that.

(Oh, I always love the moment when Victoria throws a Cybermat in her purse. First, I want a 500-Year Diary. (It's like a *Gravity Falls* manual thing.) Second, she keeps souvenirs. Delightful.)

The Tomb of The Cybermen

Episode Three

Episode 172: (September 16, 1967) The Cybermen attempt to assimilate the humans. There are troubles.

Cliffhanger: Klieg and Kaftan are out of the testing room. Klieg fires the X-ray laser at the Doctor.

It's time to mention the behind-the-scenes kerfuffle happening around now. Gerry Davis is gone. Yes, he wrote this story and he will be back at least once more. But he is done. He started around "The Ark" and his script editing duties wrapped up on "The Evil of the Daleks." Innes Lloyd is ready to go too. But he is merely on vacation here. Peter Bryant, who had assisted as script editor, produces this story. Victor Pemberton, who played Jules in "The Moonbase," is script editing here. Things are beginning to get a little wacky. It's odd because the "base under siege" scenario isn't fully in place yet. This season is the one where almost all the stories are variations of base under siege. And yet, we think of Lloyd and Davis being the ones who did those. In the end, they instigated. The confusion of producers and script editors after them just continued what they were doing. Season Six will begin some variation again. The Lloyd/Davis template will hang on for a while. How is it doing in this episode?

First, I don't understand the Hopper and Victoria exchange about "To Be A Woman" and "How would you know, honey?" I never have. I can make guesses about what it means. But, those are only vague guesses and don't really amount to much. Anyway...

Why do they lock Klieg and Kaftan up in a room with weapons? I don't know. All I can say is that maybe the Doctor is up to something again. Maybe he did it deliberately. Maybe he didn't expect Captain Hopper to show up and free them. Maybe he had a plan all along and that involved them getting back into the Cybertombs. That's all I can come up with. Otherwise, it makes the Doctor seem a bit dim. And it makes everyone who goes along with him and doesn't make suggestions seem dimmer.

I have a question about the way the Cyber controls work. How do the Captain and his second-in-command break into the Cyber hatch by simply following the wires? Why is it a big logistical hoo-hah if one can just unscrew the panel and follow the wires? That makes no sense. If the Cyberguys are looking for higher intellects, how do they know they won't be invaded by a bunch of rednecks who can hotwire a car? Is that the way this technology works? It doesn't seem terribly efficient. Unless they can also use people that can hotwire cars. Then, it all makes sense. The show is known for having a bunch of weird inconsistencies. If you look at them from another viewpoint, maybe they make sense. Look at the fact that they want to convert Toberman. They make a big play about only wanting the smartest. Then they pick the big, dumb guy. Well, he's strong. Surely, the Cyber Race need a couple strong guys to enforce their power. (Although, I thought they were all made stronger by the process.) Maybe a Poindexter isn't as strong as an actual strong guy. I don't know.

I'll wrap this up with two things: 1) The Cybermat attack is well done. One can't imagine an attack like that using multiple cameras and shooting live could work. But, it pretty much does. That is a thumbs up to the director, the editor and the visual effects gang. 2) The scene with the Doctor and Victoria chatting. (Remember that the Americans call her "Vic.") The Doctor and Victoria have a sweet chat about the Doctor's age, her father and his family. We know so little of the Doctor's family apart from Susan. It's a lovely chat. The Doctor is so sincere and it works so well. The scene is stuck in there like the island chat in the X-Files episode "Quagmire." It's just as important and just as lovely.

The Tomb of the Cyberman

Episode Four

Episode 173: (September 23, 1967) The Doctor must close the tomb.

Cliffhanger: Onto their next adventure.

"This door is closed."

In the novelization, The Doctor and Jamie are yelling at Toberman to get away from the door or he will be electrocuted. It happens much quicker in the televised version. (Although Toberman seals the Cyber controller in and the book is done a page later.) In the televised version, Toberman has three lines. All great. It gives him a bit more of a heroic flare. The character isn't without problems. Like Kamal in the previous story, (the novelization refers to him as "The Turk" whereas I see him as a big Jamaican guy) he's there for strength. He says very little. He seems dumb. He is under the control of the more "intelligent" people in the story. In the end, he joins the side of good (although Toberman is really fighting for Kaftan, who was bad) and helps. It is problematic. Others have gone into greater detail than I will go into here. His end though is a powerful one. That shot off him in the foreground with the door and the Cyber Controller on the other side really works. His final moments are good ones. As a storyteller myself, I applaud that ending. As someone who is wary of the way non-whites were treated back then, I'm a little grossed out.

Having said that, I have watched this serial many times. Quite often it doesn't do much for me. Episode 1 meandered about for far too long. Episode 2 picked up the pace nicely. Episode 3 had a few too many dumb moments. Episode 4 involved the Cybermen just going back in their tombs and it ends. Much like "The Tenth Planet" there's a really feeling of "Do these people know how to structure a story?' This time, however, I thought it worked quite well. I can still see the flaws. Klieg and Kaftan are persistent, but annoying, villains. Toberman is a problem. The rest of the cast don't really register, including Victoria and Jamie for most of the time. It's basically the Doctor, the Cybermen and the bad guys. Looked at that way, it works. The ensemble assemblage of the two previous Pedler/ Davis stories kind of lost the Doctor in the shuffle. Here, it works nicely.

And yes, it has seemed like the Doctor was deliberately doing all of this. In the end, he has found the Cybermen. Found them circa 2570. He has assessed what they have at their disposal. And he can safely seal them up so they will never harm anyone again. * Hooray! If we look at the whole story from The Doctor's point of view, that is what happened. He landed there at the same time as this expedition because, frankly, he needed people who could be sacrificed if necessary. Thought of like this, this is a much more manipulative Doctor than ever before. Also, this is a Doctor who can control the TARDIS. Maybe he can. Maybe the regeneration freed up something in his mind. Or maybe, it was all an accidental landing. Maybe it was all a coincidence. Or it was the TARDIS taking him where he needed to be. It's tough to say. Maybe it's all these things. Let's see where they land next.

*I do like that we learn what the Cybermen were up to in "The Moonbase." They say they are there to take control of the Gravitron, which is true. But they are mainly there because their body parts had dried up. They needed access to more humanoid bodies. The Cyber Controller does mention that they are "humanoids." I assumed everyone was from Earth. Is something else happening?

THE ABOMINABLE SNOWMEN

By Mervyn Haisman and Henry Lincoln

Directed By Gerald Blake

Episode One

Episode 174: (September 30, 1967) The TARDIS lands in Tibet. The Doctor must return a bell to a monastery. But there's something odd going on here.

Cliffhanger: The Yeti advances on Jamie and Victoria, trapped in the cave.

We're in the early 20th Century. Tibet. The serial opens with a man seeing something killing his friend. Classic Horror film style stuff. Classic Hammer Film horror. In 1957, *The Abominable Snowmen of the Himalayas* hit theaters starring Peter Cushing as Doctor Who (I'm kidding). It was written by Nigel Kneale of Quatermass and lots of other things fame. (He wrote the original script for *Halloween III: Season of the Witch*, which is a film I truly adore.) Kneale's work, like H.G. Wells, is a precursor to *Doctor Who*. So, it only seems right that, after a time, the show would take on one of the tropes he examined: the Yeti. The Abominable Snowman.

I'm a huge fan of the Sasquatch myths and all related. When I heard this title, I immediately fell in love. Then, I discovered that most of it was missing. All but the second episode, in fact. This is not a fast-moving story. It is very deliberately paced. It is, as you can see, the first of six six-part stories in a row. (Remembering that "The Dominators" was originally six but got cut back to five at the last minute.) For a series that spent most of the last two years doing four-part stories, this is a big change. They did seem to have the knack of the four-part stories. As "The Faceless Ones" showed, they could do a six-part story but the pacing could be off. So why six of these in a row? I honestly am not sure. Inflation maybe? Confusion within the production team? Possibly? Maybe someone just loved the long stories. Regardless, we've got a long stretch of long stories ahead of us. Let's have a look at the first episode of this one.

I like the long scene with the TARDIS crew looking for the ghanta. The Doctor's inability to tell them what's up is fun. The moment where the Doctor finds a strange object and is glad to see it but can't remember what it is is lovely. I like Victoria and Jamie rambling around the countryside. The Doctor's rambling around while looking for the monastery is nice too. I just wish we could see it. The model of the monastery looks fine. In the animated version, there's a lovely spaciousness to everything. Apart from a few very static shots (like the "looking for the ghanta" shot), the color version is epic and spacious. The black and white animation is moodier and creepier. Probably feels more like the original episodes.

Where the episode loses me is when the monks immediately believe Travers and imprison the Doctor. Why doesn't the Doctor show them the ghanta? Why do they put him away so quickly? I know Khrisong is security but it seems forced to me. When Travers talks to the Doctor, that gives a little background but one can't help but think the whole time... "Doctor, show them the ghanta or show them the psychic paper. This is silly." It's too convenient. They don't really seem like good Tibetan Buddhist monks to me if this is what they do when someone comes to their monastery. The Meddling Monk was more accommodating!

Anyway, it's a nice set-up episode. Since we can't see the original, try either of the animated versions. Both have their charms. I'm not fond of the way the Doctor is treated but I think we're going to have to get used to that this season. I think that will happen often. We'll see. Another base under siege is slowly about to begin.

The Abominable Snowman

Episode Two

Episode 175: (October 7, 1967) Jamie and Victoria run from a Yeti. The Doctor is tied to the front of the monastery as Yeti bait. We meet the Abbott and the master of the monastery. They're great and they're intelligent. And something is going on...

Cliffhanger: The spheres begin to move on their own.

I do love that this episode exists. Because of the deliberate pace of the show, it doesn't really do much. In a modern-day episode, the stuff that happens here wouldn't take more than 10 minutes. So, once you can grab the groove of it, once you can get into the pace, it works. We are in a monastery for most of it. Put yourself in a church-like frame of mind. Leave out the folk singers trying to pick up the pace and you've got this episode.

There is a Yeti attack. Two Yeti Attacks, in fact. One at the beginning and one at the end. The Doctor spends the majority of his time tied up outside the monastery looking uncomfortable. * I still think he should be a bit louder about the ghanta. He mentions that Khrisong already convicted him of murder so how could he explain the ghanta. I don't know. Maybe he should have tried to explain the bell. It would have saved some time. But, as mentioned, we are amid a series of long stories. So, things that may have been cut short or left out of previous seasons may be back here. Because they've got an extra 50 minutes to fill out.

Again, I don't dislike the episode. It just moves at a very deliberate pace throughout. Even when Travers is pointing a shotgun directly at Victoria and Jamie, it moves slow. And boy that Travers, huh? Are we supposed to like him now? He accused the Doctor of murder. He left and the Doctor became Yeti bait. Then he strolls in and says "Oops! The Doctor didn't kill anybody." At that point, if I were Khrisong I would have given Travers a quick knee to the groin. But I'm not the holiest of holies.

I won't go without mentioning the Abbott and Padmasambhava. Pad is the Master of the temple. A disembodied voice that vacillates from kindness and gentility over into a sharp hiss and vague talk of a Great Plan. He also speaks of the Doctor's intelligence and that they have been waiting for a very long time. Something is happening here. Especially when the thing that might be evil knows the Doctor of old. At least no one has to play the Trilogic Game. Although, those spheres are stacked in an orderly Trilogic-esque triangle. The spheres clearly seem to fit inside the Yeti as the ambushed one has a sphere-shaped hole in its chest. Are Pad and the Yeti and the spheres all in cahoots over something big? Over something great? We'll find out. It won't be the next episode.

*One of the tricky things with the episode is the line between outside the monastery and inside, or the entrance to the place. It's like "The Tomb of the Cybermen." We had the whole tomb set on the film. But only the first two levels were in the studio. So, everything felt much smaller when the tomb was in the background. Here there is no transition between the two. There is a shot sowing what's outside the building. Then, there is the entrance. Everyone does their best. And I bet on 405-line TV (which won't be the case in a few months) it was very forgiving. Here, it's like when someone enters the TARDIS and there's that hang time before they enter the console room. "Here comes the yeti!" Pause. There's the yeti!

The Abominable Snowman

Episode Three

Episode 176: (October 14, 1967) The Doctor tries to examine a sphere. Victoria tries to get inside the inner sanctum.

Cliffhanger: The chained and "dead" Yeti begins to come to life in front of Victoria.

Ouch. I don't want to say that this episode is a classic example of "Middle of a 6 parter that's running in place" but that's kind of what it is. Even with the animation, it kind of ends up that way. This episode introduces the concept of the giant board with a hand moving the action figure Yeti across it. Cool animated image, and also when it was just in my mind. This episode has a lot of Victoria creeping around. It has a lot of Travers watching the Yeti. It has creepy Padmasambhava stuff. (They keep his face suitably shrouded by curtains.) The animation, in general, keeps it pretty subdued. *

I think a quick run-down of what mainly happens in this episode gives away the slow game here. Victoria speaks briefly with Padmasambhava. He tells her to go. We learn from Pad that their Great Plan may not be something the Doctor will like. The Great Intelligence is looking for a place to take corporeal form and it will be here. And that's about it. I just finished watching the color animated episode and all I can remember is lots of Victoria wanting to see the Master of the Monastery and Thonmi saying "No" repeatedly. Plus, a long shot of the defunct Yeti laying prone surrounded by wires.

That's too bad. I'd like to think that the serial improves as it goes. But this one stymies me a bit. It's just not exciting. Everything gets in everyone's way of anything happening. Khrisong doesn't want this. He doesn't want that. This can't happen. That can't happen. After a time, you kind of wish for the big cliffhanger and for the episode to end.

At this point Peter Bryant is now the Script Editor and Innes Lloyd is working on getting off the series. So, I feel like maybe Innes isn't really caring so much anymore. And Bryant must love the six-part stories. Maybe he grew up with over-elongated serials in his childhood. I'm not sure. Regardless, this season could become problematic if all the stories are structured like this.

The problem is: What do you talk about? I've no interest in relating the padding that's here. You can feel that there is a big, exciting story lurking here. But this episode isn't going to let it happen yet. So, instead, we sit for 25 minutes and watch nothing go on. It's not incredibly boring. It's just not incredibly exciting. It really is just running in circles for 25 minutes with a revelation or two not quite being enough.

*There is one moment I really loved. When Victoria and The Doctor are questioning the guard outside the monastery, the front of the monastery is behind the guard. Whenever we cut to our time travelers, they have the beauty of the Himalayas behind them. I'm fairly certain that things wouldn't have been this grand in the original version. And I like that they did this.

The Abominable Snowman

Episode Four

Episode 177: (October 21, 1967) The Great Intelligence's plan begins in earnest. The Doctor comes up with a plan of his own. The monks are asked to leave the monastery. The Yeti stand by

Cliffhanger: Victoria enters the Inner Sanctum. She meets Padmasambhava.

This one sort of picks up the pace. Regardless, it is fun to watch the Doctor and Jamie goofing around with the yeti. "I'm going to bung a rock at it." I kind of wish we'd gone inside the TARDIS but we don't. I always find it fun when we go back inside The Ship during an adventure. You can really see here how Jamie and The Doctor have grown into an excellent team.

Victoria and Thonmi are also a decent team. Thonmi's acceptance of the Doctor being able to take the bell 300 years ago but still be alive is nice. The gentle acceptance of a believer. I kind of wish Victoria hadn't used the "Oh, I'm sick. No, I'm not!" thing to free herself from the cell. The episodes aren't loaded with excitement here. So, to use that old trope seems like tired writing. The first two episodes went along strong but these last two have been running in place. Even the Yeti seem reticent to attack in case that's too much going on too far from the ending.

Regarding the animation, it is nice to see images move (in color or B&W) The direction is kind of awkward. A lot of lengthy long shots. There are several scenes where a little extra movement or a few more shots would have helped. (I'm thinking of the scene with the sphere and the Yeti and the TARDIS. It's mostly one long shot that ends up feeling odd.) The fight with Thonmi and the Yeti in the beginning always seems to be using the wrong angles. Also, there are a few moments without dialogue where the animation should be revealing what is happening but doesn't quite. Having said that, I do love having images there even if they're not exactly how I would have done them. Anyway...

Travers still seems a bit of an odd character, even this late in the story. He sees the pyramid and the Yeti. He sees something weird bubbling up from the pyramid of spheres. And he goes loopy. He got in the way in the beginning. And now, he's just kind of meandering around. I'm glad he went to the cave and saw the weirdness happening. But he seems oddly disconnected from the story. "Professor Travers got lost somewhere in the middle of our six parter."

It is cool to hear the phrase "Great Intelligence." At first, it just seems like whatever it is describing itself. "I am a Great Intelligence." But that's its name and it will haunt the Doctor several times over the years. I'll talk about it here since most of the episode was build up with that quick Yeti attack. The Intelligence is some sort of sentience that can survive for a very long time with no corporeal form. In fact, we learn eventually that it exists outside of our universe. In the place where similar beings come from. The Animus is one of these. The Nestene Consciousness is also from this sort of space. The Fendahl might be. The Gods of Ragnarok. Maybe that Devil thing in "The Satan Pit." The interesting thing with these sorts of monsters/ forces is that they really can't fully take hold. Once they do, you're done. Look at Vortis. The Animus wrecked that place. Don't Let Them Out of their Lovecraftian dimension. The Great Intelligence and the Nestene never get they want because humanity would be dead. Thank goodness the Doctor is there.

The Abominable Snowmen

Episode Five

Episode 178: (October 28, 1967) The Doctor speaks with Padmasambhava. He learns of the Great Intelligence. The Yeti attack the monastery.

Cliffhanger: As Travers remembers what he saw in the cave, stuff begins oozing forth from it.

Well, the pace hasn't picked up that much here. There are things to recommend. There are also some issues. The first issue being that the monks and the monastery are kind of in the exact same position at the beginning of the episode as at the end. In the beginning, they're planning on evacuating. The Yeti are standing by waiting to attack. At the end of this episode, the Yeti have attacked. They've left. The monks are still kind of hanging around. Stuff has happened in between there. But so little has happened with the monks that I would now declare it frustrating.

At the start of the episode, Padmasambhava speaks through Victoria. He says what we already knew was going to happen. Evacuate. The time has come to leave. Good-bye and so on. The monks say yes, we must evacuate. Although, we knew they were planning on it anyway. But first, we must meditate and then we'll go. Just go already! Get somewhere safe and then meditate. (Isn't there something strange about how these are peaceful Tibetan monks and yet Khrisong chastises himself for being a bad warrior? He wasn't shown a prospectus before he joined.) When the Yeti do attack, they seem like a bunch of thugs hired to smash up a place and not hurt anyone. Rather than, say, advanced robots controlled by a multi-dimensional force capable of destroying the planet.

I know that a bunch of stuff happens with the Doctor and Victoria. Jamie stands around goofing and Travers does very little. (Although, I find that cliffhanger very eerie. The way Travers slowly speaks and then it cuts to the cave expelling the whatever it is.) The Doctor's chat with Pad is excellent. These two old men meeting up after 300 years. Except Padma took the long way round. It's a nice talk between the two. The Doctor's realization that the Master's (Pad, I mean) astral travelling hooked his mind to this Great Intelligence is well done. I wish I could see Troughton's response. I'd love to know if there was more of a "Oh, my poor old friend" feel to the scene, since much is made of the Doctor's return. It's tough to gauge from the dialogue.

Luckily, the Doctor does get some background into what's happening. He does triangulate where the main control unit is. (You got it. It's with Pad in the monastery.) He does get those fun scenes with Victoria. She gets possessed. She has a great overwrought line she delivers to the Doctor repeatedly. The story is doing well in building to some sort of climax where, possibly, it has to be the Doctor versus the Great Intelligence. What's going on can only be resolved by these two. I like that quite a bit.

The problem I have is the continuing feeling that this should have been four parts. I don't ever remember reading that it was. So, Haisman and Lincoln wrote it like this. Some of the deliberate pacing does work. The fact that there is no incidental music adds to the feeling of being in the middle of nowhere, far away from everything. The closest to music that we get is the synthetic noise of the spheres. (That sounds close to music to me.) But the choice to have no music score makes it eerie and does kind of point up the longueurs that hover over the story. But episode 6 is here. If I'm not mistaken, there should be an end in sight.

The Abominable Snowmen

Episode Six

Episode 179: (November 4, 1967) The last battle between the monks and the Yeti begins. As does the first battle between The Doctor and The Great Intelligence.

Cliffhanger: Jamie asks the Doctor to take them somewhere warmer. We'll see…

Things happen again. Quite a few things. Although, it still takes a while for the monks to leave the monastery. I really don't fully understand why it takes so long but it does. They get out in time for those remaining behind to have their final battle with the Intelligence. And what a battle it is. The Doctor faces Pad. The Intelligence mentally attacks him. The Yeti storm around. Jamie and Thonmi smash things up. After a time, it all ends.

The good thing is that it seems like (the images help) a big, pitched battle that I'm hoping was fun to watch. It sounds like a more desperate and dangerous version of the end of "The Savages" where everyone destroys the laboratory. It all begins with the Doctor meeting the Intelligence and letting out a horrifying scream. I don't think we'd ever encountered the First Doctor at a point like that. There are certainly a few desperate First Doctor moments. But an outright chilling scream is something he never let out. Even up against the Animus, he just fell to the floor. The scream really states that "Now, it's happening. Finally."

One thing that doesn't really happen though is the Yeti attack we've all been expecting. Oh, they're there. And they are threatening. But all the buildup and build up doesn't come to a whole heck of a lot. As if the writers spent so much time putting the Yeti off and putting them off that they forgot them at the last minute. "Oh heck! We don't have the Yeti do anything!" "Let's hope no one notices." I only noticed because I'm writing about it. Maybe in the actual moving episode they do more. They basically attack as you think they would but it feels a bit afterthought-like.

I also like how it seems like The Doctor has a plan. But he's really kind of winging it. There's a whole lot of "Try this! No try this!" kind of thing going on through the battle. Having said that, this Doctor is a bit of a manipulator. That is his thing. I wouldn't be surprised if he knew exactly what he was doing.

In the end, it's a fascinating story that seems like a "base under siege" but, like "Tomb of the Cybermen" the evil is coming from inside the house! As it were. It just looks like it's coming from elsewhere. Peter Bryant is now script editor. Innes Lloyd is back as producer. I get the feeling that this sort of story, structured in this way, is what they really like. I don't know though. There's something about waiting a week for a 25-minute installment of something and having almost nothing happen that seems a bit perverse. I would have kept hanging in there. But I'm certain there must have been plenty of people who thought "To heck with this! I'm watching whatever is on the other station." As far as deliberately paced stories go, this is one of the better ones. I just wished its plotting and story had been sharper and more immediate. Just because the monks love to meditate doesn't mean we had to base the structure around that noble exercise.

And to conclude it all, Padma's final word is a whispered "Doctor." Followed by The Doctor saying goodbye to his old friend. That's nice. Travers chasing a Yeti and Jamie wishing for somewhere warmer is fun. The poignant moment wins out. (At least there isn't a hilarious moment where they all laugh at something and the image freeze frames. That would have been too much.)

THE ICE WARRIORS

By Bryan Hayles

Directed by Derek Martinus

ONE

Episode 180: (November 11, 1967) It is the year 3000 AD. A new Ice Age has begun. A valiant group of scientists and technicians use an ionizer gun to melt the oncoming glaciers. Meanwhile, a scientist finds a man (?) buried in the ice.

Cliffhanger: The Ice Warrior comes back to life.

This one takes another twist to the "base under siege" saga. If the previous one fooled us by putting the siege within the base, this one has the base under siege before the base properly comes under siege. The "siege" is usually led by whomever/ whatever the monsters/ aliens/ bad guys are in the story. The base is going about its business. Somewhere in there the Doctor and friends land. Then, the siege begins. Here, the siege will happen from The Ice Warriors later. The base is already besieged by glaciers constantly swarming towards them. We don't really see the glaciers. Well, not much of them. But their presence is felt, which makes for a doubly disconcerting adventure.

I am intrigued by and slightly confused by exactly where the main computer set is. It's a huge circular space with computers all around, mainly manned by ladies in the shortest skirts yet. In the middle is a big computer that the leader Clent talks to and it talks back to him! (He's not a nut.) This is one of those societies that is completely dependent upon a computer telling it what to do. That's why their main computer expert, Penley, abandoned them. (We'll talk more about him and his friend Storr later.) The room is in a Victorian mansion. The concept being that this is the base where they set up the ionizer. I think that's cool. But one thing confuses me.

The TARDIS lands on its side on a snowbank and slides off it. The gang must get out on their sides, which allows for some physical comedy. * (They also mention the previous story, which is a nice bit of continuity. Although, if it's so cold and unpleasant, why not just leave? There's nothing saying they must stay there.) They are near a giant white circular door/ entranceway thing. It's tough to gauge if it's huge or if it is just what we're seeing. Some scavengers rush out. (Important later.) The TARDIS crew step in through the door and we see the image of a mansion. Is that image meant to be the actual mansion somewhere in the distance behind the door? Or, since the mansion is an historical site, is it an image of what they're about to step into? The way it's shot and the characters enter the space it's kind of impossible to tell. I remain confused.

I love that they are not immediately distrusted. Clent gives them a test. The Doctor solves it and everyone is on the same page, sort of. We don't have to have all the normal distrust and annoyance. Clent seems to understand that people will be running away. He doesn't seem happy about it but he seems resigned to it. When someone like the Doctor comes along, he welcomes the help. But Clent does prefer the computer. And, let's be honest, The Doctor is cool here as he runs around saving the day and then figuring out problems. When will he get his own exciting jumpsuit, I wonder aloud?

Oh, and they find this strange thing in the snow, a la *The Thing From Another World*. What could it be?

*I love this opening for the crew because it's made to be to remembered. It's a variance on what normally happens. This is a time in TV where formula was king. So, when a show tweaks its formula, however slightly, it is well remembered. Trust me. The kids of the 1960s remember the TARDIS landing on its side on the snowbank. Just a minor change, just a little extra effort can make the episode that much more memorable.

The Ice Warriors

TWO

Episode 181: (November 18, 1967) Varga the Ice Warrior is free from the ice. He kidnaps Victoria and plans to bring his fellow warriors back to life.

Cliffhanger: Varga begins to unfreeze his Ice Warrior shipmates.

I know that the leading ladies character's name is Miss Garrett. And I know that one of the most beloved shows of the 1980s was *The Facts of Life*, which featured a character named Mrs. Garrett. As far as I can discern from all my research, they are not related. Although, there is some decent fan fiction in there. I can feel it.

The difference between this and "The Abominable Snowmen" is that there is no mystery here. In Tibet, the attacks of the Yeti were a mystery. The spheres were a mystery. Everything was a mystery. In the end, all is revealed. It takes an exceptionally long time to get there. And there's only so much time the writer can hold back the reader/ viewer from learning what is happening. I think, "Abominable" goes a bit too far. It stretches everything a bit too much. On the other hand, we have "The Ice Warriors."

Varga, our main Ice Warrior, spills his story to Victoria pretty quick. We're Martians. We came here some time ago. We got frozen in ice. There are five of us. Help me free my fellow warriors. Then we might leave or we might take over the Earth. It's all straightforward. Nothing hidden away. Now, it's just a question of stopping the Warriors before they get out of hand. Will the Doctor and his gang be able to do it? (Yes, I do know that they are not actually called "The Ice Warriors." Some guy calls Varga that and it sticks. I can't be held responsible for names people like.)

So, this is about suspense and excitement and trying to stop something from happening. But everyone doesn't know what's happening yet. Victoria and Varga do. The others are just trying to figure out what's going on. Clent may have brought the Doctor in to help. He does quite a bit of that "What? What are you talking about, you foolish man?" kind of chatter regarding the Ice Warrior and the Doctor's thoughts on it. Don't we ever get tired of that. I'm positive we can produce some better way to have the characters interact than like that. Can't we?

Then there's Penley and Storr. Penley is the scientist who abandoned the base. He's not gone full on caveman but he refuses to live in a world that treats him like a machine. Wise man. Varga knocks out Clent. The Doctor and Penley help Clent recover and have a calm chat together. Two smart men who don't think like everyone else discussing what's going on. It's civilized. It's shared discussion not just dismissing what one person is saying. It's quite good. So good, in fact, that you can see that Mr. Hayles is playing around here. Clent acts the way he does because the computers control his life. Penley is more human, is more pliable, is a better person because he can think for himself. That's what this society needs. Will this society figure that out before it gets crushed by glaciers or destroyed by Martians?

On the flipside of those two, we get Storr. The Scottish man with the big beard who distrusts scientists. He lives in a cave with Penley. He grows tomatoes (or something like that). He hates technology and complains a lot. He is injured in an avalanche and the drugs Penley gets for him saves his life. Storr just keeps complaining. Somehow this character seems very familiar to me. Distrusting those "darn scientists and their medicine or tech." Distrusting anyone smarter than him and deciding to follow his own ignorant path rather than someone with experience. There must be a reason Penley is helping him (Penley doesn't seem to like him). Maybe all will be revealed soon. To be honest, Storr can take a leap for all I care. Let's see some more Ice Warriors roaming around.

The Ice Warriors

THREE

Episode 182: (November 25, 1967) The Ice Warrior team is free. But not much happens.

Cliffhanger: Victoria is radioing the base and the Warriors are going to stop her.

They got the Warriors out of the ice and now they don't seem to have much for them to do. Varga says "Zondal" a lot. He's one of the warriors. He says that name a lot. Good Old, Zondal. I was hoping Zondal might be the funny one. Not really. Not huge on laughs, these Warriors. In fact, that's almost kind of a Doctor Who thing, isn't it? The villains are generally the ones without sense of humor. Even The Celestial Toymaker isn't much of a jokester. And his clowns… let's not talk about them. Clent is a lot like the Warriors here, huh? Penley has a sense of humor. I feel like Miss Garrett would be up for a laugh. Clent and the Warriors are 100% sticks in the mud. They wouldn't laugh if it rained banana peels down on them and everyone fell over one another. That's comedy!

There isn't much going on in this episode. Unlike the previous two, it feels a bit long. The Warriors do very little. The glaciers don't seem to be hanging around much. There's a brief skirmish with the Warriors, Jamie and Arden. Arden is killed. Jamie is knocked out. But, mainly Victoria yells. In fact, she yells basically "You killed him" for the second episode in a row at someone that they haven't killed. Maybe that will be her catchphrase. Remember when the Doctor used to keep saying "I would like a hat like that." Anyway, the episode is more about several conversations between the main characters. Further cementing their relationships in the way they interact with each other.

Let's get Storr out of the way. He's the exact opposite of Clent. His utter lack of humor and contempt for, well, everything is as obnoxious as Clent's total belief in his computers. I mentioned it previously and I'll probably mention it again. Maybe when Penley and Storr met it was in a "meet cute" moment. But there's nothing to recommend about Storr here except as an obvious character type.

Miss Garrett's visit to Penley is a nice one. This episode, like the last one, is animated. So, we can't pull emotions from the actor's faces. It's clear that Miss Garrett and Penley had some sort of relationship in the past. Clent makes a point of calling her "Miss Garrett." The Doctor wants to use her first name. Penley definitely does use her first name, "Jane," when they speak. It's a nice scene, interrupted by the annoyance that is Storr. But the chat between the two of them expands Penley's reasons for going and really brings the characters closer together. They're not just random cyphers, like say the monks in the previous story. They feel like real characters dealing in some unbelievable circumstances. Penley's description of Clent and men like him ring true today. Mediocre bureaucrats are always going to win out over creative people with no need to control others. That's why Clent will always somehow be in charge, even when he's no good at it. I like this scene.

The Doctor has some nice moments with Clent. Constantly reminding the Commander that he is helping them but he's not an employee. There's some great business with the Doctor writing all over the place trying to figure out assorted ways to fix the ionizer. Miss Garrett is impressed. Clent might be too. But he's clearly jealous of anyone with any sort of creative spark, any sort of "genius." He takes solace in his boxed-in, boring world where everything is done by the book and he always comes out on top. A place where his mediocrity always wins. It defeated Penley. Even animated Penley is clearly more interesting than Clent, and it's not just his slowly growing beard. Mediocrity is always contemptuous of the creative.

The Ice Warriors

FOUR

Episode 183: (December 2, 1967) Everyone wants to know what the Ice Warrior propulsion unit is made of, except for Storr. He dies.

Cliffhanger: The Doctor is in the airlock and the air is slowly being removed.

This episode contains two people deciding to go and have nice chats with the Ice Warriors. At least, The Doctor goes in with some sort of swagger. (Until he gets caught in that airlock, of course.) He's trying to find out about the engine and is attempting to be direct. Storr just goes there to talk to them because they're against the scientists and the ionizer. He decides that they'll be great pals because of this. As in life as in death, he was an idiot. Although, it doesn't speak terribly well of the Doctor either.

The main thrust of the episode is "What are the engines of the Martian ship made of?" That's really it. As you might imagine, it doesn't make for the most exciting episode. Much like "The Abominable Snowman" this story has kind of run itself into the ground. It doesn't even have the fun discussions of the previous episode. It has Victoria hiding in plain sight from an Ice Warrior named Turoc. It has the Ice Warriors gabbing on for a while, not accomplishing much. The Doctor, Clent and Miss Garrett chat for a bit. We see that Miss Garrett is now wearing very tight shorts instead of a very small skirt. Again, I applaud whoever oversaw this century's ladies fashions. Jamie is unconscious. Victoria runs around. Because we can see it, it seems a bit more exciting than episode four of "Snowmen" but it's doing nothing.

I'm not sure what the ice Warriors are doing here. I was expecting the "base under siege" element would have ramped up around now. But no. Nothing. The glacier's movement is the only real forward push of the episode. Lots of snow collapses down on people along with big chunks of ice. That does give the episode a bit of suspense and excitement. But once you realize that "They aren't going to do anything in this episode," all the fake ice dropping on people's heads in the world can't bring it back to life. Again, at least they killed Storr. (My favorite Stupid Storr moment is when Penley mentions the advanced weapons the Ice Warriors have. Storr sneers and says that they're probably "scientifically designed." No Storr. They were pieced together by the finest bakers on Mars so once you're done taking over the base you can eat them. Idiot.)

So, let's talk about something else. The fun opening. Instead of the title and the writer credit and the episode number appearing on top of the credits, we get something more creative. Remember the computer lettering of "The War Machines?" This is cooler. We see great images of a Tundra-like landscape. Some eerie Dudley Simpson music plays. And we see the title, the author's name and the number. "FOUR" or "FIVE" or... You know the numbers. It's a nice way to differentiate everything.

Another thing that comes up on the DVD Production Text and in the history of the show is that Season Five was always known as the "Monster Season." Apart from "The Enemy of the World," (which was seen as an aberration for many years because there were no monsters in it), we get two Cybermen stories, two Yeti stories, an Ice Warrior Story and the Killer Seaweed. In the text, it does say that production crew was really trying to brand Doctor Who as "The Monster Show." Even having a tie-in with *Blue Peter* to design your own monster. (You're going to have to look *Blue Peter* up yourself.) So, not only were they standardizing the storylines but they were removing all the subtleties, all the differences, all the things that made *Doctor Who* such an interesting show. Unless, of course, all you cared about where the Monsters. You might be surprised at how many people only did.

The Ice Warriors

FIVE

Episode 184: (December 9, 1967) We find out what kind of engine the Ice Warriors have. Also a BEAR ATTACK!

Cliffhanger: Zondal triggers a sonic blast!

Clent turns out to be a petty little man. (Maybe if he got the chance to wear some super tight shorts things might have been different.) Penley arrives with a wounded Jamie. In fact, Penley's been attacked by a bear so both the guys are wounded. Clent treats Penley awfully. There are two moments here that sum up the sort of person Clent is: 1) Miss Garrett and Clent are arranging something as led by the Computer. Clent is excited while doing it and says to one of the men that this couldn't have been what he envisioned when he volunteered. Of course, the worker was drafted. 2) Clent's eyes gleam when he realizes that Penley is no longer his superior. He's just some scavenger. He treats Penley accordingly. I can't say I'm a huge fan of Clent. (I do like Miss G.) By this point, I just wanted something to happen.

The Doctor does find out what kind of engine the Ice Warriors have. The whole hubbub revolving around the engine is whether it will melt the glaciers or disrupt the ionizer or… if they shoot it, is it nuclear? Or something? To be honest, in this episode I forgot everything. I was watching it and things were happening. Varga laughed a bit, sort of in a variation of the Cyberman's "Clever, clever, clever." All the other Ice Warriors just seemed to stand around. The Doctor did what he could. The info he gets does lead to stuff happening back in the computer room. However, it doesn't lead to much else.

It's odd. The scene with Clent and Miss G assembling data has a bit of a thrill to it. And the Ice Warriors are menacing. But the main big scene here is the bear attack. It's the scene shot on film. It's the scene that really feels like it's set during an Ice Age. Derek Martinus apparently asked for a bigger studio so he could give the thing a sense of space. And it works. Plus, there's a bear. It's not like the elephant in "The Ark." It doesn't enter the shot with the actors. It gets a nice POV attack in though. Apparently, choosing to attack the human who is fit rather than the paralyzed one.

The whole episode feels odd. Episode 5 of "The Abominable Snowmen" had a sense of dread building. It had a sense of "What the heck?" even when it was running the story in circles. "The Ice Warriors" seems to have kind of stalled in Episode Three. Time is simply passing. People talk. People move around. The Ice Warriors don't do much. Jamie hasn't done anything really in two episodes. Why isn't stuff happening? I remember reading this novelization several times as a kid and loving it. When this episode ended, all I could think was "We're only here? How much stuff happens in Six?" The problem too is that as my interest wanes, my ability to keep the focus also does. (See my next paragraph.)

Finally, there's the Computer. They have some discussion regarding whether the computer could destroy itself to stop the movement of the glacier. And it's interesting. But the mix of everyone's costumes, Clent's limp and Miss Garrett's wig made me almost instantly forget everything they were saying. I found it very tough to concentrate on their discussions. Not least of all because by this point, I thought something should be happening.

Something I learned: The production text says that the polar bear is higher up on the food chain than humans. It actively hunts and eats humans. I did not know that. The loveable buggers!

The Ice Warriors

SIX

Episode 185: (December 16, 1967) The Ice Warriors try to take over the Ionizer base but the Doctor has a trick up his sleeve.

Cliffhanger: The Doctor, Victoria and Jamie leave.

In the end, it's Penley sitting down at the controls. It's Clent and Miss Garrett overriding the computer. It's humanity teaming up to destroy the Ice Warriors and their ship before the Ice Warriors destroy them. Hooray! The base and the ship both take a pummeling during this episode. The Doctor sends some sort of pulse at the base. It knocks the humans out and disorientates the Ice Warriors so much that they leave. It is interesting to see the very clinical, very stark white and bland computer room strewn with rubble and bodies.

Is this episode a satisfying end to the serial? It felt like it when I read the novelization several times as a kid. As far as the televised version goes, I'm not so sure. Clent's confusion and shock when he sees Varga on the viewscreen always makes me think "That's right. He hasn't really met the Ice Warriors yet." When the Warriors storm the base, that's a nice moment. As I mentioned, it's not really "base under siege." It's more like there are two bases in close proximity and some characters move from one to the other. The Doctor's big moment where he zaps the Base is one of those Second Doctor moments we're seeing more and more of. Like when he blew out the electrical system in "The Power of the Daleks" or began fiddling with everything in the Cybertomb. These things he's doing seem rather reckless. I mean, he could have killed everyone in the base. He didn't. He could have.

As mentioned, it all comes down to the final meeting between Clent and Penley. With Penley's clear thinking saving the day. In fact, it's so clearly about these two that no one else really does much. The Ice Warriors storm the base but then run away before much has happened. The Doctor sends the pulse but that's about it. In fact, when Penley and Clent look around for the Doctor and friends in the end, I'd forgotten that they were still there. Jamie and Victoria do almost nothing. It's very odd. After six episodes, this is the big ending we get. It's more controlled than the ending of the previous story. It has less of a crazy supernatural thing going on. It's more of a straightforward sci-fi thing. The constant presence of the glaciers is still felt. But the actual big ending itself just sort of happens. It's not bad. It's just not much.

Overall, this story would have been a much better 4-parter I think. It lacks the mystery of "The Abominable Snowman." All it has is a lot of time spent with Clent believing in his computer and an inordinate amount of time spent wondering about those darn Ice Warrior ship engines. That goes on and on. Why did I remember this one being so much more thrilling? It's kind of underwhelming once it really gets going, which is too bad.

One thing I noticed and that I will probably notice more of as the seasons go on: Miss Garrett changed again. Everyone else is in the same outfits throughout, especially Clent. He must have a dozen of those jumpsuit things. Miss Garrett started in a short skirt. Then for a few episodes, she was in tight shorts. Now, she's in a skirt again. I wonder why no one else changes their clothes like she does. Maybe it's the Computer's decision?

THE ENEMY OF THE WORLD

Written by David Whitaker

Directed by Barry Letts

Episode One

Episode 186: (December 23, 1967) In the not-too-distant-future (around 2018), the TARDIS crew lands on a beach only to be attacked by some fellows who recognize the Doctor. A woman named Astrid Ferrier rescues them. She explains that the Doctor looks just like a would-be dictator of the world. A man named Salamander.

Cliffhanger: The Doctor does his first Salamander impersonation using the word "Bruce."

Welcome Barry Letts to the land of *Doctor Who*! He will be with us on and off for the next year or two. Then he will lead the show through the first half of the 1970s. Previously he was an actor, after a stint in the Navy, but he's meeting us here through his Director role. He's a fine director. He's got a decent grasp on action scenes. (He's no James Cameron but he keeps the energy level up.) He does some good suspense stuff. (Although, I've no idea what Astrid is doing hiding behind that easy chair. Does she think she's part of the People's Front of Judea?) And the scenes with just dialogue are directed well enough. He's not a stellar director. Derek Martinus is, I think, better. Douglas Camfield certainly is. (Although, see "Inferno.) Letts keeps things moving and interesting and that's what we want. In future times, his producer side will come out along with his writer side. In at least one story, all three. Usually, we don't get that on the show so it's very welcome.

Also, David Whitaker is back! The one person who really seemed to be able to nail how to do one of these 6-part stories has returned for the third six-parter in a row. (It's starting to be a bit too extravagant now.) He certainly brings the excitement in this episode. Setting us in this "futuristic" world! (Yes, I know. "The Tenth Planet" was set in 1986 and made in 1966. This was made in 1967 and is set in the vicinity of 2018. Some things don't quite match up with the history I remember.) There's a hovercraft! (Man, I love hovercrafts.) There's a helicopter! This first episode feels bigger than the first episode of any episode of the show since everyone ran around the airport in "The Faceless Ones." (OK. Maybe the destruction of the Daleks in "The Evil of the Daleks.") The Cybertomb felt big but it didn't have the production value of the helicopter swooping in and the hovercraft hovering around. This feels like proto-Pertwee *Doctor Who* to me. Letts taking a Whitaker script and putting a future stamp on it and it's fun.

Now, why the Doctor, Victoria and Jamie*don't run back to the TARDIS when they see danger, I don't know. The Doctor is so excited by the beach that he rushes down there and gives a wave to the hovercraft guys. Is he high? Why isn't he more careful? Unless he knows what's happening and who he looks like and he's doing that to draw attention. That makes more sense than what's on the face of it. We get a helicopter ride. We get a nice chat between the Doctor and Astrid about what type of Doctor he is. We get the Doctor getting angry when he's told those guys hate him. And we get the reveal of the "Evil Doctor" Salamander! Or they think he's evil? We don't quite know yet. Hell, we never figured out the Abbott of Amboise. I think we'll do better here.

Overall, it's a good starter episode. My only worry is that the last two stories had good starter episodes too. At least, we have all of "The Enemy of the World" and we can judge it fully and properly. Yes, we will talk about that shortly. First, what brings you here, Bruce?

*Yes, those two are dressed in matching outfits. And it's adorable. They seem more touchy feely with one another in this episode than ever before. Jamie (or Frazier Hines) is doing a lot of clowning, even when it's off to one side. Focus on Jamie throughout. It seems like he's always trying to engage in some sort of silliness no matter what's happening.

The Enemy of the World

Episode Two

Episode 187: (December 30, 1967) Jamie and Victoria are going to get jobs in Salamander's mansion. Salamander predicts a natural disaster, which comes true.

Cliffhanger: Fedorin lowers his head in shame as he realizes that Salamander has him completely under his control.

I forget how much of Fariah there is in this story but I like her. Her and Astrid. As adorable as Victoria is, these two have the feel of mid-1960s Bond girls all the way. Astrid is the cool, hip gadget strewn one. Fariah is the more mysterious one who has somehow gotten mixed up with the bad guy. But she's wearing a very short skirt and I do love fashion. The scene where she speaks to Fedorin about being Salamander's food taster is great. Salamander's line after "Why did you become his food taster?" is wonderful. ("She got hungry.")

The story is very much emulating James Bond films. Currently, there had been five of them. The most recent one *You Only Live Twice* took us into outer space, sent us to Japan, had a hideout in a volcano and featured dozens of ninjas. That series had gone from a sort of low budget espionage series to a true globe-hopping phenomenon. "The Enemy of the World" is clearly trying to follow Bond's lead. And, after the last run of stories, it's a breath of fresh air. For some reason, I always find the scene with Denes and Astrid hiding under a dock very charming. We've never seen anything like it before. It doesn't completely shed its studio bound feel but I'm pretty darn convinced. Denes mentions that he hasn't hid somewhere like this before and it does feel almost childlike. Maybe the whole thing is meant to be.

The way Jamie ingratiates himself into Salamander's clan is a bit too pat for my tastes. Basically, Jamie breaks into the house, throws a radio telephone into a field and it explodes. (I do like the use of the space around the mansion. They're on a studio porch area. But the explosion (on film) looks like it is in the distance. Well done. The scene where Jamie is walking towards the ladies on the bench is similarly decent.) Jamie claims that he'd heard there was a bomb nearby. So, Salamander gives him and Victoria a job. Hooray! I guess it makes sense.

One thing you will notice is that after the huge blowout at the start of Part One, there isn't so much going on here. A couple of rooms, a park bench, a dock, a porch. That's about it. The scope is still there, especially when they cut to the natural disaster. * It's slightly underplayed until it happens. Then, when it does, it's a big moment of devastation. They all seem to know that Salamander did this but how the heck are they going to prove it. Troughton doesn't have much Doctor in this episode. His Salamander impersonation is pretty good. When he becomes Salamander he definitely exudes the crazy, dictator style evil that we've all come to know and love over the last few years, circa 2018-ish.

*Yes, it is stock footage. But it does have a wonderful sense of demolition behind it. Luckily, we never see any people get hurt. Just buildings go. How did Salamander predict this? Why didn't Denes do anything? And just how strong are those binoculars? We may or may not find out in future episodes.

The Enemy of the World

Episode Three

Episode 188: (January 6, 1968) Denes is kept in a hallway. Victoria, Astrid and Jamie try to start up a diversion to free him.

Cliffhanger: Bruce suddenly realizes that there may be a Salamander impersonator out there. And not a funny one.

Two big things happened around this episode: 1) It was the only episode that existed of this show until 2013. So, from the Troughton Years VHS in 1994 to the full DVD release in 2014, this was the only portion of the show that survived. It colored many people's views of it. 2) 625 lines. The big switch from 405 lines to 625 lines hit all BBC shows at the beginning of the year. * The station was prepping for the upcoming switch to color so they needed more definition in the picture. Keep in mind when you're watching the show prior to this point, things looked primitive. There were times when you had to strain to see what was happening. Now, things will look better. Oh, there might be a third. Griffin The Cook!

Griffin is only in this episode but everyone remarks on him. Rightly so. He's a charmer. A chef who is clearly a good chef. (Salamander wouldn't keep him if he was a rotten chef.) But he has a wonderful sarcastic, bleak outlook on life, which is genuinely funny. You can tell he's funny because he lets loose with the zingers but he doesn't laugh at them. Everyone else does. Always be wary of someone who always laughs at their own jokes.

A lot happens in this episode. Although much of it is set in a kitchen or a hallway. Yes, they keep Denes prisoner in a hallway. The show knows that they're keeping him there so it's one step ahead of you. The Doctor only gets one scene. The extra-slimy Benik enters Kent's caravan and has his guard smash everything. It's petty, sadistic and gross. You learn that Kent had all the evidence to stop Salamander. Salamander intercepted it all and replaced it, thereby ruining Kent. The man who was right is no longer believed by anyone. In fact, the Doctor doesn't fully believe that Salamander is a bad guy yet. I'm not sure if the Doctor is being obtuse or not. If Salamander looked like a Cyberman, he'd leap right in there. Salamander looks like the Doctor so he is taking forever to get involved. (As of this moment, it's not bad though. He is waiting on Jamie to get back to him with proof. And the story has plenty of activity in it so nothing's slow.)

Victoria and Jamie get a bunch to do here, which is great. I sort of felt like they didn't have much going on in the last few stories. Victoria's time with Griffin is fun. Her scene with that guy in the hallway has a creepy vibe to it. (Well, that guy has a creepy vibe.) I'm hoping our gang can get out of there safely before Salamander and all his gang get them. All I can think with these episodes is "How do you live like that? So much intrigue. So much worry about people attacking the place. Worry at every meal. Guards everywhere." I guess it takes a very special personality to live like that. And it ain't me, Jack.

*Actually, the lines thing is true-ish. 1967 was the start of 625 lines in preparation for color programming, which was not too far down the line. However, the first two episodes of "Enemy," once found, were also in 625 lines. So, the last 405 was Episode Six of "The Ice Warriors." Go and watch them back-to-back. See if you can spot the difference. It was huge then. I'm not sure if it matters much now.

The Enemy of the World

Episode Four

Episode 189: (January 13, 1968) The Doctor decides to help. Benik and his goons attack Giles and everyone with him. Salamander locks himself inside the Records Room.

Cliffhanger: The Doctor, dressed as Salamander, sees someone enter.

Ferrier and Fariah? Really? Are you guys doing this on purpose? When Benik says "Fariah" repeatedly at one point, and he's just said "Ferrier" a few moments before, it sounds like someone is goofing around with us.

Overall, this is a great episode. The Doctor finally decides to join them. Victoria and Jamie have the week off. As they were captured, they are spoken of but we don't see them. That adds very nicely to the suspense. We don't see them and we wonder what might be happening. The attack on Giles's office is nicely done. (I do wonder who that woman with the baby carriage is though. I thought she might pull a gun on the guards.) The death of Fariah is unexpected and rather nasty. Her final conversation with Benik is kind of gross. Then, there's Salamander's trip to the center of the Earth.

Before that, isn't Benik great? What a nasty piece of work. He's so slimy. So self-serving. I love the feeling that he doesn't care who is in charge or who he must suck up to, he'll do whatever because he just likes that power. He likes yelling at guards and being unpleasant. He'll be a character who will die and we will cheer. Anyway…

Salamander has a lot of money at his disposal. Presumably what we see in this episode is some of the stuff that Kent found out about but got covered up. Because… here's the big zing… Deep, deep in the Earth, well it seems that way, there are a bunch of very British (as opposed to the mix of nationalities we've seen throughout) thespians that Salamander has been using. He has them operating big racks of computers and causing natural disasters. So, up top, he looks like he's the only one who knows what is happening and he should be in charge. The people underground seem pretty content with their life, except for one guy who wants to go up top. The story has been realistic for *Doctor Who* up until this point. The moment he enters that underground base the whole story starts to go a little wacko. But wacko in the best possible way. The most unexpected way. Salamander predicts the volcanic eruption earlier but it seems like some kind of weird prognostication. To find out that he is causing them with a group of people underground who are being told that war is ravaging the planet is deliciously screwball and instantly makes the next episodes something one has to watch.

My one problem at this point in the story is that I (and the Doctor has this a bit) have become a little vague on what exactly Kent and his people want to do. They want Salamander arrested and probably killed. The Doctor is going to help. I've forgotten how. Did we know how? It's taken such an inordinate amount of time for the Doctor to agree to their plan that I've forgotten the plan. (Why does the Doctor take so long? Because he has to impersonate? I guess.) Luckily, at the time that the Doctor's wishy-washy behavior reaches its peak, we get Salamander and his Jules Verne journey. That changes things.

The Enemy of the World

Episode Five

Episode 190: (January 20, 1968) The Doctor and Bruce go into the research center. Salamander brings Swann up to the surface.

Cliffhanger: Astrid finds the dying Swann who whispers one word: "Salamander."

"Received wisdom" is a rough thing. "Enemy" was dismissed for so long. Originally for its non-monster synopsis and then for Episode Three. Well, episode three is a lot of fun. Episode Four is better and this episode is better than four. So, for decades we really clung on to how lame the serial seemed to be. The episode takes place in a hallway for Heaven's Sake! One of the problems is that the writer and director had passed away long before the story was rediscovered/ found. So, some of the main people involved weren't here to tell us why they did it. Creative people will do things that they aren't thrilled about. We must make money. We must survive. The world isn't made for the creative. It's made for the business minded, the people who think that money is all. That leaves us in the dark here. One episode that is light on everything but charming and no one to fight for it.

However, I would think anyone with a bit of creativity would see this as a sharp story. Would trust David Whitaker. He's a great writer. Remember that first season? The one where the show was fighting for its life? He was the writer that guided us through. Now, his stories didn't become great until later but that doesn't mean anything. Terrance Dicks is sort of in the same space. He wrote his best stuff for the show right before and long after the show. Always trust a good writer. Always trust the name of a good writer. Even if they are knee deep in a writer's room, their magic will still shine. Mr. Whitaker is making it happen here.

The episode pushes the story forward in a way that the last two stories did not. Things are getting bigger and more dangerous. The Doctor is now Salamander. Salamander is down below with his people. Swann discovers a discrepancy and things might be going wrong. Benik almost tortures Jamie and Victoria. The TARDIS gang reunites. It's all a hell of an episode. After two that were slow but, like "The Power of the Daleks" very important, now we are moving towards the ending. It's nice that we do go out in the open during this episode. Things were getting a bit claustrophobic recently. But now, the world seems the world again.

I think the expansion in the last episode really has made this story something special. Salamander using all the public funds to build this huge hideout is awesome. And it's something that we never used to really understand back in the day when we read synopses. I just looked at the Jeremy Bentham synopsis from *Doctor Who: A Celebration* and to be honest it's laughable. It dismisses the show outright because it does not have monsters. Then, it presents a plotline that isn't quite right. The serial is a good one.

I love how Bruce, who seems to be Salamander's guy, gradually shifts his leanings over to the Doctor and friends. The moment when the Doctor hands Bruce his gun is kind of a mini-Doctor Who staple. Gain the confidence by turning over your weapon. The fifth Doctor did that in "Warriors of the Deep." And here, it's a heck of a moment. We know what Bruce is like. We know what everyone is like now. It's too late to back down. It's nice to see the Doctor still doing his best to not get caught up in the awfulness of what everyone is doing at this time. 2018! You stank!

The Enemy of the World

Episode Six

Episode 191: (January 27, 1968) All hell breaks loose. The Doctor meets Salamander.

Cliffhanger: The TARDIS doors are open in flight! Everyone is going to get sucked out into the vortex.

There's a clue right at the beginning that something went wrong in the production of this episode. It's in the length. The average episode length for 1 through 5 is 23-24 minutes. This episode is a little under 22. Why? It's got a lot to wrap up. How could it be shorter than the others? It's a lode-bearing episode, as it were. There is a production problem. In the end. Barry Letts originally planned on a much more extensive split screen battle between Salamander and The Doctor. But the technical end let him down. (That would happen often to Letts, especially when CSO hit.) So, the episode was trimmed and the big ending confrontation comes off as very rushed. Which is too bad.

The rest of the episode is fantastic. It doesn't feel rushed. Bit by bit, everything that needs to be taken care of is dealt with. Salamander is finally caught out. Benik is arrested. The research center is rocked to the ground. Most of the decent people survive. Bruce finally decides which side he's on. Jamie and Victoria don't have a lot to do. They're basically sent back to the TARDIS. The rest of this wraps up well. I think only the sixth episode of Whitaker's "The Power of the Daleks" does it better.

Yes, there is one outstanding question that doesn't quite hit until afterwards. How does Salamander know about the TARDIS and where it is? It seems like odd plotting. The Doctor knows about Salamander because he's been shown speeches and people have told him all about the dictator. Salamander knows nothing at all about the Doctor. The story seems to go under the theory that as the Doctor knows about Salamander so Salamander knows about The Doctor. It's almost like a two-way stream. I'm thinking of "The Girl in the Fireplace." The Doctor investigates Madame De Pompadour's mind and she investigates his. But, of course, it shouldn't work like that here but it does make for a tense and interesting, if too brief, scene.

In fact, it's quite nicely done until we have a Troughton fight. That's when it clips around oddly. Seeing the TARDIS on the hill by the beach in the dark with Jamie looking out is cool. And Salamander, determined and looking eviler than ever, approaching the ship is also cool. The Doctor in the doorway = cool. The whole scene is rather audacious and fun. Salamander, briefly, has control of the TARDIS. Oh boy! It's too bad we had those tech issues.

Great story well told. It avoided almost every one of the issues that the previous six-part stories had. And it exists! All of it. That's so nice. Maybe they need David Whitaker to write more for the show. We're more than halfway through the season now. We have three more 6-parters, none of which exist in full. Let's see how this goes.

THE WEB OF FEAR

Written by Mervyn Haisman and Henry Lincoln

Directed by Douglas Camfield

Episode One

Episode 192: (February 3, 1968) The Yeti are back in Modern day London. In the Underground. The Doctor, Jamie and Victoria investigate! Oh, Professor Travers is back as is his daughter, Dr. Anne Travers.

Cliffhanger: The webbed explosives sort of explode, knocking the Doctor off the platform.

Innes Lloyd is gone. Peter Bryant is now producer. Derrick Sherwin is now script editor. Things don't seem much different. Especially with the Yeti, Dr. Travers and the London underground under siege. The first thing one notices though is how great the Underground looks. And they were all sets! The underground wouldn't let them film there so it's all in the studio. Everything really looks great. It's like the caves in the movie *The Strangeness*. If you hadn't told me they were fake caves, I would never have noticed. Looks so good.

This is a bona fide sequel. It jumps ahead about 40 years in time. It is the Great Intelligence's second attempt to take over the Earth. They have a more extensive plan. They're forcing London to evacuate using thinner Yeti that have web guns that cover anything. They're lurking in the Underground which is, of course, where the Doctor and his gang land. There are soldiers, scientists and reporters a plenty. And there's Travers blustering around. And his daughter being sarcastic. And the Doctor's eyes opening super wide when he sees the Yeti. Here we go!

Plus, we have Douglas Camfield directing. One of the show's best directors. A man who knows how to do the action and how to build the suspense. Haisman and Lincoln have us land in the same dramatic spot where we were in "The Abominable Snowmen." Although, one doesn't really question it but the thought does come up: Why use Yeti in the middle of London? Why not make your robots look like something different? It doesn't matter though. Just keep watching.

There's a lot of nice movement and introduction of characters here. It has a very claustrophobic feel to it, in contrast to the previous story. This one is dark and shadowy, with little shelter-type rooms. It has an extended opening in the TARDIS. First, of course, we must conclude last week's cliffhanger. (Spoiler: Our gang is OK.) Then, the TARDIS is caught in mid-air (mid-space) by some sort of web that holds it there for a while before letting it come to Earth. I like the thought of the Intelligence spotting the Doctor on the way and then stopping him before he can get there. Only allowing him out when it feels ready. The Intelligence has learned a thing or two.

Your mileage may vary with the opening scene. Travers arguing with Silverstein over the Yeti. Apparently, Travers sold this guy a robot Yeti that he brought back from Tibet. The sphere contacts the Yeti and a whole new invasion attempt begins. Does this scene happen before everything else? Is there meant to be a big jump in time between here and the Underground stuff? I didn't see it mentioned in the story and I can't find my novelization. Hmmm...

Fashion alert: Victoria wears another miniskirt in this episode. (Minidress?) And she looks great. Plus, in and amongst the soldiers and other guys (this one has a lady in it who isn't Victoria!), Anne Travers is also in a miniskirt. And a thumbs up there. I'd be flirting with her too if I were a soldier boy down there. I love her sarcastic frame of mind. Victoria's always fun but her and Jamie have sort of got lost in all the other characters from the last few stories. There's been very little time for the two of them to truly stand out.

The Web of Fear

Episode Two

Episode 193: (February 10, 1968) Victoria and Jamie meet up with Prof. Travers. Everyone thinks the Doctor stopped the explosion from happening. But the Doctor is missing.

Cliffhanger: Jamie and a soldier are trapped in a tunnel filling up with foam.

The Doctor is absent from this episode. But luckily, people talk about him a lot. Back in Episode Four of "The Enemy of the World," Victoria and Jamie were gone. We knew they were being held prisoner. There was a tension there. Last time, we saw the Doctor he was being abruptly knocked to one side by the web-covered explosion. (The webs contained the explosion.) The soldiers who investigate find this but not the Doctor. So, we know the Doctor is up to something. Most likely doing what the first Doctor did in "The Dalek Masterplan." Investigating off to one side so no one gets in his way.

The show has evolved so much from early on that the Doctor's missing presence is felt throughout. And not in a great way. More in a "We're waiting for the most interesting person to show up" kind of way. That's too bad. Because it tends to make the episode drag a bit, which is a problem for a six parter when we're only in part two.

The scene where Victoria realizes who Prof. Travers is and they reunite is lovely. It's nice to have a character recurrence like this because it rarely happens in the original run of the show. It's just not the way the show worked. But here he is! And here's his daughter. Poor Victoria is left to talk to her and explain their time machine. Luckily, Anne is whip smart and interested, if skeptical. The trickiest moment of their conversation is the dating. (Follow me into the next paragraph for that.)

Of course, for those of you that are huge UNIT fans, we can begin the confusion of "UNIT Dating" here. The very basics behind this are: The production team at that time (well, in the next season) were setting up the idea of UNIT, a slightly futuristic group that The Doctor would get involved with. In the team's mind, these shows were set a bit in the future. But, in the minds of later production teams, these stories are set very much in the present. And the battle raged on! A certain generation of *Doctor Who* fan always believe the UNIT stories, with their basis here, are set in the future. Another generation is fine with them being in the present. And here, we get the first bit of confusion. I thought that "The Abominable Snowmen" was set in the 1920s. When Prof. Travers says that their adventure was "40 years ago," that made sense to me. It was around 1926/ 1927 or 1928. Somewhere in there. But Victoria and Anne specifically say that it was "1935." That means this story takes place in 1975, the future. Granted, "The Tenth Planet" took place in "the future" as did the previous story. The next "UNIT" story is the proper first one, "The Invasion." Things will only become more confusing from there.

I spent some time on that because the episode, while charming enough, is running in place until the Doctor returns. Everyone gets a little bit more to do. A little extra character stuff. We learn a little bit more about what's happening. But nothing ever goes too far where, if you missed this episode like Troughton did, you'd be in bad shape when you returned. Hopefully, when The Doctor returns, we can get back to the business of moving the story ahead.

Weird thing: People keep casually saying: "The Doctor sabotaged the explosives." And yet, the explosives are covered with the web. Don't they know the Yeti spray the webs? Why does no one mention the webs? Surely the conversation would go like this: "It was the Doctor." "Yes. The explosives were covered with webs." "It was the Yeti." "Oh, yes. That's right." No one ever quite says that. It's not as annoying as "How come no one can find out how the Ice Warriors power the ship?" Still annoying.

The Web of Fear

Episode Three

Episode 194: (February 17. 1968) We meet Colonel Lethbridge-Stewart who takes command of everything and holds a big meeting. There's a traitor in our midst. Who might it be?

Cliffhanger: Prof. Travers is attacked by a Yeti.

In some ways, this is such an important episode. In others, it's a good episode in the middle of a six-part story. It gives us the background we need. We learn about the mist and the Yeti and the webs. We learn that it probably was that sphere in Episode 1 that started this. If I was Professor Travers, I'd be dying of guilt. But, then some of us don't get as guilty as others. Now, we know what's going on. We don't know why though. There is a traitor in our midst. The remaining explosives are dowsed in webs and destroyed.

Someone has a Yeti action figure that they're manipulating around the place. Also, the webs are closing in around them. Our gang is looking trapped. Uh oh.

But the Colonel is here! Colonel Allistair Gordon Lethbridge-Stewart, that is. Soon to be The Brigadier. One of the longest running supporting characters in the history of the show. A fixture in the first half of the 1970s and a welcome returning character over the years. Here, he shows up holding the Doctor at gunpoint. He takes quick charge of everything and throws the 1968 equivalent of a PowerPoint meeting. (It's tough to say exactly but The Doctor looks like he wants to run away when a meeting is announced.) He puts Chorley, the reporter, in a separate room and acts like he's giving him something to do but doesn't. (Victoria goofs that up by mentioning the TARDIS to Chorley. Chorley wants to get in on that!) He takes the Doctor on as a sort of advisor. And he keeps everything running proficiently even as it's all falling apart.

The drawback to the episode is the obvious one. We still don't have it. The rest of the story was found in Africa in 2013. But. The 3rd episode "vanished" in between when the gentleman found the episodes and when he went to pick them up. The people who had them claimed that they never had Episode 3, which, I believe, is baloney. A private collector was contacted and offered the people who had the episodes a lot of money. So, they hid it. So, some a*shole now owns the only existing copy of this important episode. And we'll never see it. Never let anyone tell you that life is fair. Anyway, the episode is lost. The reconstruction on the initial DVD is fine. It's a little light on captions, especially when Jamie and Evans are walking amongst the tunnels. The animated version works better but still, once you see The Brig (or the Colonel), one can't help but be saddened by the fact that one person's greed prevented all of us from enjoying it. Well, I guess I should take my own advice: Budnik, suck it!

I do like how they do the "traitor amongst us" thing. Because once you realize that there is a traitor out there, everyone suddenly becomes suspicious, even The Doctor. (What was he doing in the previous episode?) Suddenly, one thinks "Where did The Colonel come from?" Evans vanishes in the tunnels and then returns. Staff's character changes a bit. Who is this Chorley? What is going on? Who has the Yeti action figures? It's nicely done. The whole episode is well handled, even though nothing really happens. They almost blow something up. But don't. Jamie and Evans almost escape but they don't. The Intelligence seems to be pressing them into a smaller and smaller space for some purpose. I think we may soon find out why.

The Web of Fear

Episode Four

Episode 195: (February 24, 1968) The Colonel leads a bunch of troops to try and get into Covent Garden to get the TARDIS. It doesn't go well. Evans complains a lot. Victoria kind of does too. The Doctor and Anne try and build something to stop the Intelligence.

Cliffhanger: The Yeti enter the room with Travers in between them.

The episode is a very strong one with two drawbacks. 1) Evans. He was fine when we couldn't see his face. He complained a lot. Whatever. There are a lot of other characters. Now that we can see him, if he is the traitor then he's the goofiest looking traitor around. He's constantly complaining and he's always trying to back out of whatever he has to do. Plus, he's constantly making faces like Huntz Hall. What on earth is that about? Did Douglas Camfield really request that he do those ridiculous faces? It's mighty distracting. Which is too bad because it's such a good episode that that bit of overacting really mucks it up a bit. There's always something. Evans certainly can't be the traitor, can he? Not with those faces.

Having said that, the traitor is impressive. Follow the paths of all the little Yeti. He's sneaking things into people's pockets left, right and center. That's good work! It almost gets a little silly when we see the Colonel and we hear the beeping. And we're thinking "Is that the Yeti or does he have one of those Yeti things?" It's kind of too bad that the army had this big sneaky strategy planned. The traitor just dropped a Yeti in the Colonel's pockets and that put paid to everything. Doesn't the Colonel ever check his pockets?

The other problem, sadly, is Victoria. Jamie has fallen into a weird place where he generally gets lost in and amongst the supporting cast. He's never going to develop character-wise in any way. The most fun thing to do with his character is watch Frazier Hines trying to add as much comedy as he can to the proceedings, which he and Troughton are becoming bored with. Maybe they should have gotten rid of Jamie. It's not like he gets smarter or learns anything. He's pretty much the same Jamie from around "The Underwater Menace" that he is here. But he's not really a problem. It's just that the inertia factor is high. With Victoria, there's a real sense of "We don't know what to do with her." First, she tells Chorley about the TARDIS. (They think he's going to steal it. What?! And how?! I know the Second Doctor can seem a bit irresponsible but right after Salamander got on he surely remembered to lock it.) And here she just kind of whines uselessly and a lot. The moment when she doubts the Doctor saving the day is especially odd. She has no faith in the Doctor? Weird. She's still cute but her character is screaming too much. Whining too much. I feel like the production team might have known this. She doesn't have a whole lot of time left with us.

Otherwise, this is a suspenseful and harrowing episode. The attack in Covent Garden is very nicely done. We haven't really had anything like this since "The War Machines." (At least, that we could see.) It gives a nice sense of desolation to the story as we see no one on the surface. Sticking to the Underground tunnels is fine. It's nice to get up above for a while. This was the perfect spot for this because it gives a feeling of "How are they going to win?" At the same time it makes one glad the Monks weren't attacked by a bunch of these things in Tibet. They would have been completely slaughtered. In the tunnels, things are getting worse. The Doctor takes a sample of web. Two soldiers try to go through the web and are immediately killed. Anne gets thrown around by a Yeti. And, in the end, the survivors are trapped in a room with the Yeti. Finally, we're going to learn what is going on.

The Web of Fear

Episode Five

Episode 196: (March 2, 1968) The Great Intelligence gives the humans 20 minutes to turn over the Doctor. Then, the episode chronicles the next 20 minutes.

Cliffhanger: The wall of one of the offices bursts open and the fungus pours in.

Again, what in the hell is Evans up to? It's bad enough that he's overreacting and mugging horribly. Douglas Camfield keeps cutting to close ups of him. Is he meant to be the comic relief? If so, someone needs to re-write the definition of what "comic relief" is. He's just annoying. And there's that weird moment where he says, "Let's give the Doctor to the Great Intelligence." which is disgusting. (But, understandable for a mealy-mouthed coward such as himself.) But then, ten minutes later Anne and The Doctor are joking with him! What?! Oh, he's horrible. Why did they kill off Knight but not this guy?

The realization that this episode will be in real time is awesome. They stick close to it. It's more like 19 minutes. If we include the closing credits (with that cool web effect over it), then we hit 20 minutes. Watching Anne and The Doctor work together is delightful. Watching Jamie and the Brig/ The Colonel trying to save the day is fun. It's interesting to see Jamie get mad at the Doctor, claiming he's not doing enough. Both Victoria and Jamie have doubted the Doctor in this story.

It does seem like maybe The Doctor and Anne aren't doing that much. They are though. Getting themselves a sphere that they control so they can place it inside a Yeti is a good idea. What precisely they have up their sleeve we shall find out. But it's the Doctor so we trust him. Meanwhile, Victoria and Prof. Travers hang out in a tunnel. And Staff returns from being inside the web... Hmmm.

I like a good "real time" episode. Luckily, this is a good one. It's very casual about it. There's no ticking clock at the bottom of the screen. There are just a few reminders here and there. The episode rolls ahead. It cuts between everyone so cleanly that it seems like it could take place over a longer time but everyone has their own thing. Seeing something like this in a show like this in 1968 seems odd. I'd love to know if there was some other show at this time that may have tried something similar. It seems odd that the story would suddenly go to a micro level like this. It means that there is a real focus here because every minute means something. It's also something the show at this time never did again. I've never seen anything written about why they did this. And, of course, in the novelization, one wouldn't necessarily know that it was real time or as suspenseful as it gets here. It's kind of a brave move. The previous episode had that big shootout with the Yeti on location. This one diddles with story structure. What is next?

The Web of Fear

Episode Six

Episode 197: (March 9, 1968) The Doctor meets the Great Intelligence.

Cliffhanger: After the web, it's the fury.

The second fight with the Great Intelligence ends with the Doctor almost removing that evil force from the universe. Jamie's assistance keeps the Intelligence alive. So, flash forward ahead to "The Snowmen" and beyond. Everything is Jamie's fault. We saw in the previous episode that he didn't think the Doctor was doing enough. Here, his use of the good Yeti to attack the bad Yeti, thereby ruining the Doctor's plans, follow up on that scene and lead on... remember this: that when the Intelligence ravaged the Doctor's timeline and Clara had to dive into it to save the universe, it was Jamie's fault. Well, Jamie isn't going anywhere soon. So, we just shrug our shoulders, nudge him in the ribs and say, "Maybe next time."

The reveal of the rogue element happens in this episode. I so wish it was Evans. It's Staff Sgt. Arnold. It turns out that Evans was just a jerk after all. I'm thinking of "Voyage of the Damned" right here. There's nothing horrible about being an ass. But maybe there should be. This was a great serial. Very claustrophobic. Expansive when it needed to be. It feels better than "The Abominable Snowmen." (Even if I prefer Terrance Dicks's "Abominable" novelization to his "Web of Fear.") It feels like a wonderful extension of the first story. The whole premise here is that the Intelligence does this to bring The Doctor to it so it can assimilate the Doctor's experiences and life and intelligence. That's awesome. The Cybermen, for example, have basically ridiculous reasons for returning. The Intelligence's return is intelligent. I understand what the writers were doing with the ending. Keep the beast alive. But, also, I wouldn't have minded something more definitive. It does make the Second Doctor seem a bit iffy and whiffy. Maybe that's why Jamie is unsure. He doesn't quite save the day in Ice Warriors. He doesn't see him too much in Enemy. Others seem to be sealing the deal around the Second Doctor. The problem in this one is that the Doctor can't trust anyone so he can't tell anyone his full plan. And that's what scutters his attempts to banish the Intelligence in the end.

That was a heck of a paragraph. But it's a great episode. It assembles everyone with Yeti all around them. It builds towards a strong ending. And the ending is strong. It just goes wrong for the Doctor. We see a big pyramid. We see Chorley being nuts. We see more of Evans, unfortunately. And we see the story bring itself to a close. Much sharper than the first story. It could be because we can see most of it. It could be the script. It could be The Colonel. (We shall see more of him very soon.) But it works. Deep into this season of base under siege stories, this serial does a very straightforward example of one and it works. Heck. The web/ fungus is constantly hemming them in throughout. It really is a base (as weird as the base is) under siege. This formula works. The tricky thing is that the next two stories will repeat this formula. Will it continue to work?

We say goodbye to Professor Travers and his daughter Anne. To be honest, I would have loved it if the Doctor took Anne with him and left Victoria with Professor Travers (Not so weird as one might think.) Anne is delightful and exciting. Victoria is really the pits here. She is the screaming female companion that Susan degenerated into at her worst. Something needs to switch it up soon here. The companion team is beloved. However, when you watch them closely, they really don't amount to too much.

FURY FROM THE DEEP

Written by Victor Pemberton

Directed by Hugh David

Episode One

Episode 198: (March 16, 1968) The TARDIS crew land on a beach. They examine a pipeline. They are knocked unconscious and taken into a facility where they are questioned. Meanwhile, something is lurking in the pipes.

Cliffhanger: A foamy, weedy thing menaces Victoria.

If you haven't seen any of Season Five or missed most of Season Four, * than "Fury From The Deep" might seem like a wonderful example of *Doctor Who*. As it stands, it seems to be lots of fun. ** The Doctor, Jamie and Victoria land in the water. Literally, the TARDIS appears in the sky and homes in on the ground, which is water. They ride a little dinghy to land. The Doctor uses the sonic screwdriver for the first time. (What?!) To the disappointment of some, it's not the catch all name for the device that does everything for the Doctor. *** The crew gets knocked out. They get questioned. They get imprisoned. Classic *Doctor Who*.

To anyone who might have been watching the show regularly, oh, like, maybe us... this episode feels very tiresome. Well, tiresome might not be the completely right word. When Hobson or Robson or whatever his name is starts yelling at everyone, your first thought is "Why is this guy in charge of anything? I understand that he gets stuff done. But everyone here hates him and he's such a jackass." In fact, the thought of spending more episodes with this guy really makes me tired.

The episode really is about bringing the TARDIS crew into the base that is about to be under siege and then isolating them so nothing can happen. The evil (whatever it is) can now build up as our gang sits helpless. We get to see the inter-dynamics of the employees in the pipeline facility. Isn't that something you've always wanted to see? Yes, there is something inside the pipes. And it may have a heartbeat of sorts and be frightening and deadly. But we're left listening to the people outside the pipes. And, man, have we seen them all before!

Except for Maggie, the wife of one of the scientists that the man in charge doesn't listen to. (What, in fact, is the point of having the scientists there if Robson dismisses everything they say?) Maggie's a breath of fresh air. Someone from outside all of this. In the previous sieges (and we've seen a lot of them), it was all working people. She's the wife of one of the employees. That's a nice addition. Too bad Robson can just yell about her too.

Do I need to talk about Robson? Do you care? He was out on a rig for four years straight. That seems very irresponsible of someone. No one should be out there for that long. Did they forget he was there? Did they just leave him there? That sounds right to me. That's what I would have done. So, they put him in charge of this facility where his only motto is "Keep everything running." Even in the face of smart people telling him not to. Even in the face of actual evidence. (Although some evidence is stolen by a mysterious person... how does the mysterious person show up right at that moment?) He yells and yells at the TARDIS crew. I guess we're getting used to that by now. Maybe this is what Troughton and Hines were getting tired of having to do because I'm getting tired of having to watch it. I think things might improve with whatever is in the pipes. Let's go to the next episode and find out.

*Up until recently this was very easy to do. Animation is a wonderful thing.

**Animation is wonderful but is not the actual episode. So, I'm making some guesses here.

***Let's be honest: By time we reach the 13th Doctor and she's using that device to do readings of everyone and every place, it's not a screwdriver anymore. It's simply what she calls it. A hamburger has no ham in it. And yet it can be eaten and enjoyed even when you know that. So, to everyone who complains that the sonic screwdriver does too much, yes. If it was a screwdriver, it would do too much. That's just what she calls it.

Fury From The Deep

Episode Two

Episode 199: (March 23, 1968) Maggie meets Mr. Oak and Mr. Quill. Robson yells a lot. Something evil is waiting in the foam.

Cliffhanger: Van Lutyens says that there is something in the pipeline, alive and waiting.

Here's a bit of nice turnaround: Robson is still annoying. One still can't imagine why anyone would work with him. * Once you can put aside his awful moments, and really, he's no worse a character than Evans was, he fades into the back as the weirdness with the pipe and the foam builds.

And it does build well here. The scenes in the Smith's ugly (did I say that?) apartment (with a patio!) are rather harrowing, especially with the foam building up outside. And especially when Mr. Oak and Mr. Quill appear. And yes, you're meant to think of an Evil Laurel & Hardy. But you can also think of the two assassins from *Diamonds Are Forever*. They're obviously very creepy guys. One of the existing clips we have of the episode is them attacking Maggie with their methane breath, or whatever it is. In true *Doctor Who* fashion, it is rather scary and rather silly at the exact same time.

This weed is going to be trouble. I can feel it. The joy of the episode is how easy it is to disconnect Robson's idiotic ravings from the steadily mounting terror. Remember that the previous stories had all featured some sort of monster or alien race. Some sort of tangible something. And the last base under siege was obviously a sequel, as "The Moonbase" was. This one, though, is different. It's been two episodes and we've got nothing. No Yeti. No Ice Warrior. Just random bits of strange seaweed and foam. Yes, one might say "Hey! The Great Intelligence are back!" because of all the foam and whatnot. Not only are names getting very similar but some modus operandi is seeming the same.

Overall, it's an episode that overcomes the sameness that is beginning to infect the stories no matter how hard they try. There is a distinct lack of imagination in this season. It's weird because the limiting factors that the show has now were placed by the previous producers. Innes Lloyd and Gerry Davis are gone now. Maybe it's time to try something a little new. It's one thing to limit yourself a bit to see what you can do within your new confines. It's another to confine yourself and then struggle. You can easily get out of this by expanding the formula again. Why aren't they? It's weird. I thought maybe having new folks in charge with Peter Bryant producing and Derek Sherwin on script editing would change the show a bit. But, it really hasn't. Luckily, the concept of this seaweed and the foam and the weird Oak and Quill are keeping everything moving nicely. I just wish we could see the story. The animation helps. But this is one of those stories that really works best if you don't know about the other stories before it.

*Although, there's always one guy. Whenever you're in an environment like this, whether in a factory or an office, and there's someone who is unpleasant and in power, someone who no one can stand, there's always one person who shrugs and says "They're not that bad." "Oh, Mr. Robson, sure he yells at everyone and doesn't listen to anything anyone says. Sure, he insults everybody including people's family members. But I like the cut of his jib. I don't mind working for him." "Thanks, Ron."

Fury From The Deep

Episode Three

Episode 200: (March 30, 1968) Robson goes mad and gets attacked by the weeds. The TARDIS gang do some research in the TARDIS itself and think they've found the source of the problem.

Cliffhanger: Maggie Harris tells Robson that he knows what he needs to do. She steps into the sea.

Robson blathers a lot in the first half of this oddly short episode. * It's nice to know that the horrible behavior he exhibited in the first two episodes is basically him at the end of his tether. They talk about his four years on the rig. They talk about their boss, Megan Jones, trusting him implicitly. He seems to get the job done. There's only so long you can just ram everything threw and verbally abuse people before it's over. (The worst moment here is when Harris says he needs an ambulance because his wife is sick. Robson replies "Does she have a hangover?" Harris is a better man than I. I would have punched Robson right in the kisser for that sort of shi**y remark.)

The best part of this episode is when Harris forgets to pay attention to the Doctor, Victoria and Jamie who are still, technically, prisoners. The TARDIS crew grab some seaweed and take it back to the TARDIS for experimentation. I love that we spend a large chunk of the episode inside the TARDIS lab experimenting. It's unlike anything we've seen before this season. It's our heroes being allowed to do their thing without anyone bothering them and I find it refreshing. The other thing I love here is the Doctor's book of

Monsters. It shows the giant Weed Creature from 18th century seaman legends. As a kid, I adored this kind of stuff. I always wanted a book that had all the monsters in it. There are a few books out there like that. (I have one called *Monster's Who's Who* that I adore.) But I've never found the perfect one. The one that mixed reality and fiction perfectly. I had a Movie Monster book when I was a kid that I carried around with me in case monsters attacked because it listed weaknesses. That was a comfort. This is why I love The Doctor. He does his research. He checks his book of monsters and then he presents his proof. And people generally believed him!

As much as I dislike Robson, the final scene is chilling. The synth score in this story is very fantastic. Whenever it starts up, it puts us in a very different space, away from the complaining humans, bitching and moaning. And watching Maggie and Robson speak on the edge of the sea is chilling. It ends with her strolling directly into the sea. That's a heck of an ending. Despite some annoyance early on, this is, in fact, becoming an excellent story.

One last thing: In deference to the previous companions, Victoria beings to express some discomfort and disenchantment with the life she is living. She screams a lot in this episode, which means something. She is being set up to say goodbye here. It's nice because this hasn't been done since, let's say, Vicki. And that was about two-and-a-half years ago.

*I had a look around in the books written by my betters to see if anyone mentions why this episode is just 20 minutes. When the last episode of "The Enemy of the World" ran short, it was due to technical issues. I didn't see a reason for that here. I thought maybe it was shortened due to something else being on afterwards. I couldn't find anything. The episode moves along fine and is maybe helped by being a little shorter.

Fury From The Deep
Episode Four

Episode 201: (April 6, 1968) Megan Jones arrives. Van Lutyens disappears into the impeller shaft. The Doctor and Jamie almost follow. Victoria is ready to end her TARDIS travels.

Cliffhanger: The Weed Monster is in the impeller shaft. The fight is on.

Megan Jones arrives! She's the woman who put Robson is charge. So, she might not be the best person to speak to. She calls the Doctor a "half-wit." There's always something weird about doing something like that. Have you seen the first season of *The X-Files*? 24 episodes. Throughout, whenever Mulder and Scully arrive on the scene, the local authorities laugh at them. Now, we know that they're going to save the day. (Generally.) And, practically, we understand why the authorities must think these two are nuts. But, man, does that trope get tiresome. Mulder knows his stuff. Scully knows her stuff. By time you get to the end of Season One, that becomes the worst part of the show. Luckily, as we go on, writers begin to deal with that. They dismiss it convincingly. Or don't bring it up. Kolchak in his show dealt with that so often it becomes something we're meant to laugh at by the end. But, Kolchak like Mulder and Scully save the day. So, hearing the people who are wrong laugh at them becomes super grating. It's just as bad here.

Especially because at that moment the Doctor and Jamie have gone down the impeller shaft to try and save Van Lutyens. They're saving the day! Half-wit? Your mother! Sorry. I thought I'd like Megan Jones. By the end of the episode, she seems more rational than Robson. Robson, throughout the episode, is presented as strangely incommunicado. I like that. Oak and Quill have a bunch to do in this episode too.

Who are they and where do they come from? I couldn't say. I like how it seems like they might be weird outsiders that wandered into the factory.

Anyway, Megan Jones is here. Van Lutyens has gone missing. And the Doctor and Jamie encounter the Weed Creature. From the images we have, from the drawing and animation we have, the Weed Creature seems to be an awesome force. The Yeti is numerous and strong but always a little too cuddly. The Ice Warriors didn't really do much. The Cybermen are less energetic than they should be. But, this force, this weird Weed thing seems to be a powerful enemy. As the Doctor says, it is fighting for control of humanity. I'm glad Megan doesn't call him an idiot when he says that because, frankly, Doctor maybe it should be toned down slightly when dealing with the bureaucrats. Harris recommends blowing up all the rigs at one point. Even I thought that was crazy.

So, the Weed is approaching. The misdirection of Robson's craziness has kept us looking in one direction while this craziness built up. I think its nicely done. Yes, I was annoyed/ am annoyed by a bunch of it. But we are here now. There is a crazy monster trying to take the rigs. Let's see what happens.

The other big thing here is Victoria's story. She really, really is done with the travelling. Jamie is all for leaving and going to a new place that's just as crazy and just as dangerous. But Victoria is tired of it. She didn't join the crew willingly. She joined it because she had to. And I feel like, as much as she loves The Doctor and Jamie, she simply can't handle this anymore. I like that. This hasn't been a fun time for the TARDIS crew. Well, maybe the Doctor and Jamie have been enjoying it. But these base under sieges are more oppressive and far less varied than what we are used to. She can't handle the Innes Lloyd/ Gerry Davis format. To be honest, I think there are others that have the same problem. When this is over, she wants to go. Even if it means leaving her two best friends. As Megan goes on and on, as the weed attacks, as the Doctor plans on how to save humanity again, this really is the topper. His best friend, Victoria, doesn't want to do this with him anymore. One would have never thought this was an option when travelling with the Doctor. Isn't this fun? Isn't this fantastic? Sometimes you don't always recruit the right person. Victoria needs a way out. It's time. Let's take care of this Weed Creature and go our separate ways.

Fury From The Deep

Episode Five

Episode 202: (April 13, 1968) The Weed attacks the base. Robson kidnaps Victoria and flies her out to one of the rigs.

Cliffhanger: The Doctor and Jamie enter a foam-filled control room on one of the rigs. Robson rises out of the foam declaring that they have been expecting The Doctor.

A good hang tight sort of episode. The episode doesn't advance the story that much. We get more from Victoria about how she's ready to leave. We get more of Oak and Quill creeping around. We get a lot of Megan Jones saying "Well, let's trust the Doctor. No one else seems to know anything." We get Robson and the kidnapping. We get what looks like a great attack by the Weed and foam in the main control room. It's always a big moment in the base under siege stories. The moment when the main set is overtaken by the evil.

There's something that feels very satisfying about this because it's all that weed and foam. Granted, the previous story had the HQ being overrun with foam. But this seems larger. This seems messier. As if this wonderful antiseptic world is being over-run with awfulness. This living Weed deep from the deep.

Trying to take over the world. In similar news, the Weed Creature seems to know who the Doctor is. Victoria mentions at the start that they seem to keep winding up on Earth. Is the TARDIS bringing them back repeatedly to face these threats and come up against these forces that want the Doctor? Is the TARDIS deliberately doing this all at once to get these threats out of the way? So, next season, we can do something different?

Hey! I like that. If, as "The Doctor's Wife" implies, the TARDIS herself guides the Doctor to the places he needs to go to, they could be going to all these bases under siege because this is the perfect team to do this. Think about the ending of this one? Why bring Victoria? Because she will stop all this. I like this idea. Jamie's up for whatever the Doctor is up to and this is the Doctor (Moreso than the first one) who seems most suited to this kind of story. So, this is the Optimum team for "base under siege." Just as the First Doctor was optimum for all those historical trips. I like this theory very much.

Anyway, that seems like an idea for another book. The Third Doctor was best suited to take care of those attacks on Earth during his tenure. So, the TARDIS sent the Second Doctor, Jamie and Zoe to the planet of the War Lords where he had to contact the Time Lords and he was exiled to Earth and had his face changed. Now, I like it too much.

Double anyway, the episode has a nice pace. We do seem to be moving towards an ending much speedier than some of the previous stories. The foam and the Weed seem to be a fantastic combination. I'm not sure about the seaweed sticking out of Robson's turtleneck when he's on the helicopter but I can't love everything. And I really like that the Doctor and Jamie head out to the rigs. There's something so isolated and alone about that. It just works perfectly. Flying directly into the heart of the evil. Or whatever the Weed Monster is.

Fury From The Deep

Episode Six

Episode 203: (April 20, 1968) The final battle between the humans and The Weed. Victoria stays behind.

Cliffhanger: The TARDIS launches itself into the sky as Victoria remains on the Earth.

A fine ending to a story that struggled to rise above all the tropes that the show has introduced over the past two years. Sometimes it succeeded. Often it didn't. In the end, it worked. It has just enough variation to make itself stand out. Just enough to make it a story that stands out amongst all these other similar adventures. Per my previous review, I like to think that since Victoria is gone that the "base under siege" stories will now be wrapping up. (In fact, they are.) We've got to find another way now.

The first half of the episode has the feel of the last episode of "The Abominable Snowmen." Lots of chaos, (lots of screaming, obviously) lots of foam and lots of craziness. The animation brings it to life nicely but we still can't really see it. And I'm not terribly familiar with the direction of Hugh David. So, I'm not sure if this sequence looked like chaos or just felt chaotic. I'm hoping the latter because it seems like a heck of a good time. The image of the giant hand-like weeds flailing around out of the foam is wonderfully creepy. The kind of scary images that I love.

There is something perverse (Rob Shearman had previously pointed this out) about Victoria wanting to stop doing this because she's sick of being scared and now she's being forced to scream at the top of her lungs to save the day. Over in "Delta and The Bannermen," the shrieks/ screams that save the day are supplied willingly. Here, Victoria doesn't want to scream and scream. It's odd because in one way you can understand why. She's sick of it. She doesn't want to do it anymore. But she knows that the only way to kill the creature is her screaming. (Odd that sound defeats the evil here in the story that begins with the sonic screwdriver.) So, the fact that she's struggling to use her screaming makes her seem a little selfish while we understand exactly why she's doing it. It's interesting and probably not something the writer thought about at all.

The Weed Creature is defeated. And, for one of the few times in his tenure, the Second Doctor stays. In fact, they stay an extra day because they want Victoria to have time to decide if she wants to remain or go. I don't know what the Doctor does in that time but surely there's a short story or an audio in there somewhere. The final scene between Victoria and Jamie is heartbreaking. We understand Victoria completely but we don't want her to go. Has she been the most effective companion? I don't know. After my previous review, I think she was the perfect companion for this time. And she will be missed. I like that the Doctor says she must choose for herself. It's very Doctor-like. You can see Jamie strain against it but the Doctor is right.

The closing sequence on the beach. With everyone waving goodbye to one another is the less dramatic, but also less sentimental version of the end of "Doomsday" and even "Journey's End." RTD does know how to milk those big moments. Here, we say goodbye. That's the way *Doctor Who* works. You say hello. And then, before you know it you say goodbye. That's why you should always be wary of a "fan" who wants previous teams brought back. They're not doing it right. (Call it gatekeeping if you like. I was born when the Tenth season aired. The show set its format in stone long before I was here.) Watching the TARDIS fly away as Victoria stands on the beach is a sad moment. It comes at the end of a weird raucous story where even Robson gets redeemed. He'll be back to his normal self in a few days but hopefully he's a bit wiser now. Oh well. Victoria, we shall miss you. The closing conversation between Jamie and the Doctor is heartbreaking. Let's get involved in a big, dumb adventure to take our minds off all of this. Shall we?

THE WHEEL IN SPACE

By David Whitaker

From a story by Kit Pedler

Directed by Tristan De Vere Cole

Episode One

Episode 204: (April 27, 1968) The Doctor and Jamie land on a small spacecraft where they eat strange "SPACE!" food and the Doctor hits his head.

Cliffhanger: The Wheel is going to destroy the Silver Carrier.

I'm not sure if David Whitaker does this on purpose but this episode is put together almost exactly like a Hartnell first episode. When "The Ark In Space" does this in 1975, we think the show is sort of looking back. Harry, Sarah and The Doctor apparently alone on the ark for one full episode. It makes one nostalgic for past times. In fact, for many of us, we'd only heard or read about these times. And it's an exciting episode. This episode does almost the same thing.

It isolates us in this small ship, after the opening scene in the TARDIS, with only the Doctor and the Jamie and a clunky-looking servo robot. Both Jamie and the Doctor are still thinking about Victoria. They wonder what she's up to. Jamie asks where she is right now. And the Doctor speaks of time being relative. There's almost kind of a laziness to it, which is nice to see. They get attacked by the robot, sort of, at one point. It's really the weird scene with the small silver globe things that are sent sailing through space that makes one think "Huh? Is the Great Intelligence back?" (Not this time.)

The TARDIS has gone screwy and kerflooey and it involves mercury and fluid links, just like out of "The Daleks." The Doctor removes a very powerful Time Vector Generator that shrinks the interior of the TARDIS. They need that mercury! But, as no one seems to be there and they keep missing the Servo Robot, everything seems calm. It's kind of a nice feeling. We know that something will be happening soon but the return to the past style of episodes gives us breathing room, especially after losing Victoria.

It all culminates in the last three or four minutes. We see a larger spinning "wheel" in space. And just at the point where we thought "Where's my colorful cast of characters for this story's base under siege? And where's the base?" It suddenly appears. There's the big control room. There's the colorful cast of characters. Unlike the regular way these stories work, we haven't gotten to know them over the course of the episode. We have no idea who they are. All we know is that they're going to try and destroy the ship that the Doctor and Jamie are on and that's not good. It feels odd, and rather fresh, to hold off so long on showing us the standard sort of group. It's nice to have the Doctor and Jamie just together for a while. (Sure, the space food scene is tiring but the rest is great.) It's Whitaker going back to a previous template of the show to try and refresh this one. I don't know if it fully works but it makes for an intriguing episode this late in the season.

The Wheel In Space

Episode Two

Episode 205: (May 4, 1968) The Doctor is out cold. Jamie meets Zoe. The Wheel plans on destroying the Silver Carrier with the TARDIS inside.

Cliffhanger: We see inside one of these silver eggs. Is that a Cyberman?

A Doctor-less episode. This one works pretty well. It's the second episode and we're just now getting to meet all the people in the Wheel. There are a lot of names; there are a lot of people. I remember Gemma and Bennett. I remember a lady talking about her nose. I remember a guy talking about plants. At this point in the season, these characters really all have sort of run into each other. Gemma stands out. Bennett doesn't quite stand out because we know that he's going to do something crazy-ish soon what with being in charge. I like Gemma. She's a smart, sharp woman who seems like she'd get along very well with the Doctor. If only the Doctor would get up from his coma.

We meet Zoe. She is the "librarian" on the ship. But really, it's a bit stranger than that. She's a part of this futuristic society. An almost robotic part of this society. We see it a little bit here. There's that odd pause when Zoe and Gemma are talking. Zoe suddenly does something else within the call and it feels strange. If you've seen it, you know what I mean. Zoe is some weird, futuristic super smart person that they use for knowledge and info. It's nice when she meets Jamie because there seems to be the promise of some fun there. She laughs at Jamie's kilt. He threatens to spank her. It's all good stuff. And it portends that Zoe might be joining us in the future.

Jamie on his own is a first. He doesn't handle himself particularly well. He's very worried about the Doctor and the TARDIS. He tells some silly lies. He says the Doctor's name is "John Smith" from a piece of machinery. That will stick with the show. It seems very silly and obvious when he does it here. He does seem lost without the Doctor. It is kind of too bad that he doesn't seem to have picked up any smarts as he's been on all these adventures. In fact, he almost decimates the crew while using the Time Vector Generator to signal to them at the start. And then, when he finds out about the Silver Carrier going to be destroyed, he immediately goes to the power room. He's going to do some bad stuff there. It's weird I really thought he would have handled himself better during a time like this. He doesn't.

Luckily, all this narrative stuff keeps everything moving as the Doctor is out of the way. The crew talk a lot. They think Jamie and the Doctor might be saboteurs. They talk about everything in general. It is nice to have all these intro bits and bobs 1) pushed into the second Episode and 2) happen without the Doctor. It gives the story an extra push. When we see the silver egg with the Cyberman inside, my first thought was "End of Episode 1." Then, I thought "Oh no wait…" So, it's decently put together. Just enough to keep the story moving and just enough to keep us a little further ahead of everything than we think we should be. I look forward to the Doctor waking up in the next episode

The Wheel In Space

Episode Three

Episode 206: (May 11, 1968) The invasion of the Space Wheel by the Cybermen has begun.

Cliffhanger: The Cybermen on the Silver Carrier have taken two of the Wheel crew hostage.

After the loss of Victoria in the previous story, I am very happy that this episode exists. We get to see the new team of Zoe, The Doctor and Jamie working together. They're funny. They're charming. Zoe is smart as a whip. The Doctor is occasionally a bit condescending but he has just come out of a concussion. To be honest, Zoe doesn't seem to care. Their scenes together are fun. That's a good team in the making.

This is one of two episodes from this serial that we have. If you watch it standalone, it doesn't amount to much. A lot of characters. A strange scene with a guy getting attacked by Cybermats. Jamie committing sabotage. Cybermen sitting around. But, in the context of the story, it's a great Episode Three. Whitaker's delaying tactic in episode one really keeps the story moving along nicely. I mentioned my confusion at the cliffhanger in the previous episode. Something similar happened in this episode. As Bennett is berating the man who kept the Cybermats a secret, I thought that this felt like an episode two scene. The man in charge is beginning to start yelling. It's at about the halfway point. We're about to enter the second half of the story. Whitaker's shifting of the structure has bumped everything just enough so that the story, timewise, is ahead of us. And I like that.

It reminds of a filmmaker named Michael O'Rourke. He made several films in the late 1980s and early 1990s. They were mainly horror movies, mainly slasher films. His two big films, *Deadly Love* and *Moonstalker*, fiddled slightly with the structures of these sorts of films. They added extra material at the start. When the film settles into its formula, we aren't 5 minutes or 10 minutes or 15 minutes in, we're 30 minutes or more in a 90 minute or less film. So, when we get to the formulaic part, his adjustments have reduced the time we need to be in there. Everything feels quicker. Everything feels sharper. This episode has that feeling. The unfortunate thing, though, is that the next two episodes are missing. It's tough to figure out if he keeps this going when we can't see the episodes.

This episode, luckily, has a heck of a lot going on in it. One of my favorite conceits is that the Doctor and Jamie are 100% spanners in the big Cyberman plan. Their plan is to send this rocket reeling. It approaches the Wheel. They send the cybermats on board. The cybermats corrode the bernalium that powers the laser. The Cybermen blow up a star and the meteorites are flying towards the defenseless

Wheel. The Silver Carrier has what the Wheel needs so they send spacemen over to get controlled and... well, we don't know all the plan yet. But it is a hell of a plan. And the Doctor and Jamie are complete variables who sort of help the plan at one point. Jamie sabotages the laser before it can destroy the Silver Carrier. Were the Cybermats meant to take out the laser before he did? It seems like a bit of a slip-up in their plan. The Carrier is not destroyed at the start of the episode because of Jamie's sabotage. Of course, the TARDIS would have been in trouble too. Now, we wouldn't worry about the TARDIS. It would pilot itself to the Wheel. Back then, we were a little more troubled.

And Leo definitely bawls out Zoe here for not being quite "human". She shrugs and goes on with her business. But that is a definite feeling that she has been raised in some ways that the others find uncomfortable. Tanya and her nose probably wouldn't approve.

The Wheel in Space

Episode Four

Episode 207: (May 18, 1968) The Cyberman is brought over in a box of bernalium and things will never be the same.

Cliffhanger: The Cybermen are on the Wheel.

It's nice to see the Doctor get a little flirty with Gemma. I think they'd make an adorable couple. Wouldn't you watch them get in a series of fun adventures? I know I would. I'm not 100% sure about the scene where the Doctor is trying to convince Bennett that there are Cybermen out there. The Doctor is just a bit too whiny for me. "Come on! There are Cybermen! Come on! There are too! Shut up!" I know he was recently concussed but whining isn't his best point. Another interesting thing is that he's basically been in the sick bay since the start of Episode Two. But, again, because of the way Whitaker has structured everything, you don't really notice it. When you finally do, it hasn't been a real problem and you're ever so much closer to the end. I would bet cash money it was Whitaker's idea to do this to the story. As great as Kit Pedler's idea may have been, I don't think story structure was something that really seemed to come to him that easy. Or at least, not yet. *

Jamie and Zoe are getting on nicely together. The scene where Jamie discovers what a tape recorder is is a good one. The scene where Zoe really wishes that she could be more than just the 'librarian' on a Wheel is telling. Victoria (created in a previous Whitaker story) unwillingly becomes a member of the TARDIS crew. Zoe is practically saying "If someone here has a time/ spaceship, please take me away." I like it. We still haven't had someone from "Modern Day" Earth on the show for over a season but still. This bunch looks like they could be fun. (Luckily, most of their season exists.)

I love Bennett in this. At first, it seems like he's going to go the way of Robson and become a screaming maniac. Gemma does mention that, basically, cognitive dissonance has set in big time. The scenes of Bennett walking around, asking if everything's OK and then immediately saying that of course it is before walking away are very funny. They're a definite blessing after Robson's histrionics in the last story. But, of course, Bennett doesn't have as big of a part in the story as Robson did. Because of the structure he never fully takes hold. But he's OK. He is funny when his mind goes out to lunch. I guess it takes all kinds to run a base under siege. Although, this siege is certainly a calm one.

Overall, this is a very good middle episode of a Season Five serial. It doesn't move particularly fast. The menace isn't as strong as it could be. But it isn't boring. Yes, maybe the character of Chang isn't great. We can't see the episode so we don't really know if it was incredibly racist or just a bit. The moment when the Cybermen casually dumps him in the incinerator seems like it's kind of a rough one. I mean, dumping a human in an incinerator is never nice. Especially a character we just found out about. And especially the Asian guy on the ship. Thank goodness he wasn't wearing a red shirt. Anyway, the episode is running a bit in place. But it's building nicely. I think Whitaker seems to have a grasp on how to do this 6-part base under siege thing. Now, granted, we're pretty much at the end of this cycle. But thank goodness someone figured it out.

*-Kit's on the line. -What's he want? -He's got an idea. -What is it? -Cybermen attack a space station in the future. -Pay the man and call in Whitaker. -Whittington? -Whitaker? -Gotcha, Chief! – Don't call me Chief!

The Wheel In Space

Episode Five

Episode 208: (May 25, 1968) The Cyber invasion has properly begun. For real.

Cliffhanger: Jamie and Zoe, floating in space, are in the path of the meteorites. Meanwhile, right before that, Gemma is killed.

We'll talk about the cliffhanger in a bit because a lot is going on in this episode and some of it is tough to gauge because the episode is lost. It feels expansive. Humans are being taken over by the Cybermen. The Cyber Controller has said they will take over the Wheel. And the folks on the wheel lock themselves in the main control room. They set up a forcefield around themselves. The meteors are coming. And...

I love this... The Cybermen who wanted the laser taken apart must put it back together again. Because they'll get destroyed by the meteors if they hit the wheel. * I like that. They do have the plan worked out well. Everyone does sort of figure out what the plan is in this episode so that works out nicely. There's a weird claustrophobia (that may or may not be because of the recon) throughout this episode.

We really have no concept of how big the Wheel is in truth. We can see the model. It looks big. But how big is it? It's like The Enterprise over on *Star Trek*. How big is that thing? I mean lots of people live there. They have huge engines. We mainly see the control room, which is a not-very-big room right at the front. What does the rest of the place look like? (Same could be said for the TARDIS. But I think she reconfigures herself every once in a while. So that might be different.) Same for the Wheel.

The Cybermen are going to poison the air in the Wheel at the end. They mention that there are several sections (12?) in the Wheel. Each one with its own air supply. So, this is a big place. I wish we had more of it to see. More to absorb. Because the Cybermen do really seem to be overtaking everything.

Then, of course, we get the scene where Jamie and Zoe are sent to the Silver Carrier to retrieve the Time Vector Generator rod in the middle of the crazy meteorite shower. That seems odd to me. Leo yells at the Doctor. Leo does love yelling so that doesn't seem terrible. But he's right. The Doctor sends Jamie and Zoe deep into space during a harrowing shower of huge rocks. That doesn't quite seem like the Doctor to me. Maybe he's still got some concussion? Who knows? The more one thinks about it, the crazier it seems.

The big blip in the episode happens right at the end. It's a bit tough to unpack. In Terrance Dicks's novelization, Gemma is killed but it doesn't seem like the Doctor sees it. In the episode, using the recon, it seems like the Doctor sees her die on the viewscreen, which is horrible. She has taken control from the loopy Bennett. She is killed in her first journey out as Controller. It's heartbreaking. It's shocking.

And it immediately cuts to Jamie and Zoe where a more regular cliffhanger is happening. An odd moment in the show. Strangely mature amid all this good time Cyber silliness.

Overall, again, it's the end of the season and Whitaker has kept the excitement up. The Cyber invasion isn't huge. But it's in such a controlled space and there is that meteorite storm. Things seem pretty darn harrowing from where I'm sitting. One episode left in the season. Let's see how this goes.

*It seems pretty desperate on the wheel. What with all the meteorites and floating spaceships and Cybermen and Cybermats. I know I wouldn't want to take a job there. But then, I write. We're pretty solitary. The Wheel seems oddly crowded for being (possibly) so huge.

The Wheel In Space

Episode Six

Episode 209: (June 1, 1968) The Cybermen don't quite take over The Wheel.

Cliffhanger: The Doctor shows Zoe "The Evil of the Daleks."

The Doctor only gets one scene with the Cybermen in this one. He didn't really get a scene alone with them in the previous stories. It was always a group scene and, generally, he was in the background. But here, the Doctor's reputation precedes him. (As it has through a lot of this season.) The Cybermen know that he is the one who has kept everyone on the Wheel alive for this long. He hasn't amassed as much of a reputation as he would. But they know him. I love how the Doctor plays coy in this scene. I always love the way Troughton uses his hands. And then, when the Cybermen come for him, he has a trap laid out for them that they can't through. That's one for the Doctor! I suppose it's a good thing the forcefield was up. He would have been shot down quickly. I'm thinking of "The Doctor Falls" here. Troughton's a good runner, though. But he doesn't seem like he'd be as nimble as Capaldi.

Otherwise, a lot happens in the episode. People pass from the Wheel to the Silver Carrier as if it were no trouble at all. Zoe, somehow, sneaks aboard the TARDIS. I'm not sure how she does that. And, in fact, no one seems to care. I understand that Zoe went over there to help make sure they took off OK. But we see the Doctor pouring in mercury. Re-loading the TARDIS. Somehow, she got in before that. How? Anyway. Zoe's part of the team now. We'll talk about that in a moment.

It's kind of an interesting ending. The Cybermen end up helping themselves out by repairing the laser that is used to destroy them. The Doctor uses the rod of the time vector generator (which has gold in it) to boost the power of the laser. And then they blow up the Cyber ship and everything is done. It is a tad anti-climactic. Blow it up! The Doctor has the Cybermen tell him their plan. But he must have known it since he had Jamie and Zoe get the generator. To be honest, a favorite part of the episode is when the Doctor tells Leo to operate the "sectional air supply." It's right after Gemma dies and he is clearly broken up by it. (Seeing her dead body on the monitor isn't helpful.) So, he clearly calls it the "sexual air supply." Making Love Out Of Nothing At All, that's our Second Doctor. (I also love the way he peers out of all the monitors he winds up on. Very commanding.)

Then there's the ending. The story is that there was a 9-week gap between this episode and the start of Season Six. They had Wimbledon for two weeks but no replacement show for the other 7 weeks. So, they used the end of this episode to link to a rerun of "Evil of the Daleks". So, This season ends with Zoe being shown "Evil" and then the next season begins with "So, what did you think of 'Evil of the Daleks,' Zoe?" Well, not quite. One thing that does become immediately noticeable is that with Zoe onboard suddenly the "base under siege" almost completely vanishes. Zoe is here to engage in different types of adventures. That will be Season Six.

Season Five is certainly an interesting one. As I mentioned earlier, to fans of a certain age, this is the "Monster Season" and the pinnacle of what *Doctor Who* is. I would put forward a theory that this is the pinnacle of what *Doctor Who* is at that moment. Each story starts off with a lot of promise. Then, they almost all turn out to be "base under siege." Then, we see the writers do their best to tweak the formula while stretching out the shows to six episodes. Sometimes they worked. Sometimes they slowed down so much it was kind of amazing. I suppose it's a classic season of the show. But I preferred the show when it had a bit more verve and unpredictability. Here the unpredictability comes with "Oh! They didn't do that thing the exact same way again!" That's not really unpredictability. Gerry Davis and Innes Lloyd are gone. Derrick Sherwin and Peter Bryant are in charge. Let's see where we go next.

SEASON SIX

(1968-1969)

THE EVIL OF THE DALEKS

I'm Kidding!

THE DOMINATORS

Written By Norman Ashby

Directed by Morris Barry

Episode One

Episode 210: (August 10, 1968): The Dominators land on the pacifist plane Dulcis. Stuff happens for about 25 minutes.

Cliffhanger: We meet the Quarks! And the feeling we get matches the overall feeling of the episode.

("The Evil of the Daleks" repeat has finished its run with a two-week break for Wimbledon. Technically, there are no Dalek stories for 4/12 years. The rerun had to have been a treat for everyone. We don't get repeats often (or really at all) during this time. So, in this episode, at 8 minutes in when the TARDIS lands and the gang steps out, the Dalek story is mentioned briefly and then the excitement begins!!)

I'm goofing. This is "The Dominators." "Excitement" isn't on an anybody's mind. I know what you're thinking. "Another 6 parter!" Then, why is this story 5 parts? It's written by Mervyn Haisman and Henry Lincoln. (pseudonym party!) So, why isn't it 6? There is a story behind that. I'll tell you later. Suffice it to say, Derrick Sherwin seems to make his first real executive script editor decision here. And it's a wise one. (I would have gone further but it's still a wise one.) Anyway...

The Dominators sure look tough. Rather butch guys with big shoulders and tiny robots named Quarks. They are part of a large group of spaceships that break off and land on "Death Island" on Dulcis. They are about to do something on the island. But preparation is needed first! Much preparation. Who knows what that consists of? You got it! They walk around a lot. The best part of the episode is that they absorb all the radiation on Dulcis (which is just on this island). So, everyone expects everyone else to be filled with radiation but no one ever is. Oh boy!

The Doctor, Jamie and Zoe arriving eight minutes in kind of shows off something that really began to happen in the previous season. We're going to spend time introducing the world before the TARDIS shows up. In fact, in this one, I kind of forgot to expect the TARDIS until it arrived. This trend in the show will culminate at the end of the season. (And, also, possibly, in the "Doctor-lite" episodes from the current run.) It's nice that it gives us a pile of what we need beforehand. But, also, the "where the heck are we?" of stories like "The Wheel In Space" are gone. One gets the feeling that no one quite knows what to do with the show now.

The death of the three people that Cully brings to the island is something. We get the doubting guy. We get the "Let's get going" guy. We get the cute gal who keeps giving Cully the eye. Then they rush towards the Dominators and they get killed. We will see the way the Dulcians are characterized throughout the story. Peaceful people with no curiosity. All I think when they rush the Dominators like a group of hippies is "If the Dominators had hockey masks on, would I have stopped short?" These guys seem scary.

Of course, the Dominators are interesting. More or less. There's the lead guy who yells at his subordinate. There's the subordinate who does whatever he wants until his superior yells at him. You get away with whatever you want until you get caught. So, there's a group of people in tutus going up against sadistic killers with homicidal robots. This should go well.

Note: The production text of the DVD points this out but I think it's something worth mentioning. Zoe has been with the Doctor and Jamie for a very small time. They met on the Wheel. They watched "Evil." They've been on Dulcis for half an hour. But when, the Doctor and Jamie leave the base to check on the TARDIS. Zoe decides to stay at the base and chat with Cully and everyone else. Why? Yes, to split them up. I get the narrative convention. But, why? Maybe because she prefers to be with a group rather than just a couple people? Who knows? You think she'd go with the people she came with. Although, actually, we know very little about her. Don't we?

The Dominators

Episode Two

Episode 211: (August 17, 1968) The Doctor and Jamie are put through tests. The Dominators argue. The Dulcians do the opposite of arguing.

Cliffhanger: Cully and Zoe are in the base when it gets bombed.

In the "Making Of" documentary on the DVD, Derrick Sherwin, the script editor, says that the problem he had with this story was that it was crap. The first episode isn't stellar. * This episode is less stellar. It has some funny moments. You can feel Troughton and Hines doing their best to liven things up. But, oh boy, is it repetitive! However, it's not repetitive like Sideshow Bob getting hit with rakes. It's repetitive in the way where you want to go on top of a building and have a jump. It seems like the writers had one idea and they're determined to beat it into the ground. The Great intelligence and The Yeti were amorphous and weird. They could handle extended serials. The Dominators are obvious. To make them repetitive is to make everyone sleepy.

The Doctor and Jamie test scenes have their charms. They go on for too long. But they're fun though. As mentioned previously, you can see the actors having a good time. The script, though, should provide something. This really feels like the script gave them nothing and they are working their behinds off to entertain. They are so good at being stupid. The Dominators check out Jamie and he only has one heart. The Dulcians have two hearts. I think we know someone else here that has two hearts. I'm glad they didn't check the Doctor. We are less than a season from the Doctor getting specific biological traits.

It's the repetitive stuff that begins to really drive the story into the ground. The Doctor and Jamie's tests all seem the same by the end. Whenever we see Dulcians they're so boring, that it gets tiresome. I think that is the writers' point. The endless "Oh, Cully! What are you up to?" routines are quickly more boring than all the base under siege stuff from the previous seasons. This story is at the end of a block and the start of this season. One hopes there might be some change but it's all a big shrug. A big, boring shrug.

What about those Dominators? The writers don't seem to have anything to say about the pacifists. They seem to have less to say about the Dominators. Stupid, sadistic, running in circles. The Quarks are awkward creations that keep needing to be recharged. The Dominator's smile when he's destroying the base should be rather chilling/ sardonic. Instead, all I can think is... "He's going to get yelled at for that in the next episode." It's weird. I think Sherwin might be right. This is crap.

Note: For a story that seems to be about condemning pacifists, there's an odd moment with the Doctor. The moment when he's holding the laser gun in the museum. He's acting like he doesn't know what it is. The Dominator asks him about it. He says it "It's a gun. It kills people." That line seems out of place for the story. I can't imagine someone who wrote this throwing in an aside like that. Mr. Sherwin?

*And, in a world where season openers and closers are huge, it seems like a ridiculous way to being a season. Guys with big shoulders! Effete men in tutus! Perfect! Maybe there was another show in another world that could handle this. *Doctor Who* looks odd doing it.

The Dominators

Episode Three

Episode 212: (August 24, 1968) The Dominators use the Dulcians to clear a drilling site. The Dulcian council debates. The Doctor and Jamie keep going back and forth between assorted boring locations.

Cliffhanger: The Quarks blow up a room with Cully and Jamie in it.

Have I mentioned how ridiculous the costumes are? When Tensa, the Dulcian leader, enters the debate about what they can do stop the Dominators, he is the only Dulcian who doesn't look like a complete buffoon as he speaks. His tutu thing is much longer than everybody else's so that helps. * Haisman and Lincoln really felt like they were making a point. And, originally, apparently, they thought all this stuff with the Dulcians sitting around in their tutus acting effete and ineffectual was hilarious. But, guys, if you really think pacifism is stupid (look at your previous stories for more straightforward appreciation of calls to violence), maybe try to find an alternative.

Especially in a show where your lead character is meant to solve problems by using their brain. If your response to pacifism is, it doesn't work. Then, I guess we always must resort to violence. In the context of *Doctor Who*, this is grotesque. And leads one to re-evaluate their other stories. "The Web of Fear" is made great by Douglas Camfield's direction and the set design. The story is meandering and a bit muddled. "The Abominable Snowman" has its moments but it also has a group of peaceful monks. Except for one monk who wants to resort to violence and it turns out that he's right. I'm kind of glad Derrick Sherwin angered them to the point where they left. And the Quarks are stupid.

OK. I guess the Quarks are menacing. I keep hoping that a Chumbley will show up and blow them off the planet. They look so cumbersome. They constantly need re-charging. Every time Rago has them do something, the other Dominator yells at him. Why did the Dominators make robots that look like this? And why can they never stay charged? I know the show was after the new Daleks. But no. Maybe they could have made a neat wind-up toy, galumphing along with their arms moving in and out, running out of energy when you need them the most.

As far as the episode is concerned, it's basically watching a bunch of actors haul fake rocks around as if they were heavy. Alongside the Doctor and Jamie, going to the mainland and then back to the island. The arguments between the Dominators are the same as before. The Quarks are still tough to understand. Cully is still the only Dulcian who has any fight in him, which means in a land of peaceful people the angry, violent jerk is the hero. (Although, the other young guy is starting to show some fight.)

I don't know. The ideas behind it make me shake my head. But some of it is OK. The Dulcian arguments are old already. The rock moving gets dull fast. But it picks up at the end with some exploding Quarks. And the Doctor and Jamie are doing everything they can to goof around and have a good time. Heck, if Zoe hadn't inexplicably decided to stay with the Dulcians in Episode 1, they could all just go home. As it is, this grinds on for another two episodes. Won't you join me?

*I wonder if that's some sort of sign of leadership or dominance within the Dulcian community. It's like Batman having a thicker batpole than Robin in the 1960s TV series. (Yes, I know exactly how that sounds.)

The Dominators

Episode Four

Episode 213: (August 31, 1968) The Dominators visit the Dulcian council and tell them what's up. The Doctor and Zoe begin to figure out what's going on.

Cliffhanger: A Quark is about to kill the Doctor.

This is probably the best episode of this serial. It's repetitive, sure. There's a long sequence where the Dominators threaten one another. We know it's going nowhere but it works out well. It happens in front of the Doctor and friends so we can see the problems within the ranks. And it brings up: Is this a race of beings? Is it some sort of super assemblage of Dominator-themed people? Who are they? Where do they come from? I've never read the novelization. (Seeing the serial first stopped me from spending the money.) But one wonders: who are these guys? They control the ten galaxies, but later they control a galaxy. I don't know. They seem like a bunch of jerks who have some ships and some weaponry and have declared themselves "Dominators." I don't think it's an actual race.

The episode is the best of them because there's so much going on. The Dominator visiting the Dulcian capitol is a really good scene. Just to see him sneering (what a bunch of sneerers!) at the Dulcians is interesting because they can't really come up with a defense. They will simply lose. So, I'm happy the Doctor has stayed. And I'm happy that he and Zoe are checking everything out in the Dominator's control room.

I love the scenes with Zoe and the Doctor looking through the control room. Yes, Zoe is adorable in her little skirt thing and with dirt on her face. But I love the two of them working through what's happening. The Doctor could have done the same with Susan and Vicki. Maybe Barbara. But it's been a long time. He pulled Victoria on as an orphan. She seemed to be with them for a while but I don't think she ever really fit. Zoe is the first companion to really WANT to be on the TARDIS. We will get more of those as time goes on. She is really the first one who wants to be there and do whatever it is that the Doctor does. (Jamie's intro is best left vague as far as I'm concerned.) So, the two of them together are a joy. When they examine the ship, it's two smart people overriding the pacifism and the sadism that has overwhelmed this story. It helps and it makes this episode better than the others.

The scene where Teel is tortured by Rago as they try to learn who destroyed the Quark is another strong one. They really are just bullies. Watching him bully the young gal and torture Teel is kind of sickening. We had the character of Benik in "The Enemy of the World" who was a sadist. This is different. It seems to be horrible people banding together just to beat down others. It's kind of tough to watch and unless the show can bring us some relief in the last episode then maybe we should abandon this and carry on. (There's a reason why the next story is called "The Mind Robber.")

When the head Dominator visits the Dulcians, there's a real frisson there, I think. Because he believes completely that since he has firepower, he rules the roost. And, I'll be damned, he's probably right. However, I would have liked it if we had found some way to work with the issue rather than just murder and sneering. Heck, the cliffhanger here is an excellent one because the old guy gets killed and the Doctor is threatened. I still ask, "What is this all in aid of?" The story is too repetitive. The story isn't providing any answers. What is the response of pacifism to this sadism?

The Dominators

Episode Five

Episode 214: (September 7, 1968) Do the Dominators succeed?

Cliffhanger: Lava overwhelms the TARDIS. What can the Doctor do now?

The Dominators plan comes to an end! It's one of those endings where the bad guys think they've won up until the very last moment. (The ending always reminds me of the ending of "Underworld.") So, the Dominators remain as arrogant and as awful as ever... right up to the five seconds before they blow up. And it's the Doctor who makes them blow up For Heaven's Sake. There's not much else he can do, though. There's nowhere else he can put the Dominators' bomb but in the Dominators' ship.

After watching this story again, I have discovered the perfect way to watch it: Treat it as if everyone in it, apart from the Doctor, Jamie and Zoe, are all between ages 10-13. The Dominators are the bullies. The Quarks are the big dumb guys who love picking on the little kids. The Dulcians are the smaller kids or the smarter kids. The ones that the bullies pick on. The only way to get around a bully is outwitting them, which is what the Doctor does. Think of Dulcis as a schoolyard where all the kids got along. Then, some new kids came to the school and tried to ruin it all.

Like a lot of the stories from this time, * when the final episode begins, it seems like there's too much to be done. Stuff happens in episode one. Then, the middle episodes are a lot of back and forth. Then, things get resolved super quick in the end. Even the very ending feels rushed. With a volcano erupting and the Doctor and the crew rushing into the TARDIS quickly. (Although, the Doctor does seem to forget what's going on rather quickly.)

Most of the other books mention this so I feel I should. The Doctor's little bombs that everyone throws around are made with Number 9 tablets. In the Navy, the Number 9 tablet was a laxative. I'm not sure if that pertains to this story but it might.

So, the first story of Season Six is done. There's really nothing else to say. We do get a cliffhanger ending. Let's see what's next.

*This serial was originally in six parts. Sherwin cut it down to five. He and the newly arrived Terrance Dicks did the re-writing. Apparently, according to the DVD production text, the original writers never actually made it to the point of writing the last episode. It was just sort of re-written before it was written. Maybe that's why the pace is sharper than the other episodes. At 4, this story might have been worth it. Or more watchable. 5 is still too long.

THE MIND ROBBER

Episode One

Written By Derrick Sherwin

Directed by David Maloney

Episode 215: (September 14, 1968) The TARDIS leaps outside of reality into a white void filled with odd white robots.

Cliffhanger: The TARDIS explodes and the console spins off into space.

The consequence of cancelling the 6th episode of "The Dominators" meant "The Mind Robber" needed an extra episode tacked on to it. (They were at the end of a production block.) But they couldn't tack it on to the end. So, they had to do it at the beginning. Script Editor Derrick Sherwin created this episode which is the Doctor, Jamie and Zoe along with the TARDIS console room and the power room. Plus, a white void. The budget for this episode was very low. (As the DVD production text notes, it had the budget of "The Dominators" Episode 6. In serials, the last episode always had the smallest budget because things had been paid for already.) The use of imagination in this episode makes for fascinating viewing.

It's simply a very weird episode. They step out of reality and some force is trying to separate them from the TARDIS. Some force in the white void that shows images of home. Some force that eventually blows up the TARDIS. That closing sequence is something. After an episode of something trying to get them out, it just decides to blow everything up. That's a cliffhanger! Where on Earth do you go after you blow up the TARDIS?

One of the things I love here is the strong felling of "the unknown" pervading everything. There really is a feeling of 'What the heck is happening?" The white void has always looked great. It's too bad DVD clarity is so good. On PBS, when this originally aired, you couldn't see the back walls or the edges of the white studio. In certain shots of the DVD, you can see the walls and the floor. It's OK. It means it is not an endless void. It's a void with some boundaries. I'm all for that.

Because of having to expand the story, it is one of the shortest episodes in *Doctor Who*. This episode is 21 minutes and 19 seconds. The entire 5-part serial is a little under 100 minutes. In contrast, "The Dominators" is 121 minutes. There's almost an entire episode missing. It does make for faster paced episodes than we've had in the show for a long time.

This was, famously, the episode that eventually got the number of episodes in the seasons reduced. Patrick Troughton was not happy about the three regulars having to lead the entire episode by themselves. They did a good job. The Doctor has a nice sense of worry and reassurance to him. I love the lava in the opening scene. The white robots are fab. Zoe's catsuit is awesome. I do hope Jamie has more than one kilt. Where can we go from here?

Oh, in the Closing credits "The Master" appears. Could it be…?

The Mind Robber

Episode Two

By Peter Ling

Episode 216: (September 21, 1968) The TARDIS crew end up in a strange forest, filled with a traveler, some children and an obsession with words.

Cliffhanger: A unicorn charges Jamie, Zoe and the Doctor.

In the first episode, the Doctor and the gang enter a world outside of reality. A force in this world finds the Doctor and wants him brought to it. It gets the Doctor there at the end of that episode. In the second episode, we see the back of a man monitoring a series of monitors, working on bringing the Doctor and friends to him. We learn that this world is obsessed with words. The highlight moment is when the Doctor is surrounded by riddle-telling children. (I like the Doctor's reaction to them. He seems amused and then annoyed.) One child seems to threaten the Doctor with a sword, a weapon. The sword becomes words, a dictionary. The real weapon in this place. In fact, they are in a forest of giant letters, that become words, that become sayings. It's an odd land.

And "The Master" is mentioned for real. The Doctor doesn't recognize the name. So, presumably, the fellow we will meet in two seasons had a different name. (Or something else is going on.) There's some clever camera stuff going on here for the time. With all five cameras in the studio being used during the scene's in The Master's lair. It's casually done but when you look at it and think about everything that's happening, it's very smart.

I will save talk of "The Stranger" until the next episode. But, if you know your literature, you will probably guess who this gentleman is. The unicorn and The Stranger bring in the next element of the story, which is Fiction. But again, that's for the next episode.

A bit of serendipity before this episode began shooting gives it one of the wonderfully oddest moments in an episode to date. Frazier Hines had chicken pox and could not appear in the episode. (He is in a sequence at the start that they shot several weeks later.) Jamie is shot by a redcoat and becomes a stand-up 2-dimensional figure with his face removed. The Doctor must replace his face and he does it wrong. So, for this episode and the next Jamie is the same but with a different face and that's good comedy. And that's a fun, imaginative way to fix a problem. Derrick Sherwin is working on all cylinders here. (Plus, he now has Terrance Dicks helping him out.)

This is the longest of the 5 episodes at around 21:48. It goes by very quick. The forest of words here is much more tangible than the odd white void. The white void seems/ seemed a bit like an odd waiting room. A space leading towards possibly assorted worlds in this non-reality. This Master pulled them into this one for whatever insidious reasons he had. It's a fun episode. It puts us in the thick of this weirdness. (I think the word puzzle thing is particularly odd.) Zoe gets put in a jar. Clockwork soldiers follow them around. Something weird is going on. With the biggest moment of relief being, thank goodness we're not on Dulkis anymore. But where are we?

The Mind Robber

Episode Three

Episode 217: (September 28, 1968) The TARDIS crew begin to maneuver through a maze as fictional characters accumulate around them.

Cliffhanger: Medusa is about to turn Zoe to stone.

This episode is under 20 minutes. That's a rarity in the land of *Doctor Who*. And, in fact, this review and the next two might be shorter than usual to match the episode length. Or maybe not. Let's see.

As I mentioned in the previous review, the fact that the first two episodes put us in such different places is, I think, cool. Things are weird. Things are atypical. Things have a nice flow to them. In this episode, we get the "fiction" element added. We get several fictional characters, including Rapunzel. The Stranger is officially named as Gulliver, deep within whichever travel this is. We get several fictional beasts and creatures. We also get Jamie getting his face back. My problem with the episode, as charming as it is, is that it works best if I just name everything that happened because it doesn't have the strange flow of the first two. It becomes repetitive rather fast.

So, Jamie gets his face back. The moment that Zoe realizes that the Doctor put his face on wrong is the funniest moment in the episode. Jamie gets chased by a clockwork soldier, scales a tower using Rapunzel's hair and meets the Princess. That's a lovely little scene. I do wish Jamie was a prince. The moment that's a real zinger is when he hops into the castle and it becomes the Master's control center. We keep seeing the Master watching the TARDIS crew's progress. (In this episode, we get an elaborate cave-type map thing.) Jamie discovers the computers sending out ticker tape which is telling the story that we are watching. And this starts to look like some big, crazy what the heck thing. What is all this? What is it doing in the center of this non-reality? How did The Master get there? What is going on? But that doesn't get answered here.

Let's talk about the Doctor and Zoe. The episode is short. But it does get repetitive, which is too bad. And I'm not just counting the cutting from The Doctor and Zoe to the Master in his chair. I'm talking the structure of it all. The episode begins with the unicorn rushing our trio. We get a classic "I deny this! This is not real!" sort of thing and the unicorn becomes a cutout. That's fine. It doesn't quite make the menacing things menacing though if all you have to do is yell that. (The next episode will deal with that.)

What makes it tricky is that we get that "denying the reality of the creature" thing three times in twenty minutes. It's fine the first time. The second time, especially with Zoe refusing to acknowledge it, is a bit "I think we just saw this." But then, the third time is the cliffhanger and all I can think is "Isn't the same thing going to happen here that happened twice already?" (We'll find out shortly.) But it doesn't bode well, unless the next episode shifts everything in the way the first three did. It just feels too much like they thought of one thing and then they just drove it into the ground. The first two episodes are so imaginative that the repetitive elements of this one make me think we might be out of ideas.

If this were one of the six-part stories from the last season, I'd think "Ahh, they're playing for time." But this is different from those. This is more imaginative and this is the first episode dealing with this portion of the story and it seems to say that "There isn't much to this portion of the story." We'll have to see how the next episode goes. I've always loved the concept behind this story more than the execution. I think this could be the root of why.

The Mind Robber

Episode Four

Episode 218: (October 5, 1968) They meet The Master, the man who tells the stories in the Land of Fiction. He wants to have the Doctor stay.

Cliffhanger: Jamie and Zoe get closed in a book.

Yes, *Batman* did a similar cliffhanger two years before. The Bookworm closes Batman and Robin in a giant book. There, it's a simple trap. Here it's more of an existential thing. If they get shut up in the book, they become fiction. Oh boy!

Anyway, the episode builds nicely from the previous one. Apart from a few awkward moments with Zoe fighting the Karkus and the moment when Zoe runs through the photoelectric lens, generally this episode is quite good. I like the way that they resolve the Medusa thing. It is NOT the same way it was resolved in Episode Three. They end up using the myth itself to stop Medusa, rather than wishing her out of existence. Because Zoe can't admit it's not real and the Doctor has a sword. It's nicely done. And it lends itself to the thread that if they succumb to the fiction of this world, they become fiction themselves.

The scene with the Karkus is a nice twist on the events of the previous episode. Zoe knows the Karkus from comic strips when she was young. But the Doctor doesn't know who or what this is and honestly can't say that he is fake. It's nicely handled. It's not as if the episode is bullet paced but there is just enough happening here in variations to keep us moving.

What about that poor Master of the Land of Fiction? An older gentleman with gloves and a tendency to foam at the mouth a bit. For a brief time, it feels like the Great Intelligence might be back. The Master mentions the intelligence. This intelligence brought the Doctor there. One might think that this locale, this area, is the real home of the Intelligence. It makes sense, I think. The Intelligence did always have a thing for the Doctor. But, as far as we know, that is not what's happening here.

All the questions I asked in the previous review still hold here: Who built all this? Who oversees it? I don't know if we'll get an answer. I do know that enough happened here to keep things moving nicely. And, you know what? Another short episode. And this is a short review.

The Mind Robber

Episode Five

Episode 219: (October 12, 1968) The Doctor and This Master have a battle of the minds.

Cliffhanger: The Land of Fiction dissolves around everyone. The TARDIS reforms.

The story ends with a big battle. The Karkus, Blackbeard, Sir Lancelot and so on and so forth. They all storm around fighting on the turrets of a castle as the Doctor tries to save the world. I'll be honest: That's something I always forget. I thought the Computer that controls everything just wanted the Doctor to take over. I forget that it wants to transfer all of the inhabitants of Earth over to their planet and then take over the Earth. Making the Earth a fictional place. I'm not 100% sure where that comes from. It seems a bit out of place but what are you going to do?

It feels like maybe someone thought that the original concept behind what the Land of Fiction computer wanted wasn't enough. It is, basically, what the Great Intelligence wanted in "The Web of Fear." So, they thought "Let's up the ante here." Even the Doctor looks a bit like "What are you planning on doing?" Maybe the games of The Celestial Toymaker weren't enough?

Troughton is fun to watch as he goes head-to-head with this Master. Jamie and Zoe are scary and delightful. Having everyone together in one big hog pile is fun. Seeing Gulliver one more time is great. In the end, the "sabotaging the computer" thing seems a bit too familiar. I wish they could have come up with a clever way, within the story being told, to save the day. The Doctor can't say his name in the story because then he'll become fiction. I wish they had maneuvered the story to have him win without a "Sabotage the computer!" thing. But everyone did their best and victory was won through creativity.

In the end, it's a fine story. Much much better than "The Dominators." I don't know if I'd quite call it a classic. The structure works for the first two episodes. But the last three never quite get as exciting as the first two. The mind fight between the Doctor and the Master is charming but it's never incredibly exciting. It just sort of is. Jamie and Zoe acting weird and fictional is great. Whenever a new fictional character appears, that's cool. But this episode never really feels as strong and as engaging as I think it should be. The fourth episode picked things up a bit. But, in the end, the whole thing is never quite as great as I think it's going to be. It's atypical and there are stellar moments. Don't not watch it. Watch it twice! Prove me wrong.

I do like how the Computer wants to take over the Earth. The very end of the fifth episode is kind of ambiguous. And then we see "Next Episode: The Invasion." Oh boy! This is going to be good.

(The delay in air dates between this episode and the next is due to the 1968 Summer Olympics in Mexico, which took place in the fall. The 12th to the 27th of October.)

THE INVASION

Written by Derrick Sherwin

Directed by Douglas Camfield

Episode One

Episode 220: (November 2, 1968) The TARDIS gets shot at by a rocket on the dark side of the moon. Soon after that, Zoe is in a fashion photo shoot and the Doctor and Jamie meet one of the world's most important electronics experts.

Cliffhanger: Tobias Vaughn smiles happily at a shiny, lit-up thing.

(Note: This episode and four are animated on the DVD. The VHS had brief linking scenes from The Brigadier, Nicholas Courtney.)

I will give this episode some kind of reward for covering possibly the most ground we've ever covered in one episode, especially one on Earth. And not quite Earth. We begin the story with the reformation of the TARDIS. (Yes, Zoe is technically wearing the wrong thing in the animation. She should be in the catsuit. We'll let it ride. Be happy that you have the animation.) They get shot at by a rocket on the dark side of the moon. * They land in a field with a cow where the TARDIS becomes invisible. They meet a suspicious lorry driver. They find out that they are on land owned by International Electromatics. They learn that this is one of the biggest corporations in the world. ** The lorry driver is killed. They meet Isobel Watkins who takes pictures of Zoe. Jamie and the Doctor end up at the Electro etc. headquarters where they harass a computer and talk to Vaughn, who is not what he seems.

That is something! The animation gives it a feel of scope. Gives it a feel of sweeping along from one big moment to the next. As the Doctor and friends learn bits and bobs about what is going on in this world, they're also trying to get a circuit on the TARDIS repaired. The Doctor seems very optimistic that Travers might be able to help or Isobel's uncle, Professor Watkins. Somehow, I get the distinct feeling that the Doctor knows something might be happening and is after information. (The rocket attack from the moon probably primed his curiosity.) The animation does work well here. As the serial was directed by Douglas Camfield, I am guessing that it probably flowed nicely. ***

I like the episode. It doesn't quite cohere as much as it thinks it does, unless you pretend like the Doctor already knows what's happening and is doing this to learn more. But, if you let it flow, it works nicely. Suddenly, you're here. Suddenly, you're there. We meet Isobel and we meet Benton. In the next episode, we will re-meet someone very important to the show. Derrick Sherwin has done a good job here of dipping us deep into this familiar, but not quite, world.

We meet Tobias Vaughn. He seems a bit familiar, maybe like a certain oddly colored gentleman from the future. That's cool because he has the same feeling of menace. We can see the actor doing his thing for most of this story so the lost episode doesn't detract too terribly. Only episode four also remains lost. (Of course, that's the one with a big reveal at the end.) It's nice to see Vaughn here and I love his sadistic henchman, Packer. Just kind of a jerk who likes to bully people. We haven't seen anyone like that since "The Enemy of the World."

*And here we are not too far out from the actual landing on the moon. The belief that there is a 'dark side of the moon' is still an exciting thing. Seriously, who knows what the heck is over there? Am I right?

**This certainly implies it's in the future right. They, at least, think it's set after "The Web of Fear" because they're hoping to meet Professor Travers again.

*** Although, the Second Doctor doesn't feel completely right in all this. The same way the First Doctor didn't seem completely right in the "base under siege" scenarios. This is set up for future Doctors, kind of.

The Invasion

Episode Two

Episode 221: (November 9, 1968) The Doctor and Jamie meet Lethbridge-Stewart who now runs UNIT. Zoe and Isobel are captured by Vaughn after destroying his computer.

Cliffhanger: The Doctor and Jamie are caught! Again.

Back in the day, this was the first episode of the show that we saw. The Brigadier! Benton! What was that cyber-looking thing that Vaughn was talking to? How many times will I see Zoe's underpants? How many shots of legs in short skirts will I see? To be honest, as a young man, I was much more interested in the ladies then I was in the scenes with the guys. However, the episode did seem to promise that this story would be big. Nicholas Courtney's VHS intro for episode 1 was sufficient for me. It seemed very straightforward. Let's do this!

The problem with having the first episode animated and being able to watch it in (basically) real time is that this episode can't help but mirror the first episode. Go back and watch them again. Well, wait... before that, let's discuss the Brig. Here he is! We saw him in "The Web of Fear." We figured we'd never see him again. * Here he is and the Doctor and Jamie are instantly happy to see him and that's awesome. I love that he has set up this paranormal organization within the British military to look out for weird stuff. I do wonder how many weird things have popped up since the Doctor left. Probably enough to justify this. Regardless, it's great to see him. The future!

In the production text on the DVD, they say that Kit Pedler's original plot breakdown only covered four episodes. Derick Sherwin got special dispensation to make it into eight. Stories were a problem in this era of Doctor Who. That's why they're almost all overlong. And that's why this episode is so repetitive. We meet UNIT. We see Vaughn with his metal pal. But that's about all. The rest of it is basically repeating the first episode. The Doctor and Jamie meet up with mysterious figures. They go to Isobel's place. Isobel and Zoe have gone to where they were. They get caught. The Doctor and Jamie go to where the gals were and they get caught. I need to re-read the novelization to see if Ian Marter kept the same weird cyclical pattern. The episode is just a repeat of the first one. We get a few added extras. But, if the serial is eight episodes, this doesn't bode well.

Vaughn watches a sliding door open about 3 times in this episode. I don't know that it's terribly exciting for anyone after the first time. Even Vaughn must want to go and grab a coffee as it happens. The fun thing with the silver structure behind it is… the episodes where we might have seen something like that are lost to us now. But possibly, people watching might have recognized what was going on there. They do a sharp thing by saying that they know the Doctor from "Planet 14." When we learn who this is, it makes us think… "Was one of the stories we saw set on this planet?" "Is it a story they didn't show us?" "Is it a future Doctor story?" It's intriguing. And it's done specifically to hide what the "monster" is in this story.

*The Brig says this is 4 years later. 1979?

The Invasion

Episode Three

Episode 222: (November 16, 1968) The Doctor and Jamie learn more about Vaughn's setup. And then, there's an exciting escape!

Cliffhanger: Jamie is hiding in a capsule with… something.

I do love the reveal of Vaughn's other office. It's the exact same as the first office we've seen him in. It's presented as office efficiency. It's obviously budgetary efficiency. It's also very Vaughn. It also highlights something about this episode that kind of drives me up the wall. At least, we don't spend much of the episode watching that door go up and down.

So many episode threes in this period feel like this. We kind of meander around. We learn a little bit about what's going on but not much. Things we kind of thought we knew get repeated and repeated. Things are shoved along to the point where we want something to happen. The episode, like all Camfield's, moves along quite well. But what is it moving around?

Vaughn captured Jamie and the Doctor. UNIT watches them. We learn a little about what's going on. Jamie and Zoe are still under wraps. Watkins is threatened. (Prof. Kettlewell. No!) And not much happens. If there is an invasion going on, it hasn't happened yet. In one respect, I applaud the fact nothing happens and it's interesting. Think of this: The previous episode ends with those big coffin-type container things. And we almost find out what's in them. This episode ends with Jamie and the Doctor hiding in them… and we almost find out what's in them. I will grant you that, at my day job, a lot of it is repetitive. And, in an invasion of earth there is bound to be some repetitiveness. I accept that. But there really is very little happening here.

Calling the story "The Invasion" really puts one in the mindset of "This is the big one." If I knew, when this aired, that it was 8 parts, the second longest story ever, than I would think "This IS the BIG one." But, oh heck, we are running in some circles here. Even the novelization, like "The Web of Fear," has a feeling of "running in place." We've nowhere to go yet. Maybe something will happen next time.

We really need the back half of episodes to kick in here because this has gone on a bit. Everyone's fine in the episode. I'm so glad we have it. There's some excitement here and there but it is a question in playing for time. It is a question of stalling. So, I'd like to go onto the next episode. It's animated! By the people who did *Danger Mouse*! Penfold!!!!!

The Invasion

Part Four

Episode 223: (November 23, 1968) The Doctor, Isobel, Jamie and Zoe are freed from Vaughn's headquarters.

Cliffhanger: A Cyberman breaks loose!

Of course, this happens. This is the sort of thing that always happens in life, right? The thing you need, the thing you strive for suddenly isn't there. Everything around it is there. Everything you want is nearby. Then, the thing we need to happen, happens. And we're not there. Or we're not looking. Or who knows what...

That's this episode of The Invasion.

This is the big one. The big escape episode. UNIT joins in and crazy stuff happens to free Isobel and Zoe. Helicopters. Climbing the sides of huge buildings. Shootouts! It's the birth of the Pertwee era, after three episodes of... sort of "base under siege." Now, we're there! Excitement is happening. Craziness is going on. The Doctor and his gang are freed. They're discussing things with the Brigadier and we finally learn who oversees all of this.

Not "in charge." Vaughn might be. But he has the Doctor's TARDIS as a backup. Sort of. I do wonder why the Doctor gave those circuits to him. It seems odd to me. In compensation, we get Crazy Good Times excitement throughout this episode!

However, the episode is lost. It's animated. On the DVD commentary, everyone enjoys it. I enjoy it too. This story's missing episodes were the first ones that were animated. They take a little more liberty with them than they will later. And it works for me. (For example, when the Doctor is back in the UNIT plane, the scene starts with someone eating a sandwich. In the animated version, it doesn't. There is a lot of people eating in this story. I like that. It gives a weird, rooted feel to everything that's happening. This may be a crazy invasion. This may be when the Cybermen (sorry, spoiler?) take over everything. People still need to eat.

I wish this episode existed. This sounds like the first episode of "The Enemy of the World." That was big and fun and crazy. Of course, the director of that, Barry Letts, will oversee the UNIT era. So, he was right there alongside it all, ready to go. I just wished we had this episode. I'd love to know if it gave us a sort of catharsis that we needed after three episodes of back and forth and back and forth.

The ending has the Doctor and the Jamie in a canoe. Riding down a river towards the place where the Cybermen are kept. I've seen stills of it. I've never seen it. I'm thinking of "The Talons of Weng-Chaing."

Riding down the Thames. The show is getting bigger and bigger. I love that. But I'll be damned, we keep sort of missing those big moments. We keep missing the bits where we expand and must rely on animation. But there is a Cyberman! The Doctor has defeated them a lot though. And they're not as dangerous as Daleks. How will this go? We're in the second half of the serial now. Oddly enough, this is not the longest serial of this season. They really did have trouble getting stories for the show that worked.

(Another very UNIT-like moment is when Vaughn calls the Minister of Defense. "Is it a man or a woman?" says the minister. Neither. It's Tobias Vaughn. Bad guys using bureaucrats to interfere. That's a *Doctor Who* theme.)

The Invasion

Episode Five

Episode 224: (November 30, 1968) The Doctor and his gang are now free. They begin to figure out how to counteract whatever Vaughn is up to.

Cliffhanger: A crazy Cyberman approaches Isobel, Zoe and Jamie in the sewer.

A lot of upskirt action in this episode. Mainly from Jamie. It's something to remember if you're the sort of person who remembers that kind of thing.

Something happened here. By removing the "good" side from the captivity of the "bad" side, the story got freed from its back-and-forth shackles. Note: We're still going back and forth. But now we go from the bad guys doing their thing and the good guys doing theirs. The story is no longer cyclical, capture and escape, anymore. "The Invasion" has suddenly become a great story. I know we're halfway in. I know it took about 100 minutes to get there. But here we are! There is actual tension in the air. An actual feeling that something is going to happen. It helps that the allies are revealed. It is the Cybermen again. For whatever reason, they're never as dominant as the Daleks. But we've grown to be a bit afraid of Vaughn and having his allies be a force we know ratchets that tension way up.

On Vaughn's side, he has a tense scene with the Minister of Defense. He brings Vaughn the info about UNIT snooping around. In the original script and in the novelization, Vaughn gets the Minister to shoot himself. Here, the Minister is left alive. But sweaty and shaky, as most Ministers are. The best bit here is watching the Cybermen revitalized and sent into the sewers followed by the Cerebration Mentor test. That is what Isobel's uncle has been working. It basically reverses the Cyberman's emotionless state. They hook one up and set Fear at 11. The Cyberman basically goes crazy and runs into the sewers. It's bad enough to have all these Cybermen there in the first place. But to have one that's mad is a whole 'nother kettle of fish.

Meanwhile at UNIT's plane, the Doctor is examining the little chip in Jamie's transistor radio. They all know that something is going to happen soon. It involves Vaughn's electronics and it's going to affect the world. But what the heck is it going to be. (Again, after all the running around, there is a palpable feeling of approaching danger and disaster.) Meanwhile also, Isobel and Zoe want to do something so (with a lift from Benton and with Jamie in tow) they head down into the sewers to get a picture of the Cyberman. They meet a cop from *Dixon of Dock Green* and then all heck breaks loose. In separating everyone and not having them all locked up, finally, everyone has something to do. Excellent.

Overall, this episode makes you really want to see what's going to happen next. The cliffhanger is excellent. The thought of a Cyberman driven crazy by emotion is super cool. But more than just the cliffhanger, the story itself has put us in a position where not watching is not an option. No way.

The Invasion
Episode Six

Episode 225: (December 7, 1968) The Invasion begins. The Cyber force is released.

Cliffhanger: The Cybermen are all over London.

The Invasion begins! The Doctor fits everyone he can with little things for the back of their necks that stops the Cyber signal from breaking through. Most people are knocked loopy. So, as the episode ends, it looks like the Cyber force might win this one. The episode almost ends with the classic shot of Cybermen walking down the steps of St. Paul's cathedral. (Recreated at the end of "Dark Water.") Oddly enough, the episode doesn't end with that shot. I always forget that it doesn't. It ends with a low angle shot looking at group of Cybermen walking along the sidewalk. I wonder why? Surely the Cybermen at the Cathedral is more exciting? Oh well, I guess not.

The opening sequence in the sewer is nicely done. The continuity seems slightly off. Isobel, Jamie and Zoe come down the ladder. They walk a little. There are two sane cybermen behind them. The crazy one in front. It passes them and heads towards the others. Jimmy and some soldiers come down the ladder and yell for them. The trio are afraid to yell in case there is a Cyberman approaching them. Then, suddenly, the crazy cybermen appears behind the other two. But it was in front of them. How did it get back there? What's going on? Otherwise, it's a good scene.

There's a great bit of *Doctor Who* frugality here mixed with some confusion. Look at the bits with Watkins and Gregory. There is a long scene with Jimmy on the radio. He and the Brig set up an ambush to try to get Watkins. It sounds like it's going to be very exciting. Lots of soldiers and artillery. Oh boy! We immediately cut to Vaughn's office and a close up on Gregory's face. (This happens so fast that it is rather confusing.) Gregory explains what happened and how Watkins got free. Then, Gregory is shown getting killed by Cybermen in the sewer. What?! I understand that *Doctor Who* does have to take a "tell don't show" route at times. This is ridiculous. In fact, it's almost incoherent. It's like "Where did the Ministry of Defense guy go?" I'm certain that the first time I saw this I had no idea what was going on.

The rest of the episode is Vaughn excited about the upcoming invasion. Using the Cerebration Mentor on Watkins. Oddly enough, they act like they haven't used it before but they used it in the previous episode. I am confused. The Cyber Controller thing is very calm but you can tell how excited Vaughn is getting. The realization of his plans! Control of the Earth. What he'll do with the Earth? Well, it's tough to gauge.

It's great to have the Doctor doing his scientific thing and helping. He draws a nice diagram here. He posits the Cyber plan. And the Invasion hits. Of course, now, we're going to see exactly what can be done against these Cybermen, hidden away in the sewers. I bet they smell great.

The Invasion
Episode Seven

Episode 226: (December 14, 1968) The Invasion continues. The humans may have a way to stop it.

Cliffhanger: Zoe's plan has destroyed the first Cyberfleet. The Cybermen are taking over the invasion from their ally. What does Vaughn think?

The Invasion has begun. Most of the world is knocked out. There's just this small group of people in the London area with the Doctor's help that have made it. (Possibly there are some other groups somewhere who have resisted the control but we don't hear about them. And, obviously, I would think groups of people without electronics are not affected. It's just another day. It could take years before they realize that there is an invasion.) Vaughn and Packer learn that a group is free from control and won't let them have Watkins back. Bits of the invasion are starting to look a little shaky over on Vaughn's side.

The interesting thing here is that there are cybermen everywhere. There is a bit of a scene in the sewers. There's talk of the invasion fleet. But, apart from the opening of the episode and the recap from last week, I don't remember seeing any Cybermen in this episode. There is the constant threat of them being there. But they're not actually onscreen. That's pretty clever. And, again, is an example of *Doctor Who* implying something huge while not showing it. Just letting everyone run around and be crazy.

Jamie gets shot! It's only a wound in the leg but the moment when he gets hit does worry a bit. Remember the last time companions got damaged. That was in a very long story too. That didn't end well for many. Hopefully, this will go a bit better.

Zoe is great in this one. She's back in her catsuit and cute as ever. She helps revive a group of Cyber controlled soldiers. Not one of them looks at her and says, "Who's the catsuit-wearing cutie?" (That's what I would have said.) The scene where she figures out the calculations for the anti-missile missiles to destroy the fleet is great. The Brig really does have faith in this trio and that's cool. Because he is super military and super by-the-book. It portends a nice time together in the future. So, hooray Zoe!

And the big moment of the whole shmegegge arrives in the second half. When the Doctor returns to Vaughn's office, which they're got a lot of mileage out of, and tries to talk Vaughn out of his invasion plans. It's a quiet, calm conversation between two intelligent people. And it is an example of the show talking its way towards an ending. Of course, they do mix in the Cyberfleet being blown up to keep all age groups awake throughout. (Or maybe they mix in the talk to do that. I'm not sure.) Regardless, it really does feel like the climax of the story. Vaughn's response to the end of the episode is going to be the big turning point here. But also, maybe, the big moment when the pace shifts a bit. (If we know the ending is on its way because of his choice…) We shall see.

Overall, since the end of Episode Four, it has been an excellent adventure. One has almost forgotten the running around of the first half. Well, you don't need to forget. You can flip back a few Episodes and read about them again. Let's see how we end this "Invasion" and see where we go from here.

The Invasion
Episode Eight

Episode 227: (December 21, 1968) The Invasion ends.
Cliffhanger: The Invisible TARDIS becomes visible again. The crew heads out on a new adventure.

A lot happens in this episode. We don't really see much of it. We spend a good amount of time in Vaughn's office. We spend a lot of time watching people watch things. Camfield's direction and the convincing acting keeps it all moving. The Cybermen sort of become a threat. There's a great melee in a sort of alleyway type thing with the Army and UNIT fighting away. Vaughn and the Doctor run around zapping Cybermen with the emotion machine. But there's a starling amount of things NOT happening.

Watch the scene with the Doctor and Vaughn. What happens? They run around a lot. They shoot Cybermen with that emotion machine. They go up. They go down. Then, Vaughn is killed and the Doctor is attacked. The military appear and fight the Cybermen. They beat the Cybermen. Then, we cut to the next scene where it's announced that they stopped the radio signal to the Cyber ship. We don't see it happen. We just hear about it. Same with the cyber bomb being blow up. At least, we see the cyber ship getting hit, but even then, there's some oddness.

I think what I'm trying to say is that, while the episode moves nicely and is fun to watch, it's got some strange dramatic ideas. Having one scene where we sit and watch people watch something happen is fine. But then, doing it again an episode later just feels weird. Surely, they could have come up with something different to do here. Then, Vaughn and the Doctor finally team up. It seems like they're going to accomplish something. They do shoot a bunch of Cybermen and run a lot. However, they don't do what they mean to do. They only do because the military show up. The Doctor says to the Brigadier that the two of them must rush in because there isn't time. It turns out there's more than enough time. It's an interesting episode because it is so much fun. But it's so oddly done. There's a constant feeling that everything we're looking at isn't the actual thing we should be looking at at that time. Misdirection sci-fi.

Everyone gets something to do. (Except Jamie who only appears in the end.) Everyone gets to cheer. Romances are kindled. UNIT continues to impress the world. And a new era in Doctor Who is beginning.

Overall, it's a fun serial. But something interesting does happen. At the end of the DVD commentary, everyone agrees that this was a solid serial. There was no running around. There was no feeling of padding. It used its eight episodes well. I stand by what I said a few reviews ago. By time you get to the end of episode eight, you've completely forgotten that the first three and a half episodes consisted of running around and lots of filler. But it's OK. That's the way it works here. It fooled you into thinking you saw what you didn't see. It also fooled you into forgetting when it wasn't at its best. That's some clever *Doctor Who*! And we see the Brig and Benton a lot!

THE KROTONS
Episode One
Written by Robert Holmes
Directed By David Maloney

Episode 228: (December 28, 1968) The TARDIS lands on the planet of the Gonds where their rulers, the Krotons, may not be as nice as we're led to believe.

Cliffhanger: A giant snake-thing is about to do something to the Doctor.

As everyone points out, the opening shot of this one is a small hatch opening. A man reaches inside to retrieve a scroll. But the hatch gets stuck halfway open. The guy must sort of reach around it. To some, that's seen as a sort of reason why this one isn't great. I think that's foolishness. Look at how awesome that snake thing is. No wires. It's being operated from cables inside it. That's sweet stuff. Should David Maloney have done a second take of the hatch not opening? Yes. Can we survive it? Yes. Why? Because this episode has more incident in it than three episodes worth of many of the previous stories. And that's something.

This is the first four-part story since "The Tomb of the Cybermen." * And we all call that story a classic, regardless of whether it is. But the plotting in it is atrocious. Here the plotting is comparable to a Sylvester McCoy story, especially something from Seasons 25 or 26. That's amazing. There's no slow build. There's no being captured for two episodes or more. Halfway into the first episode, the TARDIS crew have kind of overturned the beliefs of this whole society. That causes students to rebel and smash up the establishment's equipment and... Yes, the story is sharper and better than history says it is.

To me, most of that is the Robert Holmes script. We are now meeting one of the four or five best writers for *Doctor Who* ever. Holmes's script is continually one step ahead of where we think it is. That's why it goes so fast. That's why it accomplishes so much. Go back and watch any 6-parter from the 5th season. More happens in this episode then... The first four episodes of "The invasion," for Heaven's Sake. There was a reason why 4-part stories were so big in the 3rd and 4th seasons. You could tell a better story. Only people like David Whitaker and... maybe Victor Pemberton (ish) could handle the six-part stories with aplomb. Even Robert Holmes wasn't huge on 6-part stories. A good six-part story really needs major shifts to keep it going. (Of course, we're about to leave one era of 6-parters and enter another big era of 6-parters/ long stories. We'll see how they deal with those.)

In the end, the best thing about this story is this weird realization that, if they had found writers like Robert Holmes earlier, they could have possibly done more fast-paced, more sharply drawn stories earlier. I love *Doctor Who*. From the most sharply paced episode to the slackest bit of episode you've ever seen. "The Krotons" sneaks into a, basically, six-episode era where there are only two four-part stories made. And Holmes's script shows that this is the way to go.

The Gonds might not be the most interesting race of people. (Which is probably the big issue.) They are interesting enough. And things move fast enough to keep it all alive. Let's see if the story keeps this going. Let's see what happens in Episode 2. The first Episode aired in 1969.

*Remember that that was the last story of the fourth recording block. That means that the fifth recording block, out of which arose 46 episodes, did not have a single four-part story.

The Krotons
Episode Two

Episode 229: (January 4, 1969) Zoe and the Doctor accidentally revivify the crystalline Krotons. Nothing will ever be the same
Cliffhanger: Jamie is under scrutiny from the brain drain thing and it's draining his brain.

Yessir. The pace stays strong here. It starts off with that snake attack and it ends with the Krotons being completely revitalized. This would have been the end of episode three- or four of a six-part story. The fun now is that since the Krotons are here we can learn what the heck they're up to and what the heck they are. We can see that they are crystalline. But we can also see that they have some kind of hover skirt on. What does that cover up? What's up the Kroton's skirt?

I love the voice of the Krotons as it booms over the loudspeaker. It has a distorted tinge to it. But it's also just the accent being used. I will admit that I always like the image of the Krotons I have in my mind more than their actual appearance. I like the shapes. I like the curves and the indentations. But they do look a little too plastic for me. I don't mind the skirt thing but they just look like their texture is incorrect. Which is too bad.

The Gonds honestly aren't up to much so far. I think they'll be doing a bit more as the episodes go along. It's been mainly The Doctor, Zoe and Jamie. But, to get us through two more episodes there must be more to this.

The scenes in the learning hall are very funny. The Doctor's babbling and then missing questions is great. The back and forth about how much of a genius Zoe is is delightful. It's nice to see that Zoe has become such a strong part of the group here. Kind of in a way that Victoria didn't quite. She was always a bit screamy and never quite had her own way of doing things. She was just kind of there.

We're halfway through this story. That's so odd. It's been so long since we've had a story move like this. The tricky thing is that the swift pace doesn't allow for too much analysis. Yes, the Gonds are a rather wet bunch. If I felt bad for the Krotons, I would feel bad here. They landed their root spaceship and chose a group of people who were never going to be smart enough to revive them. That's too bad. I like the Doctor's response when he realizes that he and Zoe have started everything rolling. In the first episode, they shake the foundations of Gond society. In the second episode, they bring the dormant Krotons back to life. I'm afraid to see what they'll do next.

Note: Something I realized here. That the Krotons do seem to recognize the Doctor. Zoe mentions that it's as if it knew them. I always thought that it saw the Doctor as "the leader" because he seemed to be the one leading things when the Krotons were looking. But the thought of the Krotons having met the Doctor before is intriguing. It certainly could be in the Doctor's future, of course.

The Krotons
Episode Three

Episode 230: (January 11, 1969) The Doctor has some ideas on how to stop the Krotons. The Gonds have their own idea. It's not great.

Cliffhanger: The Kroton's structure collapses all around the Doctor.

When the Doctor and Zoe step out of the TARDIS, there's a feeling that we rarely get this early in a *Doctor Who* story: A feeling that the Doctor knows how to solve the problem and is close to the solution. This is kind of the way they should have been using Zoe and the Doctor all along. They're being smart together and solving the problem. Sulfur, tellurium. Using the elements that the Krotons are constructed of to work towards bringing them down or putting them back in their soup. Now, they get interrupted by the Kroton who thinks it has destroyed the TARDIS. (Oh the HADS! That will come into play again a long time from now.) Then, he gets caught up in the Gonds and their "bad idea." And it's nice because, we know he knows how to take care of the problem. The obstacles don't feel like time wasters or filler. We know the Kroton is coming for the TARDIS. The Gonds aren't just going to sit around and do nothing. Setting all that aside, the joy of knowing that the story is moving quickly is wonderful. Heck, there's only one more episode after this.

I hadn't quite known what/ who the Krotons reminded of me before. Because they look the same, it's tough to gauge this. But it's the Dominators. There's a Commander and there's a subordinate that complains. These just have big eyeless-crystal heads, which are fun. They're also one of those interesting creatures that is revived but then almost immediately begin to run out of energy. Sort of like how the Quarks never have quite enough energy. If I thought Robert Holmes had encountered "The Dominators" scripts, I would almost say that he's making fun of them. Bad guys who do nothing but argue and constantly complain that they never have enough energy. I get it with the Krotons though. The point is that they need the energy to live and they're not getting it.

Jamie doesn't do a whole heck of a lot here. They gauge that he's not as smart as The Doctor and Zoe. (May I just say the Doctor and Zoe cavalierly saying how they made it out of the Kroton's space is lovely.) I like when he attacks the Krotons. That flame thrower thing is something.

The Gonds, yes, are not the most interesting. They're not super dull like the Xerons or the astronauts in "The Sensorites." The thing is that the story is moving so quick that all their ideas seem superfluous. One feels that the Doctor is already on it. But the Gonds can't sit around and do nothing because it is their world. There is talk of a massacre when they first arrived. The place is currently evacuated, which one must pay attention to in order to really comprehend. The people who storm the base of the Kroton ship are the only people in the town at the time. So, the Gonds are going full bore. Let's see what happens.

The Krotons
Episode Four

Episode 231: (January 18, 1969) The Krotons need The Doctor and Zoe to leave the Gonds planet and return to their battle fleet.
Cliffhanger: The TARDIS leaves.

And "The Krotons" ends. And one can be forgiven for all the people in the past who denigrate this story while puffing up the stories around it. The Doctor and friends come in, do their thing and save the day. There aren't entire episodes where nothing happens. They arrive and they assess the issue and they save the day. (I can't help thinking of the Doctors advice to Vicki in "Galaxy 4".) It is so different from much of the Troughton era that it can feel weird.

People have nitpicked at the Krotons quite a bit. They're pretty cool though. They don't get much backstory but what they do get is good stuff. They are ruthless. They are not carbon-based so eliminating anything carbon-based (i.e., us) is nothing to them. It just happens. I like them. They don't do much. But let's reflect back... The Ice Warriors kind of did less in a six-part story. So, to denigrate a story for being well-told and well-paced but you think the monsters are a little wonky, makes you sound a bit like a douche. Lighten up. Enjoy yourself more.

Because this is a fun final episode. When Selris does a roll into the Dynatrope to get Zoe and The Doctor the sulfuric acid, it's very cool. The way things were shot at that time means it's a bit less cool than it could be. We can work with it. We can see how it's awesome. It's like that one rebel who picked a fight with Jamie in Episode One. He led the destruction of the Dynatrope in Episode Three. But then blames Eelek, here. Classic crappy human being/ Gond.

I do wonder what the show could have been like in this era if it had become what it was at the end of the Hartnell era and the start of the Troughton era. This four-part story is not an absolute classic. It's not something incredible. It's just a fun adventure, well-written and paced. When the Doctor and friends leave in the end and we cut to the TARDIS dematerializing, it doesn't feel like an effort. It's effortless. And it's fun. Look, I'm just saying that this serial is a treat. We have a big one ahead. The final proper "base under siege" stories of the 1960s. One with one of our favorite (ish) monsters returning.

THE SEEDS OF DEATH
Episode One
Written By Brian Hayles
Directed by Michael Ferguson

Episode 232: (January 25, 1969) The TMAT headquarters on the Moon is taken over by...
Cliffhanger: The Ice Warriors are back!

The fun thing about the Ice Warriors returning here is that they're coming at us from a different angle than in their first story. In that one, it was four warriors that had been frozen in the ice for ages. They're fighting for their survival during an Ice Age. In this story, the warriors are an actual battalion of Ice Warriors (or whatever they call themselves) with a plan to take over Earth. This story takes place in the 21st century. "The Ice Warriors" takes place long after this one. So, we get to see The Ice Warriors doing what it is they do. They're never on the back foot here. They are large and in charge.

We are right back to 6-part stories. We are right back to a "base under siege"-esque story. With the group at TMAT on the Moon, under control of the Warriors. The Warriors that we don't see in full until the end of the episode. I wonder if people would have known what was there just from the voice. It's tough to say because they have a voice that is all their own but a bit like a lot of other voices.

This is an interesting and slightly stunted version of Earth. It's odd that at this time when humanity is about to land on the moon... we get a *Doctor Who* story that said we never bothered to go past the moon. There were rockets, sure. There were people who wanted to go but couldn't. Because TMAT, a teleportation system, made everything so efficient and easy that people became complacent and all attempts to explore failed. Professor Eldred is the sign of what was.

The man who has been building his own rocket. The man who has a space museum. The man who other scientists laughed at. That's Eldred. He represents the only creative force here. The only person with a willingness to look beyond the Moon. He is this script's version of Penley in "The Ice Warriors." Penley gave up on an over-scientific and heartless society to go out on his own. Eldred has been forced into his unfulfilled life by the world. Meanwhile, over on the moon base, we have the weaselly guy, Fewsham. The guy whose sole purpose is to do exactly what the Ice Warriors want to save his own skin. This will be another thread through the serial: How far will you go, how much will you connive with evil, to keep yourself safe? As the story is six episodes, we can take some time (maybe too much) exploring this idea. How long can you be a quisling before it's too long?

The Doctor, Jamie and Zoe are back to not doing too much. They don't show up until a third of the way into the story. They spend time looking at the museum exhibits. They talk to Eldred. They stand in the background a lot. I hadn't really missed this style of Doctor Who storytelling. But here it is again. If falling back into this old rut bothers you, at least, you can giggle at all the silly outfits that the TMAT men wear. Especially the gentleman with the briefcase and that odd jumpsuit that looks a bit like it's fitted with a diaper. Well, they are very efficient. Who has time?

The Seeds Of Death
Episode Two

Episode 233: (February 1, 1969) The TARDIS crew ride a rocket to the moon.
Cliffhanger: The homing beacon for the rocket turns off. Bad news!

Well, so far, at the end of two episodes, things are moving along nicer than they were in "The Ice Warriors." They get a rocket into space. * Miss Kelly makes it to the moon. There is some fun Ice Warrior stuff. The Doctor and friends do something weird to their faces, which I think is meant to simulate g-force. And, overall, the episode moves along at a decent pace. "The Krotons" was paced faster. (For example, you can really feel like that quisling's plotline is going to go on until at least Episode five. Whereas everything happened so fast throughout the previous story.) I like it though.

It does feel kind of weird to go back to this sort of story though. After the epic in two halves of "The Invasion" and the weirdness of "The Mind Robber," this story feels a bit like a leftover. As if Brian Hayles couldn't write fast enough (or as fast as Haisman and Lincoln) and this episode should have been in the previous season. When all we had to watch were the existing sixth season stories, this one was a fun breath of fresh air after the other ones. It seemed to imply that the Troughton era was as eclectic as the Hartnell era. Now, having journeyed through the whole era, this feels like a step back. Suddenly, all those story styles that we experienced are flashing back. And it does feel as if, maybe, we didn't have to see those again. But they're back and maybe for the last time? We'll find out.

The spots that could be padding are the arguments between Eldred and Radnor. They go on for a while. We know that they're going to use the rocket. So, maybe those scenes could have been a touch more succinct. Again, variation on characters from "The Ice Warriors," they do their thing. But the point they're making isn't as defined as it is in the previous story. It ends up reminding me of a variation of some scenes from Alfonso Brescia's *Star Odyssey*. Where the government is trying to convince a genius professor to help them save the world from a Darth Vader-like jerk. That goes on for a bit. And we never think that the Professor will not help. But then, that movie has an IQ of 11 and is pure fruity goodness so it is in a different realm.

The Doctor, Jamie and Zoe are sort of peripheral and important at the same time. They do go up in the rocket. I did get a little scared for them. The Doctor and Zoe generally don't seem worried. They do a lot of hanging out in the background with clipboards. I almost feel as if the story has forgotten that they're meant to be the leads in the show. But then, that happens during these "base under siege" stories and, again, didn't really happen during "The Krotons." If this story is saying goodbye to your standard base under siege... then I guess I'm OK with it. Just don't get boring!

Oh, I don't know if this is too obvious: One third of the way in. What are the 'seeds of death' exactly?

*The one thing that always makes me kind of giggle is that they act as if Eldred's rocket is a secret. But then when we see it's a regular huge rocket. How was it a secret? Did he have it under a big tarp? Did he build a silo around it so people though it was a structure filled with grain? Was it in a bunch of smaller bits he had in a field covered with hay? I don't get it. But I love it.

The Seeds of Death
Episode Three

Episode 234: (February 8, 1969) The Ice Warriors plan is revealed. They are sending some sort of inflating and exploding seeds around the world via TMAT.
Cliffhanger: One lands at main control and begins to inflate.

This episode and the next three were mainly written, in their final form, by Terrance Dicks. He's the script editor now. Peter Bryant is listed as producer and Derrick Sherwin is on the other stories of the season. I won't go into it here because it doesn't quite fit the purview of the book: but this was a crazy time for the show regarding scripts. That's why so many of them are so long. It's easier to come up with a good idea and to keep expanding it rather than coming up with three or four good ideas. I don't really think it will be until the Tom Baker era that things calm down properly in this department. But, regardless, it's nice to have Terrance Dicks writing some of the show. He'll be back. A lot.

The Second Doctor gets a wonderful iconic chase here. Very slapstick. A bit Chaplin. A touch of Keaton. Zipping around the moon base, running through a hall of mirrors. Ice Warriors around every corner. It's a fun sequence. That might make one think that this sort of thing happened in this era often. When, of course, it didn't. It's an odd scene that is clearly filler but also clearly delightful. And I love it. And I think, with a crowd, it would be an uproarious time. The Second Doctor has really taken the show to his own place. It's too bad that they seem to kill him at the end of the episode. That's not good.

The quisling continues to be a quisling. He has a moment here that seems a bit much even for a quisling. Fewsham has set up the TMAT to be under complete control by the Ice Warriors. They know that they're going to do something horrible. Miss Kelly berates him because he's going to destroy so many lives. Fewsham basically responds with 'Well, if we don't do this, we'll be killed." So, you're going to destroy the population of the Earth to save three or four people on the Moon base? That makes sense.

Anyway, the rocket lands. I'm glad it does. I'm fairly convinced of its landing. The models here are pretty good. Sometimes they do have a bit of a feeling of "A guy is holding the rocket up right out of frame. Don't worry because it's all right." I like this regardless.

I always enjoy when the Doctor encounters an old villain/ monster. He's playing it coy here. He met Varga and the others a couple centuries from this point so they couldn't know who he is. I always like when he slips out bits of info here and there. Little bits of "I know who you are..." to keep everyone intrigued. And having Slaar the Ice Lord here gives a sort of warrior class system that we didn't quite anticipate from the previous story.

It's nice that the seeds have finally arrived. What they are exactly is still unknown. But we'll get more information on them soon. Soon, soon, you're a balloon.

The Seeds of Death
Episode Four

Episode 235: (February 15, 1969) The seeds are sent around the world.
Cliffhanger: Zoe is about to be zapped by an Ice Warrior.

The Doctor is on vacation. Is this the last episode (until the "Doctor-lite" episodes of the modern-day run) without one of the main characters? Yes, they do do something clever here. They pre-recorded a scene with the Doctor being TMAT-ed out into the universe. That's fun. That makes one think this isn't what it is: A Doctor-less episode. But it is. The Doctor is out of it. The last time he was gone was when he got knocked unconscious in "The Wheel In Space." Here we think he's dead and then we think he's dead again. He's not dead because he's the Doctor. The rest of the episode does its very best to run around this and make one feel like no one is missing.

Those Ice Warrior attacks help. Ice Warriors killing everybody. Pods exploding. Foam! Oh, have we missed the foam? I guess we have. There's plenty of it in this episode. If you haven't encountered the foam in the previous season, this is a lot of fun. If you have seen the foam from the previous season, you may or may not be thrilled by all of this.

Everyone, like I said, does do a nice job of moving around and making everything feel important and making every moment count. Radnor and Eldred really do a good job here. Although, there is that great cost-cutting moment. Radnor runs out. Then, he runs back in announcing that all the guards are dead. That saved some cash.

The others run around on the Moonbase trying to stop the Ice Warriors from being awful. There are only a few moments where one thinks "Where'd the Doctor go?" But, by the end you're thinking "It'll be nice to have him back." There's a little too much "hiding in plain sight" in this story for my tastes. Let's go onto Five and see what's up.

The Seeds of Death
Episode Five

Episode 236: (February 22, 1969) The invasion continues. Fewsham does something noble. The Doctor learns what destroys the fungus filled seed pods.
Cliffhanger: The Doctor is about to be overwhelmed in foam and fungus.

Unlike "The Ice Warriors," there is a definite feeling of movement here. The Ice Warriors attack is getting larger. There is a bit of a global feel to all of it. The approaching Ice Warrior fleet (using the same sort of homing signal the rocket used in episode 2) seems to portend bad things for the people of Earth. I have to say that it must have something to do with Terrance Dicks's influence. Especially when you read the information text on the DVD. It details what Brian had planned for the third through sixth episodes. It seems far less interesting than what we have going on here. A lot more running around. I know the show as aired has a lot of running around. But it seems a touch more aimless in the original story. Dicks brought something extra to it. It's not a world beater but it is fun.

I like the character of Sir James. Another blustery old white guy who doesn't know what's going on and doesn't seem to believe anything that's happening around him. We'll see more of this type during the

Pertwee era. And we certainly saw some like him in the past. But here, he does nothing but bluster and look silly. We're already knee-deep in an invasion that is occurring. It's happening. So, to have this old guy in his goofy outfit trundling about expressing disbelief at what is happening right at this moment in the world is funny. Luckily, he doesn't get a chance to cause a lot of harm.

Fewsham gets to prove himself a decent human being here. Helping save Zoe's life at the start. Getting everyone else off the Moonbase. And then, in his final act, allowing the people on Earth to hear the Ice Warrior's plan and their rocket signal. Which can be used against them. He dies. And when he dies, he dies with a bit of triumph on his face. He's not been such a jerk after all. The moment when everyone has left the base and it's just him is excellent. The camera slowly tracks in on him as he stares at the TMAT booth knowing that he will never go home. He turned out heroic in the end. Granted, his cowardice indirectly caused some deaths. But that happens!

After being gone for an episode, the Doctor does a lot here. I feel like, possibly, Troughton is hamming it up a bit. He knows he's leaving. He's decided now is the time to have a little more fun with the part. From the chase in Episode Three to his lolling around in the foam here, he seems to be indulging his silly side. His time is fast approaching the end so let's goof around. Again, for some time, this was one of few stories of his that existed. A lot of people thought that's how his character always was. Not so.

The story is moving nicely into its final episode. With a few exceptions here and there, it has justified the five episodes so far. Will the final episode close things off nicely? Will it be a rushed mess of confusion? Or will it be something else?

The Seeds of Death
Episode Six

Episode 237: (March 1, 1969) The final phase of the invasion! The Ice Warrior fleet arrives. Cliffhanger: Onto the Space Pirates!

Well, the Doctor runs around in this one with a giant light-flashing thing that kills about three Ice Warriors outright. Normally, you don't see the Doctor going around killing like that. There's a first time for everything. The set-up looks cool on the Doctor. Two big lamps. One in each hand. When the power is thrown, they release super light at the Ice Warriors. When I was a kid, that was fun to see. We rarely got to see the Doctor with a weapon. So, it was certainly interesting. Plus, he and Jamie have a sort of action scene with Slaar and the remaining Ice Warrior at the end. Leaping onto computer banks, trying to tackle Ice Warriors. All that sort of thing. I wonder if this was Terrance Dicks's contribution.

The story wraps up nicely. The first half of the episode is securing the Weather Station and getting it to rain. There's some more running around. It's not as much fun as in episode three but it is fun. The Doctor does seem to be out in the foam for an incredible amount of time. I got a little worried about him. They stick a lot of extra material into there, in the space between when the episode begins and where the cliffhanger goes. The suspense builds nicely. The best part being when Zoe throws open the door. Tons of foam with the Doctor mixed in there fall into the room. The Doctor falls. Zoe is clearly seen laughing. (I would imagine they couldn't do it again.) That's a fun moment. And I did enjoy watching the Doctor covered with wires and fixing the equipment. Although isn't Jamie getting more stubborn and impatient as time is going on? Maybe that's just me.

The second half is the Doctor going up to the TMAT Moonbase station on his own to turn off the homing beacon noise thing and get the Martian fleet to follow his faked-up signal, which will put them in permanent orbit around the sun. So, that means that whole fleet is dead huh? Usually, when they blow up big ships and things, we don't spend a lot of time dwelling on it. It just happens. Here The Leader in the spangly headpiece is clearly very distraught. A simple misdirection destroys the entire fleet. These are not like the Cybermen with their faceless, similar characterization. Each Ice Warrior is a different character. The Doctor gets pretty bloodthirsty here. Maybe he knows the end is near and he's trying something new? It does come up a bunch in this episode. I do know that The Ice Warriors are also bloodthirsty. The Doctor isn't usually. Really. Is he?

The story ends and we say goodbye to the Seeds of Death. It was pretty darn good, I thought. It didn't even really get too stuffed up in the middle. If the "base under siege" had to go out on this serial, it's not a bad one to say goodbye to the format. We've got a new format on the way anyway. But, first, we have an odd story (and the last one with missing episodes) followed by one of the series epics.

THE SPACE PIRATES
Written by Robert Holmes
Directed By Michael Hart
Episode One

Episode 238: (March 8, 1969) In the future, space cops hunt down space pirates. The TARDIS crew get mixed up in all of it.
Cliffhanger: The beacon separates the Doctor and friends from the TARDIS.

One of the odder episodes of the show. Ever. Really. You won't hear people mention it often but it's true. Robert Holmes's name on it implies that we're entering classic Who sorts of stories. (Holmes must have made a mark on the show because he writes the first third Doctor story. And it is a very Robert Holmes type story.) This episode, though, just seems very strange. It's a weird reconstruction and it just seems weirder when you can focus on the recon. * There are a lot of screen-full text heavy moments describing lots of space action that we're not seeing. Most of what we see is bits from Episode 2 masquerading as bits from this episode. So, it's tough to gauge if this is good. I feel like it is. But, heck, it's tough.

In this episode, a group of pirates are breaking apart beacons made of argonite, a very valuable mineral. There is a rather prissy group of government something or others after them. We see pirates (we see nothing really but help me out here) take apart the beacons. They were assembled in sections and they are blown apart in sections, which makes for a nice effect. Possibly someone in charge should have noticed that this might happen in the future but that's not a future I live in.

The story shows us an interesting future. The government ships filled with bureaucratic space police float around keeping an eye out for chicanery. There are those beacons, floating through space and keeping stuff in intergalactic storage. And then there are these pirates. The thing I love about them is that they're not "Yo Ho Ho" pirates. They're like hi-tech pirates who seem to be having fun, mostly. When you see the Space Cops, the people in charge at this time, you instantly think "Why wouldn't you be a pirate in this universe?" I don't like those "cops" at all. If they're in charge, they can shove it. I'm going to Pirate Town.

Regarding the visuals, which we can't see, others have pointed out that this was the time when the Space Race was showing their best footage. And it's very much like watching a car chase on modern TV. It's exciting and it's enthralling. But not much happens throughout. There will be big "Oh boy!" moments. But, in general, it's more about the anticipation. It's about waiting to see what's happening. The space race was like that. Slow rocket movement. Lots of people in "Houston" saying stuff. Lots of standing by. All part of the fun. All part of the package. That's why people loved it. It's like the world's longest climb on a roller coaster. You get to a point where you don't even care when you go over the top because the anticipation is so killer.

The Doctor, Zoe and Jamie arrive about 15-16 minutes into the episode. They get separated from the TARDIS. I like Zoe's new outfit.

*Yes. This story contains the final recon episodes. 1, 3, 4, 5 and 6. Unfortunately, this is a very visual story as I will mention. The novelization is OK. It's one of Terrance Dicks's later ones. That era where he was still doing good work but not the great work he'd been doing in the 1970s and the early 1980s. Things become a bit rote. It could be because the story is lost. "The Smugglers" has that feel. He's working off limited materials and doing his best. I will say this: At some point, I watched "The Space Pirates" quite well. It worked for me. I don't remember how I did that or what my frame of mind was while watching. This time is not that time.

The Space Pirates
Episode Two

Episode 239: (March 15, 1969) The government guys meet Milo Clancey and think he's the head of the Argonite pirates.
Cliffhanger: Jamie is shot by a pirate stepping onboard their section.

Here is where we meet Milo Clancey. He speaks like an old Western prospector. He makes some eggs using a new-fangled solar toaster. He has a goofy mustache. He seems like he's out of a comedy. The government guys might be a little camp. The Commander constantly calling his second-in-command "Ian" feels a bit silly to me. The pirates are the rough guys. Milo is sort of a hero with a bit of goofiness to him. Is this a pantomime? It's not Christmastime anymore. No one making this would have expected it to be aired anywhere again. Yet, it all feels a bit silly.

It does create its world rather nicely though. Parkin and Pearson's *AHistory* places it around 2135. I'll go for that. We have spaceships. We've had a time where it was very much like the Wild West. * But now, the government have taken control after the initial pioneers have done the work. And the people in control now are boring and stifling. That's something I always think about. The people in charge seem like jerks to me. Clancy is dismissive of them and their rules. But I would be too. Bill Murray could play Clancy in a remake of "The Space Pirates.'"

Then, we meet Madame Issigri and she has a big golden helmet on her head. The commander is clearly enamored of her. Well, why wouldn't he be? She has a big helmet on her head. And it's gold. Apparently, her father worked with Clancy. I am sure that that will mean nothing in the future. I'm sorry. There's a lot of exposition going on here but her head helmet thing is getting in my way.

Actually, there really is a lot of exposition here. If this were Robert Holmes in the mid-1970s, I'd say he was parodying the space opera genre. He has ridiculous heroes named Ian. (Who seems to have appropriated one of the Ice Warrior's helmets.) We have Wild West rogues getting up to no good. We have a stiff upper lip guy in charge who is clearly an idiot. We have a leading lady who seems all right except for that weirdly distracting gold helmet on her head. Now, we do have a female voice making noises on the soundtrack that reminds me of "The Ice Warriors." But the voices feel different in space rather than on ice. Maybe if this story were on ice, it might have a little more verve.

The story does have energy. We do know who the pirates are. We can cheer on Clancy. We can boo the government guys for being dummies. We can boo the pirates for being evil. Although, they do have some good plans. We can cheer on the gold headed lady because... why not? Let's cheer her on. And we can hope that The Doctor and Jamie and Zoe are all right.

Oh yeah. They're in this. Aren't they great? Preserving oxygen and talking about magnetics. Hey! Look out. Jamie gets shot in the end. By a pirate. This can't be the end, can it? Especially because we're two episodes in and they've done nothing. Holmes! I think he's warming up for "Spearhead In Space." I could be wrong though.

*In some ways, a great way to watch this story is as a Western. Milo Clancy is one of the original frontiersmen. The pirates are people trying to usurp land. The government are the clueless bureaucrats who are never going to be able to control the land, try as they might. And the Doctor, Jamie and Zoe are... You got me. They're in this.

The Space Pirates
Episode Three

Episode 240: (March 22, 1969) Milo Clancy and the TARDIS crew hide out on the planet Ta. The Space Force (or whatever they're called) are still after him.

Cliffhanger: The TARDIS crew, being chased by Caven, fall down a hole or something. It's a little tough to say. (And impossible to see.)

You can spot Robert Holmes in this writing. In the same way, that the aliens in his first story were named Krotons, i.e., croutons, in this story one of the head pirates is named Dervish, as in 'whirling'. Holmes is about to being re-shaping the way *Doctor Who* stories can be told and that's exciting. Unfortunately, I'm having a bit of trouble getting through "The Space Pirates."

The story does seem to have its charms. Milo is cool enough. He's a little annoying but I do like him flaunting the Space Guard guys. Hermack and his group are a bunch of goofballs. Clancy's trick to stop Ian's ship, by shooting millions of copper pins at it that clog up its systems, is very clever. The pirates are generic but, apparently, Caven is a rough guy. Madame Issigri and her golden hair helmet thing amuse me every time I see them. A sign of status! The recons, though, make this episode feel about 45 minutes long. It spent all that time in Episode 1 setting up the world but it's still barely introduced the Doctor and his companions into it. And, really, all they want to do is get back to the TARDIS.

I looked at "The Seeds of Death" as a goodbye/ return to "base under siege." A type of story we hadn't seen in a bit. That was fun to watch. Generally, the story acquitted itself well, especially when Terrance

Dicks took over on the writing. In some ways, I almost looked at this story as being a "return to recons." "The Wheel in Space" was the last one where we had a lot of non-animated recons. And, in general, that one worked well. Very much helped by the fact that two episodes (middle and end) existed. But "The Space Pirates" only has episode two. The story is still building up at that time and it hasn't given the recon people a lot to work with.

As I mentioned, there are quite a few screens that are just filled with text describing what's going on as music plays. That's always a sign that we're in trouble. It means they don't have enough reference materials from the episode itself to show. All they can do is tell. And that makes for me being glad we have these reference points over the audio but it doesn't do much dramatically. Then, when we start to see the images they're using, it becomes a little discouraging.

Long conversations where they intercut between the same three or four photos show us what everyone looks like but isn't, again, thrilling. Then, there's the realization that quite a few of the images we're looking at are not from this story. Zoe is in little shorts throughout. But, on Milo's ship, she's in a jumpsuit. Oh wait, that's the rocket trip footage from Episodes two and three of "The Seeds of Death." And they use it a lot. A lot. In fact, most of their time in Milo's ship is from "Seeds," which is necessary, I know but almost makes me want to start tallying up how long they do this, in minutes and seconds. Then, when they land on Ta and start creeping through caves, there's a sequence with pirates chopping up bits of beacon, which we see none of and most of the "cave" shots used… are from the forest of words in "The Mind Robber." Again, I thank the people who did this work. But this story really could use animation or a miracle where we find the five episodes. Because the recon isn't cutting it. It's making me kind of wish I could just skip the next three episodes and go right to "The War Games." I won't though.

The Space Pirates
Episode Four

Episode 241: (March 29, 1969) Creeping around on Ta, the Doctor and friends meet a guard named Sorba and get in some gunfights.

Cliffhanger: Sorba is gunned down. Craven now has Clancy. Madame Issigri is not on the good side of things.

I really think I'd enjoy this story if I could simply see it. * Not much happens in this episode. The pirates go hunting for the missing chunk of the beacon that the Doctor shot off into space. Ian goes after them. The Space Corps doesn't do much. We do get the revelation at the end that Madame Issigri is involved but then…. The Beta Dart discussion in the previous episode is sort of a giveaway but maybe not really. Much of the episode is the Doctor and the gang trying to get out of the hole they've been trapped in.

It's a holding pattern episode. But it feels a little sharper and a little more interesting than other ones. There's certainly more going on, incident-wise, than in other holding pattern episodes. The weird thing with this show though is that the Doctor, Jamie and Zoe never really got into the story. So, we're two episodes from the end and they haven't quite made it in yet. (And the sixth episode is a very special kind of thing.)

Now, six-part stories like this won't end here. Seasons eight through eleven will be filled with them. Some wonderful and some padded. It is interesting though that in the 60s it really is true… the episodes go at a steady pace and it barely feels like things are being padded. They're just going slower. So, as far as I can tell, this episode really doesn't have padding, per se. it's just moving slowly. Whereas when the 70s begin, and the Action Doctor arrives and we're in color, padding seems to be the way we would describe an episode that doesn't advance much but does something.

May I point out that both Zoe and Jamie seem to constantly be rolling their eyes at whatever the Doctor's up to? They were a bit like that in the last few stories too. In fact, Jamie seems to be sort of sick of all of this. He's constantly saying the Doctor doesn't know what he's doing. Zoe is constantly chastising the Doctor. But then, in the previous episode, The Doctor kind of made fun of Zoe when she presented her projections on where the TARDIS portion of the beacon would be. It's weird. I never quite thought this before. It kind of does seem like this TARDIS crew are getting tired of one another. I feel like Jamie is sick of the meandering around. Zoe thought that these journeys would be something different. She stowed away expecting something from these travels. But she isn't getting it. And the Doctor is starting to wonder if he can go back and pick up Ben and Polly. I've never really thought this with a TARDIS crew before. It seems like it's time for everyone to go their separate ways.

*Oddly enough, as I was watching the episodes for these reviews, I kept having odd flashbacks. Remembering watching the episodes quite clearly a few years ago. I'm not sure where these images came from. I kept thinking I had somehow seen the story properly. All I can think is that maybe… the last time I watched these recons, I did it as I read Terrance Dicks's novelization. (It is one of his last and one of the very last "older" stories to be novelized.) So, I had vivid images from the novelization in my mind meeting up with the audio and the available images. However, I can't vouch for that. It occurred to me that maybe these episodes do exist. But, in my mind.

The Space Pirates
Episode Five

Episode 242: (April 5, 1969) Madeline Issigri is involved with Caven. Space Corps is ready to attack pirates. Pirates are ready to escape from Space Corps and Dom Issigri is still alive.

Cliffhanger: The LIZ starts to take off and the Doctor is caught in the backblast.

This one is making me really wish for the end of the recons. We discover that Dom Issigri is alive. Clancy is overjoyed as he talks to his old friend. His old friend that Caven has locked into an old study. The man seems to not be well at all. His memory seems off. His health is bad. The scene where he meets with Clancy again seems like a nice one. But, again, it's tough to tell. Especially because the image the recon uses for Dom Issigri is of the actor who plays Eldred in "The Seeds of Death." And they keep using a distracting screen shot of him sort of leaning over so it looks like he's in pain. It's distracting and takes away from any of the drama. We know something big is going on. I find it impossible to connect with it in the recon.

Something weird happens here too… The Doctor, Jamie and Zoe are in this episode a bunch. The Doctor gets the cliffhanger. But we know from records and history, that for the next episode Patrick T, Frazier H and Wendy P will be on location for the next story "The War Games." So, they are not actually in the studio for that episode, just pre-filmed inserts. We'll talk about that more when we review the next episode but it makes for a strange feeling in this one. "Mission to the Unknown" is the only other episode where the main cast wasn't there for the studio filming but we knew why. Here it seems odd to think about.

Because they do help. The Doctor is always trying to arrange stuff to free them. Zoe helps. Jamie complains. And we do get a wonderful moment that really does seem to portend something. Jamie complains and the Doctor says quietly "Jamie, sometimes I don't think you realize how much I do for you." I think the two worst things about this story being lost is 1) I feel like there's a lot of great Robert Holmes stuff happening here that just having the audio isn't fully revealing. 2) I feel like we may be setting up something here. (as unplanned as it was.) The companions and the Doctor are fraying a bit at the edges. Jamie has been there so long. He's taking everything for granted. I think he has no way to get out and now the Doctor is like an uncle who was fun to hang out with for a while... but the eccentricities are now getting annoying. I wish we could see it though.

The rest of the episode does have a lot happening. Caven and Madeline argue a lot. A lot. She doesn't want violence to happen. Gradually Caven takes over everything simply because he uses violence. Madeline has an interesting chat with Dervish about why he's doing this. Caven sets up a plan to destroy the Space Corps ships. It's all very exciting. Maybe I should re-read the novelization. Maybe that would give me the spark. Darn it, I feel like I should really like this story. I'm just barely hanging on. One episode left, everybody! The last missing episode.

The Space Pirates
Episode Six

Episode 243: (April 12, 1969) Everything turns out OK. Although our main cast doesn't seem to be that involved.
Cliffhanger: Everyone laughs and it's fun!

The Doctor, Zoe and Jamie are only in pre-filmed inserts throughout this episode. I don't know if people watching it then would have gauged what was happening. Because they do seem to be in it quite a bit, which is nice. Participating in the final bit of bomb-related excitement. Trying to stop the Space Pirates. It's an exciting Episode, I think. I also fear that maybe the TARDIS crew aren't quite as intertwined in this episode as I think they are. But that's OK. I really don't think people would have gauged that back then.

Anyway, I think The Doctor and his companions are in this quite a bit. The recon keeps using the appearance of Troughton at the very end of The Tenth Planet as its stepstone for "the dying Doctor." I applaud them. They have done their best. This story was one of the last ones that was novelized. It was also, it feels like, one of the last ones reconstructed. They did their best. Does it make the episodes better? Not really. But they hold the episodes in a place where we can experience them decently and try to work out what happens.

The first episode of this story is the one that takes the longest to bring the TARDIS crew in. They seem like an afterthought. In some ways, they are. In some ways, this is a story that deals with all those serials where the crew only interacts because they need the TARDIS back. This story keeps them away as long as possible. Jettisons the TARDIS away as soon as possible. And really limits their interest in the finale. That's amusing to me. I don't know if Robert Holmes was huge fan of the show. But this story really does feel like a flip of the middle finger to other serials like this within the format.

The Doctor is part of the story but never really. It's always about the Space Corps, Madeleine, Caven and all their machinations. The TARDIS crew is always right outside of it. Milo Clancey is kind of outside of it at the start. He gets in when Dom Issigri appears. Clancey seems like a goof until he becomes important. But Jamie, Zoe and The Doctor are all left out. They got involved in "Seeds" when they flew that rocket. They were never fully a part of "The Krotons" apart from instigating everything. It brings up the thought of how much is this TARDIS crew really involved with everything that's happening. In this story, "very little" would be the response. They help. They look for the TARDIS. In the end, we get everybody laughing and happy… but they're still not at the TARDIS. Is this Robert Holmes goofing around? Maybe.

From what I can hear and the little I can see, there is definite peril and excitement in this episode. It doesn't go out like a lamb. It goes out with a full-on kick in the pants. But, of course, the Doctor and friends aren't really near it. They seem to do a decent job and we do have the final story looming. This isn't quite like "The Smugglers." That story was sort of re-affirming William Hartnell's necessity while also preparing a goodbye. In this story, the companions and the Doctor seem to be a little uninterested in what's happening. The story itself seems to be slightly outside of the world. If that makes sense.

THE WAR GAMES
Written By Terrance Dicks and Malcolm Hulke
Directed by Derek Maloney
Episode One

Episode 244: (April 19, 1969) The TARDIS crew land in WWI. In No Man's Land. Things go badly. Cliffhanger: The Doctor is shot by a firing squad.

I love "The War Games." Malcolm Hulke is here from "The Faceless Ones." Terrance Dicks's hidden work on "The Seeds of Death" sets up this episode nicely. It begins fast and it moves. It moves like "The Krotons" moves. It moves like very few episodes before it has. That's why it's awesome. And no, the Doctor doesn't die at the end.

Back then, people knew that Patrick Troughton was leaving. I'm not sure if they knew he was leaving in this story but this episode has the feeling of that. It has a feeling of darkness to it. It has a real feeling of the story getting out from under the Doctor. It did that in "The Space Pirates." But that story was set in an indefinite future. This story seems to be set in WWI. A time when things were rough. One thinks of the 12th Doctor saying that the soldier in "Twice Upon A Time" is from "World War One." And the soldier says "One?" This is a rough time. Jamie shouldn't know it. I'm surprised that Zoe doesn't. But then, she didn't know what candles were a few episodes ago. Maybe we don't know Zoe as well as we should. Regardless, the wonderment of this episode is that it truly feels like the end has begun at a point in the show where that doesn't really mean anything yet. And it hangs over the episode. And the Doctor is shot in the end. That's not good.

The Doctor doesn't die at the end. (Or does he?) It's not for me to say here. But, boy, Derek Maloney really brings an awesome feel to this episode. The Opening sequences feel so WWI. The mud, the trenches, the barbed wire, the bombs. The randomness of it. In a later world, Wonder Woman would have run across everything and taken them all down. But here, we have the Doctor, Jamie and Zoe. Oddly enough, they're having a great time. They step out of the TARDIS and they're delighted. But, maybe, they should have a look around more. The barbed wire and the exploding things and the mud seem to be a giveaway that this isn't a nice place.

The episode moves so swiftly. The arrest, the court martial and then suddenly the firing squad. The crew get caught up in this military hierarchy long before they can climb out of it. I love when Zoe tries to save the Doctor but it ain't happening. Things seem oddly predetermined. Then, when we mix that with the General and the strange monitor, that Zoe sees, and his odd hypnotizing glasses, there is obviously something else going on here. But the tide of the drama carries everyone along until they can't get out of it. Until they are watching the Doctor get killed.

The design and the acting and everything about the episode are so WWI! That is awesome. Every time a weird moment appears, it does feel legitimately weird. It feels like "What the hell?" It really does kind of sink into the story. What feels like a regular war episode might be something bigger. It might be something crazier. And, in fact it is.

The War Games
Episode Two

Episode 245: (April 26, 1969) Things get weirder in WWI.
Cliffhanger: The ambulance goes through mist and everybody encounters... Romans!

This episode does have quite a bit of running in circles at its core. Terrance Dicks, on the DVD commentary, mentions that one of the things you really do have to do with a story this long is keep everything moving while accomplishing very little. * We've seen that a lot in the Troughton era. Here, it feels a bit different though. We get just enough to keep us moving along. The strange TARDIS-like machine that appears. The Redcoat clearly out of time. The mist that everyone keeps talking about. The growing strangeness of no one remembering how long they've been here. And the feeling that all this is being watched... The cliffhanger is icing on the cake.

It really does have a large, epic, end of the season, maybe end of the era feeling to it. Much more so than "The Tenth Planet" did. That story felt disjointed. That story felt like it had moments of obvious padding, even though it was only 4 parts. Only at the end did it seem to become big and, of course, that's the episode that we're missing. "The War Games" does feel very weighty, even if it does feel a bit repetitive.

The BBC is always great at period costume drama so everything and everyone looks right. (On the commentary, they mention that the Romans seem a bit camp. Possibly. Who's to say that Romans weren't naturally camp?) This story really has that dirty, trench-filled feel of WWI down pat, which helps greatly. Although, I do have that question: Why didn't the TARDIS crew immediately turn around and go away when they saw where they were?

There is a weird thing that happens in this era. The TARDIS lands and they get out to explore. Regardless of where they are or what is happening, there is the odd feeling that once they land... they must explore. On occasion, Jamie wanted to turn around and go. But the Doctor won't let them. Does this mean he knows that wherever they land there is something there that they need to investigate? So that's why he always goes out? I don't think this is something that they thought of much but it is something. Sometimes they do think it through like the Hartnell era. Separating them from the ship in the last story. Turning the ship invisible in "The Invasion." The Doctor really needs to do a lot of work on the ship. He's not kidding. I wonder when he's going to get around to it.

A solid episode. Not quite as good as the first one. But it moves things forward, a bit. And it gives us just enough bits and bobs to keep things intriguing and to keep us wondering. It's laying the groundwork for something big and earth changing. That doesn't happen for a few episodes though. Let's see what's going on with these Romans first.

*Dicks also mentions that this story came about when a 4-parter and a 6-parter fell through. I don't know where they were getting their stories from at this time but things were just continually going wrong. That's a crazy thought. "Hey, we lost a 4 and a 6. We need you to do a 10." "You want me to do what now?"

The War Games
Episode Three

Episode 246: (May 3, 1969) The Doctor and friends get a map of the war zones and end up in the American Civil War zone.
Cliffhanger: The Doctor and Zoe are inside the dematerializing SIDRAT.

I never noticed that the Doctor has a hole in his pants before. His right knee has a rip in it. He's very hip, is our Doctor. There is something about that that reminds me of the Fifth Doctor's cricket outfit getting dirty in "The Caves of Androzani." The Doctor's clothes are pretty much untouchable. Until it comes time to ruin them in some fashion. Seeing the fifth Doctor covered in mud and grime meant something. Seeing the Second Doctor with a hole in his baggy pants and a thread hanging off his sleeve is moving us towards the ending.

OK. This episode, again, is structured well. The transfer over to the American Civil War zone at the end comes at the perfect time. But there is a scene that is definite filler. And it's kind of too bad because it appears in an otherwise cool scene. The German officer is interrogating the Tardis crew. They tell him the truth and then show the sonic screwdriver in action. The officer believes them! What? Since when does that happen? (That almost gives the episode an extra tinge of excitement and specialness because that just doesn't happen normally.)

Fortunately, we get the sonic screwdriver being used to take a screw out of a revolver. Then, the head German jerk hypnotizes the officer. And, unfortunately, we get the exact same scene with the screwdriver again. It's not lengthy and you can see why they do it. But still, it's some sort of padding, even when it's important to what's going on. Dicks and Hulke really do have control of this narrative. One can't help wonder what this would have been like if it were only six episodes though. Hulke's novelization streamlines it nicely.

But in and amidst all the repeated motions and the shots of the ambulance driving along and all the captures and escapes and all the shooting, there is a story moving ahead. Of course, the ambulance breaks down, which is too bad. But even that leads them to the barn and the enemy space/ time machine. The SIDRAT. Watching it disgorge about ten Confederate troops is a little disconcerting. And yes, you can gauge exactly what's going to happen when the Doctor steps in. But it mostly works. And it means that now, the Doctor and Zoe will go back to headquarters, to the central space that is not on their cool map. Leaving Jamie and Lady Jennifer to fight or do something or other.

We meet the War Chief. He's got a bit of a sashay to him when he enters the scene. His leather dressed guards with their long guns can't top him and his big medallion. If this was a 1979 story, his shirt would be buttoned down to his waist. It's interesting that we are getting these glimpses of what is going on. Or at least who is in control of what's going on. And the War Lord is mentioned. They'll hold off a bit on showing him through. We've still got seven episodes.

The War Games
Episode Four

Episode 247: (May 10, 1969) Jamie and Lady Jennifer are in the American Civil War. The Doctor and Zoe watch the aliens in charge of all this run a conditioning exercise.
Cliffhanger: A newly conditioned Carstairs is going to shoot Zoe as a German spy.

I love those goofy glasses everyone wears in this episode. Apparently, in the script, the writers mention that the glasses are being worn because of sensitivity to the lights. Which begs the question: if this is their workspace, why can't they put in lights that don't hurt their eyes? I like the glasses with the plus signs but I also like the ones with the multiple slits in them. They don't mention in the episode why they wear them. So, it ends up looking a little odd. But then, maybe these aliens are a little odd. The head conditioning scientist certainly has a bit of a weirdness to him.

I love the way the Doctor takes over the presentation. And I love those little fun magnets that operate all the equipment. We never fully figure what they are exactly. But they look like a hoot. Like maybe it was designed for children and somehow the adults got hold of it. The Doctor re-ka-jiggering the conditioning machine will be important as time goes on. Watching Carstairs get conditioned and believing the Doctor and Zoe are spies is rather chilling. Well, chilling might be too strong of a word. Definitely disheartening.

Especially because this is the episode where we meet the proper Resistance. A group of soldiers from across the war zones. I like the thought of a motley ragtag group of goofball soldiers pushing their way from time/ war zone to zone trying to recruit others and find out what's going on. I'm not sure, without the Doctor's help, that they would have gotten anywhere. Yet, after meeting everyone, we still don't know why the aliens are doing all of this.

This episode has another "circular sequence," which is the more sophisticated way of saying "padding." Jamie and the Lady Jennifer escape from the Rebel soldiers. There's a long and fun On Location scene where they, individually, get chased by men on horses. They seem to be OK. They seem to have escaped. Suddenly, they get caught again and oh well. Back to where we started. Once you point out this sort of "circular" padding, it becomes pretty apparent in almost every episode. (Even the 10th episode has it. In that one, the Doctor kind of acknowledges it.)

The best moment in the episode is probably the War Chief seeing the Doctor and their reactions. The Doctor does quite obviously take off his glasses when no one else does. But it's a setup. And the moment the two of them see each other and the Doctor and Zoe take off running is one of the most exciting moments in the show for some time. Who is that guy? How does he know the Doctor? And what does that mean? It's an exciting moment that is as big as Vicki and Steven discovering The Meddling Monk's TARDIS. What does this portend for the future of the show? Maybe the Doctor will show him how his sonic screwdriver works? I'd watch that again.

The War Games
Episode Five

Episode 248: (May 17, 1969) Zoe is interrogated. The Doctor and Carstairs run around a bunch. The rebels hang out in the barn.
Cliffhanger: Jamie and the rebels are shot down by the guards as they leave the SIDRAT.

What's with all those nails and spikes in the Security Chief's interrogation room? After a time, I start to imagine that the Security Chief is the head of a black metal band from Norway and doesn't want to tell anyone. I could be wrong.

This is the last episode with Lady Jennifer. She doesn't join Jamie and the rebels when they go into the SIDRAT near the end of the episode. So, they just lead her away. Presumably, she'll get taken back home when all this is over. She was a good character. Sort of like Anne Travers in "The Web of Fear." I would have liked to have seen her in more episodes.

When PBS first showed "the War Games," in early 1987, they showed in it two chunks of about two hours each. The interesting thing about the way they showed it on WXXI-TV 21 was that they showed the first five episodes one night. Then, the next Saturday, they showed the next five. But, because they showed the omnibus edition, we got the big cliffhanger. The guards with their fun ray guns shooting circular psychedelic effects knock Jamie out. We've previously seen a rebel killed with the gun so we're very worried about Jamie. In the original episode, we go immediately to the credits, which roll very fast in this story. That night, on PBS, around 1 AM on a Sunday, the image of Jamie being shot faded out and the station turned off for the night. No credits, no nothing. Just ended. One week later, it began from that exact same point. No opening credits, no nothing. I always remember that very clearly because the image of Jamie on the ground is a strong one and the DVDs split the story the same way across two.

Anyway, the plan of assembling the rebels together into one big group comes to the forefront here. We can sort of begin to see where the story might go. However, that sounds like a heck of a huge plan. And, we haven't had anyone walk from their war zone into the central zone. It seems to be surrounded by some forcefield and only the SIDRATS can enter. I'm guessing a bit there. The thought of someone wandering into the mist and then suddenly appearing on one of these weird and wonderful sets is compelling.

What about the bad guy's sets? Nice use of space and darkness. Very minimal. They sort of remind me of the sets from a lot of the third Season *Batman* episodes from 1967-1968. They had budget cuts. So, a lot of the sets for the villains use darkness on the edge of the sets instead of walls and strange doorways and arches. "The War Games" is, obviously, more futuristic and looks more like a strange, swirly psychedelic place. But they come from the same mindset. Needing to save money and not being able to decorate the whole of the set.

James Bree is a delightfully obsequious Security Chief. I love his big slide projector hat thing with which he interrogates Zoe. And he has a great argument with the War Chief. I like how we get small bits and bobs of what's going on. They don't over-emphasize what's happening. There's always that fun thing where they bring up the War Lord whenever the other one gets a bit too stroppy. "I'll tell dad!" I always thought that the War Chief's pendant was some sort of immense source of power. Now, I just think it's a nifty pendant.

Now, we're entering the second half of the story. We know quite a bit of what's going on. We fear that that poor hapless scientist is going to be picked on again. We look forward to more guys in rubber or whatever with big guns and we look forward to more arguing between the bad guys and maybe some revelations regarding The Doctor...

The War Games
Episode Six

Episode 249: (May 24, 1969) Some escape from the control center. Some do not.
Cliffhanger: Carstairs, Jamie and The Doctor are being crushed inside a SIDRAT.

Now, we know that whatever this thing is, this space/ time machine which has not been named, that it is a TARDIS-like vehicle. Not only is it the noise and the inner dimensions. It's the fact that The War Chief can shrink the inner dimensions. This happened in "The Wheel In Space" but that episode is lost. We have the audio and the novelization. So, this ties in with what we hear the Security Chief and our hapless scientist discussing earlier.

We've seen Susan. We've seen The Meddling Monk. We know that The Doctor's kind of special. But now, we learn the name of the Doctor's people (or something): The Time Lords. And it's the scientist who says it. So, he knows this big, important bit of information. This info that is tossed off casually here. Not really meaning much. This is a land of Chiefs and Lords. What are we to pay attention to and what do we just let ride? Maybe we'll let this ride. Maybe it will be important later.

A large portion of this episode is taken up with the German Officer trying to hypnotize a rebel soldier from the 19th Century named Moor. Moor is played by David Troughton, one of Patrick's sons. He's very clearly a son of The Doctor. And it's a nice scene. Very tense, very well written. It's also the kind of scene/ scenes that one wouldn't really see in something today. Because it's a side story. A decent chunk of this episode deals with this. I mean, it could just be giving the star's son something to do. Both actors are good in the scene. Both are convincing. The DVD production text points out that the origins of Moor's character, which zone he might be from, don't quite work, historically. But it's fun, nevertheless. One might call it padding. Or one might call it taking advantage of the length available.

It's like a band or an artist releasing a double album. You know, a song or two that seems a bit weird or maybe superfluous in that context could be either filler or the musician is experimenting with the format. Now, I have 80 minutes of 40. So, I can put something in I would never regularly add. That's what these scenes feel like. And they resolve themselves well.

Meanwhile, the story is moving along decently. There is a feeling here of "We haven't been on location for a while, have we?" We haven't. We've been in a barn. We've been on the "futuristic" sets. But we haven't been on location since Episode Four, I believe. That's not bad though. I'm sure we'll get back to some but it is interesting when one realizes it.

I don't understand how the Security Chief and the War Chief could work together. You must have some minimal respect for a co-worker. There's just nothing here. These two clearly are at odds constantly. I don't know. That seems like a hostile work environment to me. Anyway, they argue, they argue. Meanwhile, the Doctor steals the conditioning machine. And there are some very abruptly put together scenes in the SIDRAT control room, especially the one with the gas valves at the end. But then, sometimes, one prefers to see something happen quickly rather than deliberately. I don't need to see the screw come out of that revolver again. I also don't need to see them sneak up on the SIDRAT bay. Just show up, take over and hope you don't get crushed.

The War Games
Episode Seven

Episode 250: (May 31, 1969) The rebels take the chateau. But the War Lord has a plan.
Cliffhanger: The bad guys capture The Doctor.

The last 6 or so minutes of this episode do something interesting. Something that a previous episode or two may have done. I know we're in the stretch now when Hulke and Dicks were sort of struggling to fill in all the time that needed filling. But watch how calmly paced the first 16 or 17 minutes of this episode are and then catch the ending. It's almost like a What the heck? Did someone else take over the writing of this episode?

What happens in that last fourth or so? General Smythe is killed and they discover the controls for the 1917 time zone. The Security Chief sends a contingent of soldiers to attack the chateau. The Doctor is able to place a time mist around the chateau so the soldiers can't get in. A soldier is deconditioned. The War Lord says he'll take charge. A SIDRAT (Side-rat?) appears and they kidnap the Doctor. That's a heck of a lot of stuff for a few minutes. Especially considering how much didn't happen throughout so many of the stories of this era.

Now, the opening ¾ aren't bad. The Doctor, Jamie and Carstairs stumble out of the SIDRAT. The Doctor pulls some nice shenanigans in the control room. They end up in Roman times, hoping to get back to WWI. Then, things become a little tricky. And I can't tell whether the writers are having a bit of fun or are just exhausted.

There is a moment when the Romans chase them. That's fine. But it is the exact same footage from the previous episodes. Literally. Then, they get caught in the 1917 zone and Smythe sentences The Doctor to the firing squad again. We've seen it before. And this time we don't even see a firing squad. Just the General looking down and someone yelling orders. (Apparently Patrick Troughton.) If you watch the episodes in quick succession, it feels a bit like "Oh, we're here again." Backing into the beginning of the story. However, watching it over seven weeks back in 1969, it might have felt different. And, presumably, quite a few people might not have seen the opening episodes. It might have felt like a fun callback of the sort that the show doesn't really do. It is the end of an era. Why not give a shout out? Again, I don't know that this what was happening though.

Do we need to mention how cool The War Lord is? Terrance Dicks calls it in the commentary. The War Chief is slightly pantomime. The Security Chief is kind of affected in his speech. But then, the War Lord shows up. And he's quiet and threatening. He's so good. It's Phillip Madoc who was not as threatening in "The Krotons" a few months ago. In fact, he looks completely different and he's so good. You can tell that this is like The Boss showing up and the subordinates must be at their absolute best. You can sense him just barely tolerating them. And he does put them in their place. He does take over and he does accomplish something quickly. Maybe he should have been more hands on? I don't know. But, heck, this is a villain. This is a Tobias Vaughn or a Mavic Chen. Or The Master, at his/ her best.

The seventh episode ends. And one can feel that it's only a matter of time before something big and important happens. I feel like The Doctor can sense it. But, as always, they'll do their best to not get all wrapped up in it. This time, though, it might be too big.

The War Games
Episode Eight

Episode 251: (June 7, 1969) The Doctor has turned against all that is good and right!
Cliffhanger: Or has he?

Never fear, kids! The Doctor is still a good guy. But think of it. At this time, there was talk of the show going off the air. There was talk of the show ending with this season. We knew nothing of The Doctor. What if he came from an incredibly war-like race and he'd spent the last 250-odd episodes and 6 years fighting against what he was raised to do? And what if The War Chief was his brother or something? What if he decided that now was the time… the time to follow his birthright as a Doctor of War! What if that happened here? Well, I think it would have blown a lot of people's minds. And, from what I've seen of the TV criticism of the day, a lot of the halfwits writing would have been simply confused. Luckily, this isn't what's happening.

The Security Chief recommends basically nuking the whole thing before it gets out of hand. The War Chief isn't thrilled with this. The War Lord is considering it. In fact, the War Lord continues to be pretty darn creepy throughout. One can imagine that, yes sir, he has started all of this up. It's overfunded and it's not the best idea but darn it we're going through with it and it's going to be so awesome when it's done. Probably. Sometimes I get the feeling that he never really expected it to be done. "I hadn't thought that far ahead." Sure, War Lord. Sure.

Luckily, the good guys have Zoe. There are quite a few fun scenes here of recruiting people from around the zones to help fight. Arturo Villar isn't the most politically correct character here. But he sure is gung ho. And, yes, as others have pointed out, Zoe is meant to have remembered photographically all the rebel leaders but she doesn't know who Villar is. The production text on the DVD suggests that it is dark and she can't quite see who it is. I would add that she was sound asleep and he's nudging her awake. Give her a moment. Could we please? I love pointing out errors that other people have made all the time. Sometimes your errors aren't errors. (Remember when you all thought that a bit fell off a war machine? And that Ben picked it up? We laughed at you then. We're still laughing.)

It's a nicely done episode. One side builds up one side of the story. The rebels accumulating in the chateau is nicely done. Finally, a feeling like something might be done. A feeling like these evil aliens, whatever they are, can be put down. Their abhorrent plan to take over the galaxy with the strongest warriors can be stopped. (I know. It seems a bit odd. But they seem a bit odd. Let's let it ride.) On the other end, we have the talk between the War Chief and The Doctor. We don't get a lot of info. Bits and bobs of the Doctor's background. We've known so little. We still know little but we can feel that something is going to happen soon. Certainly, that ending doesn't bode well for anyone. Luckily, for us, it keeps us hopping and keeps us thinking right up to the end.

The War Games
Episode Nine

Episode 252: (June 14, 1969) The War Games end but the Doctor can't send everyone home. He must call on the Time Lords to help him.
Cliffhanger: Having summoned the Time Lords, something is trying to stop the Doctor, Jamie and Zoe from entering the TARDIS.

The episode where things get too big for The Doctor. Maybe William Hartnell was in over his head on multiple occasions. His thing was that he could run away really well. And, if the overwhelming odds succeeded (remember The Thals ramshackle defeat of "The Daleks" in "The Daleks?") he could hang around and tell stories about how great he was and things like that. The Second Doctor really isn't like that. Some things have gotten crazy for him. But "The Evil of The Daleks" is the craziest I can think of it getting. He got lucky there because he was always sort of in step with The Daleks. They had been enemies for so long. One feels that he was right there alongside their machinations. He defeated them as much as they defeated themselves. Remember this is a Doctor who expressed confusion over saving the day back in "The Power of the Daleks" and specialized in running away before questions could be asked. But now, things were too big and things were ending.

It's also the episode where things fall apart for our friends: The War Chief shuts down the fighting. The Security Chief is killed by the War Chief. A lot. The War Lord gets pissed off and looks legitimately afraid when the Time Lords approach. The fighting ends. But none of it happens on the field. It all happens in the middle Zone, the Alien Zone. That gives it a different feel then if it had been fought out in the "real world." It ends up looking wonderfully incongruous. Seeing these dirty fighters from different years amongst the antiseptic sets is something. Yes, Arturo Villar is an acquired taste. But he's only in the story for an episode and a half so… hold your breath and he'll pass.

Overall, the episode is a good one. There's a lot of running around and a lot of fighting. I love the moment when The Security Chief leaves the Doctor alone with all the rebels and they try to rip him up. I like watching the Doctor "fake" condition everyone. A lot of stuff is packed into this episode because this is the episode where this story ends. I miss Lady Jennifer. Carstairs vanishes. All the others are left behind. It's very *Doctor Who* to me. Maybe not RTD version but Moffat definitely. When it ends, it ends. When it's over, sometimes we don't get to say goodbye.

That leads us to the ending. All the soldiers vanishing, including Carstairs. They're all gone. And it's just the Doctor, Zoe and Jamie running like mad through a WWI field towards the TARDIS. A silent field. A field with no noise. The exact opposite of the place they ran through so long ago. Now, just trying to get back. And the Time Lords have them trapped in treacle (not my words, the writers). Trapped in time. They are a powerful bunch. The Doctor knows this. The Doctor carries it with him. (Remember when he blew up a Dalek fleet in "The Time of the Doctor" with Time-Lord assisted yellow regenerative power?) And now they're dragging this missing son, this missing character, back to them. But can they? The Doctor is resourceful. Maybe they'll break free. Or maybe it's time for the trial of a Time Lord.

The War Games
Episode Ten

Episode 253: (June 21, 1969) The Time Lords put the Doctor on trial for his interference in the lives of other beings. We say goodbye to everyone. All change!
Cliffhanger: The change begins as the exile commences.

One of the most important episodes of the show. Ever. And they handle it well. From the moment the Doctor arrives on his home planet, * (possibly), we can feel that it is over. What that means specifically we don't know at this point. But we can feel that what we've seen for the past six seasons might be over now. Something might be happening to alter what we know. Maybe.

It begins with a bit of an odd sequence. We see, for the first time in ages (as far as I know), the full TARDIS set. It's nice to see it. Normally, we just get the console, the doors and a wall. But, here, it's closer to what we used to see a lot in the Hartnell era. But then, we get the Doctor doing some craziness to try to keep away from The Time Lords. We see a clip from "The Web of Fear" and "Fury From The Deep." We get a bit of a jaunt through the Second Doctor's adventures and it's nice. Hartnell never got anything like that. This is the second time the show is doing this. The second time is usually more interesting than the first because there's a precedent that can be worked within and around

I love that The War Lord does try to escape. He has one last SIDRAT and he's giving it a shot. It fails, of course. The Time Lords wave their hands and it ends as quickly as it began. But it's nice to see them try. I don't know why they never named the War Lord's planet. It does give it a real mysterious feeling though. For those interested in visiting, it's been time looped away. You'll never get there.

The Second Doctor is put on trial. Three dour Time Lords, who look familiar, listen calmly as he speaks. They are clearly some sort of gods. Aren't they? Then, the Doctor is one of these gods too. He just dresses in fewer robes as maybe we all should. I don't have much to add to the trial scene that others have said before me. It's a nicely done moment that makes sure we know that our hero for the past six years is as awesome as we'd hoped he might be. He's a good man who left this world of stasis, almost entropy, and decided he wanted to do something. He wanted to help others. And he did it. And it's awesome. Thank you, Doctor.

A brave new world lies ahead. The show does this every few years. It reconfigures itself. It makes itself into something different. That's what's happening here. My only sadness is the Doctor being forced to leave Jamie and Zoe. I am convinced that Jamie is going to get shot dead about three minutes after being sent back. I am also convinced that Zoe will remain a human computer component in her world for the rest of her life. Now, she wasn't a fan of violence. (Apart from Starsky and Hutch, who is?) And she did seem, sometimes, to be less than thrilled with her time spent with The Doctor. I sometimes felt that she thought something different was going to be happening. I think her time spent with the Doctor is better than time spent without. Same with Jamie. I always think this is worse than what happened to Donna Noble. Donna seems fine either way. Whereas Jamie and Zoe left places that weren't great to have adventures. Plus, Donna got that lottery ticket** and Jamie looks like he's getting a bullet.

Enough of that. The exile has begun. The Doctor's face has changed. Let's see what happens next.

(I have one question: What the heck is that set The Doctor, Zoe and Jamie run through when they're trying to get away? Weird white stepping squares with like a misty liquid around it or... I don't know. Is this from an episode that's lost? I can't imagine, at the end of a production block, that they built this awesome set for about 20 seconds worth of footage. It must have been for something else. Mustn't it?)

*Actually, I just realized that Season 23 (The Trial of a Time Lord) sets an odd precedent. The Doctor is put on trial there. But it's on a space station in the middle of somewhere or other. Does that mean that this is not Gallifrey? It would make sense. Why would the non-intervention Time Lords bring possible

criminals to their home planet? They wouldn't. They'd bring the criminals to a space station at a spot where the abducted can't figure out where exactly they are. Makes sense to me.

**As you know, Donna got more than that lottery ticket during the 60th Anniversary.

Final Note: Right before publication, I saw half of the colorized version of "The War Games." It was at the Gallifrey One convention in Los Angeles on February 15, 2025. I stayed to a point that coincided with early Episode Six. The color is fantastic. If colorizing is your thing, they did a great job. It was a lot of fun to watch some Troughton era footage with a crowd. I wasn't enamored of the editing to the story to reduce it to ninety minutes. It's bordering on incoherent at times. Two examples: 1) There's talk of a scene where Zoe finds a TV monitor screen in the WWI General's room. That scene has been cut but characters remember it happening. It made me feel like I'd missed something. I hadn't. 2) Jamie and all the rebels go from being in the War Zone to suddenly being captured at Headquarters. It just happens because they cut out the capture scene. That bit coincided with early Episode Six, coinciding with my leaving. I found the chaotic editing funny at times. I think it's trying to mirror modern day, super-fast paced programming. To me, it worked sometimes and felt very clumsy at others. Many people seemed to enjoy it though so I'm thinking it did its job. I'll stick with the original.

SEASON SEVEN
(1970)
In Color!!

SPEARHEAD FROM SPACE
Written by Robert Holmes
Directed by Derek Martinus
Episode One

Episode 254: (January 3, 1970) Strange meteorites land in the Epping Forest. The Brigadier recruits Dr. Elizabeth Shaw to help with UNIT. A tall white-haired man with two hearts appears near a police box in the woods.
Cliffhanger: The Doctor is shot in the head by a rambunctious UNIT soldier.

Robert Holmes's script handles everything perfectly. When the first Doctor became the second, it was within a season. One week there was one guy. The next there was another. The companions were the same and The Daleks were promised. A seismic change occurred. But they kept it rooted in what had come before. Here, that doesn't happen at all. Holmes finally truly shines as one of the four or five best writers *Doctor Who* has ever had. This episode has so much happening. It has so much going on. But it never feels like an unwieldy mess.

Liz Shaw gets a nice opening scene. She's sarcastic and disbelieving. Gradually, the Brig does start to win her over somewhat. The Brig, himself, is in his element here. Large and in charge. His excitement about seeing the Doctor again and the subsequent confusion over who this man is is nicely done. Seely, the poacher, is the skeezy version of Bernard Cribbins. The grandfather you want to run away from. Even the secondary characters are fun. Munro has a nice turn of phrase here and there. Doctor Henderson and the Nurse are a delightful duo. The fact that we won't really see them much after the next episode makes them one of those many characters in the show who appear for a bit and then leave our memories. Until we see them again and think "Oh them!" Then, there's Mullins, the porter. I love the way he talks. I wonder if the UNIT solider who says, "Mustn't they?" is a relative of his. And then there's Channing, who we'll learn more about later. Even the reporters are fun. And What about that lady with that Monty python-esque bandage over her eye? It's all good stuff.

And then there's Jon Pertwee as the Doctor. To British viewers at the time, they would have known him from mostly comedy. Broad comedy. And he's doing comedy here. But then, the Doctor is still working his way through whatever's happening. He spends most of his time in a hospital bed but he does get some wackiness going with a wheelchair. He's king of vague in this episode. The regeneration has left him wonky. But he'll become the Doctor soon.

Then, there's those meteorites. Not much happens with them. We get a little groundwork laid down. We get a little "What might be happening here?' We get a couple of weird looking guys. But that's it. The story is keeping its cards close to its chest at the moment. All shall be revealed, however.

The other fun thing we get here is Holmes re-writing (or writing) huge swaths of mythology very casually. The Doctor now has two hearts. He can put himself into a coma when he needs to. His pulse is 10 a minute. These are all little throwaway things that he adds to the story that other writers build on and make integral parts of whole adventures, which is awesome. Holmes will do this again.

Spearhead From Space
Episode Two

Episode 255: (January 10, 1970) The Doctor sort of joins UNIT. The Auton Invasion continues. Mainly Seely argues with his wife.
Cliffhanger: Munro gets attacked by an Auton.

I almost forget sometimes that this seminal story really takes its time. But it takes its time in such an odd way. Because there are several big stories going on at once. They all advance themselves along at a decent, but not a crazy pace, which is fun. It makes the viewing of the story feel off-kilter and exciting. However, this is one of those stories that I would suggest is jumbled up a bit by the fact that Robert Holmes seems to have chosen a completely odd structure for everything.

The Nestene Consciousness is about to invade. You remember "Rose?" That's them. They're like The Great Intelligence or The Gods of Ragnarök. They are outside of our universe trying hard to break in. And they are something. They are possessing plastic, which is still relevant. It's Terrance Dicks and Robert Holmes having some fun. They will have more fun in a season but here they are stretching out their craziness. Even with Derrick Sherwin still there.

The Doctor is delightful in this episode. The Second Doctor was in the TARDIS. Was safe. They got involved in a weird adventure. (Please, "The Power of the Daleks" is odd.) The Third Doctor is on our Earth. He's on our grounds. Liz Shaw is doing what she needs to do but is very blasé about it. And it makes for fun. There are some good scenes between the two of them. She is clearly doing her job. He is doing his thing. They end up encountering a mélange of people working at cross purposes for the same purpose. That's entertainment.

The moment when the Doctor arrives at UNIT HQ is fantastic. He's charming. He's charismatic, He's in charge. Yes, the Brigadier has the key to the TARDIS. But, you know, that The Doctor will get it back sooner rather than later. By whatever means. This leads to some fun scenes with him and Liz. His Delphon thing is a bit of an acquired taste. However, it all helps to make them a team by the end.

Meanwhile, we get Seely and his "Thunderball." I don't know why they named that after the 4th James Bond film but I'm sure there is an awesome reason. Seely and his wife are great in this episode. The Auton, mannequin, is cool, creeping silently through the thick woods. "The Seelys and The Auton" is a show I just conceived of and it's freaking me out.

Channing and the worker are intriguing. There's a lovely off to one side adventure happening here, which almost doesn't quite become part of whatever it is we're doing. I love how this story rolls along. And we watch The Doctor… because he's the lead. But there are all these other characters. What are they doing? Why are they doing whatever it is they're doing? It really gives the feel of a new era. A new type of story. And we all think "Will this white-haired gentleman who is clearly older than the previous Doctor be able to make everything OK?" Maybe he will. Let's dive in and find out.

(I haven't really mentioned the switch to color yet. The scene where the jeep is shunted off the road by an Auton and hits the tree is very gory for Doctor Who. We have seen blood before but in black and white. The dead UNIT soldier with his bloody head through the windshield is a whole other thing.)

Spearhead From Space
Episode Three

Episode 256: (January 17, 1970) The investigation continues. What is going on?
Cliffhanger: General Scobie's duplicate arrives at the front door.

Pour Ransome. His story ends rather horribly. He goes to America for six months to arrange some sort of deal with Americans for their new dolls. He comes back to find he's been given his walking papers. Going to see Hibbert, Ransome finds the plant is almost, but not quite, totally automated. He sees this odd man, Channing, before he is booted out. Later, he breaks in and see a mannequin come to life and attack him. It puts him in an almost catatonic state. He talks to the Brig. Then an Auton breaks into the tent and completely obliterates his body. The Nestene mean business, even though we don't know who they are yet. Or what they are.

The Doctor is acclimating nicely to all of this. I like the scene where they go to speak with Hibbert. Liz in one chair. The Brig in another. The Doctor casually leaning against a pole in the center of the room. Mirroring the ways that the 4th Doctor would join in conversations like this. The Doctor is doing his own thing throughout. Luckily, he has Liz there. She's right alongside him. The grown-up Zoe. I like that. She's skeptical and she's lees inclined to go off on an adventure, like Zoe. (And, in fact, she won't be doing that.) She's a great co-worker for the Doctor.

The whole thing looks fantastic. Having the show entirely on film (and HD) is a super treat. It gives the show a continuity that many of the color episodes will not have. The black and white ones, generally, were able to hide themselves when they went from film to video. The first episode of the next serial will show up the piebald issue very strongly. But here, Pertwee gets a nice intro. He gets a nice set of episodes that slowly reveal this brave new world to us. And slowly reveal who he is to us. It's going great so far.

Yes, the pacing does feel slightly off. There is a big invasion looming. Investigations have begun. We know there is craziness going on. But we're ¾s of the way in at this point. We only have 25 minutes left. From our knowledge of previous serials in the show, it seems like this might not be enough time to get everything done. Or we are going to be doing some major cramming. I always think the story may have done a bit better as a five partner. But then, I never really stop and argue with it as a four parter. Let's hop to the last episode of this one and see how it goes.

I do want to mention one more character. I'm not sure about General Scobie. When Hibbert says that they're automating most of the plant to cut down on human workers, he seems excited. He points out that machines can't strike. You'd rather the plants be automated and all those people be out of work? The moment they go on the dole, am I right in thinking.. you'll be the first one complaining about people living off the government and welfare? I think it's Holmes throwing in a little sarcasm/ satire. "If you automate everything but we don't have some sort of utopia where people don't have to work, what do the people do?" All I can think is that this is a few years away from "The Good Life" and self-sufficiency. People driven to this by the sort of attitude we see here. Of course, if we'd only let the Nestene take us over. None of this would matter.

Spearhead From Space
Episode Four

Episode 257: (January 24, 1970) The Nestene Invasion begins.
Cliffhanger: The UNIT era truly begins.

Yes, a lot of stuff does happen in this episode.

The most well-known portion is the Auton attack on the quiet London street one morning. A series of rather disturbing mannequins come to life in shop windows and begin to attack and kill people. (There's an attack on a line of people at a bus stop that always reminds me of the time the Frankenstein Monster attacked people in a similar line during *Monty Python's Flying Circus*.) It's a great sequence. Unlike "Rose' which has the Autons bursting through windows, the windows aren't seen to be broken here. We just hear them coming apart. But the killing is real. It's as immediate as Barbara and Jenny running through the London streets sometime in the future in "The Dalek Invasion of Earth." It's a heck of a sequence and it's done very well. Sitting comfortably within the context of this atypical serial.

Because the episode is very weird, structurally. The first half of it is calmly paced. A long portion is spent at the wax museum. Quite a bit of it. Then, Scobie and Channing reveal that the Nestene are here and we get a monster/ whatever it is that is very much like The Great Intelligence. It is something outside of our Universe that wants to come in and take over the Earth. The Great Intelligence was a bit more esoteric. It had the Yeti. But one didn't quite fully grasp what the heck It was doing. But It knew and, in the end, that was enough. The Nestene however clearly have a plan. They have control over the plastic. They have the Replicas and the Autons and they are going to take over the Earth. That's what they do.

The fun thing with a villain like this is that if it completely breaks through, we're probably all dead. So, it kind of is held at bay. (What happened to the Seeleys?) It's probably better if we don't fully grasp what it is. Because that always helpfully allows for a sequel where, maybe, we can get a bit more of what's happening. Yes, the Doctor gurning along with the tentacles at the end of this episode might not be the world's best ending. The UNIT soldiers fighting the Autons is nice, though. The more I watch the tentacles the more I don't mind them. I like the concept that this is sort of an octopus/ Lovecraftian-being in this stew pot that is trying to take over the world. Why does it have so many tentacles? What is it? Well, we don't find out here. Maybe we will sometime in the future. But just the fact that these hairy tentacles attack the Doctor makes it interesting. Is Kroll from the Nestene future? Maybe. Setting aside all these unanswered questions, we can firmly agree that The Third Doctor is here. He's working for UNIT, for now. And we're in a whole new sort of TV show.

A couple more things before we go underground: Poor Hibbert. His attempts to destroy the oncoming Nestene Consciousness are doomed but he does his best. We get a weird bit of sound structure when he is destroyed. The Auton fires at him. His body bursts into smoke and them reverses. When the bolt is fired at him, there is the huge sound of whooshing and shooting mixed with what seems like big music... but then when the smoke is gone everything stops. So, it ends up being a wonderfully over the top moment that happens too quickly and too strangely to end up being over the top. I think it's fantastic.

Yes, the structure is a bit off. But, overall, this is a fantastic entry into this era. In the same way that "The Power of the Daleks" brought us into the previous one. It's fast paced. It's more suited to color. It's more "modern." But, at the same time, it's clearly *Doctor Who*. It clearly isn't any other show. So, with the next story, the producer credit will change hands. The show will start to go in a different direction. But, I think, we all feel like we're in safe hands.

DOCTOR WHO AND THE SILURIANS
Written by Malcolm Hulke
Directed by Timothy Coombe
Episode One

Episode 258: (January 31, 1970): The Doctor, Liz and UNIT are in an underground nuclear reactor investigating some odd occurrences.
Cliffhanger: The Doctor meets a dinosaur.

With this episode, the show properly feels like *Doctor Who* of the 1970s (and beyond). "Spearhead From Space" does feel weird. It seems like the start of a brand-new show. Something new and something exciting. "The Silurians" feels like we've calmed down a bit. It feels like "yes! It's the same show but we've made a few concessions." The film of "Spearhead" and the feel of it made it feel almost like a *Doctor Who* movie. But now, the piebald regime is back. That's when the interiors are on video and the exteriors are on film. In this episode, we're almost all video. And we get our first glimpse of CSO. That would be basically what we now know as greenscreen. When the dinosaur is seen with the miners at the beginning that's CSO.

If you watch "Spearhead" and then immediately watch this episode, it can leave you with a weird feeling. First, there are no more missing episodes at this point. The Pertwee era was made in color. Many areas of Britain were still in black and white. Versions were made in B&W and color. Some episodes are missing B&W versions or color versions. "The Silurians" is missing most of its color episodes. When the show originally aired on PBS, it was in black and white. But the DVD is in color. It is more or less "colorized." Some of the color is strong. Some, frankly, is not. In fact, the overall softness of the color in this episode is such a contrast to the previous episode that only the fact that we recognize a few of the lead characters and the credit sequence clues us in to the fact that this is the same show.

It is a very distracting episode in that respect. Obviously, as you watch it, it's clearly the *Doctor Who* that we all know and love. It has the same spirit and is the same fun kind of show. And there's The Brig. And there are your *Doctor Who* types. This might even be a "base under siege." Possibly. But it's too early to say. What about that odd guy in charge who smiles at everything even when bad stuff is happening? He couldn't be deluded in any way, could he? Sorry. I hopped ahead there. It really does look very different from the previous story. However, it does look very similar to the way *Doctor Who* looks throughout the 1970s. So, it's the first story that Barry Letts has produced. It's the first one with this incredibly odd music. It's the first of three 7-part stories in a row. And it's the first one that can put a viewer in a comfy "*Doctor Who*" frame of mind. Let's see where everything goes from here. The look is slightly off-putting. Hopefully, it should turn out all right.

How is the episode? It's a lot of fun. It sets up this underground base very nicely. Introduces us to a slew of characters. The Doctor and Liz are getting on well here. It's nice to see the Brig take charge. Overall, not much happens. But it is the first episode of a seven-part story so you don't want to overplay your hand too early. You've got plenty of time. This episode gives you just enough to keep you interested. The color of it, accompanied by the odd kazoo soundtrack, keeps one slightly off-kilter. Which helps.

Doctor Who And The Silurians
Episode Two

Episode 259: (February 7, 1970) Things heat up with dinosaurs and some sort of strange lizard man who goes wandering the moors at night.
Cliffhanger: The wounded Silurian attacks Liz.

Well, there is a moment I don't fully understand in here, which might be a goof. The UNIT soldiers are in the caves looking for the Silurian. (They don't know what it is but they're looking.) Liz and The Doctor are looking at the blood they found in the cave and realizing that it's reptile blood. Then, the Brigadier enters and says they lost it, whatever it is. Darnit! Besides, it was getting dark. Oh well that… Huh? They were in a cave deep underground. They're in a facility underground. In the previous episode, someone mentions that you can't tell day from night here. And they stopped looking because it got dark. Is that some Malcolm Hulke comedy? (Somehow, he doesn't seem like the world's funniest guy.)

Thank goodness we get out of the studio and get to roam the countryside. It's gorgeous out here. Granted a lot of it is from Silurian POV. Broken into three triangles, one red and with limited peripheral vision. We get some great night footage of the heavy breathing whatever-it-is trudging through a farm and collapsing into the tender winter hay. We only see whatever-it-is briefly. The director wanted to keep it even more hidden. But we can clearly see that something is going on. The scene where the squire attacks and gets attacked is excellent. It seems to be a cut above what other BBC shows were doing at this time. That's why *Doctor Who* is always worth watching and enjoying.

The Doctor and the Brig are really becoming a nice team here. When the head of the compound comes to berate them, they treat him with respect but with just a touch of sarcasm that is quite charming. And they work well together down in the cave. With the Brig listening to the Doctor. Yes, he will probably shoot at something as soon as he can. One also feels that he will listen. They're settling in nicely. I wish Liz had a bit more to do but she will as we go along. And she gets the cliffhanger, which is always cool.

The episode lifts the pace of the first episode a bit, obviously with the whatever-it-is hunt. But it doesn't go super-fast. We see our smiley scientist friend in cahoots with whatever-it is. We get some dinosaur fun. We get Baker sweaty and attacked. We get the Doctor kind of berating the farmer's wife for info. There's a bunch of stuff going on here. And so far, we are moving forward nicely. We've not yet started to run in place like we did in a lot of the Season Five stories. I'm hoping that Episode three will keep that momentum going or at least keep that kazoo playing.

One of the joys of watching the show the way I normally do, one episode at a time, week off into between seasons, is that it takes several years to get all the way through. But there are so many moments that you don't think about for years and suddenly they happen and Proust would be proud. When the dinosaur is about to grab the Doctor (those are high caves aren't they?), suddenly a weird three note noise goes off recalling the giant beast. And the moment I heard that noise it all flooded back. For this book, I'm watching the stories much quicker than I normally watch them. I'm digesting them faster than I ever have. But it's awesome to be at this point. Apart from Terrance Dicks and Nick Courtney, everything is new now. (And both were just starting.) We've got a new era ahead of us. It is truly exciting.

Doctor Who and the Silurians
Episode Three

Episode 260: (February 14, 1970) What is out there? What is in the caves? Who is working with it? Who is against it? Will we ever see it?
Cliffhanger: The Doctor comes face to face with a Silurian or whatever they're called.

This episode has two interesting threads pushing down on it by the end: the bureaucratic thread coming from the approaching Under Secretary and the head of the company and Baker trying to get some violent action down in the caves. Alongside that is Quinn and the Silurian. That story builds up alongside the other one. With the Doctor and the Brig and Liz sort of in the middle hoping for a break on one side and for no breaks on the other. It's nicely done. There's a great feeling of tension building.

It's helped by the scenes between the Doctor and Quinn. (The scene where Liz and The Doctor are looking through his office is a good one too.) There is a lovely tension between them. The Doctor exploring the cabin and looking at the thermostat is a nice scene. Quinn tries to keep up that happy face but it's breaking. He's not going to get violent with the Doctor but… he's close. When The Doctor finally says Quinn should let him help and Quinn just shows him the door… we learn later why he does that. He wants the scientific fame. He wants to be the one who wins the day. His scientific jerkitude causes his death. Which is a shame. He was a character a bit unlike others. All the remainder of them are kind of stock *Doctor Who* characters but he will be missed. I think.

I'm glad Liz is OK. The farmer got killed. I'd like to think the Silurian isn't a complete jerk. Just scared. *
It's always a bit disconcerting to see a companion with a bandage on their face. It happens though. I like her scene with Baker here. She clearly sees the condescension of her male colleagues. Even the Doctor had a slight moment of that in the previous episode. (Although, this may be clutching at straws. I always think of the women the Doctor travels with as extensions of Susan. So, he's always erring on the side of "send in the guys with guns rather than my granddaughter." I don't think that's a particularly beloved theory. But it's one that sits in my mind. And I think it's rather chivalrous.)

The thing that makes this episode great is the gloriously excessive amount of footage on film in the first half. Swopping helicopter shots over the moors. Crowds of people. Silurians, barns, Liz and the Doctor. Pouring down rain. It's all so great. Quinn standing on a deserted stretch of road as the helicopter goes by is fantastic. As I watched, I wished that we had this footage from the negatives and/or interpositives like "Spearhead." It would look so good. Maybe sort of STRAW DOGS-like. I really think it's fantastic and gives an epic feel to everything. The Doctor and The Brig in Bessie are so cool. I know we'll be clashing soon but I am enjoying myself here. The Pertwee era sort of has set itself into place now. Studio scenes, mixed with these big film scenes where there's an epic feel that we didn't have often at all (when we left the studios) in the 1960s.

*There's always so much argument about the name of these creatures being wrong. While, technically, it is. The info text for this episode points out that Malcolm Hulke chose the name simply because he liked it. And if it sent all of us scurrying around to the history books, so be it. He got paid. We can complain all we want but it got us thinking. And the original title was "The Cave Monsters" not "The Silurians."

Doctor Who and the Silurians
Episode Four

Episode 261: (February 21, 1970) Quinn is dead. It looks like the Doctor's attempts to broker some sort of peace is ruined by Those Darn humans. (Be honest. The Silurians aren't helping.)
Cliffhanger: The Young Silurian subjects the Doctor to some third eye torture.

This is an episode all about frustration, mainly on the Doctor's part. He is trying so hard but everything is conspiring against him. His meeting with the Silurian at the start is excellent. Then a car drives up and it runs away. He's desperately trying to convince Masters to leave the Silurians alone. But Baker is acting nutty. Dawson's entrance into the meeting is timed perfectly. She's very insistent that now the Silurians should die. Of course, we know that Quinn was keeping the wounded Silurian in his cottage rather than taking it back to the caves where it could be healed. And we know that he was doing that so he could get the scientific knowledge he wanted. So, we're not sure how it happened. Maybe Quinn committed suicide? (I'm kidding.)

Isn't Geoffrey Palmer great? He's the perfect sort of character for this sort of thing. I like how the first thing he needs is a cup of coffee. And I like how he brings up the fact that Lawrence's cyclotron isn't doing quite as well as they hoped. Which leads Lawrence to nice deflection. It's a good scene because Masters isn't an awful guy. Lawrence is the one who seems a bit unhinged. Masters is very calm throughout. Then, when the Doctor and the Brig and Liz join in, we get all the sides.

In the previous seasons, with a base under siege where the Doctor had no connection, we'd generally expect the people in charge to ignore the Doctor. Look at "The Power of the Daleks." It would be frustrating but why would they listen, especially with the sort of shabbiness of the previous Doctor's appearance. Here it's a different dynamic. The Doctor has access to things here. He has friends/colleagues here. But he now must play by the rules. (Of course, he will break them as needed.) And this is not what the Doctor is used to so you can see his frustration. A bureaucrat has arrived and the Doctor is kind of helpless. It's an interesting space to place the Doctor. They will listen but he is only a small part of the whole puzzle. That's why he runs down into the cave on his own. Down there, he runs into the sort of characters we would have seen in previous seasons. He wants to help and they cage him up. That's the Silurians doing that.

Now, the Silurians are fully in it. We learn why what's happening is happening. We meet the different divisions of the Silurians. We see their third eye power. We see that they hate the humans as much as the humans fear them. And there's some great mouth movement on the Silurian masks too. Their voices are coming from offscreen, not being spoken by the actors. And they're convincing. Although, I always ask myself: Should they be wearing pants? They look like Silurian Ken dolls. They are going to need more than this little space in the cave, though, if they want "their" world back.

Another strong episode. Again, the pace isn't lighting fast but it's moving. And now we're more than halfway in. The Silurians and the humans have some plans for each other.

Doctor Who and the Silurians
Episode Five

Episode 262: (February 28, 1970) The Silurians argue amongst themselves. The Doctor tries to broker peace and Baker is infected with a virus that will kill everyone on the planet.
Cliffhanger: The Doctor and the Brigadier arrive at the local hospital. Baker dies.

This is an interesting episode. After the expanse of a couple earlier episodes, this one goes claustrophobic in more ways than one. The Brigadier and the UNIT troops are trapped in the caves. * One of them goes loopy. The Doctor and Baker are trapped in cages. They're getting sweaty. The humans in the complex are trapped in that one office. Lawrence is sarcastic. Masters is good at patience. Dawson is overwrought and xenophobic. And Liz is just trying to be as calm as she can as hell seems to be breaking loose.

That's the joy for me of an episode like this. S*it is hitting the fan. And in some spots, it's calm. In others, it's chaos. Bad things are about to begin. Only we can see it. Watching the group in the facility waiting for a report and the Brig and his soldiers is exasperating. But it's life. There are some things that happen where you can only wait. And we cut between The Doctor negotiating with the old Silurian. And the Young Silurian infecting Baker. And then the Old Silurian dies. Like the episode ending isn't bad enough, the one ally that the humans have is now dead. (I do like The Doctor reminding the Silurian and us that he's not human but he can try to make the peace.)

Malcolm Hulke is keeping things cooking even five episodes in. Yes, there is something funny about the Doctor trying to bring peace between these two races while the bureaucrat sits quietly at a desk doing nothing. Hulke making fun of the way governments and these sorts of people work. And I really like it. We've gone from the "Is anything happening?" of the first episode to the grand outdoors sweep of the third to this one where the tides change so roughly by the end. But it never feels odd.

It is interesting to me that the Doctor is trying so hard to bring peace. To prevent possible war with these two species that don't know each other but immediately don't like each other. The condescension of the Silurians towards the stupid apes. And the humans fear of anything that isn't like them. It's almost not worth it. But the Doctor does have to live here now. That must come into play somewhere.

The great thing is that we are now at Episode Six and the plague can fill an episode. Which would lead us to seven. The show tends to fluff when we hit final episodes. Not always, but sometimes. I feel like this one is moving nicely towards an ending. We shall see.

*We never really deal with how exactly the Silurians seem to do some of the magical things they do with that third eye of theirs. It's almost like a genie in their head sort of thing. When they shake, when the eye glows, when the sounds goes off, they can do almost anything. Isn't that odd? The Doctor seems to shrug it off. There's a moment where he's looking at some of their accomplishments on a screen and he is impressed. So, I think he probably recognizes the tech that looks like magic.

Doctor Who And The Silurians
Episode Six

Episode 263: (March 7, 1970) The plague spreads. Liz and the Doctor must find a cure.
Cliffhanger: The Doctor is kidnapped by the Silurians just as he finds the cure. Oh well.

The scenes out in London, the film scenes, are fantastic here. Contrasting with the wide, epic sweep of the countryside in episode three. This one is filled with people and hustle bustle. There are some nice crane shots at Marylebone station. They don't cover the landscape like the helicopter shots in episode three. But they work. When people start dropping from the virus, it feels big. When Masters succumbs, it truly feels like something bad is now happening. The show needed to have these scenes in it. This wouldn't have been a time where people in the studio getting phone calls, hanging up and saying, "two people have just died!" would have worked. It needs the scenes at the station to really make it immediate and make it right there, then and now. (Even if it's possibly meant to be set in the future. I don't know.)

The Silurians don't do much in this episode. I applaud the Young Silurian knowing where the camera is when he says quietly that he is now the leader. You must hit your mark. They are just waiting for the virus to spread and kill everyone now. Apart from zapping the Doctor in the end, they don't do much. But what they have done hangs over everything.

I love Lawrence in this episode. After the Covid pandemic, he feels exactly like quite a few followers of the President back in 2020. Refusing to believe the proof of their eyes. Refusing to believe that anything bad was going on. And refusing to care or think about anything but themselves. His first scene with Liz has a bit of menace to it as he hasn't been vaccinated. And he refuses to get vaccinated. Thereby outing himself and others in danger. But he blames Liz and the Doctor and the brigadier. (Has he been competent and sane at any point during this story?) In his final scene, he's gloriously unhinged. He still refuses to blame himself for anything. And he goes crazy. One of the moments I love is when his obvious combover of five-and-a-half episodes goes wild. That's when you know it's over. When vanity has gone out the door.

The Doctor, oddly or maybe not oddly, spends the entire episode in one room (apart from the opening "on film" moments). He's in a small lab trying out antidotes, which he does eventually discover. He mentions that he's been around for several thousand years, which does conflict with the age the Fourth Doctor would give. Maybe he was lost in the void after the previous regeneration for ages. (Which would match him being lost in the void at the end of this regeneration.) Here he is with more costume changes than any other Doctor I can think of. In the lab, being very science-filled. And that's cool. I like that. I like the scanning microscope. I don't fully get what I'm looking at but I know what I like.

And we have montages! I like a good montage. Have we had once since "The Sensorites" when the Doctor cured that plague and saved everyone?

I love Liz. Perfect companion for the Doctor. Although they haven't really travelled anywhere so I believe that appellation is incorrect. She's great right alongside the Doctor. Imagine him asking Jo Grant or Dodo or Victoria to get a blood sample. Right… you can't imagine it. Neither can I. I don't think he would have asked Zoe either. (Could you imagine him asking Jamie?) This is a good companion. We'll mention what the producer and script editor though of her later. But this is a great companion.

The introduction of the virus and the possibility of a pandemic is the perfect thing to occupy episode six. Previous seven-part stories had flagged but this one hasn't. Terance Dicks points out that the virus was brought in to keep the story from flagging and it's perfect. Because we now enter the final 25 minutes and we have a lot to do. I hope it goes OK. I'm sure it will end just fine.

Doctor Who and the Silurians
Episode Seven

Episode 264: (March 14, 1970) The Doctor faces off against the Silurians.
Cliffhanger: And the Brigadier blows them up.

This is an excellent closing episode. It has a bit of a late episode eight/ early episode nine of "The War Games" feel to it. Is the Doctor betraying everyone? In "The War Games," we were pretty darn sure that he wasn't. Here it is a little different because he's exiled to the planet. He loves humans but he has a similar love for The Silurians. So, maybe he is trying to do something to help. Think about it. He already got the antidote to the virus by the time he comes up to the reactor to help revive all the Silurians. Maybe it does really seem like, this time, he might choose different allegiance.

He doesn't. He overloads the reactor to drive the Silurians away. His plan is to put them back in hibernation and then they can bring out one at a time to negotiate. It's a pretty darn good plan. It is fun to watch the Doctor in a T-shirt attempting to negotiate how to stop the reactor from going nuts. And it is awesome to think that he has set things up where now... now... there may be a peace. Then the Brigadier blows up the caves and it all ends. * It's such a sharp final episode for such a long story. And that ending is killer. That ending is a short sharp kick right in the pants. It's fantastic.

The story ends and it is very well done. So many of these stories kind of mess it up when we get to this point. This one gets the Doctor and gets what he's up to and makes a great episode. The virus is kind of taken care of rather cursorily. I'm not bothered by that. The real story is deep in the caves and at the reactor. That's the major spot where things are happening. The show gives everyone enough to do to help wrap it all up. Overall, this is a strong story and an excellent opener for the trio of seven-part stories that we are about to experience.

*Of course. The big thing is "How does The Doctor continue to work with The Brigadier after the explosion?" We know, now, that there are more of these beings around the world. So, it's less of an issue. But, at that time and at this point in the series, it seems vastly inappropriate that The Doctor stays. Well, my theory is this: I have worked at office jobs that I didn't like. I maybe had a friend or two. The day may have been tolerable. It wasn't and never will be me. My character, my person. Feel free to laugh at me and yell "man up" or "suck it up, douchebag." I know that not everyone gets what they want. I think the Doctor here is tolerating what he must do. He tolerates the Brig at this point. He likes Liz but he's not happy with his appointed place in the Universe. Sometimes, when you're in a spot like that, the boss does something awful. And you are not able to say "See ya!" and leave. At this point, the Doctor can't fly the TARDIS and he's stuck here. So, he must work closer to the side of "Save humanity." Is that awful self-preservation for the Doctor? Possibly. He is doing his best in a situation that he is trapped in. So, let's give him a break I say. Am I wrong? Probably. But I still stand by it.

THE AMBASSADORS OF DEATH
Written by David Whitaker
Directed by Michael Ferguson
Episode One

Episode 265: (March 21, 1970) Something weird is happening on Mars Probe 7
Cliffhanger: The Brigadier is about to get shot.

Another seven-part story begins. As others have mentioned, if you treat this season as a series of possible *Doctor Who* stories that were never done beyond this initial story, they may work better. This is the second story in a row that takes place at a big government installation. There's a main set. (Although, honestly, the reactor set in The Silurians didn't really get used much.) There are the main characters in the set. And there is some sort of problem. In the previous story, it was all about energy. Atomic energy. In this one, it's about space travel. Let's go to Mars. It's about losing our astronauts. It handles itself well.

Having said that, The Doctor is fun in this episode because, obviously, he's the only one (apart from the "bad" guys) who gleans what's going on. His sequence where he yells at an unseen security guard about passes is fun. One might almost think "Doctor, come on, you live here now. Just get a pass." How long has he been here by this point?

The loud noise alien going off over and over that seems to be an assault on the senses is a cool fixture of the episode. And it's cool because once the Doctor says what it is it becomes obvious. It becomes a "Eureka!" moment. (Yes, the Doctor had one of those in the last episode too.) I love it. Especially when the noise goes off and everyone is like "There it is again!" And the Doctor points out that that noise was different. That noise was the reply. Love it.

So, we get fun outer space stuff. Which we haven't really got in the first part of the season. This stuff is like the T-MAT stuff from "The Seeds of Death." It's more hands on. It's more tactile. It's more like what people at that time would have been familiar with. And Britain has it! Not those darn Yanks! Or those Commies! It's the Brits! All Hail The Queen!

They do say that these stories were meant to be more in the future than is let on. Ten years, approximately. And this is one of the few stories ("The Invasion" is another) that really seems to be set ahead of our time. Certainly Liz is dressed as a 1970s lady. (I'm not sure about her wig.) The shootout looks like it's from the start of this decade. But the space travel is definitely from a different era. A future era that never happened. Or maybe the *Doctor Who* universe is a bit more advanced than ours.

I like the shootout at the end of this. It gives us a very different feeling than the first episode of the last story. In that one, things were slowly building. Slowly building. Here, it's an all-out melee between UNIT and these guys who are speaking to the aliens (?). It's a super kinetic ending. And it shows, resolutely, that this program can do a lot of different things. Having so much more on film here that the first episode of "The Silurians" makes for a nice change. Then, there are the touches of The Doctor choosing to involve himself with what's happening and the constant presence of the reporter at the space station that make things different. This location is very public. The last one was very not.

And then there's the opening scene where the Doctor fiddles around with the TARDIS. It's lovely to see the console. It's been a while. Yes, we don't know how he got it out of the TARDIS. It's fun to be reminded of what this show was and what it will be again. We're just in a different space now. It's like when Dobie and Maynard went into the Army! Things got different for a while. Time travel is still part of the show's DNA. We will get back there soon. But not this week. Not this year.

The Ambassadors of Death
Episode Two

Episode 266: (March 28, 1970) The capsule returns. But what's in it?
Cliffhanger: Cut it open!

The second episode continues to move along well. The Doctor gets to meet another bureaucrat. He's about as helpful as Masters, which is "not at all." But, this guy, at least, is in on the conspiracy, whatever the heck is going on. So, he, like the other people involved in whatever is happening, does what he thinks is right. Even if he's wrong. The Doctor's face when he's talking to this guy is very much "I'm so, so old and I still have to deal with jackballs like this. It ought not to be allowed."

I do like the capsule that has crashed down. It looks very impressive in the space center as they're trying to get the astronauts to come out. Out on location, in the middle of a field, it does look a bit tiny. It's not like the wonderful capsule that was featured in the classic film *Monster a-Go Go*. The return capsule in that one is hilariously chintzy. This one looks more like one of the capsules from "The Ark" that everyone took to Refusis.

We get another big, pitched battle with the suspicious guys taking the capsule from the Brig and the space center people. This one's outside so we get a lot of fun crashes, flips and explosions. It's a nice contrast to the battle in the previous episode in the confines of the warehouse. Both work well. I particularly like the way the Doctor gets the capsule back. Pretending to be a dottery old man who can't get his car started is fun. The last portion though with the capsule retrieval, the battle and the return of the capsule does all seem to happen a bit too quickly. Especially after the deliberate opening episode.

This is the episode with the Doctor doing his amazing sleight of hand with the computer tape reel thingy and Doctor Taltalian. He makes it vanish into thin air and then reappear. I think he learned a thing or two from the magic that the Silurians kept perpetrating in the name of science. It's a very odd scene. I'm not sure why it's there but it is so we must dwell on it.

Overall, a solid second episode. We get the soldier getting interrogated and then freed. We get the pitched battle. Some fun Doctor stuff. Liz doesn't do much but her presence (and wig) is felt. There are just enough very intriguing things going on here to keep one moving on into the next episode to see what the heck is in that capsule.

The Ambassadors of Death
Episode Three

Episode 267: (April 4, 1970) General Carrington steps forward and reveals what's been going on. But then, somebody steals the three astronauts.
Cliffhanger: Liz gets flipped over the railing of a weir.

I wanted to start here with a weird moment when the Brig and the Doctor are talking to Quinlan before Carrington comes out. The Brig is explaining something to Quinlan. The camera is cutting back and forth between everyone. The Doctor is in the frame listening intently. It doesn't cut away from him for a while. So, one expects something to happen. It doesn't though. It seems like we should have just had a brief shot of the Doc but it's a little too long. Odd moment.

I love the scene with the delightful bread truck or whatever it is. When you've seen this before and you know the fate of the two henchmen, it's rather disturbing. If you haven't seen it before, upon reveal, it's really a bit frightening. Whoever these people are that have stolen the astronauts are cold blooded. That main guy just casually kills and does whatever. He must get paid very well. That's a heck of a henchman! Heck, he's able to hire two guys to chase Liz around.

I also adore that crazy closing chase. The car stuff is OK. It's the foot chase that is great. Liz is a good runner in her high white boots. The scene on the weir is nice and scary. Some good stunting around. Liz or her stuntperson flipping that railing and then immediately cutting to the credits is well done. Because you're halfway through a "WHAT?!" and suddenly the episode is over. Each episode has had a nice sequence on film like this. (Plus, this also has the truck sequence.)

The astronauts are eerie. You can't see their faces through their helmets. They are so radioactive that a 15-minute ride with them in the back of a truck will cause death. But the henchman is fine with just some gloves on. I never fully understand these radioactive suits, especially the ones that are just sort of helmets that rest on your head. Can't radioactive whatever sneak in under the flap? Or is radioactivity simply not that smart? I don't know. I'm no scientist or whatever all these people are.

The episode keeps moving along well. General Carrington generally seems like a decent sort. But something is a little fishy about the astronauts getting kidnapped so immediately. Maybe Carrington has something else up his sleeve. Hopefully, whatever it is, it's not radioactive.

The Ambassadors of Death
Episode Four

Episode 268: (April 11, 1970) Liz is being forced to help Reegan and his goons with the astronauts. Taltalian blows himself up. An astronaut is sent on a mission.
Cliffhanger: The astronaut with the deadly touch is about to touch the Doctor.

Real life events were far more pressing than what happens in this episode. But it's still a good episode. This was the week where Apollo 13 got halfway to the moon when something went horribly wrong. The world waited to see if they would get home alive. Which makes this *Doctor Who* story very, very topical. With its astronauts who may or may not be trapped in space. Carrington and his people believe the astronauts are their astronauts. They just have some sort of issue with the fact that they have "contagious radiation" issues. The Doctor firmly believes that the human astronauts are still in space. He wants to get them back and find out what these other things are.

There's a lot going on here. Liz is captured at the start. Then, she escapes. Then, she hitches a ride with Dr. Taltalian, which seems a bit of a coincidence. But, if they are in the middle of nowhere, the chances of people being there who aren't related to what's going on here is probably slim. Taltalian doesn't have his French (although he's supposed to be Swiss) accent when he captures Liz. But what are you gonna do? I am sort of surprised that Liz didn't escape one more time in this episode. Third time's a charm.

I adore the opening scene with Carrington, the Brig and the Doctor. The latter two are at desks working. Carrington looks like somebody who showed up thinking his buds were getting off work but they still have an hour left. He paces around nervously. He seems to be serving no purpose. I love the way he dives into the "evidence" from the two dead guys. Neither the Brig nor the Doctor are interested.

Carrington keeps trying to shanghai everything. So obviously desperate to get the Doctor to stop his investigations. The bit with the comb is great too.

There is a bit of repetitiveness when we cut from the same sets over and over. I can tell that I might get sick of the underground lab with Reegan in it sooner rather than later. But I do like Reegan. He's one of those henchmen who 1) has no personal stakes in what's happened and 2) is competent. That's a fun mix. You don't normally get something like that. I'm not sure what sort of temp agency you use to get someone like him but this one was well chosen.

Then, there's that sequence with the astronauts entering the space center. The shot of it slowly approaching the guard with the sun behind it is classic. It's not as elaborate as the scenes from the previous episodes but it's fun to see. Heck, we get an explosion in the computer lab a few minutes before that. Now, we get a deadly touch alien running around. This serial has a heck of a lot in it. And it's still got three episodes left.

The Ambassadors Of Death
Episode Five

Episode 269: (April 18, 1970) As the bad guys continue using the atomic astronauts, the Doctor takes a trip into space.
Cliffhanger: A red disc approaches the Doctor's spacecraft

This might be the episode where I wish out loud: "I hope I never have to see that underground lab set again." Yes, Lennox does escape from it. Liz sure doesn't. Poor Lennox by the way. He gets a death nastier than those two henchmen. Someone puts a radioactive isotope on his dinner plate. The more you think about it, the nastier it gets.

Boy, Reegan knows a lot of stuff, doesn't he? This episode's segment on film is him running around some sort of refinery turning many, many wheels and things. (Caroline John asks on the commentary if those things he's turning affected the factory. She never gets an answer.) Reegan does some nice stunt work in there too. He also kills at least one guard. This guy is hardcore. In the book, it was said that he was once with the IRA. That's Reegan!

Most of the episode involves the gradual movement toward the Doctor taking off in the new Recovery capsule. It is said repeatedly that everything is being done to hold them up and delay them or try to stop them. I, honestly, think I can feel the slowdown happening as I watch. The Doctor does get into the rocket at the end and we get some fun liftoff action with Pertwee doing some flabby face G-force stuff. (It's better than the Doctor, Jamie and Zoe holding their faces or whatever that was they were doing in "The Seeds of Death.") If this were Season Five, they could have probably delayed the liftoff for another episode and a half.

The coolest moment is probably when a third capsule approaches the Doctor for the cliffhanger. It reminds me of *You Only Live Twice*. The rocket in space, by itself, suddenly gets approached by another unidentified one. You expect to see a UFO from space in the middle of a cornfield. Or sailing over your house. But a UFO from space approaching you while you're in space. That just seems crazy. And it makes for a good cliffhanger.

Now's as good a time as any to mention the opening credits. They're diddling around with them again. We get the opening few seconds with the name of the show and Pertwee's face. Then, we fade to a reprise of the previous episode's cliffhanger. Then, the rest of the opening credits. We see "THE AMBASSADORS." And then, with a smash… "OF DEATH." It's all very dramatic and kind of fun. Somehow it makes us forget that "Hey! These alien astronauts… They're ambassadors of some sort, aren't they?" Sometimes the explanation you need is right there, in plain sight.

The show is starting to slow down a bit here. They're doing their best to keep things moving. It's been five episodes. I think it would be cool to get some information soon and some resolution. OK, I'll admit it. Maybe I want to see another ten minutes of Reegan running around throwing switches. It's true. (Those wheels he turned and such didn't really seem to do much did they?)

The Ambassadors of Death
Episode Six

Episode 270: (April 25, 1970) We learn what's going on. We also learn that we don't have much time. Cliffhanger: General Carrington is our bad guy!

There's some lovely weird CSO in the opening of this episode. That strange long ribbed tunnel that the Doctor is in is fantastic. Very *2001*. Very psychedelic. When The Doctor lowers to the ground from the capsule, even he seems to going "Hey!" and "Wheee!" The whole spaceship sequence is charmingly unnerving. The alien behind the venetian CSO blinds might be moving a little funky but that could be how they move outside of the suits. (Don't forget: Liz sees one of them without their helmet, for about two seconds. It's done like a quickly edited cut of something gory in a horror movie and it makes you yearn for more. *)

And then you see Carrington who seems to be going steadily crazier. At least his hair is. He has kind of a Boris Karloff Frankenstein Monster haircut or maybe that's his head. It gets weirder as the serial goes along. The first moment when he mentions his "moral duty" is a sure sign that this guy is Bonkers, Maurice, Bonkers. And he is the head bad guy. And he hired Reegan. I still don't completely see how that gets Reegan everywhere he wants to go but… hey, let's talk about Reegan some more.

Our film sequence in this episode is another one of Reegan getting onto the space center and sabotaging something and then kidnapping the Doctor. How does nobody see him? Plus, the guards recognize him and his Silcock bakery truck. So, surely there must be a time when someone says, how come we never seem to have any baked goods around here? What is that guy delivering? Anyway, he gets the Doctor out of there somehow. I don't even want to know how he gets into the quarantine area so easily without anyone seeing him. Unless the bakery guy just delivers stuff to the quarantine area. "Oh, it's Earl. He delivers croissant to all the astronauts when they return from Mars." It could happen.

Yes again, I am sick to death of the underground lab. I am watching this episode to review them over the course of three days. Normally, I would watch them over the course of a week. Watched like that they are far more palatable. I can't do one episode a day when I'm writing a book like this. Maybe if this were a *Doomwatch* book or something I could. Over 800 episodes is a big No Way.

*I do get tempted sometimes to freeze frame there but I don't. They wouldn't have been able to back then and I probably shouldn't be doing that sort of thing now.

The Ambassadors of Death
Episode Seven

Episode 271: (May 2, 1970) The story draws to a close, with rather civilized results.
Cliffhanger: The Doctor and Liz leave as the center plans to bring the astronauts down.

General Carrington has his moral duty. As Cornish states in the previous episode, he's gone insane. What he saw on a previous Mars trip did this to him. It reminds me a bit of Luigi Cozzi's film *Contamination*. That one is about a Mars astronaut who is taken over by an alien force, returns to Earth and then slowly prepares for its invasion. Poor general Carrington. He seems to have the episode under control as he's planning his broadcast. I do like the mounting troubles that the good guys are having here, as we draw closer and closer to the broadcast.

Then we have the climax of the episode. A beautiful scene. Probably one of the best shot studio scenes of *Doctor Who* ever. The framing of the closing scene, the master shot, is superb. One alien on each edge of the frame, like a pillar. Carrington and the Brig in the center. The soldiers kind of spread out and around with Cornish leaning on a railing in the back. The long stretches of underground lab stuff where I was getting worried completely vanish during this. Carrington's final moment has rightly been mentioned before. Asking the Doctor if he understands and the Doctor saying he does. It mirrors the final scene with the villain in "Nightmare of Eden" about nine years from now. But, in the opposite direction.

Let me give a shout out: Reegan gives the good guys the idea for how to save the day. He comes away alive. Hooray! I wish they'd written a Target novelization about him. He wouldn't have to suddenly become a good guy. But if he is a mercenary, then maybe he could work on the side of good in the novel? It's a suggestion. Nothing more.

For a second seven-part story in a row, this is an excellent closing episode. The intercutting between the General preparing his speech and the Doctor and Liz still locked away is great. (Liz's line "Just get me out of here" delivered quietly is a favorite of mine. I lost all clue as to the passing of time in this story.) It ends very differently from the previous story. But here the Doctor strolls out to go and work on the TARDIS. He says goodbye to everyone, including The Brig and Liz. And we get a big CSO space center shot to close everything out. I don't know how many of these seven-part stories the show could do but right now they're doing great.

Final thing: As Michael Ferguson himself mentions in the making of for this story, they made the cliffhangers the way we know them. No long pauses. Just something happens and then the credits are rolling. Good stuff. I always worried for the actors that had to stand still as the credits slowly kicked in and started rolling, especially during the early days. You all know that.

INFERNO
Written By Don Houghton
Directed by Douglas Camfield
Episode One

Episode 272: (May 9, 1970) At Project Inferno, a giant drill is about to pierce the Earth's crust. This isn't going to go well.

Cliffhanger: Slocum rushes the Doctor and the Brig.

The third of the seven-part big base series begins. I mentioned last time that someone better than me said that these three serials are more like set-ups for their own TV shows than stories within a series. We go to different places. There are whole new bits of business going on. Two of them involve energy. One of them involves space travel. Liz Shaw and The Doctor and The Brig are the links. Benton was briefly in the previously story and he features heavy here. It's an interesting world. A place where UNIT gets sent to these sorts of places. Maybe they need a nemesis of some sort to make their assignments different? I don't know. Let's keep tuned in.

One might get a little distressed, though. Seeing a big main set and then seeing a guy who is being a douchebag might make you think "Oh, we're here again." When Stahlman begins his complaining to Sir Gold here, it feels like we're back in Season Five for a while. Stahlman is a jerk. He's like Carrington. He's like that guy from Silurians. He's like a jerk who refuses to admit that anything he's doing is a problem. I wonder if people watching it at this time had the same issues one might have watching it now… We watch things closer together now. We binge. You didn't binge back then. To those who know this didn't happen, I apologize for bringing it up. But there are ways to watch the show that work better than others. This season is one that should really be watched an episode a day.

The interesting thing here is that the Doctor and Liz are there. But they are clearly not a part of what's going on. The Doctor looks at some readouts. He saves the day at one point. He's up to something else. That's why he talks to Stahlman the way he does. Because he's not entrenched in this. The Doctor has something else on his mind.

But first, there's Slocum. The technician who gets touched by the green slime and becomes the green man. The moment he leaves the base and wanders out onto the surface is amazing. It's accompanied by 1970s synths. They make this moment feel like they are right out of a 1970s British horror film. It's nice atmosphere and it's very weird. And then when he kills someone it's so creepy.

Benton is back! He is preparing the Brig's office at the center. There is a constant and unpleasant drone at that center. Which makes one wonder why they are there. But it is a big thing going on. Sir Gold is trying to keep things under control. Petra is doing, frankly, stupid things for her boss who is clearly nuts. Greg is being a bit sexist but he also clearly knows his job. The episode is a fine installment, which we shall build from. Slocum has been infected. He has killed twice. Who knows where we will go from here?

Then, we learn what Liz and the Doctor are up to. Experimenting on the TARDIS console with the use of the power from this crazy excursion. The Doctor doesn't seem to care about everything else. I don't think I care either. But he operates the console as soon as Slocum does something to the controls. And then the Doctor goes into Crazy Town. In the original script, things were much more specific. But in the episode as aired, it's the Third Doctor mixed into a lot of weird, bendy and psychedelic effects. He has been dropped into someplace weird. If the Time Lords have removed all the info from his head, then, I applaud him for trying this. I can't imagine he thinks it's going anyplace good. This junk is too crazy.

We get the story in the drilling location. But then, there is something else going on. There's a green man running around killing people. Things are getting out of hand. There's a beautiful parallel run of storylines here. The middle of everything with Stahlman and friends. Then, there's Slocum doing something a bit different. Then the Doctor. I think things might go wrong very soon. The TARDIS trip is going to make this super odd.

Inferno
Episode Two

Episode 273: (May 16, 1970) Things seem to be getting worse around the project. People are dying. Green men are appearing. Then, something happens with the Doctor and his console from the TARDIS.

Cliffhanger: The Doctor and Bessie and the TARDIS console vanish.

Stahlman is a jerk. We can gauge that pretty quickly. How he got put in charge of anything is for another story that I, frankly, don't want to watch. The serial is odd because the UNIT crew are so secondary to everything else. The Brig has Stahlman look at stuff but it means nothing. And whatever the Doctor says means nothing. It's odd. It doesn't feel like a proper story. It feels like we're kind of vamping before something else happens. And, yes, that is exactly what we're doing.

All the characters are doing their things. The Doctor has some encounters in Stunt Town that are awesome. It is said that Jon Pertwee was not thrilled about the heights. But he does them. I know the anxiety. I know the craziness of being out there in those high spaces. The Doctor handles them well. I love the concept of this station doing this huge thing that might benefit the world. But, over to the side, there's a crazy bunch of green faced zombie type guys trying to kill everyone.

And, of course, Stahlman touches some of the green goo. It's fun to watch the main jerk guy do something stupid like that. We always try to think of our leader as someone who knows what they're doing. The problem here is that Stahlman doesn't know about the Doctor. That's the tricky thing. The Doctor may be worrying more about his TARDIS and trying to get off the planet... but he can fully keep an eye out on all other stuff. Stahlman should have kept an eye out.

This is an interesting episode because UNIT never fully quite gets involved in all of it. Benton is here. The Brigadier is here. But, unlike the previous two stories, there is a weirdness involving what exactly the Doctor and friends are doing there. Stahlman clearly hates anyone who isn't absolutely in love with him. So, the episode builds this tension of the folks we love being able to do nothing alongside the man in charge who can do whatever he wants alongside the military who are restricted but they try. There's a lot going on here.

We saw the Doctor go into a weird place in the previous episode. In this one, he seems to go full on weird. Where he goes... we don't know. But the joy of this seven parter is that it spends two solid episodes putting us in a place. Putting us somewhere where something might go horribly wrong. And then, at this cliffhanger. we are suddenly going someplace different. Someplace weird. Someplace we may have never been before. Where is that? Well, hang on.

Inferno
Episode Three

Episode 274: (May 23, 1970) The Doctor is now on a parallel Earth, where things are very fascist and the Inferno project is far advanced.
Cliffhanger: Benton threatens to shoot the Doctor.

This is, I think, an excellent episode of *Doctor Who*. And, yes, it's almost entirely because of the parallel universe switcheroo. It is cool to see characters playing the evil variations of themselves. (I've heard tell of an eyepatch story regarding the Brigade Leader's first scene but I forget how that goes now.) It's great to see Pertwee's Doctor confused and on the defensive. Wondering what's going on and how the heck he can get out of this. It's a nice twist to the story.

Because, honestly, it had to get out of the space where it was. Two more episodes at a government facility. Two more with the Doctor and UNIT being barely tolerated. Two more with another jerk getting up to stupidity. Another slowly growing crisis. The switch to the other world here accelerates everything. They're ahead on this alternate Earth by hours. The implication being that they are fascists and they get things done so much more efficiently. We're closer to whatever will happen when the Earth's crust is penetrated. It's a lovely conceit and it's well handled here.

It's not just the Brigade Leader's eyepatch, of course. They do a nice job of upping the ante all the way around. We haven't really seen Benton too much but we know that he's a generally affable sort of gent. So, seeing him rough here is startling. And Liz with an evil wig is clearly not pleasant either. Greg Sutton does seem out of place. Sir Gold would have too but he's dead in this world. Slocum is still alive. I like that. There was no Doctor around to help stop him. And, I bet, no one here believes in anything that's happening re: the monsters created from the green slime. The desperation that the Doctor faces here is palpable. Not only is this place so much closer to its fate but he's no way of getting the power he needs to save himself.

In the end, this episode is kind of a variation on the two that we just watched. However, it's a variation of the *Doctor Who* formula we've seen all season and that we won't really see again. So, to me, this is exciting. This is fun. I know the ratings had dipped at the start of this story. I do hope they pick up. I'd hate to see the show get cancelled.

There are some reviewers out there who do not like this story and I do get where they're coming from. These four episodes are padding. There's no way around that. If these episodes weren't here, we would have either had a padded 4-part story too darn close to what we've been watching or an extremely padded 7-part story. I give the creative team credit for giving it a whirl. Here, at least, it's working great.

Inferno
Episode Four

Episode 275: (May 30, 1970) The Doctor is interrogated and imprisoned. He tries to save the Parallel Earth but he just can't do it.
Cliffhanger: The crust of the Earth is penetrated.

And the very long and drawn out and harrowing end of this world begins with the cliffhanger. The next two episodes will detail this world being absolutely destroyed. It's not for want of the Doctor trying.

We do great a brief return to our time though (Or the show's regular time.) Sir Gold is going to the ministry. Stahlman is still being a jerk as his hands get greener and greener. Petra and Greg seem to be growing closer. Liz is moping about the disappearing Doctor. Things have kind of stalled. Everything sort of hanging in space and time.

The Doctor is interrogated quite brutally in this episode. Bright light in his face. People yelling questions at him. I'm sure this works on some people but does it work on everyone. I really feel like there should be some more advanced techniques on display. The Brig yells. Liz yells. Benton stands by being a jerk. It's not a great time and it is rare to see this Doctor in this position. I do kind of miss the Second Doctor putting himself into some kind of trance so he can't get hypnotized but this works nicely too.

There's a moment in the cells I need to mention. I was watching this with my stepdad a long time ago. The Doctor is locked in the cell. The technician from the previous episode is in the next cell. He's completely green and stark raving bonkers. He and the Doctor jump around a bit. Cell bars are bent. The Doctor knocks the green man over. The Doctor leaps out of the cell, pulls the bars back into place and leaves. That moment drove my stepdad nuts. "Why does he do that? That's so stupid!" I asked why. "He's just wasting time and that guy's going to pull them apart anyway." I suggested maybe the Doctor thought he was buying a little time. Stepdad didn't buy it. He left the room laughing at the ridiculousness of it all. Not a good story. Just a story.

There's a nice bit when The Doctor is talking to Liz and trying to convince her where he's from. She says that she works in security and the other Liz is a scientist. They're nothing alike! Then the Doctor says did she ever think about becoming a scientist. And you can tell she did. And you can tell she was probably forced into whatever she's doing by this garbage world she lives in. This rotten place. Petra and Stahlman both say that when this is all over Greg's "for the chop." I'm not sure if that means he gets put away somewhere or whether he gets killed. This place stinks. Only Benton seems to be having a good time and he's a sadist.

There is an interesting moment where the Doctor saves the day in the beginning. He stops the drilling from backing up. Is he simply "saving his skin" or is he just naturally trying to show what he can do? At any rate, if he had left it alone maybe, just maybe, there might have been a delay to the project. In the end, it doesn't matter. But it's always something that I forget he does.

So far, we are moving toward a big climax. Then, because of the nature of the story, we'll immediately start moving towards another one. But first, apocalypse. Doctor Who-style!

Inferno
Episode Five

Episode 276: (June 6, 1970) The end of the world. You either die or go green.
Cliffhanger: A green and hairy fist smashes through the window of the door. Trouble!

They really do a beauty of a job with this episode. Most of it takes place in the control room. (So, it has a bit of a base under siege feel.) There is a scene in the storage garage with the TARDIS console. And there's some depressing footage outside with Benton keeping his troops in line, futilely. Fairly early on the Doctor announces that "Yes, you're all dead." They shouldn't have done what they did. Weird, isn't it? Back in "The Underwater Menace," a mad scientist was going to break through the Earth's crust to drain the oceans. So, in all honesty, the Doctor kills that scientist to stop him from destroying the world. Here, one mad scientist's hubris destroys this world.

I don't know about you but I'd be extremely pissed to learn that one person's ego caused the destruction of the world. Especially someone who was such a jerk. Heck, in the previous story one man's ego almost causes a space war. It's tough to keep the loonies under control.

The episode cooks along nicely. I don't just mean because now everything is incredibly hot. Everyone gets some nice stuff to do. There's some decently filmed action done in the main control room. The moment with the blast door going up and crazy, hairy Stahlman is fantastic. And his werewolf buddies are fun. Some of them seem to be walking like zombies. That maybe should have been discouraged. But, when the gang gets locked in the room with the monsters outside, there is a wonderful *Night of the Living Dead*-type vibe. The Earth is dying. The only thing these people here can try to do is save the Doctor. A man they literally met several hours ago. I guess you could do worse than having the Doctor be the last person you meet in life.

There is something sort of selfish too about the Doctor right now. Obviously, it's the only option that makes sense but it isn't a happy one for anyone there, not even him.

Back on the Earth of the show, Sir Gold has been given the authority to shut everything down. Luckily for him, because his driver was going to shoot him but then changed his mind. But then, they get in a big accident. I can see how this scene is foreshadowing what happened in Alternate Earth. But unless what he did comes into play at the complex then I don't fully understand this scene.

Do I need to mention how much fun the "Transforming Benton" scene is? It's good and scary. It's on film. Not in the studio. I'm not sure about his vampire teeth in the last shot though. That seems like a joke shot that they accidentally put in the episode.

In the end, all of this is kind of amazing as the Director Douglas Camfield went out sick. And Barry Letts took over. Letts, as we know, was a trained TV director and had made "The Enemy of the World." But there's nothing like taking over someone else's camera script at the last minute. Fortunately, it all seemed to work out nicely. I believe he does the directing in the studio for the next two episodes too. So, he does have this under control.

Inferno
Episode Six

Episode 277: (June 13, 1970) The remaining people on Alternate Earth rush to try and send the Doctor back. The Brigade Leader isn't thrilled.
Cliffhanger: The end of the world.

I love this episode.

It may cause the final episode to be an anti-climax but I can't say that I care. By time the next episode begins, I'm as excited as the Doctor so I just want to see things wrap up without a fiery apocalypse. I've no interest in seeing my favorite characters burnt to a crisp. Which must be a terrible freaking thing. So, here we get to see variations of the characters we love, and some we've grown to love, burn and burn. It's very affecting. Seeing how hard they work, how much they run through a hell space, to try to save the Doctor.

It seems the exact opposite of everything they would have done in the fascist world they're a part of, certainly the Brigade Leader is confused by all of it. But they're doing it. From pulling out the coolant hose to going to the nuclear reactor to set everything up to going BACK to the nuclear reactor when it doesn't go right the first time. There's a crazy energy to this episode. The mix of the studio scenes to the film scenes shows an episode that is going out of control as much as the world that it pertains to is... and it's great because of that. The sense of "This is over" is as palpable as the sweat on the character's foreheads.

Watching this world being destroyed is a heartbreaker. Yes, this world isn't particularly nice. But it's over now. It ends at the end of the episode. That is scary. That is harrowing. That is sad. All these lives lost. Surely a life must mean something. Mustn't it? Surely whatever runs this crazy universe of ours doesn't create a world teeming with life simply to do something like this. "Inferno" keeps things moving nice and fast so you don't really dwell on it. The end of the world is in our face though. It's right there and The Earth Dies Screaming. There's nothing you can do. One man's hubris burns us all.

The scenes that we see, briefly, on the Doctor's Earth, in the Doctor's universe, have a feeling of "We can definitely end this" but "We'll never quite make it there." They have a slower, lazier, feel. Nothing seems to be too bad. Yet. But we know what will happen. We expect the exact same horribleness to occur on both Earths. If only the Doctor would come back. Sir Gold tried and who knows where he is? The Brigadier seems oddly impotent. I'm not sure why he's there sometimes. Regardless, the other Earth is coming to an end in a sweep of molten lava and explosions. The Doctor hasn't much time. None of us do. Now.

Note: Batman is mentioned! The 1966-1968 *Batman* series was being shown on British TV at this time so this was a topical reference. The original script mentioned Buck Rogers. In about 10 years, that reference would be timely again. Also, that reference and Gil Gerard might be giving the show some trouble in the ratings. That's in the future, though.

Inferno
Episode Seven

Episode 278: (June 20, 1970) The Doctor returns to our Earth and looks like a complete nut. Guess the world is over here too.
Cliffhanger: The Doctor ends up on the rubbish tip and we shall miss Liz.

This episode isn't as strong as the finales for the previous episodes. Those feel like they have a really lovely build towards craziness. This one, because of the structure, is different. It re-introduces us to a place where we haven't spent much time in four episodes. A month upon initial viewing. And it does an odd thing that never struck me before this viewing.

Sir Keith is shown in Episode Five as specifically being given the word to postpone and shut down the drilling until further investigation. Stahlman has Gold's chauffeur try to kill Gold. They end up in an accident. Gold goes missing. In this episode, he re-appears to tell Stahlman what's happening. And suddenly he has Zero Authority to do anything. What? He was told to shut the place down. Stahlman connived to have him killed. We have proof of all of this. Why can't he do what he's supposed to do? It seems like he's being kind of lackadaisical here or something. This man tried to kill him and all he can do is shrug and say, "I don't have authority." No, two episodes ago you had complete authority. I don't like this part of the episode. It makes no sense. And I've never seen a decent explanation for it.

The Doctor has a crazy moment when he enters the control room that is perfectly justified but odd. He spends the first half of the episode in a coma. Then, upon awakening, he slowly works out what's happened and what is happening. He's seen a world destroyed and now his Earth is about to go the same way. Upon entering the control room, he goes nuts, smashing things and shouting. Soldiers drag him away. As justified as this might be, it really doesn't feel like the way he would behave. To add to the weirdness, watch the film sequence about two minutes later where The Doctor incapacitates the guards taking him from the control room. The Doctor is now completely acting like his old self again. Film sequences were shot long before studio sequences. Pertwee probably didn't know how he would act in the later studio sequence when he was on film. Regardless, it just makes the moment weirder.

Plus, The Doctor doesn't save the day. Stahlman goes crazy with or without The Doctor. Throughout the episode, Stahlman is getting worse and worse. We had the setup for that several episodes ago. The Doctor does help save the day. But, presumably, even if he wasn't there, someone would have said "Hey! Stahlman's a werewolf!" and done something about it. But we don't know. Anyway, it is fun to watch. The episode moves. It's never slow. It puts us back into a space we haven't been in for a while. And it lets that story finish. I mean, to me it works. I just don't love it.

The serial ends with a big "Everybody laughs" scene. I grew up with these sorts of scenes. They're tricky. Because the people onscreen are laughing and laughing... but I'm a viewer. These scenes never make me laugh. So, as an adult, I don't know how to deal with them. They look kind of silly. The Doctor should have called out the Brig for what he did at the end of "Silurians.' So, to see him sucking up to the Brig after calling him out here is less funny than pathetic... let's see what happens next season. It is great to see Liz's face laughing for the final shot. She was great. She wore more miniskirts than any other companion combined and she was quite wonderful. She left because 1) the production team wanted someone dumber and 2) she was pregnant. They even each other out.

Lovely moment: the Doctor releasing that free will is possible because of the existence of the multiple and parallel earths is quite delightful. Of course, no one else here experiences that but that doesn't mean that it still isn't cool.

SEASON EIGHT
1971

TERROR OF THE AUTONS
Written by Robert Holmes
Directed By Barry Letts
Episode One

Episode 279: (January 2, 1971) The Master arrives at a circus. Jo Grant arrives as a replacement for Liz. Mike Yates appears. There's a joke about farting. And the Autons have returned!
Cliffhanger: Jo opens a large box in the Doctor's lab. It's a bomb.

Barry Letts now has complete control over the show. As he points out in his DVD commentary, he has now begun firmly putting his stamp on it. Much of the previous season was set up before he got there. He directs this one too. And it's (not counting the studio sequences from later in "Inferno") the first time we've really had this happen. The person in charge is also doing the directing thing. He's not the most dynamic of directors but he keeps things moving.

I think the problem is that some of the editing here is sloppy. The first Auton story, on film, was nicely worked out. In that one, the script got a little wonky when it hit Episode Four. In this one, the script is working very well but there are a few odd moments. For example, Jo Grant arriving at the plastic factory with the Master at it happens almost out of nowhere. How does the Doctor know that the crate has a bomb in it? The Big Top at the start looks important but then never appears again. The edit with the Doctor leaping to catch the bomb isn't the best. Also, there's no sense of time passing although, technically, a lot of it does. (Jo says "Good morning" at one point. Implying that it's now morning and previously it wasn't.) The editing is awkward. There's a lot going on but it feels a little off. Not bad. Just off. (Then, there's that odd shot where Jo is talking about the Nestene meteorite and the camera is looking at her through the Doctor's equipment. But the camera is never quite in the right spot. It's a lovely shot but it's slightly off.)

So, the Master has officially entered our story. He shows up with a working TARDIS. It disguises itself as a horsebox at a circus. (A horsebox is a trailer you put a horse in. I was confused too when I first saw it. I expected a giant box with a horse in it or shaped like a horse.) He has incredible hypnotic powers. He's very assured. He has bombs. He as a Tissue Compression Eliminator. (More about that later.) And he is there to bring the Nestene Consciousness back to Earth and annoy the Doctor.

Jo doesn't do a lot here but she is set up as the exact opposite of Liz. Liz didn't want to be there. Jo does. The Doctor wanted to work with Liz. He doesn't want to work with Jo. Liz is overqualified. Jo isn't really qualified for anything. But Jo is adorable and she is hard working and she does get herself to the right plastics factory quicker than everybody else. So, I think we've got a chance of this really going somewhere fun.

And we conclude the new characters with Mike Yates. He is Benton's superior. There were several "Captains" in the previous season. Mike seems a bit chatty. He also, if you watch him in shots when he's not speaking, prone to look a bit bored and have his eyes glaze around the room. That's a little odd but we'll keep our eye on that.

Overall, this is an excellent start to a whole new era of the show... one season after the previous "whole new era" began. That's a lot of "whole new eras." This one is a little shakier than the previous one. (Although, I think the script, in general, is stronger.) We'll see how it goes. One thing we can note: Barry Letts loves CSO. And we are going to see a lot of in this story, and this era. Some of it very well done. Some of it not as very well done. The guard standing in front of a picture of a museum trying to stop the Master from stealing the Nestene unit is probably the first of these. We'll see how it goes though. Episode Two awaits.

Best lines: "You ham fisted, bun vendor!" The Doctor thinks Jo is the tea lady. That's why he says that. I have seen folks get angry here. Thinking the Doctor is being too upper class and posh and insulting the "working class" tea lady. I say "Lighten up. It's a funny line." Also, the Doctor telling the Time Lord "Well, you better find a witty way of dealing with it" regarding the Volatizer always makes me laugh.

Terror of The Autons
Episode Two

Episode 280: (January 9, 1971) The UNIT gang hunt for Professor Phillips and they met some strange cops.
Cliffhanger: The Doctor pulls the cops face off.

This is the first of the episodes that brings us the "*Doctor Who* is too scary for kids" argument that went on for years and years. There's a gross killer troll doll that comes to life and strangles an old guy. There's a cop whose face gets pulled off. Apparently, folks in the House of Lords had a problem with this. This is the first Third Doctor story I ever saw. It was at a convention. The crowd had a ball. I don't think any of us were scared. It was 1983, not 1971. Although, with Vietnam going on and such, I almost feel like that was a scarier time. We all thought we were dead in 1983 with the Cold War. The body horror of the 1970s was worse individually. Anyway, this is an episode that is called out for being a crazy scary episode.

And it's a darn good one. I watched it this time with new digital effects on the troll doll. The initial effects are quite subtle. I didn't quite notice that it wasn't the CSO doll. But it works here. It's not Chucky, of course. It's a weirder sort of movement. And it kills an old man whose wife is screaming in front of a picture of a kitchen and that just makes it weirder.

McDermott gets the best moment here. Murder by big plastic chair. There was a *Monty Python*-esque sitcom called "No Soap, Radio" that aired on an American network briefly. I watched it as a youngster and loved it. The first episode features a chair that eats people. * Mr. McDermott dies in the same way. Crushed by this chair, followed by a great line on the phone from Mr. Wisher. A great scene. They say that Robert Holmes wrote this character only for that scene. I believe it and I love it.

The episode moves. It has a bit of a stream of consciousness kind of plotting to it. I don't mind. Because it's weird and it's funny and it's exciting. I'm glad Jo's OK. I love the tiny car that the Brigadier and soldiers show up in. I'm not sure if that's meant to be sort of a clown car kind of thing but it looks like it. The Master is as imperious as ever here. He almost slaps the old man at one point, which seems a bit much but I love it.

My favorite part is trying to chart the second half of the episode: Prof. Phillips goes missing. His car is found in a parking lot. It's where the circus was so the Doctor goes to where the circus is. The Master says he led the Doctor there. Rossini and the strongman capture the Doctor. Jo and the Doctor get free. Phillips shows up with a bomb and blows himself up. The Doctor and Jo are being attacked by Rossini and his people. They are rescued by cops. The cops are Autons.

That is some complicated scheme. Phillips is under the Master's control. As is Rossini. As are, presumably, the Autons. So, every step of the way, every twist and turn, they all involve the same person in charge. That is a large number of contingency plans. I think it bodes well for what sort of planner the Master will prove themselves to be.

*Note: To those of you who think, how can these people watch these ridiculous things? Don't they know they're ridiculous? Have you ever seen the movie *Death Bad*? It's about a possessed bed that eats people. If you go online, you will find plenty of people who will say to others "Can't you see how stupid this film is? It's so dumb? A bed eats people!" Yeah. You know what? We got it. We figured it out. It's camp. We're having fun and you're ruining our party. Go away.

Terror of the Autons
Episode Three

Episode 281: (January 16, 1971) The Auton invasion is about to begin and it involves plastic daffodils. Cliffhanger: The Doctor is strangled by the phone cord.

The image of the Autons with the giant heads passing out plastic daffodils is perfect. It's so normal. It's so bland in a slightly twisted way. And it portends something terrible. We saw only mannequins, replicas, Autons and such in "Spearhead From Space." In here, anything plastic is a problem. That troll doll is something. The chair is awesome. And, of course, the episode ends with a phone cord. We also know that the Master is evil. We meet Goodge only briefly. He talks about his wife not giving him any more hard-boiled eggs. Then the Master shrinks him to death a few moments later. Prof. Philips dies with some sort of grenade in his hand under the Master's control. And so on and so on. When one begins to think "What might these daffodils be used for?" one doesn't have pleasant thoughts.

The story keeps up its strong pace. It still has a weirdness to it though. One reviewer said that this story is more a series of set pieces than a regular, linear plot and they could be right. The circus shows up for a minute or two at the start of Episode One. It appears for a few minutes at the end of episode two. And now it's done. The plastic factory is almost done too. (They were beginning to shoot episodes two a fortnight rather than one a week. That may have something to do with it.) In fact, the scene where the Doctor and the Brig go to the plastics factory is oddly superfluous. They find out that a van/ bus of some sort has been rented, which is great. That's followed by the oddest moment of the episode. The Doctor opens a safe and there's an Auton inside. Why is it there? We never find out what's in the safe apart from that Auton. Is that the safe where they keep the spare Auton? Does it just stand in there and shoot whoever opens the door? It's a good scare moment but it makes no sense.

The scenes with the doll are great. First the Doctor does an autopsy. Then, it attacks Jo when the Bunsen burner heat brings it to life. Seeing the dismembered doll on the floor being shot at is kind of disturbing. And the discussion about making cocoa with the Bunsen burner is fun. I remember seeing that scene with the crowd back in 1983. Folks were cheering and laughing and having a great time.

They go all out for the quarry shootout scene in the beginning. The policeman/ Autons with their handguns. The UNIT people shooting all around. Terry Walsh has a great stunt where he goes rolling down a hill. I just wished it hadn't cut away before he got to the bottom. Show the whole thing. Unless there was an issue with the camera? I'm sure they didn't have him do that twice. Overall, it's a great fight scene, apart from a few odd Mike Yates moments.

Mike's kind of awkward, isn't he? He was originally meant to be a possible love interest for Jo. Luckily, that went nowhere. He's odd to watch. He seems kind of wrong next to the Brig and he's not right with Jo. The way he grits his teeth before he fires the gun at an Auton seems weird. The way he runs into the car makes it look like he's never run before. And, as others have mentioned, why does he take a long look at the phone company guy's behind? Maybe Jo was the wrong character to try to hook him up with. Regardless, the Doctor and the Master meet, finally, sort of. And it seems like now the Doctor will be strangled by the phone cord. Is it all over for the Doctor and the planet Earth?

Terror of the Autons
Episode Four

Episode 282: (January 23, 1971) The Nestene Invasion is about to begin. For real!
Cliffhanger: The Doctor looks forward to his next meeting with the Master. It won't be long.

The first Master story ends. And he escapes! Oh, he's going to be one of these types of villains. In the past, when the Doctor met a race/ monster/ whatever that he'd meet again, he always defeated them. So, when they returned, we were all like "Hey! That's back!" The Master, though is specifically presented as "He shall return!" And it's tricky because we're eight seasons into the show. Try to think of an eight-season old show that introduces a character like this. How many times did Grimes come back on *The Simpsons*? I'm sure some of the *Law and Order* shows have probably done something like this. Normally, it's not done. Yes, Shorty came back a lot in *The Beverly Hillbillies* but I don't know that I'd call him an enemy. Mostly annoying. So, the Master is set up here as a reoccurring villain. Barry Letts says in the commentary that it was a bit of a mistake to have The Master reappear so often in this season. I say, maybe that was a problem then. It's not a problem now. This is very much the Master season. * And it's a good one.

The first big scene between the Doctor and the Master happens. And it's a standoff. Dematerialization circuit in one hand. Tissue compression eliminator in the other. (William Hartnell may have had a rough time with some of these devices.) There is a wonderful feeling of history between the two characters, which is implied here and expanded upon later. The Master's hatred for the Doctor, but also the odd playfulness (that comes out especially in Missy) is here from the start. Jo is the one to see it firsthand and I'm a bit jealous.

This episode is a lovely fast paced closing to the story. It goes through almost as much as the last episode of "Spearhead From Space" did but here it seems a bit more balanced. The Nestene are coming. The daffodils are going to kill. We've got an RAF strike. We've got Jo getting suffocated by a daffodil. (That's dark, isn't it? Super clever and pure Robert Holmes right there. There's a reason why he's one of the best writers the show ever had.) There's so much happening here. Along with a pitched battle in a field. A chase up a huge radio telescope tower. (Shades of "Logopolis.") And an ending that some have problems with.

I don't have a lot of trouble with the Master switching his mind in a split second at the climax. (I have more trouble with the fact that the novelization promised a giant crab-octopus-spider thing that we never saw.) The Master is notorious for wanting to humiliate the Doctor and just play with the Doctor maliciously. They've had plenty of bad plans. In the end, this is one of them and so it doesn't bother me. It's the first of them that we see so it ends up affecting us more than others. But, once you know the Master/ Missy, you know they don't always quite think it through like they should. This is a portend of the future. In the next story, The Master will have a firmer grasp on things.

*It's also very much the "Delaware" season. That was the synthesizer that they used to score every episode of this season. Synths were new things at this time. This is the year of Who's Next and "Baba O Reilly." This was the year where the superior British blues band Ten Years After started throwing random synth noises into their albums just to liven up those old blues riffs. The music in this season is alternately otherworld, old fashioned and modern. The kazoos in last year's "Doctor Who and The Silurians" are one thing. The synths are sort of futuristic. We'll see how they shape the season as we go.

THE MIND OF EVIL
Written by Don Houghton
Directed By Timothy Combe
Episode One

Episode 283: (January 30, 1971) The Doctor and Jo head to Stangmoor Prison to witness the Keller Machine in progress. Things don't go according to plan.
Cliffhanger: The Keller Machine is scaring the Doctor to death by showing him fire.

Very different from the previous story. It's less kinetic. It feels, somewhat, more real. OK, the blinking machine that kills men with rats but not really and drowns them in rooms without water isn't that realistic. But it is *Doctor Who*. The opening with Bessie pulling up to a castle that is a prison mixed with the inmates who always seem to be rioting makes this feel certainly darker and more real than the world with the killer dolls and daffodils. Granted, maybe the Doctor's silly wave at the security camera isn't the height of serious sophistication but you can't have everything.

The thing I love about this one is that The Doctor and Jo are doing something UNIT-related while the rest of the gang are doing their thing. The Brig, Yates and Benton are dealing with an International Peace Conference where the Chinese delegate is having some issues. We meet the Chinese representative who embodies every "Oriental" cliché we had at the time. But we lucked out. She is played by an Asian actress. Thank goodness. * But we get this very important conference being threatened by a suspicious death. And it might have some link to the Keller Machine. To see The Brig and friends doing this while Jo and The Doc are elsewhere gives a feeling of UNIT spreading out. Yes, it all links in the end but it's fun to be separate for a bit.

Meanwhile, at the prison. We get Barnham, a big bruiser, getting all the evil drained from him. But then two others are killed by fake rats and dry water. What is this Keller machine about? We do get a nice long demonstration of the way the machine works. I've never been able to figure out whether I like the Doctor in this scene. He and Jo are in the front row to watch the Keller Machine, which has been around for a year, in action. All the Doctor does is talk to Jo loudly. He's basically heckling the presenter but acting like he's casually talking to a friend. It's amusing. But, also, c'mon Doctor. You've been invited here to watch. Why are you acting like this? Maybe that's why the machine goes after him later. "You're that jerk that was heckling me earlier. Watch what I can do." The Third Doctor could be arrogant at times. Very arrogant. And not always in a fun way. This is one of those weird moments where I can't figure out if I like him or not.

This is an excellent first episode, apart from that. It moves along. It cuts between the two main stories well. It builds the mystery in the prison with the constant noise of the riots in the background and the weird killings. We know that anything going wrong at the peace conference ain't great. So, we're rolling into the second episode hoping that the Doctor isn't going to die because that would ruin the show.

*Even then the show does something a little silly. The head of the prison is talking about Keller's machine. He mentions that the assistant was a young Asian woman and it dissolves to the diplomat's rep. As others have pointed out, it seems to imply that there is only one Asian woman in Britain. Maybe they were right. I'm having trouble accessing the pertinent census materials.

The Mind of Evil
Episode Two

Episode 284: (February 6, 1971) The Thunderbolt is going to be moved. The Doctor meets the Chinese Delegate. The Master is here.
Cliffhanger: The American Delegate is attacked by a dragon.

This is an episode that's a little confusing. In one respect, it seems to be moving ahead. We get The Master in another disguise. He taps UNIT's phones. He sits in a Black Maria like a gangster. He controls Chin Lee, the assistant to the Chinese Delegate. We also meet a hardened criminal who starts a jailbreak over at Stangmoor. We also prepare for the movement of the Thunderbolt nuclear missile to the ocean with Mike Yates. Sgt, Benton is knocked unconscious. Jo gives Barnham chocolates. The Doctor speaks in Hokkien and we get English subtitles at the bottom of the screen. There is a lot happening here.

At the same time, it certainly is not moving very quickly. Nothing gets done with the Keller machine, except it begins to kill the American Delegate. It turns Chin Lee into a giant pink dragon, a la a Chinese dragon at a parade. The Master appears and listens in but, apart from threatening Chin Lee, he doesn't do a whole heck of a lot. The Doctor has the chat with the delegate but really seems to get nowhere. The scene is there to show the Doctor can speak Chinese* and to pick on the Brig, And the Thunderbolt stuff is set up but the episode ends before anything happens.

It's a case of moving a whole bunch of stories forward while at the same time holding back on a whole bunch of story. There's newer stuff brought in for this episode. The stuff from the previous episode that we really kind of wanted to see move ahead ends up standing still. It makes for an oddly unsatisfying but not bad episode. One wants everything to move ahead rather than continue to pile on the new stuff. It means that when the episode does end you don't feel like there's been much advancement. It feels like we have gone two steps forward but one big step back.

The story will have a lot going on as it continues. It obviously links up the Master to the Keller machine. I think it was a great idea to hold off on the Master until episode two. It makes us wonder if he's going to be showing up. It leaves us hanging just long enough and then it starts. He's here and he has another plan up his sleeve using another strange force of some kind. He's got a TARDIS full of them. I hope this story doesn't end as the last one did. "Oh, wait! That Keller Machine is awful! Let's blow it up!" Maybe it will end that way? It's tough to say. Even the Doctor is all confused in all the chaos. Let's just keep our focus on the pink dragon attacking the Southern Senator. That's amusement enough.

I need to say this: I know prison is rotten. But, good gravy, with the Keller machine there the whole of Stangmoor seems completely unbearable. Constant noise, constant riots, constant yelling. I don't fully understand who the new guy is or how he breaks out so easily but I guess we'll learn. Until now, we just have to wait until next week to find out what's happening. Maybe that guard will play some checkers with us or Barham will share his chocolates.

*The TARDIS must not be working. It would normally translate the delegate's speech and we wouldn't need the subtitles and the Brig would look less like a boob. Oh well. Also, the Doctor mentions being friends with Mao Tse-Tung. Really, Doctor? That could be just small talk but this Doctor does like naming names and showing off who he knows. Half the time, he seems to know jerks.

The Mind of Evil
Episode Three

Episode 285: (February 13, 1971) The Master's plan is revealed. Take over Stangmoor. Steal the Thunderbolt and blow up the Peace Conference.
Cliffhanger: The Doctor is subjected to the Keller machine again.

The thing I always find most surprising about this episode is, well, two: 1) that odd CSO shot of Benton standing in front of a picture of the Thunderbolt yelling at soldiers. (that happened due to some location film being lost) and 2) the song that The Master is listening to on his transistor radio while he sits in his car. It's a song called "The Devil's Triangle." It's an 11-minute song from Side 2 of the 1970 album *In The Wake of Poseidon*, the second album from prog rockers King Crimson led by Robert Fripp. (You may have seen Robert Fripp and his wife Toyah Wilcox's pandemic videos, which were hilarious.) They are known as the inventors of progressive rock with their first album, 1969's *In The Court of the Crimson King*. Their second album is not as beloved but I sure like it. And "The Devil's Triangle" is basically a Bolero-esque song with a rhythm played over and over as mellotrons and other instruments swell around it. (The song after it is called "Peace.") The thing that I find surprising is that Crimson, like Led Zeppelin, almost never show up anywhere. They keep a very close eye on people using their music. To hear them in an episode of our favorite show, even for only about 10 seconds, surprises me. The Master is cool.

The rest of the episode proves that the most interesting stuff here is the prison stuff but even that is getting a touch repetitive. It reminds me of Episode Four of "Ambassadors." We catch Liz. She escapes. We catch her again. In this one, the prisoners have the prison. The good guys take it back. The Master shows up and the bad guys take the prison again. This will happen several more times in this era. It's a Terrance Dicks thing. Remember "The War Games?" How many episodes in that had big things happen but then, when they were over, the state of play had not changed at all? That's what happens here. It is great to see Jo kick ass and take names. But it comes to nothing in the end. Is that padding? I don't know. When I watch a horror movie, the stakes can change from moment to moment. Same with an action film. In retrospect, it is padding. This is the middle of the story. In another respect, it's just the story. The story being told.

The material with Chin Lee leads us from one plot point to another. More elegantly than the previous story but not as interestingly. I do love the moment when the Doctor says "God go with you also" to the Chinese delegate. I feel like The Doctor met God somewhere. Or maybe I'm thinking of Doctor Strange. Anyway, this leads him from one spot to the next and to his first meeting with the Master. He does seem to already realize that an over complicated scheme and ridiculous nonsense is the Master's thing. In one way, we love the Master for his suave. In another, we kind of agree with the Doctor. The Master is already overdoing it.

The Pertwee era is not my favorite. But when I really get into it, I get ensconced in there, I really like the space it uses. I like the world that's created. Whether it be with Liz, Jo or Sarah Jane. It's a fun spot to be in. You can tell those that made it felt the same way by listening to all the commentaries on the DVDs/Blus. Infectious. In a good way.

The Mind of Evil
Episode Four

Episode 286: (February 20, 1971): The Thunderbolt is hijacked. The Keller Machine begins to move on its own.
Cliffhanger: The Keller Machine materializes before the Doctor and Jo.

We get a great moment where the Master must confront the Keller Machine. It calls out his biggest fear. And that's the Doctor. A Giant Doctor laughing at him. Over the course of the series, we will learn a lot more about their relationship. A lot more about what happened back on Gallifrey. But at this point, we don't have much. We don't know much. All we know is that they have a past together and the Master wants to make the Doctor's life on Earth miserable. * And he's doing it because he's afraid the Doctor will lord over him and laugh and laugh. And The Master would probably be super pissed when he learned that the Doctor's fears don't involve him at all. Jealous.

The Keller Machine really comes into its own. The mind parasite inside the machine begins to teleport itself around the prison. Which is good because it really wasn't the most mobile and exciting villain. Just sitting in one room and only hurting people going near it doesn't really do too much. Now, it's become active and evil. It's a wonder it doesn't pick off the whole population of the prison in a few minutes. And why does it go after the Doctor and Jo? Surely, they'd be the last people you went after in a prison full of hardened felons. Or maybe not? That's the Keller Machine for you!

The Doctor is very damaged by the attack the Keller Machine. He goes into a coma like he did at the start of "Spearhead From Space." But he does snap out of it after a time. I like that they bring us back to this point though. It kind of solidifies that the Doctor is healing himself here. He is making himself better by putting himself into the coma.

It's nice to see the Doctor and Jo running around together inside the prison. They've rapidly become a fun team. More fun than Liz and The Doctor but there was a very different dynamic going on there. And, as we know, Katy Manning could barely see anything so they get closer because she'd run right into walls if they didn't.

The big sequence in the second half is the stealing of the Thunderbolt. It's an epic adventure scene a la the big scenes in "The Ambassadors of Death" or the search for the Silurian from this director's previous story. It's filled with lots of fun stunts and explosions. It looks like most of the budget was spent doing this. That's probably true. It's too bad though that Mike Yates isn't the most convincing soldier out there. And that moment when he runs up to the hangar, he's so clearly in everyone's line of sight that they should have shot that scene again. But they probably didn't have time. Regardless, the episode ends with the Master in charge of the Thunderbolt and the Keller Machine moving on its own. That can't be good.

*It's interesting that the Master first appears in the show only after the Doctor is exiled to Earth. He doesn't go after The Doctor when the Doctor can go anywhere. (Maybe because the Doctor is never sure where they're going that he doesn't want to follow. I don't know.) Now, that the Doctor is stuck in one place for a long time, now is the time. One can imagine The Master really saying "Now, I'll get The Doctor. I'll destroy his beloved Earth and make his life miserable." That's the Master for you.

The Mind of Evil
Episode Five

Episode 287: (February 27, 1971) UNIT storms the castle, as it were. The Doctor tries to stop the Keller Machine,
Cliffhanger: Mailer is about to shoot the Doctor.

Like the underground lab in "The Ambassadors of Death," I am frankly a little tired of the that cell where they're keeping the Doctor and Jo and that staircase leading down to that cell. Is that the only cell at the bottom of that staircase? Doesn't it seem like it? The lonely little spot at the bottom of the stairs. Architecturally, it does seem odd. Because you then go up the stairs, across a walkway and then back down some stairs to get to the main area where the Keller machine is. Weird? I think so.

The Delaware synthesizer continues to be the sole provider of music for this season. Dudley Simpson provides some nice themes throughout. He also puts in a wistful one when The Doctor is telling Jo a story about being in the Tower of London and we crossfade to a van pulling up to the prison. It reminds me of Mort Garson's work from around this time. He did the all-synth score of a very odd and quite wonderful film called *Didn't You Hear?* Starring Gary Busey and Dennis Christopher. A lot of great bouncy synth lines alongside some eerie ones. This was a heck of a time for synths.

The padding is beginning to show here. The production text on the DVD/ Blu-ray points out that the first four cliffhangers are all pretty much the same. The Doctor, or someone, is threatened with the Keller machine. It's different in this episode. But this episode uses a cliffhanger trick that is older than time itself. It's OK though. There is a new character introduced since Yates and Benton are elsewhere for much of the episode. A rather silly Captain or something. It's too bad when you have all the regular characters there but write yourself into a corner where none of them are available. It happens.

The attack on the prison is fun. I think it works better in black and white. This story was the last one of the Pertwee era to come out on DVD because it was the only one that was all black and white. They colorized it. Like many of the colorized episodes, it can tend to look a little odd. But this is the only one that is pretty much all colorized so it does have a strange look. Luckily, the next story is in full color. You can, especially on the Blu, compare and contrast. For years, I saw this in B&W. I sort of got used to it, even though I knew that wasn't its original state. Parts still hold up better in the shades of grey than the colorized world.

Anyway, it's nice to see the Brig doing his working-class character with a van full of grub. (Actually, a van full of UNIT soldiers but they are both scrumptious.) A lot of violence in the shootout. A lot of people are getting shot down in this serial. Mailer shot a ton of people back in Episode three. And the Brig and his men shoot a lot of people here. Quite a few of them in the style of *The French Connection*. You know what I mean. Guys on staircases realizing they're done for and getting shot and falling. It's all very dramatic and it's more grown up. I didn't count the number of people shot but it's pretty darn hefty.

The Master and the Doctor gang up to try to stop the Keller machine, at least for a while. The Master really seems to have no idea what to do to stop it. Where'd he get it from? Why can't he control it? He says he built it himself but that's baloney. The Doctor does get in there and stop it for a while. Things will go bad again soon. We know they will. But, on either side of that sequence, we get the lovely scene where Jo beats the Doctor at checkers and Jo and The Doctor eat some floor toast as the Doctor tells stories. I like that. They have become a good team very quickly. Of course, if Mailer shoots and kills the Doctor, that friendship will be over fast. We'll see.

The Mind of Evil
Episode Six

Episode 288: (March 6, 1971) The Doctor almost completely saves the day.
Cliffhanger: The Master is free to roam. The Doctor is not.

We don't get a lot of characters like Barnham in *Doctor Who*. A character who as had their evil removed and who can literally negate a "mind of evil." Can literally calm it down. There are a lot of sweet moments with Barnham through this episode. The looks he gives both the Brig and Acting Governor Benton are great. Watching him eat soup is delightful. In the previous episode, The Doctor and Jo ate toast. Here Barnham has some soup. His kindness saves the Master and gets him killed. I feel like there's a *Doctor Who* lesson in there somewhere. Thank Goodness this wasn't an Eric Saward story or Barnham would have died horrifically. (Not that getting hit by a car and then blown up in the aborted missile explosion isn't horrible.) He was a fun character. He shall be missed.

Sgt. Benton is great as Acting Governor Benton. The smile on his face when he gets put in charge is fantastic. When he tells Barnham to go talk to whoever he wants, I always laugh. Captain Yates doesn't do as much. His sandwich hidden in his sling has some charms. I question the Brig's choice of having Yates evacuate the area around the hangar with one arm in a sling and what he's been through.

One of the odd things that happens with *Doctor Who* stories of a certain length at a certain time is one can't help but thinking: How's the Peace Conference going? So much of the first 2 ½ episodes dealt with that but we haven't been there in ages. How's Chin Lee? How's the ambassador? How's the Senator that saw pink dragons? We understand that it's still going on. But, never going back to it is odd. I know, it's because those sets have all been taken down and those actors aren't in these episodes. That doesn't mean it's not weird. When the next season starts, we'll see that another Peace Conference has been scheduled. What that says for this one… we'll find out.

I do like the episodes like this, or the stories like this, where it feels like things are kind of over but they're not. The Brig is taking care of Thunderbolt. The Doc is taking care of the Keller Machine. It's all going to be awesome. But it all goes south because the machine is horrible and the Master is a real smart fellow. There are more stories like this and we will discuss them when we get to them. As if "freeing Stangmoor" was the most important thing here. And yet, it does feel like a sigh of relief when it happens.

Are there flaws here? Sure. When Doctor Summers enters the lab, it's too rushed. He's been gone for ages and now suddenly must get Barnham back to the sickbay so quickly that he almost kills everyone. A few moments in the final confrontation feel a bit rushed too. You know why? They probably were rushed. But it still works. It feels suitably big. The explosion in the hangar works well. I'm not 100% sure how the Master got the dematerialization circuit. (Maybe it's something to do with the way the Doctor made that reel of computer tape disappear last season?) Overall, though, it's a strong ending. Because UNIT takes control of Stangmoor early on, the pace kind of shifts towards ending the story. The fact that the Keller Machine meets the Thunderbolt to stop the Master is clever. A good story well told.

Odd Moment: After the Thunderbolt explodes, the main cast are sitting in the Warden's office. I'm not sure why as surely other policemen would have come to take charge. Are there any more prisoners here? The scene begins with a UNIT solider extra placing a tray of coffee on the table. Instead of talking beginning, the camera follows the extra as he goes to the door. Opens it. Closes it. Then, the scene continues. What was that about? Why did that happen? It feels like the editor wasn't paying attention and thought maybe something was going to happen at the door. (Nothing does.)

THE CLAWS OF AXOS
Written by Bob Baker and Dave Martin
Directed by Michael Ferguson
Episode One

Episode 289: (March 13, 1971) A spaceship lands in the British countryside. It has an interesting race onboard.
Cliffhanger: A hideous brown tentacled monster attacks Jo.

A weird episode. It welcomes a full-on new writing team to the show. Don Houghton has been here. But he's leaving to write some Hammer Dracula films, which are lots of fun. Bob and Dave are here. They would become regular writers for the show until 1978. They would write a series of big, crazy stories. Stories full of lots of different twists and turns. Moments that are crazy alongside moments of sheer blah. It's weird. They were brought on because of their proliferation of ideas. (Please, track down the storyline for this original story under the title "The Vampire In Space.") They always got trimmed down and trimmed down until it was almost silly. This is their first story for the show. It features great stuff and some stuff that seems kind of dumb.

First off, the smart stuff. The Axon ship is great. An organic artifice that buries itself beneath the Earth. We only see the opening that brings itself to life and then closes as if it were the mouth of some tapeworm. A tapeworm that everyone in the cast seems to keep walking into. The Axons themselves are clearly sinister. But they're also a lovely orange/ brown color. (Lovely might be overdoing it.) And they seem friendly. I love when the head Axon apologizes for picking a frog to expand with Axonite. Hey, we all make mistakes. The freak weather conditions are great. They add a refreshing element to everything that has already appeared in previous episodes. This is the second (semi-third) big alien invasion since the start of the previous season.

The rest of the alien invasion stuff feels like belabored overdone nonsense. The technicians watching the ship approaching is taken from "Spearhead" and that was taken from Quatermass. And here, it just feels like we should have a twist on it but we don't. Shall we talk about Chinn? Where did he come from and why did we think the show needed him?

There were so many awful figures in charge during the Troughton era. This one is clearly an idiot but he also is large and in charge. I get that he's meant to represent bureaucracy out of hand. But how is that interesting? I'm not laughing. I'm not intrigued. I'm just annoyed. The Doctor seems to be doing his best but he's treating Chinn like a roommate that no one wants. And that's not something I'm interested in at this point in my life.

Filer? Does he warrant discussion? He flirts with Joe. He's from the US. He sneaks onboard the ship and sees the Master. (Yes, he is here. But he really doesn't do anything. He's a captive in the Axon world.) Filer is so vaguely introduced. It seems like all the elements that would make him interesting got left on the cutting room floor. With the ship approaching, Chinn being a jackass and all the other incident, Filer is so secondary as to be laughable.

That's the problem with this episode. It looks like it might be epic but much of it is laughably blasé. Even the walk through the ship. It has a bit of a "Who cares?" feeling to it. There's the actual doctor who looks like he hates The Doctor. The Brig not quite caring. That weird scene where Jo, in her purple miniskirt, strolls by all the guards and goes in the TARDIS. So many things jump ahead in weird ways during this episode. It almost doesn't make sense. The episode feels edited by someone who wanted to speed everything up but edited a lot of the right bits out. The episode feels off. It feels wrong. It feels like a dumb parody of the show rather than the show itself.

Last thing: Pigbin Josh. He's the guy on the bike who gets eaten up by Axos. Where did he come from? What is his purpose? Regardless of what we learn, I've never quite figured out his purpose. In the novelization and in the subtitles, he's just talking gibberish. What is wrong with him? Is he touched? If so, should be watching him the way we're watching him? If his accent is some sort of regional thing, we all could use something to clue us into what's going on. The bike into the freezing stream is great. Everything else involving Josh seems really stupid. But should it?

The Claws Of Axos
Episode Two

Episode 290: (March 20, 1971) The humans are given Axonite. Also, all kinds of other junk happens. Cliffhanger: A giant Axon monster attacks the gang.

Let's talk Dick. So, there's a scientist here that really hates the Doctor. He seemed to hate him the previous episode and he hates him to death literally, here. Now, we've seen this kind of character in life. When I published my previous book on the Henningverse, "experts" came out of the woodwork to call me garbage to say my book was crap and give the worst review they could up online. I guess that's professional jealousy, right? People who hate you simply because you're doing your work. That's what Dick is like in this episode. I think some would call him a twat. He hates the Doctor because the Doctor maybe has a better job. Maybe because he thinks the Doctor makes more money. I don't know. It doesn't matter. He has a scientist's turtleneck on. It's pulled up to right below his chin very firmly and he condescends to the Doctor throughout. Frankly, I hate this kind of *Doctor Who* writing. I find it lazy and exhausting. This episode has a lot of that.

The Brigadier goes up against Chinn. Chinn's an incompetent buffoon that gets special government powers to take the Axonite distribution under his wing. He has the regular army under his control. And as imaginative as some of the bits of this story are… it's becoming every dumb Earth-bound adventure show that we have avoided so far. The Axons are kind of interesting. The examining of the element is kind of interesting. But it ends up being a script that we thought they had rejected in the previous season but are completely ready to make reality now. That kind of makes me tired.

Because, although this episode has a lot going on, it's kind of dull. Filer? Who cares? The Axons? I guess they're interesting. The Master? Doesn't do much. The Doctor? Argues with The Dick throughout. Jo? Looks cute in the miniskirt. The Brig and UNIT? Under Chinn's control. Watched one episode a week this probably works quite well. It probably holds up its end. Watched as I am watching it, it really kind of drags and gets on my nerves. The Axons are not much. I know they've got something big planned. There's the Filer double. There's the cliffhanger. But at the same time, it's not very exciting. I don't think any of what we're seeing is padding. However, it isn't terribly interesting at the same time.

And that breaks my heart because this seems like an exciting episode. Or like it should be. It just comes off as an average episode in the middle of a season. It's not "Meglos" dull but it feels like it should be better because these are new writers becoming part of the show. There should be a thrill to this and it is noticeably absent. We know the director can do well because of "Doctor Who and the Silurians." He's doing his best. The story just feels like a bit of a dud. The Axons are not the Autons. They don't have the flair. So, what do we do? What does the story do? Let's see what episode three has awaiting us.

The Claws of Axos
Episode Three

Episode 291: (March 27, 1971) The Doctor and Jo are captured by the Axons who reveal their scheme. Meanwhile, The Master ends up helping the planet Earth.
Cliffhanger: The Master is going to destroy Axos. He also might destroy The Doctor and Jo.

All right, things do pick up here. The Doctor and Jo are captured. Chinn has his power taken away from him. Then, almost immediately, he gets his power right back. I'm not sure about that. Filer stumbles around confused. And the Master gets into the Doctor's TARDIS, which is a mess. We haven't seen the console in this season. The last time we saw it was when it went to the rubbish tip at the end of "Inferno." The console room does look a bit different from how we remember it. But the memory cheats. Maybe it did look different.

The Doctor and Jo do little in this episode. Jo is aged almost to the point of death. Here, we get one of the few moments where the Third Doctor is completely set back, completely worried and must find a way out. You know the way that is. When something terrible is about to happen and all you can do is yell at it. It doesn't help but that is all you have. The Axons are after the time element that the Doctor has access to. He really doesn't have access to it now. I don't know why they couldn't get this from the Master. The Master never keeps a deal. Why would the Axons?

The Master takes over a portion of this episode. He becomes like the Doctor. He becomes like a William Hartnell Doctor. We see why you never leave the Doctor alone. Because he goes rogue super-fast. I like the Master picking on the Doctor's TARDIS. He must know that the Doctor didn't chose that TARDIS. Clara Oswald pointed him to it because the spirit within it was in perfect synchronicity with The Doctor. And that's cool. I don't know how the Master chose their TARDIS. Some jerk said "take this one. It rocks!" And they went. I don't know.

The episode has a lot of incidents occurring. It's nice to know that the Axons aren't evil. They're just surviving. The Autons aren't really either I guess. They're just surviving. This is what they do. But that means that a lot of these invaders aren't jerks. They just are. I don't yell at an ant or a cockroach. I just remove them from the premises. I just make sure they're not there anymore. That's what Axos is. They're not evil. They just can't be here. They just don't understand. They need to be sent away.

What the fourth episode has in store I can't say. A lot of craziness here. But less memorable madness than say "Terror of the Autons." We do have a TARDIS and time travel involved. So, this time things might go a little mental.

The Claws of Axos
Episode Four

Episode 292: (April 3, 1971) The Axons get control of time travel. Sort of.
Cliffhanger: The Doctor is a galactic yo-yo.

Someone, somewhere, has probably taken down a list of important concepts in the world of The Doctor that were done casually. Robert Holmes is the biggest purveyor of this. The Doctor's physiology in "Spearhead" is Holmes goofing. He singlehandedly creates the history of The Time Lords in "The Deadly Assassin" almost on a whim. And here, we get two of the other great purveyors of this kind of thing. Although, I always got the feeling that Baker and Martin were doing it a little more self-consciously. Here they mention the High Council of the Time Lords (No name for the planet yet) and introduce us to the wonderful world of the time loop. It starts here and features as recently as the 2022 New Year's Day special "Eve of the Daleks." It's an important concept that's always good for a few laughs. Although here, it's deadly earnest.

In a show like *Doctor Who*, it can be very easy (as the first six seasons demonstrated), to never give us any new information. To keep the show going and going without any backstory. (Heck, after nine seasons, we never learned the Virginian's name.) So, when things do begin to change in a show that's been going on for so long, it feels cool. It's one thing to have a show, like say a *Babylon Five*, where we know that things will be revealed in time. When *Doctor Who* began, there was no guarantee of any of this. Now, we're getting quite a bit of it. It's happening at a time when the format of the show has changed. Maybe it feels safe to do so now that The Doctor can't do anything but hang out on Earth.

Anyway, the Doctor uses a time loop to trap Axos forever. Possibly the Master too. Although maybe not. It's nice to see the TARDIS going again with the Doctor and the Master at the controls. For a split second, maybe not really, I did almost feel like the Doctor was going to abandon humanity to the Axons and leave with the Master. Only for a minute though.

The story ends in chaos and monsters. It ends with psychedelic effects and switches being thrown that mean that time loops are happening. It ends with a nuclear power plant, exploding, kind of. But it's OK. And the Doctor is pulled back to Earth even though he tried to escape. A lot is thrown at us in this story. I don't think (I've never thought) that it fully works. Some does, some doesn't. It's less fun than "Terror of the Autons." (I don't recall laughing at any good lines.) It's more annoying than "The Mind of Evil." (Some of the secondary characters are tough to deal with.) But it's colorful and it's weird. And it's *Doctor Who* baby. Through and through.

COLONY IN SPACE
Written by Malcolm Hulke
Directed by Michael E. Briant
Episode One

Episode 293: (April 10, 1971) On the planet Uxarieus, something strange is happening to a group of colonists.
Cliffhanger: A giant robot with IMC on the front of it attacks the Doctor.

Of course, it is wonderful to see the Doctor out and about in space and time again. 2473. The Planet Uxarieus. Jo and The Doctor have been sent by the Time Lords for some reason other. (If you know the title of the novelization, it might give something away.) Now, the Time Lords don't send him with any kind of information. They just send him. So, here's hoping he figures out the correct thing that he's supposed to do out there.

Jo, unfortunately, really doesn't want to go. She thinks the TARDIS is some sort of hobby. She doesn't believe that there's anything inside it. She doesn't know why the Doctor is always working on that dematerialization circuit. For someone who spends so much time with the Doctor, this has always seemed odd to me. * And her constant wanting to go back home is like that too. We'll see more of this with Jo. She loves being in UNIT and working with the Doctor. But she never really became a travelling companion. Her world was Earth. And you can see it starting here.

The story then does something that I've never figured out was good or bad or a joke or what the heck it was. But, the TARDIS, for its first trip in over a season and a half... lands in an old rock quarry/ clay pit thing. It looks so much like so many other places we've landed before I always think it's a joke. In a world of nothing but rocks and clay, we're supposed to find endless wonder. There is one flower. I don't even know why the colonists are here trying to grow things. It's a rock quarry. There's only one sign (apart from the Primitives who live in a special place) of non-rock life out there. Why on Earth did they choose this place? And why is the Doctor so excited?

It could be because it is his first alien world in a while. (He knows exactly what planet it is.) He's simply really excited about it. It's like if you hadn't had a donut in ages. And you didn't have one and you didn't have one. Then your first one was just a boring old donut. Nothing flashy or exciting. To someone who has never seen a donut, they might think "Oh, that's rather dull." But you're super stoked because it's a donut and you haven't had one in ages! Maybe. Maybe it's just the Doctor trying to convince himself and Jo that after all his time spent fixing the TARDIS they can't have just landed in a boring quarry. He's overselling it because he's trying to make Jo interested. And himself.

Then, there's the story. Boring colonists being boring. With bad beards and some bad wigs in there. It was almost not worth the Doctor going into the TARDIS. In fact, this time around, I got actively annoyed by the bad beards of the colonists. (Also, Jo thinking that this lot came from 1971 boggles the mind.) Watching the Doctor having discussions with the colonists about crop subsistence and such might be a social topic we could all learn from but I find this episode a little tough going. Finally! We're back in time and space! And we wound up here.

Then, to end the episode, we get the guy from the "other colony." His story is as fake as they come. I think obviously so. There is no "other colony." If the colonies were within walking distance, how come they never knew about one another. The worst thing about our fake friend is the way you can tell that he's a big liar: he has the ugliest beard. A beard that defies you to not pull it off his face. I know I wouldn't be able to resist.

*There is a very nice parallel moment here. Jo tells the Doctor he's wasting his time on the demat circuit and why doesn't he give it up. Then, the Brig walks in still hunting the Master. The Doctor responds with "Brig, you're wasting your time. Give it up." What comes around, etc.

**Colony in Space
Episode Two**

Episode 294: (April 17, 1971) The Doctor meets The Men From IMC. * The guy from the "other colony" turns out to be a big, lying faker.
Cliffhanger: Back in the dome, the Doctor is threatened by another robot.

"The Mind of Evil" had a variation of the same cliffhanger for four episodes in a row. This story, literally, has the same cliffhanger for these first two episodes. The episode isn't really doing that thing we talked about where people run around and it looks like important things are happening but everything winds up in the same place. This is an important episode. The Doctor learns about IMC. We learn about IMC's plans. We learn that that one guy from the other colony is as much of a jerk as we thought. We learn about the horrible lives of everyone back on Earth. We get a lot out of this episode. So, why does the cliffhanger take place in the exact same spot with the exact same character encountering the exact same thing? It's rather frustrating to dwell upon.

So, we get IMC in this one and they've got their "Oh we didn't know anyone was here" shtick. I don't buy it for a minute. I guess they're in real cozy with the Earth government if they are doing this as often as is implied. Caldwell seems like a decent guy, All the rest of them, including Dent the captain, are straight out of Evil Capitalist Villain 101. And if they must kill every single colonist so be it. Now, Janet Fielding in the "Behind the Sofa" featurette on the Blu makes a good point. The planet has gravity. So, it must be sizable. Why on Earth, or on Uxarieus, can't the colonists have their patch of land and IMC go to the other side of the planet to do their mining? They could have landed 500 miles away and the colonists would never have known they were there. **

What about that "other colonist" guy. Why is he so gross? Clean your beard, man! Don't talk with your mouth full. He's so obviously faking it. Why is it only Jo that notices the hairy chicanery? Are these colonists the universe's most gullible bunch ever? They're like the people on the Ark in *The Restaurant At The End of The Universe*. The Earth loaded their most useless people on a rocket and sent them away.

So... their engineer, and they've only one, spends a lot of his time fixing their power unit. He has a Primitive assistant. They're pals. The "Other Colony" guy insists that all primitives are evil. He asks the other colonists a dozen questions about the power unit, their scientist and how it all works. Then, he kills the scientist, kills the Primitive and destroys the power unit. He brings everyone over to the power room and makes up a story about the Primitive attacking. No one says, "These two have been working together for months without a problem. You show up and almost kill one of the Primitives while complaining about them. You ask all about our power source. And then, about ten minutes later this happens. That's too much of a coincidence." Instead, they wonder why the Primitive did this and buy this greasy gentleman's story wholesale. Put them all in a bag and fling them over the moon.

Unfortunately, much of the episode gets me in the same way. There are so many questions. The fact that the show isn't going to answer them just leaves me annoyed. If I could, I'd give you the final word on the whole story but I must review all the episodes. Please let Three be better than the first two. They're all so competently made. If they were inept, we could laugh. Let's go Three!

*The Interplanetary Mining Corporation

**Yes, the colonists do get on my nerves. We hear about how bad their crops are growing. And yet we never see any of the crops. Everything we see is clay, dirt and stone. What sort of farming are they doing? "Bad Farming," one might guess. Where are they farming? In the stones? In the clay? There is no sign of arable land anywhere here. In fact, it looks like what it is: a quarry. For mining. So, maybe the colonists should leave.

Colony In Space
Episode Three

Episode 295: (April 24, 1971) Jo and Winton try to get info from the IMC ship and end up getting taken prisoner by IMC. So, the Doctor and everyone else storm the ship to save the day.
Cliffhanger: Jo is entering the Primitive City.

Following up on something I said in the previous review, the IMC ship lands near the colonists and they hear the ship land. That implies that they didn't hear the ship where it landed originally. Why didn't they just stay where they were and mine? Caldwell says that their ship was a "few kilometers" from the colonists. They were able to do all their mineral checks in their original spot. Why do they have to bother the colonists? I don't understand.

Something I just realized; it's been three years since I last saw this serial. About a year before I'm writing this, I read Mac Hulke's novelization, which I really enjoyed. But, for some reason, I'm not enjoying this. Hulke was great at streamlining the stories. In the book, he gives this one a nice feeling of movement throughout. The televised serial has a lot of movement. But it's kind of aimless. And the stuff that happens in this episode, I'm sorry to say, teeters into stupid.

I won't list them all but I'll mention a few. The Doctor was literally attacked at the start of the episode. The plan was to kill him. Yet, somehow when the Doctor tells Dent all of this, it's treated very nonchalantly. No one acts like it means anything. Yes, when Dent has Jo, he says The Doctor will get her back if he doesn't testify. But Dent didn't know that Jo was going to do what she did. It's not like he kidnapped her to get some leverage. If IMC just arrived, how come no one seems to wonder how Dent and The Doctor know one another? It seems like some lines have been left out.

Then, there's the bit where Winton and Jo storm the IMC ship. It seems like a dumb idea when it's suggested. You can't imagine that they'll go through with it. Then, they do and, thanks to Norton warning Dent, they're caught almost immediately. And it's so stupid. In fact, when Jo says she has an idea of something they can do and is asked what and she says this... I laughed. You can't be serious. It only seems to happen so they can have Jo as a hostage and try and get leverage from the Doctor.

But, to add insult to injury, The Doctor and others storm the ship and take it over, mainly to try and get Jo back. This time it seems to work but you know it's not going to be for long. Again, it's idiotic. There's an Adjudicator on the way. Surely once they hear what the colonists have done, it's not going to be good. They don't have real proof of what IMC is doing. They're going to look like the bad guys.

Then, they throw in the "Primitive City" stuff. One gets the feeling that, finally, we're getting to the point of why the Time Lords sent the Doctor here. But, mixed in with all the stupid stuff, the City stuff gets lost. It feels very secondary to all the nonsense going on. And the cliffhanger is just confusing. Jo takes a step into the Primitive City. We don't see anything but her face. I can't tell what she's thinking. I think it's meant to be "awe" but truly I've no idea. It's not a great cliffhanger. The moment leaves the viewer with a "Whatever" sort of feeling. What the show needs now is love, sweet love. The show needs a kick in the pants. It needs to shift to somewhere else. Quickly.

(One more odd thing: Do you remember the first thing we see that aren't rocks on the planet? A giant mining robot of some sort. A huge, unwieldy thing. Presumably that's an IMC robot. Do none of the colonists ever see that? Is that just something the director included to make us think "Hmm, what's that?" It's tough gauging where everything is in relation to one another. They seem to get from one spot to another very quickly. But then, there are times, like the Doctor being driven back to the dome in the previous episode, when things seem to take forever.)

Colony In Space
Episode Four

Episode 296: (May 1, 1971) The Adjudicator arrives. He quickly becomes Master of the situation. Cliffhanger: During a gunfight, the Adjudicator decides the Doctor and Jo might get shot.

Yes! The Master arrives! Yes! We spend some time in the Primitive city. That's what we need. The moment the Master shows up as The Adjudicator we can guess at what he's going to do. All the other stuff becomes kind of superfluous. Which is helpful.

The Master arrives in a spaceship that lands in a weird way. That may be a clue. Or it might not. He's here. He has his TARDIS. He has everything that this era of the Earth requires. The Doctor and Jo, as travelers, don't have the bureaucratic junk that is needed. One would have thought that the Time Lords might have given them what they needed. Hell, they should have, right? The moment the Master shows up that must mean something. That must mean that the Time Lords knew what was happening. And they didn't give Jo and the Doctor what they needed.

The trial sequence here is kind of a shrug. Once we see the Master, we know that the IMC will win, regardless of what's happening. There's too much back and forth going on. It's a bit of a drawback to the story. We can't quite nail down what this story is because of this. Norton is still here. And he's still discouraging everyone. Why is he flipping here?

Norton has his big moment where he is uncovered by the brother of the man that IMC killed. There's an odd scuffle that leads to the final fight, which leads to the cliffhanger. It's odd because we've been here before. We've been here so often in this serial. These obvious bad guys and these monsters are just getting in the way of everything.

Power changes hands often in this episode and the one before. They happen too often to be realistic. Not that I want the show to be realistic, per se. But I want to feel like I'm happy where I am. I want to enjoy the spaces that we are in. This story leaps around in such a screwy fashion that I don't know anymore.

But then, the Doctor and Jo go to the Primitive City. Things go really weird there. We see several different versions of these people. We see scrolls on painted walls describing that they were big and important at one time but something happened. And we get the best part of this episode. The moments when the Doctor talks to the Guardian. The small character who lets the Doctor and Jo go after they tried to escape. This being who lets them go to try and save this world that they once ruled. It's a fantastic moment. We'll have to see where we go from here. The Master, obviously, is hanging around.

Colony In Space
Episode Five

Episode 297: (May 8, 1971) IMC gets control of everything again. They order the colonists to leave in their rocket. Meanwhile, the Master and the Doctor begin to explore the Primitive City.
Cliffhanger: The men from IMC have broken into the Master's TARDIS. That means death for Josephine Y. Grant.

The visit to the Primitive City is taking longer than expected. The Master is here for what's in that city. That's obvious. He holds out on the Adjudicator thing as long as he possibly can. In fact, he convinces the colonists that he has more cred than the Doctor because the Doctor doesn't have "papers." (The colonists don't think to check the Adjudicator. But IMC does. I like them a little bit more with each passing episode.) The Master has a lot of plans. He has a lot of schemes. He has an elaborate trap set up in his TARDIS control room where gas pours out to fill up the room, to incapacitate or maybe kill. I don't know about you but that strikes me as an accident waiting to happen. The Master is sleepy one morning. He hits the wrong button. Suddenly, the console room is filled with gas. You can overplan something. It feels like the Primitive City storyline is going to be more interesting than the colonists thing. But it's taking so long to get there. And, when IMC gets control again, that storyline becomes interesting.

We know that IMC are awful. They really take the cake here. They leave the planet and come back and take control. (Once again, someone on the planet has done something stupid. Ashe doesn't allow anyone to carry around guns. So, IMC gets them back.) Dent's stoic face when he orders the colonists off the planet immediately is great. The scene with Mary and Caldwell is as good as Joanna and King Richard back in "The Crusade." As this episode ends, the colonists versus miner story has finally hit a very dramatic point. I'm interested to see where it goes.

Now, it's not all great here. Remember at the start of Episode Three when Winton and Jo stormed the IMC ship in a starling display of stupidity? Well, we get a variation on that here. The Doctor and Jo break into the Master's TARDIS. There is a very prominent electric eye that they sneak under. The Doctor is looking around. Then, the super dumb thing happens. *About Time* described this the best. So, I won't try to top what they've said. But Jo, in her excitement to get back to the colonists not only runs through the electric eye… but SHE STANDS IN IT! Just stands there. A few minutes before, they made a big deal about sliding underneath it. Now, she does this. And that's stupid.

It's stupid because that's how The Master gets his hold over the Doctor for the rest of the episode. In the same way, that the colonists compromised themselves in Episode Three because of Jo's dumb idea, it happens again here. She forgets something very important and they get caught and she's held hostage. Imagine if that hadn't happened. It's so contrived that it kind of hurts. Surely, they could think of a better way to get the Master and the Doctor working together here. Or maybe not. It's just really dumb. For a story written by Mr. Hulke and edited by Mr. Dicks it feels a bit like end of the season exhaustion. We can't come up with anything else.

Now, I love Jo. I think we all do. But Jo said it best herself in "Death of the Doctor." She asks the Doctor if he thought she was dumb. The 11th Doctor doesn't reply. And Jo agrees that she wasn't the smartest. After Liz, who was so smart and Zoe who was even smarter but naïve, Jo, as a dumb companion, takes us back to… I'm not sure. Victoria wasn't dumb. She was generally out of her time. Dodo wasn't dumb either. Jamie was kind of dumb and the Second Doctor travelled with him the longest. Hmm, maybe that's something. Maybe it isn't.

Anyway, we have one episode left in this story. Hopefully, we will learn what the Master is after, why the Time Lords sent the Doctor and see the ending of the colonists versus miner battle. Maybe it's time we returned to Earth. There's not a lot of intelligent life out here.

Colony In Space
Episode Six

Episode 298: (May 15, 1971) We learn what the Master wants. The colonists and IMC clash one more time.
Cliffhanger: They return to Earth and to a bemused Brig.

The story ends. And the colonists versus IMC bit wraps up nicely. Jo somehow gets lost a bit in the mix but the way they work through the story here is nicely done. That knockdown drag-out fight in the mud and clay is really something. There's a real desperate go for broke feeling in that scene that is so much more real than pretty much everything else in the story. It's because we know that if Winton doesn't take down the guard, the colonists are all dead. No more back and forth. No more "we're in charge and now you're in charge." This is a fight that means something.

It is nice to see the colonists win and send IMC away. But, by time the end comes and the TARDIS has been found, I just wanted us to get out of there. Presumably what the Doctor and the Master went through in the Primitive City is related to why the Time Lords sent the Doctor, although it's never really brought up again. The whole thing ends with a joke involving the Brig. There's no real discussion of

"What was all that about?" For all we know, those colonists could have been the reason the Doctor was sent. We just don't know.

Mixed in with the colonists final fights, we get the second visit to the Primitive City. And we get the big reveal. The Hulke novelization is called "Doctor Who and the Doomsday Weapon," which is a cool title but misleading. In the novelization, Hulke adds a brief mention of that at the start and it kind of sits in the back of the reader's mind so when we get to the conclusion it's there. In the televised version, it's a surprise. It helps make a lot of sense of events and the realization that the Weapon infects the ground and is ruining the crops is excellent.

However, the closing bits with the Doomsday Weapon feel like such an afterthought. So much of the story has been this endless back and forth between the two groups. The Primitive City has always been hovering in the background. Then, when they finally decide to make the City important, they're intercutting it with the best moments between the colonists conflict. And to see these characters getting so desperate intercut with another hare-brained Master scheme kind of brings both down. I never got a feeling of threat from the Doomsday Weapon. It was too little, too late. That should have been introduced earlier and been shown to be a threat. I like the line about the Crab Nebula being their test subject. But the Master just ends up looking like a doofus, again. Our first sojourn into space could have easily taken place on Earth except for the Doomsday Weapon stuff. I still stand by the novelization as being excellent. The rest is, to quote *The Discontinuity Guide*, "like watching socially aware paint dry."

THE DAEMONS
Written by Guy Leopold
Directed By Christopher Barry
Episode One

Episode 299: (May 22, 1971) The Devil's Hump is about to be excavated. The Doctor isn't too happy about it.
Cliffhanger: The Hump is open and it looks like the Doctor is dead.

As others have pointed out, this is a story where suddenly The Doctor, the person speaking out for science and rationality, seems to be interested in witches, the Devil and even festivals like Beltane. In fact, he seems a bit deranged right at the end of the episode. As he and Jo run through the night past barbed wire and the camera crew to stop the Devil's Hump from being excavated. Barry Letts, producer and co-writer has said that he was deliberately futzing around with the format trying to see what they could do with it. This is a nice opening episode to the closing story of this sometimes wonderful, sometimes exasperating season.

The Doctor and Jo do make a fun couple. She's speaking about the Age of Aquarius. He's making Bessie drive on her own. She's got her cute purple hat on. He's in fancy dress. (I do love when the people in the pub refuse to answer a simple question and accidentally make fun of the Doctor's outfit and his "wig." Jo charms them there so that's a good scene.) I do wonder how much time has passed. We do know that it's April 30, Beltane. But we don't quite know when the previous stories were and was there a one-year gap between "Terror of the Autons" and "The Mind of Evil?"

The Master is back! This time he has a living stone gargoyle and a bunch of black robed followers. There's a lengthy Black Mass-esque sequence here, which is a mix of real stuff, fake stuff and probably

Pat Gorman. Our favorite villain has got a good gig here as the local vicar. As the White Witch, Miss Hawthorne states, their previous vicar vanished in mysterious circumstances. If the Master can impersonate an Adjudicator or a famous professor who specializes in some sort of mind control, a small village vicar must be super easy for him.

The episode, overall, is quite good. It's got a swift pace. It introduces the setting quickly and does it well. It's a great village and we shall be seeing a lot of it in the next four episodes. It has a wonderfully gothic, spooky atmosphere in sharp contrast to the weird atmosphere of, say, "Terror of the Autons." This is the end of the season and the show's being produced with great confidence.

May I just add how much I enjoy Benton and Yates hanging out and watching TV. Catching some of the dig, watching some of the football highlights. Eating some corned beef. Giggling at the Brig in fancy dress. This story is the height of the UNIT family in more ways than one. The next season will only have two UNIT stories and large portions of those will take place elsewhere. This is the end of this ensemble being such a regular thing. It's a little sad. But, first, I think the Doctor's been frozen solid. Let's see.

The Daemons
Episode Two

Episode 300: (May 29, 1971) Things are getting strange and demonic in the village.
Cliffhanger: A gargoyle attacks Jo and The Doctor at the Hub. (They should stay away from The Hub.)

I love this episode. It is an episode where the Doctor is absent for much of it but he's not on vacation like during the 1960s. He's out of it because the force (of evil or whatever it is) knocks him for such a loop. In an episode that is around 24 minutes and 20 seconds, the Doctor (yelling "Eureka!") doesn't enter the episode properly until 14:52. That's a long time. And, luckily, by this point, the UNIT family has become such a part of the series that we almost forget it happened. It's great to have the Doctor back but we almost forget that he's there for a while. *

While he isn't there, Jo and the villagers get some nice moments together. Her grief at almost losing the Doctor is palpable. You can feel how saddened she is. Which makes it worse when he returns and he chastises here for not knowing Latin. She looks very sad and distressed that he speaks to her like that. Hey, if the Doctor's going to be a jerk maybe they should stay in the coma.

Yates and Benton get the best stuff here. They get to ride in in a helicopter. They get to see the giant cloven hoof marks in the ground. They get to meet up with Jo and get involved in the adventures. It's nice to see them here. There's an expansion of their characters, which never quite gets followed up on but is lovely to see. You can feel Barry Letts, Terrance Dicks and Robert Sloman working towards expanding the characters. Although, at the same time, we knew that Letts and Dicks didn't like this format. So, I'm always a little confused.

Benton gets to team with Miss Hawthorne. And they're a fun couple. The fight between the verger and Benton in the cavern is good stuff, especially when Benton stands in the mandala. May I say? This verger is a jerk. I'm not a fan. And there's some good background, if you hunt it down, for why they set the "Satanic" mass deep in the cavern rather than in the Church itself.

My favorite thing in this episode, I think, is the Heat Shield. The moment where the truck stops and then bursts into flames is fantastic. It's more dramatic that the shield in "Pyramids of Mars". Certainly more Satanic. I love the Brigadier approaching it and losing his swagger stick and a rock. Some have said that maybe The Brig should have been trapped inside with them. I agree. Maybe Yates should have been outside the shield. I'm not sure. It makes for some interesting adventure in the next few episodes.

Yes, the Doctor does seem to be believing in, to some extent, the supernatural, the Devil and the occult. I think we know in our heart that this isn't quite what's happening here. The show is expanding, as it always does. As it does when it is at its best. When the people in charge are fascinated by having all of time and space in front of them. The gargoyle is interesting, certainly. But, the first visit of Azal, unseen as it is, sits in the mind. Something is here. Something huge that travelled in a tiny spaceship. Only the Doctor and the Master really seem to know what's up. Or do they?

*In the Season Ten Blu-Ray set, Steven Moffat makes a brilliant point that only someone who ran the show for 6 seasons could say. He applauds the creation of the UNIT Family and the addition of all these characters. But, at the end of the day, try as hard as you might, people want to see The Doctor. Sorry. It's true. They're the best.

The Daemons
Episode Three

Episode 301: (June 5, 1971) The Doctor reveals what is going on. The Brigadier tries to get through the heat barrier. The Master rallies the town together.
Cliffhanger: Azal rises for a second time. The Master cowers before him.

The third episode begins! There are some great scenes in here. We get some more helicopter stunting. That seems to be a trademark of the action in this era. We get Yates on a motorcycle. We get the Doctor and Jo on Bessie. Explosions and craziness. We get a huge heat dome covering the town like that giant dome that covered Springfield in *The Simpsons Movie*. This is some fun stuff.

We get The Master taking control of an entire village. Not by hypnosis. But simply by getting some intel on the villagers. He knows about Azal. He has control of Bok. And he now has all these people on his side. The good guys number five. The bag guys are legion. And the indeterminate ones are huge and made of stone. Again, this is fun stuff.

This episode has a fantastic scene where the Doctor explains what's happening. And, eventually, he ends up getting picked on by all assembled. We learn the very *Quatermass and The Pit* style story here. We learn that the Deamons were an ancient race that has boosted humanity along. And now, Azal has arrived (or has been waiting) to judge the experiment. OK, so the Doctor seems to know a bit more than he should. But he's the Doctor! Who else is going to know this stuff? The Doctor has slides and occult books. They mention the Rakshasa, an Indian demon. If you know your *Kolchak, the Night Stalker*, you'll be familiar with that one. It's the one that takes the shape of your most trusted person and then kills you. You can tell that Barry Letts and Robert Sloman did their research here.

Oh, did I mention that "Guy Leopold" is Barry Letts and Robert Sloman. (If you knew this bear with me. If you didn't know this, I've got a great story about eye patches from "Inferno" to tell you.) They used a pseudonym constructed from their father-in-law's first names. Barry Letts would use the closing story from this season and the next three to really put his stamp on the show. If you are completely interested in seeing exactly how Mr. Letts thought the show should work, these four stories are the stories to watch. Interesting stories they are too.

How often does a story have the villain cowering in fear from the big, scary thing? Not often. In fact, I can't remember it happening but here it is. The Second Coming of Azal is upon us. The Third is nigh.

The Daemons
Episode Four

Episode 302: (June 12, 1971) Azal is prepping for his third appearance. The good guys are trying to stay alive until then.
Cliffhanger: Azal appears for the third and final time.

This episode is about the Master trying to kill the Doctor before Azal appears for the third time. The legend says, although I guess it's not really a legend, that Azal will appear three times. He will either destroy the experiment or bestow his powers on someone who is in the experiment to carry on. The Master and Azal have a little chat where we learn that 1) Azal might be giving up his powers to someone. 2) he might not 3) it might be the Master 4) it might be the Doctor. So, when Azal goes away, the episode becomes "Kill the Doctor."

The Master seems to be in charge of whenever Azal will appear. He begins to assemble his coven back into place. Surely, he will wait until the Doctor is dead, right? Well, we've seen the Master quite a bit throughout this season. We know that he may not be the most hinged person. We'll see how this goes.

There is a quite a bit of business involving Osgood not being able to get the UNIT convoy through the heat barrier. The Doctor is being super advanced and expecting a UNIT boffin to take care of it. Apparently, Pertwee and the actor playing Osgood didn't get along. One can see why. The Doctor is so high-handed here. He needs the Brig in there to save his friends, especially Jo. So, everyone else is treated like an as*hole. It's not pleasant to watch the Doctor do that. I'm not sure why Letts and Dicks thought it was. You don't want your hero shoving his superiority in another's face especially when he is relying on that person. I like the heat barrier. This portion of the script, however, drives me up the wall. We'll see how it goes in the next episode.

After heat barrier stuff and Jo escaping from rooms onto ladders, it becomes about a weird Mayday celebration with Morris dancers. I'm not going to go into Morris dancers here. Every country has something that they're kind of embarrassed about. We might be at that point with England here. But the Doctor does get tied to a pole. The Bible is invoked. And he might have been burned at the stake if it wasn't for some sharp shenanigans by friends. It's a fun scene. It might be padding. Or it might be, as I said, the Master's big ploy to get the Doctor killed before Azal returns. I can't quite say.

At the end though, the best review of this episode is in Elizabeth Sandifer's TARDIS Eruditorum volume 3. I won't go into what she says because you should own the book. She perfectly nails down what this episode is doing. The moment you read her assessment it becomes clear. And you can't quite watch the episode in the same way again. I'll say this: Remember when we talked about the Terrance Dicks/Malcolm Hulke thing where lots of stuff seemed to happen but when the episode ended nothing had changed... keep an eye and ear out everyone.

The Daemons
Episode Five

Episode 303: (June 19, 1971) Azal appears for the final time. The Doctor, Jo and The Master chat with him in The Cavern. Meanwhile. UNIT fights Bok in the graveyard.
Cliffhanger: May Day has arrived.

OK. Well, the big discussion between everyone in the Cavern is pretty good. Azal is unmoved by everything. He just wants to follow his rules. The Master keeps saying "Give me the power!" While The Doctor is trying desperately to have a discussion amongst all the echoes and the booming voices. If I was The Doctor, I would ask Azal to bring it down a bit. If he can be minuscule or huge, surely there must be a middle ground. One that doesn't involve such a large amount of yelling. Apparently, that's not true but we don't see the Daemons again. Maybe they're just a bunch of yelling jerks? It's tough to gauge.

Anyway, the ending isn't the best. The production text mentions a *Star Trek* episode with a similar sort of ending. I don't doubt that. I don't remember the episode. But I'm a fan of *Next Generation* and the movies not TOS. So, as far as I'm concerned, this is just fine. But, yes, it is odd that Azal dies as he does. He and his people created this world and self-sacrifice confuses him? I think Barry Letts and Robert Sloman are the only people who are convinced by the ending.

The rest of the episode is entertaining. Bok is a fun, if slightly silly, guardian of the cavern. It's probably the tongue-sticking out that does it. *Doctor Who* has a long history of doing things that make you pause and go "Why that?" The plunger on the Dalek is very functional for the first Dalek story. After that, it can confuse people. "Dalek" makes the plunger a threat. Thank goodness for that. But, Bok, if he were to return, would be more like a Weeping Angel. Thank God none of them were sticking their tongues out.

The episode begins with the threat of the huge Daemon Azal. It works itself out all right. Even giving five minutes at the end to wrap up the Master threat and to have a wonderful UNIT family moment. It's quite sweet. "Maybe there is magic in the world after all." The camera zooms back and we see Maypole dancers and Morris dancers and assembled people watching everything. They do look a bit like an assembled group watching *Doctor Who* being filmed. But, in the story, a church just did blow up. So, that would have brought in plenty of people to goggle at things. And the Maypole dance is a tradition. Yes, the Doctor is a bit too tall for it. It still goes well and ends the serial on a high.

Overall, it's a strong story. We had that weird pacing/ plot thing in episode four. Some of it is a bit clunky. However, this is the producer's vision of the show. Enclosing a British village in a heat dome with a demon and a crazy Time Lord works quite well. Apart from a moment here or there, the story moves. (Overall, apart from much of "The Colony of Space," the season has strong pacing.) There's a genuine sense of climax and ending to this episode. I do wish UNIT had defeated Bok. He is destroyed because Azal is destroyed. Oh well. That's nitpicking though.

A fine season. Maybe CSO got overused. Some say The Master was. From now on, we won't see him this much again. Nor will we see the UNIT family this much. We see the Master twice in the next season, once in the Tenth. Then he's not back until the 14th. If you want to complain about him being too prevalent in this season, remember that he only appears occasionally from now on. (Not counting Missy.) I prefer the previous season's stories. The joie de vivre of this season makes it special.

SEASON NINE
1972

DAY OF THE DALEKS
Written by Louis Marks
Directed by Paul Bernard
Episode One

Episode 304: (January 1, 1972) Ghosts are bothering a UN level negotiator. UNIT investigates. Cliffhanger: The Daleks announce the extermination of anyone operating one of those time machines.

The new season begins! As with the other Pertwee seasons, something big happens. The Daleks return! And they return in an intriguing time travel story. As much as *Doctor Who* was a time travel show back in its original run, it didn't do a lot of time related stories. We had the time loop in the previous season. We jumped a timeline in "The Space Museum." But, generally, there wasn't a lot of big-time stuff happening.

At this point, we are completely ensconced in the Letts/ Dicks/ Pertwee/ Manning era. The show is being enjoyed. People are getting a kick out of it. * And they have brought the Daleks back. Yes, there are only three of them. Yes, their voices are wrong. And yes, they only appear for about a minute. Some of that can be explained away. Some of it... not so much. Having the Dalek first appear at the end of episode one is classic. But then, why does that one Dalek appear for a split second 13 minutes in? (On the commentary for the DVD, Barry Letts misses it.) To me, that's the director throwing in a bit of a teaser. Some have called it a mistake. I presume that they mean an aesthetic mistake because this shot is clearly chosen. Is it a good idea? Well.... not so much.

We haven't seen the Daleks since the Summer of 1968 in the repeat of "Evil of the Daleks." We haven't had a new story since the Summer of 1967 with the original airing of "Evil of the Daleks." Pop culture-wise, that's a hell of a leap. We've gone from the time of James Bond, hippies and flower power. We're now in the land of prog rock, Norman Lear sitcoms, Dirty Harry and Shaft. Things are very different. So, what do the Daleks mean now? They were very specifically haters of everyone who wasn't them in the past. Will things be different now? It is tough to say as they don't do much here. They seem the same.

The Doctor and Jo are charming. They have a scene where they meet themselves in the beginning. The Doctor has some lovely wine and cheese. Jo gets flustered. But she looks adorable and that miniskirt is one of my favorites. Benton and Yates get some cool stuff to do. The Brig is large and in charge. But, if one knows the show, one also knows that this is kind of the last "regular" UNIT story like this. "The Time Monster" is all over the place. "The Three Doctors" is something special. "The Green Death" leaves Yates out for a bunch of it. And then we go into other realms. Even this story has large chunks of it outside of the present day. It's a tricky thing: The UNIT era. It ends rather quickly. Dicks and Letts have said that they didn't particularly like this setup. This season begins their deconstruction of it.

The episode itself is a good one. The guerilla aspect is intriguing. The future world with the strange silvery faced people is odd. The Ogrons are charming. Especially the one who doesn't know at what speed to deliver his lines. And the Daleks appearing means that something big has happened. That's why the Daleks were added to the story. They weren't originally in it. They were added to open the season stronger. You see the Daleks and you know that we're all in trouble. What sort of trouble though? What the heck is happening here? Let's keep watching.

*Although in true British fashion, one of the people who quite enjoyed the show in the previous season derides the tiredness of the show now.

Day of the Daleks
Episode Two

Episode 305: (January 8, 1972) The Doctor and Jo go to a Dalek-led future.
Cliffhanger: The Doctor, in a tunnel, sees some Daleks.

The Doctor and the Daleks meet again! Albeit briefly. But that's got to be an interesting feeling. The last time he saw them he had declared it the end of the Daleks. Timewise, for all intents and purposes it was. But, in a story about time, it makes sense that the Daleks would return. Because it's no longer the end anymore.

Although, this is a pretty rum bunch of Daleks. In the Special Edition DVD, Nick Briggs does the voices. He's the man who has done all the Dalek voices since 2005. In the original televised version, the voices are lame. In a similar fashion to the TADRIS materializing so oddly in "Colony In Space," the team seem to have forgotten how Daleks talk. And maybe what they're like in general. There are only three of them. Are they some sort of breakaway group who somehow got control of Earth and forget how to talk? They're startlingly unmenacing in this story. They don't do much but yell at the Controller. Now, they do go to our Earth time in the end. But they haven't done much yet.

Meanwhile, the Ogrons and the Guerillas are running around shooting each other with disintegrator guns. And then, the Doctor joins in on the action. I think if I were younger, I might not have said "Hey! The Doctor just disintegrated two Ogrons!" Now, as an older fellow, I find it a bit odd. It's so casually done though. Everyone's doing it! And, in the Special Edition, the "disintegration" is a "disintegration." I guess if there was a Doctor who'd do this it would be this one. But, then the Second Doctor did evaporate Ice Warriors in "The Seeds of Death." Sometimes when the action gets going the morality goes out the window.

Jo gets to meet the Controller. We should know something's wrong when he described the Ogrons to her. It can't be good if these giant brutes are basically their "police force." They have a nice conversation in which Jo seems incredible gullible. Maybe it's his very comfy chair. I wonder if he's the only one that's allowed a comfy chair. (Also, the strange coincidences of time travel are multiplying here. Jo holds up the time machine box at the moment it turns on. The Doctor rounds a corner at the moment the Dalek appears. Time Coincidences!) She seems oddly charmed by this silver faced man. I guess as long as he's not an Ogron, right? My favorite moment is when they're done talking and Jo leaves the room. Where's she going? She just got there. Is she going back to the spot where she materialized? It's weird. They finished talking and she leaves. Jo, come back! We didn't tell you to go anywhere. Time Disorientation!

Overall, an excellent episode. Things may slow down a bit with the guerillas in the middle. But, generally, there's always something happening and we're slowly getting bits and bobs of what was going on and what the time travelers are up to. We still have more to learn though.

Note: I don't know how interesting this is but reading the novelization of this one several years before seeing it taught me the word "guerillas." Now, the cover of the book had a drawing of an Ogron on it. I thought that the Ogron was some sort of gorilla. And I thought "guerilla" was the British spelling of "gorilla" and that the "guerillas" in the story looked like that. I checked a dictionary eventually and it all got cleared up. Hey, I think that was kind of interesting.

Day of the Daleks
Episode Three

Episode 306: (January 15, 1972) The Doctor meets the people in charge of this incorrect future. He doesn't like them. The feeling is mutual.
Cliffhanger: The Doctor is having his mind probed while the Daleks yell at him.

Again, what we asked in previous Dalek stories where they take over a world is: what are they up to? I know that we got a fun explanation in "The Dalek Invasion of Earth." But what are they doing here? We don't yet know how they took over the Earth again. Maybe it was just three of them that got lucky. What we see is three of the dullest Daleks ever repeating themselves and saying nothing of importance over and over again. There's a scene where they talk to the Ogrons and its hilariously not so good. I'm glad the Daleks are back. But someone should have taken a moment and checked with somebody who had made one previously. Where was Douglas Camfield when you needed him?

To me, this is all some sort of satire on the way corporate Britain/ America/ maybe anywhere works. You know the supervisors, like the one-way traitor guy. You have the person in charge of the department, like the Controller. Then, you have "upper management" who are so disconnected from day-to-day reality that they think pushing people toward death is A-OK. As long as their profits are good and the stockholders are happy. This episode has one of my favorite things in it. The Daleks note that production has dropped. The Controller points out that they're pushing people too hard. People are too old or too young. Upper management doesn't care, in fact they raise the work quota by 10%. I have heard that more times than I care to say. You're pushing the workers to failure or, in some cases, death. When you try to reason with those in charge, they don't want to hear it and they probably wouldn't understand or care if they did. The poor Controller with his grapes and his nice wine thinks he means something. No. He's in charge of a bunch of old people who spend their days hauling around stones. The scene where The Doctor calls him out on it is a great one. (The scene where the Doctor is being mistreated by the guards is also great. Some good Pertwee acting in this episode.)

All but the recap and very start takes place in the 22nd Century. So, the shift here is interesting. Two episodes of trying to murder Styles becomes: How did the Daleks get in charge of the planet? In fact, Styles is almost gone from the episode, as is UNIT. And the guerillas aren't particularly interesting here. The one who keeps complaining is particularly tiresome. I love how we are 3/4s through and we still really don't know exactly what happened.

OK. The chase on the trike thing, which I had just seen one of in *Diamonds Are Forever*, that's filler. Watching the Ogrons trying not to catch the Doctor and Jo on this slow-moving vehicle is amusing. I wish he could take it into the past.

Day of the Daleks
Episode Four

Episode 307 (January 22, 1972) The truth about this future is revealed.
Cliffhanger: The Doctor tells Styles to bring world peace.

In this episode, it becomes very apparent that there are three Daleks and that's it. The DVD production text notes that there are 3 ½. The half is used when one Dalek is blown up. The scene with several Ogrons and three Wobbly Daleks approaching Auderly House is a decent one. But it's clearly just three Daleks. The Special Edition does a sweet job of covering this up by adding more heft to everything. However, it does seem strange to me that they would do a Dalek story when their Dalek resources were so limited.

Luckily, the story itself is excellent. Normally, exposition doesn't hold out this long. Normally, at this point in the story, we're working to wrap up everything up. Here we get the big twist about 14 minutes before the end. It is a good one. The guerrillas caused their own future. Hopefully, it's changed now. It's a wonderful moment. Because there is a great weirdness when the Daleks don't quite explain how they are there. They don't quite make it clear what happened. *About Time Volume 3*, both editions, have an excellent essay during this story about How Time Works? It discusses whether the Daleks invaded the Earth and discovered it was in ruins. Or whether they saw the Earth was in ruins and invaded. It's fascinating. I do like that we get a sort of explanation for the constant mining and factory stuff. The Dalek empire is expanding and they need an influx of raw materials.

It's not much of a Dalek story, as many have said. But it's a hell of a good *Doctor Who* story. I also learned the word "quisling" here. And it's nice to see The Controller calmly changing sides and accepting his death… because if The Doctor succeeds than none of this will have ever happened. Again though, putting the Daleks in here is as important as putting them in "Power of the Daleks." We know the power (sorry) of the Daleks but we also know the Power of the Doctor and having them here makes the stakes so much higher.

I love a good time travel story. So far, the Letts and Dicks brigade is doing some good work here. And, no, I'm not talking about Jo's red knickers. They do make some odd choices here and there. (The scene on the trike. The lack of actual Daleks.) But this still works well. I do wish there was a bit more UNIT. I'm starting to miss them already. But now we know that the Daleks are out there again and the Master is in prison, it bodes well for some craziness in the future.

Note: I always remember reading the novelization and loving the closing scene in it. The Doctor and Jo appear at the TARDIS console in the opposite version of their opening scene. I can see why they cut it from the televised version. Watching the House blow up, knowing that that whole future timeline has now changed. Knowing that the Daleks are now not the rulers of Earth. And hearing the Doctor's plea for peace is much more dramatic. But, gosh, I liked that scene anyways.

THE CURSE OF PELADON
Written by Brian Hayles
Directed by Lennie Mayne
Episode One

Episode 308: (January 29, 1972) The Doctor and Jo are sent to the medieval planet Peladon as part of the Federation. Mr. Spock is not involved.
Cliffhanger: The statue of Aggedor begins to fall on the delegates.

Another adventure off Earth. The Doctor has the TARDIS console inside the TARDIS sometimes and sometimes it's in his lab. As I mentioned in "Colony in Space," The Time Lords are in their own special space in time. So, it's not "lucky" that the TARDIS is sent to Peladon at that time. The Time Lords would have waited until the Doctor put the console back inside and then they would have sent him. * Anyway, the Doctor and Jo are sent to the planet Peladon.

The Federation are arriving. The King (played by David Troughton) and his two advisors await the delegates. There is a curse in the Kingdom, a giant bear thing called Aggedor. The High Priest wants Peladon left alone. He doesn't want the Federation near the planet. The adviser doesn't. The adviser is killed almost immediately. (Dammit, one week from retirement!) The delegates arrive. Alpha Centauri, who is tough to describe, is one. (Once you've seen them, you can't forget them.) Arcturus is another. I think he's awesome. His people look like weird octopus/ Medusa heads in glass cases getting sprayed with liquid. (This would be handled a bit better with Sil.) And then there are the Ice Warriors.

But the twist is that they're good here. A "monster" from the previous era has become good. Granted, the ones in "The Ice Warriors" were trying desperately to get off Earth. So, we've no real concept of how they acted previously. "The Seeds of Death" ones were not nice. Here they are part of the Federation. And, of course, we see how that happens in "The Empress of Mars," a long, long time from now. (I wonder why the name "The Doctor" didn't carry down as he was the one who introduced them to Alpha Centauri.) It's a great twist and one of the great moments in this episode.

The other one comes when the TARDIS falls off the cliff. It dropped off a cliff or a hill or something in "The Romans." We don't know how far that was and the Doctor keeps reassuring everyone that the TARDIS will be fine. Here, we see the TARDIS topple in slow mo. It's a beautiful shot as the drop seems to be forever. Also, isn't the castle model on the side of that cliff one of the coolest things ever? It gives us no concept of how this world, or this land, works. Having a castle so precariously perched so high up on a mountain is a fantasy conceit. And I love it. Anyway, this is the episode where the Doctor outright says that the TARDIS is "indestructible." Which is something I've always loved.

Overall, it's an interesting start to a story. Some court intrigue, some interesting monsters, Jo pretending to be a Princess and flirting with a King. Also, like the first episode of "Colony In Space," it makes one think "Where are we going from here? Here's hoping, things will get more exciting." We'll find out.

*How he gets the TARDIS console inside and outside is, of course, a question that we can't answer. Especially when "Colony In Space" has a moment where the Doctor asks how the giant lizard got through the small door.

The Curse of Peladon
Episode Two

Episode 309: (February 5, 1972) A series of misadventures and red herrings and suspects and things litter this episode. Ending with a moment that is either super annoying or super dramatic.
Cliffhanger: The Doctor is sentenced to death.

The first episode had a very *Star Trek* feel to it. It's known that Terrance Dicks enjoyed the original series when it aired on the BBC. Talk of the Federation mixed with the general set-up and feel of everything is, to me, very Trek. I'm not a huge fan of the Original Series. I quite enjoy the six movies and Next Gen. But the original series isn't a favorite of mine from that time. I'd rather watch *The Wild, Wild West*. It's just as repetitive as Trek but more fun. I find the original Trek to be rather stoic, stodgy and kind of dull. That's what the first episode felt like. Luckily, Brian Hayles seems to have a different plan here.

At this point, this is very much a mystery. Someone is up to something. Granted, Hepesh clearly wants the Doctor to be killed. In fact, he basically says so. There is something else happening. Arcturus is attacked. Jo finds something incriminating in the Ice Warriors room. The Doctor is led by Grun through some dark caverns. Jo encounters Aggedor. We learn that the Ice Warriors are no longer warriors. So maybe it's time that they changed their name. Alpha Centauri does little. But something is working here to foment trouble amongst the delegates. And it works. It transforms an episode that could have bogged down, because the story isn't terribly dynamic, into one that's in a far more interesting space.

I think that's down to the direction, personally. This is the first all studio show we have had since... I don't know. (I wish I'd included an index.) This medieval/ cave strewn world of Peladon wins me over even when the story doesn't do much for me. I wonder if the shenanigans of this episode are important to the overall adventure. Or whether they're just some fun filler? Or whether they were originally the point of the adventure? I have not read either of the novelizations but I'd like to think they maybe have a little more for us. One of the things they always say is how this show was about the British Empire entering the Common Market at that time. That's great. As someone who enjoys history, it is interesting to me. I can see how other people wouldn't give a care about it. So, it's an odd episode that is fun but also seems to be goofing. It's not a farce but it almost is. When Jo ends up on a ledge outside the castle, I sense farce around the corner, which doesn't happen. But it's still interesting.

Now, whether you like the ending of the Episode, as I mentioned, is up to you. I find it abrupt and annoying. I'm sure there are some who find it super dramatic.

The Curse of Peladon
Episode Three

Episode 310: (February 12, 1972) The intrigue increases. The Doctor must fight Grun in a pit. Cliffhanger: The fight is over. Guns are drawn.

I thought I'd start this review with two bits of interest. Again, they're things I find interesting. 1) The ratings for this episode dropped by three million, which is rough. There was a reason for that. Britain was in the middle of a miner's strike. For episodes three and four, the country was in a state of emergency and there were many power cuts. So, it's not as if people didn't want to see it. They simply couldn't. 2) This was the first *Doctor Who* story shot out of production order. Today, that happens all the time. But, back then, this was the first. They had two off world stories and two on-world stories. The Earth ones were being shot first. So, we got out of order serials. That will happen again.

As far as the episode goes, it's another good one. Again, I don't find it utterly spectacular. There is just too much meandering around hallways and caves. I love those torches that unhook from the wall and open secret passages, I also love ice cream and I'd be sick if I ate that all day. The political machinations continue. It is great seeing the delegates argue without the Doctor there. There is something very "Only in *Doctor Who*" about it. But it also has that kind of blah that the original *Star Trek* had. It hasn't shed that. I think because, unlike the previous story, it's starting to feel like this may have been a great three-parter. As it is, the meandering is going on just a touch too long.

The best scene is probably Jo talking with the King. Poor guy. He sentences the Doctor to death and then asks Jo to marry him. He keeps stumbling over social niceties that continually appall Jo. I think this is one of Katy Manning's best scenes in the series. (Later on, when she breaks up the Doctor trying to hypnotize Aggedor, we get a bit of the Annoying Jo.) Her and Mr. Troughton are excellent together even if the hairstyles of the people of Peladon will never leave my mind and not in a great way. There is a very worthy story here but sometimes one prefers a little more pizzazz. And the final fight is a good one.

Lennie Mayne isn't a dynamic director. That happens a lot throughout the 1970s and the early 1980s. When the show should be moving along fiercely, it's a stage play. I know how they shot it. Look what Graeme Harper did with "The Caves of Androzani." That was shot the same way. So, it's not the way it was made, it's the director. Everyone seems to have nice things to say about Mayne. So, I think he ran a fun ship. But it can be tough to stay focused, especially during the repetitive bits of this story.

The final fight, on film, in a pit (actually a water tank) is pretty darn good. The enclosed space. Terry Walsh giving it his all as Pertwee's stuntman. Some good flips, some good falls. It's all followed by a cliffhanger ending that seems to make little sense but will when the next episode gets rolling. There are a few too many quick cuts and "What?!" moments this time around.

And, oh yes, the Doctor gets a fun scene with a giant bear thing. Aggedor! The Doctor sings a Venusian lullaby to Aggedor as he hypnotizes the bear. It's cool. Then, as mentioned, Jo shows up. But this bodes well as a future ally for the Doctor. One episode left, let's dive in.

The Curse of Peladon
Episode Four

Episode 311: (February 19, 1972) The intrigue builds to a breaking point. Will Peladon collapse and take everyone with it?
Cliffhanger: The real Earth Delegate arrives. WHAT?!?!?

I think the real American influences shine through in this episode. They do so in a way that I am not 100% sure I can explain but I'm going to try. First off, this episode is one of those where it seems like, at the start, that things are wrapped up. At least for a moment. They're not. Because of a big event at the cliffhanger (or slightly later in the episode), the focus of everything shifts.

Arcturus and Hepesh are in cahoots. Arcturus is killed. Hepesh escapes. But he has not been relieved of power so he assembles a contingent of guards to take the palace and overthrow the King. The Delegates radio equipment has all been destroyed. * And the episode takes on a more immediate feel than the other ones. Although, The Doctor and Grun recruiting Aggedor isn't particularly zippy.

That leads to my thought. Many American shows from this time, specifically hour-long ones, do a thing where for quite some time I'm not that interested. But, somewhere in there, as I'm watching, I fall in love with the episode and I've been moved. An example: *Tales of the Gold Monkey*. 1983. There is an episode called "Ape Boy." It is about a boy on an island raised by apes. Sarah, Corky, Jake and Jack arrive and meet him. There are also some people from a circus trying to capture him. When I heard the premise, I was not that interested. For about 15 minutes, I wasn't interested. But then there were a few twists, the character development kicked in and, by the end, I had a tear in my eye. I couldn't forget those first fifteen minutes but by the end it had won me over. "The Curse of Peladon" does the same thing. To me, that's very American. If "Day of the Daleks" episode one had been like this story's episode one, I don't know that I would have kept watching. I'm interested to see this feeling comes up again. I don't think of Doctor Who like that. I think of it as generally more entertaining overall. Let's see. Every new regime on the show does something new. That's why they're the "new regime."

Setting that aside, it's a decent episode. There's a fun fight scene in the palace. The Doctor and Aggedor become pals. The Doctor and Jo discuss the Time Lords controlling him. The King and Jo have one last scene. And Amazonia, the Earth delegate arrives to goof everything up. It really does have a ton of stuff going on, not counting the giant one-eyed, six-armed green thing with the high-pitched voice. Overall, it's kind of a triumph in its own way.

And it all ends with a great shot of Amazonia, the Earth delegate, mouth wide open watching the TARDIS disappear... while, out of focus, to the left, we see Alpha Centauri's huge eye. All I can say is: I hope the Federation is going to be as beneficial as they say they will be. Only time will tell.

*The production text makes a very good point here. In *Doctor Who*, the Doctor and friends always landed on the planet or wherever. The Enterprise (as far as I can recollect) never landed on anything. They beamed people down. In other shows, shuttlecrafts were sent. In this serial, the ships of the delegates are in orbit and they travelled down to the planet via whatever. The Ice Warriors assume that she has a ship up there. This isn't *Star Trek* and she sure doesn't. There's an odd blue box somewhere around here. They'll leave in that. Thank you very much.

THE SEA DEVILS
Written by Malcolm Hulke
Directed by Michael E. Briant
Episode One

Episode 312: (February 26, 1972) The Doctor and Jo go to visit The Master on a prison island. Then, they visit a sea fortress where weird happenings have been reported.
Cliffhanger: The Sea Devil meets the Doctor and Jo.

A new story begins on Earth! Oddly enough, there's no sign of the Brig or the rest of the gang. And oddly enough this episode is very much split in two parts. 1) Visiting the Master and 2) Visiting the naval base and the sea base thing. That's a lot more incident than the first episode of "The Curse of Peladon," which makes this episode feel more like current *Doctor Who*. And I'm all for it. A one-off like the last story is fine but the show must be the show.

It's nice to see the Master again. The director has chosen a great location. An old castle-esque building on an island in the middle of nowhere. There's a ridiculous old bureaucrat in charge and a bunch of guards dressed as... I don't know what. French Foreign legion? The Doctor and The Master have a brief, but nice, chat. As always, throughout the history of the show, they can have chats like this but the Master always has something evil in mind. We know that. It's the Master!

I love how, once the Doctor and Jo leave, it is immediately revealed that the Master has complete control over the island. The UNIT family goes through all that trouble. They chase the Master all around the world. They get him sent to the most secure island in the world. And he probably had them all hypnotized within fifteen minutes. Plus, he gets a color TV! Which many of the viewing public wouldn't have had. And he watches "The Clangers" on it! I've never seen "The Clangers" but it looks fun. There is no justice.

The Naval scenes are entertaining. I've always liked the head guy's secretary. The Doctor still refusing to carry a pass after all this time is either the height of arrogance or honest to goodness laziness. And we're getting a nice mystery off to one side here. When the Master appears, we think that that will be the story. How wrong can we be? There's going to be a lot more happening here. And some of it will involve a great rig thing.

Isn't that rig thing/ sea fortress fantastic? This giant round metal thing parked in the middle of the North Sea. What a place. I'd love a proper tour of it. I'm convinced by the sets but those are sets. I'd love to know what it's really like. There's such a nice feeling of covering more than one space in this story. It's nice to be back on Earth. But this is a six-part story. Let's see if filler begins to set in. "Peladon" didn't really have filler, apart from some walking through corridors. It just moved slow. This episode moves very fast. I'm interested to see what will happen next.

The Sea Devils
Episode Two

Episode 313: (March 4, 1972) The Master's machinations increase. The Doctor discovers that everyone at the prison is on the Master's side.
Cliffhanger: The Master throws a knife at the Doctor.

This is going to be one of those stories where we're able to get from places that seem to be quite some distance from one another in moments. From the rig to the Naval base to the prison. It all takes seconds. That's OK though because it keeps everything moving along nicely, even if possibility is stretched. I'd forgotten that the big Scotsman who goes delirious and yells about "Sea Devils" played the original Jabba The Hut.

Anyway, the Master and the Doctor have a lovely swordfight together. In and all around the prison cell. The Master is so convinced that he's better than the Doctor at everything that he thinks he can win the fight. He's losing from moment one, pretty much. There's a moment on the table where they speed up the image slightly. That's obvious and too bad. What are you going to do? I do like the Doctor eating a bit of sandwich as he fights the Master. It's just like finishing his wine as he's beating up guerillas in "Day of the Daleks." This is one suave cat. Although, I think the outfit probably gave that away.

Question: how does this happen? Whenever the good guys order gates to be closed and for no one to be let off a base, the bad guys always seems to be able to sneak off right before that happens… but when the bad guys do the same thing, the good guys can never get away? Trenchard and The Master get off the Naval Base. But Jo ain't getting off the prison grounds. Evil is more efficient, I guess. They keep those buses running.

Then there are the Sea Devils. The Doctor quickly gauges who they are. And he calls the Silurians, the Eocenes. (Because Silurian was wrong but apparently Eocene is wrong too. So, it's a lose-lose.) The Sea Devils and Silurians get to join the ranks of villains/ monsters like the Ice Warriors and Chumblies. They get named by someone else but keep that name. The Ice Warriors in the previous story say that they aren't warriors anymore. But they are still called "The Ice Warriors." That's unfortunate. Anyway, what we see here of the Sea Devils looks very promising.

Possibly my favorite moment of this episode, though, is the Doctor making the transistor radio into the two-way radio. There are some topical jokes. There's some technobabble. Then it ends up working but exploding in the Doctor's hands. He pulls a great face when that happens. And we'll leave this episode there. Knives out!

The Sea Devils
Episode Three

Episode 314: (March 11, 1972) The Doctor is arrested by Trenchard. Jo runs around the prison grounds. A nuclear submarine is put out of commission. And...
Cliffhanger: The Sea Devils rise from the waves.

Classic cliffhanger time! The Doctor and Jo are being chased across the prison grounds. They rush out onto the beach. The Master and Trenchard are on a hilltop. The Master has a gadget. A dune buggy with guards pulls up in front of the escapees, blocking them from the water. The only other direction is through a minefield. (It all made sense until the minefield. Did an 8-year-old come up with that?) Then, the Master operates his doodad (no laughing) and a Sea Devil rises from the water.

Doctor Who cliffhangers are an integral part of the show. That's why we still have them today. That's why Chris Chibnall loaded "Flux" with the craziest cliffhangers he could come up with. Others have discussed the way cliffhangers work on the show. But I'll just mention it briefly here. There are cliffhangers that are shocks. There are cliffhangers that are big reveals. There are more subtle cliffhangers that change the balance of a show. This is a shock reveal. The Sea Devil rising from the waves under the Master's control is always going to be awesome. The previous episode's cliffhanger was a good old-fashioned "How's he going to get out of that?" The first cliffhanger was a shock. The Sea Devil! Or what the hell is that?

So, this cliffhanger is an excellent one. In an episode where the Doctor is mainly tied to a chair and Jo mostly creeps around, that's nice to see. Has anyone ever rated the cliffhangers? On a scale of 1 to 10, say? That would be interesting. How will they get out of that? What's going to happen next? What the heck just happened? What was that? All parts of the repertoire. It's something to think about. The Cliffhanger Rating Index. (Volume 3?)

The rest of the episode is fine. The introduction of the nuclear sub that is pulled to the bottom of the sea is an interesting touch. It's nice to have this additional group of people involved. Going back and forth between the Naval base and the prison was starting to get a touch of strain. (I did like Trenchard giving the Naval Captain the bum's rush though. Oh Trenchard!) We don't really know who these people are on the sub so it's a little tough to care. Time will tell. It always does.

Jane at the Naval Base is Maggie from "Fury From The Deep!" That's where I sort of recognized her but not really as only one scene with her in it exists from that story so I forgive myself.

The Sea Devils
Episode Four

Episode 315: (March 18, 1972) The Doctor and Jo get back to the naval base. The Master summons a group of Sea Devils. The Doctor decides to go underwater to find the missing nuclear sub and the Sea Devils.
Cliffhanger: The diving bell is pulled up and the Doctor is gone!

The Doctor escapes with Jo by running through a minefield. And they're OK. The Doctor uses the mines to repel the Sea Devil brought up from the sea. There is a moment here when the Doctor drops himself onto razor wire to protect Jo from it. It looks crazy to me but it turns out to work OK. I guess you have to land on the wire just right. Or maybe he has enough layers on to keep himself from being ripped up. The story goes: The second time the Third Doctor leaps down on the wire... Jon Pertwee bruised a rib. He bruised his rib early in the shot and it goes on for some time. That's a trooper. Watching his face throughout, I think you can see that he doesn't feel great.

This could account for the way The Doctor acts towards Jo later. He's very rude to her when they get back to the Naval Base. When she tries to explain what's happening, he says to leave the explanations to him. When she's brought sandwiches, the Doctor intercepts them and eats them all. Even giving some to others and he seems oblivious. He knows exactly what's happening and he's being a jerk because his rib hurts.

Meanwhile, the Master activates his thingy machine and the Sea Devils arise. Trenchard dies fighting. Fighting something he really doesn't seem to understand. He's an interesting character because he dominates so much of the first three episodes. Then he's killed by the Sea Devils and no one really cares. There are certainly characters like this in the show and in life. He was misguided but he thought he was doing the right thing. Godspeed, Trenchard!

There is a lot of wonderful Naval footage shown within the episode. Well, stock Naval footage shown within the episode. It's incorporated around The Doctor, Jo and Captain Hart being taken up to the huge ship. Plus the diving bell stuff. Lowering it, extracting it. The closing shot of Jo in the bell and no one else being there. It feels like the sort of shoot that some people would have gotten seasick on. And that's exactly what happened. But it's still awesome. I'm glad Barry Letts pushed for the Navy to help them. There are a few moments where we forget what we're watching and just enjoy seeing machinery and equipment most of us are unfamiliar with.

At the end of the episode, things don't look great. But, luckily, thanks to the intro of the sub guys, things are going along OK. The Sea Devils have not fully and properly entered the story. And the Master's schemes will become known. Where did the Doctor go?

The Sea Devils
Episode Five

Episode 316: (March 25, 1972) The Sea Devil invasion has begun. They have shanghaied the sub. They have spoken to the Doctor. Also, the guy from the Ministry has arrived. He will be useless.
Cliffhanger: The Sea Devils are here.

Walker, I think, is the straw that broke the Doctor's camel's back here. Walker arrives as the representative of the government. Malcolm Hulke specifically represents him, (I have not read the novelization) as a gluttonous and stupid piece of garbage. Someone that somehow got into a position of power, probably through a family connection, and now has the exact same outlook as Trenchard but in a far more powerful position.

As mentioned, he is a glutton. Constantly shoveling food into his face. There is a fun Belgium film from this time called *The Devil's Nightmare*. It's about a succubus killing a group of people in a mansion. The people represent the Seven Deadly Sins. The glutton meets a particularly gross and greasy end. I wish Walker would've had a similar experience. No matter what happens here, he will be fine.

There is the moment where the Doctor asks Walker to allow him to broker a peace with the Sea Devils. Walker says, "You didn't do so great the first time." The Doctor pauses and then basically says the same thing again. That is, for me, a very weird moment in the show. The First Doctor would have lashed out. The companions may have tried to restrain him. He would not have taken that lightly. The Second Doctor would have looked at Walker without saying a word and then done his own thing. This Doctor looks at Walker and basically capitulates. "Please let me try again."

I think it's time for this Doctor to start wrapping up his constant peace with humans.

Otherwise, the nuclear sub escapes. They never quite made an emotional connection with the story, which is weird. But they are part of it. The Doctor gets them free. Also, I mentioned this earlier but it becomes a big thing now, it's very strange to me that everything seems to be within walking distance of everything else. Watch the Doctor go to the Sea Devil base and then get freed and then go to the Naval Base. It almost seems to be in real time. That's not a story issue. It is a pacing/ editing issue. Once you realize it's happening, it's tough to pay attention to anything else.

The rest of the episode is good. The Master is a jerk. The Doctor is being the best. But then, humans crap all over it and he is suddenly in the wrong and the Master is in the right. That seems very Human Being. Even though human beings are barely involved in this transaction. It's a very good story. It's the simple version of "The Silurians." But, even simplified, it still generally works. Mainly because it keeps that pace going. Let's see what the finale has for us.

The Sea Devils
Episode Six

Episode 317: (April 1, 1972) Chaos reigns supreme. The Sea Devils are everywhere. The Master is near victory. And the Doctor tries to stop the madness.
Cliffhanger: The Master escapes in a giant hovercraft.

Walker is what we call a "douchebag." I will leave it at that.

It occurs to me that this is the last of the "exile" stories that takes place entirely on "modern" Earth. "The Mutants" goes out into space. "The Time Monster" spends an episode on the TARDIS/ in the void and two episodes in the past in Atlantis. And "The Three Doctors" is mostly in the world of Omega. So, this is the point where everyone got sick of this, not just the Doctor. The UNIT era, as it were, goes by rather quickly in hindsight. We still will get Earth UNIT stories, at least three more. (Four if you sort of include "Planet of the Spiders.") This is the first signpost of the end of this era. (Of course, not having UNIT in it is certainly another sign.)

This episode is as anti-climactic as the last episode of the Silurian story is climactic. It's obvious that the Sea Devil and human peace isn't going to work. Especially with the Sea Devils attacking the naval base in force at the start. The whole second attempt to broker peace feels like a waste of time. Normally, the filler in a story like this is in the middle. Here, it's the ending. We're 95% sure that the Doctor won't succeed. Having the Master hanging around doesn't help. Everything we think will happen is what happens, except this time the Doctor doesn't really seem to care.

The other thing that makes this doubly anticlimactic is that we're pretty sure the Master is going to get away. Again. So, the storyline is: The Doctor attempts to broker peace with the reptiles, again. He fails, again. They get blown up, again. Then, he and the Master have a wild jet ski chase and the Master escapes, again. The whole thing feels like we could have just let the Master escape at the end of the last episode and Walker could have just blown everything up.

As great as it is to see Cowardly Walker, his intro near the end of this serial isn't as interesting as the virus storyline in "Silurians." You can see what they're doing. This character can speed us towards the jumbled ending faster than any other one except the Master, but we don't want him succeeding. So, they bring him in and he wrecks everything, getting us to the climax. We've seen far too many characters like this over the past few seasons. I can see that Hulke was making Walker into a powerful glutton who couldn't oversee a Shoe Town in the mall let alone be in a true position of power. Hulke seems to have given up too. There's no way the Doctor will succeed so let's go crazy.

The episode is entertaining. It's just anti-climactic. There's plenty of shooting and explosions. Lots of Sea Devils flipping through the air. Boat stuff. Jet ski stuff. This, that and the other. A lot of sound and fury. It was probably (I believe it was) well-loved by the kids of the era. I can feel the drag though. If you watch all six episodes in order, it really becomes obvious. (So, really, don't watch them that way.) At least, Barry Letts got to play with Naval stuff.

THE MUTANTS
By Bob Baker and Dave Martin
Directed by Christopher Barry
Episode One

Episode 318: (April 8, 1972) The Doctor and Jo go to the planet Solos. They are sent by the Time Lords with a mysterious box thing meant for... Who knows?
Cliffhanger: Ky and Jo vanish in the teleporter.

Solos! The Skybase! A mysterious container! We're on an adventure around the year 3000. We're 5 hundred years after the world of "Colony In Space." At that point, the Earth Empire seemed to be at its height. Here, it's a bankrupt mess. They're giving independence to Solos after apparently gutting it and leaving it a slagheap with the people on it mutating due to the Earthling's interference. (This certainly doesn't bode well for the Peladonians, I think.)

We meet the Natives in their fun robes and long-haired wigs. We meet the Earth people in their dull outer space outfits. We meet the Marshall, obviously the bad guy. We meet Varan and Ky, the two opposite sides of the natives of this world. We meet Cotton and Stubbs, two guards. We meet the Administrator, who gets killed almost immediately by a smug looking guy holding a brown rock. We wonder why the Time Lords sent the Doctor to a Skybase filled with people to deliver a package. But, they didn't tell him who the package was for. I don't know. That seems a bit remiss.

The episode does a nice job of setting up the world. It gives us the history nicely. Stubbs might overdo the exposition in his first scene, though. We get the whole colonial history of the place and we learn that they are being given their independence. Not because of any magnanimity on the Earthlings part. But simply because they're out of money. No way to run their Empire anymore. Varan isn't happy. The Marshall isn't happy. Ky and his bunch want it to happen immediately.

It sets up the world nicely and then drops the Doctor and Jo into it. Clearly, though, the reason why they aren't given the addressee is because they want the Doctor to get involved in some fashion. We learn that the box is for Ky at the end. They only learn that because he bumps into them. So, maybe The Time Lords knew. Who knows?

It's not a particularly fun episode. All three of the off-world adventures of this era have had dull first episodes. They're there to set up the space. There's a bit too much of the politics of this world. One was hoping for a bit more excitement. But, having seen the opening, hopefully it will get better. Ky overacting and The Marshal being kind of silly might not get in the way. Or they might. It's one of those stories that go great or go south very quickly.

I think the thing that sums up this whole episode is the opening scene. An old Man rushes towards the camera. As noted everywhere, he resembles Michael Palin's "It's..." Man from *Monty Python's Flying Circus*. So, you can enjoy that or not. We see he has some sort of weird vertebrae, not human in other words. That immediately cuts to a fat guy in an ill-fitting uniform wearing a weird gas mask yelling "Mutt!!" Like I said, this could go either way.

The Mutants
Episode Two

Episode 319: (April 15, 1972) Things on Solos heat up. And yet, the Doctor still has no idea why he's there.
Cliffhanger: Varan attacks the Doctor with intent to kill.

A lot happens in this episode. (Check out the DVD production text to read the story of Terrance Dicks almost going crazy as the ever-odder scripts were turned in.) From the surface of Solos, with Ky and Jo being chased by Overlords. Jo doesn't have an Oxymask. They're weird looking things. To the Doctor basically being blackmailed into helping The Marshal and Jaeger the resident mad scientist. The bad guys basically want to change the atmosphere of the planet, kill all the Solosians and bring Earthlings here. The murder of the Administrator before he could make his announcement last episode means that independence has not been officially declared yet. And the world is under Martial Law, Marshall law.

That's what all the setup was for in the first episode. Now, Marshall has complete control over everything here. Until Earth can send someone, which will take some time. The Marshall, I'll be honest, isn't the most terrifying villain. He's played by the guy who played The Squire in "The Smugglers." We have so little of that story surviving but he wasn't terribly terrifying there either. He does seem suitably mad. He knows that his career is over when Solos is given back to its people. So, he's going to do whatever he has to do keep it.

The Skybase is one of those interesting ships where it seems huge but we never really seem to go anywhere but the same couple of rooms and the transmat area. We do get a room with plants and such in it here. That's a nice touch. But it's got Varan in it. Whether or not you like that is up to you. I wish we could see more of the Skybase. Maybe see a little bit more of how these people live. That's not going to happen though.

Especially when we see the lab. Stretching up to the ceiling with a strange U-shape to it, it's a decent room. Many of the buttons and such around there must be extremely sensitive to touch because they don't look like you can really press on them too hard. It's a nice room. Like a base under siege main set. Enjoy it. We'll be here a lot.

So far, we're still moving ahead proficiently here. We get some clue as to the Marshall's plan. We get Ky telling his version of what the Earthlings did to his people. Jo hurts her ankle. She is having a rough time in the air of Solos. She has a chat with Ky about Earth. While it isn't as naïve as the one she has with Mary in "Colony In Space," it borders on it. She only seems to remember that she's travelled in time at the very end of it. I'd like to find out what's in that container. That's making me a little antsy. Because one or the other of them always must carry it around, it's becoming unwieldy. The Time Lords have a strange way of doing things.

The Mutants
Episode Three

Episode 320: (April 22, 1972) Danger in the caves. Mutants, psychedelic caves, silver men and gas bombs.
Cliffhanger: The Marshal sets off his patented brand of gas in the caves.

A lot of great cave work in this episode. Fantastic locations. The Doctor, Ky and Jo holding torches aloft, exploring. Mutts everywhere. The Marshall and his gas bombs letting out fetid, dangerous odors all over the place. And that weird, weird cave… along with "What's in the box?"

Tablets. Ancient stone tablets. That no one from Solos can read. What and why? Because when the Earthlings arrived, they started Solos's history from Day One. As Jaeger points out, seasons on this planet last for 500 years. The humans haven't been there that long. So, they don't know what happens when Solos Winter ends and Solos Spring begins. So, might these tablets help? Again, one must question the Time Lords here. First, we didn't know who the container was going to. Now we do. The correct person has it. But the information is useless to them. This Time Lord scheme, frankly, seems half-assed. And I'm not even sure if Time Lords have proper asses. (Although, when the Doctor was in the shower in "Spearhead From Space," the other Doctors who gave him a long look would have mentioned if something was wrong, ass-wise. "I've got three cheeks.")

Luckily, someone does know of a man named Sondergaard who might be able to help them. But where is he? And who is this strange being in the silvery space suit? (You see what I did there.) It is one of those stories that is either parsing out its information perfectly or testing the patience of the viewers. An episode of "Who is this for?" An episode-and-a-half of "Let's get this to him." Now, who knows how long of "Who can figure out what this even means?" Baker and Martin are crazy or geniuses or crazy geniuses.

The mutants in this episode go from being kind of scary to kind of goofy to kind of sad. Varan's scene with the old man and his discovery that he too is changing is a great moment. Especially when Varan seems to be put in touch with something and his mind begins to go weird. What are these changes? The great James Acheson did the mutant costumes himself. That's *Doctor Who*. That's DIY, baby.

My favorite parts here though are 1) Ky seeing the cavern and having some sort of primordial response where he knows what this is but can't fully pull it together and 2) Jo in the psychedelic cave. It comes out of nowhere. It's extremely weird and it ends with a silver man approaching her. The mix of the filmed caves with the video effects, yes, throws me back a few years, in a psychedelic manner. But it also has the feel of "Jo, get out of there please. This isn't safe."

It's an excellent episode three that keeps things moving nicely. It uses the interesting caves rather than the slowly growing dull Skybase sets. We've got questions to be answered. But we must deal with the Marshal's pungent gas first.

The Mutants
Episode Four

Episode 321: (April 29, 1972) The Marshall gets crazier as the Doctor discovers more of the planet's history.
Cliffhanger: The Marshall shoots a hole in the Skybase. Trouble and floating ensues.

Varan is getting a bit tiresome here. But he has a lovely moment where he spins off into space in the end. Not the best way to die but it looks majestic, especially since he seems to vanish in front of the Crab Nebula. Well, that cliffhanger is crazy anyways.

Sondergaard collapses as he and the Doctor are trying to get out of the cave. (I almost typed 'grave.') The rockets are launched that will change the atmosphere of the planet. And, the Marshall, Varan and everyone blow a hole through the side of the Skybase. Although, that seems like strange engineering. Surely if everyone has the same type of blaster and they're on this ship, shouldn't the walls be resistant to a stray shot? If someone fires within the Skybase, what if they hit the wall? Does the Marshal have a bigger gun? That would make sense. Anyway, if you want to encounter a perfect example of the Baker and Martin craziness, that's this cliffhanger.

The rest of the episode is quite a thoughtful and interesting one. Mainly from when we meet Professor Sondergaard. A very bald man who lives in and around caves filled with radiation. I like the moment when he's talking to Ky and Ky seems genuinely surprised that his people and Sondergaard lived in peace and harmony for a while. Sondergaard does say that Solos was a slave colony. The people of Solos have said this. The Earthlings have always assured everyone that they were living in peace. Now, here is an Earthling saying "Nope. Slaves." That's a powerful and understated moment.

Can I just say: I know the Doctor's OK with the radiation. I'm still worried about him. Especially if you know the way that this Doctor dies. You want him out of that cave fast. It's a great scene though. The colors are great. And that odd white pedestal with the crystal on it is something. Obviously, it was placed there by a part of the civilization that has not been here for a very long time. The radiation cave is the place the Solonians go to speed along the mutation and final evolution. To make sure it goes safely. But now, it's either not working or forgotten. Either way, it helps no one.

It's nice to see the Doctor working with Sondergaard. Someone he takes to and can work with in an instant. Watching them decode the meaning of the tablets is great. We heard Jaeger mention the Seasons in episode two but I doubt anyone would have remembered that two weeks later. Plus, the Marshal dismisses it so quickly. I like the concept here. And now, as we move closer to the end, I want to see it in practice.

I do get worried that an Earth investigator is approaching. First, one must wonder if it's the Master. Second, it smacks a bit of Walker in the previous story. Someone we're bringing in at the start of Episode Five to help expand it and, possibly, not in the most interesting way after what we've learned. However, the episode awaits us. Let's see what The Bristol Boys get up to.

The Mutants
Episode Five

Episode 322: (May 6, 1972) An investigator is on his way. The Marshall is having a great time. Cliffhanger: Jo, Cotton and Ky are about to be awash in radiation.

I knew that the Earth Delegate was approaching throughout this episode. But, for some reason, I really wasn't interested in seeing him in this episode. I kept thinking "I'm fine with what we've got right now. Let's meet this guy in the next episode." Somehow, the story knew. The Administrator approaches but does not arrive yet. I breathed a little sigh of relief.

The rest of the episode is filler. Jo, Ky, Cotton and Stubbs getting caught after escaping and then escaping again and getting caught later. It is the "Run around a lot but accomplish very little" episode of this story. The Marshall, who is startlingly inept throughout, constantly keeps being given one more chance. Really, if the Time Lords had just had a little more foresight here, we could have wrapped everything up ages ago. Maybe there was a sticky note on the container that fell off. "For KY. Tablets establish seasons and evolutionary change." Now that's some assistance. I imagine the people from "The Savages" watching this on their galactic TV and thinking the same thing.

At this point, the Marshal stuff is feeling like running in place. He rushed the rocket launch, which failed. Now, he's trying to rush a particle reversal of the planet. Please, Marshal. Knock it off. Although, the best exchange in the story might be here. The Doctor: "Marshall, you know you're quite mad." Marshal: "Only if I lose." I don't dislike "The Mutants." I just think that if they had put a 4-parter in between the previous story and this one it would have been a nice little break. A story that had more forward momentum, a story with more push. We started off so strong with "Day of the Daleks." Now, where are we? And let's not even talk about spending more time at Skybase. *

The only thing about the episode that is starling is the death of Stubbs. First, he and Cotton were not a great duo but they had their charms. Second, the actor who plays Stubbs is clearly better than Cotton. Cotton's accents and inflections on some of his line deliveries make for some rather amusing moments. Third, normally, a character like this makes it to the end. A generally lovable, slightly hapless character usually can be guaranteed to see through until the end. But Stubbs is gone. It's very surprising. And it seems like Cotton is going to really act for a moment when he finds Stubbs dead. Nothing happens. In fact, when the camera cuts from Cotton to a long shot, he's not doing anything. Was that the best choice? I don't know. It's certainly an affecting moment as we move into the final episode.

*Having said that, at the end of the day, one of the things I do love about these stories is that all the production design does have a different feel in each story. As much as the Skybase and all those hallways are not favorites of mine, I will miss them when we move on to Prof. Thascales and the giant crystal of the next story.

The Mutants
Episode Six

Episode 323: (May 13, 1972) The Earth Administrator arrives. All good things come to an end... as Solos's spring begins.
Cliffhanger: Heading back to Earth for more Earthy adventures!

The final mutation happens. Ky becomes a beautiful floating psychedelic being. He can move through walls. He can travel via teleportation. He can send out rays that destroy people. He speaks telepathically. Ky adapts to it quickly. This is a strange race of beings, isn't it? What do they become when summer hits? And then autumn? 1500 years from now, when winter returns, do they really turn back into those proto-Vikings that we just spent 5 ½ episodes with? Presumably, as I mentioned earlier, the Spring Solos people would never have let humans near them. It seems strange evolution to have a phase be where your people are all-powerful omnipresent beings and then have another phase where you're barely smarter than cavemen.

Do they become like this to handle the atmosphere better? The Doctor had a tablet for each season. So that presumes a change for each of the seasons. What on Earth would they become for summer? How could it be better than what they become for spring? I would love a return to this planet (maybe in a shorter story) where we see the other changes. The implication is that they're going from caterpillar to butterfly. The further implication is that they eventually become caterpillars again. Isn't that odd?

The episode itself is OK. It moves fast enough even if it's a bit clunky. The Investigator arrives. He believes whatever they throw at him. Sort of. Basically. It's obvious that the Marshal is completely nuts at this point and yet The Investigator always seems to believe him (up until the very end). And the Investigator always ends up believing the Doctor and Sondergaard in different ways that allow him to change his mind again. It's cluttered but at least it moves fast enough.

It is fantastic to finally get to see the Solos transformation. The mutant phase is a very quick one. It seems to be sort of there to hold the interior of the being together until they can let out their inner light. It is interesting that when the story starts Ky has a bit of a smug, superior attitude. Gradually, that is toned down as he gets to know and interact with others. Then, the change happens and his smugness is justified. Must be a race memory. (Could you imagine if Varan had achieved this stage? Oh boy.)

The Doctor and Jo head out from Skybase. To fight another day. Cotton is put in charge. Good luck with that. Sondergaard is going to help the rest of the Solonians. The Doctor makes a joke about clean sweeps when Jo mentions that they're in the broom cupboard. And this assignment from the Time Lords ends. A lot of chaos. A lot of destruction. But Solos is safe and will be free. Although, if, in a few hours, they'll all be like Ky, they could eject the Skybase and everyone else with the simple wave of a hand.

THE TIME MONSTER
Written by Robert Sloman
Directed By Paul Bernard
Episode One

Episode 324: (May 20, 1972) There's a crystal. There's a Woman's Libber. There's the Master. There's another big season finale serial.
Cliffhanger: Come Kronos! Come!

The second of the four Letts/ Sloman season closers. Big six-part stories that signposted Letts and his thoughts on what the show should be doing. If "The Daemons" was his very 1970s take on mixing the occult with sci-fi, this his attempt to make something that mixes mythology with sci-fi whilst trying to make it seem like the sci-fi might be a bit on the "harder" side. It's a time hopping, space hopping story that is truly an epic. It also features the magic of TOMTIT.

Look, I knew TOMTIT was an embarrassing acronym when I was 10 years old. I knew that there must be some way that they could have come up with a different one. Maybe it was a joke? I've always thought so. I've heard nothing to that effect though. As a kid, the second half of that acronym made me giggle like an idiot. Then, I learned some Cockney Rhyming Slang and I saw an episode of "The Royle Family" where the Dad grabs a newspaper and heads upstairs to take a "Tomtit." Surely Letts and Sloman knew that? Is the name of the device meant to imply that The Master doesn't know it's going be some sort of useless garbage but we know it is? I've never understood that. It would be like naming your experiment "The Douchebag" or something. And, you know what? It doesn't help the story at all.

And yet, there's so much more here. Yes, the Master does seem to be doing something big. And, again, he's got himself ensconced deep within an institution. There's an implication that a lot of time and money has been spent. Either these Master stories take place over the course of many years or there are several Masters on Earth at any one time up to assorted and nefarious schemes. This one seems to involve a volcano and Atlantis. Didn't Azal create Atlantis? Maybe, maybe not. Could this be a sequel to "The Daemons?"

It is nice to have the UNIT gang back. Yes, the story feels almost like a UNIT parody but that's not terrible. Maybe it is. What makes the episode tough to watch are the ancillary characters of Ruth and Stu (along with some random bits of awful dialogue). I'll talk more about Ruth and Stu later but... wow! They're not good characters. Ruth is hardcore feminist to the point of comedy. Stu is a leftover hippie. How the Master put up with the two of them for so long without shrinking them with the TCE is beyond me. They are cringeworthy characters of the sort that seem shoehorned in. They don't seem accidentally cringey. They feel as if Letts and Sloman were trying to make a point about something but left most people nauseous.

As for the Doctor and Jo? The Doctor gets a dream that's a variation on the Master's fear scene in "The Mind of Evil." The rest of it is a variation on the first episode of "The Daemons" but without the same sense of urgency. The Master's plan with the giant crystal is pretty vague. Yes, Benton explains what interstitial time is but that doesn't make it any more interesting or exciting. Luckily, the Doctor gets to use the inertial control thing he was working on in the previous story so that's a bit of nice continuity. Really though, the episode is about keeping the main characters out of the action. Because if they were in it, they'd see who the bad guy was far too quickly.

The Time Monster
Episode Two

Episode 325: (May 27, 1972) The Master is keeping UNIT at bay as he works out his latest crazy plan. Cliffhanger: The Old Atlantean appears.

The first episode of this serial is almost a parody of the Third Doctor era. At this point, we are more than halfway through it. So, it has a signature. It has certain things it does and certain things that happen. The previous episode seemed to be laughing at it all. (Elizabeth Sandifer's idea that the perfect 3rd Doctor parody is the "Science Fiction Sketch" from the first season of *Monty Python Flying Circus* is far more interesting and funnier than the previous episode.) So, when the second episode began one could imagine being a little bothered. The commentary text says that Jon Pertwee didn't like this story. He thought it was nonsense. In this episode, however, you'd never know it because he's fantastic. He really nails down his Doctor. Intelligent, charming and always pushing on to try to find out what's happening.

The moment that Stu becomes an old man the dynamic of the episode changes. In the previous one, Stu and Ruth were insufferable. The "We did it! We did it! We did it!' sequence is the least funny thing the show has ever done that the show thinks is funny. * When Stu becomes old and Ruth joins the Doctor the dynamic switches. Ruth becomes like Liz Shaw. But the Doctor still has Jo there to be his connection with humanity. (In the way that Clara oversees the 12th Doctor's emotions.) I love it. I think if they had had a Ruth-like character at UNIT while Jo and the Doctor ran around the previous seasons might have been better. That's just hindsight. It doesn't mean anything.

I love that the bulk of this episode is cutting between the Doctor and Ruth (mainly) trying to figure out what went on and the Master and his lackey (in the lackey's office) trying to do the same thing. There's a wonderful linking moment in the dialogue that shows that someone was on top of it. It's all still a little theoretical and a little tough to follow but it's getting interesting.

It clearly introduces another one of these *Doctor Who*... I won't say villains... but adversaries, beings, I don't know... that can't really be let loose in our galaxy because it would tear everything apart. (Doctor Strange encounters a bunch of these. And it's all very Lovecraftian, although I don't feel like the *Doctor Who* crew at the time would have been very familiar with his work.) It's the concept that there is another universe, another space, outside ours... sometimes intermingling with ours. It contains beings that would shove us in a bag and fling us over a rainbow with zero effort. The Great Intelligence is one that picked on the show until it was finally destroyed. The Nestene seem like one of the most interesting but we've never really got a great full-fledged Auton story. They always seem to be in the background. (I would have loved to know what Robert Holmes had in store for "Yellow Fever And How To Cure It.")

I think it's quite a good episode. From the Brig taking charge in the beginning to the Master belittling the Headmaster to Benton's creeping around on ledges to Jo comforting Stu to the Doctor reviewing mythology, it's quite well done. I do wish the first episode had been as good. But I think we might find that this story exists in a weird, weird space outside of time where episode quality can vary like the weather.

*Keep in mind whenever people complain about "Doctor Who not being done seriously" and they refer to Tom Baker or Sylvester McCoy…. This scene needs to be answered for. It's neither funny, in any way amusing or fun to watch. It's embarrassing and, frankly, dumb.

The Time Monster
Episode Three

Episode 326: (June 3, 1972) The UNIT brigade approaches. Interstitial time holds them at bay. Cliffhanger: Has Yates just been bombed?

The big moment in this episode for me is when the Doctor's doodad thing explodes. So, the Doctor spends several minutes setting up a weird revolving thing. It seems to be nonsense. No one believes in him. Not even the Brigadier who was there when the Doctor saved them from the Yeti in the Underground. They watch him put together a weird bit of weirdness. And it works! The tea leaves do it. That seems very English. But it doesn't last long. Long enough to annoy the Master. * But then he goes full on Time Crazy.

And the moment is this one… Once the gadget explodes, Jo leans back in shock as does Benton and the Brig. Ruth leans in and gives the Doctor a kind of from the back hug. She leans in and gives the Doctor comfort when everyone else leaps back. Ruth is Liz! There should have been a Liz-like character there the entire time. The Doctor could have travelled and fought with Jo. But Ruth/ Liz would have been the person who was alongside him drawing up the theories and doing the business. I can't believe I disliked Ruth in the first episode. (Granted, Young Stu comes back in this episode but the whole show dynamic has changed so they don't have as much to do together.) I want a Doctor/ Jo/ Ruth UNIT season. Now.

The episode builds on the last one nicely. The Master has control of the crystal. We know that the base of the crystal is somewhere in ancient Atlantis. So, the Master had access to a heck of a lot of power. Neither of his helpers seem to do much. But that happens with the Doctor so we can't imagine that that wouldn't happen with the Master. He just has to go ahead and fight the Doctor and Yates and the UNIT armada approaching. Obviously, the TARDIS must not arrive at all costs.

The ending sequence is one I remember reading about in *Doctor Who: A Celebration* when I was young. Jeremy Bentham (and his Panopticon) went into detail describing the craziness of it. It's not quite as mad as it could be but it's a heck of a film sequence for a series that had a heck of a lot of great film sequences. Knight in shining armor. Roundheads attacking. (Prompting me to look up English Civil War history.) And the Doodlebug dropping from the sky.

The moment where that explosion tears through the trees is incredibly good. The Brig calling for Yates, and then calling for Mike is fantastic. (We also do know that the TARDIS is over there somewhere. But, because of Peladon, we know that it is indestructible.) It's a dark, worrisome moment. I know the viewers at the time didn't know what was happening with the show. We know that the exile is up at the end of the next serial. So, might one have been worried about Yates? He's rather left out of this story. I don't know why. The Brig was sort of left out of "The Daemons." I don't know how contracts worked and things but here… it feels like something bad has happened. We will see. The Master needs to be stopped. UNIT may not be part of it.

*In fact, it lasts for such a brief time that it does seem like filler. Charming filler. (To some.) but filler.

The Time Monster
Episode Four

Episode 327: (June 10, 1972) The Doctor and Jo engage in an inter-TARDIS vortex battle. Time Ram! Cliffhanger: The Doctor vanishes into the vortex. The Master sends Jo following him.

I remember reading about this episode a long time ago. It was the Doctor and The Master matching wits, TARDIS to TARDIS, in the time stream. It was exciting. It was something we'd never seen before. It was the most TARDIS action we'd got since Episode One of "The Web Planet." This story was groundbreaking. In some respects, that's true. The TARDISes are intermingled here. Like in the first episode of "Logopolis." But it's all much brighter and less ominous than the first episode of "Logopolis." That episode feels like the beginning of a funeral. This episode feels jaunty. And it's not quite as thrilling and there's not quite as much TARDIS as one expected. But it is still interesting.

I love the TARDIS in the ditch. The Doctor and Jo climbing in and going on their adventure. There's something about that that gives the story an epic twist that I appreciate. You know, there's been a battle. The good guys are down. Our heroes climb into the ship and take off. I'm glad Yates is OK. It was a little dicey there.

I like the Stu, Ruth and Benton team. When Ruth tells Benton to just stand there and look pretty, I laughed. Awesome. That's how you do the Women's Lib thing. Give it a twist. Their attempt to free the Brig and UNIT from the time trap they're in was nicely done. And look! It's Baby Benton!

The Master is particularly nasty in this one. Jodie Whitaker's Master is close to this. He's going to possibly destroy the universe but Who cares? He's having fun and it's all or nothing. The way he sends Jo off into the void at the end is nasty. He seems to be going crazier as the stories go along. As his plans are failing, he seems to be ripping up the universe behind him. He also has his new friend: The High Priest of Atlantis and apparently, he has control of Kronos. This might be the most dangerous that the Master is in this era. He banished the Doctor and then immediately does the same to Jo. That's not nice.

The Doctor and Jo's exploration of the interlocked TARDISes is great. And, of course, who doesn't like the mention of the Time Ram? Jo's underpants match her boots. That's good planning! And this is the infamous coccyx episode. Where they wouldn't let Katy Manning say that word. Although, apparently, she originally said that she bruised her bottom and she is rubbing her bottom when the Master arrives.

It's an episode which is setting new precedent for time travel in the show. And at the same time being maybe a bit too silly. The Doctor speaking backwards. Jo rubbing her behind. Where are we going with all of this?

Atlantis.

The Time Monster
Episode Five

Atlantis was huge at this time. In books and documentaries. This was the Speculative 70s. This was the time of *Chariot of the Gods*. The time of the wonderful Leonard Nimoy- narrated *In Search Of*. After the attempts at social change of the 1960s, many people decided to go cosmic or otherwise. (By otherwise, I think I mean Bigfoot.) The world was intent upon finding other explanations for what was going on. Other places where things were happening. Atlantis was one of those places. * And we go there!

But yes… Azal did mention Atlantis at the end of the previous season. He said that his people destroy their failed experiments. So, let's keep a look out for Azal here. And… wait… didn't Zaroff and the Second Doctor tussle in Atlantis during "The Underwater Menace?" Yes, yes they did. But that Atlantis was already under the water. So, maybe Azal had done his thing to them. Maybe we're all just confused.

They do a classic gag here. "Jo. Jo grant." "Well, Jojogrant, welcome to Atlantis." That's where comedy sits and that's where comedy is waiting for you.

The Master is so very aggressive in this episode. Basically, seducing the Queen. While the Doctor makes the mistake of not seducing the Queen and talking to the old king. This won't go well in the next episode. But it is nice that we are moving towards the ending. One can't imagine this going particularly well for everyone involved. Kroos hasn't been the kindest of bird gods.

Jo gets a great wig here. I guess they just have them lying around waiting for a head to fit them on. She looks fun in her Atlantean gown. Although I do prefer the miniskirt.

This review has been as disjointed and crazy as this episode. To introduce a new element at Episode Five is normal. To restart the show in a whole new place is craziness. But it is the end of the season and it feels like a good craziness. Let's see what the minotaur does for us.

*If you've seen *Ancient Aliens* or its spinoff *In Search of Aliens*, you know that everyone is still looking for Atlantis. The concept being that Plato's description is so exact that it must be real. My thought is: That's how creativity works, boys and girls. There's a John Barth novel called *The Tidewater Tales*. It's a fantastic novel. The first 60 pages or so is a very in-depth, very detailed family background and life background to the two main characters. It's so detailed that one can lose the thread of what the book is about. As detailed as it is, it's all made up. We love Plato because of the detail of his dialogues. To deny him imagination is foolishness

The Time Monster
Episode Six

Episode 329: (June 24, 1972) Atlantis falls. Kronos introduces herself.
Cliffhanger: The season is over and Benton is nude!

Not a lot happens in this episode. They find the crystal. The Master calls out Kronos. It ends with Atlantis going under the sea. Luckily, it doesn't feel anti-climactic like "The Sea Devils" and it has more of a forward push than "The Mutants." I don't know if it properly works. But it closes off the season in a grand manner.

The best moment here is the Doctor and Jo locked up in the cell. The Doctor's story from his past is the longest anything we've heard about from his past. We got bits and bobs in the past. Susan describes the home planet. The Second Doctor tells Victoria about his family. But here, the Doctor, knowing that it could all be over soon, tells a lovely Buddha story about a man and a flower. It's very Barry Letts. (And I think the opposite of Terrance Dicks.) It's a great way to end the season.

The Master, as always, makes things go crazy. He destroys Atlantis and he kills so many. Then, he grovels like a jerk and gets away Scot free. In *Tardis Eruditorum*, Elizabeth Sandifer says here that the Doctor shows a ridiculous amount of mercy. The Master has destroyed so many. Killed so many. Hurt so many. And he gets away with zero consequences. 23 seconds of groveling is not proper punishment. I've said on one of my podcasts that some villains need a proper "kick in the shorts." The Master needs that here. It's funny that no version of the Master after this ever mentions the point where the Doctor prevented them from being tortured by Kronos for all eternity. Whenever I see the dentist who pulled my wisdom teeth, I thank him even though it was 20 years ago. The Master is awful. I get a weird feeling that the production crew haven't quite figured that out yet.

The Minotaur isn't great. Yes, it is Darth Vader. Mileage may vary. The scene is nicely shot in a film studio. But it isn't terribly thrilling, especially because it's basically the Doctor and Jo revealing something for the Master. That's kind of what the Episode is about. Jo even offers to sacrifice herself like in "The Daemons" so this is all beginning to feel a bit familiar. It moves well and it's fun. So, I won't take that away from it. Although, maybe, the Master should have gagged the Doctor and Jo while he was revealing Kronos. That's a suggestion though. I don't want to bother his holiness The Master.

And Season Nine ends. The ratings are sweet. Season Ten is automatic. But it's also in the tenth anniversary of the show. Maybe something interesting will happen? Anyway… This season was an interesting one. It sheds a lot of the UNIT family stuff while also sort of keeping it on occasion. I have started to miss them. They were a fun bunch and they're not in the show as long as we think they are. The Brig isn't in this story much. Yates is barely in it. Benton is in it the most and some of that time he's a baby. It's at this point where the show begins to change. The anniversary is approaching. It's time to send the Doctor out into time and space once again.

SEASON TEN
1973

THE THREE DOCTORS
Written by Bob Baker and Dave Martin
Directed by Lennie Mayne
Episode One

Episode 330: (December 30, 1972) UNIT is under siege from some strange blobby antimatter stuff. Reinforcements are needed.
Cliffhanger: Jo and the Third Doctor are zapped away to... somewhere.

A new season begins. The end of one era is commenced and the start of a new era doesn't quite happen until we've got a new Doctor in the show. The title is a big giveaway to what's happening, unless you don't know that there were two previous Doctors. Then, you might expect it to be something where Pertwee is cloned or duplicated. Or maybe two other Doctors, like actual doctors, show up and help him out. But it's not that. It's something that had been suggested to Barry Letts for a while: it's the Three Doctors, as we know them.

Except, unless you saw that title, you wouldn't know this was happening until over halfway into the episode, which I like. The story seems to start off as a regular UNIT story. * No Yates but Benton is there. You can tell it's Baker and Martin because there's a yokel. There's also a slightly arrogant scientist. Both of those guys vanish when something sparkly and very video-like makes them vanish. We get to see Jo's underpants again. There's some fun fiddling around with science stuff. There's talk of a black hole. And then, the big blobby Gell Guard things appear and we realize that they're after the Doctor. So, the Doctor contacts the Time Lords who send himself. Twice.

It is nice to see the Second Doctor back. As many have noted, he doesn't seem quite like himself. They have him act like a Victorian grandfather or uncle, rather than the slightly crazy and skittish character we knew for three seasons. However, it's nice to have him here. It's great when he meets Benton again and says Hello to Jo. The chatter between 2nd and 3rd is delightful. Pertwee was notorious for not liking Troughton's working methods. Troughton was very lax when it came to lines and movements. Preferring to improvise. Pertwee was very exact and Troughton's style drove him up the wall.

Seeing the First Doctor is nice too. In a slightly different way. He's stuck on the TARDIS console screen because Hartnell was too sick to remember lines. So, he's clearly reading lines but because of the way things are set up it often looks like he is looking back and forth at his other selves. The question has been asked: How does the First Doctor have the knowledge that the others don't have? If he had the knowledge, wouldn't they automatically, have it? Why do they sort of defer to him, when each of them is far older than he is? He just looks older. Oh well.

Regardless, it's a fast-moving romp. There are explosions, monsters (more or less) and a few fun twists and turns. I've always liked the X-ray with the face screaming on it. And I do hope they get Bessie back. It's got a good cliffhanger too. Where are the 3rd Doctor and Jo going now? We get to see the Time Lords, however briefly. They're still overdressed but they seem to be enjoying themselves. The First Law of Time is "You're not allowed to meet yourself." That could be important down the line.

Oh, the Gell Guards are awful. One of those *Doctor Who* monsters where from the moment they appear to the moment they stop appearing you hope you never have to see them again. The UNIT soldiers are doing their best to battle them out on the lawn. It's a decently staged battle. The Gell Guards look ridiculous though. One wants them to go away. Immediately.

*They're in a new location here. This one is out in the countryside and lovely. It's Top Secret but there's a huge sign out front saying what it's for and who's in charge. Maybe that's a gag sign another rival top-secret group put up to razz them.

The Three Doctors
Episode Two

Episode 331: (January 6, 1973) The Doctor, Jo and Doctor Tyler are brought into a great castle in the land of anti-matter. The Brig meets the Second Doctor again and, briefly, the first.
Cliffhanger The whole of UNIT HQ is thrown into the black hole.

It's great to see the Doctor (Second) and the Brig meet each other. Yes, the Brig seems mostly confused mentally by all of it but it's nice to see anyways. Benton gets a lovely moment where he throws a gum wrapper at the anti-matter thing and almost causes big problems. Meanwhile, the Third Doctor and Jo wander around a quarry. It has bits of UNIT headquarters randomly sitting it. There's a nice eeriness to that. In "The Five Doctors," they would all be sent to a much more picturesque place but the quarry seems to suit this era.

We briefly see the gentleman who brought them there and the sort of ceremonial/ ornamental robes he's wearing might remind you of some other elements in this story. He's an all-powerful being but he couldn't have made anything better than those Gell Guards? Their eyes are cool. Their claws aren't bad. But you spend every moment waiting for one of them to run into the walls. Shades of The Zarbi, I guess. Others have pointed out the fairy tale feel of some of this. The Wizard of Oz, Aladdin and so on. And there is a feeling of that. That, unfortunately, isn't the biggest feeling I get out of this story.

The first episode had a nice push to it. The first episode had a lot of excitement and questions. Then, the other Doctors were introduced and the ante was upped considerably. This episode starts strong. But then, somewhere around the time the Second Doctor, Benton and the Brig rush into the TARDIS until the end. It's all padding. And the tricky thing is that part of the padding is the classic Terrance Dicks "have someone make a daring escape only to get caught again" ploy. That's fine and dandy in a six-part story or longer. In a four-part story? One that we're not even halfway into? That's a problem.

The story really does have a feeling that it was built around the cliffhangers and whatever padding was needed was shoved in. They could have revealed who the man in the castle was in this episode. We could have learnt something. Instead, we get an inordinate amount of padding. We get Doctor Tyler suddenly acting like a complete jerkball. We get the Doctor spending ages fiddling with the Brig's radio to accomplish nothing. In a big anniversary show like this, we shouldn't be getting loads of padding halfway into the second episode. We just shouldn't. Why are we? This was the way I used to write *Doctor Who* stories when I was a kid. Think of a cliffhanger and fill up the pages until it happened. I believe a lot goes on in the next two episodes. Doing this here is kind of inexcusable. It makes what should be a big, big story kind of dull.

I always forget that this story does this. I always try to remember why I don't love it as much as I should. The first episode always confuses me. But then, I remember all the padding. Are they out of money again?

The Three Doctors
Episode Three

Episode 332: (January 13, 1973) We meet Omega and we learn of his vast powers.
Cliffhanger: The Dark Side of Omega fights the Doctor.

The sets of Omega's main throne room and the singularity room are interesting, aren't they? They're big. They're not as high as they seem to think they are. (Hence, the moments when you can see the top of the set because Omega is so tall.) They contrast with the hallways that feel like a couple random corridors that accomplish little. But, at the same time, there are those green streaks on the wall. What are those? I always use to take any inconsistency here as being this: This is all created in Omega's mind. So, he simply doesn't care about how some things look. Or maybe he likes the green streaks. I don't know. Anyway, it's the big set in the episode and Omega treats it as his garish home.

I like Omega. Although, when I was a kid, I always pronounced his name wrong. He has a huge helmet, which seems impractical but if he's OK with it who am I to argue. He seems to have a definite grudge against the Time Lords and probably not one unwarranted. (I always wondered this: if Omega harnessed the black hole which the Time Lords used to create time travel, how did he knew the First Law of Time? Surely, they wouldn't have written up laws if they hadn't harnessed the power yet? Maybe.) Anyway, the Doctor revers him as a hero. Omega himself thinks he's a god. This isn't going to go well. The story is kind of vague (maybe too much) on what exactly Omega is up to by bringing another Time Lord here but we'll learn in time.

This is the episode where many people think that the Brig finally goes around the bend. He's been so in charge of himself and UNIT stuff for so long. Now, he's been inside the TARDIS. He's seen two other Doctors. And UNIT HQ has been transported to an anti-matter universe that he thinks is Cromer. He's doing his best. He gets to recruit Hollis the yokel. He's doing his best.

Benton is really handling himself well here. Better than you'd think. That's kind of because he is replacing Jamie and Jamie would have done this a ton of times by now. Regardless, Benton and Jo running around is fun. Dr. Tyler is fine. He doesn't do much for me. There are enough characters we know and love here without giving away time to character that we'll never see again after this story. But that's just me wanting to hoard the time with the Second Doctor.

It's lovely to see the two Doctors working together. Their creation of the door is a great moment. The realization that the Doctors can harness the same power as Omega is a smart one. Their slow creep towards the Point of Singularity is delightful. The Third Doctor not wanting to play the Second Doctor's coin toss game is fun. The Second Doctor constantly mentioning the recorder seems like an annoyance but does become important.

The episode is an interesting one. In some respects, it is sort of big and epic. But in others it is a pantomime bit of fun. I guess the references to Aladdin make that concrete. We'll see how things go now. We've got a big ending coming up. I think. Well, it's an anniversary ending anyway.

The Three Doctors
Episode Four

Episode 333: (January 20, 1973) Omega meets his match with a well-placed recorder.
Cliffhanger: The dematerialization circuit is back! And Mr. Ollis asks if "Supper's Ready"? *

A good ending to the story. It's not terribly exciting. It's got a clever ending moment. It's sad to say goodbye to the two Doctors. But, when we see the dematerialization circuit arrive, it's a joy. It's a breath of fresh air. I don't think the show had become stagnant where it was because the previous season shook it up pretty good. But, as Katy Manning points out in the commentary, it is a sci-fi show and it does need to escape the confines, as it were. So that's cool.

The best moment here is the "Walk Through The Singularity" scene. Hollis and Tyler don't mean much to us. But the other three do. (I think one of the problems here is that the extraneous characters do amount to pretty much nothing.) The Brigadier has a lovely moment as he steps in and salutes the guys. It's a great moment. It really does make one feel like this might be the end. It isn't. Everyone knew it wasn't. This was the start of a new series and they'd probably already seen ads for the next serial. However, for a few moments, it feels like it could be over.

It's nice that the First Doctor joins the guys for a bit of a mind meld. Always wishing he'd done more. He never quite feels like the First Doctor but he almost does. So, it's cool to have that one more time. And he is the one Doctor who has been well-portrayed by others.

Really, this story was about seeing the Doctors again. Some of the script seems to forget that. "The Five Doctors" will rectify that. In an anniversary show, the anniversary characters should be featured. Here they sort of are but maybe not quite as much as they should be. It's still early days for this sort of thing. The show is one that will gradually begin to revel in its past and the world its created. And rightfully so. You create a rich tapestry and sometimes you want to hang out there. But, this story, very nicely, doesn't quite do that. The Three Doctors are prominent but it isn't all about them doing their bits and everyone cheering. That's something that hasn't really happened yet. It will be the 1980s when this really kicks off. Here, it's being birthed.

After all that, it was about more Time Lord mythology. Not that we have a lot of it currently. But we are slowly building. The concept of the man who flew his ship into a black hole to engineer the power within for time travel is wonderful. Disney's *The Black Hole*, which I adore, takes a very different and less practical approach. But, at this time, black holes were still very young and new. It's exciting. It expands the world the Doctor came from. And the fact that he never interacts with them, makes him slightly outside of all of it even though he is clearly inside.

In the end, it was great to see the Second Doctor and the First Doctor again. It's a suitably epic story done in a not quite epic fashion. But it's fun all the same. Let's see where the Doctor and Jo go now that they have free reign again.

*I know. As a Genesis fan, you're thinking what I am. "Walking across the sitting room/ I turn the television on/ Out in the garden, the moon seems very bright." In 1972, the band released their fourth album, *Foxtrot*. The height of progressive rock's first wave. Side Two of that album is 24 and a half minutes long. The first minute and a half is a beautiful Steve Hackett acoustic guitar piece called "Horizons." The remaining 22:58 is their epic "Supper's Ready." A wonderful, weird, shifting churning mother of a song. (In the studio, it's something. Live, I think it's better. No matter who sings lead.) So, when this story ends with that, I think "Bob or Dave, Genesis Fans?" The commentary doesn't help.

CARNIVAL OF MONSTERS
Written By Robert Holmes
Directed by Barry Letts
Episode One

Episode 334: (January 27, 1973) On a strange planet, strange people do strange things. While Jo and The Doctor look around the S.S. Bernice… and there's a dinosaur.
Cliffhanger: A giant hand grabs the TARDIS.

The first of the post-exile stories!

It's been some time. I like that the Doctor's first trip is to the Acteon Galaxy. To the planet Metebelis 3. (In some cut dialogue, Shirna and Vorg mention that they are in the Acteon galaxy so the Doctor tried, even if the Miniscope got the best of him.) This is one of those wonderful Third Doctor era continuity moments. We have the future Earth stuff. Now, we have the Metebelis 3 thing. Now… it is Robert Holmes goofing around.

There are so many great things going on here. The split stories are fantastic. The point behind this was that the production team were trying to keep things cheap. So, they did the stuff on the planet and they did the stuff on the *S.S. Bernice*. In the end, I believe, it didn't really matter. The producer was directing it and I pretty much think that he would let everything go and be as expensive as it needed to be.

The scenes on the boat are great. The very 1920s British bunch being very British… but then they get attacked by a dinosaur. That is awesome. Jo and the Doctor wander around it trying to figure out what's up. It is Jo's first non-Time Lord led journey. She seems convinced that none of this is going to be outside of our world. But maybe it is? I don't know. We'll find out.

On the other side, we have the people on Inter Minor. The Doctor was trying to get to Metebelis 3 but he got shanghaied, or did he? They are a very grey Group of people. They're not so much fun. They're very bureaucratic. And they're bordering on goofy as they try to keep themselves together. Shirna and Vorg are great show people that just distract them terribly.

So, the viewer watches and thinks how do these two things correspond? Robert Holmes's original script had the whole thing set on the ship. When we see the hand grab the TARDIS it's an even bigger crazy moment. I love that concept. But I think either way works. I think both have the spirit of the show within them. I think both are crazy and weird. That's *Doctor Who*. That's how we roll.

The masks of some of the aliens are junk but most of it works. Let it pass. There's a lot going on. The exile has lifted. The Doctor is free. This is a new world.

One of the things that makes this episode feel weird is that the Doctor is free to travel. We have travelled with him in a free state. But Jo hasn't. So, it's an odd feeling where the viewer is more familiar with this stuff than the companion But, it's not a new companion. Jo has been here for so long. Liz never travelled with us. Jo always seemed a bit uninterested in the travel. They make it work here. Jo is travelling but… as much as she might love the Doctor, she doesn't really love this. We haven't seen that before. People travelling with the Doctor learn quick that they need to travel. But this Doctor can get us back "home" so it feels odd. A different sort of set-up for the show. That works and that makes sense. We are ten years in. We are over 300 episodes in. We need to change it up. That's what they're doing. Luckily, we have Robert Holmes leading us. I don't know that he ever knew how awesome he was but I don't want anyone else leading us.

Carnival of Monsters
Episode Two

Episode 335: (February 3, 1973) The Doctor and Jo are trapped in the Miniscope. While Shirna and Vorg deal with bureaucrats…
Cliffhanger: Welcome the Drashigs.

The blue-faced Inter-minor bureaucrats are delights. They are the sort of people that you can really love as long as you don't have to spend any time with them. They are self-serving. They are stupid. They are the sort of people where you think "who in the name of the Lord put them in charge of anything?" They are in charge. They are ruling over the oddly faced beings that live here and we must deal with their decisions. Even though they are idiot decisions. Even though they are decisions that hate the world. We watch them and obey them.

A Robert Holmes trope here. Stupid people suddenly get put in charge of everything and the rest of us must bow our heads and bend over while they declare what is best for us. Why is Mr. Holmes one of the best writers for the show ever? Well, he never was self-conscious about it. He was right in the middle of it. He was writing to make a living. He had the imagination of Ovid. And he wasn't afraid to move everything ahead if there were no other ways to do things. He is one of the best writers ever. We'll talk about him more when he takes over the scripts for the show. But, for now, remember this: The producer of the show decided that this was a show he wanted to direct. Not the anniversary show. Not something with The Master or the Daleks. But this weird show in between everything. (Not even the show he co-writes at the end of the season.) This is the show he makes his own. And it is a beautiful vision of what he felt the show was under his leadership.

Meanwhile, The Doctor and Jo meander around the *S.S. Bernice*. And then wind up within the framework of the Miniscope. It's a fantastic concept. We haven't had them meet the Inter-Minor people yet. They met the crew of the *Bernice*. It's such a strange story. It's such an oddly constructed story. It's also a fantastic story for The Doctor and Jo. It's a wonderful story to welcome them back to the world of time travel. Welcome them back to a place where everything is so weird so much of the time.

It's a great episode. One gradually learns what is going on. Pertwee's Doctor gradually learns what the heck this strange place is and why it is. You hope the Doctor and Jo can get out of it. You imagine they can but maybe they can't. And then… we get those last moments. The cave. The marshes. And the Drashigs! Holy Heck! Will we be all right?

Carnival of Monsters
Episode Three

Episode 336: (February 10, 1973) On the run from the Drashigs, the Doctor and Jo pass through the workings of the Miniscope.
Cliffhanger: The tiny Doctor falls out of the Miniscope.

The Drashigs are here! And they're fun. Not the world's best monsters. They are, however, relentless and they do cause lots of trouble. I love the way they invade the entirety of the Scope. There's a small hatch for maintenance in a cave. The Doctor and Jo go through it, the Drashigs catch their scent and oh boy! Plus, we get the second appearance of Vorg's hand in the Scope.

This is a weird story, isn't it? Blue-faced men arguing endlessly. A group of people running through the same hour of their lives repeatedly. The Doctor and Jo crawling from segment to segment. In some ways, it's like a crazier version of "The Mind Robber." Someone is watching them go through a series of assorted bits of trouble. I kind of prefer this story though. I think it's sharper written. I think it's much funnier too. The fact that Inter Minor is such a drab planet that all we see is basically the customs area of an airport sums it all up.

We also get a nice little bit of the Doctor's past here. He fought to get the Miniscopes banned and succeeded. The Time Lords listened to him. Prior to "The War Games," the term "Time Lords" never came up. Now, people can't stop bringing them up. I guess that's the way this works. Even Hartnell's Doctor talked about them in the previous story.

Then, there's poor Vorg and Shirna. Just trying to make a living. They sure went to the wrong planet. Did they mean to come here? I don't remember. They're certainly not welcome. What sort of a planet is Inter Minor anyway? Everyone's blue grey and everyone is a bureaucrat of some variety, even the dumbest of people. I wish we got to meet President Zarb. That's a fun name for someone in charge of something.

Jo's interaction with the crew on the boat is great. That moment when the young woman almost remembers what's happening every hour, when she almost remembers that they are trapped in this loop is nice and eerie. But it's lost. And they all fight the Drashigs and a dinosaur. Jo is doing her best not to be annoyed by all of this. She's clearly struggling. It's such a strange almost atypical story. It's such an odd choice for the first serial after the anniversary show and the first one where the Doctor is free in over three years. It shows how Robert Holmes took the formula, the world, the tenets of the show and made them completely his own.

Then, there's that cliffhanger. The Doctor lowers himself to a point where he breaks out of the Scope and suddenly, he's on Inter Minor. Finally, after three episodes, the worlds meet! Life will never be the same. Especially with the Drashigs still having the Doctor's scent.

Carnival of Monsters
Episode Four

Episode 337: (February 17, 1973) The Doctor meets the people who have been watching him. The Drashigs do wild.
Cliffhanger: The Doctor and Jo head out into space and time... and not right back to UNIT headquarters.

This is how you do a four-part story. Barry Letts isn't the most dynamic director. But he takes care of everything that he needs to take care of. The "split the story into two distinct parts" thing is a great conceit. It works well. With the people on the S.S. Bernice being returned home never having known what happened to them. * And the owners of the Miniscope not caring. The Scope is confiscated by the Doctor in the end. Vorg and Shirna will carry on as long as people around the universe love gambling. The climax is an interesting one. It's basically: A dumb politician lets out a giant carnivore that eats him. While The Doctor and Jo rush to escape the Miniscope. The monster attack is all too real. (As real as the show gets anyway.) The Scope stuff is more conceptual. Watching the two clash is fun.

You can see why this story was chosen for one of the first Jon Pertwee DVD releases. It's exciting. It's funny. It's weird as heck. And it, in the end, is delightful. The Drashigs should have made an appearance in the new series. That would have been fantastic. I'd like to see what a modern-day designer/ monster maker does with them. Evil caterpillars with teeth. I'd watch that. "The Drashig Conundrum!" It's a very atypical Pertwee story. It's like "The Celestial Toymaker" or "The Mind Robber." But better than both of those. It's on par with "Warriors' Gate" or "Ghost Light."

The episode has an excellent pace. The blue-skinned boobies are still going about their business. However, it all seems kind of foolish now. The Doctor so easily puts forth and exudes authority that bureaucracy can't really handle it. They get some great lines here, concluding with the one about not wanting to be eaten by monsters even if it's while making a political point. Sharp dialogue all the way around. "The Three Doctors" is fun. But, this story, completely devoid of anything steeped in the mythology of the show (except for a shot of an Ogron and a shot of the Cyberman, the only time this Doctor meets the Cybermen within his own era). A lot happens here. In fact, at times, it seems like there might be too much going on. It eats through the story like a modern-day episode and it works.

It even has a slightly extended coda. Probably because there's no evil genius to stop. Probably because there's no war. There's nothing but freeing Jo and a blue guy with thoughts above his station. As it were. So, the last few minutes very calmly wrap up storylines, while sort of putting the Doctor and Jo to one side. The closing shot of Shirna smiling at the TARDIS dematerializing is fantastic. It's not a group of people standing around laughing at a bad joke. It's not a forced bit of business. It's just a young woman leading a crazy life who just met the Doctor. She'd be a member of LINDA if she could.

(I also love when the Doctor seems genuinely upset that he's not on Metebelis 3 in the Acteon Galaxy. As mentioned earlier, in the original script, Shirna mentions that they are in that galaxy. So, technically, the Doctor isn't too far away. I guess that's why the guys are kind of blue. Metebelis 3 is the blue planet. This is the Blue-Grey planet.)

A new era of the show begins. Jo is on her first series of travel through time and space journeys. We'll see how she feels about all of it when she gets back home some time from now. It's interesting because this season is structured like the last one. Two four-part stories followed by three six-part stories. We saw how strange all that was. Let's see what they do here. Anything could happen. But, in the end, it might be a little more expected than expected.

*Although, the young lady for a split second seems to remember it all. She doesn't quite though. Her dad does get to finish his book, which is a beautiful moment.

FRONTIER IN SPACE
Written by Malcolm Hulke
Directed By Paul Bernard
Episode One

Episode 338: (February 24, 1973) The Doctor and Jo are in the Future Earth timeline again. Cliffhanger: The Doctor and the Jo are traitors!

The fact that this story is the third in the "Future Earth": saga is my favorite part of it. It's like RTD's "End of the World," "New Earth" and "Gridlock." Except in this era, they do them out of order. "Colony" is when Earth is at its height and things are starting to become a little much. "The Mutants" is the empire at its end. Worn out, bloated and exhausted. (No, I'm not describing myself.) The current serial takes place at a point where the Empire is so huge it has encountered another empire as huge and things are getting a little unpleasant. The Earth Empire and the Draconian Empire. Neither of them seems to be worth our time. But, like "The Curse of Peladon," the folks in charge have been watching *Star Trek* and getting ideas. I do wish they'd stop doing that.

The tricky thing with the episode is that I feel like we've been here before. Immediately, the Earth space pilots see the Doctor and Jo as Draconians, as enemies. Jo keeps telling the Doctor that they should leave before anything happens. The Doctor's wanderlust has returned and he won't budge. They end up getting imprisoned and some Ogrons steal the TARDIS. It's one of those episodes where you think "Oh no. How long will it be before the people in charge here listen to the Doctor and Jo?" The answer here is: Quite some time. Weird that the first two times the Doctor landed in this Empire, the Time Lords sent him. The Third and Final time the TARDIS brought him. Or did she? It would be just like the Time Lords to give the Doctor one free trip and then tighten the reins again without him knowing it. Especially because the Master is involved. (Sorry, spoiler.) Along with another evil race.

Hulke is doing his absolute best at creating a universe here on a grand scale. The Draconians and the Earth people distrusting each other. We learn that the Ogrons are causing the distrust but it's a bit early to say why. They're hired hands. Mercenaries. Who hired them this time? There are some interesting politics here and there. For the first time in this trilogy, we are on Earth. Not a settlement. Not a colony. Not whatever. We're on Earth. The lady President looks distressed. She has an arrogant general who always seems to be around. The Draconians seem just as arrogant.

In the end, I do like this story. But it seems so much like other stories from the history of the show. The moment the pilots mistake them for "dragons" my heart always sinks. We need the psychic paper here and we need it badly. There are some moments I like. The Doctor's response when he opens the cell door and the pilot appears. The first few minutes before everything starts changing. The "DANGER" lettering on the cargo of flour. Is flour normally a dangerous cargo to haul? I guess if the thing breaks open and it gets all over everything it could be hilarious. But dangerous? I don't know about that. And I like the fact that this is another story set in that Empire I find intriguing. I'm just not sure I'm up for all the imprisonments followed by escapes followed by more imprisonments that lay in our future. Or maybe I am. Let's see.

Frontier In Space
Episode Two

Episode 339: (March 3, 1973) We'll cover the plot in the review. This one's kind of special.

Cliffhanger: The Ogrons capture the Doctor and Jo.

Remember how we discussed before the Malcolm Hulke thing that he passed on to Terrance Dicks involving a lot of escaping and recapture. It makes it look like things are happening when things aren't really happening. We saw it in "The War Games." We saw it in "The Faceless Ones." (Although, that story was extended at the last minute. So, there's a chance that the original script didn't have any of that.) We saw it in "Colony In Space" etc. and so on and so forth. Until someone points it out to you, it's something that might occur to you but it might not be a trend you recognize.

The way they try to distract you here is when Jo and The Doctor are locked up on the flour ship (again) and Jo begins to go through every trick they use to escape, especially the "I'll pretend to be sick…" There should be a moratorium put on that one. Imagine if the Doctor had the psychic paper here. The ship would have immediately been sent after the Ogron ship and the story would have been two episodes. The padding of the six-part stories is no more apparent in the whole of *Doctor Who* than it is in this episode. Not necessarily this story. But this episode.

The episode itself moves at a fast pace, which goes to show that Hulke's idea was correct. But, in the end, it accomplishes nothing. They had to move some of the start of the episode to the end of part one. That means this episode has an overlong recap and a feeling that it doesn't have quite enough going on. We learn a bit more about the Draconian and Earth troubles but not much. They talk about Mind Probes a lot. But nobody is seen to use one. I think the most interesting way to watch this episode is to just move through exactly what it does:

-On the ship, the Doctor and Jo are completely ignored and disbelieved, even though the story the pilots tell make no sense.
-Back in the prison room. This time with a guard nearby. Jo goes through the possible escapes.
-On Earth, the Doctor and Jo are brought before the President and General Williams. They are disbelieved and threatened.
-They are imprisoned for a while. The Doctor tells a story.
-They are brought back before the President and General Williams. This time, the Draconian ambassador is there. Jo and the Doctor are supposed to be spies. That comes to nothing.
-They are imprisoned for a bit more.
-As they are being led back to the president again, the Draconians attack them and get the Doctor.
-The Draconians question the Doctor. He is not believed in any way. He escapes.
-Jo is brought before the President and General Williams. They still don't believe her.
-The Doctor is captured by the humans.
-The Doctor and Jo wind up back in prison.
-The door blows open. This time, it's the Ogrons and they're prisoners again.

Are you kidding? This is either the laziest episode ever or one of the most chutzpah-packed ones. Your tolerance for it is in how often you can watch Jo and The Doctor get caught, questioned, not believed and then imprisoned. Rinse and repeat. The rest of the story, I believe, isn't completely like this. But it could be. It's a strange way to put a story together. It moves fast but accomplishes nothing. It's intriguing and maybe a little too repetitive.

Frontier In Space
Episode Three

Episode 340: (March 10, 1973) The Doctor is sent to the Moon. Jo meets the Inspector from Sirius Three. He looks familiar.
Cliffhanger: The Doctor and The Professor are in the airlock together. Their air tanks are empty and the air is being pumped out.

Ahh, we calm down a bit here. The Earth people continue to not believe the Doctor at all but at least, after the Ogrons attempt is thwarted, all the escape and such is done. Ish. Jo doesn't do much. The Doctor gets to brawl with a Mind Probe. The Earth government are really the worst. If the President and General Williams are the best this Empire has to offer, it's a wonder the whole thing didn't blow itself up ages ago. They do become tiresome.

Luckily, the Doctor is sent to the Moon. He's surrounded by political prisoners. Prisoners of the Peace Party. They seem like a pretty run bunch to me. I feel like this is Malcolm Hulke creating his group of people here. He was a Communist. He believed the east and the west could live together in peace. I like the concept that most of the people he would side with would be locked up forever and ineffectual. It's kind of fun but we won't be here for long. So, enjoy your time with the men on the Moon.

It does feel a bit like a "standing in place" episode even though the Moon prison colony is introduced. Because once we meet the Master we know that things are going to go his way. It was lucky that the Ogrons grabbed the TARDIS. All this might have all gone in a very different way.

Again, I always applaud the Master's planning. For however many times, he's set himself up perfectly with complete credentials to do something big and crazy. Last time he was trying to control all of time. This time, he seems to be trying to start an interplanetary war. It really does feel like the Time Lords sent the Doctor and Jo here at this point. It only makes sense. All the other times they met the Master was on Earth. Now, here, a couple hundred years in the future, they run smack into the Master. Not a coincidence, I think. But we've still got a lot to learn about what the Master's up to and why he's doing the weird things he's doing.

I like the Doctor's swagger even when they put him a silly robe like he's heading into some sort of eternal yoga class. It's nice to see that all he's thinking about is escaping, even from moment one. The thought that the trustees in this prison are hardened criminals rather than people who are actual prisoners shows what kind of world this is. Not a nice place to be. At least, I wouldn't want to live there. None of the "Earth Empire" stories paint any sort of a picture of a world where I would like to live.

Frontier In Space
Episode Four

Episode 341: (March 17, 1973) The Master imprisons The Doctor and Jo on his ship, until some stuff happens.
Cliffhanger: The Master contacts the Ogrons.

I just realized something. How many times have I watched this story? How many times have I watched this era? * I just realized the big similarity between this Master story and the previous one. The structure. The first three episodes go in one direction. Take it as far as it can go. Possibly too far. Then, the last two episodes go in a different direction, ish. But the fourth episode is basically time spent with Jo, The Master and The Doctor.

"The Time Monster" was quite a bit of TARDIS fun. The three characters and, yes, that high priest. But he mainly stood there gawking in amazement. In this one, after they get on board the rest of the ship and until the Draconians arrive, it's basically the three of them. It's quite an interesting way to tell the story. Three episodes full of this political intrigue. It's all feeling like it's building towards something. And then, we take the time off. Three old friends hang out. (When you know the immediate future, you'll really appreciate it.)

Much of the episode is The Doctor talking for a long period of time... and then Jo talking for a long period of time... "Thank you, Miss Grant. We'll let you know." Does it become a bit much? Possibly. But, again, when you know the future, you'll know that this should be relished and enjoyed. The Master reads "The War of the Worlds." Jo talks and talks. The Doctor sneaks around the ship in a space suit. Classic Doctor Who stuff. Not really classic third Doctor *Doctor Who* stuff. Because of the exile. But here, it's lovely to see.

I like how Jo, in her improv ramblings, says that when they get back to Earth, she's never going in that TARDIS again. Jo never seemed to like the TARDIS and time travel much. I think, no matter how crazy things got, she really felt home on Earth in her time. (Whenever that is. I was going to say the "early 1970s" but some might argue. But, when else would Jo have been doing this. The Disco era? The time of the punks? She ain't New Wave, baby.)

There's not much happening in the episode. One might call it a filler episode. No. It isn't. I love the Master's tease about his employers. And we might possibly be starting to think of where this is going to go but maybe not. It's all very intriguing. As we near the end of the story, it starts to become a little sad.

The final thing to applaud is the fact that the episode took time off from the intergalactic conflict. Then, when they meet the Draconians we learn that all diplomatic ties are cut off. We learn that while our trio goofed about the universe began to teeter on the absolute edge of a galactic war. You can never take a day off, can you? (Jo does mention that the Doctor shouldn't try to save the universe by himself, which is an interesting thing to say considering he just got out into the universe two stories ago. And his first story involved dismantling a Miniscope.)

*I'm being rhetorical. If pressed, I'd say "eight."

Frontier In Space
Episode Five

Episode 342: (March 24, 1973) Let's meet the Draconians.
Cliffhanger: The Master turns on the fear button.

This is one of those Pertwee era stories where about a thousand things happen. If you look at where we are at the start and where we are at the end, it's kind of crazy. It's a very modern pace. It's a bullet pace. But, at the same time, the show couldn't have run like this all the time. They had the time to set up the serials and they had their specific budgets. Things did what they did in the space and time they had.

The interesting thing about this episode is that the structure makes it move so quickly. The structures of so many of these six-part stories have been odd. This one has a reason for it. Others have written about it in more detail. But, basically, the first episode of this story was edited very tightly. It wound up being short. They had to move up scenes from episode two into episode one. This routine happened all the way through the story. That's why these episodes are a bit shorter than some of the other episodes around it. For example, the closing scenes in this story on the Ogron planet and in the Master's cave, were meant for episode six. The real cliffhanger was General Williams finally conceding that he'd been a jerk and saying he'd lead the expedition. But the constant moving of scenes meant that everything is slightly off. That's why the cliffhanger of the previous episode is hilariously underwhelming. Things kept moving. There's fascinating stuff going on like this in many of the stories from the original run.

The Master and The Ogrons are an interesting group. We see the Daleks fight with the Ogrons but not do much else. It's the Controller who works with them. The Master, however, is surrounded by them and he is clearly frustrated. There's a particular moment when he yells at Ogron that always makes me laugh out loud but I'll let you find it.

The scenes in the Draconian throne room are fun but brief. The constant berating of Jo for speaking is very early 1970s. But Jo speaks and she makes sense. There is a great untelevised adventure mentioned. The Doctor was here 500 years before helping stop a plague. (Somehow, I thought of "Timelash.") That's excellent. The Master expounds on how much he loves peace, which gets a great response from the Doctor. It's a fun scene. It's well done. "My life at your command!" It gets more done story-wise, due to the Ogron attack, than 2 ½ Episodes with humans. That's saying something.

This is one of those episodes where everything is so epic. It feels like in that in the previous story but really, it's not. Here, it is epic. Hulke did the same thing with "The Sea Devils." That strange feeling that everyone lives on the same street and just needs to walk next door to get something done is here. It feels a little unreal but the quick pace is appreciated.

Then, in the end, Jo resists the Master's hypnosis. She has grown as a character. She has evolved. In "Terror of the Autons," she fell immediately. Here, in her karate outfit, she's strong. Something feels like it's coming to an end in this story. It wasn't meant to. But it is. However, we've still got a big episode ahead of us. A big reveal. Some awkward things and saying goodbye to someone. Let's check it out. The Ogron planet isn't for everyone but I think you might like it.

Frontier In Space
Episode Six

Episode 343: (March 31, 1973) We meet the Master's employers.
Cliffhanger: The Doctor is shot and the employers escape.

It's a weird episode. I don't think anyone watching would have expected a cliffhanger that this episode brings us. The super surprise is a good one. The extension of the story over the weeks would have made the surprise something few would never have spotted. But, at the same time, the Doctor and the good guys spend half the episode on a ship approaching the planet. The reveal is excellent. The lead up to it maybe goes on too long. I feel like the second half of the episode is cashing a check that the next episode didn't know about.

It's not bad in any way, shape or form. It just feels a little off. "Frontier" does feel like it's setting up the next story. The weird thing is that the next story doesn't feel like it was being set up by this one. The next story feels very different from what's happening here. Almost as if any story (or no story at all) could have preceded it. That leaves us with an odd feeling. Because as much important stuff as is happening, one can't help thinking that this is all a little askew.

The Daleks are here! They are the mysterious employers. Their reveal is fantastic. One really doesn't expect it but it kicks butt. It's a great moment. It elevates everything. We love the Master but currently he has become a bit of a goofball. The Daleks, however, are still mostly shrouded in mystic stuff from the 1960s. The "Day of the Daleks" Daleks were kind of different. But they are back and the Doctor must hunt them down at the beginning. That's something major. That's something big.

The Story is this: It's the 10th season. Letts and Dicks are working on something to make the season truly epic. They decide to remake "The Daleks' Masterplan" A story that hasn't been aired since 1965/6 and probably will never be aired again. So, they make it. But they keep the Daleks hidden until this point. And it works. In some ways. "Frontier In Space" is not the most exciting story the show has ever done. The pacing is all over. The structure is weird. But, in the end, it does what it needs to do. And it leads us to the big Dalek story. Bigger than the last one. Bigger than any one since 1967. It's going to be a humdinger.

But we have to say goodbye to the Master here. At least for a while. Roger Delagdo dies in a car crash soon after this episode. The Master is last seen wielding a gun and that's about it. He was a great Master. All the way around. At this moment, we don't know that he's going to be missed. Now, we do. It hurts a bit because he's so darn good. He seemed to know that he was a mustache-twirler. He seemed to know that he was a crazy fun villain. That's why we loved him. He's gone too soon. And left us with... well, we'll find out.

PLANET OF THE DALEKS
Witten By Terry Nation
Directed by David Maloney
Episode One

Episode 344: (April 7, 1973) The injured Doctor lands with Jo on the inhospitable planet Spiridon. There are others there.
Cliffhanger: Some of them are Daleks! Invisible Daleks.

Terry Nation is back! And he hasn't watched the show since he worked on it last in 1965. He originally gave the six episodes individual titles. Per the DVD information text, this episode was called "Destinus" because the planet they landed on was named that. Now, it's named Spiridon, which is a much more sinister name for such a gross planet. A planet that could be Kembel! A planet that could be Mechanus! A planet that could be any one of several Terry Nation planets from previous Dalek stories. I don't think he's come up with any new ideas since 1965 either.

It's an odd episode all the way around. It doesn't really seem to relate to the previous episode in any way. The Doctor puts himself in one of his comas. Jo speaks into a cassette tape, which is very interesting technology. She talks to herself, into the tape, a lot. It's a tremendous amount of chatter.

Again, Terry Nation seems to not quite understand that plants are alive. He's also missed some very important TARDIS-related information.

Nation's ideas on what the TARDIS is like inside are hilariously silly and should have been vetoed from the story. Unless someone higher up really got a kick out of this. Here's what this episode posits re The TARDIS interior: It's like a big closet. It's not a huge inter-dimensional space. It's like you're in a submarine or something and there's an oxygen supply. Somehow it pulls in oxygen from the outdoors. The Spiridon plants have covered the exterior of the TARDIS in a fungus so no air is being absorbed to the interior. The Doctor has backup oxygen supplies but they're almost empty. So, he's going to suffocate inside the TARDIS. Lots of questions to be asked there. *About Time* asked most of them. My favorite is: How does all this work when the TARDIS is in space or in the Time Vortex? I know there's no air in space and I'm guessing there's very little in the Time Vortex. How do we work here?

Now, setting Terry Nation silliness-aside, which granted was much more delightful ten years before this. (Before the Space Race really began and we went to the Moon, this was all very charming.) Now, it feels like someone didn't get an important memo about something. The rest of the episode has the regular Nation-style plotting. Separate the Doctor from his companion and have them meet the two sides of the story. Don't mention the Daleks by name until the very end, even though they're in the title. Do everything you can do to make the reveal fun. An invisible Dalek! That's a good one. I will give him that. Of course, he had invisible people in "The Daleks' Masterplan." And there's probably another invisible thing I've forgotten.

It's nice to see some Thals. it's been a very long time and these are very different sorts of Thals. Warrior-like and desperate. Well, with all these spitting plants I can't even imagine how they lasted so long. It seems like it might be impossible. But it is nice to have the Doctor team up with them again, although it'll take some getting used to. We've got Daleks. We've got Thals. We've got a hostile planet. We have the Doctor and Jo. As much as this seems very familiar (but only if you've been watching these episodes like we have*), it does seem like fun.

*Remember that 1965-1973 is a very long time. Many kids watching would have had no contact with the earlier Dalek stories. So, for now, Nation can get away with something like this.

Planet of the Daleks
Episode Two

Episode 345: (April 14, 1973) Daleks vs Thals! Plus, some invisible guys.
Cliffhanger: There are 10,000 Daleks on the planet.

This is a good episode. Now, that all the "they" and refusing to say "Dalek" is out of the way, Nation can begin telling his story. It's got something to do with invisible Daleks and possibly something to do with a bacterium. It's standard Dalek stuff. But we do get one really dark, but casual for the Daleks, scene. They blow up the Thal ship. (Don't worry another one lands at the end.) The Doctor believes Jo is still inside and tries to stop the Daleks. He gets his legs shot at for his trouble, shades of Ian. We know (well we're pretty sure) that Jo is no longer in there but, regardless, it remains a good scene. The Doctor really looks devastated by what's happened.

The Doctor is in chatty form throughout. He has a long talk with Veber, which I quite liked. It doesn't feel like padding. It doesn't feel like "We're running three minutes short. Add something." It feels like a well-done, well-earned conversation. His chat with the doctor of the Thal group in the cell is a good one too. The Doctor isn't about speechifying, well this one really isn't. But Nation gives him the speeches here. All I could think of was the First Doctor telling the Thals that he never gives advice back in the last episode of "The Daleks." And then he proceeds to give advice. Maybe the Thals, since they were the first non-cavemen they met at the start of the adventures, makes him break into speeches. Regardless, I do like how, at the end of his courage, speech, the Thal says Thank you but that he's not convinced.

Jo meets Wester the Spiridon with his cool purple coat thing. She spends most of the episode slightly dazed but that's what the Fungoids do to you. It's nice to see that she's not dead. The Doctor gets to hear Jo's voice thinking it's the last time they'll meet. I do hope they reunite soon.

The Daleks are charmingly ruthless throughout the episode. Casually ruthless. There's a weird sequence that I'm never sure what to think of about halfway through the episode. The Doctor is taken hostage. He is being led through the corridors of the Dalek base/ city to the prison. For about a minute, it's the Doctor and the Dalek walking through corridors. "To your right. Forward. Left. Forward. Left." It goes on like this for quite a while. For some reason, I could have watched it all day. I know we're showing how deep and cavernous the place is but I found it charming.

May I point out that I do love the cliffhanger? They make a point of saying "Ahh, there are about a dozen Daleks." Then we get the zinger. I kind of wish it was delivered more dramatically. But the slight zoom into Taron's face when he does a bit of "Holy hell!" is great.

Something weird is about to happen with the next episode. Keep in mind, until the DVD release, episode three was only available in black and white.

Planet of the Daleks
Episode Three

Episode 346: (April 21, 1973) Everyone is trying to escape from the Daleks.
Cliffhanger: The Daleks are about to break through the door. Will the Doctor's parachute thing work?

The episode is about the Thals creeping into the Dalek base and passing an icecano, which is lots of fun. It's also about The Doctor and the Thal doctor trying to escape. And Jo and Wester entering the Dalek base. There's a lot of hallway acting. There's a lot of crawling through ductwork. There's some interesting science with the allotropes and the creation of the parachute thing. The episode begins with the Thals being told there is a huge Dalek force on the planet. It ends with the Doctor seeing hundreds of Daleks frozen underneath the base. Things aren't going well.

But it is a Nation runaround so things never feel as dark as they did in, say the previous episode. We know Jo is alive. The Doctor doesn't. He's running himself ragged with the Thals here. Desperately trying to get themselves out of the base and back to the hidden Thal explosives. But the Daleks know where the explosives are. Oh, the chicanery!

It has a bit of a feel of the fourth episode of "The Daleks" from so long ago. With the Doctor and the Thal escaping from the cell and trying to get out. We get a door being burnt through. We get all the classics here. Alongside the ductwork with the Thals. Even though I always think this episode is going to drag, with all the running around and accomplishing little, I don't mind it. In fact, I quite like it. I think there's a reason.

This episode was the last Pertwee episode I saw. Many years after the rest of the story. So, even though everything around it is very familiar to me, this episode has a slight freshness even though there's nothing fresh about it. This was the episode, alongside Episode 1 of "Invasion of the Dinosaurs" that was only in black and white for some time. That meant that when PBS aired the story in an omnibus version for the first time and beyond in 1987, they left this episode and Episode 1 of "Dinosaurs" out. Literally, "Dinosaurs" begins with Episode 2. "Planet of the Daleks" skips Episode 3. We get the announcement about the Daleks and then it cuts to the Daleks cutting through the door and the Doctor and the Thals floating up the shaft.

The odd thing about the first time I watched it was that I don't think I noticed that the episode was missing. I didn't know how they were going to handle it. I knew it was in black and white. I expected the show to go to black & white and then switch back to color. But they just left the episode out. It wasn't until the show ended and I noticed that it was around 20 minutes shorter than it should have been that I thought "Oh heck., that's right. Episode three wasn't there." But it doesn't feel like anything is missed. I don't know whether that's a good or a bad thing for the story. Someone can leave out one full episode and it isn't noticed. That's odd, isn't it?

It wasn't until the first DVD release that we got a color version of the episode. Like I said, it doesn't really advance or detract from the story. It's fun and it moves us closer towards the ending. Now that we know what's up, we'll see how the Thals handle the Daleks and vice versa. I'm looking forward to The Doctor and Jo meeting up again.

Planet of the Daleks
Episode Four

Episode 347: (April 28, 1973) The Doctor and Jo are reunited.
Cliffhanger: Take him to the Daleks.

Odd cliffhanger on this. The hotheaded, argumentative Thal steals the last two bombs and plans on blowing up the Dalek base himself. He has just enough time to hide the bombs before getting caught by The Spiridons. They announce "Take him to the Daleks" and the episode ends. I guess we're meant to care more about the fact that the bombs are lost, rather than he's been captured. He has that chat with the Doctor in Episode Two, which was nice. But, to say that he's been "one note" since then is an understatement. It occurred to me that the Episode Four cliffhanger for "Frontier In Space" was also very underwhelming. Maybe it was a conscious decision. Four? Cliffhanger? Make it lame!

The rest of the episode reunited Jo and the Doctor, which is lovely. Jo is super ecstatic and mumbling, stumbling through her words. The Doctor takes her to one side and they have a chat. They talk about landing here and why. It doesn't quite connect with the previous story or the start of this one but it's close enough. We also get a chat between the leader and his lady. They're in love! Nation is doing a pretty nice job of doing his darndest to give us some character development here. We even get to meet the young Thal here who takes an instant shine to Jo. Could there be sparks in their future? And I don't mean from hitting rocks together for fire.

I think back now to how strong the Daleks are here. And how the Thals clearly seem to be getting stronger and stronger. Then, I think to the fact that they share the same planet. Skaro – Home of the Daleks... and the Thals. That's an interesting combination to have on the planet. You wouldn't think the Daleks would allow the cohabitation. But the races seem to have been in some sort of harmony for years. Or something. Has that ever really been explored? You would think the Daleks would never have let the Thals develop to the point where they are. The Daleks have to be cheesed off in this serial. They leave their planet to put a base on another one... and the Thals follow them. "Leave us alone. Our business is not yours."

Moreover, the Daleks are beginning another round of preparing a bacterium to destroy everything but them and the Spiridons on the planet. It's a fourth episode added twist. Look out for that bacterium! Nation loves his bacteria. It's like he's never been away.

I like the stone place where they're relaxing. Something huge and unseen flies overhead. Lit up eyes stare at them from the darkness. It's the wildlife wanting to take access of the rocks. It's a wonder there aren't dead animals strewn everywhere unless the animals get on so well together because of the plants. Odd, we haven't really seen any "wildlife." It's all been the plants. Where is the wildlife throughout the day if not in the jungle? Something I've never really thought about. And something Terry Nation probably never did. It doesn't matter though because we are, probably, moving towards the end now. A big ending. Thousands of Daleks. Here we go.

Planet of The Daleks
Episode Five

Episode 348: (May 5, 1973) The Thals and The Doctor and Jo come up with a plan to get inside the base by stealing Spiridon purple outfits. They learn something disturbing: The Daleks are about to release a bacteria that will kill them all.
Cliffhanger: Someone's boot is visible beneath the Spiridon robes. A Dalek calls out an alarm.

We are gradually moving towards the end. This episode has location footage, which is very welcome. This era has lots of location footage. But, ever since the start of this season, it's been really limited. Quarries and a lake in "The Three Doctors." Marshes and boats in "Carnival of Monsters." Futuristic houses and quarries in "Frontier In Space." And the weird marsh quarry whatever the heck this body of water is here.

It's effective. They basically shove two Daleks into a small body of water that is related to the allotrope, so it's very cold. The Daleks don't do well in very, very cold. They shove two Daleks in so they freeze up and then get access to one of the Daleks. Again, very Terry Nation here. David Whitaker and Louis Marks didn't do anything like this. Terry Nation seems to enjoy a bit more freedom with what can be done to the Daleks. And, as I said, the location works. It's miserable looking. It's dangerous looking. The cut from video to film isn't terribly convincing. But it doesn't need to be.

Most of this episode involves us looking at the purple coat things of the invisible Spiridon. There's a little eye hole area. And there's a great jump moment when one of the Thals thinks the Spiridon approaching is a colleague. It's actually an invisible Spiridon. I like their big purple outfits. They sort of remind me of grimace from McDonald's if he were a sasquatch. They also remind me of a purple version of Mr. C from *The Letter People*. There's something very odd about them. No matter how often we see them.

Vaber tries to invade the base with the bombs but he fails. We lose him. But his loss gives the rest of them the courage to try their plan. One of them in a Dalek. Three of them dressed as Spiridons. We are approaching the final episode so let's get it moving. There is a bit of a disconnect in the sort of spatial realm here. I'm a little vague on where everything is in relation to everything else. But that's happened before. Everything, in daylight, seems much closer than I thought.

The Doctor and Jo spend much of the episode at the rocks. Trying to keep away the animals and just talking. The animals, yes, are made up of lights with pupils. But I don't know if it's the Blu-ray that did this, I quite liked them this time. The eyes have more character the better you can see them. I liked it. I did forget though how much of the episode leaves the Doctor and Jo out. Nation seems to be shooting for something like a Thal spinoff here. The Doctor joins the heroics in the second half. But he's semi forgotten before that. Jo and Patel get more to do. That's OK though. If Nation thought he was still writing for Hartnell, then it makes sense.

Then there's Wester. I love the moment when the Doctor thanks Wester for saving Jo. The Doctor doesn't quite know if he should try to shake Wester's hand or what. Then, Wester goes and sacrifices his life so that the Daleks can't use the bacteria. That's a good guy. We don't really get to know the Spiridons and we don't really get to know Wester that well. We can feel that they're part of an enslaved race under the Daleks. We applaud his bravery. Now, let's see how the Thals do as the ending looms.

Planet of the Daleks
Episode Six

Episode 349: (May 12, 1973) The last desperate attempt to stop the Dalek army is underway. Cliffhanger: The Daleks have simply been delayed. Jo wants to return to Earth.

The epic 12-part story draws to a close. Terry Nation returns to the fold and he gives us a straightforward but generally fun Dalek story. A bit of a runaround but not without its charms. Its pace is a good one. Like "The Daleks" and "The Dalek Invasion of Earth," the action ends some minutes before the ending to allow time for clearing up some bits of plotline.

This time we get Jo being asked by Latep to go back to Skaro with him. They look like a sweet couple and that might have been interesting. However, 1) Jo clearly misses Earth. That's where she wants to be. 2) Skaro? Home of the Daleks? Come on. That makes the suggestion instantly unappealing. But the way Latep responds to Jo's "no" makes it sort of seem as if he was half joking. This does portend events of the next story. Look out for those.

The Doctor gets to make a speech about war. This Doctor was never big on the speechifying. Here though, he does go to town. Pertwee does a good job with it. Although again, his immediate response to Vaber when the speech is done makes it seem like maybe he was half-kidding. Regardless, he's still got Jo. Even if she doesn't want to travel the universe.

This episode gives us a yellow Dalek Supreme/ Superior. Basically, he's the worst boss ever. He rolls in, takes command, kills the current Dalek in charge... but then does no better than that Dalek in trying to stop the resistance. It is nice to know that he (it/ they) do recognize the Doctor in the end. I always like when that happens.

The sequence where the Doctor must crawl on top of Daleks to get the bomb back is nicely done. Because it's in studio and because it's shot live with multiple cameras it's not as suspenseful as it could be if it were on film. On film, they could have done close-ups, raised the tension. Here, you just keep thinking "Gosh, I hope the Doctor doesn't break one of those Daleks." Nation's original script had the Doctor drop down and then climb back out on them. That might have worked better. Anyway, it's a nice moment. These are reviving Daleks, still too loopy to do anything. But it's like moving through a snake pit. Hoping you don't exasperate anyone.

The icecano drowning the Daleks is nicely done. It never looks like anything more than some sort of colored water in slow mo whooshing over toy Daleks but it is effective. I particularly like the CGI shot (added on the Blu) of the tops of Daleks poking out from the goop. The whole sequence with the bomb and the wall and the constant smokiness of the cold is well done. It's never through the roof crazy suspense but it works well enough. And there is a definite feeling of some sort of victory when the Daleks are buried.

Poor yellow Dalek. The Thals steal his ship and he's left with a bunch of incompetent boobs. I do like their final chase of The Doctor and Jo. It keeps the excitement and the danger going right up until the very end, which is pretty *Doctor Who* to me. Now, we're back to Earth to close out the season. One final story before things really change.

THE GREEN DEATH
Written by Robert Sloman
Directed by Michael E. Briant
Episode One

Episode 350: (May 19, 1973) Global Chemicals. The Nuthuch. Green dead men. Metebelis 3, the famous blue planet of the Acteon Galaxy.
Cliffhanger: The mine car is plummeting into the mine with Jo onboard!

And so, the big one begins. Well, the third big one. But the first big one that has major consequences. For the third season in a row Barry Letts and Robert Sloman put forward an epic six-part story that will affect the show. Yes, we do get the visit to Metebelis Three. This is the an example of a Robert Holmes joke becoming an important part of later mythology.

The Doctor lands on the planet and is assaulted from every single direction. The giant pterodactyl feet are my favorite. He ends up taking a gorgeous blue sapphire and then running for his life. It's an interesting scene. The contrast is between Jo taking an interest in her Earth and leaving behind the Doctor who is more interested in the universe. We see Metebelis Three twice in the series. Neither landing is great. I'm not sure why the Doctor wanted to go there so bad.

Jo is now officially of the Earth. She has travelled the universe and not liked it. She wants to fight for her planet. She's grown up. She's so different now from the gal we met three seasons ago. And everything here feels like the beginning of the end of her travels with the Doctor. It's nice to have the Brigadier back. He can't handle the universe either so these two work well together. The Doctor, oddly enough, seems out of place.

When Pertwee became Baker, the UNIT era ended. The 4th Doctor is not going to hang around here any longer. The 3rd Doctor wants to be around his friends. He also wants to travel the universe. And he wants Jo to join him. Liz never had the chance. But everyone else, apart from Ian and Barbara, joined him to travel the universe. To see the sights. And Jo, who he's spent so much time with... doesn't care. She isn't impressed by the universe. The Doctor's dream of being able to see it all is now achieved after much fighting. And his best friend doesn't care. She's not mean about it. She just doesn't care. And there's something heartbreaking about that. The format of the show has returned after a break of a few years. And the Doctor's best friend wants to be on another show.

She wants to be in *Doomwatch*. And that's a heart breaker.

The rest of the episode does its thing. We meet Stevens from Global Chemicals. He's clearly up to something not nice. He's polluting Wales and the world and doesn't care. We meet Professor Jones. He and Jo get a very lengthy "meet cute" scene. It does resemble her first scene with The Doctor. But things are different now. I'm not a huge fan of hippies. I'm all for stopping pollution and trying to halt global warming if we still can. So, I'm with Prof. Jones. We get the miners. Just wanting to live. And we get the man whose body goes green. Portending something else.

We get a lot in this episode. And, in fact, the episode is long. It's 26 minutes. This will be a long story. A lot will happen. Mostly, it's the Doctor saving us all again and trying to keep his friend. The moment she meets Professor Jones, she's lost. That doesn't mean we can't have fun though.

Note: This is my "birth episode." I was born two days after this aired. Although, I did not see it until 1987 when I was 14. (I suppose the next episode might actually be my "birth episode." I'll take them both.)

The Green Death
Episode Two

Episode 351: (May 26, 1973) Rescuing Jo and Burt! Cutting equipment discussions!
Cliffhanger: Giant maggots burst through the wall and threaten the Doctor and Jo.

I quite like this episode. There are so many episodes of the show where The Doctor and Jo gradually meet the people involved in the story. We go over here. We go over there. Eventually we meet everyone. Both sides of the story, etc. "The Green Death" does something different. Something sharper. Something that feels more mature in the way it's telling its story than previous serials.

The whole episode is based around trying to rescue Jo and Burt. One of Steven's guys fiddled with the lift so the duo plummet to the ground. The Doctor, The Brig and Dave stop it. Only just. Because the mine is shut down, they don't have the necessary cutting equipment to fix the lift so they can bring them up. The episode becomes about trying to get equipment. In doing so, The Doctor meets the protagonist and the antagonist. Jo discovers what Global Chemicals is up to. By the end of the episode, the whole focus has shifted.

The suspense is kept up throughout. Burt insists that there is another way out. So, their time underground will, hopefully, end at some point. They just need to keep going. The Doctor arrives as the lift is descending. So, he's thrown right into it. The constant upping of the ante makes it exciting.

The lengths Global Chemicals go to do prove that they don't have cutting equipment is insidious. They (we don't know how yet) hypnotize one of the employees to lie about cutting equipment. They threaten the Doctor with guns. And they make sure to clear out the garage where they keep the cutting equipment. What a bunch of jerks! They honestly are going to let Jo and Burt die rather than jeopardize the nasty stuff they've been doing in those mines. *

The Doctor meets Stevens. He's all axel grease and peach butter. But it's obvious he's evil. We've seen enough villains on this show (and James Bond villains) to clue us in. Professor Jones is a little arrogant. However, he and the Doctor become best mates when they're both fighting to help Jo. The Doctor knows knows the full lay of the land. And it's been done in a heightened suspense atmosphere, where he gets to do some Venusian aikido. Could the Sloman/ Letts stories be getting better plotting? Will they improve from here? Join me for episode three... next.

*It's interesting, if you think about it. The mine has been active for decades, Then, it's closed. Right after that, Global Chemicals moves into the area and claims that their process is almost waste free. And it is. If you don't count all the waste that they're pumping into the mine that's now closed. Here's hoping no one decides to open the mine again.

The Green Death
Episode Three

Episode 352: (June 2, 1973) Jo and the Doctor escape from the mine. Stevens is put in charge of investigating his own company's malfeasance.
Cliffhanger: The newly hatched maggot is approaching Jo.

Another fine episode. The first one puts everyone out into the world. The second one brings everyone together with a crisis. This episode resolves that crisis and gives everyone a bit of a breather. So far, this is the best Sloman/ Letts script. We are halfway through and there don't seem like a lot of questions to be answered. But there are a lot of things to do.

First, we get a dinner party. How often does that happen in the show? It's like seeing the Avengers party in *The Age of Ultron*. You don't expect it but it's lovely to see. I like that the Brigadier is hanging with all the scientists at the Nuthuch. Professor Jones and Jo have clearly hit it off. (Jo's dismissal of the Doctor's sapphire from Metebelis 3 is where we know things are sliding downhill fast. All change.) The Doctor tells an anecdote that seems pretty much incoherent. And the brig eats some fungus. (I do kind of wish that UNIT would show up quicker. If Jo is leaving soon, I'd like everyone to get together ASAP.) We get Jones's talk about travelling down the Amazon to find a unique toadstool. Jo, who didn't like travelling the Universe, suddenly being very interested in travelling the Amazon. *

We get the Brig being put in his place by Stevens, The Minister of Ecology and the prime Minister. (I'm not sure if the writers thought having the ecology minister (who, if he's backing Stevens, is an idiot) insult the Brig was a hoot. I don't find it particularly funny.) Poor Brig. He goes in, asserts his power and then, as I said, they basically hand the power over to the person who is causing the trouble. That would be like if the Doctor was in a room with The Master and there were a bunch of tiny bodies around. The Doctor says "I'll take charge." But then The Master gets the Prime Minister to say "The Master is in charge." This investigation isn't going to go well for anyone and it might be one big waste of time.

The scenes in the cave with the maggots and the mine car gondola are suitably gross. Some of the CSO is pretty dodgy. But, if there are gooey maggots around, things are always fun. Second story in a row with frequent and scary life of some kind that can kill you just by being touched/ sprayed with plant venom. Dangerous places. And the shot of the pipe filled with maggots is super gross. I love it.

The death of the employee who was brainwashed is rather disturbing. But it doesn't seem to register with anyone. It just kind of happens. I do like how Stevens calls The Brig "sentimental." Then the Boss calls Stevens a "sentimentalist." Twice. But Stevens has no problem driving this man's brain to the point where he casually leaps off a walkway to his death. The Prime Minister put the guy in charge of that company in charge of the investigation. Oh boy.

Overall, the episode works. The break in the action doesn't slow things down as one might worry would happen. Instead, it just gives our friends a chance to take a breather. Of course, the bad guys never rest. Stevens is working 24 hours. His goon is on the same schedule. Can you get a degree in Goon?

*I'm sure the Amazon is awesome. I know it mainly from horror films/ cannibal films. It's like Australia. Everything there wants to eat you.

The Green Death
Episode Four

Episode 353: (June 9, 1973) The mine is blown up, releasing the maggots. The Doctor gets inside the Global Chemicals facility and meets the Boss.
Cliffhanger: We learn the true identity of the Boss.

Another excellent episode. This one starts off strong with the resolving of the cliffhanger. Moves quickly into the mine being blown up. We get the great scene with Stevens berating the Doctor and then brainwashing another employee. Then, there are maggots everywhere and the Doctor goes back into the facility to meet the Boss. Plus, Mike Yates!

It is nice to see Mike. We've seen so little of him since Season Eight. It's odd. I always remember him being in the show more but not really. He's in 4 of the 5 stories from Season Eight. He's in "Day of the Daleks" and "The Time Monster." But he isn't really in either one that much. He's almost an afterthought in the latter. After this serial, he gets two more. I know he was originally created as a possible love interest for Jo. I'm glad that didn't happen. I do wish he was in this a bit more though. He's here as the Man from the Ministry that the Brig has sent in undercover. He gets to have a nice scene with the Doctor where the Doctor is dressed up as a cleaning lady. It's been since "The Highlanders" since we've got some good Doctor drag. Fun.

I like how the episode resolves itself to blowing up the mine. It happens very quickly and you know it's going to be a rotten idea. I do love how angry Stevens gets at the Doctor. I think it's probably a mix of worry and arrogance. Everyone else jumps when Stevens says, "Do whatever I want." The Doctor does not and in fact goes against him all the way. Stevens is clearly going nuts here is the long and the short of it. Just the fact that he seems to be so willing to hypnotize his own men and make them do what he wants is a clue to that. Is this really the ultimate model of capitalism?

Well, the fact that his Boss is a computer probably means it is. Now, this computer does seem to have a sense of humor and some emotion. He calls Stevens a Nietzschean. He is disappointed that the Doctor doesn't realize what he is, or it is. Yes, the BOSS is a giant computer that takes up the top floor of the building. It's a nice reveal. The BOSS had been so vague in the previous episodes that this works well. It's not bad enough that the maggots are out but now there's a nutty computer too.

And the maggots are everywhere. They are invulnerable, of course. The rash decision to blow up the mine sends the maggots everywhere ese, including the Global Chemicals pipe. And coming up out of the ground and in caves and everywhere. With, of course, speculation of what the maggots will become. (The Brig calls them "caterpillars," which always seemed a little ludicrous to me but I get what he means.) The maggots have full on become a creepy, relentless killing thing. Still infected with the "green death." I do always wonder what exactly happened to the goon that gets bit at the start. Stevens claims that the Doctor is lying about the maggots. But, what about the goon? Do the people at the Nuthutch just compost him? I'm not sure what's happening there.

Another strong episode. We have two left. The Doctor has met the computer. UNIT is fighting the maggots. Jo has gone to get a maggot for Professor Jones. That last one seems like a bad idea to me. But Jo is determined and she's not going to be with us for too much longer.

The Green Death
Episode Five

Episode 254: (June 16, 1973) The maggots are getting out of control.
Cliffhanger: Yates is caught out by Stevens.

Oh no, Mike! He falls under the BOSS spell in this episode and tries to kill the Doctor. That's not good. But then, Jo tried to blow everyone up back in "Terror of the Autons." So, it's not an unknown thing. But, here, with Yates dressed in a suit and not looking like his normal self, it feels a bit weird. It feels a bit like something that wouldn't have happened with Yates when he was at his best in Season 8. It feels, again, like we're nearing the end of an era. The blue crystal from Metebelis 3 helps him. I'm glad The Doctor made that trip after all. I knew it had a purpose.

Jo and the Professor spend quite some time on a slag heap surrounded by maggots. This brings up a weird thing about the episode. (The info text insists that this was meant to happen.) The UNIT guys are out in the quarry or wherever the heck they are. Jo and the Professor are in this broken-down cave area. The cutting between film and video become obvious here. The shots with the Brig, Benton and some soldiers in front of obvious CSO backdrops immediately switching to actual location shots is very jarring. I'm not sure why they did it that way. Maybe to make the linking from the base to the cave a little easier to take? I don't know. Regardless, it's odd looking. Oh, and the Professor ends up starting to turn green.

When I was growing up, *Doctor Who* taught me lots of stuff. Occasionally, it would teach me a word. Interregnum. Galumphing. In this episode, it's Serendipity. Jones whispers it to Jo before he passes out. It's a good word. It's one of those words that... if you say it, it feels like its meaning. You know what I mean? Squeegee is another. But here, I learned about serendipity. I learned about serendipitous events. Chalk that up to another thing the Doctor taught me!

Mixed in with all this, the Doctor is able to defeat another mind probe-related thing. Poor BOSS. First, the Doctor confuses him with a conundrum. Then the Doctor defeats the attempt to probe his mind. BOSS has his charms. I'm not sure how he works exactly. It's said to be hooked up to a human mind (Stevens) so it can replicate the mistakes or the odd slips of mind that humans have. That makes it stronger. I think it makes sense. I'm not as certain as I could be but I think it does.

We are finally moving towards the ending. Jo will be leaving us after the next episode. Things are kind of moving along so quickly that there's no chance to stop and breathe. What with Yates, and the maggots, and BOSS and everything else. Also, BOSS threatening to release some sort of chemical that will put him in control of people. A lot happening here. It is odd, though, how streamlined Malcolm Hulke's novelization of the serial is. This episode takes up about 11 pages of his 136-page book. In contrast, the first episode takes about 32. Hulke was a heck of a writer. I think his novelizations might be better than the scripts. He has a way of making everything work perfectly by, sometimes, removing huge chunks of story. For example, all the rescue stuff with Jo and the Professor is excised from the book. It gets a paragraph. A paragraph after the fact. It's fascinating. Anyway, the end is nigh. We will say goodbye to Jo and finally learn what these maggots eventually become.

The Green Death
Episode Six

Episode 355: (June 23, 1973) The final battle with the maggots and BOSS.
Cliffhanger: Goodbye Jo.

Here endeth the lesson. Jo Grant will marry Professor Jones and become Jo Jones. (Yes, there is a jazz drummer also named Jo Jones.) They will travel down the Amazon, have lots of kids and grandkids and spend their lives trying to make the world a better place. * That's where she ends up. Here is where it really starts. It's rare to have a *Doctor Who* companion where their life after the Doctor is the exciting one. Usually, once you save the Universe, that's it. But not with Jo. She was a companion that the Doctor, per Hulke's novelization, "learnt to love…very deeply. He found it difficult in his heart that he might never see her again." (I know. That should be "hearts." But, like Romana said, "One for casual, one for best." Two hearts breaking at once can't be good for anyone.)

How about the rest of "The Green Death?" Really, by this point, it's all about saying goodbye to Jo. They set it up early and it pays off. (Unlike say, our next travelling companion. Although, she gets a special deal years later.) The episode, like all of them, is a little longer than a regular episode. But the time is well used. They figure out how to defeat the maggots. The solution is with them all the time. It's the fungus they've been eating. Tastes like beef! Kills toxic maggots! That's something you can put on the side of the package. "It's a substitute for meat! It kills maggots!"

We get to see a giant fly. And, heck, they do their best. It's giant and practical. It whizzes around the field they're in. The Doctor gets to do what he did with the Minotaur in "The Time Monster." He loves that trick. It works on all species. To be honest, the fly is much better in the novelization where it feels as vile as the maggots. You knew they had to give this a try in live action though, regardless of whether or not they could pull it off.

BOSS almost succeeds in his big plan. He's going to make mind slaves out of everybody... in the world! In the end, it doesn't work. The final moments as Stevens basically kills BOSS are quite affecting in a psychedelic freak out kind of way. But then BOSS seems to be lost in his own form of freak out throughout his final moments. He is the chattiest computer around. And he loves his classical music. I wonder what it feels like having no limbs though. Oh yes, and in the end, everything blows up. That seems to be a 3rd Doctor thing. We don't really know it's over until everything blows up. Amen.

Goodbye Jo. The season was as uneven as the others from this era (from this TV show). But this was a great way to go out. You saw the Universe. You made your choice. The Earth is a better place because of it. Even if the Doctor misses you terribly.

A good anniversary season. A season that showed off the type of stories the show does and does well. The Blu-Ray set is excellent, by the way. I recommend it highly. Now, things are about to change. And I don't mean just the fact that skirts are about to get much longer.

*Thank you RTD and "Death of the Doctor" Parts 1 and 2 from *The Sarah Jane Adventures*

SEASON ELEVEN
1973-1974
(Mainly 1974)

THE TIME WARRIOR
Written by Robert Holmes
Directed By Alan Bromly
Episode One

Episode 356: (December 15, 1973) We meet Sarah Jane Smith and a Sontaran. Cliffhanger: Linx takes off his helmet. We see a Sontaran for the first time.

There's a lot happening in this episode. A heck of a way to start a new series. Jo, of course, is gone. The Doctor is by himself. We first see him being sequestered away with a bunch of other scientists under UNIT surveillance. We see the Brig, which is nice. We see that the Doctor's hair is getting bigger and taller as time goes by. He has a lovely aloofness in this episode. When he speaks with everyone, including the newly introduced Sarah Jane Smith, he seems to be in a different place. On a different plane. Very much the way the Doctor is in the current series when they've been left to their own devices too long. With Jo gone, the Doctor seems to be hanging out on Earth just because that's what he's been doing. He doesn't seem to be really enjoying it. Until he sees a Sontaran halfway up some steps. Then, the game's afoot!

We don't learn much about Sarah Jane here. She's obviously not her aunt Lavinia. (Again, a throwaway Holmes moment becomes something that part of *K9 And Company* will base itself around. That guy had the zingers.) She's there as an investigative journalist. Obviously, she's about 100 times more qualified for doing whatever it is she's doing than Jo was... the thing Sarah is missing. An influential relative? (At the end of the day, that's probably what most good people are missing.) But she's there doing her thing. Professor Beamish (who, luckily, is charming rather than annoying) knows that she's full of baloney. The Doctor doesn't care. He's enjoying acting odd and being the Doctor. Sarah's reaction to being transported through space is to think she's not been transported through time. That's interesting.

Then, there are the gang from the Middle Ages. Irongron, Bloodaxe and Linx. They're a fun bunch. The guys are so dumb. They're almost charmingly dumb. Having taken a castle because of the Crusades, all they do is argue and fight and act stupid. Holmes likes them so much he gives them the first 6 minutes of the episode. We haven't really done that in a while. Then, they meet Linx. The strange silver warrior from somewhere beyond the stars. Something strange begins to happen in the basement of the castle. Irongron and his men remain dumb throughout all of this.

It's a great story. Holmes didn't want to write it. But he does a beauty of a job. There's so much going on for one episode. So much stuff happening. Plus, Sarah Jane. Plus, the Sontarans. This is a big episode. It's the start of what will be this creative team's last season. They made the show hugely popular again and now things are breaking up. So, why isn't it a great episode?

One word: Direction.

In the commentary (more about that elsewhere), Barry Letts says that Alan Bromley was good at grouping people in frames and picking faces. But everything else in his direction came from his previous experience: live TV. "The Time Warrior" should be fast paced, exciting and weird. As it is, the 24 minutes feel like 44. A lot happens. But it doesn't fly past. It feels like a lot happens. Rather than carrying us along, it moves right alongside us. Barry Letts was supposed to direct this before *Moonbase 3* got in the way. He should have done it. He's not the most dynamic director but he does a good job. Bromley points the camera and lets it happen. If this was a Buster Keaton film, that would be OK. Here, it makes for an episode that should be brilliant in practice and ends up being brilliant in theory.

The Time Warrior
Episode Two

Episode 357: (December 22, 1973) The Doctor and Sarah get more embroiled in the Middle Ages. Cliffhanger: You don't hit Irongron.

Now, we're completely back in the Middle Ages. The time jumping of the first episode is gone. We have Sarah Jane Smith, not realizing that she's a companion, accusing the Doctor of terrible things. We have the Doctor meeting with a Sontaran and saying, for the first time, the name of his planet. * We have robot warriors. We have Hal the Archer. And we have the story slowly moving along. Possibly slower than it should.

It's not a bad episode because everything that was great about the first one continues to be great. Just, please, don't ask Mr. Bromley to direct an action scene. I don't know when the last time it was that he directed something action-related but he seems mostly at sea here. There is one nice shot. The overhead single shot of the Doctor running through the courtyard at the end. It doesn't quite work but it almost does. I think I know what the director was emulating here. Have you seen *You Only Live Twice*? There's a sequence in that where James Bond runs along the rooftop of a warehouse as a group of guys attack him and he fights back. It's mostly done in one huge overhead, helicopter shot. The camera rises and moves along the rooftop as Bond fights. We see the bad guys rushing up to him. We feel the excitement. It's a heck of a scene. It almost works here. 90% I'd say. It isn't quite as kinetic and exciting but almost.

It's fun to see someone who we are imagining as a potential companion for the Doctor thinking of him as a jerk who is up to something sneaky. She's full of piss and vinegar throughout the episode. But there does come a point with Irongron where you have to think "Am I part of some Renaissance Fair or is something else going on?" She says she hid onboard his ship. But she doesn't mention the fact that his ship was enormous on the inside and small on the outside. Are gals in the mid-1970s so blasé? It's amusing and I like it. (She doesn't get the obligatory "it's bigger on the inside" moment.) I look forward to the Doctor and Sarah Jane properly becoming friends.

Linx and The Doctor have a great scene in this episode. It's interesting to see. In and amongst all the Middle Age squalor... even amongst Sarah Jane and her 20th century squalor... we get this. The first mention of the Sontaran-Rutan war. Something even the new series hasn't really presented us with. The first mention of Gallifrey, the name of the Doctor's home planet. The Planet of the Time Lords. This is big stuff here. A major element of Doctor Who mythology being hid amongst what looks like a regular, OK slightly odd, story. It's great.

Again, the pacing is nothing to sing home about. I feel every minute of this when I watch it. That's too bad. But it's intriguing. The implications that the Sontaran would just as soon wipe out all of Earth rather than not doing so is an element to keep you focused and watching. Holmes has something up his sleeve even if Bromley has nothing up his.

*Again, it's a Robert Holmes slightly goofy name that sticks.

The Time Warrior
Episode Three

Episode 358: (December 29, 1973) The Doctor and Sarah stop an Irongron attack on the castle. Linx prepares to take off and leave the Earth.
Cliffhanger: Linx shoots The Doctor full in the face.

If you can get in the groove of it, this episode really moves along nicely. Again, a lot of stuff happens. And, again, when something exciting is meant to be happening, it doesn't quite. The siege on the castle is fun to watch. The Doctor lighting up the stink bombs and flinging them over the turrets is great. * Sarah's conviction that the Doctor is throwing some crazy poison concoction over the walls is great. She is really determined to believe that he has some craziness up his sleeve even after she believes him.

It's a nice scene when she finally believes him and then helps him out. He states his case. She believes him. There aren't episodes full of going back and forth and this that and the other. He is believed because he's The Doctor. Probably the way to go. They have an exchange where the Doctor delivers one of my favorite lines. Sarah is incredulous that he comes from another planet. She says, "Are you serious?" "About what I do? Yes. But necessarily the way I do it." There's the spirit of the show.

The episodes moves better than the others. Now that the Doctor and Sarah are teamed up there seems to be some extra excitement here. She isn't really the new companion yet. But she's definitely here and helping out. Heck, she gets dressed as a monk to join the Doctor heading back to Irongron's. Let's see what they're up to.

Then, there's that great moment where the Doctor figures out the rhythmic beat to take the scientists out of hypnosis. "Polka time!" I've always loved that. Knowing that the Doctor can keep the beat for Polka Time makes me very happy. And I like that Rubeish can keep it going. Lert's be honest. How many people listening right now expected to hear "Polka Time!" yelled out? Very few, I would reckon.

I guess I must be getting used to Bromley's direction. It wasn't dynamic here but it wasn't bothersome. The episode did feel like it moved faster than the others and that was helpful. I'll be honest; Linx and Irongron's conversations are getting a bit repetitive. Honestly, that's what they would have been like anyways so I'm not bothered. I'm just hoping that all is leading towards a heck of an ending. Because we all know that Linx is leaving soon.

*Continuing a Robert Holmes thing. There's the stinky swamps of the Drashigs. Goodge and his hard-boiled eggs. The planet of the Gonds and the strong smell of sulfur. He had a thing for stinky smells. Another reason why he's awesome.

The Time Warrior
Episode Four

Episode 359: (January 5, 1974): Linx is leaving. The Doctor has some lives to save.
Cliffhanger: The Doctor takes Sarah Jane back home.

"The Time Warrior" wraps up satisfactorily. Luckily, Holmes has written a lot of stuff into the episode so it is constantly moving along. It's one of those final episodes where you think "How are they going to fit everything into here?" They do, in the end. The Doctor gets the long sequence as the robot warrior, getting chased around by bullets. It's a funny but rather sadistic scene. Irongron's men are all given guns and told to shoot the Doctor, who is up against a wall. They keep missing because they don't know how to use the guns and the Doctor keeps dodging. But it's really harrowing, in theory. Again, as with much of the serial, the direction is off.

This one has my least favorite directorial moment. Well, maybe my two least favorites. The first is Hal removing the swords from Irongron's sleeping men. That could have been a little more exciting. It's basically Hal moving quickly around a table and pulling swords out of sheaths while the camera kind of follows him. There could have been more suspense there. And the moment Linx is killed always disappointed me. Barry Letts said that the director's thing was to always go for the easiest and quickest way. This scene is the perfect example.

Linx is at his controls. He is about to take off. Hal sees him and the probic vent. The door to the ship begins to swing shut. Hal is shown prepping his arrow. We see the door closing and think "Is Hal going to be able to shoot into that space?' Then it cuts to Linx with the arrow in the vent and he dies. First off, that's a "Blink and you'll miss it" moment. In fact, I think I turned away for about 6 seconds the first time I saw this and did just that. Second, it's so unexciting. Why show the door closing if it has no bearing? Why bother showing Hal getting ready? If you're going to do it that way, why not just show Hal looking at Linx and then Linx with an arrow in his vent. It's sloppy.

Overall though, the good definitely outweighs the bad here. I don't particularly want Alan Bromley back directing but there are no big bungles. The effects work. The costumes are great. The story has a lot going on. There are some great jokes. (Sarah telling the other women that they're "still living in the Middle Ages" is great.) And it wraps up decently. An excellent season opener, I think.

There is a feeling of melancholy in here though. The Doctor's first adventure with Jo was on "modern" Earth. UNIT was everywhere. There was a feeling of family being assembled. And that lasted for some time. With Sarah things are more "regular." There's no feeling of family here. The Brig hasn't been around since episode one. No Benton or Yates. The Doctor and Sarah don't seem to be fully friends here at the end. Although, they seem to be getting close. There's a feeling of the show about to enter a new phase. Unfortunately, the old phase is going to have to be put to rest first. And the people in charge don't quite want to let it go yet. Luckily, the next group won't be interested. We're at an odd crossroads here. Next up: Another UNIT story.

INVASION
Written by Malcolm Hulke
Directed by Paddy Russell
Part One

Episode 360: (January 12, 1974) Sarah and The Doctor return to London. London is now deserted. How long have they been gone and what is going on?

Cliffhanger: Dinosaurs!

In the previous season, Jo reviewed what they do whenever they get caught and how they get out. In this one, the Doctor and a looter pick a fight to get themselves freed from detention. We haven't seen that one in a while. It's funny whenever you hear "Classic" Doctor Who people talk about how the sonic screwdriver is used far too much today. When the "pretend to be sick" or "pretend to fight" thing was far less interesting and generally almost always annoying. I bring this up because this is the last UNIT story of the Pertwee era. One really gets the feeling that the era has now officially run out of ideas. (Although, there is one good one here.) Malcolm Hulke the writer mentioned that exiling the Doctor to Earth left them with only two types of stories. Luckily, there were more than that. But, at this point, it does seem like they're running a bit in circles. That's too bad because Pertwee generally seems pretty game for whatever, Sarah Jane is there and they can travel anywhere in time and space.

As I mentioned way back in the intro to this book, the very first story of Doctor Who I remember watching is "Planet of Evil." The very first story I encountered was this one. In the novelization by Hulke with the T-Rex in front of the Capitol building. It was called "Doctor Who and the Dinosaur Invasion." And I loved it. I'd read half of it before I saw a Doctor Who episode proper. The one I saw had Sarah Jane in it but the Doctor didn't seem to match up. There began my first moments of confusion with the show. Plus, if you read the Hulke's novelizations, and I've mentioned this before, no one could condense a story like Hulke and keep everything important in there. The novelization of this story was no different. When I finally saw this one, my initial (well, it lasted 6 years) interest in the show was fading. I was in high school. I was watching lots of horror movies and I was listening to lots of music. The Pertwee era killed off my absolute interest. And the 11th season kind of cemented that.

Which is too bad because this episode is quite good. They even went so far as to call it "Invasion" rather than "Invasion of the Dinosaurs" to keep the monsters hidden away. Granted, a pterodactyl files at Sarah halfway into the episode so that kind of messes that up. But, still, their hearts were in the right places. (It reminds me of the first episode of "Day of the Daleks" and the odd reveal of the Dalek that should have waited until the end.) But there are dinosaurs here! And, apparently, they're random?

The episode wins because of the wonderful job they've done to make London desolate. The opening shots of empty streets with toys and dogs is nicely done. The Doctor and Sarah Jane just not knowing what is going on is great. No matter how much they wander they can't seem to get the info they need. When we see the Brig, Benton and friends, it's nice. They are a breath of fresh air here. But then, there's that Army general causing problems. Plus, there's the scene in the school gym where the Doctor and Sarah are kept prisoners. It really creates a strong feeling of a world having fallen apart.

And through it, the Doctor smiles. He and Sarah Jane joke around. They try to find out what in the name of the heavens is happening here. The Doctor's mirth over getting his mugshot taken shows that he hasn't lost his sense of humor. He mentioned to Sarah his MO in the last episode. Here he lives up to it. Let's hope he doesn't get eaten by a dinosaur.

INVASION OF THE DINOSAURS
Episode Two

Episode 361: (January 19, 1974) The Doctor and Sarah Jane make it to UNIT and learn what's going on. Mike Yates has gone traitor. I think.

Cliffhanger: A T-Rex appears to threaten the Doctor. (Different from the previous time.)

This s a good second episode. When I say "good," I'm not sure I'm including the dinosaurs. We can talk about them later. The episode gives us the background on the world we're currently in. It gives the Doctor something to do. It has Yates, Benton and the Brig. Yates is now working for the General but that's Yates for you. And then we have the General.

Oh, the General. He dismisses everything the Brig wants. If he must acquiesce to anything, he's really pissed off. And he can't handle anything the Doctor is saying. We've seen this character so many times in the past. * You can almost speak his lines before he says them. How do people like this get put in charge of things like this and why do they always end up on *Doctor Who*?

The time eddies are a nice touch. The way the episode presents time is fun. At least this era has done some fun time stuff. The dinosaurs are brought here through some sort of time displacement. When they leave, it sends time back slightly and no one (but the Doctor) can remember what happened. They just know there was a dinosaur there but now it's gone. The Doctor's vulnerability to this is cool. And the scene where the peasant from the 13th Century appears is a nice "The hell?" moment.

And there's Yates. As I said, working for the regular Army now. He has a weird conversation with Sarah Jane where he seems to think she's Jo Grant. Sarah doesn't know who he is or Benton. I'm not sure why they're talking so friendly. Especially when she says she might chat up Yates. She already has. Hasn't she? Poor Mike. When he starts talking about how wonderful London is without people, we can gauge something has gone a bit wrong. It's odd seeing a character we've grown to enjoy winding up with the "bad guys." It is nice to see the Doctor have a civil conversation with someone from the Ministry though. The gentleman who wants a greener Earth. Some more of Letts and Dicks doing their thing. It's not too obvious. I'm kidding. It is.

We're also getting some rum comedy in here. The scene where the Doctor is trying to build his weapon thing and everyone keeps asking him what it is starts off amusing. But then, Pertwee lets out a face that's a big "No, Jon. Don't." for me. We are getting near the end of his time though. He's keeping the spirits up.

Well, shall we talk about the dinosaurs? They're not terrible. OK, maybe they are. The show is doing its best. The tricky thing is that I never would tell a creative show like this that "Hey! Maybe you shouldn't try this on your budget." I would never limit what they could do. When I think that, I remember an interview with Paul McCartney were someone asked him about playing drums. And he basically says that he doesn't play them great but he plays them well enough. So, he only gives himself drum parts that he knows he can do. He would never give himself a series of Neal peart-style fills because he can't do that. In the same way. Barry Letts hasn't had great success with giant lizard-y monsters. So, why base a show around them? Granted, they're not in this a lot. But, when you're a kid, you want dinosaurs. And they need to look better than this.

*Yes. I know, Mr. Hulke has something up his sleeve. But it's up to you decide whether it's worth spending so much time with this sort of character again.

Invasion of the Dinosaurs
Episode Three

Episode 362: (January 26, 1974) Sarah Jane investigates power sources in Central London. The Doctor tries to monitor a T-Rex but someone keeps sabotaging him.
Cliffhanger: Sarah is on a spaceship travelling across the galaxy. How long has she been there?

Great, great cliffhanger on this episode. It really expands the story beautifully and confusingly. I'll start here. Sarah Jane is investigating whether there is some sort of fallout shelter in Central London that may have a power supply capable of bringing on the dinosaurs. It turns out that the Minister is involved and Sarah is hypnotized/ sent to Unconscious Town. When she wakes up, a young man shows her the view of outer space from a ship. She left Earth six months.

It's a great moment because 1) What the hell? And 2) Sarah has been gone for six months! That's very much a modern-day TV storytelling kind of thing. "Six Months Later…" "Two years later…" Several shows, including this one, have done it. When the credits roll, we really do believe that Sarah could be six months in the future. We may become disabused of that notion shortly but right now it's strong in our mind. And a great cliffhanger to add to the show about halfway through. Just enough to keep it moving and throw in a nice twist. Well done, Mr. Hulke.

The rest of the episode involves watching over a T-Rex and Yates continuing to sabotage things. It's pretty good. We know what's up but the good guys don't yet. There's a lot of talk of Prof. Whitaker and his time travel experiments and as mentioned, Sarah does a lot of investigating, which is fun. Apparently, Elizabeth Sladen was not a big fan of this element of her character but she pulls it off here. She even seems to charm the charmless general Finch.

The dinosaurs still aren't great. But, that T-Rex is in the background of the airplane hangar shot so long, it becomes like a cute little doll relaxing. Also, as much of a great journalist as Sarah Jane might be, she really didn't see a 17-foot-tall T-Rex stand up right next to her? It seems odd. Although the T-Rex is clearly fake (they couldn't get the use of a real one), the scene where it keeps trying to get into the office and get to Sarah is well done. (Although, as the Doctor and Sarah run away, it's obvious that Pertwee's back is really bothering him.)

In the end, it's another good episode. Yes, some of it is repetitive. Some of it does feel familiar. And the dinosaurs are shaky as heck. Hulke is brining just enough to the game. This may be his "Last Album" as it were but he's handling himself well. Using the tropes we expect but moving them around deftly enough to make it interesting for the viewer. Now, can we keep this up for three more episodes. We shall see.

Invasion of the Dinosaurs
Episode Four

Episode 363: (February 2, 1974) Sarah is causing trouble on the Ship. The Doctor finds the underground base.
Cliffhanger: The bad guys make a dinosaur materialize near the Doctor and General Finch accuses the Doctor of being the monster maker.

Well, the introduction of the Ship was a great twist. I'm perfectly fine going with the story when it jumps back to the regular timeline. Many say "Well, it's ruined because we see the Doctor in the same timeline so she can't be in the future." I'm fine because the Ship storyline gives away the act quick., Sarah still has a cut on her forehead from the previous episode. So, we know it's chicanery. But the three people she meets really believe they've been there for months. When did they get woken up? Why is Sarah on there in the first place? Maybe the Minister takes a shine to her but it does seem strange.

Do we honestly want the people we see on this Ship taking charge of anything? When the lady bypasses "pollution or war," to roar against moral degradation and permissiveness, we know that these are a bunch of prudes in a ship. How on Earth are they all going to survive? Won't they need to reproduce? Two of the three people we see are older people. I've seen *Moonraker*. You need to bring the younger people along. Who wants to spend the rest of their lives building a planet with the worst school administrator ever? I do like the "Reminder Room" though. It's like that room the Miners in "Colony In Space" put The Doctor into. This is Hulke speaking here. It's weird because you would have thought these might be people he liked. Idealists leaving a rotting Earth behind. But they're kind of presented as dopes. And Sarah gets to state, full on, that she should have been allowed to choose. Someone made a boo boo.

The rest of the episode is tricky. In the Ship, stuff is happening. A new world is promised and they are moving towards it. In London, if you like watching the Doctor sneak around, then this episode is for you. Oh, the Whomobile! We get the Whomobile! Personally, I prefer Bessie. If you haven't seen the Whomobile, it looks like a spaceship with fins and it seems to hover along. Actually, it looks like a moving piece of merchandise.

The bad guys do get a little sloppy in there, don't they? General Finch's proclamation that the Doctor is their monster maker seems ridiculous. You almost want to laugh into that cliffhanger. I think we're meant to take it seriously and bemoan the fact that UNIT might be about to arrest the Doctor. It's so silly though because it doesn't make sense. The bad guys pull together this plan hilariously fast and the cliffhanger just sort of drops out of the sky. It's amusing but not what I'd call terribly exciting. This episode is starting to show the mid-story slowdown big time. Let's hope the next one picks it up.

Invasion of the Dinosaurs
Episode Five

Episode 364: (February 9, 1974) The Doctor is on the run as Operation Golden Age approaches its conclusion.
Cliffhanger: The Doctor encounters more dinosaurs.

The Doctor is under arrest! He's a Monster Maker! UNIT is sent to hunt him down. Benton has a lovely moment where he lets the Doctor give him a blast of Venusian aikido. Yates is a bad guy. The Brig kind of stashes himself away so General Finch won't get in his way. And most of the Doctor's time here is spent in a chase. I wish I could say it was a super exciting chase like something from a James Bond film. Sadly, it's not. It's a lot of shots of cars passing by. Then shots of cars turning around and going in a different direction. Generally, it's not an exciting car chase. You need to work at making a car chase exciting. There are so many of them. They're like drum solos. You need to make it dynamic and exciting. Simply bashing away does very little. This car chase, while it's nice to see The Doctor sort of alone and on the run, feels like it goes on for a very long time.

Sarah Jane leaves the Ship. It's not a real ship. Is Salamander in charge of all of this? For her, there's a good deal of sneaking around, like the Doctor did in the last episode. She then discovers that ANOTHER person she's met is a traitor. "Oh no. Not you too…" equates to "Oh no. It's everybody…" The repetitiveness of this has really built up. I'm very happy the next episode is the last one because I'm not sure I'm up to having this happen again.

It's odd. The first three episodes were quite good. Ever since the dinosaur action has begun to really die down, this story has become kind of bland. They're going from over here to over there. The Doctor finds his way in. Sarah finds her way out. The Doctor being called a traitor is a big moment and it's kind of interesting. But not incredibly so. As others have suggested, this is Hulke sort of critiquing what has come before in the Pertwee era and finding the era coming up a bit wanting, if not a little light on fun. That could be true. It also could be that this is his 6th story in 6 seasons (7 if you count all his work on "The Ambassadors of Death.") and he's simply worn out. Everyone is running around in endless circles.

At this point, the story is basically The Doctor, Sarah, Brig and Benton versus everybody else in Central London. The "everybody else" has control of a bunch of dinosaurs. They have a Timescoop that can roll back time to a "Golden Age" for the Earth. These all sound like hippies. I wish they had just taken up self-sufficiency instead. Regardless, we are now on the cusp of the final episode. The last episode written by Malcolm Hulke. We will lose a creative force after that episode. I'm hoping it goes out with a big bang.

Invasion of the Dinosaurs
Episode Six

Episode 365: (February 16, 1974) Operation Golden Age draws to a close. Who stays and who goes? Cliffhanger: Sarah and The Doctor are going to take a trip to Florana.

The last Pertwee era UNIT story ends. Benton beats up Yates. The Brig and The Doctor blow a hole in the London Underground. And the Doctor walks through a time eddy and saves humanity. Plus, a triceratops shows up. It all seems a bit sad and solemn. But this era is ending. This time is ending. Pertwee is still wonderful but he's starting to feel slightly off in his own show.

The great thing here is the great thing of many 3rd Doctor stories. They diddle around throughout a lot of the 4th and 5th episodes. And suddenly there's a thousand things to do in the sixth. Suddenly, the sixth episode becomes insanely sharply plotted and almost modern in it structure. This has happened several times. One thinks "Are they going to be able to wrap everything up in this one episode?' The answer is: Yes. But it's going to be tight.

There is a great moment in the information text on the DVD. It asks you to count the seconds from when the people on the ship get to the main control room in the Underground hidden base. It's awesome. There's a nice space in between when they leave there and when they arrive in the place with the misguided people who want to help them. The people who think it would be better to negate the entirety of human history rather than let it continue. Look, I'm not a big fan of human history right now. And there are certain stretches that should be wiped out. But we must learn and we must move forward. The wonderfully odd thing about all of this is that Professor Whitaker and his assistant always seem so aloof from everything else happening. They never seem fully connected to it. It's an experiment to them. That's some goofed up science, baby.

Sarah kicks butt in this episode. Re-entering the ship. Telling them what's up. Making them bring Grover over. (Grover over?) She is fantastic. And she gets the crowd assembled in the control room. That causes the assemblage of people leading to the ending. She's a good companion, Doctor. Keep her on.

It's nice that everything is wrapped up here. The pace is sharp and fast. It dovetails into a great Doctor moment. It leads us on to the next story where they may or may not go into space again. If you've seen the title of the next episode, you can make a decent guess.

DEATH TO THE DALEKS
Written by Terry Nation
Directed by Michael E. Briant
Episode One

Episode 366: (February 23, 1974) Strange thing are happening on the planet Exxilon.
Cliffhanger: The Daleks arrive.

I do like this episode quite a bit. It has elements of "Planet of the Daleks" and "Colony in Space" along with elements of all the other Nation Dalek stories. Most of the episode is wandering around a weird landscape. Wandering around a hostile place. Forced into it because of a problem with the TARDIS. Now, back in the day, the TARDIS went screwy because the Doctor drained the fluid link or it got buried. Here, it's because an Ancient and crazy city has drained all the power from it. Doesn't that work much better than the Spiridonian fungus things making the TARDIS into something ridiculous? In here, the Doctor says that the TARDIS is alive and amazing. So what is draining the power? This works much better than last season's story. The tricky thing is: It's so much like last season's story. Terry Nation hasn't grasped the concept of variety.

A dark episode. The BBC wanted to issue a warning to children at the start. Apparently, the head of the BBC said that that's ridiculous because why would you make a show for kids and then warn them away from it at the start. It does have dark moments. The quarry is not as lit up as usual. It is a darker space. A more threating space. And the robed creatures are rough. The fact that one of them gets inside the TARDIS is crazy! That simply doesn't happen. We got a Zarbi in there back in the day but that got confused very quickly by its surroundings. This truly does feel like a strange, unpleasant world. The fact that it was supposed to be Florana makes it worse.

The City is a bit of gorgeous South American strangeness. The mutant guys running around are their own brand of weird. That crescendo chanting thing they do is enough to give anyone the whim-whams. It's good stuff. The episode just notches out the start of "Planet" because the jungle there seems so cliché. Wherever we are here has a bit more mystery to it. A bit more wonderment around what is happening and why is it happening. It's a great intro episode.

The human beings are an interesting (I think) bunch. Tough guy, wimpy guy, lead and lady. The Doctor amiably bumbles his way through a chat. Now, let's see what they have in store for us.

Death To The Daleks
Episode Two

Episode 367: (March 2, 1974) Everyone is taken underground. Sacrifice is instigated.
Cliffhanger: A giant metal snake-thing is about to cause some major problems.

And the Daleks have arrived! And their guns don't work. They are truly unthreatening when they have no ability to kill anything at any time. Now, yes, they do arm themselves with guns, regular bullet firing guns and they become a threat again. But, for half an episode the Daleks are not a threat. They're just another race looking around for Exxilon's Parrinium. It's a sharp idea, I think. Yes, the previous cliffhanger lingers too long on the Daleks guns not working. It does become obvious that something is messed up. It doesn't matter. The Daleks are here! And they're in a shorter story than usual so we should hopefully have some stronger pacing than we did previously.

There's a touch of oddness throughout the episode. It is strange to see the Daleks down in the Exillon caves as they are sacrificing Sarah. Seeing the humans there? Not so much. We're used to seeing humans and beings like that in places like this. But having the Daleks locked away is a new thing. Especially in the presence of those weird Exxilons. Their masks aren't terribly convincing. It's the robes and the set and that weird ass chanting. At one point, I thought I heard Jon Pertwee in the chanting. I know he did lots of funny voices so that amused me.

The episode moves through moods quite nicely. It goes from Dalek horror when the ship lands. Then, to a trek through the quarry and a well-executed Exxilon attack. Then, to the cage. The Doctor attacks the Exxilons. That seems very much a Doctor thing to do. And, given the amount of people there, not really a Doctor thing to do. He's getting impulsive in his last days is this one.

I can't say I'm thrilled by the Dan character. A gruff old Scotsman without a brain in his head who wants to lead. The commander, in his dying words, says he shouldn't lead and someone else should. And then he dies. I'd hope I have better dying words myself. The Commander did his best. I like that Dan has no idea what to do. When the Daleks take over, he looks befuddled. When the other humans talk to him, he acts like he had something to do with what's going on. He's a jerk. This may not end well.

The Daleks have little TARDIS models that they shoot at for practice. That is to be loved!

I like when Sarah Jane and The Doctor drop into the cave. Out of the frying pan. Sarah keeps up a sense of humor throughout as does the Doctor. There is a wonderful sense of menace. That is bolstered by the mention of a renegade group of Exxilons that the Daleks are going to exterminate.

Overall, it's a fun episode. Especially one for the end of an era like this. I think it may have something to do with the fact that, at this time, Terrance Dicks was re-writing "The Monster of Peladon" and so turned over the script editing duties to Robert Holmes, who was soon to take the job. I just like the way Holmes tells his stories. Even if, like this one, it isn't incredibly original. But it is very fun. Now, we're in a cave. There's a giant snake thing and a little grey guy. Let's see what happens next.

Death To The Daleks
Episode Three

Episode 368: (March 9, 1974) The Doctor and a new friend enter The City.
Cliffhanger: There's a floor with squares of different colors on it!

Yes. The cliffhanger is bad because they had to adjust some scenes due to running times of the episodes. We can say it's bad or we can say it's not bad. It's up to us. As it stands, it stinks. But, maybe, that checkered floor that we see for two seconds is crazy as hell. I don't know. We'll see next episode. (Unless this is the review where you give up on the book and throw it in the fire. To you, angered reader, I would say "You're not getting your money's worth". Of course, if you have the book illegally, now's the time for you to learn this: there's a small explosive in the binding of each copy. Five seconds in the fire… you and your dwelling will explode into flames in a hilarious fashion.)

Meanwhile, the rest of the episode is the Daleks slowly taking over the planet. All those rotten slave worlds that we've seen previously… here we see them being created. Here we see them bringing on the slaves. Here we see them doing that great upper management thing where they bring on people to help… but then basically they brought everyone but themselves onboard to serve. To be slaves. If you're not a Dalek, you get the shaft.

Luckily, they are on a crazy planet that isn't playing by their rules. A planet with metal snakes in the water and the caves and the grass. A place where The City is stronger and more powerful than they are. That makes it interesting. Normally, the Daleks are the force in charge of whatever is happening but here… no. The planet is actively hostile to them in a way that makes Kembel or Spiridon look a little tame. The City is alive, my friends. Alive.

Bellal and Sarah carve a fun friendship here. He's small and glowing. She's slightly taller and not glowing. It feels a lot like an easier to take version of Jo and her invisible Spiridon friend in "Planet of the Daleks." The Doctor has the same sort of reaction to Bellal as he did to Wester. Slightly taken aback but happy that Sarah has made a good friend amid all this chaos. Remember, a few minutes before, she was drugged and ready to be sacrificed to this root monster. All the chaos has woken her up and she's ready for fun.

The great thing about this story, for me, is the structure. Most of that first episode, in typical Nation/Dalek style, is meandering around and learning bits and bobs. It isn't until the Daleks show up that things really begin moving. But this is Nation's first four-parter. So, he doesn't have time, once Episode Two, begins for a lot of his tangents and all the characters he normally introduces. By removing the Daleks' power, he puts them on the back foot for half of the previous episode. Now, at the start of the third episode, things feel like they're properly beginning. But with Sarah being sent to warn the humans and the Doctor and Bellal entering the city, there's a feeling that we are approaching the climax before we settled in properly. Frankly, I love it. We needed more stories like this in Pertwee's time. And they needed to be directed by Michael E. Briant, unlike Bromley. Briant keeps this moving and exciting, even if that cliffhanger ain't the best. The "E" stands for Excellence.

Are the worst Pertwee cliffhangers the ones where scenes had to be moved around? I'm thinking of "Frontier in Space" Episode Four here.

Death To The Daleks
Episode Four

Episode 369: (March 16, 1974) The Doctor and Bellal race to the heart of the City. Sarah Jane works with the humans to try get the mineral they need and get off the planet the moment power returns. Cliffhanger: The City dissolves.

I figured out what's most interesting about this serial for me. That's that I think it's structured more like a regular single 45-minute episode of modern *Doctor Who* then like the 1970s style. Bear with me. (Or skip to the next story.) Most modern single episode stories involve the Doctor and friends landing in a place. They catch the lay of the land. They figure out what's going on. Usually but not always, there's one big thing that they must do. One big epic thing that must be taken care of. Sometimes a second one is thrown in. but, usually, they are all working towards one thing.

In here, it's the Destruction of the City. It starts out as if it's all about the Parrinium and saving the galaxy. But once the energy cuts out it becomes something different. In the first two episodes, they get the lay of the land. And in the last two they proceed to solve the problem: Destroy the City. Only then can they get the heck out of there. (But, of course, so can the Daleks.) That's not something that happened in old time *Doctor Who*. Although, I mean, you could break some four-part stories down like that. (The small number of two-part stories are like that.) The serials at that time generally involved more going on. (And, of course, a four-parter is 90-100 minutes too.) But this story really has a modern feeling to it. Except for the lack of CGI, of course.

People have denigrated the puzzles in The City. Sure, maybe they aren't the toughest. Maybe they're a bit repetitive. I enjoy it. Did you expect, when this serial started, that that would be the bulk of the final episode? Neither did I. That's why I loved the show. It's got surprises standing by. I like Bellal and The Doctor's steady stroll through the place. I love the demon-things attacking the Daleks. I like the reveal of the Guardian that turned to dust ages ago. It's a fine scene. They balance it nicely with all the drama on the surface.

Although, I do always wonder… How much did the Doctor and Bellal do within The City? Because it isn't until the explosive goes off and destroys the beacon that power is returned and the thing collapses. Is it implied that the whole thing would have done that anyway but the beacon's destruction helped that along? Or is the destruction of the beacon the real catalyst? Maybe it would have taken years for the City to rot from the inside. The destruction of the beacon started its destruction from the outside. I'm not sure. I've always wondered.

Jill and Sarah Jane do a nice job of faking out the Daleks with their mineral replacement system. The guys climb a beacon. The sets, overall, are very nice. I don't believe there's any location work here. It's all studio. And it works. Especially at night, at the rocks or by the entrance to the City. We call it a City. But all we see are corridors and a control room. Presumably, every person who lived in that City didn't have to go through that every time they came home from the quarry. They probably had some sort of passkey or something. Like getting the Front of the Line pass at Universal Studios. (The only way to go.) Everyone else must go through the twisting and endless line. You are immediately shunted through a sideline and suddenly you're home!

I do hope the Exxilons are going to be OK. I wonder how quickly after the story ends do Sarah and The Doctor leave. My favorite moment here, in a story I quite like, is when Bellal and Sarah meet up again and shake hands. Sarah has a big smile on her face. Although you really can't tell, I think Bellal does too.

THE MONSTER OF PELADON
Written by Brian Hayles
Directed By Lennie Mayne

Episode One

Episode 370: (March 23, 1974) The TARDIS lands on Peladon. Fifty years after the last visit. I wonder how they're getting along.
Cliffhanger: The Doctor and The Queen's Champion are buried alive in a rockfall.

And as the Third Doctor's era winds down we get a sequel to a beloved (right?) story from the middle of his run. Like that story, it is the only other Third Doctor era story with no location footage. All in the studio. Like that story, we get the cave sets and the throne set and the communicator room and the shrine. * There's another person in power with a bit of a lisp. And another old guy berating everything going on. Hey! There's Alpha Centauri again. Aggedor must be around here somewhere, right? And it all feels a bit like a natural extension of the previous story. The tricky thing is that "Curse" just barely filled up its four parts. This one is six.

As much as I liked seeing everyone again and as much as I liked seeing the way Peladon had progressed after joining the Federation, there does seem to be a sense of the repetitive setting in already. The episode starts with a spectral Aggedor attack in the caves. There's another one in the middle. And a third one is the cliffhanger. Let's hope they haven't run out of ideas as we still have 125 minutes left. I think they probably have more up their sleeve.

I do love the concept of hopping 50 years ahead and seeing some consequences. That's not really something the show does. "Boom Town" and then "Bad Wolf," accidentally, are other examples. Mostly, we'll see the Doctor landing somewhere we've never been before and then we learn about a previous adventure, a la "The Face of Evil" or "Timelash." So, this is interesting to see. Especially as this was coming at a time of constant miner's strikes and energy shortages. A very troubled time for the country.

My favorite part is the answer to this question: What has the Federation done for the people of Peladon? We can see the opposite quite clearly. The mineral trisilicate is something the Federation desperately needs to fight a war. Peladon has a ton of it. So, all the miners are being forced to work and work and work to help this war that they know nothing of. What does Peladon get? Angry workers. Nobles who don't really see the point of all this. General discontent. And apparently an evil spirit attacking them. I love that they were told that joining the Federation would be excellent for them. It turns out it is excellent. For the Federation. The purpose of the previous story is rendered moot by the awful treatment they're getting here.

A lot happens in this episode. Vega Nexos is in it! And then he dies. The miners all wear dumb wigs. They were described as "badgers." I call them distracting as all get out. Let's see where the story goes.

*Wasn't the Doctor sentenced to death the first time he went in that room? Things have gotten lax since the King passed on.

The Monster Of Peladon
Episode Two

Episode 371: (March 30, 1974) A lot of back and forth between royalty and the miners.
Cliffhanger: Aggedor attacks! For real.

Well, this got ludicrous quick, didn't it? The only new thing added on here is that 1) the Doctor and Sarah Jane meet up with Aggedor in the end (which kind of goofs the cliffhanger's excitement if this is the same one) and 2) the door to the Federation refinery is fitted with psychedelic lights and noises that can drive you mad, courtesy of Eckersley the Engineer. Sarah accidentally activates the alarm when she sees something lurking around inside. And it is intense. As Alpha C. and Eck. talk about why it is so strong, it becomes obvious that they consider all Peladon to be a bunch of primitives, not just the royalty. And then royalty on Peladon considers the miners to be primitives. Miners can't win.

Something here should be sending out some bells and whistles regarding Eckersley. Or maybe it's just me. He's so blasé as all sorts of crazy stuff goes on around him. I understand he is here to do his job but this is a bit much. Even Alpha Centauri cares about what's going on and they weren't like that last time. (Although, for the first time, Centauri's voice goes so high-pitched in this episode that I found it obnoxious.) And let's not mention Eckersley's "answers" when Sarah is being questioned about her possible collusion with Ettis. More about that in a moment.

It is nice to see Aggedor. The previous story did air two years previous. So, there is a good chance a lot of people haven't seen the original. I don't believe it was repeated. At the same time, why do such a direct sequel if you didn't expect most of the people to know what it was? So, I like to think most people would giggle and say "Hey! It's Aggedor! He's a nice guy." What did they do? Just shove Aggedor back into the cave after the Doctor left. Is it the same one? How long do these creatures live? I don't know if I'm that interested in all this but maybe we'll find some stuff out.

Otherwise, this episode is rather monotonous. The question of "What was in the refinery?" notwithstanding. The worst part, I think, is the questioning Sarah Jane portion. It goes a little something like this: Ettis storms the control room. He knocks out Eckersley and takes Sarah hostage. He will kill her unless Centurial opens the armory. It does. Ettis takes Sarah with him as he leaves. They encounter the guards and Hepesh. Sarah escapes. She is immediately arrested for being in cahoots with the miners. One might say, at this point: What? That's ridiculous. And it is. It's very ridiculous. Sarah calmly tries to explain wat happened but they don't believe her. And it becomes ludicrous. Especially when they ask Sarah if she helped Ettis get the doors open. "No." "Why did Centauri open the door?' "Because Ettis would kill me if he they didn't." "Then, you did help him open the door." "No..." And Sarah is right. That's a big "No." But they go with it. That works for them. And then Eckersley, who was unconscious, kind of says "Maybe she was working with them." Then, even Centauri is unsure. It's truly a stupid moment in Doctor Who. The kind of childish writing moment you hope to never see but that does appear now and again.

What happens in the rest of the episode? It doesn't matter. Running around, capture, escape and recapture. Guys with bad wigs running around. The Queen is useless. The Doctor does almost nothing. I don't think I've encountered a story where the quality dropped so fast and so violently. Episode Three, I'm counting on you.

The Monster of Peladon
Episode Three

Episode 372: (April 6, 1974) The Federation brings in their own personal peacemakers.
Cliffhanger: The Ice Warriors have arrived.

This one does something that saves the pace here. Because we're not barreling towards excitement. This story is taking a slow and determined pace to a ridiculous extent. Luckily, Eckersley is there to give us a push. What happens is that Alpha Centauri is convinced that she must call in Federation troops. They do. And the troops cannot be repulsed or sent away.

This seems like a decent complication. But the thing that makes it great is when Sarah Jane suggest they all go and act like nothing is wrong so the forces go away. That's clever. That's why we have Sarah Jane here. That's the Sarah Jane who got her own show for five series and had great adventures. The Doctor seems a little superfluous at this point. Even though I love his outfit. He matches!

There's a lot of back and forth here. The miners, the royalty, the whatever. The plotting in this story is becoming almost childish. I'm having trouble putting together a decent review because of that. Luckily, there is a moment in the end that helps. Let's talk about something else first.

Of course. This is the Women's Lib episode of the show. We had "The Time Monster" with its pile of Women's Lib. That was an important movement. That was an important thing. But, oh boy, why is that every time TV deals with this topic it seems squirmy? There was a "The Brady Bunch" episode where Marcia gets involved in WL. It was left out of the syndication package for years because it was a bad episode. It's back in there now because we're all completists. But it's still bad. So many shows in the late 19609s into the early 1970s had awful episodes like this. This is not an awful episode of Doctor Who. But that stuff makes it dated... and not in a good way.

The Ice Warriors are back! The last time we saw them they were good guys. More or less. But here, what are we meant to think? We'll find out. We have three episodes left. I don't mean to sound tired. But I feel like everyone except Lis Sladen are tired here. I think we will see as the next three episodes go. We have the Warriors here. That should kickstart everything.

The Monster of Peladon
Episode Four

Episode 373: (April 13, 1974) The Ice Warriors take over. Things go from bad to worse.
Cliffhanger: The sonic lance explodes.

The Ice Warriors have declared martial law. They have taken over Peladon and everything Azaxyr says is law. He is the judge, jury and executioner. Gosh, I do hope the people of Peladon took the time to read their Federation warranty because this seems to be a bit much. The Federation exploits a planet. The people in charge may get something but most of the people do not. * When the Federation lands because one of their members has expressed some worry, the Federation troops take over the planet. That's garbage and nonsense. I'm glad to see the people of Peladon get pissed about that. I just wished they had better weapons.

The Doctor does what he can here. He tries to get the miners to work and they do with the help of Gebek. Of course, Ettis is a problem. But, Ettis has never been a great character. The way he goes about acquiring info and getting the sonic lance just feels tiresome. It feels like a trope, a concept, the show has done one too many times. When the Doctor and Terry Walsh must fight him at the end of an episode, it feels rote. When the Ice Warriors announce that they will just blow up the lance, one wants the story to end right here. What was a tight, sharp, whodunnit from two seasons ago, has now become endlessly elongated political drama that I can't even pretend to feign interest in.

The Peladonians are incensed by all of this. Eckersley doesn't care. Alpha Centauri is a bit remorseful. Basically, they've had martial law declared on a planet that they were meant to help. Boy, they did that poorly. It turns out all the misgivings in "Curse" were well founded. This is not good. The Doctor and Sarah do have a theory. That's that these Ice Warriors might not be from the Federation at all. That's fine. That's fun. But, please, do something about it soon. I've nothing else to write about.

*We must imagine that if there is an actual planet involved around this mountain castle... then, there are a lot of people on this planet. We are seeing such a mind-bogglingly small percentage of them. The royals in charge. Some outsiders. And the miners that are exploited. It almost doesn't make sense at all that these are the people who are supposed to be the main population of the planet. Where are the wives? Where are the men and women who do anything but mining? Where are the children? Surely there must be children somewhere. Right?

The Monster of Peladon
Episode Five

Episode 374: (April 20, 1074) The Ice Warriors continue to keep control. Things are getting worse. Cliffhanger: The Ice Warriors burst into the refinery room.

I may have shot myself in the foot here. As you may have guessed, "The Monster of Peladon" is possibly my least favorite Pertwee story. There are many reasons for that. The general feeling from everyone, except Elisabeth Sladen, of "We're all tired and we're done soon. Nobody cares anyway." permeates the whole thing. Lennie Mayne is not the most kinetically exciting of directors. I know he directed the first one, which has one big fight. I wouldn't have given him this one, which is filled with fight scenes and scenes that need to be exciting. When the most exciting things happening are "Look! An overhead shot!" and "It's Terry Walsh again!", things aren't going great.

One also keeps hoping for a real and true reason to come back to Peladon. Yes, seeing the way the Federation is using them is interesting. But, not for six episodes. Then when you learn (SPOILER) that Azaxyr and his Ice Warriors are not from the Federation. They're from a breakaway group wanting to make the Ice Warriors warriors again. You have to sigh. Am I sighing because they had a villain go good and now the twist is that they've gone bad again? (But, not really, Since, apparently, most of them are still good.) Am I sighing because one spends so long waiting for the ice Warriors to show up? Then when they do, it's not too fantastic. Am I sighing because Eckersley was quite obviously up to something from the start and now that that's affirmed... where do we go from here? I'm sighing because there was no real reason to do this story, apart from the Federation thing... but these aren't beings from the Federation. Alpha Centauri is and no one else. We're just watching the clock tick away here.

The Doctor gets in another fight, gets involved in another explosion and doesn't die. The miners try to continue to pretend like they're acquiescing. Azaxyr is still a jerk. Eckersley is still slimy. We still only have three real sets, apart from hallways. It's nice to be inside the refinery. But, boy, am I sick of those other sets. The problem with the end of the episode is this: It's completely unmemorable. It's people over here doing this. People over here doing that. Some more people doing this other thing. None of it is going to amount to anything until later in the next episode. By then, I think we'll all just want it to end.

"The Smugglers" and "The Space Pirates" were also not great penultimate stories. But almost all those episodes are lost. So, some of our knowledge comes from other sources. Here we can see all of "Monster." My only thought is "Let's wrap this up."

The Monster of Peladon
Episode Six

Episode 375: (April 27, 1974) A lot of running around and then it ends.
Cliffhanger: Heading back to Earth.

The Peladon saga comes to an end amongst immense devastation. In the end, when the Doctor and Sarah leave, the only people in the throne room are Gebek and the Queen. I think that's because everybody else is dead. *About Time* was the first publication to note that this story is kind of a bloodbath. Dead Ice Warriors, Dead miners, dead royals, dead everybody litter the caves. What seemed like an end of an era attempt at a romp has a body count as high as "Resurrection of the Daleks." It does make the ending, especially with Aggedor's death, much more funeral-like that we expected. * Although the Doctor's line "A tear, Sarah Jane" when she thinks he's dead will become much more powerful in six episodes' time.

The one thing with the episode, unlike say the last few stories, is that there's not much to do. The Miners, with the Doctor's help as he controls Aggedor, stop the Ice Warriors. Eckersley grabs the Queen and sets off through the tunnels. (In probably the most harrowing moments of the story, Eckersley is legitimately unpleasant as he drags the Queen through the caves.) He's stopped. The Federation war with Galaxy Five ends and it's all done. So, the episode spends a very long time with the Doctor being bombarded by the colorful, psychedelic mind probing rays of Eckersley's alarm system. We know the Doctor's going to be OK. This isn't "Planet of the Spiders" or even *Interference* Book Two. He has dealt with mind probing things like this before. It kind of seems to be this Doctor's specialty. And it's nice to see it crop up one more time.

The episode basically rotates through the three main sets and a couple of caves. There isn't a tremendous amount of pressure or anxiety. So many miners are killed that it becomes, not comical, but like watching a lost cause. Luckily, the numbers of the miners outlast the numbers of the Ice Warriors. Things could have gone badly if they didn't.

Eckersley is probably the most surprising part here. Throughout the story, he's had this odd feeling to him. He was always a bit too diplomatic as long as it served him. He seemed to be up to something slightly different than everyone else. In the end, he was. Selling out the Federation and the Peladonians for lots and lots of money. The Ice Warrior warrior faction hooks up with a simple greedy human being. Match that up with the humans in "Invasion of the Dinosaurs" and it seems like the era is souring on the whole concept of human beings. They all seem to be nasty.

The penultimate 3rd Doctor story ends. It's not great. There are a few fun moments. If you space the episodes out enough, it works better as the whole thing is just too darn repetitive. I'm not sure if they're still actively trying anymore. I do know that they are actively trying to clear the decks. Next up, Metebelis 3's saga concludes.

*And even the Doctor seems done with it. When Eckersley and Aggedor both hit the ground dead, The Doctor quickly checks Eck's pulse and then shoves him aside to check on Aggedor.

PLANET OF THE SPIDERS
Written by Robert Sloman (and Barry Letts)
Directed By Barry Letts
Episode One

Episode 376: (May 4, 1974) At a retreat, men are doing strange things that involve big spiders. The Doctor begins investigating psychic powers.
Cliffhanger: That's one big spider!

I like this episode quite a bit. We know it's the end of this era. Barry Letts will stay on for one more story. Terrance Dicks will write the next one. Lis Sladen will be here for ages. Pertwee goes goodbye after this serial. Letts and Sloman do a nice job of pulling some threads together here. First, Mike Yates is back. He's spending time at a meditation center where he's let his hair grow out. Of course, he can't just rest. There's some sort of mystery going on so he calls in Sarah for investigative purposes. Then, we see the Brig and The Doctor on a night out together, which is very charming. We learn that the Brig has a lady friend named Doris. Jo Grant/ Jones sends the Doctor back the Metebelis 3 crystal. Thereby, linking us back to the last season's closer and reminding us of Jo. Liz never sent us a letter. It's nice to have the reminder.

The rest of the episode switched between the Doctor at UNIT experimenting with Professor Clegg. who has real ESP. and the people at the meditation center with an actual Tibetan monk. I'm surprised Leonard Nimoy doesn't pop up at some point to discuss what's going on. But then, we are a few years out from *In Search Of*. It is all very wonderfully 1970s. And not just the fashions. It has that spirit of excitement, of looking for something beyond us that vanished in the 1980s. The fact that most of the episode is focused solely on that is great.

Yes, a giant tractor appears out of nowhere and runs Yates and Sarah off the road. Yes, a giant spider appears on a mandala at the end. Yes, the Professor is killed by the blue crystal. Mainly, it's just sort of spending time with concerns of the moment and it's charming.

I love how kind of ugly all the white guys chanting their "Oms" are. They all look a little weird. Demented guy with glasses. Weird James Mason. The guy who's pretending he's not balding. They all look like the sort of middle-aged white guys whose lives have gone off the rails and now they're doing something they probably shouldn't be... if the giant spider is anything to go by.

I like the Doctor and Sarah here. She's off doing her thing. He's doing his thing. They're back from Peladon. The Doctor seems to have lost his wanderlust. Especially if he's spending his time going to see belly dancers with the Brig, which I'm sure is super fun. I'm enjoying the thought of nothing really going on. We're all just hanging out. And the Doctor is using the UNIT equipment to do whatever. It's nice to see Benton. His joke about the Doctor getting into hairdressing is funny especially because the Pertwee bouffant is at its height here. I love a relaxed opening episode. Well, Sarah and Mike are going through stuff. But, so far, there's nothing earthshattering or crazy happening. Just life. That will change very soon.

Planet of the Spiders
Episode Two

Episode 377: (May 11, 1974) Lupton and his spider steal the blue crystal. A chase ensues. Cliffhanger: Where'd Lupton go?

It's the big chase episode. Well, we did have a big chase episode earlier in the season. * This chase is bigger. The previous time, it was the Doctor being chased by everybody. This time, it's Lupton being chased. In classic chase style (a la Harold Lloyd's *Girl Shy*), we hop from vehicle to vehicle. The Whomobile. A gyrocopter thing. (Little Nellie!) A powerboat. A hovercraft. Everything! Basically, Letts gave Pertwee one last big chase scene blowout. I'm sure Pertwee loved it.

I'll be honest: in theory and from a distance, I love it too. It's nice to have Bessie back. I'm not sure why the Doctor prefers the Whomobile to her. Fickle fellow, I guess. Regardless, The Whomobile can fly! Did you know that? It doesn't fly very well or very convincingly but, by jingo, it flies. And yes, there is a yokel. Say goodbye to the Pertwee yokel! And yes, there is a wacky cop. He does NOT get his face pulled off. It really is tough to not love. But it goes on for quite some time and it's not what I'd call incredibly dynamic. (And, again, the flying Whomobile is a bad idea.) We basically cut from one vehicle to the next to people inside them to the vehicles and etcetera. I applaud the attitude behind it while, as a chase, I don't find it terribly exciting.

The tricky thing with the episode is that about half of it is the chase. Again, I'm happy to see Pertwee get one last runaround. However, it doesn't leave much to review. There's the pre-chase bit and the chase bit. The chase bit ends oddly. I'll give it that. When the Doctor finally catches Lupton, he has disappeared thanks to the spider. Do I need to even ask the question or is too obvious? No. I won't ask it.

The pre-chase portion is fine. The spider jumps on Lupton's back and disappears. One of the members laments that he just wanted to relax. Sarah reports back to The Doctor. We learn that Clegg saw spiders in his mind right before he died. Giant spiders on Metebelis 3! Not when the Doctor was there, thank you very much. Then, Lupton walks right into UNIT HQ. I thought it was a top-secret space! Come on. Anyway, all this is what it is. The spider's voice is great. The spider itself is fine. It's kind of a mess of legs. I think the legs should be more defined. They just kind of flood the space. I like my spiders scary but they weren't allowed to do such a thing back then. So, we take what we can get.

I do wonder what the advanced level of planning was here. Metebelis 3. The blue crystal. Mike Yates. The Doctor then realizing that the spiders could come from a different time on 3 than he visited. It all coagulates within the story pot and makes it seem like there was a great Masterplan happening here. It really does help. Especially in an episode that's basically one huge chase.

The thing that's kind of surprising is this: We're two episodes in. Four Pertwee episodes left. And all that's happened is: A guy got possessed by a big spider and stole the blue crystal. It seems like, at this point, there should be more than enough to sustain the remaining four episodes. We haven't even reached Metebelis 3 yet. Come on, everybody! Let's do this.

*Episode 5 of "Invasion of the Dinosaurs."

Planet of the Spiders
Episode Three

Episode 378: (May 18, 1974) The good guys try desperately to get to Lupton. But Cho-Je and his aphorisms slow them down. Eventually, Sarah Jane and The Doctor end up on Metebelis 3. This may be a problem.
Cliffhanger: The Doctor is shot down in front of the TARDIS.

The first half of this episode is alternately very fun and alternately frustrating. It's fun because, after the big chase, everyone goes to the monastery. The Doctor knows what is going on. Sarah Jane and Mike are with him. Everyone is assembled to wrap this up. Lupton is there with some of his cronies. Lupton falls asleep with the blue crystal, which is a bit of a giveaway. All is all right. The episode is moving along.

Then, Cho-Je shows up. He is the wise head of the meditation center. He is full of aphorisms. He spins prayer wheels. He tells the people of the Western World to slow down. (Although, the Doctor is not of the Western World.) He keeps everyone waiting and waiting and waiting to see Lupton as if it's some sort of lesson. Meanwhile, all kinds of chicanery is going on. All kinds of nonsense. Including Tommy stealing the crystal from Lupton and hiding it. So, Cho-je ends up sounding like less of a wise man who knows what's up and more of a dope who think his lessons are best... but people will die soon because he faffed around. I get what Letts was up to here. He was a Buddhist. This a is a Buddhist character with a very Buddhist outlook. Sometimes when your bus is on fire and rolling out of control down a hill, you need to act fast. Endless aphorisms (even Sarah asks him what the heck he's talking about at one point) don't stop you from burning alive. There are times to go fast and times to go slow.

Yes, Tommy steals the crystal from Lupton and hides it. There's a fun farce-like scene where Sarah Jane is waiting for Tommy to show her something (the crystal) but he's taking too long and she just misses it. That is fun and frustrating at the same time. As Terrance Dicks says on the commentary, if she had seen the crystal, this serial would have been a four parter. This was a six parter. So, you needed that moment of "Darnit!" And then we go on for another 75 minutes. (The omnibus version of this story that aired right before "Robot" started does a very judicious trim of it.)

Lupton gets the best moment here. As he is freshening himself up in an indeterminate place in his room, he tells one of his colleagues why he is at the monastery. The others have said they are there for peace of mind. Lupton very clearly states that he is there for power. He tells a very relevant story about working hard for a company for 25 years and then being pushed out by the efficiency experts and the bean counters. Now, he wants to take them all down. When one watches the way he treats his companion spider, he may be able to do it. One mad man to rule us all.

And then, there's the last few minutes of the episode. Sarah Jane stands on a mandala and there is a wonderfully odd CSO effect. She is in the foreground. The Doctor rushes towards her in the background and suddenly she is in the American Southwest somewhere. It's a disconcerting effect and it really feels like Sarah has gone somewhere else. Then, she meets the people of Metebelis 3. The humans and then the spiders. Wow. Has a story ever dropped so sharply in quality over the course of a few minutes?

The Metebelis 3 village, with its huge CSO backdrop, frankly, stinks. The set is cheap. The panorama is fake as all get out. And the actors are not good. With Jenny Laird taking the cake as someone who always seems to be forgetting her lines and/ or thinks she's part of another show. The spider shows up. The Doctor shows up. And it all stinks. It's all kind of embarrassing. It is a relief when the episode ends because we don't have to look at these people and this place. For a while. Episode Four looms. In fact, here it is.

Planet of the Spiders
Episode Four

Episode 379: (May 25, 1974) The Doctor is mostly unconscious as we spend time with the fun characters on Metebelis 3.
Cliffhanger: The Doctor has been caught by the spiders.

The Third Doctor goes into a coma one last time. It started back with the first story and it continued until the previous one. Here we say goodbye to it. We know now that the Doctor can put himself into a self-induced coma to let his body heal. Although here, probably because it is his final story, it takes a little more oomph to get him out. He uses some sort of fun TARDIS machine with a switch/ lever on it. It discharges the evil Metebelis 3 energies from him. I like that.

Now, one might complain here… "Every time the Doctor goes into a coma the story stops dead." Well, you're not wrong there. Sarah cries over the Doctor a bit. He speaks slowly. Lupton and the spiders accomplish little. The humans back at the monastery argue and beat up Mike Yates. Yes, indeed. Not much gets done. Others have put forward the theory that knocking the Doctor out is just a way to put the story on hold for however long it lasts. The Doctor and Sarah Jane just got here. He can't be unconscious for too long. I mean, have you seen the inhabitants?

Let's be honest, everyone on Metebelis 3 is dull. That one old guy becomes amusing when he's in the spider's larder later. Mainly because he's wrapped in spider web and lamenting on the fact that he must die and what are you (what is anyone) going to do about it. But, boy, the rest of them are dull. The one lead guy is decent. But, when Pertwee supping on broth is more interesting than any line you might have… well, things are a little rocky down on the farm.

The issue with setting the Doctor aside for half an episode is that nothing really happens. Yes, Mike Yates is caught. Who really cares? The Doctor revives and then is caught. Sure. Sarah Jane is captured. Sure. The only thing here that is truly of interest is Tommy and his awakening. The problem here is that we know that the Crystal does this from "The Green Death" so it's not as amazing as it might be.

Tommy stares into the crystal as he's reading a children's book. The crystal shines and his mind is opened. And he can think. He can read. His disability is gone. He reads Blake! Huzzah! We knew the crystal did this though. The crystal is almost like the modern sonic screwdriver. It does whatever the plot needs it to do. Here, it clears Tommy's mind and all is well. I imagine this is going to be something big and important for the upcoming episodes.

In the end, though, the episode is a bit of a clodhopper. Metebelis 3 is dull. The Doctor is knocked out, recovers and then is captured again. I wish someone could have found a way to ring some of these changes in a better way. Here, it seems stale. But you never know, there are only two episodes left. Anything could happen and probably should.

Planet of the Spiders
Episode Five

Episode 380: (June 1, 1974) The hunt for the crystal stretches across planets.
Cliffhanger: Tommy is being shot up by the jerks under Spider Control.

The penultimate episode of the Pertwee era. It doesn't feel like it. But some things feel odd. Tommy is given the cliffhanger. Kampo, the head of the meditation center, is introduced. He seems to know the Doctor. We almost meet the Great One. The giant spider that sits at the center of everything. Sarah gets taken over by the Queen Spider. We, hopefully, leave the Metebelis 3 people behind but we probably don't. And there is a weird thing (even the Doctor thinks so) about the Doctor stealing the crystal.

That's the element that gets hammered into a lot. The Doctor stole the blue crystal from Metebelis 3. The Doctor stole the blue crystal from Metebelis 3. It comes up repeatedly in this episode. And it always felt awkward to me. Robert Holmes never followed a Buddhist pattern. He wouldn't and couldn't have cared less about what the Doctor took from where. There is a possibility in "The Green Death" that Sloman and Letts were setting this up. If so, I don't know that they set it up very well. In "Green Death," we see the Doctor land on a crazy alien planet filled with giant beasts and all sorts of crazy junk.

In that story, The Doctor is on a cliff being assaulted by the landscape. It feels very Robert Holmes to me. It's clearly a big setup for the "I'll talk to anyone" joke. So, at no point does it seem like we are punishing The Doctor. But that's what this episode is doing. He "stole" the crystal. What would Metebelis 3 have been like if he hadn't stolen it? Presumably, The Great One would have taken full control or something different… In the end, I don't think we fully engage with what would happen. Does the Doctor's taking the crystal prevent the Great One from taking over everything? Or does it delay her inevitable demise and make her reign longer? Maybe that's why the Doctor was wrong. It doesn't feel right to me, though. It doesn't feel like the Doctor had done something wrong. To say that your main character, who is an explorer across space and time, should be punished for that exploring seems like foolishness to me. I do love that Letts and Dicks were considering why the Doctor should die. He hasn't been forced. (We see with the 13th Doctor the sort of problems we get there.) He hasn't died of old age. He is being punished by the universe for something.

Also, Sarah gets possessed. The jerky ugly guys use Yates for their own cause. The Doctor kind of lets it all ride. Cho-je is killed. Things seem to be building up. But, unlike the previous final Doctor story, this one seems to be drawing in closer and closer. It's as it the Doctor himself has, unwittingly or otherwise, been placed at the center of all of this. He doesn't want to be the person that this revolves around. Most of the story seems to be resisting that, but it is happening.

I do applaud the cliffhanger. As the Doctor and Kampo are learning about one another, the indestructible Tommy is fighting off the Human Hosts of the Spiders. We've seen this back in "The Mind of Evil." But not quite as strong as this. It really does feel like things are ending. One almost, if you love Pertwee, is worried to go to the next episode. He is going to be punished. Punished for being the Doctor. That worries me a bit.

Planet of the Spiders
Episode Six

Episode 381: (June 8, 1974) The Doctor must face his fear. He must return the Blue Crystal to the great One. Even though he knows that this will mean his death.
Cliffhanger: Here we go again.

And the third Doctor era comes to an end. It's one of those Third Doctor era six-part conclusions that accomplishes a lot and does it very quickly. It's a sharp blade cutting right to the heart of the story. The Doctor's thirst for knowledge is his downfall and causes his death. * Tommy's pureness and Mike Yates's compassion save them from spider attacks. And the whole thing sort of ends by ejecting every previous storyline and putting the focus squarely on the Doctor which is, really, where it should be.

The Third Doctor gets a nice send off. Yes, the giant spider is not real. Yes, the whole space he's in (the caves) isn't real. Maybe it would better in black and white. I don't know. Regardless, it is the end. He knows it from the moment he arrives on Metebelis 3 until he enters the cave. It's not a fast death. He's dying slow in the caves. It's implied that the TARDIS took some time moving through the vortex. I do hope he wasn't dead on the ground the whole while.

It is nice to tie another element of this era together. Kampo Rimpoche, the guru, the head of the meditation center. Is the teacher the Doctor spoke of back in "The Time Monster." If you've been watching the show and paying attention, this era pays things off very nicely. Well done. Some things they never quite figured out, like how to structure a six parter. And some of their politics did go a little awry. But there are a few things they got right. One of them was giving the era a nice sense of continuity. Yes, it would have been nice to hear from Liz again but you can't have it all. At this point, it's all tying together and the third Doctor must say goodbye.

Yes, the top of the episode is wonky. Scenes had to be moved around. That means that the point of the cliffhanger doesn't occur until almost five minutes into this episode. That makes the episode beginning somewhat odd. The pacing feels off to me. Because you expect to see the cliffhanger shortly. But it's so delayed that it feels like the episode has begun late. And you don't want that sort of feeling in a Doctor's final episode.

And to top it all off they do something to make the next story easier for everyone. "Robot" will be produced by Barry Letts, his last one. It's the first official Robert Holmes script edited story. But it's written by Terrance Dicks as a farewell. So, they make sure that Sarah Jane and The Brig see the Doctor regenerate. So, we don't have to worry about a couple episode of "Who is this guy?" They do mention that his brain might be scrambled, though. That might be important.

Saying goodbye to the Third Doctor. Overall, I enjoyed his era. There are some moments I don't like. But, when I get fully and properly immersed in it, I always come away smiling. It's only when I completely treat it the way I just did (in-depth reviews on each episode) that the flaws become more apparent. My tip to you: if you don't get into this era, try watching the DVDs or Blu-Rays with the commentaries playing. They will convince you that you are watching the best thing ever. Even when you realize that sometimes you're not.

*As I mentioned in the previous review, sometimes that strikes me as weird. The Master generally goes free. Their thirst is for destruction and forced subjugation. They never seem to pay for what they've done. The Doctor goes to a planet takes a shiny rock and it's his death. I guess I don't understand Buddhism as much as I thought.

SEASON TWELVE
1975

ROBOT
Written By Terrance Dicks
Directed by Christopher Barry
Episode One

Episode 382: (December 28, 1974) The Fourth Doctor helps UNIT track down "something" stealing elements of a disintegrator gun. Sarah Jane investigates a place called Think Tank.
Cliffhanger: Sarah meets the Robot.

I always thought "Robot" was a great story to begin an era with. Others have been obscure to exciting to whatever… this one is just "Robot." There's the long and the short of it. In true *Doctor Who* fashion, they all spend the first episode hunting for something we know is a robot because we know the title of the episode. That's always weird, isn't it? Is there a story out there where the Doctor or a companion know the title ahead of time and that helps them out as time goes on? Regardless, we know there's a robot around here somewhere. I feel like the Doctor figures it out fast. When Sarah slips in some oil in the closed down Robotics Department of Think Tank, she's halfway there too.

Terrance Dicks writes his first solo episode (as far as we know) for the show. And it's a delightful 25 minutes. There's nothing groundbreaking about it. It's basically the first couple episodes of the previous story but compacted and allowing for some silliness in the first third. Instead of a meditation center, Sarah goes to a rather underpopulated think tank. We meet Miss Winters and her sneering assistant Jellicoe. Near the end, we meet the robotic expert Professor Kettlewell of the ridiculous hair. Plus, Pat Gorman as the gate guard!

The production seems to have decided that the "regenerative trauma" the Third Doctor experienced should be limited here. The 3rd Doctor takes almost two episodes to get into his role, which is why 'Spearhead From Space" has such an odd feel to it, structure-wise. "Castrovalva" would completely embrace it. "The Twin Dilemma" and "Deep Breath" would go to odd places. Post-regenerative shows were always something. Here's the first time I think they really got to think about it… they throw in some gags, some jumping rope, some costume changes. Then it's over. The Doctor really is that weird.

The investigation sequences are handled well. The Brig and the Doctor get along. But there is a feeling that this Doctor is, how should I say it, more detached than the previous one? The Third Doctor could get testy but he always seemed to be fully involved. This Doctor seems a bit like he's ready to go exploring the universe again but he's going to help his friends one more time. Note the way this Doctor sits and moves compared to the Third Doctor. The Third Doctor was always very athletic and moved around a lot. Watch the Fourth Doctor leap from the jeep (and lose his hat). Suddenly there's more energy in the character than possibly ever before. That's what we needed. This is the 12th season of the show. As I'm writing this, 12 seasons seem to be like an average for a lot of shows. Back then, 12 seasons was a rarity. Anyway, we're here now with this new Doctor. Oddly enough, he does very little with Sarah although it's she who keeps him on Earth. At least for a little while. Let's investigate the Robot and see where this leads us.

Robot
Episode Two

Episode 383: (January 4, 1975) Everyone is looking for the Giant Robot. Except Sarah. She is investigating a Scientific Organization that wants to rule the world.
Cliffhanger: The Doctor meets the Robot.

Things got pretty humorless in the last days of Pertwee. They perk up slightly during "The Time Warrior." But generally, things got dour. It felt like the party was over but no one really wanted to leave yet. And Lis Sladen felt slightly out of place because she had the energy that everyone else used to have but now felt misplaced.

Boy, things are different here at least around The Doctor and Sarah. The Brig and Benton seem a little sleepy. It's a little early to tell with Harry… yet. The two leads have brought the show fully back to life. "Robot" is, in no way shape or form, classic *Doctor Who*. Like a lot of Terrance Dicks' work it is very straightforward. But "Robot" is a little too straightforward, possibly. It doesn't have the verve of his other stories. It is here for a purpose. To set up the new world of this new Doctor. It does that brilliantly.

Watch The Doctor in the scene at Think Tank. Always moving. Always in charge. Constantly going in circles around Miss Winters and Jellico. And, of course, he knows exactly what's happening (like Sarah did at the start of the episode) and he lets them all know that he knows and it's going to escalate from there. These are not nice people. They are manipulating this robot to kill and build a disintegrator gun. That's Not Nice in my book.

I like the way this Doctor is dismissive towards the obvious jerks who have touch of condescension to them. But, when he's talking to Professor Kettlewell, he befriends him by helping him with a formula. I also love the way the director frames that shot. The Professor and the Doctor in the foreground. And then sort of a tunnel effect back to the Brig who has a look on his face of "Can we please get back to business?"

The scene with Sarah and the Robot is excellent. As is the scene with the Doctor and the robot. Sarah's compassion towards him is lovely. Obviously, we are getting a bit of *King Kong* set up here and it's nice. Then, the Doctor has the great final scene in the workshop laboratory where the robot wants to kill him. I remember that cliffhanger so clearly from when I was a kid. It's great. The robot is suitably menacing. The Doctor is protecting himself and being flippant at the same time. There's an excitement and fun to it that had kind of been lost in the Pertwee years.

Now, however, we're entering the third episode. Let's see how the show handles itself from here. I can't imagine Dicks and Holmes would let it go terribly wrong.

Robot
Episode Three

Episode 384: (January 11, 1975) The Think Tank heads into an underground bunker with the world's nuclear codes. Uh oh.
Cliffhanger: The Robot destroys a tank and then threatens to destroy everybody.

Isn't Miss Winters something? We haven't really had a good raving, crazy villain like her for a while. If she had a German accent, we'd think of her as another Zaroff. But she's good and crazy on her own. Watching her rage herself into a fury at the SRS meeting is a scene that has always struck me since I was a child. I went to Catholic schools growing up and most of the teachers were women. And occasionally, one of them would rage up like Miss Winters does. It was always terrifying. Then, they would do what Miss Winters does and go very, very quiet. When she's basically saying, "We're going to fire nuclear missiles at cities and kill millions of people" and saying it so calmly, it is chilling. How on Earth can insane people like this get put in charge of anything? But here she is. And she has a giant robot with a disintegrator gun too!

The episode has a nice pace to it. The four-part stories simply work better than the six-part ones. This one starts with the robot being chased off by UNIT. Then we get the SRS meeting, followed by another pitched battle. After a few minutes of detective work, they find the bunker and there's the beginning of the standstill. I quite like the way Terrance Dicks puts this story together. There is a sort of dual cliffhanger with the destructor codes being armed and the robot attack going on. Leads nicely into the fourth and final episode.

Sarah doesn't do much but hide and cower. She does have a good chat with the robot at the beginning. She clearly has made an impression upon the being and it's something to watch out for. The Doctor is, as always, one step ahead. It is funny seeing the Fourth Doctor standing side by side with the military. That's not something we're going to see happening a lot. He's so filled with childish glee. Especially as he blows up the mines surrounding the bunker entrance. *

The story has very nicely and rather swiftly ratcheted up the suspense and the level of danger. From a strange being stealing bits and bobs of technological equipment to a bunch of crazy scientists holed up in a bunker set to destroy the Earth to prove that they're right about whatever it is there problem is. Oh, there's also a flippin' Giant Robot. Plus, the show is the first one ever shot wholly on video for location and studio segments. So, there's a nice continuity with the picture. You don't get the piebald change when we would go from film to video to film and so forth. It all feels like it's taking place in the same place. Whether you prefer the film to the video, well that's up to you. I can't help there. But it gives the story a nice overall feeling of continuity, which is good to have when we start a new era.

*Interesting dating note: They always say that the UNIT stories are meant to be set in the near future. Whether they are or not, I can't say. But this story does have the Brigadier mentioning that the bunker is from "The Cold War Days." On Earth in 1975, we have almost 15 more years of Cold War ahead of us. In this story, it's finished. The future? Or just a different timeline?

Robot
Episode Four

Episode 385: (January 18, 1975) Final battle: UNIT vs the scientists and their Giant Robot. Cliffhanger: Harry accidentally joins Sarah and the Doctor on an adventure.

The Fourth Doctor's first story comes to an end. Somewhat like "Spearhead In Space," this is the end of the previous era proper. Terrance Dicks and Barry Letts are gone for the next story. Robert Holmes is fully in charge. (In more ways than one.) Philip Hinchcliffe is now in charge of production. And, we will see in the next episode, they both have very different ways of telling their Doctor Who stories. Which is the correct kick in the pants that the show always needs. The "Spearhead from Space" jump is much more obvious than this one, though. It's because "Spearhead" was all on film and looks completely different from 'Silurians." "Robot" and "Ark" look similar. But they're very different in terms of outlook and everything else. "Robot" bridges the gap and puts us at the gate, slowly opening before us.

The episode itself is nicely paced. The countdown to Doomsday starts up and turns off repeatedly. The countdown itself rolls along ominously. In the end, the world is not destroyed. The Think Tank people are rounded up rather quickly. The robot accidentally kills the Professor and goes crazy. Then, it bonds with Sarah and then it gets huge. All sorts of crazy stuff happens.

I like how the UNIT soldiers and gang get to do the shooting and the everything involving the Robot. While the Doctor and Harry, the scientists, are sent to devise the virus that will eat through the metal. The Doctor doesn't really break a sweat in this story. The way he types away at the destruct codes and saves the day (the first time) is pure silliness but also very Doctor-like. He has distinguished himself in someone else's era here. He now needs to go out and distinguish himself in his own.

The effects are interesting. I mean, the giant robot and all its rampaging must be the most extensive use of CSO yet. Some of it really works well. The smushed soldier. Bessie driving towards the Robot and a few other moments. They do their best to make it a Kong-style rampage. Mostly they succeed. When they use toy tanks and dolls, it doesn't work that great. I'm certain they knew it didn't work that great when they did it though. It's a hell of a go for the closing episode of this Doctor's first story. And it works. It's very straightforward. It has some pathos. And it leads to the lovely closing scene. Sarah joins the Doctor. Harry, accidentally, joins the Doctor. Where will they go next…? Read the following review.

One odd thing that this show does a lot happens twice here within in a minute: the Doctor splashes the five-story tall robot with the virus. The Brig asks if it will work. The Doctor says "Look" and suddenly everyone looks at the huge, disintegrating bright red robot. As if no one would look up at it if the Doctor hadn't said something. A minute later, the Brig says that they'll call someone in to clean up the remains. The Doctor says, "No need, look." Again, Harry and The Brig look down at the robot as it completely disintegrates. They're so enthralled by the Doctor that they can't see directly in front of them. Amusing and confusing. But soft, let's go on to the next adventure.

THE ARK IN SPACE
Written By Robert Holmes
Original script by John Lucarotti
Directed by Rodney Bennett
Episode One

Episode 386: (January 25, 1975) The Doctor, Sarah and Harry land on the Nerva Beacon in the far future. Cliffhanger: A strange giant insect falls out of a closet towards Harry.

And so the Hinchcliffe era begins. At the start of the Letts era, Dicks was in place. Your man on stories was there. Here, it's the same. Robert Holmes has been onboard for a while. Some say he did a major re-write on "Death To The Daleks" I'm one of those people. A new era has begun. It's weird to watch. Because this episode feels very familiar if one has been watching the show for 12 years. It also feels a little different. I don't know if Holmes and Hinchcliffe fully knew what was happening here. They bring in a new world by using the old. And it works. So well.

John Lucarotti was originally called in to author this story. Robert Holmes was doing what Terrance Dicks did. Trying to assemble a group of writers that could do the show. Lucarotti had written three great serials back in the 1960s and was available. So, John sent the breakdowns and the scripts.

At the same time, the production team was trying to cut down on the number of six-part scripts because, frankly, they always went awry. So, they had two six-part stories, rather than three, scheduled for this season. Alongside a two parter, which they'd already shot at this point. One of the ways that they were going to save money was by using sets multiple times. That's why Lucarotti's unusable script was reused by Holmes or at least the set up was on the Nerva beacon. The Cybermen story set for later (the end of the season) was on the same set. So, Holmes had to write a story that used the space. He does a fine job of it.

Whether or not they realized it though, they are utilizing the Hartnell era set-up. Taking the first episode of a serial and giving it over completely to the three main characters. Apart from voices, it's just them exploring the space. What a space it is. Much of it is set in that initial main room with the side room that has the teleporting bench. There are lasers. There are fun benches. There are cables that have been bitten though. There is a lot of craziness going on. But it's based in an earlier, much slower era. Look at the scene where Harry and the Doctor are under the table and moving it along to avoid the laser. That would never have happened in the 1960s. Here, it's fun and, I think, fresh. The show has been revitalized and recreated using the past and thoughts of the future. That's what makes this story such a great one.

I didn't talk much about the episode. I realize that. Simply because I love it. Completely. It's the three cast members and some voices. It's Sarah being oxygen deprived and then gassed. It's a ton of great words, including "interregnum." It's the Doctor and Harry, first time working together, trying their best to figure out what's up. It's some of the best set design the show ever had. And it's got such an incredible sense of excitement and adventure. That's what this era is going to be.

The Ark In Space
Episode Two

Episode 387: (February 1, 1975) The TARDIS crew begin reviving the members of the Ark. However, there is something else onboard and it's green and it's not nice.
Cliffhanger: Noah reveals that his arm is completely green, slimy and gross.

I've always liked that this group of refugees from Planet Earth present themselves as being so amazing and wonderful. Yet maybe they're not. My favorite ways that they don't show off their grandness are: 1) The crappy way they treat the Doctor, Harry and then Sarah even when they reveal what they're doing to help. 2) The fact that Noah shoots the Doctor dead before he has been taken over by the Wirrn. He's so assured that these people are terrible that he kills the Doctor. (More or less.) They're that paranoid. They're that unsure of what they're doing that this is their response to assistance. They don't check the time they're in or anything that might level them out. They start off pissed off and go from there. When we learn where they get their ship from, then maybe we can think... OK, these people aren't the saviors they think they are. They're a second-rate group of screwballs who should shut up and let the Doctor and his friends help. Really though, we're mainly focused on the story here.

It's nicely done. We have the giant insect thing. We have the green slime trails. We see the slug things out amongst the ship. The green alongside the stark white of everything is clearly an abomination. It's clearly a grossness when placed alongside the scientific sterile environment. Maybe that's why the crew gets so eternally pissed off. They are angry that these people have brought this green in. That's not their color. That's the Wirrn's thing. And the Wirrn are very efficient.

I love watching the TARDIS crew stand by ineffectually as a bunch of stuff happens around them. Even the Doctor feels ineffectual. Although they can help with the green monsters, they can't do much with the revivification. Who could?

It's nice to have Sarah back and doing well. It was touch and go for a bit. Harry is becoming more and more of a sailor, which is delightful. And the Doctor is continuing to be the best hero around. He is set aback at times. But here, there are so many times, where he takes complete control and just does what he needs to do. The show has very definitely changed.

In the end, this is a great episode that got one of the highest ratings the show ever achieved. And it has one of my favorite moments ever. When Noah is talking to Libri… and Dune is mentioned. Noah gets such a strange look on his face. He smiles and says "I… I am Dune." Everyone looks shocked. Then, he seems to forget that he said that. And everyone seems a bit uncomfortable and Noah goes back to being whatever he is. When I watched that as a kid, that scene confused me. Now, when I know exactly what's going on, I love it. It is eerie as hell. Maybe if the scene was darker, it would have been scarier but that's not really the point in the end. This is scary in a way the previous era wasn't. It's more desperate and it's more harrowing and it's more lost. At least, until the Doctor gets there.

The Ark In Space
Episode Three

Episode 388: (February 8, 1975) The Wirrn are beginning to take over everyone, especially Noah. It doesn't look like they'll be able to get enough humans revivified before the Wirrn win.
Cliffhanger: The Noah Wirrn approaches the Doctor in the solar stacks.

The show picks up the pace considerably here. The general feeling of emergency feeling increases tremendously. At first, there was a missing person and a strange giant insect. But now, things are going very awry. It looks like these humans are going to be devoured. Not only that, but the Wirrn born of them will be crazy and out there and devouring everything in their path. It's a very credible dark story placed very strongly at the start of a new Doctor's tenure. The Silurian story seems rather silly and low-key compared to this. (Of course, the TARDIS is working. They could all go onboard that. That's not the way we roll though.)

Noah's transformation in this is fantastic. Yes, he has green bubble wrap on him. I think it works. The way he fights his arm at the start is something. His body overtaken with the green is distressing. It leads to that wonderfully odd sequence where he begs Vira to kill him. She can't. The execs at the BBC demanded that the scene be re-edited because it was very dark. I think this might have been a sign to someone that things were going in an interesting direction.

The Doctor's linking his mind with the Wirrn is one of the most interesting moments here. He links to the brainpan of the Queen Wirrn and almost becomes a Wirrn himself. We learn that these creatures absorb the brainpower etc. of the races that they eat. And it is interesting to see this Doctor like this so early. We didn't see Pertwee's Doctor go off his main foot until the interrogation scene in "Inferno." Here, the new Doctor is doing it deliberately to try and help everyone around him. Couple that with he and Vira searching for Noah... and then his visit to the solar stacks with the larvae Wirrn smashing around inside and the giant Noah coming after him... it's all much gooier and more visceral than the start of the previous era. As others have mentioned, at this time, in horror, *The Texas Chainsaw Massacre* had come out. Along with *Night of the Living Dead*, the human body became meat. *Three on a Meathook* joins the group. *Axe. Meatcleaver Massacre*. This was the way films were going. Now we have a *Doctor Who* story where the humans are the hosts awaiting the insects to put themselves within. Nasty. It's a whole new world.

Sarah and Harry are a great duo here. Standing guard in front of the rising Ark members who are so worried. They wake up after all this time to discover that things are going wrong and their leader is possessed. It's such a great concept. We sleep. Something gets in and screws it all up. Now we're fighting for our lives. It's a great idea. It's a great way to keep the show moving and to keep the show alive. Obviously, the ratings are big here. The complaints are big too. We'll deal with that more as we go along.

I will say this: When we get to the end of the season and later in the series, the thought that these are the "last humans" is foolish. These are a "group of surviving humans." In fact, "The Sontaran Experiment," the next story shoots this concept in the butt. But there is a nice, eerie feeling when we think that these are the last humans. Remember the last time we were in an Ark In Space, it was simply an Ark in space. The titles are familiar. I'm fairly certain that those people in "The Ark" were way ahead of these people. Technically, they'd have to be. The Earth explodes in "The Ark." (And maybe another story.) Here, the planet is just ravaged by solar flares. Even Robert Holmes would deal with that concept later in his stories. However, this book isn't *AHistory*, which is the most beautifully woven history of the show I've read. But it's fun to think about some of these time concepts.

Three episodes in and we have a heck of a story going on. Will they stick the landing? History says, "Probably not." But will it be satisfying if they don't? History is up in the air about that. Just remember, if this had been a six-part story all the thrill would have been gone by now. I think we're in for a hell of a closing episode.

The Ark In Space
Episode Four

Episode 389: (February 15, 1975) The final battle against the Wirrn.
Cliffhanger: Sarah Jane, Harry and The Doctor transmat down to the surface of the cleansed Earth.

The Wirrn are defeated. The earthlings onboard are saved. At the very end, The Doctor, Sarah and Harry beam down to Earth's surface to fix the teleporter relay. They don't leave via the TARDIS. In fact, we haven't been inside the TARDIS yet this season. We won't be for a while. To leave at the end of the story, with the main cast members not in the TARDIS, does feel a bit weird. What also ends up feeling weird is something that would happen in this era a few times: Everyone's dead except the Doctor and his crew and, maybe, one other person.

Vira, now commander, is the only other person alive and awake on the ship. We never come back to the Beacon in this form. We never really learn what happens to the people onboard. I'm hoping they all got well and got beamed down to the Earth. I'm hoping that Vira didn't make everyone stay on the ship until the Doctor came back because that doesn't happen. I'm also hoping that the entire swarm of Wirrn was onboard the cargo ship. One Wirrn still onboard could have eaten all the humans. That would have probably made a more interesting sequel that never happened: The Doctor returns to the Nerva beacon to discover that one surviving Wirrn had taken the whole place apart. Uh oh.

It's an excellent closing episode. The stakes are high but it's not terribly exciting. The ending sort of happens but it does make sense. Sarah crawling through the ductwork is the most exciting part and that's handled nicely. The mix of scenes with Rogin, Harry and Vira in the rocket control room alongside Sarah creeping along the tunnels with the Doctor in the now dark and rather impregnable cryogenic room is very nicely done. The Wirrn don't seem particularly smart, which is what makes the ending a little off.

I do like that Noah/ Wirrn is given his speech at the start. We learn what the heck is going on with these Wirrn and why they've chosen the humans instead of their normal cattle hosts for the eggs. And it works. There is a nice feeling of the Wirrn being here to take their form of revenge on humanity. It kicks the story up a notch. Because the Wirrn don't normally do this. They're taking revenge. And their revenge is nasty. Luckily, they don't like electricity.

Here's what happens in the ending because sometimes I get a little confused and I want you to know that I know: The power from the rocket is being pumped into the cryogenic room. It's being used to keep the Wirrn out. The Wirrn space walk across the Ark and break into a storage hatch elsewhere on the rocket. For some reason, it's the whole swarm. (I'm guessing that's Noah's doing.) Once aboard, the humans run off and set the ship for automatic take off. It does so. Rogin is killed in a blast from the rocket. But the others are safe. Well, The Doctor, Sarah, Harry, Vira. and the sleeping humans. The rocket is launched. Soon after, Vira is contacted by Noah Wirrn who says goodbye. Then the ship blows up destroying the fleet. Somehow this always seemed a little muddled to me. But that's what happens. Trust me.

It's not a perfect story. But it's darn near perfect for *Doctor Who*. Knowing that a completely different story was planned and written. And then, Holmes had a month to come up with this as he was script editing other stories makes it even more exciting. This is the show entering a new era and flying by the seat of its pants. The next story, at two parts, is almost a little respite.

THE SONTARAN EXPERIMENT
Written by Bob Baker and Dave Martin
Directed by Rodney Bennett
Episode One

Episode 390: (February 22, 1975) The trio land on Earth, cleansed by solar flares. They find a group of astronauts and a strange robot.
Cliffhanger: A Sontaran emerges from his ship.

This is a no-nonsense story, except for one big element. It's The Doctor, Sarah and Harry arriving in the middle of beautiful countryside. Getting in some shenanigans with local astronauts. Falling down cliffs and sliding into gulleys. Then, encountering the return of an alien race/ villain from a previous season. The episode moves along very nicely. The location is really something. Especially after the last four episodes being enclosed within the confines of the Ark. Here it's endless rolling hills and it looks gorgeous. I would have preferred if it was shot on film. But the video looks fine on the Blu-ray. And video does give it a more immediate feeling. It does feel like it's happening Now. More or less.

The astronaut guys are interchangeable. They try to interrogate the Doctor. They don't do that well but there's clearly something going on within those ranks. Men are going missing. One almost wishes, in a two-parter, that they could have dispensed with a lot of the back-and-forth nonsense. But, hey, we gotta do what we gotta do to fill out the time.

I love that Harry falls down the "Whacking great subsidence" as the Doctor calls it. Harry's gradually learning how to work as a *Doctor Who* hero. He's not there yet. He does kind of vanish from a portion of the episode, as if Baker and Martin didn't quite know he was going to be in it. The Doctor spends time with most of the astronauts. Sarah spends time with one who has been tortured. Harry climbs around down in that hole and somehow comes out on the other side.

I will admit that the geography of everything here always confused me a bit. One really must keep their focus to figure out exactly how everyone is getting from everywhere to everywhere. (Or you can just let it roll.) There's some sort of entryway at the far end of the pit Harry falls into that puts us out onto the place where the Sontaran ship is. Does that mean everyone has to fall down the hill to come out on the side with the Sontaran? I'd like a good map, please.

The spot where the episode shoots itself in the foot is with that "Don't reveal what the monster/ villain is until the end of Episode 1" thing. There's a chance that people might not remember what a "Sontaran" was. We do now. But it was over a year since people saw Linx. Maybe they might not remember? Or maybe they will. But, waiting until the end of the first episode here is tricky because the story's halfway over. There is a going to be a hell of a lot to cram into the next episode. The show's not always at its best when it must do that. Hopefully, it does OK. Because the Sontarans deserve another good story. Let's see what this grey-headed one is up to. (I thought they were clones. Do they just add different head colors for fun? Maybe they're color blind? I don't know.)

The Sontaran Experiment
Episode Two

Episode 391: (March 1, 1975) The Doctor fights the Sontaran.
Cliffhanger: Returning to the Beacon.

The episode does end up being crammed full of incidents. Luckily, Styre the Sontaran (not Linx, obviously) has a straightforward mission. He's testing the human beings that are on the planet. (There are only the astronauts and our main trio.) He's doing this for a Sontaran commander and a fleet who are waiting somewhere nearby. As others have pointed out, Styre's ideas of testing is a bit weird. He does test Sarah's fear centers, which seems like something usable. But then, he has two guys hold a huge weight over another's guys chest to test the resistance of that guy's chest to huge weights. I wouldn't have thought that it would have been something necessary, especially as the Sontarans have ray guns and just shoot down whoever they want.

I love how angry the Doctor gets at Styre. It seems like the Sontarans are one of those alien races that work better when we only have a few of them around. The more there are, the less interesting they become. Styre has that exact same arrogance that Linx has. It's more concentrated than Linx's because Styre only has the one episode to be a true jackass. Of course, we do learn (as we sort of did previously) that one of the humans is helping him. When does that ever go well for the humans who are grassing on their pals. "Well, I did what you asked." "Wonderful. You can go. Have a good one!" "Thanks. It was great working for you… I wonder if I can get on the Sontaran payroll."

I like that The Doctor has met the Sontarans twice now but there is no feeling of "Drat! It's the Doctor come to foil my plans again." The Sontarans are as disposable as an old pen. This serial does nothing to dispel that notion. Styre is doing a rather irrelevant series of experiments. If there are only 9 people here… on the entire planet… what is the Sontaran army scared of? It's like the Sontarans creeping around in "The Sontaran Stratagem." Why are they up to all these shenanigans if they have millions of soldiers at their command? Send the soldiers!

There is a feeling of desperation here. Styre does hold all the cards throughout most of the episode. Until the Doctor bravely stands up to him, as heroes are wont to do. Once again, they're defeated by something that is intrinsically part of themselves. Linx died by getting an arrow in the probic vent. Styre dies because the energy he feeds on is put in a loop and the feedback destroys him. Thank goodness the Doctor was here. It does seem very, very pat but he does turn the Sontaran invasion away and fix the globes that power the transmat from Nerva.

It's an odd story. Most of the 2-parters in the original run were this way. The structure means the first episode is exploring the world. Then, the second episode is dealing with the evil. The two don't cross. We see lots of open space in the first episode. In this one, it's mainly the area around Styre's ship. Odd, the episode sort of closes in on us. It takes the beauty of this brave, new world and smooshes it down to almost nothingness. One evil Sontaran hurting a lot of, let's be honest, not very nice people. And it all ends so fast. If the Sontarans come back, they should probably get a larger story.

GENESIS OF THE DALEKS
Written by Terry Nation
Directed by David Maloney
Episode One

Episode 392: (March 8, 1975) The Doctor, Sarah and Harry are sent to Skaro to stop the development of the Daleks.
Cliffhanger: Sarah sees the prototype Dalek shoot some things up. Davros is very excited.

It feels a bit like other Terry Nation Dalek stories but there's something about it that is immediately more immediate than recent Dalek stories. First off, it's the hijacking of the transmat beam. They are not on Nerva, they are not on The Ark. They are in the midst of the 1000-year war on Skaro that devastated the planet and created the Daleks. We heard about it in "The Daleks." We will see it again in "The Magician's Apprentice." But here it feels very real and very dark and very unpleasant. This war has gone on too long. Desperate measures lay ahead.

The opening sequence is men in gas masks getting mowed down by machine gun fire. The Doctor almost blows himself up on a mine. The Doctor, Sarah and Harry are caught up in the middle of a creeping barrage. There is a dugout for a bunker with dead bodies propped against the walls to pretend like there are more soldiers there. (Remember the Doctor rigging up fake soldiers in "The Time Warrior." This is much darker.) Sarah is left for dead after a violent struggle outside the bunker. And everything just looks bad. For once the Doctor's wisecracking looks a bit like false bravado. Looks a bit like a man who is worried that this time he might be in over his head. Certainly, the Time Lord who leaves them doesn't give him much. It's not as bad as giving him and Jo the black box thing and not telling them who it's for. But it sort of is.

We meet the Kaled soldiers. Young, angry men who delight in being violent. We meet Nyder, a very sinister and unpleasant gentleman. This is Davros's right hand man and he will be one of the creepiest villains in all of the show. This is a war, as mentioned, that is so strained, is so out there, that combinations of centuries of fighting are used to keep things alive. A ray gun next to an old rifle. Barbed wires and gas masks alongside a huge dome that encases the city.

Of course, we only see the military here. We'll see some science-people next. We never really get to know the civilians. I somehow don't imagine that there are a lot of them. It really doesn't seem like there would be. Who would want to live in this world? It could be one of those wars where the civilians are all dead a long time ago and only a few people left know what's being fought for. Or not.

At the end of it all, there is a strange, wizened man who seems to be in the bottom half of a Dalek casing. This is Davros. We hadn't heard of him before. From this point on, it will be tough not to. He's the creator of the Daleks. And he and The Doctor will become nemesis over the years. Not quite like the Master but nemesis all the same. Now, we're going to spend some time with Davros in this horrible, horrible world. Sarah ends up watching the first Dalek being tested as the Doctor and Harry are sent for unpleasant interrogation. * What happens next can't be fun.

*I am fully aware that this episode has a full on "Let's escape, run around for a bit and then get caught by the same people!" sequence. It accomplishes nothing and you can tell it's going to happen because the Doctor leaves everything behind at the Kaled base. Of course, he does. Because he'll be right back. Even the best *Doctor Who* stories have these moments in them.

Genesis of the Daleks
Episode Two

Episode 393: (March 15, 1975) The Daleks are unveiled.
Cliffhanger: Sarah falls from the scaffolding.

This is a great episode. When I was a kid, I saw this story so many times in so many different forms. Episode by episode throughout weekdays. In an omnibus version on Saturday nights. The Double LP abbreviation. Terrance Dicks's novelization. This is not my favorite story from this era. (I prefer, for example, "The Ark In Space.") But it is a very important story from this era and for the series.

And there's something interesting that comes up. Notice how this season is so looking back. Daleks, Cybermen and Sontarans. Which is so unlike the rest of this era, which looks forward. The Holmes-Hinchcliffe era is almost like the Bob Haney Batman comics from *The Brave and the Bold*. Yes, Haney teamed up heroes (and otherwise) with Batman. But he always created whole new worlds within his stories. New villains, new characters and so forth. That's the Holmes-Hinchcliffe thing. That's what make this story feel big. They are revisiting the start of the Daleks because 1) no one had really done that before and 2) the BBC doesn't repeat old stories. So, doing this is bringing the Daleks to life for a generation who can't watch the original stories.

And this is a strong episode. The appearance of the Dalek (before it has been named) in the laboratory is fantastic. It recognizes the Doctor and Harry as being different and immediately wants to destroy them. That's such a horrible concept. Davros has reduced the Kaled race to a thing living in a metal casing with a gun. It kills everything that isn't itself. Does the Dalek recognize the Doctor somehow? I always thought it did but it's tough to gauge.

The Scientist who meets up with the Doctor and Harry is great. There is a feeling that all is not lost. That something might survive beyond this point. Who knows? Everything seems so lost to me during this story. The fact that this high-ranking scientist can only send the two of them into a horrible ventilation shaft with monsters at the other end is probably the best example here.

And then, there's Sarah. She gets mixed in with the Mutos. She's moving radioactive material around. She's going to die. And she's doing this for The Thals! The Thals were the good guys the last time we saw them. Now they are as awful as the Kaleds. Neither side is worth it. It's funny. When you watch this as a child, there's no differentiation between the sides. The Kaleds have the Daleks. The Thals are doing this to Sarah. It's bad and it's going to get worse.

The final sequence on film is fantastic. I love some scaffolding. Lis Sladen is really diving in there. It's a well done and well shot sequence. It ends with a freeze frame, which will become kind of a David Maloney thing. It's exciting and it's a cheat at the same time. But let's see where we're going. We're only two episodes in. So much has happened. So much ahead. I don't think this is going to go well.

Genesis of the Daleks
Episode Three

Episode 394: (March 22, 1975) Things go bad for Davros. So things go worse for the Kaled people. Cliffhanger: The Doctor is being electrocuted.

Three things to remember here: 1) Davros is willing to sacrifice all the Kaled people in order to keep the Daleks alive. 2) The Thals are willing to destroy all the Kaled people in order to end the war. 3) The Kaleds give Davros and Nyder safe passage out after they tell them this. Where are they giving them safe passage to? If the Kaleds are about to destroy everything, where are Nyder and Davros going? It's like if I said to you "Hey! Do you want to destroy my building? Here's how." "Thanks, we'll give you a safe trip home." "Thanks." BOOM! "Oh hell." In the end, it doesn't matter. Things are about to change. They're about to change because Davros's own people said "Hey, stop it with the Daleks." And he didn't want to. There have been so many times where an absolute nutjob got in complete control and all we can do is watch what happens... this isn't a good way to run the world. *

The episode goes on. The Doctor is able to convince the Kaleds to get Davros to stop his experiments but that goes nowhere. Meanwhile the Thals treat Sarah horribly as she's trying to escape. So, there's a wonderfully odd moment where we realize that no one has their hands clean here. No one is innocent. The civilians will die and they probably won't know why. And it is horrible. That feeling stretches over the episode.

We do see, if you check responses to the story, that critics and protest groups thought this was the worst thing ever. It's funny that the Daleks were fine in 1963/1964 but here… nope. We could buy Dalek Pajamas back then. There were pop singles about Daleks. There were so many things about Daleks. They were all awesome. But here, it's not good. They are the evil things that they were back then but people only seem to care now. That's generations for you. I would have suggested we all lay off. You complainers will accomplish nothing. Oddly enough, they will encounter and accomplish something in a few years but not now. It's all tiresome and it's all garbage. People need to understand that not everyone is like them. We need to respect each other. If you try to dictate over me, there will be hell to pay.

All of this is in aid of me trying to say that this is an exciting episode but one that has such an odd darkness behind it. Plus, an odd movement around it. Harry and The Doctor seem to get everywhere quickly. Davros and Nyder get there quicker. Sarah is threatened in unpleasant fashion. It's an oddly exciting middle episode that shows no sign of anything letting up. It ends with the Doctor being electrocuted and it starts with a Thal saying the Kaleds will be exterminated. If you've been watching this show closely, things are now going nuts. Let's focus in.

*When Skaro blew up in "Remembrance of the Daleks," I didn't care. It was a rotten world.

Genesis of the Daleks
Episode Four

Episode 395: (March 29, 1975) The Kaled dome is destroyed. The war is over. Oh wait. It isn't. Cliffhanger: Davros is torturing Sarah and Harry.

And the story keeps moving faster and faster. It's moving so well that I can't imagine Terry Nation did all of this. Terrance Dicks and Barry Letts began working with him on this. But Robert Holmes would have been there in the end. To be honest, I think this is so good because Robert Holmes was watching over it. It's dark and weird and strange and funny like all of Holmes's stories. Dicks is a great storyteller. But he can be very generic and straightforward. This feels more like Holmes. Heck, "Death to the Daleks" had the same feeling.

The Davros formula causes the missiles to destroy the Kaled dome. The Kaled people are all destroyed except for the military and the "elite." When I was a kid, that was sad. As an adult, it's a heartbreaker. All the regular people are destroyed by their "leader" giving them up so his scientific experiment could succeed. Awful.

Suddenly, I look back to the Thals we saw in "The Daleks." Well, there's a reason why they looked good. Because this didn't happen to them. The missile didn't destroy their defenses. Everything didn't rain hell down on them in the most horrible way possible. Maybe I'm going overboard here but I agree with me. Davros is terrible. Nyder is worse because he follows him.

That's how the Daleks were born.

Sarah, Harry and The Doctor team up again. The Doctor meets a Thal woman. Her and the Muto team up to do start a rebellion. And everything burns down around them.

As everything burns down, the Doctor is imprisoned by Davros. Sarah and Harry are brought in. Davros wants to know how his Daleks will be defeated in the future so he can negate it all. The Doctor's compassion might change the future.

One of the darkest moments in the series. Right? The Kaleds destroy themselves. The Thals begin their wandering journey. Life is not nice. And the surviving Kaleds only care about how the Daleks will survive. What will they need to do to help the Daleks survive? One can only wonder how much longer the story can last. We've got two episodes left but it feels like the climax has come and gone. It's a hell of a story. Not many of them are going to work successfully in this fashion but, sometimes, all you need is one.

Genesis of the Daleks
Episode Five

Episode 396: (April 5, 1975) The Doctor gives a complete account of the Dalek history to Davros onto a tape of some sort. The military and the scientists are turning against Davros and his experiments. The Doctor decides to destroy the Dalek incubator room.
Cliffhanger: A Kaled mutant has attached itself to the Doctor's neck.

Things are continuing to heat up, which is great for the fifth part of a six-parter. There's still story in here even though it has gone through so much already. Davros is torturing Sarah and Harry. The Doctor is giving up all the Dalek info. So now, they need to get the Time Ring back and they need to destroy that tape with the future of the Daleks on it. (Although, I always wondered why the Doctor didn't just lie. Make it up! Why not? In fact, some of the things he says do sound a bit like lies.)

It is so dark to think that the crazy experiments of this one crazy man, as brilliant as they say he is or as he says is, will not only create the Daleks but will have wiped out an entire race of people. His own people. Knowing that the Daleks are based in and around this makes them even worse somehow. When the Doctor announces that he's going to destroy the incubation room, one cheers. It doesn't seem very Doctor-like but he didn't know the full story of the genesis before. Now he does. And he knows how it goes from here.

When I was a kid, the cliffhanger to this one was an all-time favorite. This was the first time I'd encountered the Daleks. But, of course, this isn't really a Dalek story. It's a Davros story. The Daleks we see are still starting off here. They're not yet what they will be. I learned more about Daleks, during those first few years, from the novelizations. In the early 1980s, we had "The Daleks." (David Whitaker's wonderfully odd but exciting adaptation of that story). We had "The Dalek invasion of Earth" and the three Pertwee Dalek stories. (I never got "Destiny of the Daleks." Probably because I figured I would see it eventually, rather than the others). Those books gave me the Daleks everyone loved. But I saw their origin first. I saw Davros first. So, for a long time, this was the way my knowledge of them was born. It wasn't until Autumn of 1986 that I saw "The Daleks" and a very different sort of timeline.

The episode moves the assorted plotlines along just enough to keep up the excitement. At the end of the episode, we have the scenes at the incubation room. Well, the hallway outside the room. We have Davros and Nyder gearing up for something. We know that the Daleks are sort of growing in strength. We also have the Thal woman and the Muto gearing up a bunch of people to attack the bunker and try to stop

Davros. Their bombs destroyed the Kaleds. The Daleks destroyed the Thals. They'll all be back for "The Daleks." Or will they? We'll talk about that in the next review.

Whether the Doctor will destroy the Daleks, was a question that may have been up in the air when it originally aired. I would say that now we watch it to see the machinations of the creation and to meet Davros. We know they don't get destroyed before they get created. Let's see how this plays out. Will they get the time ring back, I wonder?

Genesis of the Daleks
Episode Six

Episode 397: (April 12, 1975) The Daleks are now fully born. There's no stopping them now. Or is there? Cliffhanger: The trio hold the Time Ring and begin to spin through time and space. As this happens, the Doctor talks about what they accomplished.

So, it ends. The Daleks are delayed but have not been destroyed. The Doctor seems happy with the outcome. He mentions that lots of races would join and fight to stop the Daleks so that's something. Although, I'll be honest: That always sounded a little off to me. It's sounds like The Doctor's making the best of bad rubbish. It's like saying it's OK that I didn't stop Jason Vorhees from being conceived because so many great movies would come out of these killings in later years. "No! if you get a chance to kill a crazy known serial killer, you do it. You don't reminisce on what will happen after the killings are done." Is this really the victory the Doctor wants? "Sara Kingdom and I would never have met if it wasn't for the Daleks." "She died horribly because of the Daleks." "Yes, Never would have met." C'mon, Doctor. Maybe it's vacation time. You have been going non-stop since the start of "Robot."

And then there's the great scene where the Doctor is thinking about whether he has the right to destroy the Daleks. Before he can make a choice, the meeting is announced. Whew! The Doctor doesn't have to make the choice. But then, he comes back in the end to destroy them and a Dalek passes over the wires and, I think, blows everything up. However, it doesn't stop everything. It's just a delay. And that makes sense. If the Daleks are now in charge, they'll figure out a way to get the incubator back up and running. Maybe the Doctor was engaging in a little wishful thinking when he thought blowing up that room would end it. It does seem like an odd ending to me though. They talk themselves out of it. Then, when they talk themselves back into it, it doesn't matter anyway. The thread seems to be getting lost a little bit here as the ending approaches.

Poor Davros. Never quite figured that his evil, compassionless creations would ever do something like that, i.e. kill him. "I've taken almost everything into account!" To be honest, only the Daleks and the Thals and the Mutos who seal off the bunker entrance really come out great in this episode. Sara and Harry don't do a lot. Everyone else either gets killed or must justify what they're up to quite a bit.

Not that this isn't a great story. It is. An absolute classic. I'm glad they made it. I'm glad we got Davros and the history of the Daleks was explained. I'm glad we got the giant clam. It's just the dramatics are lacking a bit here. It's almost like a show ticking off a list of things that need to happen. Rather than letting them happen organically and being a bit more dramatic. It got great ratings though and it is out there for all to see and enjoy. And it changes the face, or certainly seems to, of Dalek history from now on. For some time, Davros will be inextricably tied up in their history. I know, you think he died. Well, he did. Forget that I mentioned anything. Now that The Doctor, Sarah and Harry have the time ring back they can head to Nerva and then, hopefully, to Earth.

REVENGE OF THE CYBERMEN
Written by Gerry Davis
Directed by Michael E. Briant
Episode One

Episode 398: (April 19, 1975) Back on the Beacon, there is a plague and even bigger troubles. Cliffhanger: Sarah Jane is attacked by a Cybermat.

It is kind of odd to watch this one when you think that it had been seven years since a proper Cyberman story. That's a long time for the aliens/ monsters who became the Daleks of the second half of the 1960s. And it's even odder to think that it will be seven more years before they properly return. This is the only Cyberman story of the 1970s. Seasons Seven through 17, this is it. So, enjoy what you get. Here you mainly get a very long snake-like Cybermat and a moment with the Cybermen in their ship. Plus, we get people on the Golden Planet Voga. And more shenanigans in the Nerva Ark, which is now a beacon. Because we are hundreds of years in the past.

I love the concept that the exciting, sterile huge Ark was just a used beacon that the government probably sold off in an auction or something like that. And the people on the Ark weren't the last humans at all. They were just "some" humans. It makes looking back at that story even more fascinating because the TARDIS crew almost die for a bunch of people who are kind of jerks and NOT the last.

Anyway, this is the Ark, or Nerva, being a beacon. An infected beacon. The image of the corridors lined with the bodies, I think, is powerful. Especially because, in "Ark", they're white and sterile and have those openings to the outside. * Here, having all that space littered with bodies is the exact opposite of sterile and it is rather harrowing. Now, there is one thing that modern day Blur-Ray technology reveals: A lot of those bodies are mannequins. I don't remember that at all back in the day. But they sure are mannequins.

The human crew are fine. Pretty much standard. If you've seen "The Moonbase," you kind of know how this is going to go because it's the exact same set-up but with the Cybermats. The Doctor and gang ingratiate themselves in quickly, which I like. There won't be any more problems. Kellman is a fun sort of "Is he a bad guy or what?" kind of character. And I like his outfit. The scene where he electrifies the floor in his room to zap the Doctor is great. I love The Doctor riding the dresser door for a moment. It's a silly stunt but it's cool anyways. Something I probably tried in my house when I was a kid. And I probably ripped the door of the hinges. (I never severely hurt myself emulating my heroes or anything like that. I got some bruises and I broke a few things.) The plague on the beacon makes one wonder why the Time Lords couldn't have given the Doctor a break and sent them all back at a safer time.

Because, if you think about it, they've been on the go since the start of 'Robot' and now they're going right into another adventure. When's the last time they've had anything to eat? Surely, we could all use, to quote the great Huey Lewis a "couple days off." Well, it's not happening now. Strange shaped Vogans on a gold planet. A Cybership nearby. Robert Holmes adding mention of a "Cyberwar."

Hey, what's that strange symbol on the wall in the Vogan room there? Surely, we've seen that before... or we will see it... Time travel is tricky.

*I love how no one ever mentions them. Or stops to look out of them. Surely, if you want to see what's outside, you should look out these gigantic holes in the hallways rather than, say, looking for some sort of screen relaying something a camera may be showing you. Also, like in the DVD or Blu of "Ark," we can see far too much beyond the holes. I swear by all that is holy... Watching these on PBS, especially in black and white, you could not see anything beyond the holes except stars and darkness. Now, we can see gantries and the pattern of the Christmas lights and all sorts of things we shouldn't see. Back then, though, I thought these were some of the wildest hallways in all of outer space.

Revenge of the Cybermen
Episode Two

Episode 399: (April 26, 1975) Sarah and Harry beam down to the Vogan surface. The Cybermen take the beacon.
Cliffhanger: The Cybermen take the beacon.

Well, I put "The Cybermen take the beacon" there to make it sound like it's more of an integral part of the episode. It's not. We see them very briefly a few times. Then, they dock with the Beacon. Then, they shoot everyone down and the Beacon is theirs. It's not as exciting as one might think. In fact, it's all rather perfunctory. Shoot the three people down and it's over. Not the most exciting return for the Cybermen after seven years. But then, the first appearance of the Daleks in "Day of the Daleks" is no big shakes. They had a problem with burying the lede at this time in the show's history.

Some of that might have to do with all the over writing that these stories needed. Remember that "Day of the Daleks" didn't have the Daleks in it originally. Louis Marks had to add them in. They add great gravitas but they do feel shoehorned in. Here it's interesting because Gerry Davis's original script was set at a casino and it was much grander. Holmes had to do a lot of rewriting. Sometimes, Robert Holmes's re-writing is brilliant. "Pyramids of Mars" anyone? Sometimes it's almost great.

This is one of those stories that's always "almost great" and occasionally achieves "great." For example, the locations are great. Wookey Hole, the caves were the Vogans live, is a brilliant place. It looks dark and dangerous. You can see an entire race of beings hiding down here. You can also see an entire race slowly going mad here. Trapped away from the light. But not only that, surrounded by gold. One of the most valuable substances in the universe that they have no use for, apart from practically. The moments when they must use the studio to replicate the caves don't work as well. Going from real rock to Styrofoam rock or whatever it is lowers us back to "almost great."

The Vogans have some neat but distracting masks. I like the design of their rooms. But, then they kind of let the side down. There are some great actors in those masks but my oh my are they dull. It's the kind of dull alien race that one would hope Holmes could work around. He almost does. But he doesn't. There's the old, wise one. There's the young, belligerent one. There's the other one. They seem a lot like the Silurians. And their shootouts are nothing to go on about. Michael Briant has directed exciting stuff in the past. I'm not sure what's wrong here. It's never very exciting. Just a lot of shots, some strange looking beings falling dead and Sarah and Harry trying to run through it all.

Luckily, Sarah and Harry have some great stuff to do. Her indignation when she finds herself being carried by Harry is great. (He does save her life after the Cybermat bites her.) They're a charming duo, especially when they get shackled in the gold. Harry's response to the gold is fantastic. I like the two of them here. (I wish the Vogans were more interesting.) They have some nice interplay bouncing off one another. I don't know if it's quite warranted from their experiences but it's close enough.

The Doctor doesn't do much. We get to see him be angry. That's always good. An angry Doctor is a Doctor who wants to win and who wants to take down the bad guys. When he threatens Kellman with the Cyberman, that is excellent. I wish he had identified the Cybermen a bit earlier. He does, in the end. It's a bit too late. The script feels more interested in the Vogan conflict than anything else. And that's fine. They're just not that interesting. Put our gang back in the spotlight, please.

Revenge of the Cybermen
Episode Three

Episode 400: (May 3, 1975) The Cybermen strap bombs to the Doctor and his friends to blow up Voga. Meanwhile, Harry and Sarah are asked a lot of questions by the people of Voga. No women? Cliffhanger: Harry tries to detach the Cyberbomb from the Doctor.

This is an episode I remember very vividly from my childhood, especially the cliffhanger. One thing I don't think I remember thought is boosted by the Blu-Ray. It's something I find charming rather than annoying. Harry and Kellman are in the studio. They are in a fake cave set. The Doctor and friends are really in a cave but there are fake rocks at the top of an incline. When I was a kid, this was a big "No! Look out!" kind of thing. As a grownup, I do the same thing. But I can see the fake rocks and I can see the jump in the quality. Oddly enough, I feel bad that Kellman died. That's maturity.

The Vogans are still, sadly, not interesting. I need to re-read the novelization. I want to know if this was a race that was more interesting in print than online. Their masks may be a large part of the problem. Something about them really bothers me. Maybe the distortion of the human head/ face? I don't know. I like their Skystriker rocket though. I will watch Episode Four with the CGI effects because I'm not interested in seeing what they do with the rocket stock footage again.

Sarah and Harry are doing their best to work through the Vogan bureaucracy. It's nice that Kellman was a double-double agent. However, he did assist in causing the death of all the humans on the Beacon. So, that ain't great. Weird character. They kill him off before he can redeem himself or anything else. But, maybe, this is the Hinchcliffe/Holmes conundrum. What do we do with characters like this? Kellman is greedy. He wants the gold. He has a big elaborate con going on. We knew that early on from the radio device confusion. But what does he get now?

I do love the Cyberbombs strapped to the guys. As a kid, that was a very James Bond kind of thing to me. The hero and two others with these crazy bombs attached to them. It ups the ante so much. They try their best to get out there and save the day. But those bombs. I love The Doctor trying to get them to a spot where the gold interrupts the frequency but who knows? We didn't expect the crazy rockslides. It's so interesting and, at the same time, is it terribly interesting?

At the end of the day, I'm not sure that this is a particularly fascinating episode. The Doctor encounters the Cybermen properly for the first time since the last episode of "The Wheel In Space." Their discussion is fine. The Doctor gets in some good cracks against the Cyberleader. The Cyberleader strangles, sort of, the Doctor for a bit. The Cybermen don't seem to recognize that "Hey! It's the Doctor!" So, all of this feels a bit less than it should be. To quote the Doctor: "I'm underwhelmed."

Revenge of the Cybermen
Episode Four

Episode 401: (May 10, 1975) We must stop the Cybermen! And that rocket.
Cliffhanger: The TARDIS has returned. The Brigadier has left a message. Back to Earth!

The story and the season ends. And it ends by keeping up the rollercoaster ride feeling of the whole season. One damn thing after another. We haven't seen the TARDIS for 11 episodes and now we have to get back to UNIT stat. It's like "Colony In Space." The Brig is probably still standing in the room after the TARDIS left in "Robot." No time passes there while Sarah keeps getting older and older. It does give the season a feel of the early years. When the stories seemed to roll one into the other and there never seemed to be a break. The next season will begin by continuing from this ending. As far as we know. *

This Cyber story ends fine. A lot goes on in this fourth episode. Elisabeth Sladen says something in the DVD/ Blu-Ray commentary that I've mentioned with some of these stories. When the one group of Vogans is trying to talk with the other about the Skystriker, she says, basically, "One feels like they may not have time to finish up everything that they have to get done." I've mentioned that numerous times. Almost as if, when the show hits episode four, it doesn't fully realize what it must wrap up. Yes, things do feel a bit rushed here. Granted, I would prefer things feel a little rushed and end satisfactorily rather than ending in a mess. So, I'm OK with it. But a lot happens.

And yes, the Cybermen are stopped. One of my favorite things about this story for some time, maybe it's still true, is that these are the last of the Cybermen. That's why there are only four of them. That's why they're being so covert and careful. That's why they're "skulking about" in an old scrappy ship. They are the last. Makes sense to me. When they get blown up by the Skystriker, it is the end of the Cybermen. I can't honestly think that there are a lot of people out there that aren't excited by them being gone forever. Frankly, they're jerks. I wonder what went through their Cyberbrains right when they blew up. Something like "Well that could have gone better" but with less emotion.

Then, the question comes up. How on Earth does a small contingent of Cybermen kill so many Vogans within their own world... which is made of gold? Shouldn't the Cybermen all be falling over dead if gold clogging their breathing apparatus kills them? That would be like me walking through a tunnel made of fire and not getting singed at all. Anyway...

"Harry Sullivan is an imbecile" is a great moment. The reprise of the cliffhanger, leaving out the video moments, is nicely done. Overall, not a great story. But a decent one. Maybe if it hadn't been so soon after "Ark" and "Genesis" it would be more well-loved. Overall, a refreshing season. The holdover of stories from the previous regime impedes it somewhat. However, you can see the excitement of the new regime taking over. It's more palpable than in Season Seven, even though that had color. One looks forward to seeing what this crew will do in the next season.

*Originally, the season was meant to end with a six parter called "Terror of the Zygons." The BBC wanted the scheduling of the show changed. They wanted it back the way it was in the 1960s. Because there wouldn't have been enough time to end this season properly, we end early here. That's why it's a short season. That's why "Zygons" got pressed down into 4 parts, which was probably a better idea for everyone.

SEASON THIRTEEN
1975-1976

TERROR OF THE ZYGONS
Written by Robert Banks Stewart
Directed by Douglas Camfield
Episode One

Episode 402 (August 30, 1975): The Doctor, Sarah and Harry land in Scotland near the North Sea. Oil rigs are being attacked by something. UNIT is assembled. Strange hands twist weird dials. Cliffhanger: Sarah Jane sees a Zygon.

Back on Earth, we get the last proper UNIT story for a very long time. When this was being aired, there was a feeling that viewers felt this. So, there was a feeling of melancholy running around the episode. This would be Harry's last regular appearance, along with Benton's. The Brig will pop up a few more times but he's pretty much done here. The production crew simply weren't interested in the previous production crew's setup. Even though the previous production crew had inherited this setup from the previous production crew. You know the story.

They go out with a pretty darn good serial, though. The Loch Ness monster is in it for Heaven's Sake. When Sarah and Rose argue about adventures in "School Reunion," the "Loch Ness Monster" is the one that stops Rose in her tracks. It's memorable. And the Zygons are one of the most memorable monsters the show ever had. For years, they would appear in articles as great monsters of the show. But it wasn't until 2013 that they properly returned. (Although, there had been novels, like *The Bodysnatchers*, and appearances in other media.) They're a fantastic looking monster. The image of the first one, with the blood red body and its mouth wide open in a sort of scream, is a fantastic cliffhanger. (Compare it to say the reveal of The Kraal at the end of Episode One of "The Android invasion.")

The episode, I think, benefits very nicely from the reduction in the episodes. There's always something happening and it moves along very quickly and then suddenly it's done. The Doctor is acting very alien throughout. Sarah is charming and a bit cheeky. Harry gets almost shot in the head in a rather harrowing scene near the beach. There's a stag on the wall with some sort of camera in it. Bagpipes playing. Haggis is mentioned. (This is so we know it's Scotland.) And something is seen coursing along under the water.

It all beings with the wonderful camaraderie of this trio of travelers. I love the Doctor's Scottish outfit. I love Sarah wearing his hat and Harry with his scarf. It's so charming. But they must be exhausted right? They've been on so many continuous adventures. I'd like to think the Doctor deliberately took his time getting them back. Allowed everyone to rest if they needed. Maybe got to use the pool. Hang out a bit. Make sure everyone was refreshed before having to return to what would probably be another crazy adventure. That makes sense to me.

Overall, it's an excellent opening to the season. It sets the story up nicely. It's fun that it's in 'Scotland" and not the normal England-y places. The monster is certainly memorable. And it has a very nice pace to it that a six-part version would have just demolished. Let's see how the rest of this goes.

Terror of the Zygons
Episode Two

Episode 403: (September 6, 1975) The Zygons want to kill the Doctor. They'll do whatever needs to be done.
Cliffhanger: The Loch Ness Monster bears down on the Doctor.

Another good episode. There's a great economy of storytelling in this episode and the previous one. We learn a lot. We experience a lot. We see a lot. But it's never too much. In the end, there are plenty of questions left to be answered, things to be encountered, etc. etc. There is still a lot left for the last two episodes. Maybe we can't quite nail down what all of it is at this moment but it's something exciting and weird. It's so benefited by the reduction in the number of episodes. If this had been six episodes, about half of what we experience in this episode would have been in this episode. The other half would have been meandering about. Here everything is important and it works.

Yes, even the Loch Ness Monster works. The show keeps trying dinosaur-like things and it really can't do it. The stop motion moments with the monster work decently. But the puppet head thing or whatever it is… maybe not so much. The cliffhanger is good. Everything is working perfectly. The moor is great. The fog is elegant. The Doctor is struggling. The Monster ain't so great. However, you know me, I can deal with it. It doesn't bother me. Do I wish it was better? Sure. I get into it though. I can see what's happening. I want the Doctor to be OK. It come down to other people's reactions. I could almost show anyone this story but the Monster is going to conk it up. It's just a bit too "No. I better not."

I trust that Robert Holmes was a smart guy. In fact, I'm positive he was a smart guy. Why does he allow something like this to happen? To sneak through. How did they think they could get jt to work right? Having said that, it doesn't ruin anything. And Douglas Camfield knows to limit the shots.

The rest of the episode is excellent. Possessed Harry being chased around the village is fantastic. I've always loved how Sarah can wrangle up a group of soldiers to help her look for him. The scene in the barn is great. It's quite dark. The shot of Harry hidden amongst the bales of hay is one of the scarier moments in all of *Doctor Who*. Harry with the pitchfork is next. The screaming Zygon on its back is right after that. Great stuff. The kids were scared.

Why shouldn't they be? When we're in the control room with Harry we can get a good look at them. Their design is fantastic. They have the classic arrogant thing that all the Doctor Who monsters have. And which will probably come to something later. I love that we learn what's going on with them. We don't get their full plan but we get the basics. Generally, that doesn't get parsed out until later. They're trying something different here and it works. Plus, the Zygons are flippin' shape shifters. Come on! How are we ever going to defeat them? *

Let's not forget: The room that fills up with gas leading to the Brig being confused about sleeping on the job. There's the scene in the depressurization room. I always liked that when I was a kid. I was never fully sure what was happening. But the Doctor's cry of… agony? Anguish? …really is affecting. This is a sharp episode overall. One can only hope they can bring it in by the end. I have high hopes.

*Steven Moffatt takes this thing to its logical conclusion in "The Day of the Doctor" and beyond. Where a peace is brokered and the Zygons can live amongst us if they keep their human form. Things go wrong after a time.

Terror of the Zygons
Episode Three

Episode 404: (September 13, 1975) The good guys gradually convene upon the Zygon ship. Cliffhanger: The Zygon ship rises out of the Loch with the Doctor onboard.

It's odd. I'm looking at some other reviews of this story and most of them are kind of "Ah…" Thinking that story is OK but really isn't up to much. I don't know. I have to disagree. I always have in the past. Now, writing this immediately after watching this episode, I must do it again. Yes, the Loch Ness Monster isn't great. It's in the opening couple minutes and then it's gone. The only thing that might be a problem is that at the end of this episode there feels like there's a bit too much crammed in here. I thought that this episode ended with the Zygon shop blowing up as the Zygons went to London. Nope. There's so much more for the last episode.

Is that a problem? Too much happening in a story. Back in the day, that didn't happen often with *Doctor Who*. It happened in a bunch of 7th Doctor stories especially in the 26th Season. But that's what makes that season (well one of the things) so watchable. The pacing is almost modern. Watch "Ghost Light" or "The Curse of Fenric." They cook. So, does "Zygon." The first episode may be a bit calm but it's setting up the world. By the end, the pacing is flying.

There's a lot of chatter about the script not being very good, even when they were making it. Apparently, Douglas Camfield sent different groups of the crew and cast to look at certain scenes and see what they could do with it. Per the production text on the DVD, everyone was involved in the writing. That's fun. Maybe that's why there's so much here. I had always thought that it was because of the episode reduction. But having about 25 co-writers could be a viable option.

The episode itself, I think, is quite good. We see the Duke's house, specifically his library. Or his Loch Ness room, at least. I love that the ship has been under the castle for centuries as long as the Duke and his family have been there. Presumably, they take over the next Duke and go from there. Although, I typed that and I suddenly see problems. Regardless, it's cool.

The rest of the episode moves so quick it is kind of tough to take stuff into full account. Angus is killed by a Zygon after discovering the eyes that watch from the stag. There's a lot of fun running around. And there is the sequence I always loved, it's not long but it's cool: where Benton and the soldiers chase the Zygon through the woods. I remember being so surprised when the nurse shows up. (She was/ is the Zygon.) She has a huge streak of blood going down her arm. It isn't incredibly realistic but she's not human. That's Zygon blood. We do see it quite a bit. I always liked that when I was a kid. Until I lost my fear of the dark at age 14, that was about as much blood as I could take.

The scene with the Duke, the Doctor, Sarah and The Brig is great. Knowing that the Brig and Benton won't be around much again after the next episode, it's nice to have them featured here. Harry only shows up at the very end. There's some good stuff with Sarah not believing he is himself and even the Doctor does that. It works well. It all ends with the Doctor captured and the Zygon ship disappearing off into the distance. I remember first seeing that as a kid and thinking "What on Earth do we do now?"

Terror of the Zygons
Episode Four

Episode 405: (September 20, 1975) The final confrontation in the heart of London.
Cliffhanger: Sarah and The Doctor take off in the TARDIS.

There's a review quoted on the DVD information text that calls this story dull. It hopes that the next story will be better. I have to ask. Truly... What story was this person watching? What story is everyone who denigrates this one watching? OK. Some things do move too fast. The arrival in London at the end of this could have used a few more moments for suspense purposes. But, apart from that, what are we all talking about?

Again, the Loch Ness Monster isn't great. Again, this is *Doctor Who* not an MCU TV show. There are no computer effects here. Why can't we just enjoy what we see and let life go by? It's just meant to be entertainment. It's meant to be fun. The producer mentions on the DVD commentary that these stories rarely ever got screened again. No one (pretty much no one) in 1975 had any sort of home recording equipment. So, the actual reality of what you saw gradually fades into what your memory wants you to remember. A fun Loch Ness Monster looming above everything. Fantastic exploding spaceships. Great Zygons.

The novelizations helped everything along. The prose in those books and the covers and the imagination of the reader elevated those to a magic place. The pacing was kept up by the prose and the way the readers read them. The descriptions made everything perfect. (Heck, I remember in novelizations for big budget movies thinking that my imagination did better work. *Return of the Jedi*'s novelization provided a better Sarlacc Pit fight than I saw on screen. When Boba Fett dies on screen, it's a bit of a "Hey! That guy died!" moment. But, in the book, there's more to it. It's meatier. The whole battle is, to be honest.) It was only with home video and beyond that things got weird.

Let's not forget the updating of home video. From VHS and Beta to Laserdisc to DVD to Blu-Ray. This season isn't on Blu as I write this but it is due soon. The season before it and after it is out on lovely season sets. They do look great. Not fully proper HD but great. The higher the definition, the more mid-1970s 625-line BBC shows are going to look a little scrappy.

I don't find this story boring at all. Neither do I find it one of the absolute classics of the show. No. What it is is a damn good example of the show. An example that is also saying goodbye to a certain type of *Doctor Who*. Specifically, the UNIT era. Yes, "The Android Invasion" will bring UNIT back but no Brig. You must have the Brig there. Sorry. Goodbye UNIT.

The episode is bullet paced. The best moments are probably watching Broton and the Doctor square off. Two strong forces facing one another down. Tom Baker is on fire in this scene. (That's not an electrocution joke, by the way.) This is a different kind of Doctor than the previous one. He's less haughty. Less superior. He just seems very self-assured. The electrocution moment is something. I don't feel like previous Doctors would have done that. He basically uses his body to break the electric current that shields the Zygon shop from radio detection. It works but he almost dies. Then, he gets to run with the people from Forgill and gets to hear the Zygons yelling "Let us out" before everything blows up.

He also gets to ask how the Zygons will control the planet when there are just six of them. Which is great. (More on the way.) The Doctor overall is a bit of a smartass but a dangerous and intelligent one.

As the 4th Doctor fully takes over the show, it leaves no more room for the gang at UNIT and sadly Harry Sullivan. Now, it's the Doctor and Sarah show. And they're going to the Planet of Evil.

PLANET OF EVIL
Written by Louis Marks
Directed by David Maloney
Episode One

Episode 406: (September 27, 1975) Sarah and The Doctor follow a distress call 30,000 years into the future to a very weird planet called Zeta Minor.
Cliffhanger: The Doctor and Sarah encounter a strange monster made up of odd red lines that looks like it is going to eat them up.

This is the first time that the Doctor has travelled in time and it's felt really alien. And weird. We're helped here by the fact that there is a new TARDIS console room. There's a wonderfully odd doorway to the rest of the ship that I don't think we'll really see again. The place has a largeness to it that I really like. I believe we only see it in "Pyramids of Mars." * The Doctor is acting very alien here. Moreso that we have seen him act since... I don't know. The start of the Troughton era maybe? "The Power of the Daleks?"

The Doctor just really feels like an alien. He kind of did in the previous serial. But here he has a strangeness to him. I really like the way he talks to the Morestran crew. Clearly there is something evil going on here. Or at least something odd. He doesn't have the time nor the inclination to deal with them. My favorite moment is when the Commander says that they can learn what they need from the Doctor. The Doctor smiles and asks if that means he is going to be tortured. A great moment.

The Doctor always comes up against people like this throughout their journeys. The people who don't believe them or are immediately hostile. They all have different ways of dealing with them. This Doctor is a "No BS" Doctor. I wish he had psychic paper because it would make life easier. Regardless, I love how he goes up against these guys. The soldiers themselves are standard. I love the ship they climb off. Prof. Sorenson is clearly up to something that is going to come to no good. One hopes the Doctor and Sarah can help in some way before something goes incredibly, screwball, wrong.

I applaud the soldiers here for being able to teleport the TARDIS onto their ship. You wouldn't think that's something that could happen. Teleportation will be laughed at later in this season. It causes Sarah trouble here. I would sort of like to think that you couldn't make the TARDIS do that. Yes, you can drag it somewhere. But, to do that would be outside of the ship's purview. I was surprised as Sarah was when it happened.

Final thought: The jungle set here is incredibly good. Roger Murray-Leach was an absolute master. He did the Ark sets in "The Ark in Space." Here he designs one hell of a great jungle set. I was always convinced. And that black pool... yikes! It really does feel like we are in a place... not only far in the future... but at the edge of the universe. The whole place is harrowing. You almost expect a Dalek to show up as they'd be the only ones who could easily survive here.

*I checked. That is correct. Per the DVD info text, it got damaged. That's why they went with the wooden control room of the next season.

Planet of Evil
Episode Two

Episode 407: (October 4, 1975) Sorenson wants to take energy crystals from the planet. The ship can finally leave. The Doctor reveals the secret of this strange place.
Cliffhanger: The Doctor falls into the Black Pool.

The Doctor has a great moment here. It's when he's in the main control room of the ship. It won't leave the planet. It can't leave the planet. The Doctor knows why. Exactly why. He tells the guys what's going on and basically pleads with them to give him a moment. To let him go to the black pool and try to speak with the being that guards the gateway and they let him go. To me, this is a fantastic moment because it shows the Doctor at their best. Under the gun at one moment. But they are the only one who knows what's happening. They are the only one who knows how to save the day. And the people who were previously against him give him a moment. *

This episode or the next one was the first episode of *Doctor Who* I ever saw. One afternoon at my Aunt Rose's house, probably around early summer 1981. I remember the Doctor falling into the black pool. I don't remember whether it was at the end or the beginning. I think it was the end because I remember really feeling that this black pool was a big thing. If it had been episode three, I would have thought "Oh dear. What's he falling into?" This episode is a big one for me. The Doctor is super heroic here. They can sometimes be very flippant. They can sometimes be very put upon. Sometimes very alien. The Doctor here is strong and in charge. Even when locked up.

The Doctor's knowledge of the universe is something that really grabbed my attention. You always like your hero to be smart. The hero to be slightly ahead of everyone else. Maybe not always ahead of the villain but certainly everyone else. And that happens here. I love how he knows what the anti-matter is. I love his explanation of where they are. I love that he knows to put a little in a toffee tin. He deals quite well with this rather nondescript group of soldiers. I've always loved the colors of their outfits. They're all in blue and white and they look clean. But, Professor Sorenson, slightly disheveled and slightly crazy looking, is in an odd brown. It speaks volumes.

The explanation is fantastic. A few seasons ago, we had black holes. Here we have anti-matter. To me, as a kid and now, the concept of this story set in the year 30,000 and change on a planet that is literally at the dividing line between one universe and another is incredible. It's such a huge concept. I think the show puts it across quite well. Through the story. Through the acting. Through that creepy black pool. Through the awesome red outlined monster. (What the hell is it?) And through that incredible jungle. A jungle that seems to have been laid there specifically to make sure no one tries to get through it. I do wonder if there's another jungle or something on the other side of the people. A place that stops the anti-matter people from coming out. Zeta Major? I always wondered. Why is this Zeta Minor? Did we have a story somewhere with Zeta Major in it? It seems to be a universally recognized name. Maybe the TARDIS is translating that name into something everyone recognizes. I don't know. It's fascinating nevertheless.

*They don't completely trust him. They send the awesome "occuloid tracker" after him. That great thing that floats through the air following people and recording them. Nicely done. The jungle set is already cool enough on tape. On film, it's incredible. Especially when you see little pools of water and such.

Planet of Evil
Episode Three

Episode 408: (October 11, 1975) The Doctor brokers a deal with the anti-matter guardian. There is still antimatter onboard the ship. Professor Sorenson has it and it is infecting him in a very bad way.
Cliffhanger: The Doctor and Sarah are being ejected from the ship.

Some have said that the momentum and scares that the show had diminish here, especially when the ship takes off. I will be the first to admit that all the budget seemed to go the jungle. The hallways of the ship are dull. The main bridge is dull. The ejection room is the most interesting space. I don't mind it though. There is palpable threat here. Not just from the planet but from Sorenson who keeps becoming that monster. Also, from Salamar and his guards, who are nuts. (I always thought the way that Salamar forces Vishinsky's arm down on the handle to eject our heroes rather than do it himself was proof of how rotten these people are. I can't even imagine fully what the planet must be like that these people come from. I don't want to visit there.)

As far as the crew are concerned: Let's be honest. Any military that needs two armed guards in the control room of their own spaceship are either over-over cautious or the worst. I don't know whether these people are the worst. I say that because of Vishinsky. He is a compassionate man and can see what's going on. As per usual, he's not in charge. Salamar is bordering on crazy. Maybe he got the job because his parents were important. I don't know. He makes a wise choice to get the antimatter off the ship. I don't like when he chastises the Doctor for having a small portion of the antimatter because the Doctor is saving their lives and he was unconscious. It's an interesting group of people because apart from Vishinsky and maybe De Hann, there's no one to like. We keep watching because we love Sarah and the Doctor.

As a kid, I always wanted a flask of whatever it is Professor Sorenson uses. Whenever he becomes Anti-Man, his Hyde, he has a slug of some purple/ brown (hard to tell) liquid that makes instant steam/ smoke. It takes the edge off. Maybe it is some sort of glorious anti-hangover medicine. I don't know. He is pretty broken up when he spills it. I wonder why he can't make more. I'll have to check the Terrance Dicks novelization because this was the sort of thing he always fixed up. Does Sorenson know that this will happen to him? Is that why he has the liquid cure? Or is it just luck? If it's just luck, well, that's very lucky. But, if he prepared it just in case, why not more? It's too bad that Sorenson is completely unable to see past his own pride and his own excitement over this energy source. It's obvious to everyone that it won't work. It can't work. He's literally willing to let the Doctor and Sarah get ejected into space alive to safeguard his discovery. A discovery he knows is nonsense. I wasn't a fan of Sorenson as a kid. As an adult, I think he's an atrocious human being. But, enough about Sorenson, let's go on to the final part.

Planet of Evil
Episode Four

Episode 409: (October 18th, 1975) Anti-Man contains multitudes. The Doctor must complete his side of the bargain before the Morestran ship smashes into the surface of the planet.
Cliffhanger: The Doctor and Sarah leave. He's bringing her back to UNIT HQ.

OK, so, if this was the first story I saw, then let's have a look at that ending. * The day is saved. So many have died but Sorenson has been redeemed. The Doctor hands Sorenson a better source of energy than the dangerous one we've been experiencing. As this happens, Sarah says Goodbye to Vishinsky and it is slightly overlapped. The shots are slightly off. But it doesn't matter. The Evil (i.e., the antimatter) has passed. Everyone laughs. And it ends like so many episodes of 1970s TV, including this show with Pertwee and his comedy deliveries. Here, however, it feels different. The Doctor delivers his "joke" line but it ends up feeling weird being delivered in this Doctor's fashion. Then, we cut to Sarah. She smiles and then her smile gets bigger and then we see the TARDIS flying through space.

How is the episode? It's pretty darn good. Again, a lot happens. There is no time for boredom. We get time spent in the TARDIS, which we don't get a lot of in around now. We get a fight alongside the black pool. We get the anti-matter monster rising out of the pool as the TARDIS dematerializes. As a child, I thought that was ominous. I thought "The Doctor didn't defeat the bad thing! It's still there." As an adult, I have different thoughts but I don't know if they're right. I think the monster is paying respects and saying goodbye to a being that has understood it. After years of confusion and killing to maintain the balance, it has met a compassionate soul that understands it. It's waving goodbye as best it can. If the Doctor ever needed to assemble beings to help him in the future (if for example a good man should ever need to go to war), he can rely on that creature to help.

To me, this is a darn good story. It's well told. It keeps everything moving. Salamar goes from being overzealous to insane. Vishinsky and Sarah make a great team. The Doctor wanders deep into darkness and (luckily) can get out. This is the way the show works for me. Not that the 3rd Doctor era was wrong. Because the Doctor should always be helping and saving. It's the weirdness factor in this serial. The oddness of all of it makes for something that I truly love.

*And remember that I didn't see all this the first time I saw it. I began from either episode two or three. I missed all of the intro. All the set-ups. All of Sorenson and the last of his group doing their work.

PYRAMIDS OF MARS
Written by Stephen Harris
(Mainly Robert Holmes but also Lewis Greifer)
Directed by Paddy Russell

Episode 410: (October 25, 1975) The Doctor and Sarah land at the place where UNIT headquarters will be located. But it's 1911 and there's a different building there. There's also a strange man who has some mummies. Some living mummies.
Cliffhanger: Sutekh brings a gift for all humanity. It ain't fruitcake.

This is one my all-time favorite *Doctor Who* stories. Is part of it nostalgia? I've always loved monster movies and mummy movies, especially. (Plus, werewolf films.) So, this always piqued my interest. The way it gets crazier and weirder as it goes along elevates that interest. The fact that the final episode is a complete change of pace. The fact that (spoiler!) everyone but Sarah and The Doctor dies. It's all fantastic. I also love the way that it does a Heat Dome "Daemons" type thing but makes it rather sinister and weird as opposed to the thing that the Brig spends several episodes hanging around.

This is the first story in this era where we've had a real proper hang out in the TARDIS. "Planet of Evil" had them in the TARDIS but it was setting us up for the landing. Here, the Doctor is feeling very alien. He's feeling very disassociated from the life his previous regeneration got such a kick out of. Who can blame him? All the adventures he got caught up in were structured so strangely. I like Sarah picking the period appropriate dress that used to belong to Victoria. And get that? A reference to Victoria? She hasn't been part of the series for over 7 years. I don't think she's been onscreen for seven years. * I like the reference to her here. I love the Doctor feeling so alienated. So lost ever since the trial. I feel like the 4th Doctor would never call on Gallifrey. Although, obviously, they have called on him.

The location, that mansion, is incredible. Generally, the interior matches the exterior. Although, in such a huge place, they do seem to get everywhere relatively quickly. (Did you know that that home was owned by Mick Jagger and it was meant for his mother? I'd love to think you can see Mick gyrating around like the Silent Singer from *Psychoville* in one of the windows if you look very closely.)

The Egyptology angle is always fun and always topical. You know that *Doctor Who* is going to do something weird with all of it. But you're not sure what yet. Don't those mummies look a little odd? Who is that strange person travelling down some variation of the time tunnel from the credits? What does Sutekh have to do with all this? Lots of great questions. Lots of nice setup. Oh, and what is going on in that opening sequence?

Couple all this with the fun chase through the grounds. Yes, it might have looked better at night. But it's on film and it works just fine. Getting chased by mummies anywhere is The Worst! They're relentless and they just want to treat you wrong. This is a hell of an opening episode. The journey continues.

*Obviously, Victoria was born nowhere near 1911. So maybe they're relying on us not quite remembering when Victoria was from. "Oh, she was Victorian!" Sure.

Pyramids of Mars
Episode Two

Episode 411: (November 1, 1975) Marcus Scarman leads the mummies as they build a rocket. The Doctor, Sarah and a few others try to stop him.
Cliffhanger: Sarah is being strangled by a mummy.

I love the Poacher in this episode. Classic Pertwee style yokel. He does say "Holy Moses," which is pretty harsh language from a yokel. He's different from the Pertwee yokels. Probably because everything looks a little darker here than during the Pertwee era. Sure, the "Axos" yokel got hit by snow. This poacher though seems to be poaching in a dark part of the woods. Possibly on the edges of this estate. I love the way they introduce him by finding a mummy in one of his traps. That's something you don't see every day. We haven't had a good poacher since "Spearhead From Space." Robert Holmes has a type of yokel that he prefers. "Get me a Yokel! Make him a poacher!"

The poacher here is used to do something very clever. As The Doctor, Sarah and Laurence are trying to figure out what Sutekh's plot is, the poacher, completely innocent, wanders into a space that is then sealed off with an invisible forcefield. I like that a lot. He basically shows off something crazy that is happening. (Again, people might remember something similar from "The Daemons.") Then, Holmes kills him off. It's not the most elegant use of a character but I think it's a cool one. Holmes tended to do that. We should probably get used to it.

Meanwhile, we get Marcus Scarman appearing. His poor bother is absolutely wrought out by the appearance of his brother like this. Why wouldn't he? This is awful. And the Doctor, this Doctor, is far less interested in humanity than before. Sarah here is almost becoming like Clara in S8 of the modern run. When Clara takes over as the Doctor's carer because he can't remember to care anymore. It does seem harsh. But then, he's not fighting a goofy villain here. This is Sutekh, destroyer of worlds. Yes, Sutekh may have given himself that name but somehow, I doubt it. Let the actions dictate the name. The way that we can see how Sutekh acts through Scarman is well presented. His totally alien meeting with Dr. Warlock is great. For a moment, the humanity almost shines through. But Marcus is too far gone and Sutekh is way too strong.

This episode introduced me to the concept of a priest's hole. Now, I know how that sounds. It's a hiding place within a mansion, palace or whatever that was used to stash Catholic priests during the time when they were being persecuted. They're not that large, and, apparently, sometimes priests would suffocate within them. I guess they didn't know much about ventilation.

I'll close this review with possibly the biggest moment here for the Doctor Who continuity: The trip to the Alternate "1980." Sarah wants to leave and go back to the future. The Doctor takes her there and it is destroyed. Without them to stop Sutekh, the future will be ripped apart. (I always love the Doctor's line about the fact that people can alter the future. It takes a being of Sutekh's immeasurable power to destroy the future.) The show has never really done that before and it works. One could always ask, "Why don't they leave?" Here's why. Now get back there and save the world.

Pyramids of Mars
Episode Three

Episode 412: (November 8, 1975) Stop the rocket from taking off! If the Eye of Horus on the Pyramid of Mars is destroyed, Sutekh will be freed from his prison in Egypt and travel down the time/ space tunnel to London and kill us all.
Cliffhanger: The Doctor's distraction destroys Sutekh's ship. Now Sutekh will destroy the Doctor.

One quick thing: This was one I watched in the PBS omnibus version A Lot. Occasionally, this would happen... they goofed the edit on the cliffhanger. We see Sarah being strangled and then, suddenly, she has the ring and is yelling "Return to Control! Return to Control!" There's an important moment missing. It wasn't until I saw the VHS that I saw exactly what happened. (I read it in the novelization. But sometimes things were fiddled with in those.) I always think about that whenever I watch the start of this episode.

Things get darker and darker here as the Supporting cast is now down to the "Bad Guys" and Sarah and The Doctor. I always remember thinking this was an interesting way to do it. I honestly didn't think they would kill Laurence. He's such a nice guy. But he's a wishy-washy fellow who refuses to listen to the Doctor. Understood. He does say though that the TARDIS reminds him of something from H. G. Wells. So, he isn't without that knowledge. Plus, he does unwrap the mummy.

It is harsh to see a brother kill a brother. Granted, this isn't Abel and Cain. One brother is dead. He's being animated by the power of an ancient god, sort of. The other one is just a regular guy living in his cottage in 1911. Their final scene is rough. They cut away before Marcus really goes to town on Laurence. Laurence's cry of "You're hurting me" always gets me. It's a sad, dark moment. It kind of compounds the facts that the Doctor reiterates. Sutekh much be stopped. There's no ifs ands or buts about it. If he isn't stopped, everyone dies. If a few people die in between, then so be it.

I never thought I'd see the Doctor dress as a mummy. He dressed up as ladies a few times. Never a mummy. Especially with that odd robotic/ mechanical chest region. This Sarah and the Doctor team is remarkable. The Doctor dresses as a mummy to place explosives by the Osirian missile/ rocket. Sarah reveals her rifle skills. To be honest, I wouldn't have expected that. There's something very incongruous and very *Doctor Who* about the two of them approaching the missile. One dressed as a giant mummy. The other in a long, white Victorian dress toting a shotgun. That's entertainment!

Their hunt for the gelignite is awesome, by the way. Very atmospheric. Very suspenseful. But with a great sense of humor. "Your shoes need repairing" and "Could be a ferret" are my favorite moments. They have such a great rapport and it is getting better with each story. The cool thing is that they are not split up. Holmes keeps them together. He knew what he was doing.

In the last episode, I learned what a priest hole was and in this one I learned what gelignite is. Sydney Newman would be proud.

The ending always impressed/ worried me as a kid. The Doctor stepping into that sarcophagus time/ space tunnel and arriving in Sutekh's cell. It's so still and odd and claustrophobic after all the stuff in and around the estate. The Doctor's low whisper of "Sutekh." Followed by the god turning his head and then the great shot of the missile exploding is iconic stuff. Then the Doctor is instantly knocked to the ground in pain leading to such a great cliffhanger. I remember watching that episode on a Friday and thinking "Darn it! I have to wait until Monday to find out how that wraps up." (Luckily, I remember that I did. It got so much easier when they started doing the omnibus. It also got a little more difficult.) Where is this story going next? I couldn't guess it. Some don't like where it goes next. Ahhh, I disagree.

Pyramids of Mars
Episode Four

Episode 413: (November 15, 1975) Left without the missile, Sutekh comes up with a new idea to destroy the Eye of Horus. Can the Doctor and Sarah stop him in time? No. Can they stop him after that? Possibly. Cliffhanger: The only ones left alive... The Doctor and Sarah escape in the TARDIS as the priory burns to the ground.

I love this closing episode. Yes, it does feel very much like the last episode of "Death To the Daleks." I would suggest... only sort of. I'll talk more about that in a moment. I love the fact that the story changes. It was a Survival of the Fittest story in and around the priory and under the Deflection Barrier. It changes into a story moving from room to room on a pyramid somewhere on Mars that has a series of puzzles in it. I love seeing the Doctor taken over by Sutekh. I love the ending.

I think, if you look at much of what is written about this story, this is the point where everyone thinks the story falls apart. I don't know why. Do they think it's filler? Do they think they honestly couldn't have thought of another ending? I do. I think the producer decided, very deliberately, to go in this direction. To go to another place. It works for me, it works beautifully. Partly because the designers made sure to make the hallways and the rooms in the pyramid visually interesting. In the city of the Exxilons, everything is sterile and dull. Some of the puzzles feel super goofy. I've always felt that the puzzles here are fun, maybe basic but fun. They keep the mind moving. I always loved it as a kid and I still get a kick out of it now. You're not going to convince me to shake those thoughts.

This is the bulk of the episode. It's suspenseful, fun and funny. They do something really nice in here. They flip it around. Instead of the Daleks being right behind the Doctor, the Doctor and Sarah are behind the bad guys. That ups the excitement ante. Plus, the Doctor writing "RELAX" in the dust and dirt of the tube Sarah is caught in is hilarious. (Plus, their swift turn when the mummy turns is also very funny.) They are enjoying themselves at a point where the world could be close to ending.

Sutekh proves his power here. We have heard about him. We have seen him a bit. His big scene here with the Doctor is immediately powerful. He barely moves. He can't move apart from his head. And yet he dominates the Doctor. The Doctor does his absolute best but Sutekh just strikes him down. It's similar to the scene with the Giant Spider (The Great One) in "Planet of the Spiders." But because there isn't a giant spider in front of the Doctor it works better. It's interesting that there are two big scenes/ sequences in here that mirror Pertwee scenes/ sequences. But this story does both better.

Sutekh is a completely awful being. With his voice and his green ray, he knocks the Doctor down to size. He knows the Time Lords and thinks of them as nothing. He hypnotizes the Doctor in a moment. It's so odd to see the Doctor so completely taken over and defeated here. Which is one of the reasons why Sutekh's defeat is so awesome. When I first saw Sutekh, I knew he was trouble. He proves it here so perfectly. The Doctor's defeat of him did confuse me, like Sarah, the first time I saw it. It makes sense though. I think it's one of the Great Zing endings for a show that sometimes doesn't quite nail the landing. I think Paddy Russell's last show "Invasion of the Dinosaurs" has a very nice ending to it too.

One of my favorite serials ever ends with the priory burning down. The Doctor and Sarah leave 1911. They're hoping to hop ahead in time to get Sarah back to London "1980". It is fun to think that the Doctor and Sarah saving the world caused the priory to burn clearing the space for UNIT headquarters.

THE ANDROID INVASION
Written by Terry Nation
Directed by Barry Letts
Episode One

Episode 414: (November 22, 1975) The Doctor and Sarah land in a lovely country village named Evesham. Or do they?
Cliffhanger: A strange rhino-esque face stares at Sarah from a hole in the wall.

Barry Letts is back! Terry Nation is back! UNIT is back, sort of. And all of it feels a bit familiar. It's an episode that is, almost entirely, the Doctor and Sarah walking around discovering lots of weird things happening. It handles itself well. It even has a Third Doctor special: Right near the end of the episode, the Doctor escapes from Crawford and the guards. He's chased around for a minute. He does some heroic leaping about and such. He makes a great joke and then he's immediately caught again. I always wondered "Why didn't they just take him to the cell and lock him up? Why all the runaround?" Well, it's obvious. We must have been running a bit light on the minutes. It does feel a little odd because the last few stories have been so fast paced.

I like the episode quite a bit. I love the eeriness of it. I like that they are continuing the "Trying to get Sarah back home" story from the past two. The TARDIS is going to some odd places. In the previous story, it took them to the right location but off by about 70 years. In this one (spoiler!), it takes them to what looks like the right place but it's an alien planet that is pretending to look like the right place. In fact, the TARDIS dematerializes at one point. Why? Because the TARDIS just realized that it's in the wrong spot and it's following the coordinates it was given. It's a clever Ship. One of those little neat touches that Nation comes up with. (I think. Holmes did rewrite his last two scripts heavily. Although Nation was a successful writer for a very good reason. He was a decent writer.)

I love the slow accumulation of "What the heck?" moments. And the fact that much of it can be explained by some sort of Cold War radioactive thing. The new money. The way the people are reacting. The weird reaction of the soldier leaping off the cliff. It's a bit much but it might work. The only thing that convinces us of the fact that there might be something else happening is the title. "The Android Invasion" implies that this is not England. Maybe the Soviet Union? Maybe China? Maybe somewhere else? Maybe another title would have been appropriate. "The Kraal Conundrum?"

In true Nation fashion, a character is given a new trait just so it can be important later. (The variation of which is the something-or-other that appears in the TARDIS or something similar for a particular episode and ends up being important for that episode but never happens again or has any importance again.) In this one, the Doctor has a sudden taste for ginger pop and Sarah makes it known that she does not like it. I don't really mind it. (It's not as tough to justify as Marty McFly hating being called "chicken" in *Back to The Future 2 & 3*.) The Doctor and Sarah have to eat and drink at some point. They landed in the middle of the Doctor having a sip of ginger pop. Who knows what else is in those pockets? Having said that, the moment does seem to be screaming at us: "Watch for the ginger pop again!"

Overall, I like the feel of the episode. Even if it has the world's silliest explanation, it is fun to watch. The accumulation of odd things, like say the black coffin thing with the weird guy inside, to the almost known things, like the Brigadier is there… oh no he isn't… makes for a compellingly weird episode of the show. Let's see what this rhino thing is. Shall we?

The Android Invasion
Episode Two

Episode 415: (November 29, 1975) The Kraals are up to something. It involves androids and growling and yelling at each other a lot.
Cliffhanger: "You're not the real Sarah."

Again, I like this episode. You can tell that we're in the second episode of a Terry Nation story because things are beginning to open out. They're beginning to become larger. It looks like we have an invasion of Earth thrust upon us. Again. It looks like there's another jerk group of aliens with fun masks that are concocting some elaborate something-or-other to take over our world. And only the Doctor and Sarah can stop it.*

Some of the stuff that begins to happen here does get a bit silly. I think the calendar is probably my favorite thing. A calendar that has the exact same date on it over and over again. I applaud the verisimilitude going on all around us here but that seems silly. Unless the tearing off of the day on the calendar is supposed to be something the androids are trained on. You think they'd be smart enough to know that though. When Sarah calls the Doctor on the only phone in town, that's a bit much. You can see in the Doctor's face that he knows it too as he's piecing together what exactly is happening in this wacky place.

It is nice to see Harry and Benton. I wish it was nice versions of them but you can't have it all. When I was young, I'd only seen Benton in "Robot" and "Terror." I'd seen Harry in the others. I remember being rather taken aback by the evil version of these characters that we cared about. It is odd that the Brigadier isn't here though, right? I know Nick Courtney was not available. But the description that he's away in Geneva only works if this is Earth. The Brig should be there.

That brings about the trickiness of this story. The more and more we learn of the plan, the more and more we see what the Kraals are up to, the sillier it gets. It's one thing to slowly infiltrate. Surely this plan must involve a rocket landing and lots of hubbub. That's not infiltrating. That's making a lot of noise. All the training for the androids seems weird the more you think about it. Can't they just be programmed? Why do they have to go through all of this? And why is the owner of the pub there when no one else is? There will be more questions as time goes on.

What about those Kraals huh? Sort of Rhino-esque aliens that yell at each other. They've got one real human, the astronaut, and all the rest are androids. They have a disorientation chamber. They have doubles. They have their elaborate plan that feels like something that they never planned on ever actually having to finalize. And that's the thing that also makes this story tricky. The Kraals are basically the Zygons but less interesting looking. They both want to take over the Earth. They both consider themselves vastly superior to the humans. They both have machines that cause unpleasant reactions. The Zygons shape shift. The Kraals have androids. They send duplicates after the Doctor or one of his traveling companions. It all looks very similar. The problem is that the Kraals, while not without their charms, are kind of dull. There aren't even more than two of them. Styggron mentions working with some other Kraals. We don't see them. The Doctor's already ridiculed the Zygons for wanting to take over Earth with about six of them. This feels even sillier. It really doesn't feel like there's more than two Kraals.

That cliffhanger is fantastic, though. The Doctor seems to give Android Sarah a lot of space before he reveals that he knows what's going on. His simple speech at the end is wonderful. Sarah falling on the ground and losing her face is one of the best cliffhangers around. Also, the chase through the woods is fantastic. Barry Letts is really going all out on location. In the studio, it's all starting to feel a bit familiar.

*The next story involves the Doctor believing that the Time Lords have sent him to Karn. I wonder if they did this to him here. I also wonder if Sarah and The Doctor are ever going to get some time off.

The Android Invasion
Episode Three

Episode 416: (December 6, 1975) The Android Invasion commences!
Cliffhanger: The Doctor and Sarah don't quite get in the android casings as the rocket takes off. The G-forces start tearing them apart.

This is a weird episode.

First. Is the Kraal countdown voice the most annoying thing ever? I get the feeling that Chedaki and Styggron are leaving because they're just so completely annoyed with their own race. 5..4..3..2.. Oh my gosh. That is such an awful voice. And yes, it is rather Kraal like. I find it alternately amusing and annoying at the same time. I know it's how they sound but it also really sounds like someone's taking the piss. From the first countdown as the simulated village is being destroyed to the rocket countdown at the end, it just sounds like someone with the most annoying voice you can think of barking out numbers.

Second. As I mentioned, it's weird. We go from the village and a feeling of some space and a "real" world around us to… most of the episode taking place in a few studio sets that we've seen before. It's strange to watch the episode suddenly scale itself done from rather large to almost nothing. It's a strange choice to do that halfway through the story. It doesn't quite stop the pacing dead but almost.

Third. Why do they destroy the simulated village and where the heck is every other Kraal on the planet? Why not leave the Village Green and everything up and running so people can enjoy it? If radiation has made the planet very tough to live on, then give them this space. I don't get that.

Fourth. Crayford has lost it, hasn't he? He truly believes that the Kraals will come to Earth and live peacefully. He says the Kraals just want the Northern Hemisphere. What? Why does that seem so weird to me? It's an odd thing to say. "Yes, we'll take half the Earth. That's all we want!" What the hell happens to everyone in the Northern Hemisphere? I assure you that whatever they have planned won't work.

And, of course, they aren't planning on doing that. They're planning on genocide with a virulent virus to wipe out all of humanity. These Kraals aren't as nice as they say they might be! What with their killer android, their disorientation machines and their killer viruses. I wish they were more interesting though. They really seem like a pack of dupes.

This episode does contain a favorite joke of mine. That's the disorientation one. Doctor: I feel disorientated. Sarah: You're in the Disorientation Center. Doctor: That fits. It's nice that they're still feeling wry enough to throw in a good joke. Throughout, The Doctor and Sarah only seem to be treating the Kraals as half of a big threat. The Kraals have a vague stupidity to them that is tough to shake. They're more big bullies than anything. Styggron somehow thinking that this science he's using will help everyone always makes me laugh.

The pace flags here and there. But, in general, things keep moving. The episode ends strong. It portends the invasion about to begin. Crayford describes the plan and he seems so happy about it. We look forward to an exciting final episode. Because this one really did go weird. The scaling down of everything means that the show will re-expand for the final episode. We'll see how it does that. Hopefully, seeing everyone in UNIT will perk us all up. But I fear this may all end in some confusion. Well, maybe "some" is underselling it.

The Android Invasion
Episode Four

Episode 417: (December 13, 1975) The Android Invasion concludes.
Cliffhanger: Sarah decides to take one more trip with the Doctor because he's going to get her home.

Another weird episode.

Because, although we recognize the sets and some of the people, it's actually Earth as opposed to fake Earth. So, it feels like the start of something, which really helps the episode. The people on Earth don't know all the backstory of the three previous episodes. They don't know all the craziness, all the planning, all the chaos. Watching everyone welcome Crayford home is delightful... for them. But worrisome for everyone else. (Meaning us.)

The episode cooks around this premise. Long countdown moments mixed with The Doctor and Sarah wondering if they'll survive the re-entry to Earth. The Android Doctor and the Android Sarah together! However briefly. The Doctor and his wonderful electronic schematic and the poor engineer left to figure it out. And then there's the brawling.

Doctor Who isn't filled with a lot of fighting. It's not that kind of show. The previous story deliberately went for intellectual rather than action. This one, though, goes for out and out action. Luckily, Barry Letts is up to it. The Doctor fight in the control room is excellent. The freeze framing of everyone is always cool. (Yes, "How does the Doctor free the Android Doctor from the freeze thing?" is an issue. I'll let it ride because I'm enjoying myself.) Heck, compare Monarch's end in "Four to Doomsday" to Styggron's end here. Much more physical. (Where'd Chedaki go?)

I love the "If you see me again, arrest me" moment. That's fun stuff. And they're able to adjust for before and after the invasion. They delineate where the invasion will take place. So, we know that right now it's just in the station. And it's fun to watch. The episode really works well. Maybe Letts' best directed episode? I don't know. It has a pulp adventure thrust to it that a lot of final episodes don't achieve. It was so high rated too. Well, what can you do about that? It's a heck of a story. It's loaded with little glitches and "Wait? What?!...." moments. It also moves well and seems to exist slightly outside of sci-fi. It's almost more of a fantasy story than anything else. I won't fault it for that. It might be the weakest story of this season. Only because it's a hell of a season.

Now, what about Harry and Benton? What about how we say goodbye to them? It's tricky with these two. Harry is a one season companion, which has happened several times in the current run of *Doctor Who*. Dan anyone? It didn't happen as much back then. Or, if it did, it was a long season. Benton's last word is "What?" Then, he gets replaced by his android self and not seen again. Harry is seen as himself looking at Sarah and The Doctor after the Android Doctor is killed. Then he's not seen again. Presumably, they say their goodbyes to everyone before returning to the TARDIS. (It always worries me that the TARDIS door is open when Sarah approaches it early in the episode.) But this is a weird way to say goodbye to these two characters. Harry travelled for a full season. Benton has been around since 1968. Season 6. It feels weird. The story goes that Hinchcliffe was looking ahead. Barry Letts let us look back, briefly, one more time.

THE BRAIN OF MORBIUS
Written by Robin Bland
Directed by Christopher Barry
Episode One

Episode 418: (January 3, 1976) The Time Lords (maybe?) send the Doctor and Sarah to the Planet Karn in search of a Gallifreyan rebel named Morbius who was thought to have died.
Cliffhanger: Sarah encounters a giant headless body relaxing on a princess bed.

Back in the studio for a full story. First time since "Revenge of the Cybermen." Except this one has landscapes and a spaceship graveyard. But it's OK. We can always tell that it's always a studio. I think we can roll with it though. The cave of the Sisterhood is excellent. (Where do they live when they're not there?) The entirety of Solon's castle is great. The studio bound feeling gives the whole shebang a slightly odd feeling. The last story felt mostly real even when it wasn't because of the location work. This one always feels very alien because of the studio bound feel to it.

This story is interesting. It's a Terrance Dicks original with a Robert Holmes major re-write. You can see a lot of the Holmes in it. I'd like to think the plotting is very Dicks. It doesn't move fast but it never goes too slow. It meticulously goes through its paces and reveals this world to you. Also, the use of the Time Lords in the beginning makes sense in a Dicks script. The Time Lords would yank the Doctor way off course to clean up one of their dirty little secrets. The setting and characters feel very Holmes.

The Time Lords' "dirty little secret" is kept nicely stashed away. Morbius? He has a cult. Well, that can't be good. He obviously has people who follow him. And one who is interested in his head or, at least, getting a head for him. (The headless monstrosity in the bed at the cliffhanger may have something to do with this.) The Doctor knows who Morbius and Solon is and no one seems thrilled to have a Time Lord poking around there. Once again, this does seem very Time Lord like. Drop the Doctor in the middle of it and see what happens. But, in Holmes fashion, it's starker and more dangerous and more gruesome.

The Sisterhood don't do much here but chant and talk about their Sacred Flame. However, during one scene, they teleport the TARDIS to them. These past two seasons have had more moments of the TARDIS getting lost or put here, there and everywhere since the first season. Stranded on the Beacon. Having to wait for timelines to catch up. Vanishing to leave for the Real Earth... all these bits conspire to keep the Doctor and Sarah from their home.

Solon and Cordo are a great double act. Big dumb Cordo suspecting that something is wrong with the missing hand he is promised. And Solon... once probably a nice guy. Now he is so enamored, so entangled, with the cult of Morbius that he can't see a spot beyond his nose. That leads to a lot of funny dialogue between him and Cordo and Solon and the Doctor. Very witty dialogue throughout this episode. I just listen to the chat between Sarah and The Doctor when they arrive and I laugh. Same with Solon and the rain coming down. "Can we bother you for a glass of water?" First thing to remember are the laughs. Then, the scares sneak in there.

The Brain of Morbius
Episode Two

Episode 419: (January 10, 1976) The Doctor meets the Sisterhood.
Cliffhanger: Blind Sarah encounters Morbius's brain.

The tricky thing with this story is the studio bound setting. I know I said that was an interesting thing about it in the previous one. But here, we start to see the problem. The episode basically consists of the Doctor and Sarah (and some of the other characters but mainly them) going from one place to another. Either they are in Solon's home or the Sisterhood's cave. One or the other. And sometimes it's the Doctor here but then, oh my, he's there. And where's Sarah? Well, she's either here or... There she is.

They try to keep the pace flying along but there are only the two "locations" so it ends up feeling slightly enclosed.

Luckily, the dialogue is good and the characters are interesting. The stakes are much lower here than in the previous story. In that one, it was preparation for an alien race trying to take over Earth. In this one, there's a scientist who wants the Doctor's head for his master's brain. That's about it. The Time Lords have a weird sense of humor sometimes.

Solon is great. Just his look screams out "I am a mad scientist." His deep soothing voice makes you think "Hey! Maybe this guy isn't as mad as his facial hair would make you think?" Of course, he is nuts. Loosey goosey bonkers. Completely. And that makes his sincerity and his frankness even funnier. It's a very funny story is this.

Poor Condo. He may not be bright. But he's a decent fellow at heart. Too bad about the hook. When he gets a mean look in his eye though, watch out. I wouldn't want to meet Angry Condo in a dark corridor somewhere.

The Sisterhood are fun. Mohica and friends. The elder with her bit of facial hair has always distracted me but hey... if that's her thing, who am I to put her down. They chant a lot. I'm not sure whether I'm a huge fan of that. Oh, and they do try to burn the Doctor alive. Not very nice.

And Morbius has been reduced to a talking brain in a big old jar. I love that. Classic stuff from the dawn of horror/ sci fi time. This one has a bit of *Donovan's Brain* mixed with *Frankenstein*. The brain is trying to get a body made from it. Too bad the body's a bit of a mess. Maybe it'll work out all right. (Hint: it won't work out all right.)

So, apart from a bit of repetition in going from set to set, this is a strong story in a very strong season. The Doctor and Sarah continue to be one of the best teams this show has ever had. Will they survive their tussle with the not so nice brain of Morbius?

The Brain of Morbius
Episode Three

Episode 420: (January 17, 1976) The Sisterhood treat the Doctor poorly. Condo is killed by Solon. But, not before knocking Morbius's brain on the floor. Transplant time commences!
Cliffhanger: The Morbius Monster approaches a now no-longer-blind Sarah.

The story does move a little slower than the ones before it. I think that comes down to the studio setting. It really does feel a little less energetic than even "Android." However, that doesn't mean it's boring and that doesn't mean it's not well-written. There's a lot of great dialogue here. There are a lot of fun moments. There are also several moments that are a bit "What the heck?"

Two in particular: 1) Solon shooting Condo. The first shot hits Condo in the stomach and blood flies all around. What? It's a startling moment. Earlier in the season, we saw the Nurse Zygon with a huge streak of blood down her arm. Now, someone is shot and we see a squib of blood burst. This was the time when Mary Whitehouse and her group of goofballs were going after *Doctor Who*. It was moments like this that helped their cause. I think it's interesting to see. I also think most kids wouldn't be bothered.

But, heck, they might be. I would never censor it. However, it is a moment of blood that we'd never really seen before in the show and we have seen some crazy things happen.

2) Morbius's brain falling to the floor. To see a pulsating brain sitting in green goo on the floor is alternately very funny and super gross. It's black humor at its blackest. Philip Hinchcliffe says in the DVD commentary that he mentioned some of these things to Bob Holmes. Holmes just chuckled and insisted they should scare the kids even more. The fact that we are in the studio is deceptive when it comes to the content here.

Boy, the Sisterhood aren't particularly nice here. The Doctor gets the flame going again. So, they knock him out and take him to Solon so he can cut the Doctor's head off. Awesome! You ladies are the best. Sometimes one wonders why the Doctor even tries. I do love the way the Doctor explains his purpose there while covered in the red net. If one gets a little tired of the leaders of the Sisterhood, you can always watch the extras. There is always one who is overdoing it. Staring in a humorous fashion. Or dancing a little wonky. It's fun.

Poor Sarah. She spends the episode stumbling around blind. Condo picks her up. Solon yells at her a lot. And the Doctor isn't there. She's doing her best but it has been a long couple of weeks. She could maybe use a break. When the Sisterhood tells the Doctor that the blindness is only temporary, that's a sigh of relief. It's too bad Sarah doesn't hear it. She does get the sight back so that's cool. Does she get it back at an inopportune time? Naturally.

Overall, an episode where not much happens. We are now rolling towards the climax. The Morbius Monster is alive. The Doctor has been brought to Solon. Sarah has her sight back. We'll see what the next episode has in store. I'm positive there's nothing in here that's monumental for this timeless series.

The Brain of Morbius
Episode Four

Episode 421: (January 24, 1976) The Doctor and Morbius pit their minds against each other. A mob of the Sisterhood chase the Morbius Monster across the landscape.
Cliffhanger: The Doctor and Sarah leave Karn.

Thank Goodness, Morbius and the Doctor don't play a mind game where we see their past selves. And thank goodness that we don't see a whole slew of faces after William Hartnell's face. Because at some point in the future, someone in charge of the show might decide to use this as a jumping off point for an interesting concept that never quite fully gets dealt with before someone else shows up to take over the show who doesn't seem to care about it as much.

Thank goodness. We can just have some fun with this episode. Solon's castle is empty. Morbius is properly dead. Cordo dies saving Sarah. The Sisterhood have their flame back and the TARDIS vanishes in a bang. The studio setting of this is a bit problematic. (Remember how Episode Four of "Pyramids" is all studio while the other three are loaded with location footage.) * They do their best and it's very charming while simultaneously kind of underwhelming.

However, I quite like the scene with the Doctor and Sarah together in the laboratory thinking that they may be locked in there for ages. The Doctor releases a toxic gas into the vents and kills Solon. The

Doctor is getting a bit ruthless here. But then, if Solon wasn't so mad, he might have noticed the hazy, poisonous smoke filling up the room. That's the price of being a mad scientist.

It is nice that Morbius gets a few minutes of cognizance in his new body. I love when The Doctor and Sarah taunt him. They call him "potpourri" and "Chop Suey, the Galactic Emperor." That's funny stuff that is slightly lost in the Morbius rampaging. The mind game, as I mentioned, does what it needs to do. Morbius and his visible brain put up a brave fight but he seems doomed from the get-go. (Shades of *Silent Night Deadly Night 3* and the killer with his brain exposed.) Poor guy. He was a brain for so long and then he gets to be some sort of monster thing briefly. And then, he gets chucked over the cliff. That's just the way it is.

*I just thought I'd mention it. Does everything I write have to have a reason?

THE SEEDS OF DOOM
Written by Robert Banks Stewart
Directed by Douglas Camfield
Episode One

Episode 422: (January 31, 1976) The Doctor and Sarah head to the Antarctic to investigate a pod. So do some bad guys.
Cliffhanger: The Krynoid Human Thing strangles Moberly.

In a season when thy have been running riot over classic horror and such, this time they take on *The Thing from Another World*. The excellent Howard Hawks film from 1951. Isolating a group of people (in this case three) at the loneliest place on Earth is always a fun idea. (Well, I don't know if I'd call John Carpenter's *The Thing* "fun" but I quite enjoy it.) Yes, it does seem like a few too many people are arriving onsite by the end but that happens in this show sometimes. *

Yes, the beards on the guys in the base might distract you a bit.

I like the Doctor here. He plays it right on the edge of desperation. He's not very pleasant to the guys at the base. He's not cracking wise like he normally does. The moment he realizes what this thing is, and that there is a second one, his demeanor darkens. He does get sarcastic around Dunbar, the political bureaucrat but we expect that from him. Putting his feet up on the desk. Getting really close to him and speaking. Generally, getting up his snoot. The rest of the time though, he is rather ruthless. The question does come up: Why does the Doctor go and dig up the second pod? If one pod is enough to devour the world, why bring the second one to light? I don't think he's thinking there. He wants to see the pod and prove he was right.

We only meet Harrison Chase briefly but you can already tell that he's going to be a great villain. He's the sort of guy who lives in a huge mansion surrounded by plants. He speaks in a very affected manner. He has government employees at his beck and call. And, he has the best thing available: Goons. Hired goons. They don't do a lot here but they "accidentally" get lost in the Antarctic. Sure.

The man becoming steadily greener and greener is great. It really looks unpleasant. Yes, it looks a little lettuce-like here and there. But one ends up feeling terrible for this gentleman. Things are only going to get worse.

The last story of this season. One could see the fabric of the show shifting over the previous season. Here, however, we have the Hinchcliffe/ Holmes/ Baker/ Sladen stamp all over the show. It's funnier. It's faster paced. It's darker. It's more violent. It wears its sources on its sleeve. It is a revitalized show. It won't last long before worries about content will cause it to change again. But right now, we're hanging out in a real sweet spot. Let's see how the next five episodes play out.

*In 2025, as I type this, there is at least one Cruise Line operating that has cruises to Antarctica. I'm not exactly sure how they work and I'm not sure if you get a free Krynoid pod when you go. I bet it's fun.

The Seeds of Doom
Episode Two

Episode 423: (February 7, 1976) Scorby arrives. Trouble abounds.
Cliffhanger: The power room and the base explode.

There's not a lot of location footage here but there is some. That lends the right amount of verisimilitude to everything. Plus, the constant background threat of the Krynoid and the foreground threat of Scorby and Keeler. All combine to make this a heck of a good episode. That surprises in the end. The Episode Two cliffhanger is a hell of an explosion. But, at the same time, it's the end of the first half of this story.

This was Robert Holmes's thing to do with the six-part stories. The remaining six-part stories of this era will be structured like this, except maybe "Shada." A two parter and a four parter melded together into six. As mentioned earlier these episodes homage *The Thing from Another World*. I think they do a fine job. I think it has a very realistic, cold atmosphere. I love the sets. * The Krynoid maybe looks slightly goofy as the green man running around. But I'm convinced enough. This is a warm-up. We know that because we cut back to Harrison Chase in London. We know the story is going to continue. Chase is the main anchor in the 4 parter. I think it's some sharp storytelling because we know now that the Krynoid is dangerous and it shouldn't get bigger than it already has or else we're all in trouble.

Re: The Krynoid. We're told that it eats flesh. It eats us, human beings. But this one just lumbers around a lot. I think, opposite of the Ice Warriors, it didn't expect to be birthed in such a cold space. It hides in the power room for heat. But it doesn't really do anything. It can't because it's too cold for it. Obviously, it's destroyed in the power room blowing up but it probably would have passed soon anyway. I don't think there's enough warmth here or enough for it to eat. It will have to get much larger. That's why there are four more episodes.

Tom Baker notes in the commentary that he's playing everything very seriously. However, you get two of my favorite funny moments from his era in this episode. The bits involve Scorby interrogating them. The "house that Jack built" bit is delightful. (Sarah/ Elisabeth Sladen is wonderful in this episode. When she's with the Doctor she is able to keep her courage up. She becomes terrified when she's up against Scorby and Keeler. Why wouldn't she be? I would.) The second moment occurs with these lines: "I'm not a patient man, Doctor." "Well, your candor does you credit." That always makes me laugh. Things get desperate in this episode. But there are some moments of levity.

*In the commentary, designer Roger Murray-Leach is asked how he did these sets so cheaply, quickly and well. He pointed out that the actual structure is made in a specific way to keep the warmth in and it's all very compartmentalized. They designed it using the exact same materials the base designers themselves would have used. It looks like a set because it is based on something that is kind of a set. A set built in the Antarctic.

The Seeds of Doom
Episode Three

Episode 424: (February 14, 1976) The Doctor and Sarah trace the second pod to the home of millionaire Chase. But they're too late. The pod is opening.
Cliffhanger: Chase holds Sarah's arm out as the pod opens.

The Doctor gets violent in this episode. Some punches at the start. He leaps from a tower-thing onto an evil chauffeur and knocks him out. Plus, he does that thing where he grabs someone's head and twists it so their neck cracks. I'm told that that can really hurt someone badly. Well, back in 7th grade, circa 1986, Sam Lombardo III, who tried to bully me for a time but ended up doing a Science Fair with me at Christ the King School, was trying to push me around. I was a relatively new kid there. And I was sick of it. He was shoving me and pushing me. No punches yet. He was trying to get me to punch him. The other night I had re-watched "The Seeds of Doom." The Doctor was, and still is, my hero. When Sam rushed at me with his head slightly down, I was able to stop him for a moment. Then, I grabbed his head and twisted it. It let out a loud crack and he fell to the ground. He was hurt but fine. Everyone saw him rushing at me to fight so my response was self-defense. (Well, it was.) He was fine. I was fine. He never tried that again. The thing is that people say that violence influences kids. I disagree. And yet, there was that one time... I could have severally damaged him. A lucky break.

Anyway, this is a fun episode. The first half is tracking down leads. Sort of an *Avengers*-style (not the superhero group) thing. The Doctor and his "best friend" Sarah Jane (I always love that moment) trying to track down where the pod went. From the moment the Doctor appears with a chair on his head to their arrival at Chase's mansion, it's a kind of *Doctor Who* we don't normally get. Kind of fun. Lots of great locations. A fight in a gravel pit area with the Doctor punching a man out. A rather eccentric British woman who paints flowers. * It's a super fun half of an episode that links us very nicely back into the main story. I fear if this had been a Letts/ Dicks story this would have taken an episode or more. Holmes and Stewart keep it at a decent pace.

Then, we get to the mansion and isn't it gorgeous? Aren't those grounds incredible? There's a lot of running around here but the location is so varied and Douggie Camfield does such a nice job with everything that I can't fault it. And the interior of the mansion is great, also. Chase and his huge plant room with his atonal synth songs for the plants are nice and nutty. There is a feeling of space here, with keeler in the "annex" looking at the od. And that great rooftop that the Doctor winds up on. I've never been in a mansion this big. But I always love looking at the outside and trying to gauge exactly what certain rooms might before. Or looking at bit of roof or a gable or even a Widow's Walk. (I don't think this building has one but it has everything else.)

The Doctor and Sarah's first scene with Chase is wonderful. They've met so many crazy, casual people who think they own the world... and maybe they do. But the Doctor's flippancy keeps it fun. It counterpoints with the final scene: Sarah's arm being pinned down as the Krynoid opens. That's dark.

*That scene seems to be the backdoor pilot for *Keeping Up Appearances*. Her name is "Amelia Ducat." The Doctor calls her "Miss Duc-kett." She says that it is "Due-ca." "The Bouquet Residence! The lady of the house speaking!"

The Seeds of Doom
Episode Four

Episode 425: (February 21, 1976) Keeler mutates and mutates as the Doctor and Sarah try to get off the estate.
Cliffhanger: The Doctor and Sarah Jane encounter the Krynoid on the estate grounds.

Now things have gotten very bad again. (Not "bad" as in "this stinks" but "bad" as in "It looks like the Earth will be devoured by a Krynoid.") That giant tentacled thing rushing at the Doctor and Sarah isn't the most convincing thing around. I love it though. (OK. The little wobble thing that it does isn't terribly convincing. But maybe it's just excited to grab some more flesh.) I like that the closing scenes are at night. It's not day for night. It's video night. Film will look scary because the lighting will always be better. But putting it on video gives it a stronger immediacy and a feeling that it is happening Right Now. I think it makes for another great cliffhanger. They're really nailing them in this story.

Most of the episode, granted, is running around. It starts with the Doctor saving Sarah. We'll talk about that in a minute. Then, poor Keeler is zoinked by the Krynoid. As he grows larger and larger, eventually escaping, the Doctor and Sarah try to escape but keep getting sidelines or caught or whatever. Unable to leave the well-guarded grounds. Amelia Ducat arrives to get money from Chase. Quickly, we learn she's there to see if something odd is happening. And it is! It is a bit of a run in a circle episode for many of the characters. It is anchored by the Krynoid being fed and kept warm so it grows at a much larger rate than the Antarctic one did. It's huge in the end. There could be trouble for humanity tomorrow.

This is the episode that has the scene where the Doctor beats up Scorby, throws him into the fireplace and then wields Scorby's gun. "What do you do for an encore, Doctor?" "I win." You can see it as the show getting a bit out of control, if you wish. Or you can see it as the Doctor really under the gun here. (I know. Forgive that. You know what it means.) The Doctor is desperate. Think about it? In a few hours, the Krynoid will be huge and will germinate. Then, we're all dead. It's one thing to fight the Wirrn on an Ark that has limited access to people. Here it has access to everything.

As Hinchliffe points out, this was a Holmes thing. To take a being/ creature/ alien/ whatever that survives by doing what it does... and what it does involves eating us... he was fascinated by that. Wondering how to work with the concept of there being some creatures in space who simply eat us to survive. They're not malicious. They're not evil. They are simply being themselves. What do you do with that? It terrifies the Doctor. That's why he's running around with the gun.

The monster grows. And Chase is so excited by all of it. He's a great villain. Not least because he has the best thing ever... the giant green composting machine. It's in a tiny room off to one side. It's got a huge metal bucket area and two huge round green bladed things that spin and chop up everything for composting into the garden. I love it. The James Bond film *Licence To Kill* has something similar. There's a conveyor belt and blocks of cocaine drop into two high speed spinning blades. It also works great on human flesh. Bond spends some time hanging above it before the bad guy's craziest henchman is slowly grinded into it. It's a horrible way to go. It's just as horrible in *Doctor Who*. In a few moments, The Doctor will get ground up into mush/ mulch. Come on! This was already a hilariously violent story and now this machine appears. No one is screwing around in this one. That Darn Krynoid!

The Seeds of Doom
Episode Five

Episode 426: (February 28, 1976) The Doctor runs to get help. The Krynoid gets larger. Chase comes under the Krynoid control. Scorby and Sarah hang out a lot.
Cliffhanger: Chase locks the gang out of the house as the giant Krynoid looms.

Boy, that Krynoid grows fast. At the start of the episode, it is about tall. By the end, it's looming heavily over the house. And it's got control of all the plant life in the area. It was bad enough when the Nestene Consciousness got into your plastic flowers. But now, any bit of plant life around you can kill. Aggressive rhubarb, indeed. As the humans run around, it just keeps growing and growing and growing. Things are getting bad.

Much of the episode is Scorby and Sarah barricaded within the house, like a plant-based *Night of the Living Dead*. There's some nice chat between the two of them. At the beginning of the episode, they are stuck in a small nearby house. The Doctor and Scorby argue. Scorby makes a Molotov Cocktail. * There's some chaos and running around. There is... wait for it... a giant tentacle! Hooray! I do love me a giant tentacle. It's like movies that use a few hairy legs to convince you there's a spider nearby. (Like *Robot Holocaust* od *Ator, The Fighting Eagle*.) Good stuff. I wonder who took home the tentacle.

The episode is running in place a bit. It has the "Give us the Doctor" ultimatum that we've encountered before. It does move nicely from nighttime to morning. Chase has a lovely and weird scene where he seems to reach some sort of odd balance with the Krynoid. They understand each other. He spends more time listening to his electronic music and trying to kill the "plant eaters." I do like that little twist. Normally, we have meat eaters being attacked and devoured for eating meat. Here, it's the opposite. People are being attacked and devoured by plants for eating plants. In the end, what can we eat? Processed food has never tasted so good. Unless plastics are somehow involved.

I need to mention the music. Dudley Simpson is the usual scorer for this era. This time, Douggie Camfield brought in Geoffrey Burgon. The score he writes is fantastic. It's eerie. It's menacing. It's oddly tranquil at moments. (Like Chase meeting the Krynoid.) It also makes great use of synths in spots. I love the Dudley Simpson scores. But it's nice to have one that truly gives the show a different feel. I don't normally play these but... The DVD/ Blu has an isolated music track. Listen to it. Put it on whatever you play your discs on (which, for many of you, I know, is "on nothing") and listen to it. Just let it play. It is eerie as hell. If you put on the subtitles and let the music play, you get to see where the cues come in. You get to hear great moments when you didn't realize there was music there. Which is awesome. Give it a try.

*Yes, there were some complaints. "You just showed us how to make a Molotov Cocktail!" Come on. It does seem like *Night of the Living Dead*, doesn't it? Even down to the boarding up of everything.

The Seeds of Doom
Episode Six

Episode 427: (March 6, 1976) The final battle between the Krynoid and the humans and the Time Lord known as Tom Baker. *
Cliffhanger: The Doctor and Sarah somehow arrive in the TARDIS at Antarctica. They have a good laugh and clearly need naps.

First, I do want to point out the obvious thing that really doesn't bother me. But some have had problems with it. It's the final scene. It's a classic (one could put classic in quotes) everybody laughs as the credits roll moment. The Doctor is taking Sarah to Cassiopeia for a holiday. But they land back at the Antarctic where they started. They didn't go by TARDIS though. They went by plane. So, either that's a continuity goof or the TARDIS is playing a joke on the crew. Maybe she doesn't want Sarah to ever take a vacation or go somewhere where she might swim. (Remember "Death to the Daleks.") Anyway, it's a fun scene. And it's a silly ending to what has been a rather violent and dark story.

"The Seeds of Doom," in the end, I think, is less of a 2 parter and a 4 parter. More of 3 2-part stories. The opening two episodes in the Antarctic. Then the next two Episodes. Finding the pod. The opening of the pod and the Krynoid becoming a Krynoid. Then, the last two episodes are basically *Night of the Living Dead* in a gigantic mansion with a huge carnivorous plant monster outside. That sums up this serial the best for me.

I say this because quite a bit of the last two episodes is keeping everyone in the house out of the grasp of the Krynoid, the plants and Chase. It has a bit of a "They get taken one by one" feel. With the butler going and then the UNIT solider going (horribly in the composter) and then Scorby freaking out and leaving us. It has a nice horror film feel to it. And it gets very desperate as it goes. Does it feel a bit like they're running in circles? Occasionally. But enough incident happens to keep it going and there's that ever-present giant Krynoid flailing around over the house. Although, I do note that the last Episode here is much shorter than the others. It's barely 22 minutes whereas two were over 25. Maybe everyone was getting a little tired. It was the end of the season.

The scenes with the composter crusher thing are the climax of the serial's vicious streak. When Chase forces the UNIT soldier though there, it's awful. To be made into compost and spread across the garden is... I'm not going to think about it. And putting Sarah in there. Come on! The fight between the Doctor and Chase is nicely done. At first, it's tough to gauge what Chase is doing at the end. The Doctor is trying to pull Chase out. Chase has grasped his hand and it looks like he's trying to get out. But afterwards, the Doctor says Chase was trying to pull him in. What a jerk and what a chilling end.

The destruction of the Krynoid is rather perfunctory. By this time, though, I think we're pretty sure that the Krynoid isn't going to germinate and devour all humanity. It's just a question of: how exactly do you stop it? Luckily, there are some nice explosions to help. The drama is more from whether Sarah and The Doctor, the only ones left, will get out in time. Spoiler! They do.

Season 13 is over. The production team and the new Doctor and Sarah have settled in nicely. The ratings are brilliant. And, I think, we have a tremendously strong run of stories here. However, some troubles are looming. The Whitehouse is on the horizon. I'm not giving her more space in this book than she deserves. (Actually, I think I've already given her enough space.) The show is firing in all cylinders. The biggest trouble isn't from a crazy lady who seemed out of touch with reality. It might be something to do with events that occurred a long time ago. In a galaxy far, far away.

*I'm kidding!

SEASON FOURTEEN
1976-1977

THE MASQUE OF MANDRAGORA
Written by Louis Marks
Directed by Rodney Bennett
Episode One

Episode 428: (September 4, 1976) The Doctor and Sarah explore the TARDIS, encounter the Mandragora Helix and wind up in 15th century Italy.
Cliffhanger: Well, the Doctor's going to get his head cut off.

A great opening episode to a season where everyone feels very assured of themselves. Tom Baker is fantastic throughout. Elisabeth Sladen is wonderful, especially in her scenes with Tom. Yes, she gets separated off to be sacrificed by the Cult of Demnos a bit too soon for my tastes. (She's been here before with "Death to the Daleks") Regardless, she's still excellent.

When I was young and they showed "Robot" through "The Invasion of Time," the opening TARDIS sequence was a revelation to me. There's no sign of the TARDIS control room in Season Twelve. In fact, if I had started with "Robot" instead of "Planet of Evil," I would probably have just imagined that they all jammed into that tiny blue box. We saw the TARDIS console room in two stories in Season Thirteen: "Planet of Evil" and "Pyramids of Mars." We didn't see any of it, except the console room. So, this one starts with about five minutes of just wandering the hallways and then finding the secondary control room. The wooden Edwardian one. It's a great scene and it's a great way to open the season. If only the Mandragora Helix wasn't chasing them around.

I remember being very enthralled by this episode. Sarah and The Doctor are just delightful together. And that long diamond-y spiral whatever-it-is that the TARDIS goes through was amazing. The giant space where the Helix exists always intrigued me. It was kind of too bad that all that happens after this is kind of the Doctor's fault. But he did what he could. And there's that ominous moment where the Doctor says they were caught in a forced landing. So, the Helix had control of the Ship.

It is nice to see them back in the distant past. It's been a while. Since "The Time Warrior," in fact. *
Everything looks so great. They're in the village of "The Prisoner." The costumes are fantastic. The wigs and beards are fun. Throughout it this strange energy wave turns people into dead, blue, crusty things that always scared me as a kid. The corpses still make me think "Is that a bit too much?" They also set up the exposition very nicely with Giuliano and Marco and Hieronymus and the Wicked Count, who gets his kicks from slaughtering villagers. What kind of land does he rule over where his guards go out and slaughter people for fun? ** I like the good guys here and the bad guys are nice and evil.

Throughout it, The Doctor is awesome. Yes, he gets bunged on the head with a rock and knocked off a horse. He's definitely game for it though. Whether he's talking to the Cult members or sassing the guards, it's great. One of my favorite moments is when the Captain of the Guards is threatening his life with a sword. The Doctor reaches into his pockets for his papers. But, first, he sticks his orange on the end of the sword. It was that wonderful flippancy that made the Doctor such a hero for me. He could be deadly serious when he needed to be. But then, when needed, he could be so funny. Sarah Jane was supposed to have left at the end of the last season. It's nice that we got eight more episodes. I've always been a fan of Louis Marks stories for the show. This is his last but he goes out on an imaginative high.

*"Pyramids of Mars" is set in the past. But it's the 20th Century. I'm talking a While Ago here.

**And what exactly is that the peasants are collecting? If it's straw, it's very long straw. A cart of it is overturned and Stuart Fell is collecting some by the small pond. Is this like the peasants collecting mud in *Monty Python and the Holy Grail*? Or like lupins and Dennis Moore?

The Masque of Mandragora
Episode Two

Episode 429: (September 11, 1976) The power of the Helix is building. Court intrigue is getting more intriguing.
Cliffhanger: Giuliano is about to be attacked by the Duke's men. The Doctor is being attacked by the Helix. Sarah is re-captured by those goofballs from the Cult of Demnos.

This is one of those stories that I rarely see a lot of love for and, so far, I'm not sure why. The pace is excellent. There's a lot happening. The mystery is building. There's intrigue. There's weirdness. And, best of all, there's the Doctor being very cool indeed. In fact, this episode has two Doctor moments that I adore completely. The first is the resolving of the cliffhanger from the previous episode. The Doctor spinning the scarf around the Executioner's leg and tripping him up is impossible but cool. Well, maybe it's not impossible for The Doctor. The second one is the way he slides Sarah along the altar so Hieronymus can't stab her. A very funny Doctor moment. *

The cliffhanger here is another great one. Another fine (maybe slightly rushed) series of moments. Sarah is captured by the Cult again. The Doctor is menaced by the Helix. Giuliano is about to fight eight of the Duke's men. I don't see how anyone (Anyone!) is getting out of this. Well, maybe they will. Hinchliffe always said that he wanted the cliffhangers to all be spot on. After some of the duds of the Letts era, he succeeds often.

The rest of the episode is loaded with court intrigue and flashing lights and guys in strange masks. All the sorts of things you usually want from the show. The Duke really wants Giuliano dead. He even argues with his chief astrologer over it. There is the question of why the Cult of Demnos still exists. A bunch of strangely masked and robed men living and lurking in catacombs. There's the supernatural world. Giuliano and all the people he wants to invite to his city are the people who push the world ahead and out of the Dark Ages. But it may not happen. It's certainly not what the Helix is after.

I love the concept that the Helix has hijacked the TARDIS to take it to this point. As the Doctor says, it's the point when superstition turns to Enlightenment. The helix is an actual physical force of nature whose purpose is to keep Earth back in that dark period. Certainly, giving that wacky astrologer with his fun beard lots of power is the sort of thing only a crazed Helix would consider. I like Hieronymus's asking for more power. The Helix tells him to hold off for a bit. Even the Helix is thinking "This guy's kind of a screwjob."

Overall, another strong episode. As I said, the show is incredibly confident of itself at this time. You almost feel like it could kind of do anything. Those things will change shortly through no fault of the show's. (Generally.) It is great to be here right now.

*We've had a lot of people chanting and the like lately, haven't we? The brotherhood of Demnos and the Sisterhood of Karn love doing that kind of stuff.

The Masque of Mandragora
Episode Three

Episode 430: (September 18, 1976) The Renaissance is about to be stopped before it started. Cliffhanger: The Duke is killed by his astrologer who now has no face.

Another great cliffhanger. I remember the faceless Hieronymus scaring me silly as a kid. Even today, it's a great reveal. They've been really selling the cliffhangers in this one. All excellent. Plus, oddly enough, this kills off the Duke at the end of this episode. That's another thing that I've been noticing in the show lately. The interesting way the stories are being structured.

The Duke is the main physical bad guy throughout the three episodes. He's trying to take over the kingdom. Now, he's dead. When the next episode begins, the evil shifts completely over to the Helix and its helpers. It almost sort of begins the show again. They've done this several times over the past three seasons. Episode Three of "Robot," wraps up the SRS plotline. Most of the last episode is giant Robot stuff. "Planet of Evil" shits from the planet and the red monster to the hallways of the ship and Sorenson, especially in the last episode. "Terror of the Zygons" or "Pyramids of Mars" also do this to some extent. Once the ship moves in "Zygons," the whole thing has a more immediate feel. The Zygons are on the move. "Mars" becomes about the pyramid and the mind games and no location footage. It's interesting how many of these stories build up to the end of the third episode and then shift away for the last one.

Another thing to notice is all the possession, hypnosis and the like happening here. The scene where Sarah is hypnotized is an excellent one. It's very low-key and whispered. Sarah takes on her singsong voice. I do love how the Doctor realizes that she's under control of someone else. It's never occurred to anyone travelling with the Doctor that they don't actually understand the languages they seem to be speaking. Sarah asks. The Doctor realizes that something is wrong. It's a great moment because the question does come up amongst viewers. * How does everyone understand all this? And, again, it's one of those weird things that comes up under a Holmes or Holmes-edited script that is an important part of the show's history. I do wonder why Sarah doesn't understand Latin though.

Leonardo Da Vinci gets mentioned. Does the Doctor ever quite meet him? I don't think so.

I love the image in my mind of the Cult of Demnos swarming through the countryside. And, certainly, the sequence where they are granted their powers from the Helix is excellent. The sparks, the red, the craziness. All these nutballs are now filled with the power to destroy with a touch or a bolt. That's not good. The Doctor and the gang are going to have their hands filled in the final episode. I wonder, as I haven't rewatched it yet, if that is the episode that lets people down? Is this the episode that makes people think that this serial is just OK? Let's find out.

One more thing: This is a toilet happy episode. One person mentions that the bat droppings are said to pile as high as a man in the caves. The Duke says someone is not worthy of reading his chamber pot. I think that might be a bit of Robert Holmes addition.

*Rose does question pretty quickly. In her second episode "End of the World."

The Masque of Mandragora
Episode Four

Episode 431: (September 25, 1976) The Cult swarms the castle. The Doctor tries to stop the Helix. Cliffhanger: Off on another adventure!! The Mandragora will return to Earth late in the 20th Century.

The tricky thing about the episode is this: The location footage is almost all gone again, like the last episode of "Pyramids of Mars." There is one final scene at the TARDIS. All the rest is interiors. And you can feel it, especially with so many exteriors in the first two (and some in the third) episodes. This is almost becoming like a thing with this crew. You pull them in the first few episodes with a lot of location footage. Give them the location/ studio mix that we all know and love. (Or at least we know and tolerate.) Then, when you get to the last episode and everyone is hooked, get rid of the location footage. People won't care because they're already hooked.

The problem is that you get scenes like the description of what the Cult are doing to the people outside the castle walls. Driving everyone out of the city. Then, killing everyone with fire bolts if they don't go. Marco explains that to Giuliano. And that's it. We see some more action inside the temple. But we don't see the attacks, which take place outside. That rather lowers the excitement of the episode. The pacing is still pretty darn good (and I do think The Doctor's final battle with Hieronymus is excellent *). The masque is a nice addition. It lends a weird dichotomy to the episode. The Duke and Sarah are dancing. All the best people are there. Meanwhile, the Doctor is having a shooting match with the bad guy in the temple. I always like that sort of thing.

The Doctor's full description of what the Mandragora Helix will do to humanity is excellent. It's been vague throughout. It seems like one of those things that is probably going to stay that way. However, the Doctor really dives in and goes to town. The ambition of all humanity won't stretch beyond the next meal if the Helix takes over. At this point in time, when things are about to change for the scientific, the Helix could throw us all back down a deep, dark hole. The Doctor must wander in there alone armed with only a metal breastplate and a piece of wire.

I applaud the Doctor's idea to defeat the Helix. It's using science like (more or less) "Mars" did. In that one, it was knowing how long it takes radio waves to travel from Mars to Earth. In this one, it's guessing at what type of energy Mandragora is and that, cut off from the central core of its power which is very far away, he can drain it off. It works! And the Doctor gets a nice piece of salami. I hope they have bread onboard the TARDIS and maybe some mustard. A good story ends well as Guiliani watches the TARDIS go. The Doctor never got to meet Leonardo. Maybe next time?

Note: "The Mark of the Mandragora" featuring the Seventh Doctor and Ace would be Mandragora's return. That was featured in *Doctor Who Monthly* at the end of the 1980s.

"Especially when the Doctor tells the astrologer not to give him any "Bosch." I get it.

THE HAND OF FEAR
Written by Bob Baker and Dave Martin
Directed by Lennie Mayne
Episode One

Episode 432: (October 2, 1976) Buried in a quarry explosion, Sarah is possessed by an ancient stone hand. Things get worse from there.
Cliffhanger: The stone hand regenerates a finger and then begins to move.

The last Sarah Jane story begins. But not really. Elisabeth Sladen says on the DVD commentary that the fact that Sarah is wearing an Andy Pandy overall outfit shows how far she is removed from every day reality. I agree and I don't at the same time. Because the implication throughout her time on the show is that she is one of the few companions that can come home.

Check out her travelling itinerary. The Doctor brings her back for "Invasion of the Dinosaurs." They clear that up. Then, she goes on the "Death to the Daleks" trip that is a side trip. The Peladon trip is the Doctor's journey. Between that story's end and "Spiders," they have been back for a while. Sarah is back for a while at the end of "Spiders." "Robot" through "The Brain of Morbius" is an endless trip. But, at the start of "The Seeds of Doom" she seems to have been on Earth for a while living her life and having a good time. She chooses to go back on the TARDIS at the end of that and end up back at the Antarctic, which makes no sense but is charming. Then, her and the Doctor just seem to be travelling when "Masque" begins. They seem like a couple of pals having fun. They discover that secondary control room, which is awesome. Then we get this story, when she does want to get back home. There isn't a sign of this being forever. It's just Sarah wanting her own life and travelling with the Doctor. Steven Moffat makes this work with the Ponds. Here it does work... but shortly it will go odd.

All this is not to say the episode doesn't bring out any sparks. This was a story I watched many times as a kid. It has such an odd structure to it. Bob Baker says it was always a four partner. Phillip Hinchliffe said it was a six parter originally. That makes more sense when you watch the story. It's so oddly paced. The long sequence on Kastria. Followed by the long quarry sequence. Then the weirdness in the hospital and then the trip to the nuclear complex. It's all so wonderfully huge like the other Baker and Martin scripts. Follow the throughline of this whole thing and it's a crazy extravaganza of nuttiness and it is a wonderful story to send a companion off on. Although, in the end, that's not quite what happens.

I love the Doctor's interactions with the professionals here. He can ingratiate himself because he knows what he is talking about. He really seems to grasp exactly what he can say that will make him sound crazy and what he can't say. That's what we need. It's like his version of psychic paper. He's just charming and gets in there. How does he get the electron microscope? I don't know. But he does and it's great. That's the Doctor. He's helping a friend and trying to figure out what's going on.

What about that quarry scene? The explosion of the rock buries a camera. You can see it quite clearly. It's the ultimate quarry scene because it's a quarry scene set in a quarry that blows up a part of a quarry. Yes, I've no idea why Sarah and the Doctor can't hear the siren. But, as mentioned earlier, they have been gone for a while. I hope that stone hand doesn't cause them too much trouble. Although, I have seen the start of the next episode and I promise nothing.

The Hand of Fear
Episode Two

Episode 433: (October 9, 1976) Eldrad, whatever it is, takes over the nuclear facility.
Cliffhanger: It looks like the reactor is finally going to blow up.

This episode is embedded in my childhood from beginning to end. I remember Sarah hiding inside the reactor. I remember the hand moving across the floor. I had seen *Beast With Five Fingers* so I knew where that came from. The disembodied hand was a thing that was part of the horror world. Might Robert Holmes be the most "horror kid" of all the horror kids? Throughout his run, lasting until "The Sunmakers," his shoving of the Universal monsters/ horror genre into stories makes the show more exciting and more scary. This is a fantastic period in *Doctor Who*.

The episode is set deep inside this awesome nuclear plant. A plant that Bob Baker lived nearby. A weird place. If it goes up, everyone around there dies. The interior of it is huge. Bigger than a Bond villain's lair. Bigger than so many things. Huge spaces with staircases and turning, bending tubes and control panels but places with so little humanity in and amongst all of this. It's crazy and amazing. At the time it aired, one would imagine that people would have looked at this and thought "This is the craziest place ever. And it's going to kill us all when it breaks down. Especially when Homer Simpson gets put in charge!" Terror notwithstanding, it works. The studio scenes do also. I don't quite know why. But the studio sets seem to be the most intimate, the most important, places in the plant. The film shots make for this huge space. The dichotomy is fascinating.

The Eldrad thing is awesome when it's treated as a sort of 1970s terrorist group or evil cosmic entity. "Eldrad" seems to be the name for something bigger and crazier than mere individuals could imagine. We know what Eldrad is, of course. We know what that hand is and what it's trying to do. But before the story gives us that, the concept of "Eldrad" is something beyond the expanse of our thinking. Something that can affect us all.

The Doctor is awesome here. His "Eldrad must live" moment as he bursts through the air duct when he gets Sarah to believe him is awesome. The guy who takes over from Sarah looks exactly like the sort of person who would take over from Sarah. The person who would get invoked and enveloped by Eldrad. Insanity abounds. Eldrad is trying to use nuclear power to revitalize itself. Whatever that might be.

The Doctor and Sarah are reteamed after some worrisome moments. Something odd is happening. Something crazy is happening. It all feels off-kilter if you know what's happening in the show. If you don't, it might feel normal. Sarah has been hypnotized a lot lately. So maybe all is well. I know it isn't. If you're reading this, you know it isn't. You know that out of (our) control stuff might be happening soon. And it will. But it will be odder than you expect. And it won't come from where you expect.

The Hand of Fear
Episode Three

Episode 434: (October 16, 1976) Eldrad is revived and The Doctor and Sarah take her to Kastria.
Cliffhanger: Eldrad gets nailed with a spear.

Eldrad is here! And Eldrad is a female form in a very form fitting crystalline/ silicone outfit. I remember watching this as a kid and feeling a bit confused. Eldrad and the Kastrians we met several weeks before were all booming voiced males. They shouted everything and the bass was heavy and low. But here, Eldrad seems to be a female. As a kid, that was very interesting. It wasn't something I expected. I thought Eldrad would be a big, loud jerk. Eldrad is, basically, a female in a tight crystalline structure. It was so weird. It was a long time ago, though.

This is one of those odd episodes that abandons its previous cast members. The director of the nuclear station and his assistants (the director's wife) are in this episode. They really don't do much though. They appear. They may or may not shoot at Eldrad. And then they're gone! It's very strange plotting, in one way.

In another way, it's quite wonderful because you never quite know here the heck we're going. We have been involved with hands creeping around for a while. We've encountered possession and who knows what else… In this episode, the nuclear complex is going to explode. Twice. The director clears everyone out and then does it again. The second time he does it there is a great complacency behind everything. Because everyone is expecting the same results. Even nuclear destruction can elicit complacency.

This whole story is crazy fun in the best *Doctor Who* tradition, even if it's not one of the best stories. Trapped in a nuclear reactor with a crystalline creature being swarmed by fighter jets that accomplish nothing and risking nuclear holocaust on the English countryside. I kind of love it.

The Hand of Fear
Episode Four

Episode 435: (October 23, 1976) The Doctor and Sarah meet the real Eldrad.
Cliffhanger: Goodbye Sarah Jane.

And Sarah Jane's first tenure in the *Doctor Who* universe comes to an end. Obviously, she will be back. She had her own show for five series, *The Sarah Jane Adventures*, which was a lot of fun. She's in the 20th Anniversary special and she is in the first spinoff attempt, *K9 and Company*. She is one of the most beloved characters in the series and she will forever be associated with it. In this story, she gets an excellent closing sequence with the Doctor. We'll talk about that shortly.

I think you can see here that the story was meant to be 6 episodes because everything in the first 19 minutes of this story is incredibly rushed, except when Female Eldrad has been poisoned. That's a weird moment. She is poisoned by a dart. She is going to solidify and then shatter. They must bring her to a special chamber. The chamber seems to be about 100 miles away from where they were. I would say about 6 to 7 minutes of this episode goes by as they bring Eldrad to this chamber. It takes some time.

We don't really know Eldrad all that well. We've seen the opening scene of Part One. Sarah Jane and the Doctor haven't. So, we know that something else is going on. The Doctor seems rather taken with female Eldrad. So, it's Sarah who begins to piece together everything. She's the one who notices "Hey! Why all these booby traps? And why are they all made for silicone lifeforms?" It does seem a touch odd. I don't know if this ruins everything. Eldrad isn't very nice. He's a conniving strange being who would basically destroy his race as much as see them live. Eldrad's race hated him so much they destroyed themselves rather than have to live with him again.

It has been said that the time spent on Kastria isn't enough. It's basically similar to a modern-day *Doctor Who*. They arrive there. Learn what exactly happened and then race to the ending. It's not bad. I like the planet. It's convincing. It just seems to squander a bit too much time. Although, having said that, I don't think I really want to spend more time with Eldrad. He falls down that cliff and out of our lives. Maybe he is still alive in there. Has someone written a story about him/ her?

The story isn't the strongest but the closing scene is lovely. Sarah getting fed up with travel. Fed up with being cold and shot at and blown up and all of it. It's a nice scene. It feels like the actors spent a lot of time on it working to make it just right. Then the Doctor is hit with the zoink. He's hit with the call to return to Gallifrey and he can't take Sarah. So, she must go. They have a sweet scene where they say goodbye. (Not for forever.) Sarah leaves and she's in the wrong town. (It'll be years before we learn where she wound up.) The Doctor will go on to one of his strangest adventures. But, Sarah, you shall be missed. Until you come back into our lives.

THE DEADLY ASSASSIN
Written By Robert Holmes
Directed by David Maloney
Episode One

Episode 436: (October 30, 1976) The Doctor returns to Gallifrey with visions of the resigning President of the Time Lords being assassinated. What can he do to stop it?
Cliffhanger: The president is shot dead. Did the Doctor do it?

I'll start here: *Star Wars* loomed but wasn't here yet. The movie was being made at Pinewood Studios in England at this time. It will be premiered in late May 1977 in the U.S. It wasn't an immediate success like, say, *Batman*. It was more like *Back to the Future*. It looked promising. Some people went to see it. They went to see it again, bringing friends. The friends went to see it again, bringing friends. Suddenly, it was the highest grossing movie up to that time. It arrived in the UK at Christmastime of that year, with huge expectations behind it. *

I bring this up because of the opening scroll in this story. The show had never done that before. An opening scroll to give you the background you needed. When I first saw this, I had no clue as to what the Doctor was so when he went to his home planet, I had imagined that he had not been there before. I didn't know if it was odd to see the Doctor by himself. I didn't know how much we knew about his world and his people. I didn't know who The Master was. I really didn't know diddly about all of this. It wasn't until years later that I learned about his trial and his exile. I learned about him being sent on little journeys by the Time Lords and all that. (I did see the Time Lord in "Genesis" and saw the Doctor rail against them in "Morbius." But, in "Genesis," I didn't know what Daleks were either so...)

Anyway, it's a heck of an opening episode. All set in the hallways and small rooms of the Gallifreyan capital. Then, there's the Panopticon, which is a suitably huge looking space for the resignation. There's the humor of Runcible the Fatuous as our newscaster. The Doctor gets in some humorous moments here and there mixed into the upcoming assassination. There is a dark-looking, skeletal figure out there that knows the Doctor. The Doctor seems to know what's going to happen next. I'm not so sure.

The episode is a short one. Only 21 minutes and change. It's nice to have this sort of episode with lovely character moments, bits of history, villainy and the slowly encroaching feeling of dread. Mixed in with the characters, like councilor Borusa, who will become a semi-big part of the show to Castellan Spandrell. A Castellan is the keeper of a castle. A spandrell is an architectural term. That's Robert Holmes for you. His use of the word Panopticon is also awesome. **

It's good to be on the Doctor's planet. And it's nice, for once, to only have the Doctor to worry about. No companion to get lost. No one can threaten his companion to get through to him. No one's going to fall and hurt themselves. No one's going to scream. OK, having said all that and acknowledging that Tom Baker is fun here, I still miss Sarah Jane.

*To those who were there at the time and kids, the weirdest thing about that Christmas is that there were no *Star Wars* action figures. There were plenty of glorious knock offs. But none of the toy companies thought the movie would take off. When it did, Kenner was too late to get anything in the stores for Christmas. *Star Wars* action figures didn't invade the stores until Christmas 1978.

**Jeremy Bentham coined the term. It means "all seeing." It was meant to be used in prison/ asylum designs. The interior was circular and there were spots from which everyone could be always observed.

The Deadly Assassin
Episode Two

Episode 437: (November 6, 1976) The Doctor goes on trial for assassinating the President. Then, he goes into the Matrix.
Cliffhanger: The Doctor's foot is caught in a switch track as the train approaches.

As one might expect, the biggest moment here is the reveal of The Matrix. The Matrix is a repository, sorted on computer, of the minds of all deceased Time Lords. It is a repository with so much info it that it can sometimes predict the future. In fact, the Matrix predicts the death of the President. The Master is able to pitch the portend into the Doctor's mind, which is all part of the Master's nasty scheme.

The Doctor enters the mindscape of the Matrix in the last few minutes of this episode. It's on film. It looks better than the video. Fun in a quarry and a forest. The Doctor is in his white shirt and pants and boots. The coat, hat and scarf are all gone. It makes for an oddly rugged episode of *Doctor Who*. We encounter: A horse and a soldier both wearing gas masks. Alligators and giant spiders. A person in a samurai outfit wielding a sword. An operating table in the middle of the quarry with a Mad Doctor offering a huge hypodermic needle. And then, there's that train area. When I was a kid, that cliffhanger really got me. I spent a full day trying to figure out what the heck the Doctor was going to do to get out of that. It still sticks in my mind.

As far as the rest of the episode goes, it's good stuff. The release from the Gallifreyan rooms and halls into the Matrix is a great relief. The trial and the investigation portions of this episode work well. And we see a shrunken TCE body. The Master is back! I love when Spandrell says to the Doctor that he doesn't want the Master and the Doctor fighting in Gallifrey. He draws the line so the Doctor will do what he can. Let's not forget, the Master is really, really nuts.

Goth seems pretty gung-ho here to make sure the Doctor is killed without enough proof. Borusa comes to the forefront as he points out that they can't run roughshod over Gallifreyan law and political procedure. I think Goth might be up to something. Maybe it's the name that makes me think that. I'm not sure. Anyway, the Doctor invokes Article 17 and that makes him a Presidential candidate alongside Goth. That saves his life, for now.

I think the team of Spandrel, Engin and The Doctor is a fun one. None of the new guys are as interesting as Sarah Jane but they're not without their charms. (Obviously, that's only my opinion.) The moment where Engin says that there might be some pain before putting him in the Matrix is sweet. I'm sorry that Runcible got killed. But I think that just underlies how dangerous all of this is getting. What is the Master up to? Hopefully, the Matrix will help.

The Deadly Assassin
Episode Three

Episode 438: (November 13, 1976) The Doctor is caught in the Matrix fighting the Master's helper. Things get rough and surreal.
Cliffhanger: Goth holds the Doctor's head underwater.

A starter note: When the episode was repeated at some point in the 1970s, they edited the cliffhanger ending of this episode. The episode ends with The Doctor's head underwater and a freeze frame. If it ends with a shot of Goth saying "Finished, Doctor! Finished.", then you've got the edited one. This was the story that really got Mary Whitehouse wrangled. This was the one that was taken to the British government and caused some troubles for *Doctor Who*. (First sign of trouble: After three intensely successful seasons with some of the highest ratings ever, Philip Hinchcliffe is no longer Producer after this season.)

From *The Manchurian Candidate* to *The Most Dangerous Game*! After the Doctor gets away from the train (a cliffhanger that is sort of a cop out but also sets the rules for the lethal games in the Matrix), a couple weird bits occur. Eyes in the rock face. A clown under glass buried beneath the sand, laughing and laughing. Soon after that, though, the adversary with his mesh mask over his face (Is he a murderous beekeeper?) arrives and the games begin.

It is very much a Most Dangerous Game sort of thing here. The adversary has a rifle. He has poison. He's a troublemaker. But he does the thing you should never do; the Master knows this too. Never underestimate the Doctor. He is never more dangerous than when all the odds are against him. Things get sweatier and hazier and bloodier and the Doctor keeps pushing. Let's be honest: When William Hartnell first appeared as the Doctor, did you ever think you'd see that character doing stuff like this? The scene where the Doctor hides up the tree and blows the poison dart at the adversary is very harrowing. Especially the casual way the rifle is raised and shoots the Doctor out of it. That is the world's heaviest drop to the ground. The Doctor is getting walloped. Shot in the leg, this is tricky. I've always liked that the Doctor accepts the wounds rather than thinking them away because this is the adversary's world. (I think the adversary is doing the same thing but it's always tough to say with bad guys.)

There's very little in the episode that takes place back at Gallifrey. Occasional moments with Engin and Spandrell to remind us that the Doctor is in an imaginary world that can kill him. (The Doctor vs. Freddy Krueger?) The Master sends a hypnotized guard to try and tamper with the Doctor's Matrix visit. That seems a little like padding but I'll let it ride.

The episode sets into a nicely measured suspenseful half-hour with the Doctor being hunted through a forest. I've always loved it. If it were done today, it would be faster. It would probably be shorter. But, you know, as well as I do, that the cliffhanger must be the final brawl. "He's either about to run for his life or fight for it." We haven't had this much film in an episode since Episode Four of 'Spearhead From Space" and the story is better for it. I can see how some parents might be worried about the level of violence. But, as a kid who watched it, I wasn't worried at all. I knew the Doctor was fighting for his life. For once, using his brains would only help a certain amount. The final fight in the swamp, with exploding methane and rough brawling is a heck of an ending. Well, the Doctor's dead! What's next?

The Deadly Assassin
Episode Four

Episode 439: (November 20, 1976) The battle extends from the Matrix into the reality of Gallifrey. And the Master is nuttier than ever before.
Cliffhanger: The Master is alive and escapes in his TARDIS.

The Matrix section ends. There's a bit of confusion when the Master seems to be dead. Then, they try to re-create the craziness of the on-film Matrix stuff in the studio, where everything is done more or less live. It mostly works. Yes, it's always obvious that the Eye of Harmony thing is already there and hasn't risen out of the ground. Yes, the Master starts to scream about two seconds before he loses his grip. Whoever the stunt person is in the Master's outfit is doing a superb job. Lots of great rolling down stairs and such. Possibly the lack of many cast members helps. Gallifrey seems barren.

The Master doesn't do a whole heck of a lot. I take that back: he destroys quite a bit of the Capital here. In the end, he does absorb some of the black hole energy. * He and the Doctor have a few moments together. But, really, it kind of has the feel of when you haven't seen someone for a while that you used to be very close with... and you don't have a lot of time with them. You say a few things. They say a few things. Because you know each other so well, that's all you need. The Doctor and the Master don't need to pontificate at one another. They know what's up.

I like the political lies in this episode. Borusa's bending of the truth to make Goth seem like a hero. He does cave in a bit near the end where it seems like might actually like the Doctor a bit. Begrudgingly. (More of Borusa later.) But generally, he seems like the perfect bureaucrat who is willing to bend the truth to keep the peace. He has that great line where he tells the Doctor that our hero will never amount to anything in the universe as long as he "retains this propensity for vulgar facetiousness." No wonder the Doctor ran away.

Once again. Robert Holmes casually creates swaths of history and backstory for the show. While really, he's just trying to get from one point to another. In an earlier episode, The "Shobogans" are mentioned. They will become popular in the next Gallifrey story. We get all this talk of Rassilon (who we've never heard of before.) We get all the talk of the legends. The Dark Times. We get black hole stuff but Omega isn't mentioned. (Possibly written out of their history after "The Three Doctors.") We see the Eye of Harmony. We learn about the immense power of it. And, of course, we get the Matrix. There is a huge amount of info being relayed alongside the story. It is overwhelmingly packed with legends and myths that fellow writers can use for years and years. That's a good Robert Holmes script.

I like this story quite a bit. It is atypical. The Doctor alone. All the stuff on film. All the mythological stuff. Some of the camera angles and storytelling techniques. Everything adds up to make this quite an intriguing story in the history of the show. Although, let's be honest, the Doctor should probably have a travelling companion. In the end.

*You can tell when his TARDIS vanishes. He has flesh on his face that wasn't there before. Whether that's a regeneration in full or just a semi-regeneration of some basic flesh, we don't know and won't know for a while.

THE FACE OF EVIL
Written by Chris Boucher
Directed By Pennant Roberts
Episode One

Episode 440: (January 1, 1977) The Doctor lands on a strange jungle planet where something very weird is going on. It might involve him.
Cliffhanger: Leela shows the Doctor the stone façade of the Evil One. The Evil One looks just like the Doctor.

Welcome to 1977. The year when sci-fi (and movies) change the world over. But, right now, we're in a very sci-fi *Doctor Who* story. Much more so than others. The Gothic horror has vanished here. It's a jungle. It's a primitive tribe. (Yes, they speak English. Remember "Masque".) There are some obvious odd things going on. And the Doctor has been to this unnamed planet before. Oh boy. Chris Boucher has joined the show.

The Doctor is alone but very soon he meets Leela. And she's delightful. The mix of Tarzan style ignorance with very strong diligence. Very different from Sarah Jane. Who knows where she is from? There is a thing that will go for a while in this era. A thing where the companion is very detached from our present day. That happened throughout much of the Second Doctor's era. Here it's a little more pronounced. Leela is here. She uses Janis Thorns that kill people. She's the perfect sort of Doctor companion. Someone who is kind of out of place in their world. Someone who could benefit from travelling with the Doctor. It's funny to think of the companions who wind up, more or less, where they began and the ones who begin so far away from where they started.

I love the jungle in this one. That's another great *Doctor Who* jungle. It's not as oppressively weird as the "Planet of Evil" jungle. But it sure is something. Because much of it's on film, there's a depth of field that is not there when the sets are on video. Where the image ends on video, it ends. On film, through lighting and the use of space, you can expand it. Artificially, sure. But you can expand it. This is an excellent jungle. When the Doctor and Leela are being hunted by invisible monsters and then Sevateem warriors, it's well lensed. Let's not even mention the Doctor threatening someone with a jelly baby.

The world Boucher creates is a strong one. I do kind of wish we got more of a feeling of how they lived apart from how we see them now. I can't quite imagine their lives before and after. I can definitely see them now. I love the pageantry and the silliness. I think the technology that they can't possibly understand is fantastic. The moment the guy gongs the metal sheet with "Survey Team 7" on it is one of my favorite moments ever. Only the cliffhanger to Episode 3 tops it. This is a great show.

With one of the best things being the moment when the Doctor realizes that he's been here before and what the heck is going on? That's good stuff. We've had the people in "The Savages" watching the Doctor. We've had "The Ark" making the Doctor return. We've not quite had this happen. Interested to see where it should go…

The Face of Evil
Episode Two

Episode 441: (January 8, 1977) The Doctor's memories slowly begin to return. Meanwhile, the Sevateem are having trouble with the invisible monsters.
Cliffhanger: The Sevateem is losing the fight against Xoanon's creatures.

An episode filled with many wonderful lines and many wonderful moments. Back in the day, quite a few people used to record the show on cassette* to remember it week after week. Yes, there were the Target novelizations. Those were, sort of, one generation removed. They were someone else taking the script and the televised adventure and giving their own spin to it. Not that we didn't like that. I loved and still love them. A talented writer extracting their own special nectar from the fruit of a story that I have enjoyed. Great stuff. But the tape recordings were something else. They were something special. Because we could hear all that dialogue and all the sharp lines perfectly. We could hear all those great sound effects. One really got into the music. Dudley Simpson, Ahoy! And, during the quieter moments, it was our job to figure out what was up. That was OK, though. Because we were up for that.

So, this is a shiner of an episode. From Leela and The Doctor staring at the Evil One's statue, engraved on the side of the mountain, to the Test of the Horla to crawling into the statue's mouth to the fights involving gigantic, invisible heads of the Doctor roaring at everybody. That is a heck of a world these people live on. Of course, it is the Doctor's arrival that boosts the scary here. It is his arrival that makes everything mount and move towards… what? A climax? Whatever. It's crazy.

And Leela continues to be an awesome companion. The scene where she is dying from the Janis Thorn is great. As the Doctor scurries around for a cure, Tomas guards Caleb with the crossbow. Rattlesnake! It's all very nicely written. Boucher turns out to be a natural writer for the show. Everything is so sharp and so spot on through. There are so many fantastic lines. So many prescient and clever lines. Enough to make one so happy watching it.

So many great Doctor moments in here. His victory over the test of the Horla is fantastic. I always love when he throws the Horla on the shoulder of the guy who slapped Leela. I've seen people complain about that. "The Doctor shouldn't do that." I think we should all calm down. Imagine a friend of yours getting slapped by a jerk, you would respond in the same way, I think. Sometimes people's denigration of this show gets on my cheese, it really does. The show is better than you and your petty complaints.

I think this episode shows exactly how a program that has been on for 14 years can continue to grow. Intelligent, creative people with good ideas just wipe the floor with any worries. If you keep making it great, it's going to continue to be great. We're not even at the best part of this serial yet. We aren't in Xoanon's lair. Hold on, everybody.

*That's why we have audios for all the lost episodes. Intrepid, nerdy warriors with reel-to-reel recorders.

The Face of Evil
Episode Three

Episode 442: (January 15, 1977) Inside the Tesh ship, the Doctor discovers what happened so long ago. Cliffhanger: Who am I?

One of the best cliffhangers ever.

This is a beautiful episode. I think part of the fun is the major shift. One of the things the show has done so many times is to shift its focus heavily. If you know the production history of the show, it involves the sets. Sets take up space. *Doctor Who* isn't *Gone With The Wind*. It doesn't get the run of the entirety of the BBC Television Centre. It has a limited space. And so, things are moved around. The jungle sets took up a lot of space in the first two episodes. You'll notice that much of this episode is set in spaceship hallways and rooms. The jungle sets are gone. That's a budget thing. That's the way the show was made.

Sometimes it's obvious what they're up to. But a very good production crew can make you keep your eyes open and not quite realize that "Hey! We've shifted to here." If you think about it, a 90-minute story all set in the same few jungle sets are probably going to drive everyone up the wall. It's fun here. Because the jungle sets in the first half are such a tangible difference from the mirrored, blocked sets of the last two episodes.

The huge Xoanon set with the three big screens and that weird thing that might have had the Eye of Horus on it at one time is fascinating. It's a strange use of space. Because the jungle sets and the Sevateem sets in the first two episodes are so very basic. They're so minimal. They're so of a world of people who had technology at one time but have now lost it all. It's so disconcerting for us but they don't know it. The Doctor points out that all this is an experiment in eugenics and that's the disturbing thing. The Doctor has accidentally created something that is doing an experiment like that. That's not great and that's not nice.

The Doctor's confrontation with Xoanon is the highlight here. The computer is The Space. The computer that rules over everything is fantastic. Maybe today we might laugh at it. I think I would tell myself, if I was laughing, to shove it. This computer is wonderfully odd and all this is great. The multiple voices are eerie and disturbing. And it's tough to gauge what the heck is going on. "I will think you no longer." There's a line there. There's something to take you down a few notches. A Doctor who wasn't full of himself here would have folded early on. Luckily, we are with one of our strongest Doctors and he is kicking ass. It's a great episode.

Yes, I do like the Leela scenes too. When they're strapped to the laser table, that's classic cliffhanger stuff. When she is holding off about eight Tesh with one gun, that's perfectly awesome stuff. I love those guns. They look like black Cybermats that fire rays at you. It's so strange. And that noise... the bwee-bwee-bwee-bwee noise is so cool with the red rays throwing off of it. It's a very specific world we are in here. It feels very real for this kind of show.

The thing about this episode is that it makes me so happy to see a new voice on the show taking it to a very different space. What I mean is that this is not quite like anything we've seen in the show before. Really. Look around. It isn't. This is a strange, beautiful space. We don't know when it is. We don't know who these people are. We just know that the Doctor touched their lives. We know that this time it may have gone wrong. That's too bad because usually he's OK. Usually, he helps. This time, he didn't.

Before we go to the final episode, can I just point out that scene with Neeva? Where he recognizes the Doctor's voice. He knows what's up. Everyone here is smarter than we thought. Or smarter than Xoanon may have allowed. And it's awesome.

The Face of Evil
Episode Four

Episode 443: (January 22, 1977) The Doctor and Xoanon clash.
Cliffhanger: The Doctor has made a new friend.

Another great story comes to an end. Like "The Hand of Fear," (which I would call a "darn good" story) the actual climax is reached some time before the credits roll. But this isn't one of those stories the Doctor can just stroll out of. He caused the problem. He needs to hang back a bit and wait to make sure that all is well. Which he does. He talks to Xoanon. He offers the two sides a solution. He leaves. Then Leela rushes into the TARDIS and it all goes wacky!

No, not that wacky. I do like the thought of Leela running into the TARDIS and just hitting every button she sees. Well, she's the new companion. I wonder if anyone wonders "Where'd Leela go?" Presumably, the Sevateem and the Tesh will now die out as Leela is the only female we see and they were definitely called "human." Think about that: The first time the Doctor arrives on the planet he leaves his brain print inside the computer. The computer then causes all this terrible eugenic nightmare stuff to happen. So, the Doctor must fix his mistake. But then, he leaves and takes the only female with him so they're all dead anyway. Oh Doctor!

It brings up the point of how many of these stories are the Doctor's fault. "Masque" had the Helix hitching a ride on his TARDIS. "Hand" had them ignoring the sirens and warnings and getting hit by that rock fall. "Seeds of Doom" wouldn't have gone past episode two if the Doctor hadn't gone looking for that second pod. I could probably list a lot more. Oh Doctor.

I do love the crazy look in the assorted Doctor faces. Tom Baker is charming as a humanoid. As a big computer face, he's scary. "Destroy and be Free!" When that gradually becomes "Destroy! Free!" that is chilling. Who here is going to miss that great laser noise and those cool guns that look kind of like funky Cybermats? Unnamed Planet, you shall be missed. This is a heck of a first story for any writer on the show. This is a heck of a way to slowly ease us towards the next era of the Tom Baker run as the Doctor. Especially when one sees how very different the next story is (and it's by the same writer).

THE ROBOTS OF DEATH
Written by Chris Boucher
Directed by Michael E. Briant
Episode One

Episode 444: (January 29, 1977) The Doctor and Leela land on a Sandminer with some robots… of death!
Cliffhanger: The Doctor is getting buried alive in the sand.

A very different kind of story than the previous one. It begins with, sadly, the final appearance of the wooden TARDIS console. Wooden console, you will be missed! The story goes that it was put into storage for the winter after this serial. When they pulled it out of storage several months later, it was warped and ruined. Rather than build another, they put together the standard console we know and love. But I miss the wooden one.

The opening scene with The Doctor and Leela in the TARDIS is great. Leela doing some yo-yo action. The Doctor describing, sort of, the way the TARDIS works from inside to outside. Dimensionally transcendental. At the start of the season, we get Sarah asking how she can understand Italian and here we have a companion asking how exactly this TARDIS thing works. It's a whole new world.

Then we get the Sandminer itself. A gigantic, clunky looking thing rolling on endlessly across a sandy wasteland of a world. Looking for minerals. Everyone inside is dressed very regally, dressed very formally. One might ask what the purpose of dressing like this is. I don't know. Is it ceremonial? Are they breathable fabrics? It's the dress code, presumably. Maybe it's rank, class, status. I don't know. But, trust me, you will get asked by people why this is the way it is. And you may not have an answer. * Make one up. Have fun with it. Or pretend like you've never noticed before.

Then, there are the robots. The great robots. The Dums. They don't speak, just work. The Vocs. They can speak and are more intelligent. And The Super Vocs (SV7 on this trip). Not only can this fellow speak but he oversees much of the ship. They have great immovable faces that are alternately non-threatening and very threatening at the same time. They have a slow, methodical walk. They almost glide along but not really. They are interesting looking, especially when compared to the overdressed humans with their regal hats and strange eye makeup. We do look like bags of meat on this trip.
,
The Doctor should know better though than to make the claim about no one wanting to harm them if they don't have weapons. Come on, Doctor. Almost immediately they get arrested and put in a room. Then they find a body. If he's trying to teach Leela something about human nature, this ain't the right place or time.

That crew is a paranoid and odd bunch. No wonder the robot kills that one jerk. I would too. At least the crew don't all look the same. Then, we'd have a hell of a time differentiating anyone from anyone else. They all have fun names; they're all doing their thing. And they want to arrest the Doctor and Leela. Standard. But, what about those robots? Are they going to be killing everyone? Also, why would they be killing everyone?

*Chris Boucher and others have written further tales involving the planet that these people came from. I've never read any but I do like Boucher's writing. No complaints there.

The Robots of Death
Episode Two

Episode 445: (February 5, 1977) The robots keep killing. The Doctor and Leela must convince the crew of their innocence.
Cliffhanger: The Sandminer is going to explode.

This episode has a cliffhanger that seems to have burned into my mind. I don't know that it's great. I think the other two are better. This one is fun. A lot of sound and fury hopefully signifying something or other. It wasn't originally meant to be the cliffhanger. But this episode was apparently very, very short. There are some things moved around. Some scenes were added. Anyway, why this cliffhanger? It's because, in the omnibus version that used to air on Saturday nights, this was one where the editing wasn't perfect. Right when this episode ends, there's a split second where you can hear the *Doctor Who* theme playing as the new episode commences. There were a few times that happened with the omnibus editions. It was always fun to see. Plus, you knew this was where the cliffhanger occurred.

I like Leela's scene with D84. The talking "Dumb" robot. He's got a good sense of humor. I quite like the Doctor and Leela trying to deal with these rather desperate people on the crew. They're there to make some money, to do their job and hopefully pull in the cash. Now, something is killing them. They go a little mental going after the Doctor and Leela. Borg especially is kind of a creepy jackass. Although Uvanov can seem just as nuts.

Chief Mover Poole is an interesting fellow. He knows that Leela didn't do it. He's not what he seems. He is someone that the Doctor and Leela can convince of their innocence. The scene with "You're in a hurry, man. What would you do?" "Well, I'd call… for a robot" is excellent. The Doctor's low-key proclamation that "if the robots have gone anti-human, it's pretty much the end of this civilization" is fantastic. It would be like our cars turning against us. (*Maximum Overdrive*?) We would be screwed.

The world building behind everything is becoming very convincing. It is called Kaldor City. Boucher would go into detail later, as I mentioned. This society has just enough sketched in here to lend interest. The sets continue to be fun to look at. The Doctor and Leela have convincingly sneaked their way into the story. It's a darn good serial that has the show, again, firing on all cylinders.

*In the production notes for this story on the Blu/ DVD, it mentions that Uvanov is very, very jealous of Zilda because she is basically loyalty where they come from. There is a bit of inference ("I thought maybe we could…") that Uvanov is attracted to her. His anger and sharpness come from the fact that no matter how much money he has, he will always be considered "lower class."

The Robots of Death
Episode Three

Episode 446: (February 12, 1977) The robots continue their murder spree.
Cliffhanger: Choking the Doctor!

The mystery continues! The intrigue goes on! Luckily, the Doctor has been, more less, welcomed into this world. I don't know what I would do if he hadn't. This is not a base under siege, per se. But there is an enormous main set. However, the enormous main set doesn't quite figure into all this as fully as it might be. I'm fine with that. Because it makes this the opposite of a base under siege. It's a species under siege. Under Siege by Taren Capel.

Taren Capel is the gentleman who was raised by robots. The first time I heard that, as a child, I thought "Sure, that makes sense." But, of course, it doesn't make sense. It's one of those weird Holmes/ Boucher things that grabs the zeitgeist of the time and makes it weird. Super weird. It's the boy or girl who gets taken by wolves/ lions or whatever and gets raised by them. It's happened. But, raised by robots? Of course, that's goofy. It's kind of meant to be goofy, I think.

The story mentions the fact that this is a society that is completely dependent upon robots. It's a place that has them do almost everything. These are the kind of people who sit around casually all the time as the robots do everything around them. What happens when the robots go crazy? What do we do then? This society hasn't even though about it.

Then, there is the Laserson probe. D84 delivers a few lines about it that are just gorgeous. But then, we see the Voc being operated on and it seems like a drill is being inserted into its head. It's such a visceral moment. When Taran Capel puts his hands on the hands of the robot who is in pain, that is a strong moment of drama. This is something good. But this is also very close to the end of an era.

The Robots of Death
Episode Four

Episode 447: (February 19, 1977) Taren Capel begins his Robot Rebellion. The final humans on the Sandminer must fight for their life with the help of a Time Lord named The Doctor.
Cliffhanger: Onto the next one…

Isn't there something delightful about the Doctor carrying Uvanov as if he were a little child? I like it. Anyway..

The story ends well. The final attack in the Laserson Probe room is handled well, especially since it was shot as live. Sometimes these action scenes on video can be a bit bland or they feel slightly off. Overall, this one works. It's got a nice excitement to it. I love when the Doctor gets himself out of the restraints and gently shoves the probe in SV7's shiny silver head. That's cool. A good ending to a fine story.

I've always loved the Doctor's use of helium to help save the day. It's a very clever idea because early on it's mentioned that all the robots recognize the crew member's voices. So, hearing Taren Capel gradually have his voice go goofy and silly while he's trying to lead a robot rebellion is a nice touch.

Doctor Who is firing on all cylinders in this season. The civilization in the previous story. The world that is created and signified in this one. The overall look and feel of everything. They're deep in a stretch of excellence. Now, as mentioned, things are going to be changing very soon. Let's enjoy what we have.

As I also mentioned, there is a main control room that makes one think that this is going to be a "base under siege" story. It sort of is but not really. One does sort of notice that the other rooms in the Sandminer are generally either interchangeable or kind of small. So, I wonder what would have happened if they cut down on the size of the main control room, especially as it doesn't even feature in the climax. Oh and look out! No more wooden control room. I miss that darn thing already.

THE TALONS OF WENG-CHIANG
Written by Robert Holmes
Directed by David Maloney
Episode One

Episode 448: (February 26, 1977) The Doctor and Leela land in Victorian London and get involved with Chinese tongs, magicians and music halls. Plus, there's a giant rat.
Cliffhanger: Deep in the sewers, a giant rat rushes at The Doctor and Leela.

One of the best stories ever, hands down, receives an excellent opening episode. The atmosphere is thick, thick, thick. They took their first studio production block and made it an outside broadcast block instead. That's why the location footage in the theater is on video instead of the normal film. And it works. Using that huge theater with a large crowd raises the production value. The meandering around in the halls and dressing rooms gives these scenes a real feeling of tactile space. Granted, the constant fog outside helps immeasurably. Alongside the fact that this episode takes place in one night. It looks very cold outside. From the fight in the alley with the coolies to the dragging of the river to claim the body, it's all excellent stuff. And that old hag without the teeth is delightful. I miss my mom.

Contrast that with the interiors of the theater. Hopefully warm. I think. Chang and Mr. Sin doing their levitation shtick. The moment when Henry Gordon Joga sees the blood rolling down Mr. Sin's hand is pricelessly creepy. Mix that in with the talk of ancient tongs, Chinese gods. Throw in the Doctor dressed sort of like Sherlock Holmes alongside mentions of Jolly Jack The Ripper and you've got a hell of an homage to fictional Victoriana. (Having two Dr. Watsons in Jago and medical examiner Dr. Litefoot is a nice touch.) Add David Maloney directing at his peak. Robert Holmes contributing an excellent script. Plus, Hinchcliffe now knows that this is his last story so he's spending lots of money. It simply works.

Jago and Dr. Litefoot won't meet until much later in the story. It's nice to see them here doing their own thing for a while. Working on either side of the Doctor's investigations. They will become super fun characters once they finally meet and team up. (I have heard several seasons of the Big Finish "Jago & Litefoot" audio series. They're pretty delightful.)

It is unfortunate that Chang is played by a white British actor. That's the trickiest thing for anyone watching it today to try and get past. The fact is that in Britain, at this time, they did this. I have heard people say that they weren't really doing stuff like this anymore by 1977. That's baloney. Suffice it to say, if you can't put the story in the context of when it was made, I would skip ahead to "Fang Rock."

The Talons of Weng-Chiang
Episode Two

Episode 449: (March 5, 1977) Chang is hunting for something. Litefoot may have it.
Cliffhanger: Mr. Sin, knife drawn, approaches Leela.

The Victorian elements keep flying at us faster and faster. Chang goes into a lair underneath the theater that runs alongside the river fleet. There's a giant rat guarding it. Apparently, an ancient Chinese god lives there. Except the "god" talks about "time agents" and granting Chang futuristic powers and such. So, there's obviously something else going on. When we learn that the "god" is looking for a "time cabinet" that Professor Litefoot has... well, all bets are off. What is going on here?

The Doctor meets Jago. There's a wonderful scene where he draws Jago from his hypnosis. They go and investigate the basement. They find a big spider. We know (we can feel) there's something strange happening here. The use of the theater is brilliant. If this had been a studio, it would have been so stilted. If this had been on film, they would never have been able to do this much footage.

Check out that chase throughout the tiers of the theater with the Doctor and Greel. Lots of fun stunts. Lots of height stuff. Swinging across spaces. Curtains being divided and torn as people slide down them. I always loved this scene when I was a kid. It's exciting in a way that the scenes in "The Deadly Assassin" where. Those were on film thought and had a different feel. They were edited better. Here, the shots are longer. Occasionally, they are a little awkward. But, generally, they're exciting and lots of fun to watch.

The production text on the Blu/ DVD says that this is, inflation-wise, one of the most expensive Doctor Who stories ever. * You can see it. It feels more luxurious. Heck, when Dr. Litefoot points at all the food Mrs. Hudson puts out for him, it looks like that food is food. Now, why she put out so much food for one man is a question that I don't think has ever been answered, not even in the spin-off series. Does the man eat that much normally?

*What about the rat then, you say? The problem with the rat, as *About Time* pointed out, is that it's clean. The rat suit itself is fine. It's just a creature that lives in a sewer. It shouldn't look like it's just had a wash, rinse and set.

The Talons of Weng-Chiang
Episode Three

Episode 450: (March 12, 1977) They are so close to getting that darn time cabinet.
Cliffhanger: The giant rat attacks Leela.

This is a good time to discuss the additional effects that the DVDs and Blu-Rays have added on. In this one, there are three major digital effects added. 1) Chang hypnotizing people. 2) The life draining machine and 3) my friend and yours, the giant rat. The hypnotizing is kind of fun. Previously Chang's eyes just flashed white. Not a great effect but you got the point. Now, there is a sort of green ethereal mist percolating from his eyes towards the hypnotized. I like it. The life draining machine is the most subtle. They just kind of made the bendy weirdness of everything flow a little better than it had. It works. The rat, however, I'm not completely sure on. When I watched this with my wife, she didn't comment either way. She saw the rat slink around and then it attacked Leela. There was no laughter. There were no shrieks. There was nothing. So, I think that means it did its job because she didn't track it as an effect per se. It simply was something on the screen like Leela. There you go.

They've perked up effects and diddled with the stories throughout the DVD run. The first major diddling was all the old VHS releases in omnibus form. As I've mentioned before, that's not the way to watch the show. Unless you are watching one of the official BBC sanctioned omnibus edits, then you're watching it wrong. "The Five Doctors" edit, which we'll talk about later is similar. But, with the DVDs and now the Blus, they're tweaking all over the place. I think the replacement of the wobbly Dalek saucer plate in "The Dalek Invasion of Earth" with a fun CGI 1950s UFO was the first thing I can remember working well.

Many stories since have had tweaks done. Most of them I like quite a bit. The coolest changes, I think, is when they can correct something that's just a little bit off but recurring.

The best example I can think of are laser guns or light guns firing. "Underworld" is tough enough to watch and keep your focus on. But then, when you have to watch all the goofy laser beams and such, it can become unbearable. The digital replacement of the rays makes the show much more exciting. Even if there was nothing could do about those CSO caves. But, just to have all those laser bolts looking nice is great. To have that be something no one can complain about is worth the time.

I feel bad for Chang in this episode. Two-and-a-half episodes in and his boss is letting him go. To us, it doesn't feel quite right. It's too early in the story for something like that to happen. They've been together a while now. Greel is way too sick of all Chang's inexpert behavior. But, we've just seen this group get together and now they're done. Heck even Jago and Litefoot haven't joined forces yet and these two baddies are breaking up. It is too bad when your god tells you take a hike.

Again, Leela really takes control here. She helps save a "lady of the night" but almost ends up getting her soul drained. She winds up in the sewer in trouble. While the Doctor takes a cold collation and ends up with a Birmingham fowling piece. Things are going weird, huh? But things are still pretty darn dynamic. Sewers, the dark spaces under theaters, cackling washer women, killer dummies, all kinds of crazy behavior. And now we hit the second half of the story.

The Talons of Weng-Chaing
Episode Four

Episode 451: (March 19, 1977) The Doctor and Leela go to the theater. Litefoot keeps a watchful eye out in his home. Chang tries to appease his Lord one last time by killing the Doctor.
Cliffhanger: Weng-Chiang finally has the time cabinet.

Li H'sen Chang runs down a sewer and gets eaten up by a rat or words to that effect. Boy, Mr. Chang has tried hard. The scene with him and the Doctor on the stage is an excellent one. It's got laughs and suspense and excitement. I love when Jago goes to visit the Doctor. The fact that the Doctor never looks at him and is always looking off to one side makes me smile a lot. Jago's a good sort. If a bit of a coward. Can I just say this... I've always found it very lucky that the deck of cards doesn't fly all apart when Chang throws it up to the Doctor. Also, the Doctor walking out of the back of the cabinet and then handing Chang the swords is great. Tom Baker's Doctor is at his appealing apex here. In front of a packed house, he's matching wits with Chang and clearly enjoying himself.

Chang's story about how he first met his "Lord" is well presented. It's mainly Chang staring straight ahead, looking lost. The Doctor, Leela and Jago listen. His mind does seem to be gone. It's an evocative story. And, hey, watching his body in the sewer water being attacked by the rat is a rather inharmonious ending for the character. (If this is his final scene...)

Poor Litefoot. It really hasn't been his day. They zinged him again! Somehow, they got Mr. Sin in there. Somehow, he got knocked out. Somehow, the time cabinet was stolen. (The closing shot of the carriage with the cabinet on back is excellent. The added sounds of Greel laughing and Mr. Sin making strange animal noises is superb.)

It's nice to get Leela dressed up and heading to the theater. She doesn't seem annoyed by these clothes. Her and the Doctor make a fun couple. He's never really kind of done anything like this with a companion before. I know part of the remit was that they're doing an Eliza Dolittle thing here. It is cool to see the Doctor take someone under his wing like this. Plus, he looks generally proud to see how nice she looks all dressed up for a night out.

Robert Holmes does something clever here, character and story-wise. Chang has now been fazed out. This important character is almost completely gone with two episodes remaining. It's now going to allow us to focus more on Jago and Litefoot and everyone else. I think we're done, or almost done, with the theater scenes now. You can watch the serial segue itself into the final two episodes, the final two weeks of shooting for the season. We will see some new sets onscreen and the amount of location work will wind down. But it's still going strong because now everything has been put in place. There is going to be an epic finale. There will be some shenanigans. And the season will end with the Doctor entrapped in the Talons of Weng-Chiang. Possibly.

The Talons of Weng-Chiang
Episode Five

Episode 452: (March 26, 1977) Greel has moved to a new location. The Doctor and Leela try to track him down. Litefoot and Jago meet one another. And the time cabinet key is being hunted for by all. Cliffhanger: Leela pulls off Greel's mask revealing a face horribly damaged by the Zigma beam.

The focus of the story shifts.

Li H'sen Chang dies in an opium den. He has had one leg removed by the rat. He is enjoying some pipe of poppy before he passes. He and the Doctor and Leela have one more chat before he goes. He's been a formidable foe in a formidable story. This final scene is a good one for him. He's gone through a lot in the last four episodes. Goodbye, Li H'sen. It's time to meet your ancestors.

The Doctor and Leela are on that hunt trying to learn what exactly is going on here. Since Greel has the time cabinet, he has escaped to a new location. The thing that I find odd about his plan is this: Greel's original lair is deep under a theater in a room that has an entrance to the sewers that lead to the Thames with a giant rat guarding it. It's a shabby, dirty place. In this episode, we learn that he was also renting or sub-letting a flippin' warehouse or something or other. (It has a kitchen so maybe it's an abandoned house.) I wonder why he didn't stay there in the first place. And I wonder where he got that giant Eye of the Dragon thing from. **

Jago and Litefoot meet in this episode. They're instantly a delightful duo. Litefoot's bravery matched with Jago's general cowardice but willingness to give anything a try makes for some divine scenes. Whether they're deducing, whether they're being threatened by Greel, whether they're being crammed into a dumb waiter, whatever it is, they're an excellent duo. Instantly. One wishes that they had started working together earlier in the serial. But, as Holmes was writing this by the seat of his pants, I don't have a problem with it. He wasn't thinking "What a delightful duo that should have their own show." He was just trying to fill out six episodes and not be dull. Holmes succeeded.

OK. The dumb waiter stuff might be a bit on the filler side. But I don't mind it because the characters are worth watching. We're pushing towards the ending here. Leela's attempts to fortify the house are very entertaining. She gets another great cliffhanger. This time, it's seeing the demented, bent face of Magnus Greel. All the Doctor's random, stream of consciousness chatter about the world Greel and Mr. Sin came from is a great addition. Holmes, again, creates a fantastic world that we don't see. A world big enough to base novels and other stories around. Simply by using evocative words and keeping us slightly in the dark. All of it, though, does lead us to know that Greel is a threat and not a nice man. He must be stopped and we only have one more episode to do so.

*Especially considering that Robert Holmes wrote it in a rush. That happened a lot in this era. It's funny. When Hinchcliffe and Holmes got a bad script or something ridiculous, Holmes either re-wrote it or he just wrote a whole new set of scripts. Whereas Letts and Dicks took whatever scripts they got and did them (with a lot of Dicks's re-writing) regardless of whether they should have done so. That might be why I prefer this era to the previous ones. The scripts stretched Holmes thin. He never did a script editing job again after this one. He was the assistant for one season. The script editor for three-and-a-half. He wrote or re-wrote so much of it. He's not left the show yet. I just wanted to mention this.

**As I write this, I realize that it's amusing but I also know exactly where he got the cash from. The cult that worships him as a god must have been assembling vast quantities of money.

The Talons of Weng-Chiang
Episode Six

Episode 453: (April 2, 1977) All good things come to an end with a huge battle in the House of the Dragon.
Cliffhanger: Muffins for everyone!

And the season ends. Honestly, one of the most completely successful seasons the show has ever done. When "Masque" and "Hand" are your weakest shows, you're firing on all cylinders. It's too bad that this is Philip Hinchcliffe's last episode. Changes will be forced upon his successor, Graham Williams. And another outside force will begin pressing on the show: *Star Wars*. We'll talk about that soon.

The final episode of this serial is very good. From the opening confrontation in Litefoot's house to the Doctor and Greel discussing the future to the final battle, it has a great flow to it. A lot happens but it doesn't have that anxious "How are they going to wrap all this up?" element that some other stories have had. Everything moves along nicely. It's well acted. It's well directed and paced. Yes, Mr. Sin without someone inside him does look a little odd but the rest is great.

The Doctor has a Batmobile in his pocket! His line "Never trust a man with dirty fingernails" is a favorite of mine. Overall, he and Greel (who is finally named in this episode) have some interesting conversations. Greel is the typical "I'm always right" crazy guy willing to kill the whole world for what he wants. The Doctor must get tired of having these conversations. The future that this foe comes from, again, is very evocatively set up. The Doctor leading the Filipino army as they attack Reykjavik is an image I love. The Doctor really has gotten up to the most amazing amount of adventure.

Jago, Leela and Litefoot get good stuff to do here too. Leela brawls. Jago is cowardly but does his best to overcome. Litefoot is full of English daring do. Not even a laser beam can stop them when they've got their wits and a small rickety table to hide behind. Tally Ho!

So, the season ends. Strong, strong ratings. Great stories. Tom Baker is fantastic. Louise Jameson has fit in well as the new companion. But, in a month-and-a half, in America, a movie will premiere that most people initially don't have much faith in: *Star Wars*. It starts off slow but by the time it hits the U.K. at Christmastime, it's the biggest moneymaker ever and it doesn't show signs of stopping. Hinchcliffe and Baker are invited to an advance screening. They meet George Lucas who welcomes them. About five minutes in, Philip says something to Tom along the lines of "Well, we're not going to get away with what we've been doing anymore." They're right in some respects. Luckily, Hinchcliffe is gone before he must deal with it. But Graham Williams will have to, even as the BBC takes away his budget for assorted reasons, inflation being one. We're entering an interesting batch of seasons here.

SEASON FIFTEEN
1977-1978

HORROR OF FANG ROCK
Written by Terrance Dicks
Directed by Paddy Russell
Episode One

Episode 454: (September 3, 1977) The Doctor, Leela and something land on Fang Rock one dark, foggy and lonely night. A lighthouse keeper is killed. The other two aren't doing that well.
Cliffhanger: A ship crashes against the jagged stones of Fang Rock.

The new season begins and with it we have a new producer: Graham Williams. He was called in after the BBC moved Philip Hinchcliffe to another show. As mentioned, Williams was told to calm down the horror and the violence. He was also told not to make it too silly. Basically, he wasn't given any assistance on what it was they wanted the show to do. Which is the BBC's stumble as *Doctor Who* was one of the most popular programs on the channel. Never go into a season having no idea what you're up to. It's only going to be damaging. As we'll see when the season goes along, the ratings stay strong but level out a bit. That's because this season is very schizophrenic.

Part of that is the standard first season thing. Several of these stories were picked out by Holmes and Hinchcliffe prior to Williams joining. That happens. The difference here is that Robert Holmes is still script editor for the first half of this season. Then, he writes the first story after he leaves and Anthony Read takes over. Oddly enough, it's that story that really feels very different from the Hinchcliffe stories. "Fang Rock" and his last edited story "Image of the Fendahl" feel very Hinchcliffe. The one in the middle, "The Invisible Enemy," half does and half doesn't. We'll discuss that when we get there. Regardless, the first story of a new tenure is always looked at as a holdover from the previous one in many ways.

This is a Terrance Dicks script. Unlike "The Brain of Morbius," this one is basically his. Holmes told him to give him a story in a lighthouse and here's what we got. It's very claustrophobic. It's very atmospheric. Ben, Reuben and Vince run the lighthouse. We get the guy in charge who is gung-ho about new technology. (Electricity over gas.) The older gentleman who complains a lot. And the young wide-eyed guy who may be rethinking his career. Add Leela and The Doctor and we've got fun in the lighthouse.

Tom Baker seems to be enjoying himself. The way Paddy Russell shoots his first chat with Reuben is wonderful. Ben has died and Reuben believes they are spies of some variety. The Doctor is in the foreground, facing the camera. Reuben is being coy behind him. The Doctor makes a lot of great faces. He's in charge. I love his investigation. It's a small island. Something is out there. Possibly something aquatic. Something that feeds on electricity and kills. It's quite dark. I do wonder what the BBC heads thought when they saw this. * It seems to be the opposite of what they asked for from Williams.

Leela and the Doctor have become a great team. Her "teshnician" line may be an attempt at humor or not. Being naïve but smart. Asking questions. Lurking around on the island. They just hopped ahead about 15 or 20 years. From the Victorian to the Edwardian era. This is probably one of the smallest time jumps ever between Doctor Who stories. It works though. The lighthouse is fantastic. The monster in the lighthouse is even better.

The one thing that might let you down is the model boat that crashes into the rocks. They try their best. It looks OK but it never not looks like a model. (But then, if it were CGI, it would always look computer generated.) I say do this… watch the flares going off in the sky behind them rather than focusing on the yacht being smashed. Although, again, it's not bad. I do love the lighthouse model.

*Sadly, Graham Williams died before the influx of DVDs. So, although Hinchcliffe is all over them, Williams is only in retrospective pieces and archival material.

Horror of Fang Rock
Episode Two

Episode 455: (September 10, 1977) The survivors from the yacht are brought into the lighthouse. Things get worse with the monster.
Cliffhanger: The lights go out and Adelaide screams.

The thing that might show that someone else has taken the producer's reign here is the cliffhanger. Hinchliffe used to go out of his way to make every cliffhanger a big moment. For the first time in ages, this cliffhanger is not quite a big moment, it sort of goes back to the Barry Letts's era where you had some vague cliffhangers. It's not bad. We know that Reuben has just been killed. We see Adelaide and Skinsale reacting to the scream and the lighthouse dropping into darkness. The novelization might work better here as it implies that things are almost pitch black. In the episode, of course, they can't get that dark or we wouldn't have seen anything. It's a great cliffhanger, abstractly.

We should talk about the new characters. We have Lord Palmerdale, posh and a jerk. Adelaide, his secretary and special lady. Also posh and believes in astrology. Then there's Skinsale. He's posh. He's ex-army and he may have done something a bit dastardly. Finally, we have Harker. The bosun on the ship. Suddenly, Dicks introduces a wonderful class element into all of this. The lighthouse keepers are British working class. Three of the four people from this wreck are posh. They demand that everyone else do what they want and they're kind of jerks. Luckily, the lighthouse keepers have been trained not to engage them in this nonsense. Vince helping Adelaide first is fun, although her treatment of him as an inferior is not fun. Harker's anger is righteous and I think real enough. I love that an upper-class story has rammed right into the middle of our alien visitor story. It's a fun smash up.

Mixed in it all, we have the Doctor and Leela who are not posh or working class. They are not part of this ensemble of whatever all these people are. Both sides look at them a bit askance. In response, the Doctor has some wonderful lines throughout that show his disdain for all this pretense. I'm not going to name the lines but there are several here that I absolutely love. Lines that, for me, dictate sort of what the Doctor is and who they are. It's so good. Even though the Doctor and Leela could hop in the TARDIS and leave immediately. They stay and they fight. That's what the heroes do.

May I just say that the green eeriness of the whatever-it-is always grabs my attention. As the Doctor and Leela are exploring the island, we keep seeing the glowing green again and again, right behind them… that is fantastic. Uncanny stuff. Like the music, like the weird bubbly alien noises. There's an overall eeriness to all this episode works incredibly well. We are constantly kept just inches away from what is happening. What might be happening and it makes for a great episode. It makes for a great story.

The odd thing is that you wouldn't think this if you grabbed the DVD and went into the extras. Everyone seems to have troubles with it. The director didn't like the setting. Terrance Dicks didn't like his script as much as he should have. * No one seemed fully happy with it. Maybe it was because there was a new producer. I don't know. Robert Holmes seems to have acquitted himself well. He suggested the idea and he made, I believe, one of the best serials ever. Complain all you want. It's good stuff.

*Keeping in mind, that his original script was a vampire one that the BBC pulled at the last moment. Holmes suggested "lighthouses" and they went from there. Dicks's novelization of this story is brilliant. I'm not 100% sure where all his complaints come from. Except for the fact that he did seem to like to complain at times.

Horror of Fang Rock
Episode Three

Episode 456: (September 17, 1977) The alien continues to lay waste to the people in the lighthouse. The Doctor tries to figure out what it is before everyone dies.
Cliffhanger: The Doctor realizes that Reuben is the alien and that it can shape shift.

I like the way this episode piles on more intrigue. Palmerdale sincerely needs to get some information to the Stock Exchange by morning. He has no problem giving Vince 50 pounds to help do this. Of course, it's unethical but what's a little cash between friends. I like how his greed and his avarice sort of, kind of, lead directly to his death. He's up in the light room giving Vince the money. Palmerdale must hide in the gallery outside of the light room. The strange sperm-like green alien lassos his neck with a tentacle and pulls him to his death. There you go. Lesson learned. Of course, Skinsale wrecks the telegraph to stop this thing that isn't going to happen from happening. That's not great.

The Doctor and Leela continue to be a great team. Trying to investigate what's happening as one-by-one people keep dying horribly. It's Reuben who helps them the most. Reuben seems to have gone a bit weird and is hiding out in his room. That's when we learn about one of the alien's big advantages: shapeshifting. The Doctor calls it lycanthropy or the chameleon factor. Regardless, it is charged with electricity and it can change shape. That seems to be a ruthless group of skill sets for an alien to have. Especially if it's the spearhead of some sort of oncoming fleet.

Apart from that, there's not much else to say here. Adelaide screams a lot when she isn't being terribly posh and condescending. A favorite moment of mine is when Leela tells the Doctor that the boiler pressure has dropped and the horn will not sound. A pause. A pregnant pause, in fact. And the Doctor whispers "Harker." They dash down to the boiler room to find him dead. I've always loved that bit. It really has a frisson to it. Trapped on a small island with a killer alien and no seeming way to stop it, things are looking bleak. Soon there won't be anyone left on the island. It will all be over. The Curse of Fang Rock will have come true. Again. Unless the Doctor and Leela can come up with something.

Horror of Fang Rock
Episode Four

Episode 457: (September 24, 1977) The alien has been identified. It is a Rutan, sworn enemy of the Sontarans. The Doctor does know how to fight it. But will he have time?

Cliffhanger: Leela's eyes have changed color. The Doctor recites a poem.

The Doctor versus Reuben the Rutan. The Rutans are, of course, the enemies of the Sontarans. They've been fighting an interminable war. It makes sense, I think, that this is the Sontaran's enemy. I'd love to know why it started. * But, at this point, I guess it doesn't really matter. They're going to keep fighting and fighting. The Sontarans are a clone race that can reproduce themselves endlessly and quickly. The Rutans have great electrical powers and can shape shift. I wonder if they shape shift into Sontarans or is that against the rules of war. I'd always thought that this war would end super quick if that could happen. "Is there anyone on this Sontaran ship that isn't a Rutan in disguise?"

The Doctor and the Rutan have a lovely chat. I applaud the Rutan for continuing to think the Doctor a primitive when the Doctor knows all about their war and how to destroy it. Good old arrogance. Maybe this is a Sontaran in a Rutan outfit? (That would change the course of this thing.) I like the look of the Rutan. Weird, gelatinous with those tentacles and all a bright shade of green. "That's the empty rhetoric of a defeated dictator and I don't like your face either" is a great Doctor retort. Plus, Leela gets to gloat over killing it. Another nice moment. In fact, both have fine lines throughout. "How will you get past the Rutan?" 'With discretion."

The poor supporting cast though. The Doctor and Leela, like in "Pyramids of Mars," are the only ones that make it out. (I guess the Egyptian carriers at the start of "Mars" probably made it out.) It's pretty brutal. You think Vince will last a while. But he dies pretty darn quick at the start. I can't believe they hired the actor back just for a minute of performance. Apparently, they did though. Maybe that scene was shot to end the previous episode? Not sure. Poor Adelaide. She faints, screams a lot and then dies. It's not the most dignified way to go. But, then Skinsale doesn't meet his maker in a distinguished fashion either. He loves his diamonds.

All in all, an excellent story. A great way to start a season. But a slightly deceiving way. The rest of the season won't be going down the path of the past few seasons. In fact, the very next episode, while retaining some elements, is going to feel very different.

*I feel like we may have heard about that in a novel or comic but I'm not completely sure. Regardless, it's not in the show. The Tenth Doctor mentions that it started a long, long time ago but doesn't give a reason why.

THE INVISIBLE ENEMY
Written by Bob Baker and Dave Martin
Directed by Derrick Goodwin
Episode One

Episode 458: (October 1, 1977) The Virus Swarm of the Purpose attacks the Doctor. Things don't go well. Cliffhanger: The possessed Doctor is going to shoot Leela.

Baker and Martin are back. This episode has some nice creepy moments in it. The initial zapping of the virus cloud is semi-surreal. The first appearance of the weird, glazed faces of the possessed is startling. The "Contact has been made" repeated like "Eldrad Must Live" is haunting, at first. And then, of course the fact that the Doctor is possessed is great. That was one of the Holmes/ Hinchcliffe things: possession or androids or you know what I mean. Finally, the Doctor is possessed. Properly possessed. And it's under Williams's reign of terror.

It's an odd episode because I don't know if I love it but I like it OK. People running around possessing other people by this point is getting a little old hat. This one makes it fun by setting it in the year 5000 and having everyone run around in space station hallways. It also pours on the model work. I know *Star Wars* wasn't out in the U.K. at this time. But the model work in this episode is some of the most extensive the show has done since, making a guess, "The Space Pirates." It all looks quite good. I love the image of the crazy, hazy and psychedelic virus as the TARDIS and the shuttle passing through it. I always thought these models were darn good. This is one of the stories that adds CGI on the DVD/ Blu. Things become a bit more fluid with the CGI. However, I don't prefer one to the other.

The Doctor and Leela move back into the original white control room. I miss the wooden one but it is nice to be back. As was pointed out earlier, this is only the third time Tom Baker's Doctor has been in this control room and that was a slightly different design. ("Planet of Evil" and "Pyramids of Mars.") We haven't seen the TARDIS interior since "The Deadly Assassin." We will see more of the interior in the rest of the season than we did in Tom's first three seasons. It's interesting how some eras will use this more than others. Tom truly seemed like a man out of place because we get so few, up to this point, episodes beginning in the TARDIS. That will change now, especially when the Key To Time stories begin.

I wish I had a lot to say about the gentlemen on the space station. They're pretty bland. Lucky for them, a crazy virus thing shows up to make life a bit more interesting.

The Invisible Enemy
Episode Two

Episode 459: (October 8, 1977): The Doctor is taken to the Bi-Al Foundation to get some help. Cliffhanger: Clones of the Doctor and Leela are injected into the Doctor's brain.

Here's where things start to go a bit wonky. The strange chintzy feel of the previous episode was kept at bay by the isolation (or isolashun) of the base they were on. Once they enter the Bi-Al Foundation, things go kind of loopy. Beginning with the weird phonetic English on all the signs. Followed by the general "bordering on camp" outfits of the personnel. The strange guys with big visors zapping people and making them go all fish scaly around the eyes contribute to the off kilter feeling. Then, there's the professor with the silly German accent. The one with the robot dog.

I think my thought on this episode is that for the first time since portions of "The Android Invasion" the show feels juvenile. Yes, a bad effect here and there might bother you. Yes, a strange performance can stick out. There's something in this episode, though, that feels like a bunch of adults playing for kids. (Yes, the dog does contribute to that.) It just feels like the show is suddenly bringing it all down a notch. There is a moment when the Doctor and the Professor discuss "noetic" viruses. That seems to make us all grow up for a moment. But, otherwise, the episode feels childish to me.

The way it sort of degenerates into shootouts in the hallway mixed with clones of the Doctor and Leela being shrunk to microscopic size and then injected into the Doctor's head to stop the virus is a great sign. The episode opens with the Doctor struggling to not outright shoot Leela in cold blood. It ends with a robot dog and a female savage shooting it out with some overdressed astronauts and ophthalmologists* with scales on their face. Then, the injection and Leela and The Doctor spinning through the Doctor's bloodstream. It's either genius or a big "What the hell?"

One note: I would use the CGI effects option on the DVD of this one. The laser rays can be very off center or feeble on the original version. The CGI effects don't quite fit. But they don't look like doodoo.

Having said all this, I do like K9. When the Doctor says "Hello" to him the first time, it's charming. And, although his laser always seemed to crap out after a couple of shots, it's still cool to see him gun down his first guard. K9 is a very interesting companion. One never knew what episodes/ serials he would be in and for how long. Very erratic but generally charming. I hope you like him. K9 is going to be with us for some time.

*The helpers that Lowe recruits confuse me. The ophthalmologist is not given a proper name. But the other two guys that they zap both have last names. One of those guys is killed but then seems to return later. I don't understand the science of ophthalmology.

The Invisible Enemy
Episode Three

Episode 460: (October 15, 1977) Go on a fantastic journey inside the Doctor's mind!
Cliffhanger: The Nucleus grows to full prawn size.

One of the odd things I always forget about this story until I start to watch it again is how little time is spent in the Doctor's body. When I was young, this story was pitched as "*Doctor Who* does *Fantastic Journey*." Loved the idea! I remember sitting through the first half of it thinking "When does that happen? Most of this seems to be interminable shootouts in a hallway." Well, it does happen, for one episode. This episode. Let's enjoy it. Shall we? Shall we??

This episode does spend a lot of time in the Doctor's mind. There are some lovely, strange sets. One that looks like a maze of some sort. Weird almost-jungle-like places. The main room that the Virus Nucleus is hiding in. And, my favorite, the bridge between the mind-brain interface. Fantastic stuff. The moment they investigate the Doctor's imagination feels truly bracing and exciting. I'll admit that the nucleus itself isn't terribly thrilling. It looks like a giant beanbag with a swinging claw and one eye. It talks big but it sure looks goofy.

The one thing that the interior stuff is missing is a sense of urgency. That's because of something they do with time here. The Doctor and Leela have 10 minutes. We see a timer running out in Professor Marius's laboratory. That creates some tension except everything seems like it's going to slow. The 23 minutes of this episode are the 10 minutes they have inside the Doctor's head. Maybe things run at different speeds inside and outside. Regardless, it makes the inside stuff have zero urgency, even when being attacked by white blood cells, because we think a lot of time has passed… and it hasn't. Maybe they should have given themselves 23 minutes, like the real time feel of episode 5 of "The Web of Fear." It all ends up feeling a little off, which is unfortunate as this was kind of the selling point.

As far as the rest of the episode goes, it's basically long shoot outs with Leela and K9 in that hallway. Lots of firing laser guns. Eventually, K9 gets taken over. It's all craziness and it all feels like we saw it in the previous episode. I kind of feel like Robert Holmes's skill at keeping 4-part stories going may be running out. He has been doing this for some time. The cutting between the shootout, which is getting monotonous, and the interior of the Doctor's mind, which is never as exciting as it should be, makes for an episode that ends up as a bit of a dud. Although, I believe it should have been wonderful. I feel like they should have come up with some more stuff to do in the Doctor's mind. It's certainly more interesting than the hallways. We just never quite spend enough time there.

Well, the episode ends with the Swarm Nucleus growing to full height. Yes, it looks rather shrimpy. (I don't mean small.) Maybe it's going to be awesome and the next episode will be brilliant. We shall see.

The Invisible Enemy
Episode Four

Episode 461: (October 22, 1977) The Swarm leader is taken back to the space station for some spawning. The Doctor and Leela must figure out a way to stop it.
Cliffhanger: The Doctor and Leela leave the year 5000.

The giant prawn thing isn't the most inspiring image. It worked better when it was a voice and a crackle of energy. When you realize that the actors must carry it around because it can't move on its own, it becomes less all-powerful. Granted, it was very small a few moments before. I suppose I would have adaptation problems too. I do like the shots of its eggs or whatever they are back at the space station. They're gooey and gross. They remind me of the eggs from Luigi Cozzi's very entertaining *Contamination* aka *Alien Contamination*. A movie I've already mentioned in this book. I didn't expect that to happen.

This episode works well. The Swarm leader isn't in it that much. We return, fairly quickly, to the space station from episode one. There's some nice "science" going on as the Doctor tries to figure out why Leela is immune. There's some good sneaking around and shooting and such when we get to the station. Generally, though, they do the sort of standard *Doctor Who* thing. The Doctor comes up with a great plan. It gets messed up. On the fly, another plan is concocted and that saves the day. It moves quickly enough though. And we get K9 in the end.

As mentioned earlier, *Star Wars* isn't out in the U.K. yet. I'm fairly certain folks would have known some things happening in it. Bob Baker says that this was before they knew of C-3PO and R2-D2. I believe him. In the DVD commentary, he says that he and Dave Martin were at lunch coming up with a computer of some sort for the Professor to use. Dave said, "Why don't we give him a robot dog?" It went from there. Once you see K9, you immediately think that he is going to go traveling with the Doctor and Leela. It just makes sense. But that wasn't the original plan. Executives weren't too keen on it. They would have been kicking themselves after December if they'd said no. So, we went on traveling with a threesome again. K9's like Harry. Except Harry's more energetic.

Overall, this is a slightly disappointing story, to be honest. It has a good idea behind it. There's just too much time spent shooting in hallways. The CGI rays help a bit. But it's too much. The model work is nice. The interior of the Doctor's head is fine. (It's just the realization that they don't really have much of anything to do once they get in there that we start to see a problem.) This isn't Baker and Martin's best script by a longshot. It starts off OK and ends OK but gets a bit too waylaid in the middle. And we have K9. Some might get excited. Others not so much. Luckily, the next script doesn't have to deal with him.

IMAGE OF THE FENDAHL
Written by Chris Boucher
Directed By George Spenton-Foster
Episode One

Episode 462: (October 29, 1977) The Doctor and Leela land in a country village with a group of scientists and an ancient skull.
Cliffhanger: The Doctor can't move. Something is approaching him very fast.

In the same way that so many Doctor Who stories have taken from other genres and other places, this one is raiding 70s rural/ homespun adventures. Down the road from folk horror. There were quite a few TV shows/ movies like this in the 1970s. They used to put on Christmas specials that went into the mystic rites (sometimes pagan) of the countryside. Movies like *The Wicker Man* explored these areas. Plus, this was the time of *In Search Of* and other shows and movies that explored otherworldly things. Supernatural elements were all the rage at this time. (Oddly enough, the same time sci-fi was hitting huge in the theaters.) People were up for going down any avenue to discover something more about our world and beyond.

Well, Chris Boucher takes a whole lot of these, throws them in a sack and out comes the "Image of the Fendahl." The last story script edited by Robert Holmes and it sure feels like one of his stories. It's darker and stranger than the previous story. It's darker and stranger than anything the show will do until the first half of "The Stones of Blood" next season. It feels like a story from last season. One wishes Boucher had written more but he's being called up to script edit *Blake's 7*. I've never seen *Blake's 7*. There are those who love it and those who pooh pooh it. From what I know, it was as much Boucher's vision as Terry Nation's. I'm glad Boucher did that show. I would have loved it if he did another *Who*.

In some ways, this has a very "Stone Tape" feel to it. "The Stone Tape" was Nigel Kneale TV play about investigators in an old house. I won't go into more of it because it's quite wonderful and very eerie. This *Doctor Who* story introduces us to Eustace the ancient shining skull that keeps threatening to take over Wanda Ventham as Thea Ransome. It seems to be harnessing some mid-1970s hi-tech equipment nearby. A Mr. Fendelman (oh boy) runs this little scientific expedition. He has a buddy named Stahl. We have Thea and a guy named Adam Colby who is smart and a smartass all at once. They're a fun bunch. Throw in an old woman from the village who seems to be a bit witch-like along with the Doctor talking to cows… what else do you want?

Maybe the direction isn't the sharpest. The episode was supposed to begin with the hiker at night on film wandering through the fog. Instead, it has a brief studio scene with Stahl & Thea talking about the skull and engaging in some exposition… then it goes to the hiker. I don't know. I would have led with the hiker. The skull could still have glowed but the stuff on film is almost always creepier than the video stuff. (Not always, mind you.) So, that was a strange choice. Some of the studio stuff is sort of blandly shot. But the director seems to be going for broke in the film scenes. And he gives Tom Baker a lot of fun closeups. As always, the 4th Doctor seems mighty amused by what's going on around him.

It's a good opening episode. It has so much going on that it never quite settles itself into one spot. I like that. It also has a double cliffhanger. That's always fun. I also love how you have no real clue where it's going. We'll find out but all is hazy right now.

Note: K9 is out of action in this story. The Doctor decides to fiddle around with him a bit. He'll be back.

Image of the Fendahl
Episode Two

Episode 463: (November 5, 1977) The investigation continues. What is going on?
Cliffhanger: The Doctor puts his hand on the skull and can't get it off... pain is involved.

I love the way this episode keeps developing everything. It moves everything along swiftly. The Doctor gets locked up. Leela gets shot at. We meet new people. The old people get more and more involved. Craziness seems to be building up. Fendelman seems to be leading us to a very weird space. But, in the end, we never quite know exactly what's happening. I mean, unless we're not familiar with *Quatermass and the Pit*. I'll give you that. The little bits that Boucher puts out there to signpost what's happening are very Quatermass. Now, when I first saw this (and I first read the novelization) I knew nothing of Quatermass. I may have read about *The Creeping Unknown* in a book or two. I may have mistaken for with *The Creeping Terror*. Didn't we all? Because of that, this serial is still a weird and wonderful "What the hell?" kind of spooky adventure as far as I'm concerned.

The mix of the magical and the mystical with the scientific is nicely done. Grandma sees evil. She senses it. It's after her soul. We learn later that that's exactly what the Fendahl are up to. Is up to. It is a thing that devours souls. More about that in the next episode. Here, we get Gran and her visions. She sits well alongside Leela who works off instinct, which was such a big part of the previous story. There's a wonderful juxtaposition here of the latest in technology alongside the things people see in their minds.

And of course, there's Fendelman. His name, as the Doctor notices, seems to tie in quite well with whatever is going on here. Fendelman has X-rayed the skull. He spots the pentagram on its head. For the first time in a long time, we are going into the territory of "The Daemons." Supernatural or science? In the end, it's supernatural based off science. It's the things that visited the Earth so long ago suddenly becoming part of our mythology. Suddenly becoming part of our world and our folklore. This skull came here before people. This thing is scary. What is it?

Well, it has weird tubular monsters at its control. Or at least that's what we see on Thea at one point. The Doctor and Adam spot it. These weird monster things. It seems like Thea is in some definite trouble here. She's part of this, as intertwined as Fendelman. I always feel a little sad when she goes to visit the Doctor in the closet they locked him in and he's gone. (How the Doctor gets out is a bit tough to say. The sonic screwdriver might do it but that isn't quite what happens.) Thea goes there to see the Doctor hoping for an answer. Hoping for some help. He's already broken out though. He's already exploring the house. Her tale just goes downhill from here. She's a rather sad character. She's caught in some sort of destiny that she never fully understands. Thea will be changing very soon.

The episode ends with a favorite cliffhanger of mine as a kid. When the Doctor's hand seems to get locked onto the skull and he starts screaming, I was overtaken. That was crazy. What was happening to the Doctor? What is this thing? I think it was some time before I caught the next episode so how it got resolved was a mystery to me for ages. But, boy, that's a good cliffhanger. It hurts and it's weird. That's this story in a nutshell.

Image of the Fendahl
Episode Three

Episode 464: (November 12, 1977) The Doctor knows what this thing is but how do you stop death? Cliffhanger: The giant Fendahleen approaches the group at the end of the hallway.

The Fendahleen appears at the end of this episode. The strange green, snake-like creature that looks a bit naughty is finally seen. They've held it off for three episodes apart from a moment where the little ones appear on Thea. And, at that moment, it's very much a "What the heck was that?" sort of thing. I've always liked it. It's very odd looking and it leaves a trail of slime so who's arguing. I'm not sure what a modern day one would look like but I'd like to see. "The Return of the Fendahl!" I'd watch that story. I'd just hope it was better paced than this one. Because this episode is one of the few examples (maybe the only full example) in Holmes's tenure as script editor that is basically almost all filler. That's what I'm going to talk about now.

This episode doesn't do the classic Terrance Dicks padding trick. You remember it. It's when someone is being held prisoner. Then, they break out! And there's a big chase all over the place. Wild and crazy. Taking up time. And then, just when they might be about to escape, they get caught again and wind up in the same place where they just were. Spending some time running and accomplishing nothing. The first couple times it was a fun little diversion. Then, you catch on to it and becomes a little annoying. It becomes a little "Oh, here we go again with this." Holmes doesn't use that here.

First, the padding doesn't begin until The Doctor/ Leela and Ma Tyler/ her nephew separates and the Doctor says the almost startling "I'll see you tomorrow at sundown." (At the Priory) What is that? About 18 hours from now? Why so long? What are they all doing? If Stahl just kidnapped Thea right before this, what is he doing for 18 hours?

What Holmes does is have three things going on at once: Ma Tyler and her nephew talk a bit and have some homey chat. Then, they get to the Priory and sneak around a bit until the cliffhanger. The Doctor and Leela are in the TARDIS. The Doctor is trying to find out something but failing. There is a ticking clock feel to these scenes. Then, Stahl is preparing the basement ceremony. These scenes seem like they should take place in quick succession. But apparently, they take place from before the start of this episode until the end. Why does it take Stahl like 20 hours to set all this up? Surely, he would have done it very quickly so no one found out. It's like he kidnapped Thea. Grabbed a few zzzs. Had breakfast. Kidnapped Colby and Fendelman. Grabbed some lunch. And it went on like that throughout the day. Why doesn't it happen faster? Kidnapping and pagan ritual preparation in slow motion.

It turns out that The Doctor and Leela are on a wild goose chase. They take the TARDIS to the fifth planet where the Fendahl lived. The Time Lords destroyed it and time looped it. But the indestructible Fendahl skull was thrown out and landed on Earth. This scene is meant to increase the tension a la the "I'm from 1980" scene in "Pyramids of Mars." Instead, it's just a filler of time because it accomplishes nothing. Normally, the Doctor would remember stuff like this off this top of his head.

The problem is that this story would have made a great 80-minute standalone piece. But, at 4 episodes, it is a good 2/3 of an episode too long. Luckily, the 4th episode will pick it up. I need to check the novelization to see if Terrance Dicks fixes this somehow. It is the second shortest novelization. Most are in the 120-140 page region. This one is 103 pages. That's saying something.

Image of the Fendahl
Episode Four

Episode 465: (November 19, 1977) The Fendahl starts to rise and all hell breaks loose. Cliffhanger: The Doctor and Leela take off to places unknown.

There's a *Doctor Who Magazine* interview with the late, great Chris Boucher where he admits that this one didn't have quite enough story. He says it had something to do with holding off seeing the monster until the end of the third episode. That's way too long. No monster can live up to that amount of suspense. If you look at where episode three ends as being the ultimate buildup to the monster's reveal, then that makes sense. I still think/ wish this could have been a 3-parter but they didn't do those then. (They'd only done the one previously "Planet of Giants" and that was an accident.) This episode saves itself mainly by the fact that it moves very quickly and it is very short. 20 minutes and change. There hasn't been an episode this short for ages. The DVD commentary text says that most of this comes from trimming the Doctor and Leela running from their house at the end down by almost a minute-and-a-half. Still brevity takes the day here. *

This episode has a lot to accomplish. Kind of. Maybe not really. Watch what they do in the episode and decide for yourself. They go to the basement and free Colby. The Doctor shuts off the time scanner and programs the implosion. Leela and The Doctor go back in the basement and steal the skull. Then everything blows up. Thea is great as the evil Fendahl. The Fendahleen are menacing enough. Stahl's suicide is toned down but still rough. I just can't shake the weird pacing of these last two episodes. If I had my druthers, I would have shrunk episode three down to about five to ten minutes and then put in most of four. It worked, basically, with "Planet of Giants." It could have worked here.

Again, I don't dislike the story. Colby and The Doctor discussing humanity's origins is fantastic and fascinating. It's done as the Doctor is re-wiring everything. There is a sense of the show traipsing through human history (leaving out the Daemons and the Jagaroth). There's also a sense of immediacy to it as the Doctor is working. It's an odd episode because it's one of those sped up fourth episodes after a slower third. But there's not a ton happening. It seems like there is until you really sort of sit down and examine it. That's OK though. I don't mind. (Although, my mind does want to edit.)

Let's end with pointing out that this is the third story in a row where the Doctor and Leela have blown up whatever space they were in to wrap everything up. And the second out of three were they had to run very fast in a predetermined time to get away from everything. Not saying that Holmes may have been tired (because, in general, I quite enjoy these stories). But maybe the cliches were just too easy and readily available NOT to use when needed. Anyway, blowing everything can be very satisfying in its own exuberant fashion.

*Although, do they not go back to Ma Tyler's house? We know that the Doctor likes to leave without a lot of fuss. Yet, they don't know that Leela and the Doctor are still alive. Isn't that a bit cruel? Do they spend the night waiting for the duo to return and then mourn them when they don't? Maybe The Doctor told Colby not to worry and they're not. Still seems odd though.

THE SUN MAKERS
Written by Robert Holmes
Directed by Pennant Roberts
Episode One

Episode 466: (November 26, 1977) The Doctor and Leela land on the planet Pluto in the far future. The planet has six suns and a human colony on it. A colony being taxed to death by its ruthless leaders. Cliffhanger: The Doctor is gassed at the ATM.

And the tone and feel of the show changes again.

Robert Holmes is leaving and has one more script to write. This isn't a horror tale or a dark bit of sci-fi. It's a social satire. It's closest in tone to "Carnival of Monsters." It's the story of a horrible society and the "used to be a planet" Pluto. Where the people work endlessly underground, never seeing the light, and slave away paying taxes. While a privileged few enjoy themselves. It's as the Doctor says a story about people who "can't make ends meet." But this is a little more insidious.

There are three parts of this society: 1) the people in charge 2) the workers and 3) the underground rebels who don't really do much but complain and eat bad food. None of them seem particularly worth your time. How did the workers get here is the question I always have? I don't honestly think it matters to Holmes. This is a satire so who cares. Holmes is telling the story of what you do when the people in charge just can't stop taking advantage of you. When they just can't stop treating you horribly. And what happens when a man, a woman and their robot dog show up to help you fight.

You can tell things are going to be rough with the opening scene. Cordo trying to pay his father's death tax. * That great hole in the wall with the woman's face in it. (Looks like the cheap version of those face robots in "Silence of the Library.") I always like how she's at a height where she can't quite look down. She must peer over the hole to see Cordo. Everything in this society is about degrading people who aren't in charge. It gets worse when Cordo meets the Gatherer, probably for the first and only time in his life. There are people in the Gatherer's employ who do nothing but either stand by to hand the Gatherer files or stand by to take the taxes. What a jerk. And poor Cordo is just an insignificant smudge, driven to suicide.

The scene where Cordo is going to jump into that strange hole high atop a really depressing building is a powerful one. Who hasn't been there? At the point where you thought maybe your life would go differently. Now it's at the point where jumping from a great height and dying is the best bet. That's the best way to go. I imagine that's one of the ways they keep the workers working. "It's better than suicide!" There's a political slogan. "Vote for us! We're better than suicide!"

The introduction of the Doctor and Leela works for the same reason that the other stories have worked with these two: because they always seem a little different and a little outside the world that's in play. And they should be here. We get some nice jokes about taxes being thrown in here. (Remembering that taxes and inflation were crazy in Britain at this time.) The pompous Gatherer and his assistant Marn are the perfect people to lead this sort of thing. Feeling themselves to be the height of benevolence even when they request things that are clearly untenable. For example, Cordo only has three hours of sleep a day. The Gatherer will gladly cut that sleep time down to zero so Cordo can work extra and pay off his taxes. I'm sure the Gatherer gets his solid eight hours. Terrible treatment, terrible people. Remember where Cordo stands as he tries to jump. Someone is going over the side later. It won't be Cordo.

And then there are the underground people. They don't turn out to be a bright, shining hopeful class of people who fought against the tyranny. Nope. They're a nasty bunch of people who fight and insult one another and anyone who tries to join them. They seem like a nasty braindead militia. Even the opponents of this Company are idiots. These people could easily have overseen some part of this place. They just couldn't find their way into the bureaucracy.

Overall, a good opener. Pennant Roberts isn't the most dynamic director on the best of days. Luckily a lot of the sets help him out and that horridly wonderful tobacco plant that they shot exteriors at is enough to make anyone sad and want to leap from things.

*I didn't realize until this viewing that Cordo is a "D-grade" worker and that means to imply "degraded" worker. I guess I'm a little slow.

The Sun Makers
Episode Two

Episode 467: (December 3, 1977) The Doctor is captured but then released by the Gatherer. Meanwhile, Leela and friends are trying to start a revolution.
Cliffhanger: Leela and friends are about to encounter the guards in a long hallway.

A very good episode. Loaded with a lot of very funny lines from the Doctor. Filled with a lot of lovely satire and some great moments from Leela. It's a sharp trip. Again, the direction isn't the most dynamic. It is so much fun to watch but at the same time it feels like every moment of its 24 minutes is staring at you. The whole story is kind of like this. It's never boring. It moves at a nice pace. Unlike the previous story, we have four episodes of material here. However, you can feel the four episodes. There's never a drag to it. However, it never really moves. Which is unfortunate.

Because overall, the script for this is fantastic. Everyone is clearly having fun doing their thing. The Doctor's funny lines here are legion. "I'm going for a little hop." "Don't leave it on too long. My hair goes frizzy." To all sorts of other great moments. The scene with the Gatherer and the Doctor is very, very funny. The Pompous Gatherer who clearly has no idea what he's talking about is evil at its most banal. From his misquotes to not knowing what the Latin name for the raspberry leaf is, it's classic pompous ruler stuff. Very much a "How the heck did this guy get put in charge of anything?" stuff.

Leela gets several top-notch moments with Mandrel and the underground dwellers. She is fantastic. There's an excitement and rage to her that we don't get when she's with the Doctor. It's great to watch. Her, Cordo and Bisham make a fun team together. Plus, once you add K9, it's a hoot. Watching this awful world and breathing in the stale air of this place really makes one hope for the revolution.

The title of this story is an interesting one. The Sun Makers are The Company. The oppressors. The horrible people making a profit at the expense of everyone else. And yet, the interesting thing is that the people they oppress never see the sun. They never go out into the world above wherever it is they are and whatever it is they do. That's always a little vague here, probably as it should be. What is the Company, the Doctor will ask? What are they up to exactly?

If The Collector is the Company's main representative, we get the 1970s version of Sil. But, whereas Sil is proud to be himself, the Controller has taken on a different, more human form. Even though he's basically sitting on some sort of commode. If the Gatherer is ridiculous and a quisling, his boss is something very odd and very different. And rather unpleasant.

The Sun Makers
Episode Three

Episode 468: (December 10, 1977) The revolution has begun, unfortunately, Leela might be steamed before she has a chance to enjoy it.
Cliffhanger: Leela is about to be steamed.

The Collector leering into the steamer saying that killing Leela gives him a real sense of job satisfaction is nasty. It's quite a violent and sadistic story although the humor and the satire keep all that at arm's length. I mean, they're going to "steam" Leela. Basically, cook her like a lobster. It's horrible enough when we think of it happening to lobster. But to one of the main characters in this show? No way, man. That's crazy. This Company should not be allowed within 5 miles of living human beings. Ever.

I like how we contrast the Company people going about their business as, slowly but surely, The Doctor and everyone else begin to overthrow everything. It's kind of a calm revolution that will pick up as the next episode goes along. It's fun to see the Doctor basically pushing a revolution on. He gives a pretty darn good talking to the Underground rebels. He keeps his cool. He's a bit insulting but they are going to torture him so I'd say that all bets are off there.

There's a nice righteous anger under a lot of this. Holmes wrote it after a particularly unpleasant audit from the Tax Revenue people. So, he's leaving Doctor Who by giving the finger to not only the Tax people but also the BBC. They'd gotten on his nerves in more ways than one throughout his time there. He does have a wonderful run on this show along with a bunch of great scripts to immortalize his name. But you can feel the anger here. No matter how many jokes he covers it in.

The Collector is a fantastic villain. His scene with Leela is excellent. Leela in a straitjacket, kicking and screaming is kinetic and exciting. I like how, at one point, she honestly thinks that she can have a reasonable conversation with this thing. Of course, that's wrong. She tries. And it's kind of nice to see. The Collector doesn't care though. He just wants her dead.

Should we talk about the hallway? Again, the hallway is part of that really depressing tobacco plant whose roof they use throughout this serial. What a crazy and depressing place. The world's longest and worst hallway. Why not have a long shout in it and enjoy the echo? What else is it good for?

The Sun Makers
Episode Four

Episode 469: (December 17, 1977) The revolution is successful.
Cliffhanger: The Doctor, Leela and K9 leave Pluto.

This episode has several great moments. The scene between the Doctor and the Controller is excellent. Two great actors sparring off against one another. The Doctors delivery of "mad as a hatter" is a favorite moment of mine. Just the way he says it, in a sort of tossed off manner, is delicious. The Doctor is dealing with the bad guy. He doesn't act as if things are going to go wrong. He's there to give The Controller a chance. To see what it's been up to on Pluto. When the Usurian turns out to be as nasty as The Doctor thinks it probably is, our hero ends it.

I love that the creature is from the planet Usurius. That's another bit of Holmesian fun here. He's not happy with the people who put profit before everything else and make human beings into nothing to make that profit. I've always loved watching the Collector shrink down into his commode. And, although we never see it, I like that this thing is "sea kale with eyes." That's something to think about.

This episode also has the rather crazy scene where the revolutionaries throw Gatherer Hade off a building to his death. As a kid, it didn't bother me. He was the bad guy. His arrogance and his ego got too much for him. The people who are now in charge take care of him. I mean, he's a quisling who has sent hundreds, if not thousands, of humans to death. So, it's tough to take his death with tears in the eyes. And yet, it is nasty. But then, everyone on this planet, except Cordo, are nasty. That's what the world has done to everyone. Hopefully, these nasty people can make a better world. Who knows?

Apart from the blandness of the direction, this is a good goodbye for Mr. Holmes. It's a wonderful direction for Graham Williams to take the show in. Although, it's not going to be easy as they just lost their best writer. Anthony Read is now the script editor. Let's see what the next story has in store. Oh look! Bob Baker and Dave Martin are back.

UNDERWORLD
Written by Bob Baker and Dave Martin
Directed by Norman Stewart
Episode One

Episode 470: (January 7, 1978) The Doctor, Leela and K9 land on the P7E where the quest is the quest is the quest.
Cliffhanger: The P7E is not becoming the core of a brand-new planet. Will they ever be able to get out?

Anthony Read has now fully taken over as script editor. Robert Holmes is gone. (Granted, he'll be back at the start of the next season but he's, hopefully, taking a nice vacation.) Read's first story is with Baker and Martin. It feels like it's from the same place as "The Invisible Enemy." There's a mythological aspect to this. However, it also does feel slightly juvenile. They're basing a lot of it around mythological stories and legends, specifically Jason and the Golden Fleece. They're also using a lot of space stuff. Many ray guns. An enormous spaceship set. Regeneration. Time Lord mythology. Lots of the P7E flying around and then getting swarmed with rocks.

I think what I find kind of tricky with this episode is that… as much as I love Tom Baker in all of these… as much as I think his character is fantastic… there are some stories where he loses me a bit. Some stories where he seems to be running a bit on empty. It has been a long season. There are new people all around. He's kept the level of comedy up high and sharp. I am slightly worried when I realize that Holmes is now gone. Is Baker coasting a bit here? I don't know.

Watching Leela, apparently, flying the TARDIS is fun to see. And seeing the Doctor in a smock as if he's been painting is fun. The rest of the dialogue is just OK. Tom Baker is doing his best to be charming and delightful. The concepts here are interesting. It's always fun to hear the Time Lords talked about, especially here as "gods." Like the last serial, I can feel the moments here. But, unlike the last serial, I am having a tough time keeping interested in what's happening.

The Minyans aren't the most scintillating bunch of space people. The point is that they have been travelling so long and regenerated so often that they've left a lot of their humanity, as it were, far behind. They are exhausted but they are still going on. And they do convey that. Apart from Alan Lake playing Herrick who always seems to be angry, everyone else is just exhausted. You can feel it as you watch and it's a little tough. Because that means that the Doctor and Leela must bring all the excitement. Leela is immediately pacified and doesn't do much. Everyone's acting is good here. Everyone accomplishes their task of seeming exhausted.

It's an OK opening episode. It's main problem is that, as intriguing as the Time Lord mythos here are, the story itself just seems to be a bit of a shrug. A bit of a "Whatever." I want to know what's going to happen next but for the first time in a while, I'm kind of OK if I don't find out. Unfortunately, I don't think things are going to improve.

Underworld
Episode Two

Episode 471: (January 14, 1978) A lot of people run through fake caves.
Cliffhanger: The Doctor is being overcome by the gases sent out by the guards.

This is one of the weirdest episodes of *Doctor Who* ever, I think. For two main reasons. Well, maybe three.

1) Very little happens. The ship lands within the planet that the P7E has formed around. They begin to explore. We see some enslaved people hauling rocks and some guards shooting at them.
2) CSO. This episode begins the classically crazy concept of setting an episode almost entirely in caves without using any caves. Nothing but CSO greenscreen backdrops, which makes the whole thing look unreal and weird. The first shot of the slaves running almost sideways through the "cave" will tax your mind a bit. It doesn't improve.
3) The fact that little happens means that the episode is running short, as was the previous one. Yet, if you watch this episode closely, you'll see that every step of the way the editors are doing everything they can to slow stuff down.

The first episode sets up an epic quest. Then, upon arriving, the episode just meanders around almost endlessly with nothing happening. It's 22 minutes long and yet it feels much longer. Even the Doctor and Leela have run out of funny things to say to each other. The ship's crew wanders off. Apart from Mr. Lake, they kind of vanish. We don't get to know the slaves, apart from Edas. (A little.) And the guards are so generic as to be almost tough to pay any attention to. If they didn't have those cool guns, they'd be Nothing running across screens. It's almost like the writers and the crew didn't know what to do when they got to the planet/ ship. So, let's meander. Shall we? It's frustrating because you expect it to become better but it becomes appreciably worse.

That CSO. I applaud their attempt. The first time I saw this was on a black and white TV. A small one. You know what? I couldn't tell. When I read about it in *Doctor Who: A Celebration*, the fact that there was so much CSO meant nothing to me. (I mean, aren't quite a few MCU movies almost entirely made up of actors in front of green cloths?) It was only years later when I saw it on DVD that I really saw how nuts it was. They might have gotten away with it on people's TV screens in 1978. *Star Wars* was out by this time. And this, frankly, looks foolish, chintzy and boring. There's nothing in the images that pulls your attention in any way. Nothing that makes you want to keep watching.

The third one recalls the video version of the 1973 film *Blackenstein*. When *Blackenstein* hit theaters, it was a little under 80 minutes. It's not the fastest moving movie in the world but it moves along OK. For some reason, the video version is almost 9 minutes longer. (The Blu-Ray has both versions.) Those 9 minutes aren't character development or more monster attacks or more gore or anything fun. It's extended shots of people walking through hallways or moving from one room to another. They're extended shots of people going up stairs. They are random shots of the monster entering one building and then suddenly being in another that make no sense. For some reason, maybe to justify early VHS/Beta costs, someone felt the need to ruin the film with this. "Underworld" Part 2 is like this. Watch it on DVD with the information text on. It will very kindly lead you through all the extra bits and bobs they had to throw in to extend the Episode to the point where it was still three minutes short. Look at all the repeated shots. Look at the shots of guards and others walking saying and accomplishing nothing. It takes an episode that is already not good and makes it a stinker.

Underworld
Episode Three

Episode 472: (January 21, 1978) We see the inside of the P7E and draw closer to finding the race banks. Cliffhanger: The Doctor and Leela are dumped into a rock crusher.

Hooray! This episode is better than the previous one. There's a fun laser gun fight that is straight out of *Star Wars*. Although no one is really 100% sure how *Star Wars* influenced this was. As mentioned, that blockbuster came out in England about two weeks before this aired. This serial was made in September. The theory going round is that the script is not very influenced by Lucas's *War* but the production is. And the ray gun fight is an excellent example. It's pretty darn good. These are the best ray guns the show has had so far. Herrick's fight on the bridge is very nicely done.

This episode does have more urgency. A bit. It's odd. Because at this point, we know that The Oracle rules over everything. We know there are guards and slaves. We also know that there are robotic Seers. We still don't quite know exactly what the heck is going on in all of this. It's a bit odd, isn't it? It never quite feels like a bit of connection we need happens. They are there for the race banks. How come we don't know where those race banks are yet? How come we don't have more of a concept of space here? There's the spaceship. There's the P7E, which looks exactly like the interior of the spaceship. (In fact, it is. That's the One Big Set for this show.) There's the cool bridge. Everything else is kind of weird. At this point in a serial where so little has happened, I feel like we need more of a narrative push to keep going.

I don't count the cliffhanger here. The Doctor seems to put them in danger specifically because the ending is approaching. And when it happens, because of the sets and the way everything is being shot, for a moment I didn't know what the heck was going on. But then, I realized. "Oh, The Doctor and Leela got dumped in the rock grinder thing. Oh well."

It's odd. Normally, Baker and Martin's scripts are loaded with good times and craziness. I don't know if everyone is run down by the long season or the thought of all that CSO has made everyone tired but this is lacking in so much of their regular verve. Robert Holmes's story previously wasn't his best but it had a lot of life to it. Baker and Martin seem to be at the end of their tether. Or maybe it's the beginning of Anthony Read's tether. Baker and Martin would only write one more for the show together. It's in the next season and it's one I quite like. This one though feels like we could all use naps.

However, it isn't as bad as the previous episode. It is more exciting. There aren't as many repeated shots or shots that just go on and on and on when they should be done. But they are there. The episode is 22 minutes and change with a 2-minute recap. So, there's under 20 minutes of new stuff. Maybe this should have been a three parter? This season is having some troubles finding its way. Seasons 12-15 were the ones shown over and over in the early 1980s. Think of all the highs. Now, think of this season and think of this being the weakest Tom Baker story to date. Soon after this aired, we go back to "Robot." Sarah and Harry are back. Puts this story and the next one in an odd perspective.

Underworld
Episode Four

Episode 473: (January 28, 1978) They must get the race banks! Rather than a pair of matching fission grenades.
Cliffhanger: The Doctor makes it plain that we've been watching futuristic Greek myths.

Oh, thank goodness. After the vague "this might be OK" of the first episode and the stink of the second and the "not as bad but certainly not great" of the third, this is a fun closing episode for the show. And it's fun because there is finally a feeling of urgency. There is also a feeling of playfulness. Again, Alan Lake is a lot of fun. (His almost dazed look when he approaches Jackson with the race bank core is delightful.) The CSO finally begins to use the space decently. It features a switcheroo ending. And, the Oracle, the computer that runs all, realizes that it was outwitted and submits itself to destruction. *

The thing I always loved most about this episode was the Oracle's trick with the fission grenades instead of the race banks. The cores are two golden cylinders. The Seers give Herrick the two of them. Herrick, Jackson and the rest of the gang are super stoked. The Doctor, Leela and Edas are sneaking into the Oracle's sanctuary and they grab the real ones. The Doctor tries to get the grenades away from the ship when a guard takes them from him. Then, the guards blow everyone and themselves up. I find that a charming way to resolve it. It's basic but after all that running around in those caves it feels right.

Tom Baker apparently blocked and set up the big scene with the slaves stretching into the background. The exodus he leads them on to the ship is fun. His encounter with Jackson in the ship (when he tells Jackson that these are his people) is excellent. For the first time in the story since the very beginning, there is a real feeling of stakes. The caves suddenly become less distracting and it feels like something is really happening here that is important. Now, for all those endless shots of the guards (and endless shots of K9 apparently floating above the ground), we never really got to know them at all. I don't think we get to know the slaves either. But they're Jackson and the crew's relations. That's all we need.

I'm glad Herrick lived. They're all so happy when they finally get what they are after. No one more so than Herrick.

I do always wonder, though, at the very end: How are the crew going to deal with all those people over the course of 70 years? That really seems like that might be tricky. Especially if they don't have showers, I imagine they do. That's a lot of filthy people in an enclosed space for 70 years with nothing to do. Maybe a whole new civilization grows out of the two or three generations that travelled the ship to get back home? I don't know.

Anyway, one great episode. One good one. One stinker. And one almost stinker. Luckily, the great one got the biggest rating. Apparently the 37th highest rated episode of the original run, which is kind of astounding. How did that happen?

*Maybe the guards aren't so thrilled about that but hey... they were real jerks.

THE INVASION OF TIME
Written by David Agnew
Directed by Gerald Blake
Episode One

Episode 474: (February 4, 1978) The Doctor returns to Gallifrey to claim his throne as President. He's not being nice about it.
Cliffhanger: The Doctor puts on the Matrix tiara and gets attacked.

David Agnew is Graham Williams and his new script editor, Anthony Read, combined into one. The season ending big six-parter had fallen through so they had to come up with something quick. Williams knew that, like Hinchliffe before him, he would end his seasons with six-part stories. He wanted them to be big. Not just big as in Krynoid big but big as in somehow pertaining to the whole history of the show. This show that was in its 15th year. This show that was now competing with *Star Wars* and the new realm of sci fi that was flooding the world in its wake.

Williams produced this idea: a return to Gallifrey. A sequel, in some respects, to "The Deadly Assassin." The Doctor returns to Gallifrey to claim his rightful title of Lord President. There is something else going on. There are some other aliens there who the Doctor seems to be helping. Near the start of this season, the Doctor became possessed and we didn't know what he was going to do next. This time, he's not possessed but he is acting very unpleasantly, especially towards Leela. Anthony Read would write the majority of it while he and Williams plotted the whole thing. Surprisingly, the rush works quite well. This episode starts off strong and strange. The confusion carries the viewer along nicely.

The thing it does is wrongfoot the audience right off the bat. Is the Doctor really acting like a jerk? No, of course he's not. Is he? We haven't seen him this rude since the start of the first season. The 4th Doctor can be abrasive at times. He doesn't suffer fools lightly. We know that. Generally, though, he goes after the bad guys or the jerks in charge. Not his traveling companion. He even has K9 threaten Leela. That's not like our Doctor at all. Something is wrong.

It doesn't really bother me when he browbeats the Time Lords. We really don't know them that well. Borusa has regenerated and seems less obsequious and a bit more controlled. The Castellan is clearly a butt kisser. Damon must deal with dressing up Leela, which can't be something one looks forward to. The Doctor runs roughshod over them. The High Council didn't appoint a new President so The Doctor is still, technically, President. The Doctor hasn't looked this serious and been this unpleasant in a long time. Who are those aliens behind the big seats who have made a pact with our hero? Our "hero?"

And why do they have such a huge Star Destroyer type ship. We've said throughout the season that the show keeps possibly referencing *Star Wars*. Now, it's definitely doing so in the opening shot. A huge spaceship flies over the camera as a smaller ship shoots along to attach itself to it. That's Williams saying, "We can do *Star Wars*!" Of course, they can't. I wouldn't want them to but that movie was so all-pervasive at that time that it couldn't be helped. I'm not sure if the BBC was asking them to try or telling them to try. It doesn't matter. When the show was getting huge, huge ratings, they told the production team to tone everything down. Now they're asking the team to do something they can't do.

Luckily, the drama and the intrigue here is very involving. What is the Doctor up to? Why is he doing all this? What will happen to Leela? We've got five more episodes to find out.

The Invasion of Time
Episode two

Episode 475: (February 11, 1978) The Doctor sneaks around a bit. Leela talks to a Time Lady. And... Cliffhanger: The Time Lord's new rulers arrive on the planet.

They look like shimmering tin foil. The digital effects on the DVD are better... but not by much. We've been hearing their voices and seeing their spaceship for two episodes. When they show up very briefly at the end, it's an odd moment. Three shimmering silver shapes floating in the air. They do look like aluminum foil. Not terribly threatening but then they only show up for a moment and we have no idea what they are. And they only got in because K9 destroyed the transduction barriers that block and shield Gallifrey. So, they may turn out to be terribly terrifying. They must, right? That's why the Doctor is working with them as if they were.

We do see here that the Doctor is not working for the bad guys. He's working against them while acting like a jerk. It's cemented halfway through the episode when he hides in the TARDIS with K9. Leela is pounding on the door outside. He won't let her in. He covers his ears as the guards approach. K9 hangs his head. The Doctor really does want Leela out of their path though. As of this moment, we don't know why. Maybe he's sick of traveling with her and this is the only way he can think of to get rid of her. I don't know. I do suppose his goofing around and fourth wall breaking when he's in Borusa's office is another sign that he's still the Doctor we love. This is the episode with the famous sonic screwdriver line. (You can look it up.) So, it's alternately an episode where the Doctor seems to be at his worst and at his silliest, which makes for a weird experience.

Leela meets Rodan! The first Time Lady. We hadn't met one yet. And, in the next story, the Doctor will begin traveling with one for 2 2/3 seasons. Williams did like these Time people. I love how bored Rodan is. She's probably halfway through her shift and just wants to go relax. Or whatever they do. She monitors passing or approaching ships. She has a fun chat with Leela. She doesn't talk down to Leela or patronize. She just talks like someone who's bored. She might as well say "The quest is the quest." Regardless, it's fun to see a Time Lady. Her announcement about the transduction barriers at the end Is excellent.

Borusa is still suspicious. Castellan Kelner is still slimy. (There are moments when we seem to think his name is Castellan. That's his title.) The younger guard is hunky enough. There's a lot of hallway running but it's not out of hand yet. With the next episode, we'll up the ante. Whatever is that the Doctor is up to will be getting exposed to us soon.

Oh, I love that container of old TARDIS keys that one guard has. He should probably take off his gloves while he's trying them but he looks like he's having fun. Too bad K9 had to shoot him.

The Invasion of Time
Episode Three

Episode 476: (February 18, 1978) The Vardans take over the planet. Rodan and Leela go outside the City. Kelner takes over.
Cliffhanger: The Doctor is about to be shot.

We finally learn what's going on! The Doctor has NOT suddenly become an evil person. He's been engaging in a clever bit of chicanery for quite some time. He does say that the Vardans are the most advanced race he's ever encountered. He says that he knew the Time Lords would never be able to handle them. He says that this was all an elaborate ruse perpetrated by him to get the Vardans to Gallifrey to try to eliminate them. Horary Doctor!

The tricky thing is the Vardans themselves. It almost feels like the Doctor is lying. Maybe he's a little bored. The Collector was hardly a big amount of trouble. The dawdling around with the P7E didn't tax anything but one's patience. And a few stories ago, he defeated Death itself. So, what else do you so in your spare time? You arrange this little deal with these jumped-up goofballs and have some fun. *

Because let's be honest: The Vardans are just shimmery tin foil currently. The CGI effects on the DVD do their best. They make them into shimmery tin foil with humanoid shapes. That works a little better. It certainly gives them more life. The tin foil things are fine because they make it seem like these are inhuman something or others. But, come on: These are more powerful than the Time Lords. They don't do anything but shimmer and zap. The Doctor says they can ride the wavelengths and read minds. So what? They only get into Gallifrey because the Doctor let them in. I think if the Doctor never bothered with the Vardans they would never have got this far. There's no reason behind the Doctor doing this at all. Unless there's something else behind it all... There couldn't be could there.

Kelner turns out to be just as weedy and gross as we thought he would be. Wrangling for power in a world where it was kind of implied that that kind of thing doesn't really happen. He throws out a Time Lord named Gomer. What a pile! In the end, he uses the time to settle old scores. While mean whilst, Borusa is let in on the Doctor's plan in a clockwork office that I've always liked the look of. This Borusa is very different from the previous one. Definitely more likeable. Definitely less shiny. Will he be able to assist the Doctor? How many questions will I ask?

And even goofier? The Shobogans. Robert Holmes came up with that name from... I don't know. I want to say while doing dishes one day but I can't come up with a decent anagram. They're a rum bunch of Time Lords who don't look like they could beat anyone in a fight but themselves. Of course, who else would they be fighting really? Another tribe of renegade Time Lords perhaps? Wouldn't they all fight together? It's not implied that there's anything else out there. Ravaging monsters of some kind. Just them. So, who do they encounter? And what do they eat? It's all quarry and desert? I don't think we'll get a decent answer here.

*How long has the Doctor been arranging this? The implication is "Some time." This isn't like a "Day of the Doctor" thing, is it?

The Invasion of Time
Episode Four

Episode 477: (February 25, 1978) The Doctor unveils the final part of his plan to capture the Vardans. Will he have time to carry it out?
Cliffhanger: Oh, the Vardans weren't the main villain here! I recognize these goofballs.

The Vardans are revealed in all their glory! Oh well. More later.

I hate to harp on it. But, at this point, it feels like we're starting to run on empty again. Episode two ended with the Doctor shutting down the transduction barriers. Episode three ends with the Doctor putting a hole in the force field surrounding Gallifrey to let more Vardans in. It's kind of similar, only with fewer explosions. Also, I thought the transduction barriers where the force fields? What is the transduction barrier if it's not a forcefield? What does it do exactly? I'm confused.

It really feels like Read and Williams were rushing through this. They got to the end of Episode Two and thought "Let's reveal the Vardans." Then they decided maybe that was too early. So, they did the semi-reveal. How does this happen? Lowering the transduction barriers around the planet allow the shimmering forms of the Vardans appear. Then, we get the third episode. That advances the story somewhat. It begins to let us know what is actually happening with the Doctor.

Now, it's time for episode four. We've got the cliffhanger. We haven't revealed the villain. So, let's have the Doctor basically do the same thing. They'll be more urgency because now we know of the Vardan's power... and so many are in jeopardy. Zap. Forcefield down. The real Vardans appear. That's the third time in a row they've let us down. I don't care how all-powerful they are. It's less than convincing.

Their first appearance was after the spaceship is seen. We see high triangular-backed chairs. Maybe their heads are the same shape? We hear their voices. Not particularly menacing. More like someone yelling at you from a crowded bus. Then, the tinfoil appears. Well, that's not menacing apart from the faceless facts of it. The CGI silvery shimmery men are slightly better but nothing spectacular. Then, they appear for real. They are two tall guys in green outfits with big helmets and one small guy in green with a big helmet. Kelner is disappointed. We're disappointed. The Doctor even points out that it's all disappointing. Does that make it OK? Not really. For all they can do, we expected more. The Sontarans come off as huge reliefs when they arrive.

There is some nice aimless running about in this episode. Overall, though, it works OK especially the closing reveal. Right at the point where they are running out of narrative steam, they pump it up with the new villains. Leela and her over-upholstered friends are there. K9 is alive and well. And we all should run from the craziness of all these long, long hallways.

When I was a kid, the cliffhanger of this episode was a favorite of mine. (Kind of ruined by the cover of the novelization, which isn't going to use the Vardans once you see them.) It always made me sit up and go "What!?" But then, of course, the more you think about, the less "What?!" it becomes and the more "Wait, what?" it becomes. How did the Sontarans slip through alongside the Vardan fleet? Do they not have thoughts? They're clones, not machines. How does this work? I never figured that one out. As a grown up, I greet the cliffhanger with a mix of "Wow!" and "Really?"

The Invasion of Time
Episode Five

Episode 478: (March 4, 1978) The Sontarans are here!
Cliffhanger: The Doctor and Rodan are going to be thrown into a black star.

Boy, that Castellan Kelner is a jerk, isn't he? What an obsequious piece of dung. Are there lots of Time Lords like this? I mean, immediately... immediately, he bows down before the might of the Sontarans. He really is quite punchable. And the fact that he's going to have the people in the TARDIS vanish into a black star is super jerk behavior. What do people like this think is going to happen to them? Sincerely. I mean, when the Sontarans take over and subjugate everyone, is it worth it hoping "Maybe I will be the one Time Lord they don't do this too because I was such a quisling?" Tiresome. Hopefully, he gets his comeuppance. Although, normally, characters like this usually end up learning a lesson and turning good before dying. I don't want that to happen here. Too much blood on his hands.

The scenes between the Doctor and Borusa are very good. A great sense of respect mixed with foreboding and keeping one eye open in case of deception. Borusa pulls a blaster on the Doctor and his gang in the opening. Then, The Doctor pulls a blaster on Borusa near the end. I like when they stare each other down as the Doctor hunts for the Great Key. * Nice scene. And since Borusa has done a "Purloined Letter" with the key, it all ends in fun. Then, the Doctor gives the key to Leela! Oh boy.

Most of the time the episode is just a lot of running around. Tom Baker is doing everything he can here. However, it really feels like he is being asked to just come up with lots of material to fill in the gaps in the episode. Sometimes it works. Sometimes it feels lazy. There are some good moments in here. I like his first meeting with Rodan. However, it's all starting to feel a bit exhausted. Moreso than ever before. Maybe everyone needs a break. It's almost time anyway.

Two things I always remember about this episode: 1) Borusa saying 'Could you please let me in?" when the Doctor closes the door of the TARDIS. (Inspired by the Doctor taking off and leaving Leela and K9 behind in "The Invisible Enemy?") 2) Leela's yelling "Over here" and then her throwing the knife in the Sontaran's probic vent. I'm not 100% sure what she's doing here. If it is some hunter trick, would it work in a high-tech corridor? Maybe. I don't know.

The episode meanders around and finally wanders into the TARDIS. The next episode will be a mad chase through the Ship, which we've never really seen before. And we won't really see again. Sort of. "The Doctor's Wife" and "Journey to the Center of the TARDIS" both wander in there.
But not quite like this. We'll talk about that when we get to it.

*Yes, in "The Deadly Assassin," the Great Key was a long rod that the President held. Here it is an actual key. Well, they were in a hurry when they wrote this. Maybe they simply didn't have time to re-watch the precious story.

The Invasion of Time
Episode Six

Episode 479: (March 11, 1978) A Chase through the TARDIS looking for the great key of Rassilon. Cliffhanger: K9MKII

The season concludes. And the padding used to fill out the episode goes on for a tremendous amount of time. When I first read about this story, the review said there were two episodes of chasing around the TARDIS interior. Could you imagine two episodes of this? What about that staircase area that they walk through about 6 times? Could you imagine if they'd done it even more? Tom Baker even fakes tripping to try and make it interesting. It could have been worse. They could have done it all with CSO. Anyway…

Big ending on this one. The Doctor has Rodan build the dreaded D-Mat gun. (Dematerialization gun. It seems a bit like a deus ex machina pistol but there you go.) It seems like an odd thing to use the Key for once you've got it. But he uses it. In one fell swoop he gets rid of all the Sontarans. Hooray! Vardans and Sontarans sorted out. The Doctor conveniently forgets everything. But now, Borusa knows Rodan can be hypnotized into making the gun so who's to say that he doesn't go mad with power at some point.

The interiors of the TARDIS were all shot at a public pool and an abandoned hospital. It looks like it. I don't mind the interior of the TARDIS looking like this (On film with a lot of brick). It doesn't bother me at all. What bothers me is that apart from a few good jokes nothing is really made of all this. They're endlessly running from Sontarans until we reach the allotted running time and the Doctor gets handed the D-Mat gun. * You can see Andred and Leela's slowly growing affection for one another throughout it, which helps. We'll talk about that in a moment. Oh, Kelner gets away with his awful behavior far too easily. He'll do this again given half a chance.

Overall, it's an overlong, padded ending to a story that started off so strong and then lost its way in the corridors. Watch this one in one sitting and the TARDIS chase is interminable. Watched across six days or six weeks it is more fun. The Sontaran twist was a nice one but doesn't really do much. They tried. But, when the chips were down, they couldn't do the same sort of thing that Holmes did. That's too bad. Hopefully the next season will go off without much of a hitch.

Sarah Jane got an odd abrupt ending that is saved by the fact that she returns to the show so much later. Leela just goes. She's done. She's staying with a guy she barely knows and is keeping K9. That seems even more abrupt. The actors did try to add some signs of growing affection here. None of it is really in the script though so it's a valiant attempt that does come out of nowhere. I hope they are happy. The Doctor seems sad until he reveals another K9. He had been wanting to be alone back in the day. Maybe now is finally the time.

Season 15 ends. The ratings aren't as consistently good as they had been. But they're still pretty darn good. However, the shifting/ changing of the guard has made the show schizophrenic to say the least. I would say that Season 14 has at least three all-time classic stories in it. Four if you count "The Face of Evil." Season 15 has one classic ("Horror of Fang Rock") and one almost classic ("The Sunmakers.") One very good one in "Image of the Fendahl." And three that range from pretty good to kind of awful. (The others.) Chalk that up to Williams dealing with stories from a previous regime and still not being given clear guidance as to what the show is supposed to be doing. Hopefully, in the next season, his vision will fully take hold. As it is, this was an uneven season with no clear direction.

*I will never understand what that Sontaran who tries to jump the pool chair thing and collapses onto it is doing. Sontarans probably shouldn't be leaping around. I do like that we learn Sontarans clone at 1 million every 4 minutes. That's good facts!

SEASON SIXTEEN
1978-1979

THE RIBOS OPERATION
Written by Robert Holmes
Directed by George Spenton-Foster
Episode One

Episode 480: (September 2, 1978) The White Guardian sends the Doctor on a quest to find the six segments of The Key To Time. K9 and the Doctor are joined by a young Time Lady named Fred. * Their first stop: the wintry *Doctor Zhivago*-esque planet of Ribos.
Cliffhanger: The Shrivenzale has arisen! And it wants to eat Romana.

There's a lot going on here... Personally, this was the story we never quite kept seeing on WXXI Channel 21 in Rochester, NY about 5 times. They would cycle through (from when I started watching in 1981 to sometime in 1984) "Robot" to "Invasion of Time." Over and over. The first time through, before I had the Program Guide, I had no idea what was next. I believe I knew that the show continued but I really didn't know what that meant or what was next. After a time, I knew this story was next. I knew it was the first in the "Key To Time" ** saga and that it was written by Robert Holmes. A name I trusted. Every time "Invasion of Time" would air, we'd sit with bated breath to see whether or not Sarah and The Brig reappeared or we finally went to Ribos. I can still remember the day we made it. Sigh...

This is the first season where Graham Williams has complete control. And he comes up with a suitably, post *Star Wars*, epic theme: Send the Doctor, K9 and new Time Lady companion Romana all across time and space looking for the disguised six segments of the Key To Time. Perfect! They are sent on the Quest by the White Guardian. A being who looks an awful lot like God. The Guardian is able to pull the TARDIS out of space time. He can open the doors and flood the space with light. And he likes a nice drink by an artificial pond.*** The Doctor is being sent on a full and proper mythic quest.

The new TARDIS Team land on a wintry Russian based planet looking for something amongst Crown jewels, of a sort. Meanwhile, two guys try to swindle a gentleman named The Graff Vynda-K. (Why isn't there a band named that?) Perfect. There's a goofy monster. There are some very serious locals. There's a guy named Sholakh. The Graff gets to make long winded speeches about how great he was when he was in power, which is a sure sign that maybe he wasn't so great. The world of Ribos is set up very smoothly and succinctly. My only quibble: Same as "The Sun Makers." The direction is not doing anyone any favors. It's a bit by the numbers and bland. Everything else makes up for it though.

As for Romana, she's a bit insufferable here. But I love her. Her willingness to be called "Fred" always makes me laugh. I like how she needles the Doctor about his poor academic performance. (Again, Holmes randomly throwing in humorous asides that others base tons of material on.) She's also got a glamourous touch to her that the previous companions didn't have. And, obviously, she's as smart as, if not smarter than, the Doctor. This is going to be fun.

In closing, isn't that title great? At first, it's a big "What might that mean?" Then, when you learn the plot and what the planet is called, you realize that it's *The Sting* but on Ribos instead of Earth. Holmes may be burnt out but he's still brilliant.

*No. Her name's Romana.
**The first season to get a Full Season release on Home Video. (??)
***The place where the Guardian sits is very fake. That's the point though. This is a construct. The Guardian is as in charge of the space and matter around him as Omega. He approximates a seascape.

The Ribos Operation
Episode Two

Episode 481: (September 9, 1978) The graft continues against the Graff. They have found the segment! They're having a tough time getting it.
Cliffhanger: The Graff captures Garron, Romana and The Doctor.

Things are moving very quickly here. We know that the Jethrik is the segment. The Graff finds out that Garron is scamming him. The Doctor and Romana meander around a bit, trying to find the best way into the royal jewels chamber so they can get the Jethrik. The Graff plans to take the mineral and buy a fleet with it. And Unstoffe gets to dress up. There's some great character moments here as Romana, who is very smart, completely misreads everything else. She can operate this machine and do that procedure perfectly. But she gullibly buys into Unstoffe's con man line about the "Scringe stone" and she really doesn't like being attacked by a monster. She contains multitudes.

Unstoffe's scene as the guard is very funny. At this point, we don't quite know how in-depth this little con game is. Garron casually asks a guard facing away from us if he can explain about the blue stone, the Jethrik. And... it's Unstoffe! I didn't expect that when I first watched the episode. (Helped out by the weird fact that I only have one of this season's novelization. That's "The Power of Kroll." I really feel like novelizations from this season and the next were tough to come by for whatever reason.) Anyway, the Unstoffe Reveal is a nice moment. His story is fantastic. I want to never get the "Scringes" again. I also like how Unstoffe adds an extra bit to the con just to generate a little additional con income.

I also like how the Doctor and Romana keep popping up randomly in the life of the other two groups. No explanation. Just two people they don't recognize appearing. It's smoothly done. By the end, they have all been put under the Graff's thumb. Who knows where we might go next? I do kind of think that this is one of Holmes's best plotted stories. It moves so nicely from its initial set up to where we head to in the remaining episodes. Again, if he is burnt out, it's tough to gauge from this story.

Overall, it, like "The Sun Makers," is an atypical sort of *Doctor Who* story. It's not about space wars or monster invasions. It's about the Doctor and Romana trying to find a piece of a key. * It's about two con men trying to pull a heck of a heist. It's about an insane dictator who wants power back and feels like everyone, except his right-hand man, are garbage people who deserve death. There's some nice design. The acting is excellent. Tom Baker here is hamming it up a lot less than in the previous season. There's some gravitas there. Romana is delightful. And there are plenty of witty bits. Even the direction joins in here with the overhead shots of everyone hiding in the jewel room done very nicely.

*I know. I think of "The Keys of Marinus" sometimes too when I watch this. I'm not sure if Williams would have known about that story. He might have. The Key To Time feels like a more mature, creative journey through the same space.

The Ribos Operation
Episode Three

Episode 482: (September 16, 1978) We learn more about Garron's plan. Everyone escapes to the catacombs, Plus, we meet Binro the Heretic.
Cliffhanger: The Doctor, Romana and Garron are about to get caught in the caverns.

I really love this episode. The first two consist of a bunch of fun characters sort of moving delicately around one another. Someone's here. Someone's there. There is all sorts of intrigue brewing. Meanwhile, the people on the planet are in the middle of it all. The world of Ribos never gets sort fully developed here. It doesn't matter though. The story isn't about the people of Ribos. They're just where the story takes place. The setting for this truly delightful *Doctor Who* story. Granted it is going to take a Donald Cotton-style turn in the final episode. We'll get to that when we get to it. In my mind, this episode has two great scenes (or series of scenes).

The first is the sequence in the Graff's chambers. Garron tells his stories as the Doctor listens and Romana frets. As K9 slowly approaches, Garron regales them with stories of his escapades. All sorts of stories of chicanery. Trying to sell Sydney Harbor to a rich gentleman and that sort of thing. I love the moment when the Doctor asks why Garron is selling mines. Garron, looking upset, says that he sells planets. It's a fun scene. The Doctor laughs at Garron's jokes and engages him in conversation. The Graff is a boorish, violent lout. Garron may be a con man but he's a charmer. (As it should be, I guess.) Watching them talk is super fun. This also seems to be where the director excels. This episode flies by and most of it is just people talking. The great moment here is when Romana, smarter than the Doctor, gets exasperated because the two guys are just shooting the breeze. The Doctor's response is perfect. Basically, when you have faced death as often as he has, nice conversation is a lot more fun. Death is close and that makes the chat so much more delightful.

The other sequence is, of course, the bits with Binro the Heretic. A homeless, toothless man who probably smells and lives in a small rectangle in a wall somewhere in Ribos. It's like some sort of Japanese economy hotel room but it's awful. The guard's dismissing of Binro would be heartbreaking except Binro clearly has put up with a lot of this and has only contempt for the guard. The scene with Unstoffe though is beautiful. Unstoffe, who has been doing mostly goofy comedy and weird accents for the first two-and-a-half episodes, sits calmly listening to Binro.

The scene has been written about in so many places and that's because it's good. Binro will help in the next episode. Here, though, it's just a man who went against the status quo and is punished. The moment when he says that he did recant eventually and shows his bent and broken hands is killer. It's so sad to see what the people in charge do to people like this. But, when Unstoffe affirms Binro's thoughts that there is more to this universe than just Ribos, it's a transcendent moment. Watching this man, who is clearly more intelligent than every other Ribosian (except maybe the Seeker) out there, kiss Unstoffe's hand and almost cry is lovely. Partly because this scene isn't needed. But what it does is paint in a portion of Ribosian background. It seems like a very superstitious place. I think when we see what this society's superstitions do to the best of its people, we realize why we don't learn more about this place. They need to work on fixing themselves. The Doctor and Romana have more important things to do. You should have treated Binro better.

The Ribos Operation
Episode Four

Episode 483: (September 23, 1978) The Graff and his soldiers pursue our heroes into the Catacombs. Only one shall survive.
Cliffhanger: One down, five to go.

The story closes out with a brilliantly scripted closing episode. All the threads of the story culminate perfectly in the catacombs. Yes, the direction is still not always the best. The rockfall scene should be thrilling and harrowing. Instead, it just kind of happens and we see the aftermath. At the same time, K9 freeing Unstoffe and Garron from the rocks should be a great K9 moment. Instead, it sort of happens offscreen and casually. This is not a director for action, which this episode has a bunch of. However, most of it is confined to the small spaces of the catacombs so nothing goes terribly wrong. And the Graff exploding is pretty wittily done.

In several previous Robert Holmes stories, he seems to lose it (some say) in the last episode. Denouement time. "The Ark In Space" could definitely be one of those. Some would say "The Pyramids of Mars." They might be right. I could argue but I won't. This story however casually draws all the cords together and gives us an ending that is kind of crazy, moving and very final all at the same time. Everything in this story has been going relatively fast, timewise. This finale suits it well.

One of the most interesting story decisions is that the Doctor spends a good third (or more) of the episode dressed as one of the Graff's guards with a big helmet obscuring his face. The Doctor, sort of, vanishes for a big chunk of the episode. For a big chunk of the finale. Obviously, he does it to get himself into this world safer than if he just strolled in on his own. (Although, that makes his dragging scarf in that one shot seems a bit cavalier.) The show hasn't done anything like this with the Doctor since, technically, "The Massacre." I would say it's more like the last two episodes of "The Daleks' Masterplan." (Simply because it's never fully revealed what the Doctor was up to in the middle of "The Massacre.") In "Masterplan," the Doctor vanishes for about an episode. When we see him next, he has a plan and he puts it in action. The next time I can think of them using that (in a non-Doctor lite episode or in an episode where the actor is there) would be in "A Good Man Goes To War." The army of troops assembles to kill the Doctor but he's nowhere to be seen...

In this story, the Doctor is basically standing back and watching everyone die as he tries to figure out the best way to get the Jethrik/ Key to Time segment. Some have called the Doctor's actions here cold-blooded. He switches the Jethrik with a bomb and causes the Graff to blow himself up. I don't know. The Doctor and Romana are trying to assemble the Key To Time to save the universe. One crazy man's existence might not be as important as what they're up to. What do I know? Anyway, it's fun to have the Doctor, sort of, hidden for a large portion of the episode.

The rest of the episode is great fun. The Seeker gives us a prophecy, which I like. Sholakh and the Graff act like a**holes. Garron is shifty. Unstoffe and Binro get some lovely moments together. With Binro, especially, getting a wonderful scene when he explains why he would lay down his life for Unstoffe. Great stuff. Throw in Romana and K9 having a blast. Overall, this is such a great story. A perfect opener to the season because it's completely wonderful but... there are no crazy aliens or monsters, more or less. We can only go up from here. Can't we?

THE PIRATE PLANET
Written by Douglas Adams
Directed by Pennant Roberts
Episode One

Episode 484: (September 30, 1978) The Doctor and Romana become confused while looking for the Second Segment.
Cliffhanger: The Mentiads blast the Doctor against the wall with resonant vibrations.

Mr. Douglas Adams has arrived! At the same time this happens, he is writing the first radio series of "The Hitch-Hiker's Guide To The Galaxy." And yes, there are similarities. Mainly in some lines of dialogue and the names of planets and minerals. (Others have covered these in-depth. I'd advise you check out other books to see the similarities.) The main Adams thing is the quality of the comedy and the craziness of the plot. The comedy is evident in this episode. The plot craziness doesn't become evident for a while but the seeds are planted here.

The episode starts off somewhat insufferably but then becomes rather insidious. The spikiness between Romana and The Doctor is continuing. She is reviewing the TARDIS Type 40 Manual. The Doctor insists they don't need it. He tries to land on the planet Calufrax, the location of the Second Segment. Something goes wrong! And then Romana lands safely on the planet. It strikes me as being a very 10 years ago Women's Lib type thing that sitcoms and dramas almost always did poorly. Luckily, Douglas Adams throws a spanner into the works. Because Romana does land in the right spot. She lands there only because she can. For some reason, the Doctor (and the Bridge) cannot land. When Romana does, oddly enough, it's not the right planet. Calufrax is a desolate and icy planet. This planet clearly is not. Hmmm…

I do love when K9 suggests that Romana asks the locals what's happening. Why? Because she's prettier. The Doctor pauses and asks, "Is she?" I love the concept that the Doctor thinks he is the Belle of the Ball or something like that. K9 is right though. He's a computer. He ain't goofing around.

This episode really sets up a lot of stuff that will pay off and it keeps the comedy flowing all over the place. I do love when the Mentiad's Dad mentions "Queen Xanxia…" very casually. Who is she? Oh boy. Anyway, this is an imaginative episode. It doesn't have the subtlety of the previous story but this is Douglas Adams at the start of his career. He's up to something very different as we shall see.

The only issue here is the one that has been marking the show heavily since Graham Williams took over: bland direction. Pennant Roberts seems like a very nice guy but the direction here is not enthralling. Especially the scenes with the Mentiads and the family awaiting the Mentiads. The story hops from the Captain, his robot parrot and Mr. Fibuli giving it their all to the Doctor and Romana and K9 having a good time. The people and the Mentiads are dull. Granted, Adams doesn't seem particularly interested in them as characters. So, this could be everyone's fault. But then, there's that repeated shot of the Bridge model up the mountain. Find another way to frame that or shoot that. I get what it is and I see that it's a model. Every shot of it draws more attention to it. Luckily, the main cast are working their behinds off. The story is odd. Adams is really cooking with all of his non-family-related dialogue. That overcomes a lot here. Imagine if this had had a great director behind it though?

The Pirate Planet
Episode Two

Episode 485: (October 7, 1978) We learn the secret of The Pirate Planet.
Cliffhanger: The Doctor meets the Mentiads again.

I always forget that the running theme throughout Season 4 in 2008 is one of the missing planets. Planets that keep getting named over and over. The Doctor vaguely trying to remember why he's heard about them. This story does the same thing with Bandraginus V, the previous planet that Zanak devoured. Leaving the Doctor wondering why and when he'd heard about the planet. It's a nice tie into a future moment. And it allows an actor to pledge revenge to a piece of rock, which is less silly than it sounds.

A great episode that expands everything around it. The Doctor is sharp and smart and super cool. Romana is a lot of fun. The two of them strive in the face of the adversity, not really caring about what's happening around them and having a good time. I love when they're poking around the giant engines and talking and yelling out numbers. I always wonder why Fibuli and the Captain don't stand closer to them so they can overhear the whispering. Bad Guys with bad ideas, I guess.

The concept of the story comes out here and it is astounding. (Per a really good story, only a portion of the actual reveal.) Zanak is a hollow planet. (Whether they hollowed it out themselves or it came pre-hollowed, we don't know.) The gigantic engines that the Captain has built dematerialize the planet. It rematerializes around other planets, crushing them. Then, Zanak mines those planets and everyone enjoys wealth. (Although, the actual society is vaguely sketched in here. If everyone works for the Captain and works towards harvesting the wealth, what do they spend the wealth on? It's the opposite of a planet oppressed and working for nothing. These people are oppressed but come away from it with fabulous wealth.) Zanak will then do another hop when needed.

It's an astounding idea. It is, of course, horrid. It's so selfish and rotten. The fact that they don't just do this to desolate planets like Calufrax but also to places like BV, which is heavily populated, is an atrocity. The Doctor keeps himself calm here as he thinks about it but he will be less calm as time goes on.

It's a sharp episode that puts the fist/ claws of the planet around our main characters. It seems like such a hugely upscaled planet one almost wonders what the Doctor and Romana can do here. Of course, the guards are always screwing up so that helps. But still... this is a tricky situation. Adams's ideas are huge and crazy. This is drawing towards something big. Yes, we get the Doctor asking guards what it's like being a guard. Yes, we get the Doctor saying he'll never be mean to a particle in an accelerator again.

We also get the Captain's Nurse. She watches the robot parrot kill a man. Then she takes the Captain's temperature. (Orally.) She seems very nice. It's great that the Captain has someone on call for him. I'm sure she's benign.

The Pirate Planet
Episode Three

Episode 486: (October 14, 1978) The Doctor, Romana and the Mentiads begin to fight back against the captain and his gang of evildoers.

Cliffhanger: The Doctor drops from the edge of the plank to the ground one thousand feet below.

In this episode, we get to see that the Captain really is a tremendous engineer. Those enormous engines deep in the mountains should be a giveaway. But we get some backstory here. We learn that Queen Xanxia was horrible. * She burnt out the planet. It was the arrival of the Captain in a starship crash that provided her release and happiness. The Captain put together the time dams, powered by the forces that they acquire while destroying planets. All this death to keep this one old, pardon me, hag alive.

The Captain has set all this up. And there's a cool excitement to his museum of trophies. Although, they're not trophies. They're the actual planets suspended. It's Douglas Adams and his writing that bumps a concept like this one step up. He thinks of the fact that you just can't have crushed planets hanging around. There's tremendous engineering skills set up to balance all of this. The Doctor appreciates it. Heck, there's a moment here where The Captain invokes Clarke's Law. That is creating a bit of technology that is so advanced it is indistinguishable from magic. He's a wistful man sometimes is the Captain. As the Doctor points out, though, he couldn't run the galaxy. He'd just yell at it.

The Doctor is his charming self throughout the episode. But he gets a gloriously angry Doctor moment here. When he acknowledges, purely scientifically, that the planet balancing trick is incredible. Followed by, his anger and demand to know what it's all for. The two engineers/ scientists standing facing off against one another is beautifully done here. Because the Doctor has a great point. What is all this for? This is a terrible thing. What could justify this? In the end, we learn. It seems even more awful when we find out.

K9 gets to fight the robotic parrot here. Granted, it probably works better in the novelization (I've never read it). Or it works better in your mind. The whole thing isn't put together terribly well. A CSO parrot firing weird rays. Then, K9 firing his rays. It's a bit, to quote the Doctor, underwhelming. It is a fun concept, though. Robot parrot in a shootout with a robot dog. Of course, it brings up another Williams era problem: all those awful ray guns. The guns here shoot red circles. They make some noise. Most of the time they seem to appear randomly and someone falls. The guns don't make sense. How did the guy who has probably never used this gun before shoot down three trained guards so easily? If they're going to use ray guns, they need to do them well. This story has some bad ray guns in it.

Most of the rest of it is a lot of fun. The story is steamrolling along. The Doctor falls off the plank. The Mentiads are having their power blocked. The next planet jump will be around Earth. Let's see where this goes. (Note: I do like the moment the Captain says that he wants to see Earth. For a moment, it almost seems like "Is he going to spare it?" He doesn't but it's a nice moment.)

*Two stories in a row with horrible planetary rulers. The differences being: They were able to banish the Graff Vynda-K. We learn here that Xanxia is alive and well. We learn that all this horrible stuff is happening because of her. We will get a similar death scene in the next episode like one in the last episode of "Ribos."

The Pirate Planet
Episode Four

Episode 487: (October 21, 1978) Zanax is about to materialize around Earth. But the Doctor fell off that plank. How is the day going to be saved?

Cliffhanger: Two down, four to go.

A hell of an episode. It's already overlong. The episode is 25:17-ish. Normally, they're meant to be under 25 as the show is in a 25-minute time slot. This story is already super packed with ideas and craziness. So much so that it doesn't even have time to wrap everything up, which I kind of love. We learn that the planet Calufrax is the second segment. The entire planet. At the end, because there's so much else going on, the Doctor and Romana are going to fetch it. They don't have it yet!

Crazy episode. There's a nice circular feeling to everything here. It begins with the Planet and the TARDIS trying to materialize in the same spot and that's how they try to save the day here. Except I do wonder how they get from the Bridge down to the TARDIS in under 10 minutes. It seems a bit of a stretch to me... unless they go very fast. There is a feeling too that the TARDIS is being ripped apart in this. The moments when the Bridge and The Ship collide are nice and wobbly. They're matched up with the calm moments of the Mentiads and the Doctor floating dreamily through the engine room. It's almost too much going on but this seems very Douglas Adams to me. The previous story had just enough happening. This goes overboard but in the best possible way.

The reveal of who the villain truly is well done. It's the Nurse! She's the Queen and she's a super a-hole. I love how she takes over. I love how all the bluster goes right out of The Captain. Mr. Fibuli tries to stick by his old boss but the new boss is here. She's legitimately ruthless and unpleasant. Whereas the Captain is a windbag. That reveal is fantastic. Link that with the evil laughter mixed with the Doctor's happy laughter because he didn't fall from the plank and you have a great cliffhanger resolution. (The first two weren't the best.)

In the end, the Mentiads are still bland. But that's kind of the Mentiads' style. What are you going to do? Their outfits and their faces scream "We're dull! And we have psychic powers." They do help in the end though so that's great. Oh, aren't the guards the worst shots ever?

Overall, a very ambitious and crazy but very entertaining story. Even if the first episode gets a bit iffy with the non-main characters and even if the direction isn't the brightest thing around, this story has so much imagination behind it. Such a story. Such an effusion of fun. Even the storytelling itself is super clever. I know people don't like clever. I hear people say that "clever storytelling isn't smart storytelling." As a storyteller and a writer myself, I can tell you this. You're Wrong. Writing like this is not easy. Most writers can't do it. Never shame a good writer who can. Go back to whatever it is you do and let us writers write. Douglas Adams is here, world. Enjoy.

Oh, the way the Doctor escapes from the Bridge is hilarious genius. It's moments like this that demonstrate how a show like this can go on forever and ever. Endlessly inventive because it can be.

THE STONES OF BLOOD
Written by David Fisher
Directed by Darrol Blake
Episode One

Episode 488: (October 28, 1978) The Doctor and Romana go to the Countryside of England looking for the third segment.
Cliffhanger: Romana falls off a cliff!

A new writer is welcomed into the fold. Mr. Adams was the first. Mr. Fisher is the second. Something rare is about to happen. Mr. Fisher writes two serials in a row! Chris Boucher did that two seasons ago. That was to keep the continuity with the character of Leela. Here, it's done because Mr. Fisher is a fast and sharp writer with a great imagination and a nice eye for witty dialogue and interesting characters. He's set us down on Earth in Hammer Horror territory where general weirdness abounds.

The Doctor gets to take Romana to Earth. They're going to the countryside of England. Near the coast. Misty moors. Stone circles. Worshippers of ancient Welsh goddesses. Who, let's be honest, look more like a bunch of bored English people that decided rather than trying self-sufficiency they'd try worshipping ancient gods. The man in charge, De Vries, is great because he's the least scary guy ever. Middle age, portly with a big mustache. De Vries has a wary wife or girlfriend or whatever she is. I like his scene with the Doctor very much. Showing off a rack of family portraits that aren't there is very amusing. And, of course, adds to the questions.

Then, there's Amelia and her friend Vivian. Amelia is a classic eccentric Doctor Who character. I think Ms. Ducat from "The Seeds of Doom" was the last person like this that we'd seen. Amelia is fantastic. She has a long fun chat with the Doctor. Vivian seems a bit odd and that might be a giveaway. Great characters though. Fun to hang out with. I like that they instantly talk to Romana even though Romana is wearing those awfully uncomfortable shoes.

Overall, it's a strong opening episode. The segment is around there somewhere. They know it is. They also know that there is something weird going on. Romana being enticed off the cliff by the Doctor gives us the clue on that. The title implies something. They pour blood on a stone and it vanishes. But what else is happening there?

Something interesting to note about this story is that it's one of five Fourth Doctor stories that is shot entirely on video. The director insisted because he didn't want the jarring moment when film goes to video and back again. They've put some sort of filter on the OB camera. So, it really works. It has an almost film-like look when we're on location. Not quite if you know what you're looking for but almost. In the end, I wish they could have shot everything on film. But one or the other does the trick. Especially here where the stone circle and the woods at dusk really work.

Final note: This is the 100th Doctor Who Serial. They did shoot a scene with a birthday cake to celebrate the Doctor's 751st birthday. It was, in fact, removed. It probably should have been.

The Stones of Blood
Episode Two

Episode 489: (November 4, 1978) The Ogri attack.
Cliffhanger: Vivian makes Romana disappear.

The Ogri appear! They are giant moving stones that were standing stones and are no longer standing. And they drink blood. Yes, they do look a little strange. You know what, we're almost 500 episodes into this show. If you're honestly thinking "Living stones? Nope. Not for me, thanks." Then maybe you are watching the wrong show. Because I always liked the concept of it. We had Eldrad who was silicone-based a few seasons ago. That's stone. Why not giant stones that drink blood? (I am glad they didn't go with the original idea with guys in giant rock suits running around. Giant stones I can deal with. Ben Grimm on a *Doctor Who* budget I am not so sure about.

Another excellent episode that keeps everything moving. In Robert Holmes-style fashion, De Vries and his lady friend are killed off early on. We only have them and Vivien and the Professor as other characters. (I don't count the Ogri.) So, killing them feels a bit odd. At the same time, it does add a feeling of desperation to everything. Even if we don't fully know what that involves at the moment. Heck, K9 is torn up by the Ogri. That's not good.

The Professor continues to be a great character, Freeing the Doctor from being sacrificed, carrying around her truncheon. I like the scene with the found paintings where they all... spoiler... look like Vivian. Very "The Hound of the Baskervilles" there. Very fun. I like the little bits of mystery added to everything here and there, as this is mixed with the craziness of a Goddess on the loose and several giant stones that drink blood. This story is gradually becoming one of the odder ones out there. And what about that cliffhanger? Where is Romana going? We'll find out soon enough.

David Fisher is a welcome addition to the writing staff. There's so much fun going on in this and we have the addition of: Where is the segment of the Key to Time? I know. Maybe you do. But we're not there yet. There's too much fun happening. I do hope K9 can face up to the Ogri in the next episode. He fought the robotic parrot and won. I understand stones that weigh several tons are trickier to deal with but who knows? We shall see.

The Stones of Blood
Episode Three

Episode 490: (November 11, 1978) To hyperspace! As the Ogri are fought on Earth, the Doctor is put on trial by the Megara.
Cliffhanger: Vivian destroys the Doctor's hyperspace machine. Trapping Romana and The Doctor in hyperspace forever.

In my mind, this episode always shifts over to the hyperspace prison ship quicker. I always think it's a sort of two for two kind of thing. With most of the last two episodes taking place here. But the Doctor doesn't arrive until 14 minutes into the 24-minute episode. So, there's a lot less time spent here than I remember. The Megara trial doesn't begin until the next episode. Once again, in *Doctor Who*, there's going to be a lot more happening in the final episode that I had remembered. As always that's a good thing.

Mainly because this episode has a lot of good stuff going on. K9 fighting the Ogri. The Doctor whipping up the hyperspace machine. The scene with the campers. And then the ship itself. Just the way the whole aural landscape of the show changes when we're on the ship is notable. You go from the woods and nature and Earth to a prison ship parked in hyperspace that now seems to be dead, except Romana. She's a prisoner against her will.

The Doctor and the Professor together are very charming. Putting together the machine and talking about Einstein. It's a cool scene that helps move everything along. Plus, the Doctor gets in some great lines. "Run as if something nasty were chasing you because something nasty will be chasing you." After the slightly out of control Tom Baker near the end of the previous season, he seems to be wittier here. I'm hoping some of it is in the script but it can be tough to tell. It works nicely here though. Thank goodness.

Vivien seems to be a fun and formidable foe now that she's fully in her bad guy outfit with the feathers and the body paint and the big wand that does all sorts of crazy stuff. I like the fact that this giant hyperspace ship is directly above the stone circle but in another dimension. Never argue with the snazzy of that.

Here, the tone of the show shifts slightly. Not fully. Never completely. Because we still return to the stone circle and we return to the countryside. But now, things become more clinical and, in the next episode, things become a courtroom drama for much of it. Who expected that? One of the reasons why I love this show. Out of nowhere, it switches genres within the same episode. Who cannot love that? Well, probably a lot of people. People complain a lot.

The Stones of Blood
Episode Four

Episode 491: (November 18, 1978) The Doctor is put on trial by the Megara.
Cliffhanger: Three down, three to go.

Now the story has become a fun courtroom drama. Two omnipotent and omnipresent justice machines somehow end up going after the Doctor for breaking the seal on their chamber. They won't try to look for Cessair of Diplos, the criminal they are there for, but they go after the Doctor. The thing I find most amusing about courtroom dramas is the way (this happens on "real" court shows too) that the judges, the lawyers, the everyone can dive in and alter whatever courtroom procedure they need to in order to get what they require.

The Megara are very funny flashing star-like creatures here. They are so convinced that they are always correct that the Doctor, after a time, basically runs rings around them. I'm amused. I admit it. The big thing that always grabbed me as a kid was when they go immediately after the Doctor. They have been locked in that chamber with the seal over it for thousands of years. The Doctor, without knowing, releases them and they go after him and try to execute him. Their procedure for putting on trial the person they're actually here for is woefully under done. And very funny.

There are people out there who do not like this portion of the story. They say that it ruins a perfectly good scary story. I don't know about that. First, we know that the show has been told not to do "Gothic" stuff anymore. So doing a story that gradually slips away from that style into something rather silly and fun is perfect. And the people who complain about the tone shift/ genre shift are the same ones who complain about the Ogri looking ridiculous. I don't know. I think we can let them go.

Why does the Doctor have a barrister's wig in his coat? Because he's a Time Lord! You never know when you're going to need something like that. Let's be honest. And it's funny. It places the thought in the viewer's mind that the Doctor is ready for anything or can do anything. I think it's very charming. And his defense of himself is very funny. Especially because he does seem like he's reaching on occasion. Especially with Vivien sitting there laughing at him the whole time. Luckily, in all this, the Ogri have a presence but not a major and intrusive one. They're just something causing trouble in the background. Adding a little extra danger to a story that has suddenly become silly.

The third excellent story in a row. Graham Williams seems to be on a roll now. This is exciting *Doctor Who*. A show that is fifteen years old but still able to be relevant and exciting and fun. In the end, the only part of this that I might call out as padding is Romana and the Professor looking for some sort of weakness in Vivian. In the end, Romana shows up after everything is done. It's good that she gets the info. But it's kind of padding. And no, I don't call the sequence with the two campers as padding. It's quite horrifying for a kids show. It's the last time Doctor Who does something like that for a while. I think that's cool. Next story: David Fisher is back.

THE ANDROIDS OF TARA
Written by David Fisher
Directed By Michael Hayes
Episode One

Episode 492: (November 25, 1978) The Doctor and Romana find the fourth segment on Tara, a medieval planet, rather quickly. That's when it gets complicated.
Cliffhanger: Grendel has drugged the Prince, his pals and the Doctor.

The Prisoner of Zenda, Ahoy! I've never read *The Prisoner of Zenda*. However, if you've seen this story, you will know eventually that it is based on that novel. There's a prisoner. There's a bad guy. There's some sneaking around of a prince imposter. And it's set in Zenda. Maybe I will read the novel for this book. I've never felt it was necessary. It doesn't, to be honest, sound like my kind of book. I think I'd probably only enjoy it through the world of *Doctor Who*. And, yes, I sure do enjoy "The Android of Tara."

Fisher is back with another charmer of a story. There is a not-so-great bear monster thing right in the beginning. Once you've got past that though, the rest of the story is bad-looking-monster free. Thank goodness. Because the story has wit and charm enough to carry itself through. It's got a great villain in Grendel. A guy who is a bit of a goon but is so used to being in power, which he inherited, and lording his "superiority" over everyone, which he inherited, that he is kind of silly. But, charming. He is doing his best to charm Romana but Romana is on too much of a straight and narrow course to be anything but annoyed.

I love the way this story begins. The Doctor simply wants to go fishing. Romana can take care of finding the key herself. And the Doctor does get to do some fishing. Romana does find the segment. Unfortunately, she also finds that monster thing and runs into Grendel. If that hadn't happened, imagine how short this story would have been. The Statue Segment! Part 1 and it's ten minutes long. Oh the chicanery!

Instead, David Fisher throws us headlong into this world. It's a kind of medieval world but it also has androids. There's a distinction between the nobles and everyone else. The nobles do not do labor and can't do any sort of trade. Peasants know how to do everything. I fear that that might turn out bad for the royalty in the future at some point. However, we never go back to Tara so we'll never find out.

Meanwhile, the Doctor gets some funny lines. His indignation at having his scarf burned is great. And his line about "would you mind not standing on my chest, my hat is on fire" is an all-time favorite of mine. The Doctor is a bit flippant here. I think that's because he recognizes what story they're becoming a part of very early on. He knows what happens next and the way it ends. Maybe. We'll find out as the Coronation of the Prince (Robot or otherwise) draws near.

The Androids of Tara
Episode Two

Episode 493: (December 2, 1978) Intrigue continues as the Coronation approaches.
Cliffhanger: The Doctor apparently rams a staff through the Princess's head.

The court intrigue continues! We see that Romana looks exactly like Princess Strella. What a racket Count Grendel runs over here! He can just come in and kidnap the Princess and the Prince so he can become the head of the Kingdom? Really? Is that how it works? Kidnap all the people who are against me! It would make life so much easier. It's the sort of storyline that kind of works better in the world of fairytales. In something more "real," it's a bit much and it ends up feeling a touch foolish. Watching the Princess dutifully looming away knowing her death is near is taking stoicism a bit too far. I think.

Anyway, the episode works. David Fisher's got a nice line in charming dialogue. Much like his line in robotic justice machines from the previous story. Grendel's a fun villain. Nasty, sure? But fun. I like his calm chats with the Archimandrite (who seems a bit like a dope) and the discussion of how many times he's going to refuse to accept the crown. It's charming.

Romana doesn't have that much to do here. She gets to see the prisons and spend some time with the Prince. The Prince is clearly not well but what are you going to do? See my previous paragraph. Of course, Romana looks like the Princess. And Grendel and Lamia thought that Romana was an android of the Princess in the previous episode. So, there's all sorts of chicanery going on here.

The Doctor, of course, gets the best stuff to do. I like that he keeps calling the android Prince "George." He called Romana "Fred" earlier in the season. He's having some fun with names in Season 16. He and K9 make a nice pair in this episode. Getting involved with intrigue because he's certain he knows where Romana is. I wonder if he feels some guilt about going fishing? I hope he doesn't. He'll never take a vacation again if he starts to feel weird about stuff like that.

All in all, it's a fun installment in a story that feels very familiar. However, it slots in just enough extra stuff. Just enough accoutrement to make it entice. The Doctor is witty. There are androids. Look at that cliffhanger! And the outside looks nice and the caves aren't all CSO. There you go! Win win.

The Androids of Tara
Episode Three

Episode 494: (December 9, 1978) The Prince is now the King. The Doctor rescues Romana. Then, that goes wrong.
Cliffhanger: The Prince's android is destroyed. Grendel escapes with Romana.

The intrigue continues! Yes, Romana and the Prince/ King do use the "Guard, come quick! So and so is sick!" trope. Boy, they do use that a lot in *Doctor Who*, don't they? I guess if all the stories took place on Earth that would be a weird thing. Surely every place on Earth must know this trick by now. I think the conceit in this show is that the Doctor and friends are going around the universe. Not everyone knows this trope. Not everyone knows how it works. "Remember when that young woman with the robot dog and that strange Doctor taught us that we could escape from cells by pretending that one of us was sick?" "We were so naïve before then." I like the thought that maybe before that they would try just hitting the guard when the guard came close to the door. "Guard, come here!" "Why?" "Come here." "OK... Hey! You were trying to hit me!"

The episode has a scene I love in it with one of my all-time favorite moments in the show. That's the scene at the small pavilion in the woods. The Doctor knows Grendel has got him walking into a trap. Grendel knows that the Doctor knows that he's going into a trap. The viewer knows that The Doctor knows that Grendel knows that the Doctor knows that a trap awaits. The Doctor is in the pavilion waiting for Romana, who he knows will be an android, and waiting to be shot at. Grendel says he will let the Doctor come out and won't shoot him. The Doctor shrugs and tries to leave. Immediately, he is shot at. The Doctor dives back into the pavilion and slams the door shut behind him. A moment later, guns still blazing, he throws open the door. Yells "Liar!" And then closes it again. I do love that moment. Then, he and K9 sneak out the back. There you have it.

There is a touch of the old Terrance Dicks "Escape, Run around and then get re-captured" thing here. Romana is freed. The Doctor gets her back to the cabin in the woods. Only to have her taken again. Oh well. It certainly moves us towards the final episode.

The mix of the technology with the medieval is quite charming here. Swords with lasers. Ray guns. Castles. Princes and Princesses. Androids and tape recorders. I like this society that has chosen to be this way. They like being in Medieval Times! But they also like their nice conveniences.

Three episodes in and my thoughts on this story are usually the same. It's a good (well known) story that is well told here. It's not flashy or crazy. It's not changing the rules of the story. It's not doing anything radically different, apart from the placing of the Doctor and friends in this Ruritania. It's just a fun story. I think we all know where this is going. It's not going to end tragically. All shall be well. It's about the journey. Unlike the last story, which flipped us around and did some odd things, this one is rather comforting. Heck, they find the segment so early that what else can happen. Let's go from here and see how the story ends.

The Androids of Tara
Episode Four

Episode 495: (December 16, 1978) The final battle between the Doctor and Grendel!
Cliffhanger: Off to find the fifth segment.

The story ends. And good succeeds. Evil does go free to fight another day. Although, in the end, Grendel diving into the water around his castle and swimming away surely isn't going to keep him out for very long. The King and now Queen are not in their castle. They're in Grendel's. So, surely, when they leave, he will return. Won't he? It's not like they drove Grendel out of Their castle. Right? Or am I wrong?

The Doctor gets a swordfight! It's been a long time. The last time was against the Master in "The Sea Devils." In that one, it's clear that the Master isn't really a super expert with the sword. Grendel is proclaimed to be the best swordsman in the land. I'm not arguing. The Doctor does get to goof around a bit, which is fun. It's the Doctor! We want them to goof around a bit. But then, they take over as the fight rambles through the castles and up to the roof. Excellent stuff. I do love a good swordfight. The only thing about it that is slightly odd are the sounds. I'm used to the high adventure "Clacking" of swords in Errol Flynn movies and the like. It always confused me here. The sounds we're hearing are the real sounds of swords clanking together. It works but it's a little less adventurous than other ventures.

Yes, the King and his soon-to-be Queen kiss at the end. It doesn't happen often in this show but it does happen. Kissing is a thing in the universe. We must deal with it.

Most of the episode is build up to the wedding. Much of that build up is fun stuff with K9 and the Doctor. The Doctor's response to the fact that K9 is cutting through the door is fantastic. "A hamster with a blunt penknife would be quicker." And, when the Doctor leaves K9 and then leans back in saying "You old sea dog you" I always laugh. The Doctor barely seems to break a sweat in this story. Probably because he knows the story and realizes what needs to be done to accomplish it. It's not the most world breaking earth-shattering story but it is entertaining.

Overall, a super fun story. One of those that is never going to be a full-fledged classic. Simply because it's not that kind of story. It's a classic tale, well told here. There's excitement, intrigue, romance and a rousing swordfight at the end. And, of course, Grendel's closing line is fantastic. "Next time, I shall not be so lenient!" Solid entry in the middle of the season. Overall, the first 16 episodes of this season have been excellent. Let's go hunting for the fifth segment. Shall we?

THE POWER OF KROLL
Written by Robert Holmes
Directed by Norman Stewart
Episode One

Episode 496: (December 23, 1978): The Doctor and Romana land in the swamps on one of the Delta Magna moons. Along with some jumpy refinery guys and some green fellows.
Cliffhanger: Romana is threatened by a giant tentacle hand thingy.

And they call back Robert Holmes one more time. Maybe it was one time too many. At least in this episode.

The Doctor and Romana land on a very swampy planet. I like swamps. I'm in. Let's see what's up. This director last blessed us with "Underworld." That story certainly wasn't anything to look at visually. This episode is up to the same standard. It contains quite a bit of four guys sitting in a boring room in a refinery talking and talking. Once the Doctor arrives it becomes more interesting in there. It feels like a set for a base under siege story but it's a small set. A tiny siege awaits. And the guys in it are dull.

Then, we move outside where we meet a gun runner and a bunch of green guys. These are the natives known as Swampies. And, I'll be darned, they're more boring than the people in the refinery. But look at that scenery! Oh my... Then, I stop looking and watch as the Swampies jump up and down chanting "Kroll!!" over and over. All I can think is "How do these guys reproduce? Why are there no women here?" Is that something significant? Maybe the guys are the only ones doing this silly chant to Kroll and the women are off being productive somewhere. I don't know.

Romana and The Doctor are doing their best. This script and the direction, though, seem like leftovers from the previous season. Now, I know that they weren't. And this is Robert Holmes. You keep watching it to catch the moments of "Holmes" in here. There are a few good lines. There is a discussion of methane/ swamp gas. That seemed to be a bit of a trope of his, casually bringing up bodily functions. But, both sides of the coin here are so dull that it's tough to get a grasp on why this is worth the time.

It's not helped by the direction, which is, frankly, dull. Especially during the opening scene with the guys in the refinery. When we get on film, things get a bit snappier. But then it's a huge swamp. It's bound to be more interesting. That opening scene seems to last 10 minutes but it's only about three. Holmes seems to be shoveling in every generic Doctor Who trope he can come up with. And it doesn't revitalize or energize anything. It feels, simply, tired. That's worrisome. The director is not dynamic enough to deal with something that's subtle or might need a lift. The green guys look ridiculous. The cuts from video to film during the ritual aren't good. The refinery is more like a stage set. This is not the way the story should be starting. In fact, it's so cliched that it feels like there's a joke here but I'll be darned if I can figure out what it might be under all the familiar dross.

I'm not saying this is terrible. I'm just saying it's a bit dull. I'm saying that I think it feels a bit tired. I'm saying that it feels like maybe there was a joke in here somewhere that the director didn't get. Surely Robert Holmes delving in all these cliches and using all these boring characters must be up to something. I can't imagine Robert Holmes just giving up. I always feel like there is something more to this than we're seeing. That must be down to the direction.

The Power of Kroll
Episode Two

Episode 497: (December 30, 1978) The Doctor and Romana learn about Kroll. Kroll makes his first appearance. And the refinery guys and the Swampies talk and talk.
Cliffhanger: That one refinery guy is pulled into a pipe by Kroll's tentacle. Hawn? Is that a name?

Weird episode. I do think that Holmes's writing isn't at his best here. I do think it feels like his sole idea is "Biggest monster he can think of" and that's about it. The rest of it seems woefully underwritten. Except for the moments with the Doctor and Romana. And that's odd. Because the show really shouldn't be like that. At times, *Doctor Who* is almost an anthology type show. We must like or at least be interested in the characters that aren't the Doctor and whoever he's travelling with. If we don't care about them, then all we do is wait for the Doctor to reappear. There must be some interest in what else is happening.

"The Power of Kroll" is a story that really doesn't do that. The Doctor and Romana have a storyline here that goes entirely parallel with the other storyline but never touches it, like two train tracks. The Swampies have been given guns, defective guns, by Rohm-Dutt to fight the refinery guys. The refinery guys are getting more and more paranoid and want to destroy all the Swampies. Kroll shows up and confuses/ scares everyone* Their stories grind on like this. The Doctor and Romana are out of it for the entire thing right up to the end.

As previously mentioned, the director goes out of his way to make the studio stuff as dull as he can. There's a long scene with the refinery guys (who are only discernible because I am familiar with the actors, if this was something where everyone was a newbie I wouldn't be able to tell them apart) that is done basically in one long take. But it's not an interesting take. Three guys in the frame. The camera is at sitting level. The guys just talk. There's no lovely framing. There's no symmetry within the frame. One guy stands up and steps to the right. The camera goes up slightly and moves over slightly. It's not clever framing. It's "keep everyone in the shot" framing. It is lazy. Again, I'm not sure that this script is up to anything more than what we're seeing… but the direction is doing the opposite of helping.

Meanwhile, Mary Tamm and Tom Baker are doing everything they can do to be interesting. Holmes's script is better when they're on. The direction is the same. ** But they are learning about the Swampies history and Kroll's history. And it's all so much more intriguing and interesting than everything else going on, that it is starling. Watch their scenes and read the novelization of the other scenes. Terrance Dicks does his best and your imagination will help them perk up.

*A point of confusion: How did Romana and The Doctor not see Kroll? He's massive. He fills up the sky. He's extremely loud. At the end of the episode, as the Doctor and Romana wander from the Swampie sacrifice site, they end up in front of the Swampie village. That's the spot where they all just saw Kroll. How did our favorite Gallifreyans not see the big guy? And where, exactly, did Kroll go? Something that giant rising out of the water and then going back must have created some kind of tidal emergency. It's almost like Kroll teleported in and then out again.

**This has been a sketchy directorial season. "Ribos" was good. "Pirate" defeated boring direction. "Stones" mostly succeeds. (Although, like Romana falling off the cliff, on more than one occasion poor editing tries to hide bad directorial choices.) "Tara" wasn't exciting. It was more literary. "Kroll" is about gun running and green men and giant squids. It should be thrilling. It has less energy than *Manos: The Hands of Fate*.

The Power of Kroll
Episode Three

Episode 498: (January 6, 1979) Not much happens.
Cliffhanger: Kroll shows up again.

I thought a lot didn't happen in the last episode. A lot of people talking about nothing that's terribly interesting. The hope was that the backstory we were getting with the refinery guys and the Swampies would coalesce into something. That it would become something greater. That's what I hoped for. That hasn't happened yet. And we've only got 22 minutes of story left after this episode.

Even in the episode of *Doctor Who* were the smallest amount of stuff happens they do their best to make it look like stuff is happening. The Pertwee era is a masterclass in six-part stories with nothing happening in the middle. They load everything up with chases and escapes and excitement. It's only afterwards that you realize that it didn't amount to anything. Hopefully, you've been entertained so it doesn't really matter.

This episode (possibly this story) does something different. Once again, the Doctor and Romana are the only interesting things here. There is a super long scene with the guys in the refinery where they discuss what to do with Kroll that seems like something that should have been excised from the script or never been written. We don't care about them. We don't care about the Swampies. We don't care about Kroll. So, hearing these guys talk endlessly about this inner working stuff that we don't care about strains to hold the viewer's attention. Again, the director goes out of his way to not make it visually interesting. Someone forgot to tell him that this is not a play. It is astounding how long their talk goes on and accomplishes nothing. When the lead guy gets angry at the Swampies, it doesn't come out of nowhere.

It comes out of No Care. These guys seem so far removed from most of the story in their refinery that this all seems like so much time wasted.

The Swampies aren't worse. They're just dull. They do nothing in this episode but argue about, again, things we really don't care about. Yes, they worship Kroll. Got it. But every time Kroll appears he randomly kills a bunch of them. Maybe it's time to start rethinking the plan. I can't say that I'm interested in anything about them, except for how silly they look. Green with strange wigs on. Once again, I feel like Robert Holmes is taking the piss here. But no one realizes it. * All the dialogue is so po-faced. None of the characters are developed. None of the situations are developed. The only through line will lead us to the Key to Time segment. All the rest is Holmes either burnt out or simply goofing around. It's tough to tell.

The reason why it's tough to tell is because The Doctor and Romana are fun here. The refinery guys argue about how to stop Kroll. That's it. The Swampies prep and begin the execution of the Dryfoots. That's it. The Doctor, Romana and Rohm-Dutt are tied up to be killed, escape and run from Kroll. That's it. Every time we go to the Doctor though, it's fun. The Doctor seems to be in the story we want to watch. The one that involves finding the Fifth segment of the Key To Time. Not the one we're watching. The dull one about the guys dressed in white and the green guys in the loincloths. Luckily, Kroll is out and about. Maybe things will pick up for the (very short) fourth episode.

*There is a 1950s sci-fi film called *Queen Of Outer Space*. Richard Beaumont wrote the script as a parody of 1950s sci-fi cliches. (Which are numerous in that time, see Warren's wonderful *Keep Watching The Skies!*) No one making it, however, knew that it was a parody. So, it comes out as the straightest of straight-faced sci-fi films of that era. But at its heart it's making fun.

The Power of Kroll
Episode Four

Episode 499: (January 13, 1979) Kroll and the fifth segment are dealt with. Some dull people are involved.
Cliffhanger: The search for the final segment begins.

This episode ends up coming out a little bit better. Basically, because everything happens in it. An orbit shot is going to be launched to destroy Kroll. One of the refinery guys shoots another one. The head jerk is speared. The Doctor dismantles a rocket. Kroll attacks the refinery. The Swampies swarm the refinery. (For the first time ever, apparently. I'm not sure why they didn't do that previously.) And there's chaos. Finally, the fifth segment is revealed. Plus, there's a lovely moment at the end where the Swampies are alone in the refinery with one "Dryfoot." That should go well. If I were the Doctor or Romana, I wouldn't have stayed either.

At the end of all of it, though, I still don't give a crap about anyone here except the Doctor and Romana. When Dugeen is shot, there's a bit of an "Oh no" feeling. It goes away quick. I like that Fenner is not happy about it. But they're all so boring. I mean, until the Swampies storm the refinery it really feels like they're in a completely different story from anyone else. Almost like a "Carnival of Monsters" thing with the Doctor and Romana passing in between. But then "Carnival" was a tour de force of imagination. This is sorely lacking in imagination. Unless, again I'm not sure, this is all a goof.

Thank goodness we got the fifth segment! Tom Baker does his best to look like he's struggling with the giant tentacle. I like giant tentacles. They're fun. And Kroll is cool when he's attacking the refinery. But it's not up to much. We know the Doctor's going to make it. There's not a lot of tension here. The Doctor does get some funny moments though. (Yes, even he seems a bit bored by the "stop the rocket" thing. It's such a foregone conclusion. It really seems, again, like Holmes is mocking the formula of this sort of thing. But who can tell?) "Let's get out of here before people start putting two and two together... I can tell you're putting two and two together." Romana comes off OK. The slightly aloof character feels slightly aloof throughout. That fits a story that's almost nothing. It feels like such a trifle. The fact that the episodes are so short only adds to the fact that everyone seems out of steam here. That can't happen before the big finale. It just won't work. We need to be excited about it. Oh, the finale is written by Baker and Martin and directed by the guy who did "Tara." This could go either way.

Oh well. It can't all be a great season. Robert Holmes, as I said, either wrote a script where he was totally out of gas. Or he was making fun of this kind of sci-fi. The whole thing ends up falling somewhere in the middle. The bland direction is a real liability here. That could be the worst part of the Williams era: bland/ poor direction. This show needs action. It needs good directors back. The bunch we've had throughout most of these past two seasons aren't cutting it. A bland script can be elevated by good direction. A script that's a bit weird and needs a creative touch is going to be let down by bad direction.

THE ARMAGEDDON FACTOR
Written by Bob Baker and Dave Martin
Directed by Michael Hayes
Episode One

Episode 500: (January 20, 1979) The Doctor, Romana and K9 land on the planet Atrios in the middle of an endless nuclear war with its twin planet Zeos.
Cliffhanger: An explosion has buried the TARDIS in rubble.

The Dalek Invasion of Earth has a very similar cliffhanger moment in its first episode. Bury the TARDIS in rubble. Here it's quite different though. In the Dalek story, the burying of the TARDIS causes the crew to become part of the story. In this one, they aren't leaving the story but the TARDIS was a home base. Now there's no home base. Luckily, they still have the tracer. Without K9 and without access to the other segments, things look a little grim.

There's a sense of deep grimness mixed in with silliness in this episode. Shapp is a bit silly. The Marshall is almost silly but he's not like the Captain. He has a definite human face and he's willing to kill everyone, including Princess Astra, to get peace., A truly dangerous man. But the episode mixes in the opening scene of the jingoistic soap opera with young man "dying for it." Freedom. So, there's some satire of Cold War jingoistic nonsense. There's the Atrios side, who are clearly losing, putting up their brave face as they live underground with the constant threat of destruction. And there is the, maybe not strange in this episode but it will be soon, fact that we never see anyone from Zeos. We don't cut to their side to see what's happening. We strictly stay with Atrios. That's odd.

The Doctor and Romana are very much dropped into the center of someone's war here. After five segments of searching, they do seem slightly weary. They are still doing their best though. The Doctor gets off some good quips and Romana is as fun and aloof as ever. I, like them, must start to wish though that these segments had been out somewhere more pleasant. Really only the fourth segment was somewhere calm. It was just bad timing on Romana's part that led to that adventure.

The episode has a nice mix of impending doom alongside some romance, with Princess Astra and her Doctor boyfriend. There's been more romance in this season than we normally have. And that's nice. I wonder if that was part of Graham Williams' thing. This is Anthony Read's last script edited story. He's been half and half. But most of the season has been stellar. Let's see how he closes everything out. Oh, and yes, Princess Astra does look familiar. You just wait a bit.

The coolest thing that this episode does though is a subtle director touch. It's something akin to a *Happy Days* thing. In that show, the gang hangs out at Arnold's Drive-In. They sit down in the same booth episode after episode. That booth is against a wall. But, as the diner is a set, there is no real wall. We pretend like there's a wall there. (Sometimes we do a good job of pretending. Sometimes not-so-much.) We are always looking into the set from that wall, like a stage. Occasionally, though, a director will throw in a reverse shot so we see the wall next to them. (The invisible stage wall.) It makes the alert viewer sit up, saying "Hey! There really is a wall there!" Although sometimes it happens so quickly, it's tough to spot. That happens in this episode of *Doctor Who*. The War Room is a big place filled with people and screens and tech stuff. In the center, the Marshal's chair sits facing us. Facing the fourth invisible wall of the set. In the beginning, the Marshall and Shapp stare towards us monitoring a screen where a battle is taking place. Then, we SEE the wall they're looking at. We suddenly are behind them! It's a great moment that doesn't happen again in the episode. It does something important though. It gives us a true feeling that this is a real Room and not a set. That can be very important.

The Armageddon Factor
Episode Two

Episode 501: (January 27, 1979) The Marshall tries to get the Doctor to help him fight Zeos. As things get odder.
Cliffhanger: The Doctor is in the transmat to Zeos with two Green guys.

One of the complaints I see about this story is that it has the typical "end of the season and we have no money!" thing happening. Well, yes, I can sort of see that here but not really. *Doctor Who* has always been cheap. It's always been a little light on cash. * It gets through everything with ingenuity and imagination. That happens here. The episode takes place in a few hallways, on a conveyor belt, in a wrecked room and the control room. The control room is the only one that looks like it has some money behind it. The rest looks like what it is: wrecked rooms and spaces. Destroyed by war. It never bothers me. Some people take this for excessive cheapness. What if it is? It works for me.

I find this episode to be delightful. The Marshall is clearly nuts. The way he keeps rocking back and forth between insanity and hatred and being pleasant to the Doctor and Romana is great. Watching the Doctor watch the Marshall watch the battle is a great scene. One of those great *Doctor Who* moments where something big is happening and we see it all through the point of view of someone watching it. Saving money? Sure. But it's much more to the point and it shows off how pathetic this fighting group have become. The Doctor's response to the Marshall is the best. Basically, he says he has the perfect deterrent. What is it? Peace.

I will say that the bit with K9 and the furnace is a bit rote. It's like when you think Mel is going to get dumped into the furnace in "Terror of the Vervoids." It doesn't amount to much. It is slightly harrowing hearing K9's voice sort of shut down as he goes. I never thought he was going to burn up. Besides, the Doctor can just make a new one. As he will do in the future.

Two episodes of this is enough. Now, it's time to open out the story. The cliffhanger implies that that is exactly what will happen. That's why I like it. We got two episodes of Atrios. Now, it's time for Zeos. Sometimes I worry about the Baker and Martin scripts. This one, though, I like.

I think the thing that makes this episode so great, to me, is that we're two episodes in and there's a real feeling that we've only scratched the surface. I don't mean in a "The Seeds of Doom" or "The Invasion of Time" way. I don't mean that suddenly the whole focus will shift to something else leaving the previous story behind. I mean, that there is a lot going on here. The Marshall calls the Doctor "The Time Lord." Now, that ain't common knowledge. Especially on a planet like this. So, what is going on? And how does the Marshall know about that transmat directly to Zeos when no one else does? And what is the mysterious force in between Zeos and Atrios? There are a lot of questions to be answered here. To me, this story answers them and answers them well. It really is an excellent conclusion to the series. But we're still some distance from that so bear with me.

*I was watching an episode of *Poirot* from 1989. There's a scene where Poirot and Hastings talk to a woman by a beach. A band plays in the background and people mingle in period garb. Poirot and Hastings walk up some stairs get in a car and drive away with all of this in the background. I thought, I bet that 3- or 4-minute-long scene cost more than an entire episode of *Doctor Who* in 1989. Maybe two.

The Armageddon Factor
Episode Three

Episode 502: (February 3, 1979) We go to Zeos. I think.
Cliffhanger: The Marshall is about to launch a final strike against Zeos.

I love this episode. Yes, it is in the same weird, cheap space of the previous episode. Maybe there is a bit too much wandering around. You could say that *Alice's Adventures In Wonderland* has too much wandering around. It has too much vague meandering. Not enough actually going on. It's a series of odd moments amongst the meandering. I wouldn't argue with you there. I love Alice and I love this episode. Because after the first two episodes paint a picture of these two planets, after they paint the picture of their never-ending war, it also shades in something else happening in the background. * Then, this episode proceeds to give us some, but not all, the answers. And it advances the Marshall's storyline while giving him less to do.

One of the things I truly love about this episode is the odd misdirection at the beginning. The Doctor is told that the transmat is to Zeos. He arrives in a place where a strange, green man wants to take over his mind and then torture him. We think, "Is this Zeos?" Very quickly, we learn that it is but this person is not a Zeon. What? Then, the Shadow vanishes when he realizes that the Doctor won't be so easy to take over. Leaving the Doctor on Zeos with everyone else. But then, we see Princess Astra. And she's under The Shadow's control. On Zeos? No. A million miles away. What? What is happening? There is a third place. And the Shadow zapped over from there to Zeos to see the Doctor and now he zapped back. It's slightly confusing. But, also, not really. It's rather exhilarating.

Especially as the episode goes along and the Shadow tells the Marshall that there will be no more Zeon attacks. Then, the Doctor asks K9 to ask Mentalis, the Zeon computer commander, about the war. "The war is over." What? The Marshall, of course, takes this as a moment to go after the Zeons. To launch a final attack using their last ship. And that's the cliffhanger. The Marshall about to attack Zeos, where all our friends are, knowing that Zeos will not attack back. It is kind of confusing, isn't it? I like it though.

Is there too much wandering around in halls? I don't know. If it's interesting, who cares? Does it look cheap? Probably. The reveal of Mentalis is alternately a "Wow!" and a "that's it?" moment. K9's excitement over having another computer to talk to is fun. The gradual realization of who the people of Atrios have been fighting and what for is nicely and slowly revealed. Now we must find the sixth segment. It's something to do with the princess. But what?

*We know almost immediately that something is happening here because we finally hear the voice that the Marshall is hearing. It's not a nice happy-go-lucky voice.

The Armageddon Factor
Episode Four

Episode 503: (February 10, 1979) A time loop stops the Marshall for a while. But The Shadow is slowly winning.
Cliffhanger: The Shadow now has control of K9. Things don't look great.

There is a lot more running around in halls and such in this episode. It might be reaching the point where it feels like too much. It doesn't. it doesn't because of what's at stake here. The fact that the bad guys had the wherewithal to send their agent to the end of the line* and wait for the Doctor and Romana to get there is pretty tricky. And a very "bad guy" kind of thing to do. Could you imagine what would have happened if the Doctor was just sent to the end of the line to wait for the bad guys to collect everything else? Nothing would have ever been done and the whole balance of the universe would have fallen apart. Why does the Shadow and, presumably, the Black Guardian want the Key anyway? The premise is that the evil/ the darkness is winning. The key must be obtained to restore balance. I guess the Black Guardian either wants to speed along the imbalance or he doesn't want good to get the chance to fix things. I guess. Regardless, the Doctor and Romana did all the work. The Shadow wants to profit from that. He hasn't even found the sixth segment, for Heaven's Sake! What a load.

There is something oddly dark and large about this episode. Not just the deteriorating time loop. Not just the computer ticking down towards Armageddon. There's a couple who are in love betraying themselves. Watching the surgeon fall into a trap because of Princess Astra under evil control feels stronger than usual here because of all the season that went before. The Shadow implies that he's been observing the Doctor's adventures. I imagine that means he's been watching *Doctor Who* but I'm not sure. Then, there's the kidnapping and reprograming of K9. That's good stuff. The ending with The Shadow petting K9 and K9 calling this thing "Master" is a great cliffhanger. Like the previous one, it anticipates bad stuff about to happen without completely being bad stuff happening.

The story saves itself from having that mid-six-part slump through the time loop and the use of the Key To Time. When I first watched this, unlike some other stories of the time that I had read the novelizations of or read big synopsis of, I didn't know what was going to happen here. The moment when they jury rig a sixth segment is fantastic. That two- or three-minute period when they have time looped the entire universe is rather thrilling. Even realigning the loop to just include what they need is great. I love the shots of the repeating timer. I love the Marshall saying "Fire!" over and over. There is something truly epic about this serial. Although it doesn't have massive space battles or huge sets. It's got a clever story that gives us just enough info to keep us moving and just enough to keep it all interesting. And now, it's moving us towards the Shadow's spaceship. The lair of the evil. What will happen now? K9 has already moved over to the Dark Side. Who's next?

*Are the segments numbered the way they're numbered? Could they have got the fourth before the second? Maybe it has something to do with how they're assembled? Maybe they can only be put together in the proper order. Of course, they could still get them out of order. They just couldn't assemble it.

The Armageddon Factor
Episode Five

Episode 504: (February 17, 1979) The Doctor is imprisoned with a strange man named Drax. Romana is tortured. The sixth segment is still being hunted for as the time loop breaks down.
Cliffhanger: Drax shrinks himself and the Doctor.

The story kind of takes a bit of an odd twist here. One that I kind of like but always kind of surprises me. That's the introduction of Drax. He's got a Cockney accent. He's very much a working-class kind of guy. Into repairs, fixing things. He's been trapped on the Shadow's ship for five years. * He clearly likes it there or he would have tried to get out. He does put out that distress signal, which, oddly enough, only the Doctor hears. I know that (from the info text) Baker and Martin had wanted this character to appear a long time ago. They finally got him on the show here. It's interesting to have another Time Lord appear. And he gives the Doctor a name: Theta Sigma. Baker and Martin had been wanting to name the Doctor since "The Three Doctors" when they wanted to call him OHM. (Flip it upside down and read it backwards. It's a step above "Alucard" I'll give it that.) I'm never sure whether the introduction of Drax works or helps the story. It's a nice bit of lightness in the encroaching darkness. But then, The Doctor's always been able to keep us laughing. I think it's having a character introduced who isn't involved with any of the hunting for the key. To me, his shenanigans are a breath of fresh air so near the end. I think.

Most of the episode is wandering about or being held prisoner in the Shadow's lair. The supporting characters from previous episodes are pretty much gone. There is a sense of dread looming over us here that I think works well. It also, I think, makes us sort of forget that nothing really happens in this episode. K9 is under the Shadow's control. But, like the furnace bit, it doesn't come to much. Romana is tortured but it isn't as bad as it seems like it should be. The Shadow seems content to just park it and be sinister. Meanwhile, the Doctor is trying to find the segment, save the day and figure out how to keep the decaying time loop going while inserting the sixth segment. He's had a long day.

In one respect, the intensity of the last few episodes has calmed down here. I'm not sure if the Shadow knows about the time loop or not. But that is pretty much only given lip service here. Most of the episode is the Shadow being ominous, Drax being a goof and the Doctor trying to figure out where the sixth segment is and what the heck is going on. The Doctor has met his opposite self-according to the Black Guardian and he is slightly confused by it. One episode left.

*I applaud the Shadow for really sticking with a theme. He's on a spaceship but he makes it look like a series of caves. That's why I don't have a problem if any of the stones or cave hallways look fake here. They are. It's a spaceship. This is all affectation. The Shadow has a Goth feel to him. It comes with his style. Look at his guards! I hope they don't have to provide their own outfits.

The Armageddon Factor
Episode Six

Episode 505: (February 24, 1979) The Key To Time is assembled. What happens next?
Cliffhanger: The Randomizer has been fitted and the TARDIS crew are off to new adventures.

The Saga comes to an end. Possibly a little too pat. I have a personal story to relate at the end of this review. That personal story always endears me to this episode. I think the first half of the episode is more stalling. But then, we're 26 episodes into the whole shebang. You know, in modern *Doctor Who* there are so many big two-part finales where the first part is nothing but build up to the huge cliffhanger leading us to the finale. I'm a big fan of "Sound of the Drums" but, really, it's all just kind of faffing around until the big, crazy cliffhanger. "The Stolen Earth" is the same but less interesting. This Key to Time saga is sort of doing the same thing.

If you think about it, the first thirteen minutes are basically: the Shadow sends someone into the TARDIS to retrieve the key. Astra becomes the sixth segment. The Doctor grows and blasts light at the Shadow and the good guys run away. That's about it. Then there's some more rushing around and dismantling Mentalis and deflecting the Marshal's missiles. The true thrust of the episode comes in the meeting with Guardian. I think the thing at the end of the day that is tricky is that the Shadow seems like a potent nemesis. But, in the end, he's just as dopey as most of the villains the Doctor meets. He's just got a longer time to plan everything. Once the plan is complete, and he has the Key, things fall apart swiftly. The Doctor being shrunk goes from a "What?" thing to something helpful. The Doctor can remove himself from half the episode and still save the day. Well done, sir.

I do wonder at what point the average viewer figures out that Astra is the segment. I get the feeling that we may not have thought of a person as the segment before. So, it may have taken some time. I can't say for certain though. The "sixth this and sixth that" speech I think delivers the message clearly. But, again, I don't know if "the segment is a person" would have been something we thought of. As the episode ends and the Doctor realizes which Guardian he's talking to, it does make the whole thing feel weird. When the Guardians chose the pieces, there must have been compromises. The White Guardian chose the Jethrik and the statue. The Black Guardian chose the planet and the person.

And the season ends. I loved it. "The Power of Kroll" is not great. Or maybe it is great. But the rest of the season ranges from entertaining to wonderful *Doctor Who*. The show at its best. A great duo in the TARDIS. A companion who is smarter than the Doctor. I love Mary Tamm's performance as Romana. Bristly at first but then so much fun as the season goes along. (I love the moment when the Doctor's eyes roll back and he seems to be corrupted by the power of the Key. Then, he reveals he was kidding. And Romana punches him in the arm. It's delightful.) A travelling robot dog who turns out to be quite wonderful. And a series of stories filled with invention and adventure. I love the season. After the iffiness of Fifteen, Sixteen turns out to be delightful. I would have liked to have seen what Anthony Read got up to outside of the umbrella concept. But he's consorted himself well here. It's almost all change as the next season begins. Same Doctor and same producer. New Romana. New K9. New Script editor. And high, high inflation as we approach 1980.

The final reason why I love the closing scene so much relates to the first time WXXI aired this around 1985, after we had been waiting for ages to see the season. I had Timer Recorded it on the old Betamax. I always gave extra time at the end. Unfortunately, there was a technical issue at the start. The show began late. The moment the Guardian appeared on the TARDIS scanner… my copy ended. It was about a year-and-a-half before they showed it again and I finally saw it. For some reason, the scene always is extra special in my mind because of that extra-long time I had to wait.

About The Fella

Daniel R Budnik lives in Los Angeles, California. He is the author of *'80s Action Movies on the Cheap, From Beverly Hills to Hooterville* and the children's novel *Arthur, Bertrand and Constance*. He is co-author of *Bleeding Skull: A 1980s Trash-Horror Odyssey*.

When he says "read," read.

(Is this a weird spot to put this? I thought it seemed fun.)

When I say "Rest"...

Rest

Rest

Your Destiny continues in Volume 2.

www.ingramcontent.com/pod-product-compliance
Lightning Source LLC
Chambersburg PA
CBHW081004180426
43194CB00044B/2759